Seville, Granada & Andalusia

LUCAS PETERS

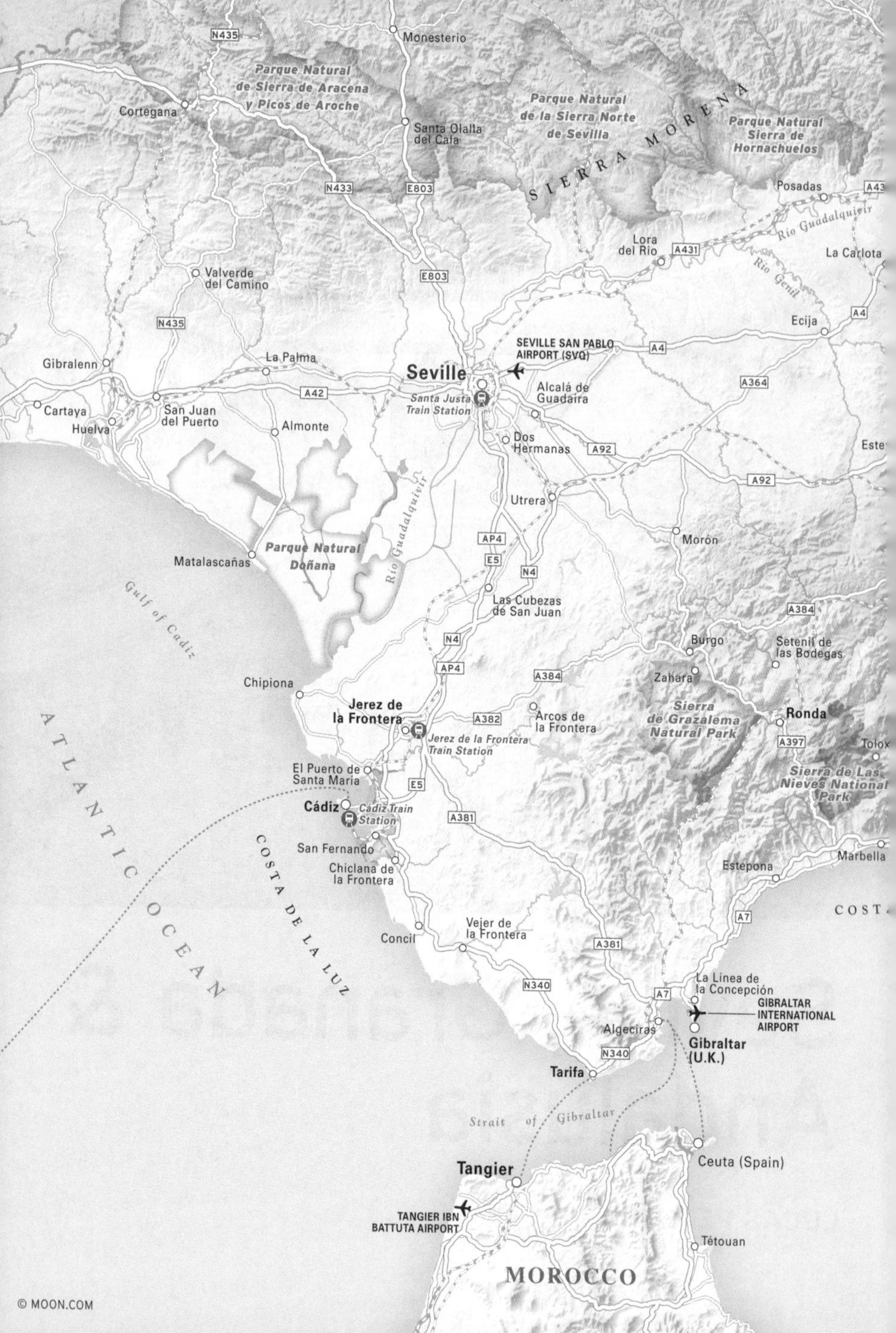
N435
Monesterio
Parque Natural
de Sierra de Aracena
y Picos de Aroche
Cortegana
Santa Olalla
del Cala
Parque Natural
de la Sierra Norte
de Sevilla
SIERRA MORENA
Parque Natural
Sierra de
Hornachuelos
Posadas
N433
E803
Lora
del Rio
A431
Río Guadalquivir
La Carlota
Río Genil
Valverde
del Camino
E803
N435
Ecija
A4
SEVILLE SAN PABLO
AIRPORT (SVQ)
A4
Gibralenn
La Palma
Seville
Alcalá de
Guadaira
A364
Cartaya
A42
San Juan
del Puerto
Santa Justa
Train Station
Huelva
Almonte
Dos
Hermanas
A92
Estepa
A92
Utrera
Río Guadalquivir
AP4
Morón
Matalascañas
Parque Natural
Doñana
E5
N4
Las Cubezas
de San Juan
Gulf of Cadiz
A384
Burgo
Setenil de
las Bodegas
N4
AP4
Zahara
A384
Chipiona
Sierra
de Grazalema
Natural Park
Ronda
Jerez de
la Frontera
A382
Arcos de
la Frontera
Jerez de la Frontera
Train Station
A397
Tolox
El Puerto de
Santa María
Sierra de Las
Nieves National
Park
E5
ATLANTIC OCEAN
Cádiz
Cádiz Train
Station
A381
COSTA DE LA LUZ
San Fernando
Marbella
Chiclana de
la Frontera
Estepona
COSTA
A7
Concil
Vejer de
la Frontera
A381
La Línea de
la Concepción
N340
A7
GIBRALTAR
INTERNATIONAL
AIRPORT
Algeciras
Gibraltar
(U.K.)
N340
Tarifa
Strait of Gibraltar
Ceuta (Spain)
Tangier
TANGIER IBN
BATTUTA AIRPORT
Tétouan
MOROCCO

SEVILLE, GRANADA & ANDALUSIA
N420
Bailen
Linares
Andujar
A4
A32
Montoro
Ubeda
Córdoba Train Station
A4
Bujalance
Porcuna
A44
A316
Parque Natural de la Sierra de Cazorla
Peal de Becerro
Córdoba
Jaén
Martos
A315
Granada Geopark
Castro del Rio
Fernan Nunez
Pozo Alcon
A316
Baena
Alcaudete
Montilla
Cullar de Baza
A92N
Baza
Alcala la Real
Granada Geopark
Lucena
Priego de Cordoba
A44
A92N
N432
Parque Natural Sierra de Baza
A92
Guadix
Rio Genil
A45
A92
Granada Train Station
FEDERICO GARCÍA LORCA GRANADA AIRPORT
Loja
E902
Granada
A92
Parque Nacional de Sierra Nevada
Gergal
A92
SIERRA NEVADA
Antequera Train Station
Antequera
Durcal
El Torcal de Antequera
Parque Natural Sierra de Tejeda
A45
A44
Almería
Málaga Maria Zambrano Train Station
Vélez-Málaga
El Ejido
A7
A7
A7
Motril
Almunecar
Adra
Roquetas de Mar
Málaga
MÁLAGA-COSTA DEL SOL AIRPORT
COSTA TROPICAL
COSTA DE ALMERÍA
Torremolino
Mijas
Fuengirola
A7
EL SOL
Mediterranean Sea
Isla De Alboian
0
20 mi
0
20 km

Contents

BARCELONA

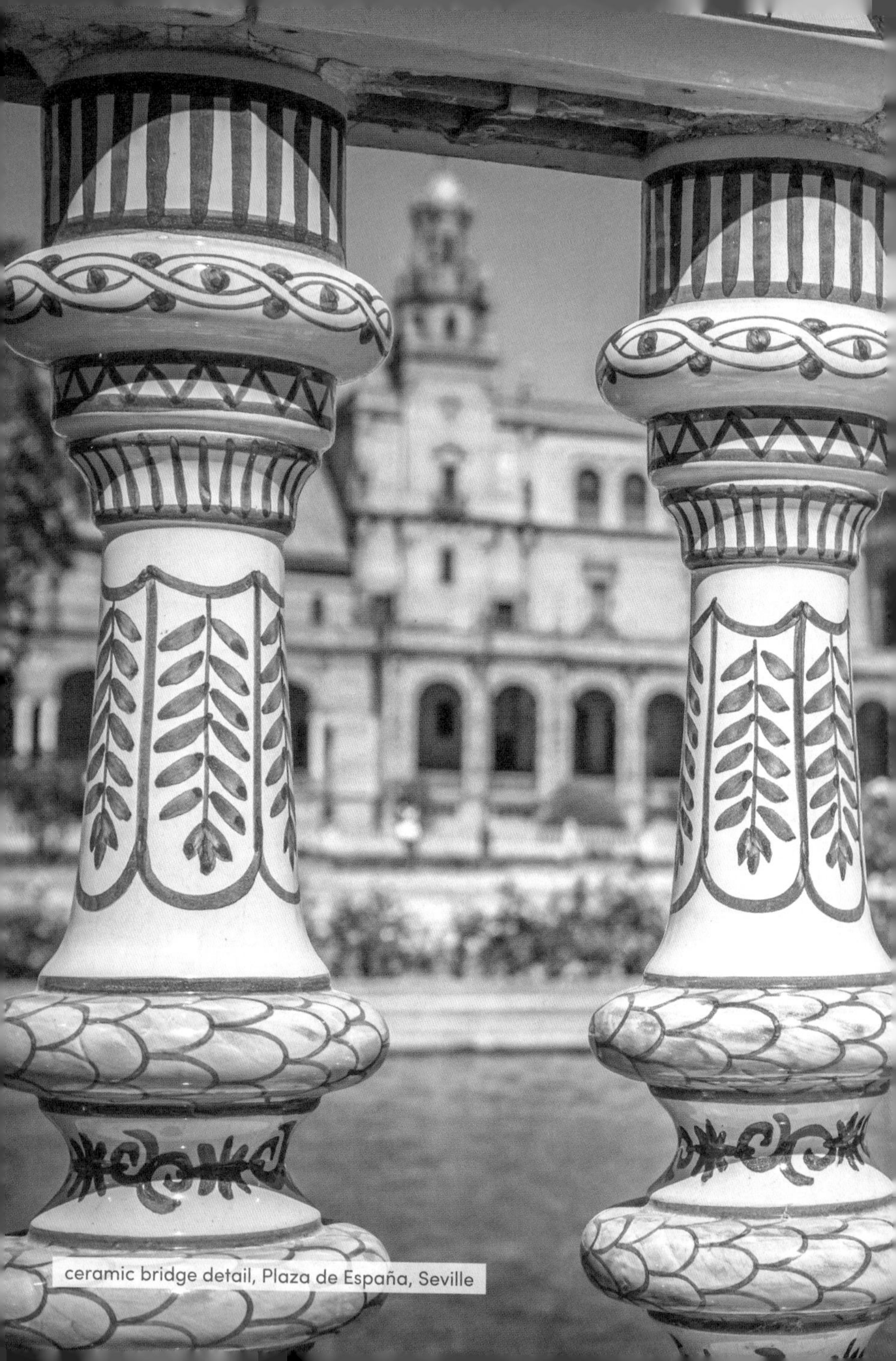

ceramic bridge detail, Plaza de España, Seville

WELCOME TO

Andalusia

Andalusia is a region that loves to celebrate. Whether it's the Patio Festival of Córdoba, the Semana Santa processions in Seville, or the weeklong Feria de Agosto in Málaga, it seems like every day there is a fiesta taking place somewhere. When people talk about the passion or spirit of Andalusia, this is what they mean.

In a way, the geography of Andalusia is the cause for all of this. Located at the southernmost tip of continental Spain, hugging the north face of the Strait of Gibraltar, staring down Africa to the south, with rivers flowing to both the Mediterranean Sea and the Atlantic Ocean, its geopolitical importance over thousands of years has fashioned vibrant cities, charming towns, and a picturesque countryside filled with colorful festivals, iconic architecture, and mouthwatering cuisine.

At the heart of Andalusia is the golden triangle of cities—Seville, Granada, and Córdoba—each with its own distinct character and appeal. Seville, the capital of Andalusia, is a city of contrasts, where ancient monuments and narrow alleyways meet modern art galleries and trendy restaurants. Granada, with its stunning Alhambra palace, is a cultural and architectural gem that has been drawing visitors for centuries. Córdoba, with its UNESCO-listed Mosque-Cathedral, is a city where the histories of Christianity, Islam, and Judaism intertwine.

From this triangle of urban exploration, you can continue your travels through rustic white villages like Ronda, chill on the beaches of Cádiz and Tarifa, or explore big nature in the mountainous national parks. To say nothing of evenings witnessing the intensity of flamenco performances in historic tablaos (flamenco venues) or days in centuries-old markets getting down with the locals.

With its warm climate, friendly people, fantastic cuisine, incredible history, and endless array of experiences, Andalusia is guaranteed to light the passion in your wanderlust soul.

Caminito del Rey

10 TOP
EXPERIENCES

1 Exploring the intricate palaces, lush gardens, and mesmerizing courtyards of the **Alhambra** as you witness this masterpiece of Moorish architecture (page 143).

2 Ascending the iconic Giralda tower for panoramic views of Seville after a morning in the awe-inspiring **Seville Cathedral,** the largest Gothic cathedral in the world (page 47).

3 Strolling through Seville's expansive and picturesque **Plaza de España** and marveling at the intricate ceramic tilework representing the different regions of Spain. Take a boat out on the moat for a romantic moment (page 55).

4 Immersing yourself in the architectural wonder of the **Mosque-Cathedral of Córdoba,** experiencing a unique juxtaposition of Islamic and Christian design (page 93).

5 Roaming the enchanting streets of Ronda and the nearby **white villages,** where charming, whitewashed buildings perch atop dramatic cliffs (page 287).

6 Hiking along the **Caminito del Rey,** an exhilarating pathway suspended along the steep walls of the El Chorro Gorge with stunning views of the rugged Andalusian landscape (page 313).

7 Savoring the flavors and nuances of Andalusia's liquid gold during an olive oil tasting at **LA Organic** (page 300).

8 Soaking up the Mediterranean breeze and vibrant atmosphere on the **sun-kissed beaches** of the Southern Coast (page 37).

9 Feeling the cultural heartbeat of Andalusia in the passionate rhythms and soulful melodies of traditional **flamenco** music (page 69).

10 Indulging in **tapas,** a diverse array of small, flavorful dishes that showcase seasonal specialties and the best of Andalusian cuisine (page 31).

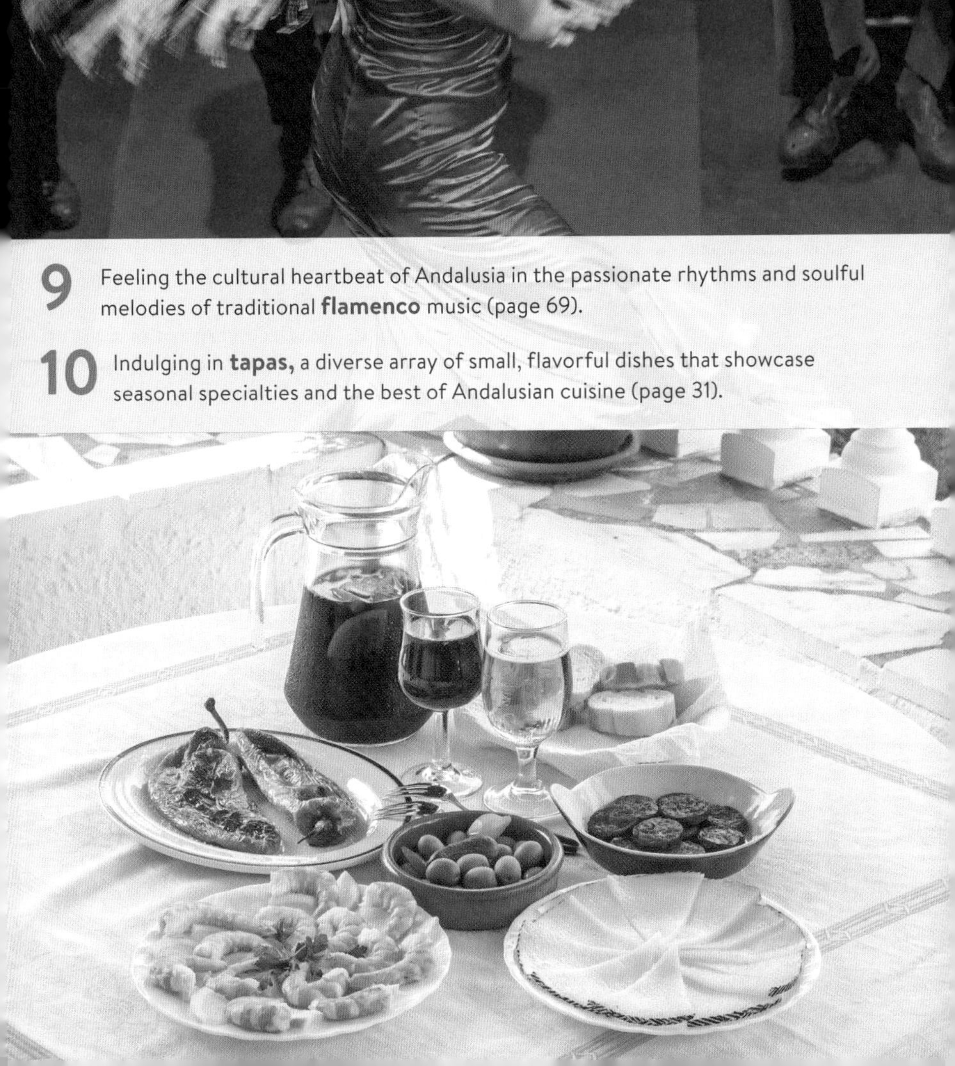

Planning Your Trip

WHERE TO GO

Seville

Seville is Andalusia's most vibrant, and most touristed, city. From flamenco to tapas bars, you'll find all the elements of Andalusia distilled here. There is a busy festival calendar as well as a slate of annual conferences, so pre-trip planning will go a long way in dodging the biggest crowds. Nearby, the Sierra Norte de Sevilla Natural Park is a haven for hikers.

Córdoba, Antequera, and El Torcal Nature Reserve

Córdoba boasts numerous World Heritage Sites, including its famed mosque-cathedral, as well as the lesser-known ruins of Medina Azahara, which, for a few decades, was the greatest city in all of Andalusia. In Antequera, you'll find traces of prehistory in the largest megalithic structures in continental Europe, while El Torcal Nature Reserve takes you even further back through time, into the last ice age when this region was under water.

ruins of Medina Azahara

Granada and the Sierra Nevada

The majestic Alhambra is the most popular site in all of Spain, and rightfully so. Reserve your tickets well in advance, but be sure to explore the rest of Granada. Though you can find tapas everywhere in Andalusia, no place does it like Granada. Nature lovers and those looking for a touch of the Andalusian countryside would do well to explore Sierra Nevada National Park, particularly the Alpujarras region, where charming villages dot the mountainside.

Málaga and the Southern Coast

Málaga has the seaside charm of an aged port town. If you can dodge the cruise ship crowds, you're in for a great time where the fresh catch and beachside vibes rule the afternoon. The home of Picasso has plenty of art and culture for a multiday stay to keep even the most erudite travelers engaged, though perhaps this region is most known for its many golf courses and beaches. You'll also be able to quickly cross the Strait of Gibraltar to Africa and the city of Tangier, Morocco, from the surfer town of Tarifa. Cádiz, the westernmost city on the coast, is well-connected with Seville and Jerez de la Frontera by train and can make a great coastal break from either location or as part of a larger exploration of the region.

Jerez de la Frontera and the White Villages

Accessible from either Cádiz or Seville, Jerez de la Frontera provides a glimpse into sherry and the horse culture that the south of Spain is renowned for. The famous white villages (pueblos blancos) are speckled throughout the mountains, each with its own long history and earthy nature. Ronda, with its impressive bridge, is perhaps the most famous. Throughout this area you can expect to be in touch with the farming, agriculture, and local festivals that truly lend soul to Andalusia. Nearby, one of the greatest walks in Spain, the Caminito del Rey, is tucked in the folds of this mountainous region.

WHEN TO GO

Andalusia is truly a year-round destination, though the interior region, including Seville, Córdoba, and Granada, can be extremely hot from April to October and quite cold, particularly at night, from November to March. Besides weather considerations, you will likely want to also look at the calendars for upcoming festivals, holidays, and even large conferences as these can impact your planning, whether you want to enjoy the festive atmosphere or avoid a location for crowd considerations. April, May, and August are typically the months with the most festivals on the calendar for towns and cities in the region. Surprisingly to some travelers, Christmas isn't as

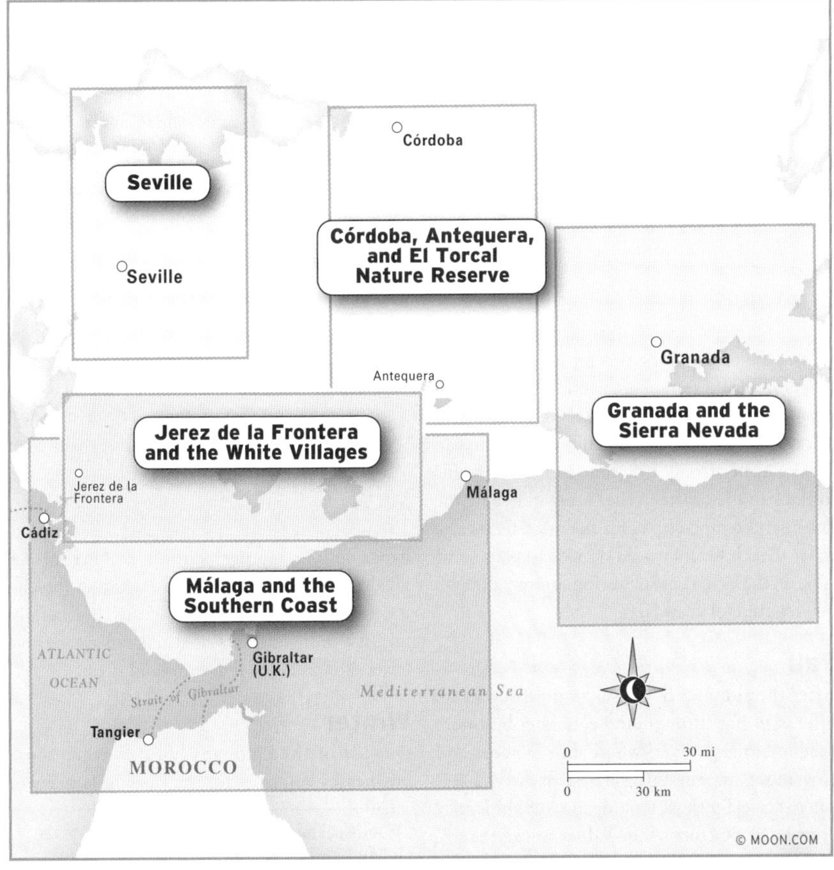

big of a holiday as Holy Week (Semana Santa, the week before Easter) and Epiphany (Día de los Reyes Magos, January 6), when many businesses will either be shuttered or have shorter hours for these celebrations.

Spring

When spring is sprung, count on more holidays and festivals than you can wave an abanico (folding fan) at. The biggest spring holiday is Holy Week, celebrated in the week leading up to Easter. Most businesses will have altered hours, and life comes to a standstill in most cities and towns for daily religious processions. One of the largest draws on the festival calendar is the Feria de Abril (April Festival) in Seville, where everyone is dressed to their most colorful nines. Nearly every town will have a version of a spring festival. In Córdoba, the month of May brings the annual Patio Festival, which is another huge draw. Earlier in spring, mountains will just be having their last snows, and toward April and May the fields will erupt in bloom. Along the coast, the beaches will be warming up, though the Mediterranean will still have its winter chill.

Summer

Inland, temperatures often soar over 40°C (100°F) during the day, making way for long, lazy afternoons where the notion of the traditional Spanish siesta truly starts to make sense. Granada is usually cooler as it is at altitude, though the sun can still be quite strong. Everyone in Europe seems to flock to the coasts in the summer, fleeing the hot inland temperatures for the more temperate coast. Beach lovers would do well to plan some time on the Costa del Sol during summer, though be prepared for crowds.

Fall

After the summer holidays, autumn settles in, often still hot throughout September but more moderate nearly everywhere into October and November, making this the best all-around season to travel for those looking to avoid the largest crowds. Into October, the Mediterranean Sea still hangs onto its summer warmth, making this an ideal time for quieter beaches, while in the cities, the lack of big holidays and festivals generally means a more business-as-usual experience and fewer crowds in the museums and sites.

Winter

Outside of the Epiphany holiday, when most businesses will close for the week of January 6,

If You Have . . .

THREE DAYS

Prioritize either Seville or Granada. Either of these cities has more than enough to keep you busy for three days. If you like a busier travel schedule, consider using one day to venture to one of the larger nearby towns, such as Jerez de la Frontera from Seville or Antequera from Granada.

FIVE DAYS

With five days, add in Córdoba. Be sure to allot time not only to the mosque-cathedral but also to the ruins of Medina Azahara. If you are driving, you will be able to connect through some smaller towns and villages—such as Montilla, Montefrío, Lucena, or Priego de Córdoba—on a road trip.

ONE WEEK

A full week gives you the opportunity to do three major cities, such as Seville, Córdoba, and Granada, as well as a smaller town or two. If you are driving, consider a circuit that takes you through Ronda and the white villages.

TWO WEEKS

With two weeks, you can easily spend 2-3 days in each of the major cities (Seville, Córdoba, Granada, and Málaga) as well as some time in the smaller villages, in the mountains, on the beaches, or even ferrying across the Strait of Gibraltar to dive into the continent of Africa at the up-and-coming port town of Tangier, Morocco.

1: Seville Cathedral **2:** traditional flamenco dress at the Feria de Abril festival **3:** Setenil de las Bodegas

1

2

3

some will be closed for Christmas. You can expect even fewer crowds than in the fall, though there's a higher likelihood of wet weather. The mountains will receive their annual snowfall, making the Sierra Nevada National Park an ideal destination if you want to make time for some snow sports with your travel companions.

BEFORE YOU GO

Passports and Visas

UK, EU, Australian, New Zealand, Canadian, and US nationals need to present a valid **passport** upon entry. Your passport should be valid for at least six months from your planned date of departure from Spain, though you will not need to present proof of return. Customs officials will stamp a valid **90-day tourist visa** in your passport on arrival.

For all nationalities, for stays of longer than 90 days you will need to request a visa from the nearest Spanish embassy or consulate in your home country. Students and employees traveling to the country for studies or work should be assisted through the visa process by the Spain-based university, school, or employer, which generally happens before you have entered and at the nearest Spanish consulate.

ETIAS Registration

https://etias.com

Beginning in 2025, all passport holders that do not require a Schengen Visa (i.e., US, Canadian, and British nationals) will need to enroll in the ETIAS program. The European Travel Information and Authorization System (ETIAS) is a travel security program to identify potential risks. Enrollment is €7 and will be obligatory.

Transportation

Air

Most travelers from North America, Australia, New Zealand, and elsewhere will likely connect through one of the European hubs, such Madrid or Paris, before connecting with their destination city in Andalusia. UK and EU travelers have a selection of direct flights with connections from most major European hubs to Seville, Granada, and Málaga.

For travelers renting a car, it will likely make the most sense to plan on an arrival/departure to/from Málaga, as car rental prices there tend to be much less expensive. Those preferring to travel by public transportation can benefit from Spain's high-speed rail network and consider a round-trip connecting with Madrid; from Madrid connect by train to one of the major cities in Andalusia.

Train

Two types of trains traverse all of Spain, including Andalusia: high-speed trains and normal, slower trains. High-speed trains are fast, efficient, and inexpensive, though they only connect to major cities, while the slower train network connects to many of the smaller towns and is generally even less expensive. Various companies run the different train services, though they all use the same track network of over 3,100 km (1,925 mi), the largest in all of Europe. Renfe (www.renfe.com) is the national rail service and operates a low-cost subsidiary, Avlo (https://avlorenfe.com), while OUIGO (www.ouigo.com) and iryo (https://iryo.eu) are private alternatives. Your choice will likely be based on availability more than anything else.

Bus

The bus network across the region will get you into many of the harder-to-reach villages that are not connected by rail. Alsa (http://alsa.com) is the largest bus company and operates the most extensive network, though in some regions you'll find that Transportes Generales Comes (www.tgcomes.es) or Flixbus (https://global.flixbus.com/bus/spain) has better options. Often this is the least expensive way to travel between destinations.

Car

For many travelers, renting a car is the way to go. As long as you hold a valid driver's license with your photo, you will not need an International Driver's Permit (IDP), though some rental agencies may require this. For what it's worth, I've never been asked for an IDP in over 20 years of traveling Spain and have been pulled over numerous times (speeding . . . always speeding), and my US license has been just fine. Drivers tend to be more aggressive than what you may be used to at home, and in the historic centers of major cities and smaller villages, there is always a confusing network of one-way streets. Parking is usually easy to find and the roads are mostly in fantastic condition. Rental cars, particularly in Málaga, can often be had for a bargain, with a small sedan costing as little as €10 a day. While driving between cities, keep in mind that there are sometimes tolled freeways, all of which accept either credit cards or cash, as well as non-paying autoroutes.

What to Pack

What to bring will be largely dependent on when you visit. Andalusia is a seasonal destination with very hot summers and surprisingly cold winters, particularly inland. Travelers should pack accordingly: lightweight, breathable clothing in the summer, jackets and sweaters in the winter. Comfortable walking shoes are essential, as is sunscreen, any time of year. Religious sites usually require shoulders to be covered, so a packable shirt, scarf, or shawl to go with sleeveless outfits can be handy.

A reusable water bottle and reusable shopping bag will cut down on waste, and you'll want a European plug adapter (two rounded pins) or two for charging your devices.

ski slopes of Sierra Nevada mountains

BEST OF Andalusia

Seville, Córdoba, and Granada

This highlights tour takes you on a whirlwind seven-day journey across some of the iconic palaces and cathedrals of Andalusia. Of course, you'll still have time for plenty of tasty tapas, interactive encounters, and dynamic experiences, such as the quintessential flamenco performances the region is known for. This is a tour you can easily do by rail.

Seville

Day 1

Spend your morning visiting the iconic **Seville Cathedral,** the largest Gothic cathedral in the world, during an informative cathedral tour. Following, head to the historic **Royal Alcázar of Seville,** a stunning palace complex with intricate architecture and beautiful gardens. After a morning of sightseeing, you'll be famished, so enjoy a leisurely lunch at **Sal Gorda.** In the afternoon, wander through the charming **Barrio Santa Cruz,** known for its narrow streets, colorful patios, and historical charm. Follow this with a sunset boat tour along the **Guadalquivir River** and enjoy the views. For dinner, consider **Veneria San Telmo** for some classic Andalusian offerings.

Day 2

Head to **Hispalis Café** to fully caffeinate for the adventurous day ahead. Start with a morning **bike tour** that takes you through the **María Luisa Park** and historic, picturesque **Plaza de España,** an architectural masterpiece showcasing a semicircular building adorned with colorful tiles representing different regions of Spain. Check in your bike and get ready for a culinary treat on a market tour of the lively **Triana Market** to experience a variety of fresh produce and local delicacies. In the evening, head over to the happening **Macarena neighborhood** and ascend the **Metropol Parasol** with its panoramic views of the city. Keep it hip for dinner and head to **Abantal.**

Day 3

Head out of Seville this morning for a day trip into Roman history in nearby Santiponce. Here you will discover the birthplace of two Roman emperors in the once powerful city of **Itálica.** Head back into Seville for tapas and a lazy stroll along the **Guadalquivir River.** Breathe in your last moments in Seville and consider taking in a **flamenco** performance at one of the many storied tablaos (flamenco venues). Cap off your time in Seville with dinner at **Maria Trifulca,** enjoying a blend of modern and traditional Spanish cuisine.

Córdoba

Day 4

Start your day with a Spanish breakfast and coffee, then take a train from the Santa Justa train station 45 minutes to Córdoba's central station. Visit the **Mosque-Cathedral of Córdoba** and explore the **Jewish Quarter** on foot, including the **Synagogue of Córdoba.** Have traditional tapas for lunch at **Bodega San Basilio.** In the afternoon, visit the **Royal Palace of Isabella and Ferdinand** and walk along the **Roman Bridge.** Enjoy organic wines with your dinner at **Restaurante La Boca** before sauntering home.

Day 5

Directly after breakfast, head to the archaeological site of **Medina Azahara,** a stunning medieval palace-city that offers a glimpse into the city's rich history. Spend the morning exploring the well-preserved ruins and marvel at the Islamic architecture. Afterward, return to Córdoba for a leisurely Arab-inspired lunch at **Restaurante Damasco.** In the afternoon, visit the **Calahorra Tower** and stop by the **Association of the Friends of the Patios** to glimpse a few of the famously flowered Cordoban patios. Treat yourself to updated Spanish cuisine at **Regadera** before striking out for an evening promenade through the **historic city center** to take in the city at night.

Granada

Day 6

From Córdoba's central station, take the high-speed train 1.5 hours to the Granada station and head straight to the majestic **Alhambra,** a UNESCO World Heritage Site, for a day of exploration. Pay special attention to your time of entry for the **Nasrid Palaces.** When you need a breather from exploring everything from the **Generalife gardens** to the **Alcazaba fortress,** have a cool ajo blanco soup at **Restaurant du Parador de Granada** and enjoy the views. Take a walk down through the **Alhambra Forest** to town, and as night falls, have a relaxing dinner at **Poetas Andaluces II** before tucking in after a long day.

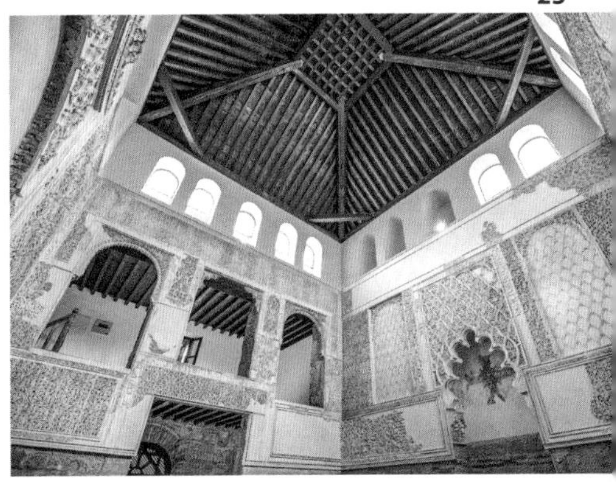

Synagogue of Córdoba

Day 7

Pick up a coffee and pastry at **Atypica Coffee,** then meet up with your guide for a private walking tour of the **Albaicín Alto** and **Bajo districts,** the old Arab quarters of Granada, which feature narrow winding streets and a Moorish influence. In the afternoon, visit the **Granada Cathedral** and maybe do a little shopping in **La Alcaicería** next door. Take a stroll up the **Carrera del Darro,** soaking in the charming atmosphere. For dinner, consider a self-guided tapas tour along **Calle Navas** or head to **María la Canastera** to experience the heart and soul of flamenco over a lovely meal in the famous **Sacromonte caves.**

1

2

IN THE SPOTLIGHT

Islam in Andalusia

The early 8th century marked the beginning of Islamic rule in the Iberian Peninsula, when Umayyad forces crossed the Strait of Gibraltar and established the caliphate of Córdoba. For nearly 800 years, Andalusia thrived as a beacon of cultural exchange, religious tolerance, and intellectual advancement under Muslim rule. Córdoba, the capital, became a center of learning, housing libraries and universities that attracted scholars from across the known world. The Great Mosque of Córdoba, with its intricate architecture and splendid artistry, is an enduring testament to the flourishing Islamic civilization that once graced the region.

Beyond religious institutions, the influence of Islam is evident in the art, cuisine, and daily life of Andalusia. Arabesque designs grace the architecture of contemporary buildings, and the echoes of Islamic poetry linger in the traditional flamenco music. The Albaicín district in Granada and Barrio de la Villa in Priego de Córdoba, with their narrow winding streets and whitewashed houses, preserve the ambience of medieval Moorish neighborhoods, offering a glimpse into the historical coexistence of diverse communities.

While the history of Islamic rule in Andalusia is revered, the contemporary Muslim experience in the region is not without its challenges. Issues of cultural integration, religious understanding, and social inclusion persist, particularly in the face of societal changes and global events. However, the Muslim community actively engages in dialogue and educational initiatives to foster understanding and bridge cultural divides.

Architecture

- **Royal Alcázar of Seville:** The royal palace of Seville is over 1,100 years old. It was built for Abd al-Rahman III, the first ruler of the Andalusian caliphate, and enjoyed by rulers of Spain for a millennium (page 47).
- **Mosque-Cathedral of Córdoba:** This masterpiece of 10th-century Islamic architecture was once one of the world's largest mosques (page 93).
- **Barrio de la Villa:** This knot of geranium-lined, whitewashed walls is perhaps the best preserved medieval Islamic neighborhood in Andalusia (page 112).
- **Alhambra:** The Alhambra complex is without a doubt the crown jewel of Islamic heritage in Andalusia (page 143).

Art

- **Alhambra:** The Partal Palace, a section of the Alhambra, has some of the only known examples of Nasrid-era paintings in the world, with *The Ten Nasrid Kings* being of particular importance (page 143).
- **Laguna Taracea:** This workshop builds intricate re-creations of ornate wood furniture that once decorated the Alhambra (page 148).
- **La Alcaicería:** This touristy bazaar has countless artisanal goods from Morocco, from pottery to leather bags and poufs. Exploring the bazaar is a great way to get a sense of the artistry of the Islamic world (page 152).

Cuisine

- **Restaurante Jaima los Llanos:** For a cultural lunch outing, try family-run Jaima los Llanos, where you can expect a halal menu and enjoy Arabic music and art (page 197).
- **Chez Hassan:** It doesn't get more down-to-earth delicious than at this classic streetside café with seasonally fresh Moroccan tajines made fresh on order (page 255).

1: detail of Córdoba's Mosque-Cathedral **2:** the Court of the Lions at the Alhambra

Grand Tour of Andalusia

For those with more flexible travel schedules, more time means more ability to get out of the main travel hubs and into the diverse landscape of greater Andalusia and the famed white villages of the mountains. This itinerary is a great mix of urban exploration with rustic landscapes and plenty of experiences to get you as culturally immersed as possible in the time you have. This a tour best done with a private driver or by renting a car, though if you are renting a car, know that you will leave your vehicle at the border crossings for Gibraltar and Tangier. With some additional planning, you could also do this tour using the local train and bus systems.

Seville

Day 1

Make the most of your time and take a fun, informative private tour that includes the **Seville Cathedral, Royal Alcázar of Seville,** and a walking tour of the **Barrio Santa Cruz.** Continue into the **Triana Market** for lunch. Stay around Triana to enjoy a flamenco show at the **Teatro Flamenco Triana.** Make your way across the Guadalquivir River for fine dining at **Abantal.**

Day 2

After coffee at **Hispalis Café,** take a long walk through **María Luisa Park,** which holds the **Plaza de España** and **Plaza de América.** Plan on a picnic lunch in the park. In the evening, head over for a tapas tour through the **Barrio Santa Cruz.**

Jerez de la Frontera and the White Villages

Day 3

Dip into some churros con chocolate at **Café Catunambu** and drive (or take the train) to Jerez de la Frontera. Explore the **Cathedral of San Salvador** and the **Alcázar of Jerez de la Frontera** before viewing the Baroque dressage at the **Royal Andalusian School of Equestrian Art.** Enjoy some traditional tapas at **Tabanco El Pasaje,** and follow up with a sherry tour at **Bodegas González Byass.** Consider stumbling through Jerez's famous walking sherry route, nibbling your way through dinner.

Day 4

In your car, cross the **Puente Nuevo** over the **Tajo de Ronda** gorge into the old town of **Ronda.** Park and, after a morning of exploring the city on foot, head to **Pedro Romero** for a traditional paella lunch. Following, head out to **LA Organic** for an olive oil tasting and enjoy a sunset paseo (walk) with the locals in the **Alameda del Tajo park.**

Gibraltar and Tarifa

Day 5

Make your way out of the mountains and down to the **Costa del Sol.** Park your car in La Linea and cross the British border on foot onto UK soil for a day trip into **Gibraltar** and the impressive **Rock of Gibraltar,** where you can visit macaque monkeys and delve into World War II history. After a fish-and-chips lunch, return to your car and head to **Tarifa.** Explore the small old city of Tarifa and stroll along **Tarifa Beach** to work up an appetite. Enjoy a breezy barbecue at **Braseria Vaca Loca** before turning in for the night.

Tangier

Day 6

Leave your car at the port in Tarifa, and board the morning ferry for **Tangier.** Spend the day exploring the **kasbah** and **medina.** Be sure to include a stop at the **American Legation.** The **restored synagogues** and **Church of Saint Andrew** are also interesting stops in this Muslim country. Afternoon tea at **Café Hafa** is a must, while **M Restaurant** is a good choice for dinner for French-Moroccan fusion.

1: sherry pour at Bodegas González Byass **2:** Ronda
3: El Torcal Nature Reserve

Day 7

Explore the **Donabo Gardens** and **Perdicaris Park** this morning to keep it active and get a feel for the nature of the area. Lunch at the storied **Villa Mabrouka** before relaxing into a luxuriously steamy hammam at **l'Abyssin de Tanger.**

Málaga

Day 8

Ferry back to Tarifa and continue to **Málaga** by car. Lunch at **Restaurante José Carlos Garcia** with a focus on freshly caught seafood. Walk off your lunch starting at the **Gibralfaro Castle,** making your way downhill to explore the **Alcazaba of Málaga** and nearby **Roman Theater.** In the evening take in Málaga's **historic center** and the **Picasso Museum.** End your day at **Malagueta Beach** for a sunset stroll and beachside dinner.

Day 9

After grabbing a coffee at **Mia Café** head over to the **Atarazanas Market.** Spend the morning checking out the market goods and stick around for lunch. Málaga is an enjoyable walking destination, so stroll the **Alameda Principal** and continue along the port and the sea. At the close of the afternoon, head to the rooftops of the **Málaga Cathedral** for sunset. For dinner, head to **La Deriva** for a taste of contemporary Andalusian cuisine.

Antequera and Granada

Day 10

Hop in the car and head to **Antequera.** Tour the **Alcazaba of Antequera** and the **megalithic dolmens** of Antequera in the morning. Lunch at **Arte de Cozina** for delicious, hearty Andalusian cooking and then walk it off beneath the natural rock sculpture formations of **El Torcal Nature Reserve.** Time allowing, consider a howling good time with the wolves of nearby **Lobo Park Wolf Sanctuary.** Plan on arriving in **Granada** just before dinner.

Day 11

Make the most of your time and splurge on a private guided tour of the **Alhambra.** With a guide, you can easily see the **Nasrid Palaces, Generalife gardens,** and **Alcazaba fortress** all before lunch. Linger over lunch at the **Restaurant du Parador de Granada** before walking down into Granada through the **Alhambra Forest.** For dinner, consider asking your guide for a private **tapas tour.**

Day 12

In the morning, visit the **Granada Cathedral** and neighboring **La Alcaicería.** Pause for lunch and some people-watching at **La Auténtica Carmela.** Take a stroll up the **Carrera del Darro** and continue on to the **Albaicín Bajo district.** Enjoy sunset views of the **Alhambra** and street musicians on the **Plaza de San Nicolás** before heading to the **Sacromonte neighborhood** for a flamenco performance and dinner at **María la Canastera** in the caves.

Córdoba

Day 13

Stop into the archaeological site of **Medina Azahara** on your way to **Córdoba.** Once in Córdoba, energize over lunch at **Casa Mazal Restaurante Sefardí** before taking a walking tour of the **Mosque-Cathedral** and **Jewish Quarter.** Enjoy dinner at **Regadera** and, if you're staying at **Palacio del Bailío,** dip into the baths for an ideal end to a long journey of Andalusian exploration.

Day 14

Have one last churros con chocolate for breakfast before either taking a taxi or returning your rental car at the **Seville Airport** and connecting with your flight out. You could also easily take a train up to **Madrid** and fly out from there. Bid adios, or better yet, hasta pronto, to Andalusia!

Tapas, Tapas, Tapas!

While in Andalusia, or anywhere else in Spain, you will undoubtedly come across the sometimes confusing world of tapas. Tapas are small dishes that can be served cold (such as slices of aged cheese or Iberian ham) or hot (like fried chorizo in garlic or baked clams). The menus and ordering system vary regionally, from city to city, while even some bars have their own sort of tapas culture.

ORDERING

In some bars and cafés, with each drink order, a tapa will automatically come free. In these establishments, there is usually no choosing. You just get what you get. This is very typical in Granada and the surrounding towns. In some places, such as Seville and Málaga, you may have to pay a nominal amount (€1-3) for a small tapa, though you will be able to choose which tapa you want.

Seasoned travelers should come prepared with a few words in Spanish. Simply learn to say, for example, "Una caña y una tapa, por favor! Gracias!" One small beer and a tapa, please!

You should know that draft beer generally comes in three sizes: caña, tubo, and jarra (small, medium, and large), and a bottle is a botella. Wine comes by the chato (glass) with your choice of vino tinto or vino blanco (red or white). Two of the more popular types of reds come from Rioja and Ribero del Duero, though locally Montilla (near Córdoba) has some great wines as well.

COMMON TAPAS DISHES

- **Queso:** semi-hard cheese, usually cured in olive oil; generally queso manchego
- **Jamón ibérico:** Iberian ham
- **Aceitunas:** olives, usually stuffed with anchovies or red pepper
- **Bacalao:** salted cod
- **Boquerones:** white anchovies cured in vinegar and garlic
- **Ensaladilla rusa:** potato salad, often with tuna and vegetables
- **Patatas bravas:** fried potato cubes, usually served with a spicy tomato sauce
- **Tortilla española:** a type of frittata with fried potatoes and onions

ANDALUSIAN SPECIALTIES

- **Rabo de toro:** literally "bull tail," this oxtail stew is a classic traditional dish (throughout Andalusia)
- **Cazón en adobo:** marinated, fried fish cubes (Seville)
- **Patatas a lo pobre:** slow-fried potatoes in garlic, pepper, and often chorizo (Granada)
- **Flamenquín:** deep-fried pork rolls (Córdoba)

WHERE TO TRY TAPAS

- **Seville:** La Casa Fundida (page 78)
- **Córdoba:** Bodega San Basilio (page 104)
- **Granada:** Braserito (page 166)
- **Málaga:** El Mesón de Cervantes (page 224)
- **Jerez de la Frontera:** Tabanco El Pasaje (page 285)

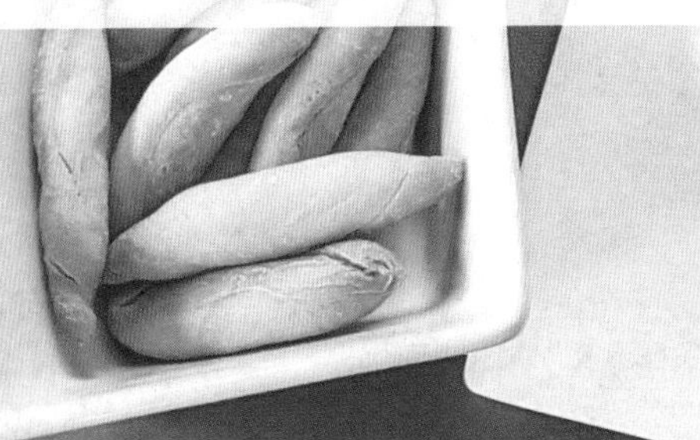

Family Adventure for Fun-Seekers

Welcome to Andalusia, where every corner unfolds new adventures for the young and the young at heart.

Picture this: vibrant flamenco beats, the scent of orange blossoms wafting through the air, and a burst of color that'll make your family photos pop. Andalusia promises laughter, learning, and loads of family fun, especially at the following destinations.

ART

In **Málaga,** the birthplace of Picasso, the inner artist in you and your little ones will be united. Channel your family's creativity at the Picasso Museum, where the art of the master meets the budding talents of your mini-Picassos.

HISTORY

In **Granada,** the whimsical Alhambra will send exploration into high gear as the kids Indiana Jones into ancient palaces and mystical gardens, and maybe discover a secret passage or two. Who says history can't be an adventure?

CULTURE

The culturally curious can hop on a ferry and cross into Africa, where the busy markets, exotic scents, and vibrant street life of **Tangier** will transport your family to a world where adventure meets cultural discovery. Don't forget to haggle for some souvenirs!

BEACHES

Of course, beaches are usually an easy win for kids of all ages. The long stretches of beach along the Costa del Sol, from **Málaga** to **Cádiz,** offer plenty of sandy stretches to build towering sandcastles, join a beach volleyball match, throw the Frisbee, or simply lounge into some old-fashioned sunbathing.

NATURE

The mountains of Andalusia beckon nature lovers with numerous national parks and nature reserves, dotted with crisscrossing trails and even ski slopes in the winter. Smaller city parks, like the Parque de la Negrita in **Antequera,** provide a pleasant green space for little ones, while the Lobo Park Wolf Sanctuary near El Torcal Nature Reserve can make for an educational encounter with elusive wildlife.

ADVENTURE

For more active families, there is plenty of thrill-seeking in **Tarifa.** Trade your family sedan for a windsurfing board, as this coastal gem is Europe's wind capital. Release your inner daredevils, catch some waves, and make memories that will leave you all windswept and grinning.

And have you ever seen dolphins dance? Head to **Gibraltar** for an unforgettable dolphin safari. Your family will be treated to a spectacular show by the ocean's acrobats, complete with giggles, gasps, and maybe a splash or two.

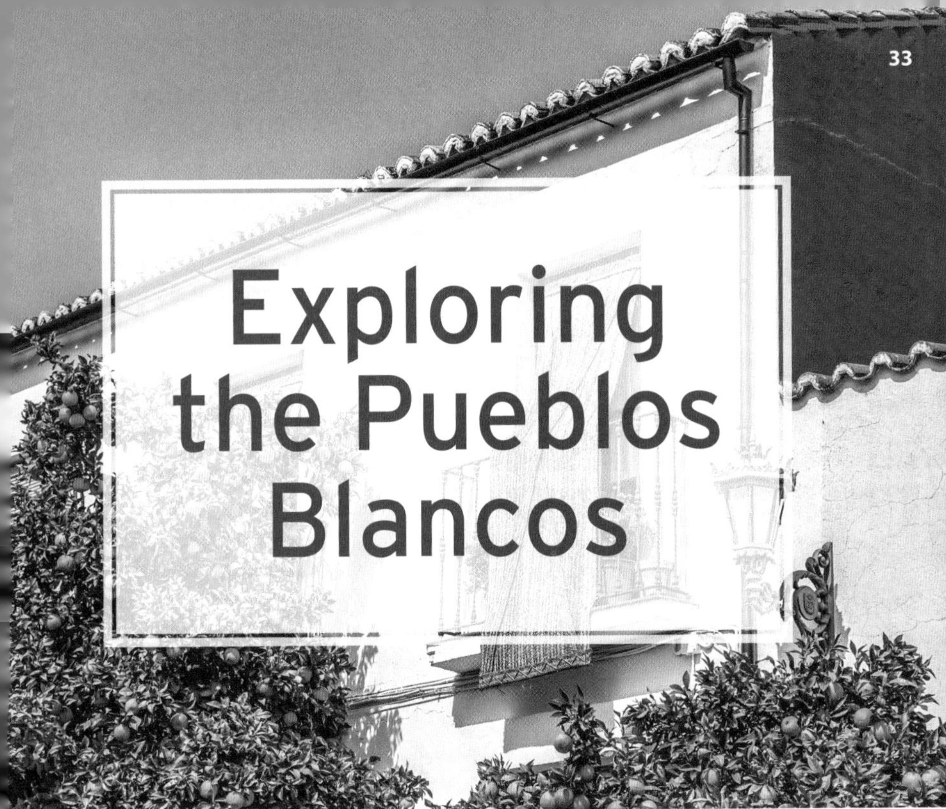

Exploring the Pueblos Blancos

The warmth and charm of Andalusia is perhaps best felt in the numerous rustic pueblos blancos, or white villages, that dot its mountainous interior. A few days exploring this countryside will connect you more with the salt-of-the-earth people, their traditions, and their ways of life, not to mention some of the most spectacular nature found in all of Spain and one of the most incredible walks along the Caminito del Rey.

Ronda

Day 1

Cross the **Puente Nuevo** over the **Tajo de Ronda** into the old town of **Ronda.** After a morning of exploring the city on foot, head to **Pedro Romero** for a traditional paella lunch. Round out your exploration at the **Casa del Rey Moro** and descend the stairs of the Puente Nuevo to get a view looking back up at Ronda.

Day 2

Enjoy a quiet morning over some churros before heading out for an olive oil tasting at **LA Organic.** Afterward, take a paseo (stroll) through the **Alameda del Tajo park.** Rub elbows with the locals at **Lechuguita** over tapas for a light dinner.

Setenil de las Bodegas and Grazalema

Day 3

Start off in **Setenil de las Bodegas,** where you can discover the charming village and its cave houses built into the cliff surrounding part of the village. **Gloria Bendita** is a good spot for lunch before you head on to **Grazalema.** Be sure to give yourself some time for a short hike into **Sierra de Grazalema Natural Park.** You'll want to head into **Cádiz el Chico** for a wild jabalí (boar) dinner.

Caminito del Rey

Day 4

Plan on spending half of the day hiking the heights of the **Caminito del Rey.** You'll likely spend 2-3 hours on the hike, and if the weather is warm, take a relaxing dip in the **Guadalhorce Reservoir.** A light lunch along the shores with the locals will be just the thing. Tuck into one of the famous countryside **haciendas** or **fincas** for your last night in the mountains.

Sierra de las Nieves National Park

Day 5

Get in touch with the Andalusian countryside. To complete your stay, head out horseback riding or consider a longer hike into **Sierra de las Nieves National Park.** Whatever you do, prioritize connecting with nature and enjoying some of the more rural, heartfelt hospitality of the region.

1: Ronda **2:** hiking in Sierra de las Nieves **3:** Caminito del Rey

Costa del Sol Road Trip

The sun-kissed shores of the Costa del Sol, a stretch of coastline in southern Spain known for its golden beaches, vibrant cities, and cultural diversity, is best from spring to fall, with the summer months busy with tourists from around Europe. In less than one week, you will visit three countries on two continents, all while enjoying some of the Mediterranean's finest beaches. Though you could do this tour using the confusing network of local buses, having a rental car would give you more flexibility, even if you do have to leave it parked in Tarifa for a night or two for the crossing into Tangier.

Málaga

Day 1

Start your exploration in historic Málaga, visiting the **Gibralfaro Castle** and admiring the views before heading downhill to the **Alcazaba of Málaga** and the nearby **Roman Theater.** Head over to the **Atarazanas Market** for lunch. Walk through the shady **Málaga Park** on your way to **Malagueta Beach** for an afternoon stroll or lounge on the sand.

Day 2

In the morning, strike out for Málaga's **historic center.** Admire works from the master in the **Picasso Museum.** Lunch at **Restaurante José Carlos Garcia** and then pick another local-favorite beach, like **Maro Beach,** to enjoy the sun.

Gibraltar and Tarifa

Day 3

From Málaga, make your way down the **Costa del Sol.** You will cross into the United Kingdom for a day trip into **Gibraltar** to see the **Rock of Gibraltar** and the resident macaque monkeys. Dip into **The Clipper** for some British pub fare

Roman Theater in Málaga

for lunch and then move on to **Tarifa.** Watch the kitesurfers zooming while you stroll along **Tarifa Beach,** and enjoy **Braseria Vaca Loca** for dinner.

Tangier

Day 4

Get ready for a day on the water. In the morning, strike out from Tarifa for a **whale-watching** exploration. **Bossa** makes for a nice lunch stop before catching the **ferry to Tangier.** Once in Tangier, you will want to enjoy Moroccan dining at **Restaurant Rif Kebdani** before tucking into a local riad for the night.

Day 5

Take a private guided tour of the **kasbah** and **medina** with stops at the **medina souks** (markets) and the **American Legation.** Take an afternoon tea at **Café Hafa** before heading on to explore the Atlantic Coast with the **Caves of Hercules** and **Cap Spartel.** Time and weather allowing, enjoy a walk in the **Donabo Gardens** or **Perdicaris Park** before relaxing in a **Moroccan hammam** and then catching **a late ferry** back to Tarifa.

Cádiz

Day 6

Wake up in Tarifa and stop by **La Tarifeña Bakery** for some treats before heading on to Cádiz. Start your exploration of Cádiz with an inspired **tapas tour** with Adriane (Adri) Anderson for lunch. Spend the rest of the afternoon exploring the **Cádiz Cathedral** and **Torre Tavira** in the historic Casco Antiguo. Round out your day with a seafood dinner at **Restaurante Cádiz Taberna Almercén.**

Day 7

Slip on your swimsuit and head down to **Santa María Beach** to enjoy some fun in the sun. When you feel nibbly, strike into the new town to **Bar El Cucharón** for tapas before heading back out. For a grand finale to your Costa del Sol exploration, spelunk into **La Cueva del Pajaro Azul** for one of the finest flamenco performances in Andalusia.

Cádiz

Best Beaches of Andalusia's Southern Coast

Sun. Sand. Surf. What more could you ask for to unwind while traveling around Andalusia? This entire region is spoiled with some great beaches. Some are wild. Some are urban. And all of them promise to deliver a few hours of fun in the sun. Just don't forget the sunscreen, beach towels, and bottles of water.

MOST CONVENIENT

Malagueta Beach: You basically walk across the street from the historic center of Málaga and you find yourself on this fine stretch of sand. With all the amenities you might want and great dining options within just a few minutes' walk, it's hard to argue with the convenience of this beach (page 220).

BEST FOR FAMILIES

Palo Beach: The natural protection offered by the small half-moon bays along this beach results in calmer waters for the young ones to splash and paddle. There are lifeguards always on duty, showers, and bathrooms, as well as delicious options for barbecued goodness that cater to all ages. Here you'll have an easy day out with the kids while on vacay (page 221).

BEST FOR THRILL-SEEKERS

Tarifa Beach: Hop on your board, grab your kite, and find a draft to pull. This beach is a kitesurfer's mecca. With near-constant stiff breezes shooting through the Strait of Gibraltar, this is a spot for those who like to grab life by the control bar and take flight (page 239).

BEST FOR A WORKOUT

Valdevaqueros Beach: Travel just 10 minutes from Tarifa to find yourself at this charming little beach, popular with locals. The distinctive dune formations alongside the forest, sea, and mountains offer various hiking possibilities. It makes for a great day out (page 241).

BEST VIEWS

La Caleta: Located at the northwestern corner of Cádiz's Casco Antiguo, La Caleta offers views of the San Sebastián and Santa Catalina castles to the north and south. To the west, you'll find rippling curls of the Atlantic Ocean—and one of the best places to catch a golden sunset in Spain, if not all of Europe (page 263).

Seville

Seville, the capital of Andalusia, is a city that will take your breath away with its rich history and stunning architecture. With a history dating back to Roman times, Seville is a city of many layers, with influences from the Moorish, Christian, and Jewish cultures. The city is perhaps best known for its UNESCO-listed cathedral, the largest Gothic cathedral in the world, which houses the tomb of Christopher Columbus. Adjacent to the cathedral is the famous Giralda tower, which was originally built as a minaret during the Muslim rule of Andalusia.

Seville's old town, known as Barrio Santa Cruz, is a maze of narrow cobblestone streets and alleys, dotted with orange trees and charming plazas. The Royal Alcázar of Seville, a palace built in the 14th century,

Highlights

Look for ★ to find recommended sights, activities, dining, and lodging.

★ **Royal Alcázar of Seville:** This palace complex boasts stunning architecture, beautiful gardens, and rich history (page 47).

★ **Seville Cathedral:** As one of the largest cathedrals in the world, the Seville Cathedral is a must-see for visitors. Make sure to climb the Giralda tower for views of the city (page 47).

★ **Metropol Parasol:** This futuristic wooden structure in the center of Seville offers breathtaking views of the city from above (page 52).

★ **Plaza de España:** This grand square in the sprawling María Luisa Park is a beautiful example of Spanish Renaissance Revival architecture and is home to a lovely canal (page 55).

★ **Triana Market:** Across the river from the city center, Triana is a lively neighborhood known for its vibrant nightlife, flamenco culture, and beautiful ceramic tiles, though the biggest draw is its traditional covered market. Visit popular local eateries and vendors selling seasonal legumes, Spanish cheeses, and cured meats (page 57).

★ **Flamenco Shows:** Seville is the heartland of flamenco. Flamenco is more than just dance; it is a way of life that shows the soul of Spain. Make sure to check out a flamenco show while in town (page 69).

★ **Tapas Bars:** Numerous tapas bars in the historic Jewish quarter of Seville, the Barrio Santa Cruz, highlight Sevillian cuisine (page 74).

Greater Seville

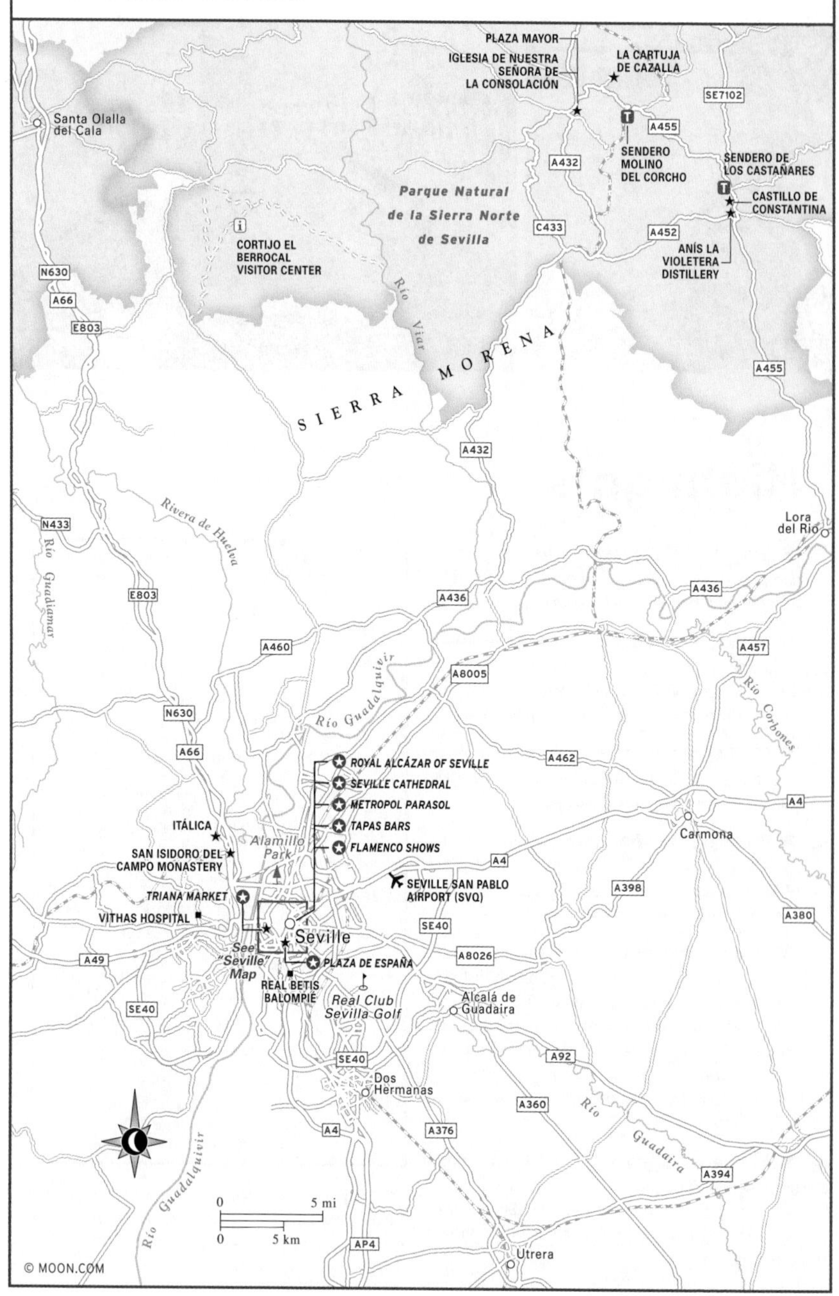
PLAZA MAYOR
IGLESIA DE NUESTRA SEÑORA DE LA CONSOLACIÓN
LA CARTUJA DE CAZALLA
Santa Olalla del Cala
SE7102
A455
A432
SENDERO MOLINO DEL CORCHO
SENDERO DE LOS CASTAÑARES
Parque Natural de la Sierra Norte de Sevilla
CASTILLO DE CONSTANTINA
C433
A452
CORTIJO EL BERROCAL VISITOR CENTER
ANÍS LA VIOLETERA DISTILLERY
N630
A66
E803
Río Viar
SIERRA MORENA
A455
A432
Rivera de Huelva
N433
Río Guadiamar
Lora del Río
E803
A436
A436
A460
A457
A8005
Río Guadalquivir
Río Corbones
N630
A66
A462
ROYAL ALCÁZAR OF SEVILLE
SEVILLE CATHEDRAL
METROPOL PARASOL
TAPAS BARS
FLAMENCO SHOWS
A4
ITÁLICA
Alamillo Park
Carmona
SAN ISIDORO DEL CAMPO MONASTERY
A4
SEVILLE SAN PABLO AIRPORT (SVQ)
TRIANA MARKET
A398
VITHAS HOSPITAL
SE40
A380
Seville
A8026
See "Seville" Map
A49
PLAZA DE ESPAÑA
REAL BETIS BALOMPIÉ
Real Club Sevilla Golf
Alcalá de Guadaira
SE40
A92
SE40
Dos Hermanas
A360
Río Guadaira
A4
A376
Río Guadalquivir
A394
0 5 mi
0 5 km
AP4
Utrera
© MOON.COM

is a stunning example of Mudejar architecture and is a must-visit attraction. The palace's lush gardens, fountains, and courtyards offer a peaceful respite from the bustling city streets.

Seville is also famous for its flamenco performances, which can be enjoyed at several venues throughout the city. The Triana neighborhood, across the river from Barrio Santa Cruz, is home to several flamenco schools and venues and is considered by some to be the birthplace of flamenco, though of course this history is very much debatable.

To the north, you can find one of Seville's best-kept secrets, the wooded Sierra Norte de Sevilla Natural Park. The oak and holm forests transform with their autumn foliage, making for distinct natural beauty in this part of Andalusia that might have you reflecting on New England. For nature lovers, a day trip to explore the park and its villages is a good companion to the urban exploration of Seville.

HISTORY

Welcome to Seville, the vibrant gem of Andalusia! Prepare to embark on a captivating journey through history, where tales of conquerors, explorers, and flamenco melodies intertwine. From its ancient roots to its modern-day allure, Seville is a city that begs you to explore its rich history and culture. Hop aboard your metaphorical time machine and set off on an adventure!

Our voyage commences in the mists of time, as we uncover the city's ancient foundations. Seville's history dates back over 2,000 years, with evidence of settlement by the Tartessians and Phoenicians. It later flourished as a Roman metropolis named Hispalis, boasting impressive structures like the grand amphitheater, whose ruins can still be admired today.

Fast forward to the 8th century, when the Moors swept across the Iberian Peninsula. Seville quickly became an important center of power within the Umayyad caliphate of Al-Andalus (Andalusia), with the Umayyad emirs and caliphs establishing their capital here. The reign of the Umayyads lasted until 1031, after which Al-Andalus fragmented into smaller taifa kingdoms. Under the Islamic rule, Seville thrived as Isbiliya (pronounced "ees-bee-LEE-yah" in Arabic, derived from the original Roman name of the city, Hispalis) and became one of the great intellectual and cultural epicenters of Europe. Subsequent dynasties, including the Abbadid and Almoravid dynasties, continued Seville's rise to prominence. However, it was under the Almohads, a Moroccan dynasty that conquered the region in 1171, that Seville saw its grandest architectural projects, including the Giralda minaret and great expansion of the Alcázar. No visit to Seville is complete without a visit to these two architectural marvels that epitomize Andalusia's Islamic legacy. Stroll through the charming narrow streets of the Barrio Santa Cruz and let your imagination transport you to this Islamic era of bustling souks, graceful palaces, and opulent gardens.

In 1248, Seville was finally captured by Christian forces led by Ferdinand III of Castile as part of the larger Reconquista. This marked the end of Islamic rule in Seville, and the city became part of the Christian kingdom of Castile.

Seville's role as a gateway to the New World played a pivotal role in shaping its destiny during the Age of Exploration. In the 16th century, the city became the epicenter of Spain's maritime empire as fleets laden with treasures from the Americas docked at its port. Seville's golden era is embodied by the iconic Torre del Oro, a watchtower that guarded the Guadalquivir River, and the mesmerizing General Archives of the Indies, a treasure trove of historical documents.

Seville's vibrant cultural heritage extends beyond its architectural splendors. The city pulsates with passion, and nowhere is this more evident than in its soul-stirring

Previous: view of Seville from the Metropol Parasol; flamenco dancer performing; taking a boat out on the moat at Plaza de España.

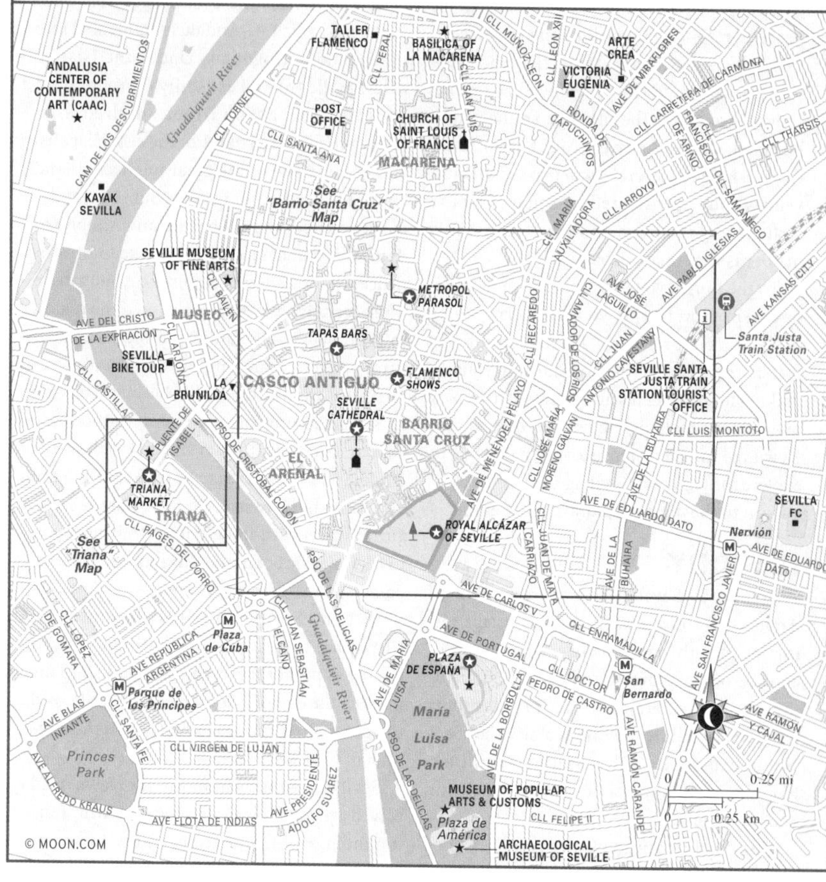

flamenco music and dance. Immerse yourself in the raw emotion and rhythmic beats of this art form by attending a flamenco show in one of the local tablaos (flamenco venues). Seville's calendar brims with lively festivities, none more famous than the Feria de Abril. Experience the exuberance of this weeklong celebration as the city comes alive with flamenco dresses, horse-drawn carriages, and endless festivities. Join the locals in dancing sevillanas (a traditional Andalusian dance), indulging in delicious tapas, and savoring the joyful spirit that characterizes this enchanting event.

As we bid adios to the past and embrace the present, Seville continues to evolve while cherishing its heritage. The city harmoniously blends tradition with modernity, boasting contemporary architectural gems like the Metropol Parasol, affectionately known as Las Setas (The Mushrooms), the largest wooden structure in the world.

ORIENTATION

Nestled in the southwestern part of Spain, along the banks of the Guadalquivir River, the radiant capital of Andalusia unfolds. The vast majority of sites of interest are found in the historic neighborhoods comprising the Casco Antiguo, or old city, of Seville. These interconnected pedestrian-friendly neighborhoods are where you'll find plenty of accommodations, restaurants, and experiences to enjoy while in Seville.

The Seville Airport, north of the city, offers international and domestic flights, providing a convenient gateway to explore this enchanting destination. The Santa Justa train station, situated in the eastern part of Seville, connects the city with high-speed rail services to major Spanish cities, allowing travelers to arrive swiftly and seamlessly. With these transportation hubs connecting Seville to the world, your journey into this cultural haven is just a flight or train ride away.

From Seville, the Sierra Norte de Sevilla Natural Park is a short train ride north, a popular day trip for locals.

Casco Antiguo
(Historic City Center)

Along the east bank of the Guadalquivir River, the historic center of Seville comes to life, where the cobbled streets lead you through a labyrinth of charm and history. Alternatively referred to in Spanish as the Casco Antiguo or Centro Historico, this is the old town core of Seville, featuring many medieval, Renaissance, and Gothic structures that provide a glance back in time.

The network of narrow streets of the historic center can be divvied up into three barrios (a Spanish word meaning "quarters" or "neighborhoods"): Santa Cruz, El Arenal, and Museo. From the historic center, nearly all the monuments and sites are within a brisk 20-minute walk; the vast majority of them are located right in the Barrio Santa Cruz.

Barrio Santa Cruz

Seville's most famous barrio, Barrio Santa Cruz, is where most of the attractions, accommodations, and classic flamenco bars of Seville are found. As the most popular neighborhood, often "Barrio Santa Cruz" or just "Santa Cruz" is used interchangeably to mean the entire historic district. This is the middle neighborhood, the hub around which the other neighborhoods coalesce. You'll find the cathedral as well as the Alcázar in this barrio.

El Arenal

The Arenal neighborhood kisses the banks of the Guadalquivir River just southeast of Barrio Santa Cruz. El Arenal is most distinctive for its unmissable bullring, though you

Seville

will also find the Torre de Oro here, as well as a wonderful river walk that connects with Triana on the other side of the river.

Museo

North of El Arenal, along the river, is where you'll find the Museo quarter, unsurprisingly home to the Seville Museum of Fine Arts. A few cafés and restaurants nestle along its quieter streets, and a river walk connects with El Arenal. If you cross the river, you'll find yourself right at the Triana Market.

Macarena

Beyond the historic district and bordering the north end of the Barrio Santa Cruz is the hip Macarena neighborhood, offering quite a few trendy bars and restaurants. Macarena is home to the Baroque Revival basilica from which it takes its name.

María Luisa Park

Abutting the southern borders of Barrio Santa Cruz and El Arenal is the María Luisa Park, which includes the famous Plaza de España. This is Seville's haven of large, green spaces. This park is the size of most neighborhoods in Seville and also includes the Plaza de América and the Museum of Popular Arts and Customs.

Triana

On the west bank of the Guadalquivir River, the lively Triana neighborhood pulsates with flamenco rhythms and ceramic workshops. A popular foodie must-experience is the Triana Market.

Santiponce

A testament to the area's rich heritage, the remnants of the ancient Roman city of Itálica lie 14 km (8.5 mi) northeast of Seville's historic city center in Santiponce. A more recent history can be enjoyed at the San Isidoro del Campo Monastery, which features Mudejar design elements.

PLANNING YOUR TIME

Seville is the sort of city where you could just as easily spend a couple of days as you could a lifetime. That said, for most travelers, three days is ideal. The summers can be blazing hot, so it's best to visit in fall, winter, and spring, and even then, sometimes the afternoon heat can be a bit much. If heat is an issue, it's best to plan your days so mornings and evenings are given to explore the outdoor sites and neighborhoods, like Plaza España, Las Setas, the Barrio Santa Cruz, and the Roman ruins of Itálica. Visits to primarily cooler indoor sites, such as the Alcázar, Seville Cathedral with the Giralda tower, and various museums, are best saved for afternoons during the hot months.

Nights in Seville, particularly in the hotter months, are often lively. Locals tend to stay out late at with friends and family in the tapas bars around town, perhaps ducking into the occasional flamenco show.

For most, the Sierra Norte de Sevilla Natural Park is best thought of as a day trip from Seville, though nature lovers who would like some time in a natural park could book one or two nights to enjoy some of the hiking possibilities. Stay away from the park during holidays and weekends, though, if possible, because the local crowds can detract from the natural beauty.

Itinerary Ideas

DAY 1

1 Start your day at the awe-inspiring **Seville Cathedral.** Marvel at the intricate architecture and explore the multi-religious past of Seville. If time and energy allow, climb the Giralda tower for breathtaking panoramic views of the city.

2 Explore the **Royal Alcázar of Seville,** a magnificent palace complex with stunning gardens, lavish courtyards, and exquisite Moorish architecture.

3 Enjoy a delightful lunch at a traditional tapas bar like **Sal Gorda,** savoring the local flavors of Andalusian cuisine.

4 In the afternoon, take a leisurely stroll through the charming **Barrio Santa Cruz,** getting lost in its narrow streets, picturesque squares, and hidden patios.

5 In the evening, catch an authentic flamenco show at **Casa de la Guitarra** and let the passionate music and dance captivate your senses.

DAY 2

1 Discover the **Plaza de España,** a magnificent square adorned with beautiful ceramic tiles in the María Luisa Park. Take a romantic rowboat ride in the canal for unique views.

2 Visit the rest of the **María Luisa Park,** a sprawling green oasis filled with lush gardens, charming pathways, and peaceful ponds, as well as the other famous square, Plaza de América.

3 Cross the Triana Bridge and venture into the bustling streets of **Triana,** known for its artisan workshops and lively tapas bars.

4 Explore the **Triana Market,** where you can indulge in a gastronomic adventure, sampling fresh local produce, seafood, and regional specialties.

5 End your day with a relaxing stroll along the **Guadalquivir River,** where the lights of Seville shimmer and dance upon its gentle waves. Enjoy the enchanting views from the riverbank or aboard a scenic river cruise.

DAY 3

1 Start the day with a journey to the past at **Itálica,** just a short trip from Seville. Explore the ancient Roman ruins, including the grand amphitheater and impressive mosaics.

2 Head back to Seville and wander through the streets of the Macarena neighborhood, soaking in its authentic atmosphere and visiting the **Basilica and Gate of La Macarena.**

3 Treat yourself to a contemporary Spanish dinner at **Abantal,** a Michelin-starred must for foodies.

4 Head up to the **Metropol Parasol,** an innovative architectural structure that offers impressive panoramic views of the city at night.

Itinerary Ideas

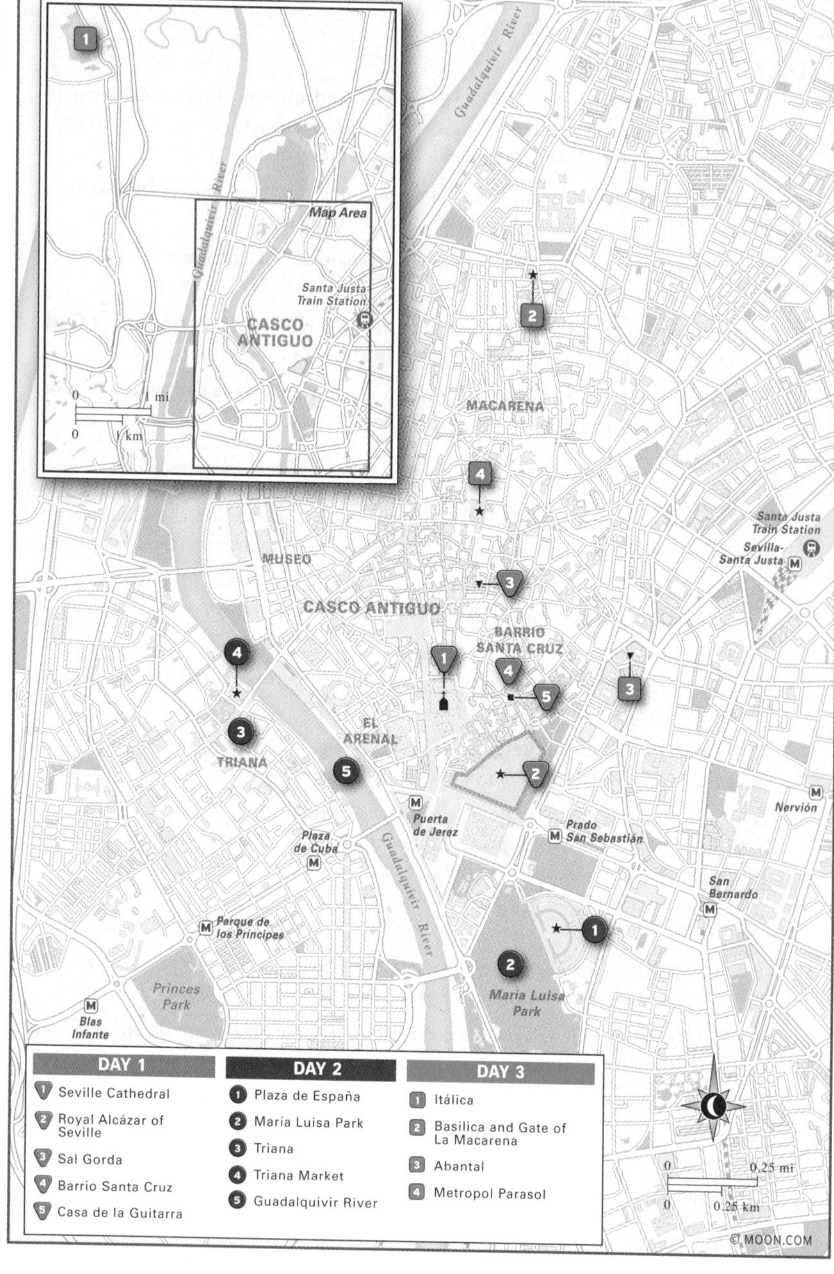

Sights

BARRIO SANTA CRUZ

The historic neighborhood of Barrio Santa Cruz was once the Jewish Mellah, or neighborhood, of Seville, though its history goes all the way back to the Romans in the 1st century. The characteristic medieval winding streets and patchwork of little public squares, the footprint largely dating from Roman times, once served a real purpose: to confuse invading armies who breached the city walls. These days, the confusion is felt mostly on us poor travelers. A late afternoon stroll through the barrio as the temperature begins to cool is just the thing to transport you back in time, particularly in the spring months when the smell of orange blossoms wafts down the narrow cobblestone lanes.

★ Royal Alcázar of Seville (Real Alcázar de Sevilla)

Patio de Banderas; tel. 912/302-200 or 610/649-410; www.alcazarsevilla.org; 9:30am-6pm daily Nov.-Mar., 9:30am-8pm daily Apr.-Oct.; €13.50

The Real Alcázar is a vast compound of competing architectural styles showing the evolution of Andalusia for over 1,000 years. The whole of it encapsulates what is so fascinating about the rich, incredible history of this region of Spain. Founded by the caliph of Córdoba, Abd al-Rahman III, in 913, the Real Alcázar has long been the home of kings. The Abbadid and Almohad dynasties continued to build onto the palace, cementing it as a seat of power for the region and as one of the more ornate and diverse examples of Moorish architecture in Andalusia. After the Reconquista, the Castilians kept the palace as a royal residence. Over the years, various schools of architecture and design have added to the palace, from the Mudejar palace of Pedro I in the 14th century to the Baroque halls of Charles V built in the mid-18th century. The entirety of it spills out over the palace gardens, which have been carefully tended for centuries. The ponds, pavilions, fountains, and waterways make this an enchanting, quiet corner of Seville.

TOP EXPERIENCE

★ Seville Cathedral (Catedral de Sevilla)

Avenida de la Constitución; tel. 954/211-679; www.catedraldesevilla.es; 11am-5:30pm Mon.-Sat., 3pm-7pm Sun. Sept.-June, 10:30am-5pm Mon.-Sat., 3pm-7pm Sun. July-Aug.; mass daily at 8pm and Sun. at 12:30pm; €11 online/€12 ticket office

The unmissable Gothic masterpiece Seville Cathedral is gigantic in proportions and dominates the city skyline. Expect to spend at least a couple of hours in the cathedral, perhaps longer depending upon your tour or interests. The Seville Cathedral is the world's largest Gothic cathedral, constructed shortly after the Reconquista in the 15th century and built over a former mosque. The **Giralda** bell tower is all that remains of the 12th-century Muslim minaret. At nearly 97 m (320 ft), this was once the tallest monument in the world. Visitors are allowed to climb the many, many stairs to the top of the bell tower and enjoy the views over Seville. Another reminder of the cathedral's Islamic heritage is the midha, an octagonal fountain in the Courtyard of Orange Trees at the entrance of the cathedral. The Muslim faithful would ritually wash in this fountain to cleanse themselves before performing prayer. In the cathedral, be sure to stop by the south transept to view the tomb of Christopher Columbus, as well as the main chapel to see the massive, intricately carved, gilded retablo altarpiece.

General Archives of the Indies (Archivo General de Indias)

Avenida de la Constitución; tel. 954/500-528; www.cultura.gob.es/cultura/areas/archivos/mc/archivos/agi/

Barrio Santa Cruz

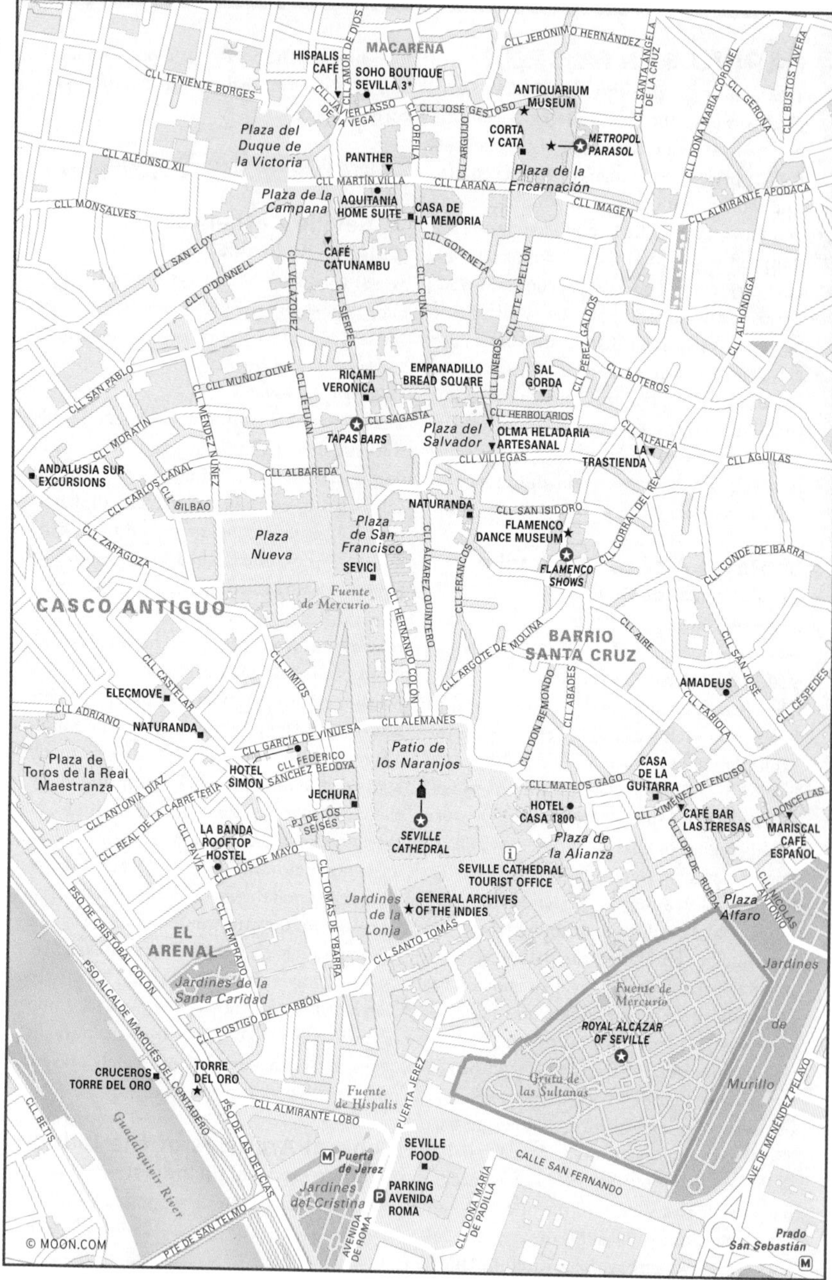

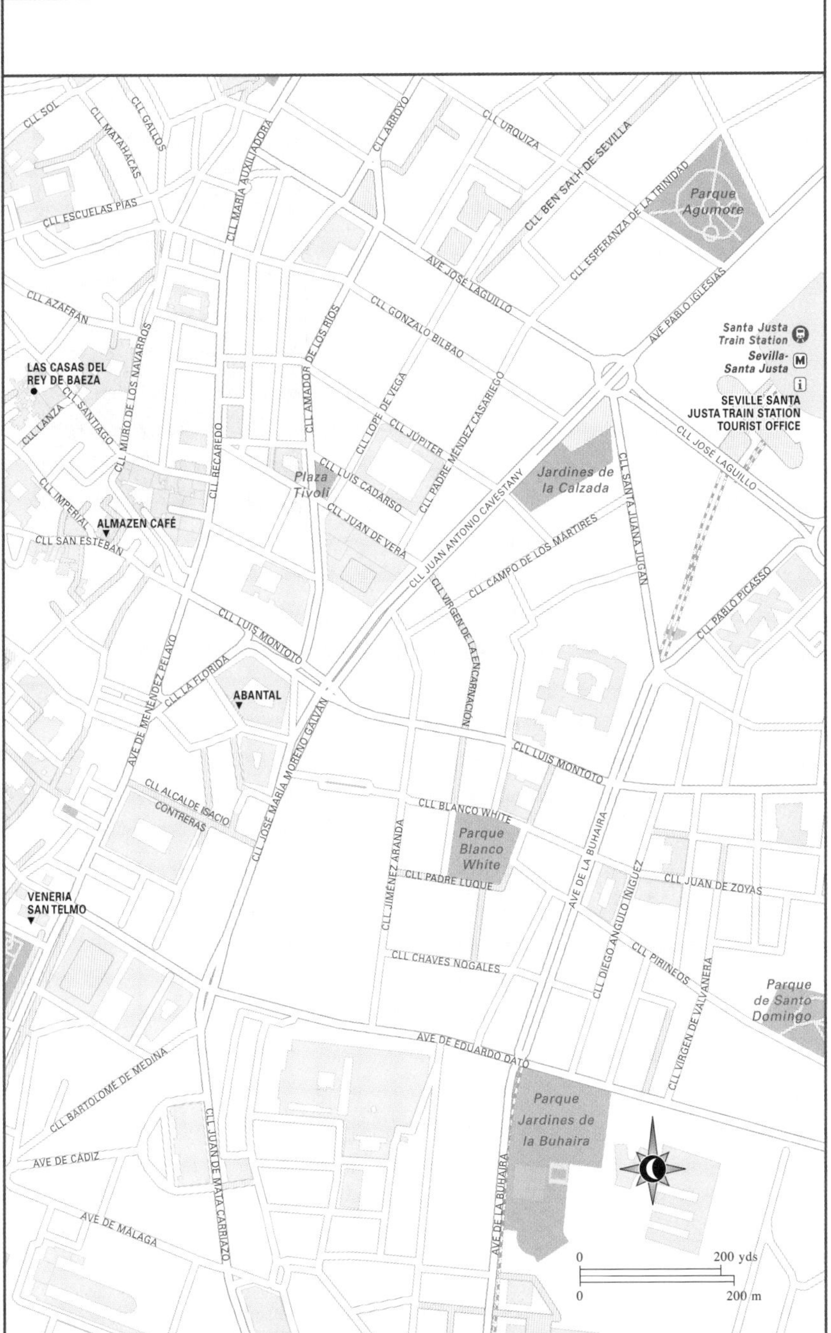

CLL SOL
CLL MATAHACAS
CLL GALLOS
CLL ESCUELAS PIAS
CLL MARIA AUXILIADORA
CLL ARROYO
CLL URQUIZA
CLL BEN SALH DE SEVILLA
CLL ESPERANZA DE LA TRINIDAD
Parque Agumore
AVE JOSÉ LAGUILLO
CLL AZAFRÁN
CLL GONZALO BILBAO
AVE PABLO IGLESIAS
Santa Justa Train Station
Sevilla-Santa Justa
SEVILLE SANTA JUSTA TRAIN STATION TOURIST OFFICE
LAS CASAS DEL REY DE BAEZA
CLL AMADOR DE LOS RÍOS
CLL LOPE DE VEGA
CLL PADRE MÉNDEZ CASARIEGO
CLL LANZA
CLL SANTIAGO
CLL MURO DE LOS NAVARROS
CLL RECAREDO
CLL JÚPITER
CLL JOSÉ LAGUILLO
Plaza Tívoli
CLL LUIS CADARSO
Jardines de la Calzada
CLL SANTA JUANA JUGAN
CLL IMPERIAL
ALMAZEN CAFÉ
CLL SAN ESTEBAN
CLL JUAN DE VERA
CLL JUAN ANTONIO CAVESTANY
CLL CAMPO DE LOS MÁRTIRES
CLL VIRGEN DE LA ENCARNACIÓN
CLL PABLO PICASSO
CLL LUIS MONTOTO
CLL LA FLORIDA
ABANTAL
AVE DE MENÉNDEZ PELAYO
CLL JOSÉ MARÍA MORENO GALVÁN
CLL LUIS MONTOTO
CLL ALCALDE ISACIO CONTRERAS
CLL BLANCO WHITE
Parque Blanco White
AVE DE LA BUHAIRA
CLL JIMÉNEZ ARANDA
CLL PADRE LUQUE
CLL DIEGO ANGULO IÑIGUEZ
CLL JUAN DE ZOYAS
VENERIA SAN TELMO
CLL PIRINEOS
CLL CHAVES NOGALES
CLL VIRGEN DE VALVANERA
Parque de Santo Domingo
AVE DE EDUARDO DATO
CLL BARTOLOMÉ DE MEDINA
CLL JUAN DE MATA CARRIAZO
Parque Jardines de la Buhaira
AVE DE CÁDIZ
AVE DE LA BUHAIRA
AVE DE MÁLAGA
0
200 yds
0
200 m

Seville Cathedral Tours

Because of its sheer size, you could easily spend nearly an entire day in the Seville Cathedral. One of the best ways to balance your time is to take advantage of the guided tours. There are three types, each with its specific focus. Tours are available in English and other languages, last about 90 minutes, and include general admission to the cathedral and possibly the Giralda tower. Prices (€16-20) are only a few euros more than the general admission ticket (€11-12), making them a great value.

view from Giralda tower

ROOFTOPS TOUR

My favorite, the Rooftops Tour, takes you up multiple flights of stairs and outside of the cathedral onto the roof, where you come face to face with the many flying buttresses and learn a lot about the actual construction of the cathedral. Views over the city are unbeatable. You won't climb the Giralda on this tour, but you will see it about as close as possible from the facing rooftop of the cathedral.

STAINED-GLASS TOUR

The Stained-Glass Tour takes you up along the balustrades encircling the upper part of the nave. From here, the vantage point on the historic stained-glass windows of the cathedral allows you to admire the craftsmanship while learning about the stories told in each of the intricately patterned windows. This is a particularly attractive tour to take before and after midday, when the sun beams through the strongest.

MAGNA TOUR

The Magna Tour takes you through the interior of the cathedral and behind the scenes (to places that are closed off for general visits) on a deep dive of the history of this house of worship and the art that adorns it.

BOOKING YOUR TOUR

Tours of the cathedral and tower are best booked online via the cathedral's official website (www.catedraldesevilla.es). Click on the red "comprar entradas" (buy tickets) button on the top right of the home page. Select the EN icon on the top right of the page for English, and then scroll down to choose your tour.

portada.html; 9:30am-4:30pm Tues.-Sat., 10am-1:30pm Sun.; free

Historians, book lovers, and those with more than a passing interest in the European discovery of the Americas will want to take a moment to meander through these great halls. You'll find documents on display, such as the Treaty of Tordesillas, letters from Elcano, and the contract for Columbus's first voyage. Even if you are not prone to long library visits, the quiet, cool charm of the 16th-century building and clean facilities make for a nice escape from the heat.

1: Royal Alcázar of Seville **2:** courtyard of Royal Alcázar of Seville **3:** dome of the Church of Saint Louis of France **4:** Seville Cathedral

1
2
3
4

Flamenco Dance Museum (Museo del Baile Flamenco)

Calle Manuel Rojas Marcos, 3; tel. 954/340-311; https://museodelbaileflamenco.com; 5pm, 7pm, and 8:45pm daily; €25

There is perhaps nothing more associated with Andalusia than the art of flamenco. Flamenco music and dancing is at turns sensual and passionate, tragic and solemn. In Seville, Cristina Hoyos, the world's most decorated flamenco dancer, opened a museum that not only takes the uninitiated through the art of flamenco, but hosts nightly shows where spectators can enjoy an hour-long show. There are two types of performances available. The Dreams show takes place in the outdoor patio while the more intimate Poems show happens in a 5th-century exposed-stone Roman centenary vault. Olé, indeed!

★ Metropol Parasol (Las Setas de Sevilla)

Place de la Encarnación; tel. 606/635-214; https://setasdesevilla.com/en; daily 9:30am-midnight; €10

Now that you have spent a day getting up close and personal with Seville, head to the Setas de Sevilla or the "Mushrooms of Seville" for some spectacular panoramic views. From atop this wooden fungi-shaped monument, thought to be the largest wood structure in the world, you see across all of Seville. The intricate structure makes for an incredible photo op. Get there early to beat the crowds and beat the heat. There is a fun 15-minute panoramic experiential film that touches on some of the highlights of Seville and includes some of the magical scents of the city. It's a nice diversion before or after you have seen the views.

Antiquarium Museum (Museo Arqueologico Antiquarium)

Plaza de la Encarnación, 37; tel. 955/471-580; 10am-10pm Tues.-Sat., 10am-2pm Sun.; €2

Visiting the Antiquarium Museum offers an opportunity to immerse yourself in a remarkable collection that encompasses Roman, Visigothic, and Moorish history, unveiling the intricate layers of Seville's past. The museum, located right under the Metropol Parasol, is made up of a large hall spanning 3,000 sq m (32,300 sq ft), which can be accessed through the plaza's staircase.

The main hall features glass flooring, offering a view of the extensive archaeological site below. Within this site, you will discover fish-salting tanks, vats, and seven houses boasting impressive mosaics, columns, and wells. The museum also provides informative audiovisual screens that offer additional details and photographs from the original excavation. Noteworthy highlights include the House of the Columns (Casa de las Columnas), characterized by a pillared patio adorned with marble pedestals and a magnificent mosaic floor. Seek out the laurel wreath, symbolizing triumph and glory, as well as the kissing birds depicted in a reconstructed mosaic on the museum wall, serving as the symbol of the Antiquarium. Additionally, be sure to admire the Medusa Mosaic, showcasing the mythical figure with serpentine locks. Lastly, explore Bacchus's house, where an intricate mosaic floor featuring elaborate drinking vessels pays homage to the god of wine.

EL ARENAL

Plaza de Toros de la Real Maestranza

Paseo de Cristóbal Colón, 12; tel. 954/147-503; www.realmaestranza.com; 9:30am-9:30pm daily; €10 to tour the building

Seville's historic bullfighting ring should not be overlooked. Though the violent spectacle of bullfighting itself is very much at debate in contemporary Spanish culture, this hopefully will not prejudice you too much in enjoying the art and architecture of the Real Maestranza. This is not only a place for bullfighting but also a symbol of Spanish cultural heritage. The Plaza de Toros de la Real Maestranza is one of the oldest and most prestigious bullrings in the world. Built in the 18th century, it is a stunning example of the Mudejar style, featuring intricate details and a majestic circular arena. With a seating capacity of over 12,000 spectators, it is also

Seville Like a Local

dining at a local tapas bar

Seville is a city that lives and breathes with an unrivaled passion. By embracing the local way of life, you'll unlock the true essence of this captivating destination. From savoring traditional tapas to immersing yourself in the art of flamenco, every step will bring you closer to understanding the soul of Seville. Be warned: You will likely have to adjust your sleep schedule!

MORNING

Many sporty Sevillians start their day with a stroll along the **Guadalquivir River.** The gentle breeze invigorates your senses as you take advantage of the cool morning air. Cross over to the Triana neighborhood and explore the **Mercado de Triana** (page 57), where locals still gather to buy fresh produce. While you're at it, don't be shy. Ask for samples of cheeses, olives, chorizo, and anything else that looks appetizing. Work on your Spanish with the vendors. If you're lucky, you might discover a secret or two about Andalusian cuisine.

AFTERNOON

Lunch is typically the biggest meal of the day in Seville, as it is throughout Andalusia. Sevillians often take their time when it comes to lunch. They prefer to savor their food and engage in conversations, rather than rushing through a quick meal. Lunchtime is seen as an opportunity to unwind, recharge, and connect with others. Take note and have a long, leisurely lunch with your travel companions. **Sal Gorda** (page 75) and **Café Bar Las Teresas** (page 74) offer up local flavor in spade.

Seville embraces the tradition of the **midday break,** and you'll feel a part of the local rhythm as you relax and soak in the warmth of the city. Siestas, though not as common these days, are still enjoyed by many Sevillians. This is especially true during the hotter months and when they are gearing up for a big evening. Taking a siesta, or even just a little quiet time, can help you recharge for the night ahead.

EVENING

As the sun begins to set, make your way to **La Macarena** neighborhood, famous for its vibrant nightlife. Lose yourself in the narrow streets lined with colorful buildings, and discover charming plazas brimming with locals socializing over a glass of local fino sherry. Venture into a **peña flamenco,** such as **Casa de la Memoria** (page 69), an intimate venue where you'll witness passionate performances by talented musicians, singers, and dancers. Let the fiery rhythms and soulful melodies transport you to the heart of Andalusia.

Afterward, continue your journey through the night with a visit to a local **tapas bar,** like the ever-lively **La Brunilda** (page 77), and revel in the joyful atmosphere as you engage in lively conversation with fellow patrons and your travel partners. Sevillians love to celebrate life, and the night is just getting started! Embrace the lively spirit and join locals in a late-night stroll along the iconic **Calle Betis** in the Triana neighborhood. Allow yourself to get lost in the rhythm of the city, joining spontaneous street performances or dancing under the moonlit sky.

a popular venue for musical performances. Outside of events, €10 will allow you entry to tour the building, while concerts and other events are priced depending on performance. Check the website for regular updates, events, and tickets. Hours vary depending on season and events.

Torre del Oro

Paseo de Cristóbal Colón; tel. 954/222-419; 9:30am-6:45pm Tues.-Fri., 10:30am-6:45pm Sat.-Sun.; €3

The Torre del Oro, meaning "Tower of Gold," is an iconic landmark situated on the banks of the Guadalquivir River. Built in the 13th century, the tower served as a watchtower and defensive structure during the city's Moorish era. Its name is said to originate from the golden glow that the tower cast on the river's surface. Today, the Torre del Oro houses the Naval Museum of Seville, which exhibits a collection of maritime artifacts, models of ships, and historical documents. Visitors can climb to the top of the tower to enjoy panoramic views of the city and the river. The Torre del Oro stands as a symbol of Seville's rich history and is a popular attraction for tourists interested in exploring the city's heritage as well as a good landmark along the river walk at which to meet up with your travel companions.

MUSEO

Seville Museum of Fine Arts
(Museo de Bellas Artes de Sevilla)

Plaza del Museo, 9; tel. 954/786-498; www.museosdeandalucia.es/web/museodebellasartesdesevilla; 9am-9pm Tues.-Sat., 9am-3pm Sun.; €1.50

Founded in 1835 by royal decree in a 17th-century former convent, the Museo de Bellas Artes de Sevilla has long been a home for many of Andalusia's masterworks. Behind the Prado in Madrid, this is the most important art collection in all of Spain. Spend a cool afternoon perusing the permanent collection, including paintings by Velázquez, Goya, and El Greco. One of the true charms of the museum is its incorporation of the traditional arabesque open courtyards and patios alongside the Christian church, the ornate star of the museum. It is here that you will see some of the defining works by Sevillian Baroque painters, such as Murillo, Herrera el Viejo, and Zurbarán.

MACARENA

Basilica and Gate of La Macarena

Plaza de la Esperanza Macarena, 1; tel. 954/901-800; www.hermandaddelamacarena.es/la-basilica; 9am-2pm and 5pm-8pm Mon.-Sat., 9am-2pm and 5pm-9pm Sun. Oct.-May, 9am-2:30pm and 6pm-9:30pm Mon.-Sat., 9am-2pm and 6pm-9pm Sun. June-Sept.; free

In many ways, this basilica, a Baroque Revival Catholic church, is the hub around which the rest of Macarena spins. Opened in 1941, it is a popular venue for weddings and funerals as well as daily masses in a way that the more touristed, historically important churches and cathedrals are not. Right in front of the church is a large archway, the Gate of La Macarena. Like the church, this is done in a Baroque Revival style. If you like a side of kitsch with your church-hopping, this is the spot.

Church of Saint Louis of France
(Iglesia de San Luis de los Franceses)

San Luis, 37; tel. 610/100-879; www.dipusevilla.es/sanluisdelosfranceses; 10am-2pm and 4pm-8pm Tues.-Sun. Sept.-June, 9am-5pm Tues.-Sun. July-Aug.; €4

This 18th-century Baroque church is a more contemporary answer to the Gothic hulk of the Seville Cathedral. If you like the look of the elaborate facade, you would do well to take a peek inside to check out the ornate interior. Mudejar-influenced carved stucco work and gilded arches rise to painted murals on the ceiling that hearken back to Michelangelo's famous series in the Sistine Chapel, while the dome gives light and height, making for a grand effect.

Bullfighting and the Plaza de Toros de la Real Maestranza

Many travelers visiting Andalusia are unsurprisingly curious about bullfighting. The passionate, violent spectacle of bullfighting has woven itself into the fabric of this vibrant culture. From the legendary Plaza de Toros de la Real Maestranza in Seville to the sun-soaked plains of Córdoba and beyond, this timeless tradition evokes both admiration and controversy. With a storied past stretching back centuries, bullfighting has produced legends that still resonate today.

a matador

SEVILLE'S BULLFIGHTING TRADITION

The **Plaza de Toros de la Real Maestranza** is an emblem of Seville's bullfighting heritage. Here, beneath the watchful gaze of centuries-old walls, bullfighters face their fears, dancing an intricate tango with mighty beasts. It is a place where the echoes of great matadors such as Juan Belmonte, Manolete, and El Cordobés reverberate, their daring and artistry forever etched in the annals of bullfighting history.

Traditionally, a good bullfight is considered an intricate ballet of elegance, courage, and precise technique. The matador's graceful movements, the flamboyant capework, and the lethal dance between bullfighter and beast all contribute to the spectacle. The audience holds its breath, captivated by the high-stakes drama unfolding before them.

HEMINGWAY'S INFLUENCE

No mention of bullfighting would be complete without acknowledging the influence of **Ernest Hemingway.** The American literary giant was enamored with the art, immersing himself in the bullfighting culture of Andalusia and penning vivid accounts of his experiences. His passionate writings brought the intensity and beauty of bullfighting to the world's stage, forever intertwining his name in the Anglophone world with the timeless spectacle.

CURRENT DEBATES

Around Seville, particularly during the bullfighting season (spring-autumn), witness the fiery debates in tapas bars throughout the city about its place in modern Spanish culture. The local population is quite divided, some seeing bullfighting as heritage and others seeing it as a relic of an ancient past at odds with contemporary values.

MARÍA LUISA PARK
(Parque de María Luisa)

TOP EXPERIENCE

★ Plaza de España

Avenida Isabel la Católica; tel. 955/473-232; 8am-10pm daily; free

With colorful traditional tile work and delicate columns set in a half circle around a moat, and bridges meeting at an impressive public fountain, it's no wonder that this expansive picturesque plaza is featured in so many movies and television series. Built in 1928 for the 1929 Ibero-American fair, it still has a touch of fairground atmosphere. In truth, there is not much actually to do here. You walk around. You take photos. And, if

1
2
3
ESPECIAS Y LEGUMBRES
JAMONERÍA
QUESERÍA
4

you're feeling adventurous, you head down to the barquitas (€5) and take a little canoe to paddle along the moat, beneath the bridges. That said, this is the gathering point for wedding photos, travel photos, festival photos, product photography, and so much more. It's said that if you haven't spent a late afternoon on the Plaza de España, you haven't been to Seville. Visually, it is a feast for the eyes. Toward the end of the plaza, there is a small **archaeological museum** with a permanent collection of Roman antiquities taken from the nearby ruin of Itálica—if you did want a touch of erudition to go with that selfie.

In early 2024, the mayor of Seville announced a much-criticized plan to start charging a fee to visit the Plaza de España. Details as of this writing are unknown, but a €5 charge may be in the near future.

Plaza de América

Avenida de Don Pelayo; 8am-10pm daily; free

In the southern corner of the park, a short walk from the Plaza de España, you'll find the other great plaza, the Plaza de América. This part of the park is known more for its pigeons than anything else. However, if you are staying in the park for a picnic lunch, something of a Sevillian pastime, this is the place to look for that shady spot under a tree.

Museum of Popular Arts and Customs
(Museo de Artes y Costumbres Populares de Sevilla)

Plaza de América 3; tel. 955/035-325; www.museosdeandalucia.es/web/museodeartesycostumbrespopularesdesevilla; 9am-9pm Tues.-Sat., 9am-3pm Sun.; €1.50

Right next to the Plaza de América you'll find an impressive neo-Mudejar-style building. From the exterior, this is maybe the most beautiful museum in Andalusia. These days, it houses a collection of ethnographic materials showing the history of Andalusian life in this region under various influences and powers. Though the collection may not be of interest to everyone in your travel party, the interior architecture and courtyard very well might be, as well as the promise of air-conditioned interiors during those hot months.

1: view from the Metropol Parasol **2:** Torre del Oro **3:** Triana Market **4:** tile detail at the Plaza de España

TRIANA

★ Triana Market
(Mercado de Triana)

Calle San Jorge, 6; tel. 674/074-099; www.mercadodetrianasevilla.com; 9am-5pm Mon.-Sat., noon-5pm Sun.; free

After climbing up the Mushrooms of Seville (Metropol Parasol), why not head across town and shop for a few of the edible fungi at Seville's oldest, most entertaining market. The market, named for the district it is located in, was built over the remains of the Castle of San Jorge, an important seat of power during the Spanish Inquisition. The castle dates back to 1171, when the Moors ruled this part of Spain. At the market, be sure to pick up some fixin's for your own little picnic in the park later in the day. Time and budget allowing, consider taking a one-hour tour of the market with a local. **Taller Andaluz de Cocina** (https://tallerandaluzdecocina.com) offers small group tours starting from €12.

Andalusia Center of Contemporary Art (CAAC)
(Centro Andaluz de Arte Contemporáneo)

Calle Américo Vespucio, 2; tel. 955/037-070; www.caac.es; 11am-9pm Tues.-Sat., 10am-3:30pm Sun.; €1.80

North of the Triana Market you can find this monastery-turned-contemporary art museum. Created in 1990, this center has quickly established itself as one of the premier contemporary arts centers in all of Spain. It boasts a program of activities that, with a clear educational intention, tries to further the study and promotion of international contemporary artistic creation in its most varied expressions. Temporary exhibitions, seminars, workshops, concerts, meetings, recitals, film series, and conferences are always changing. For those

Triana

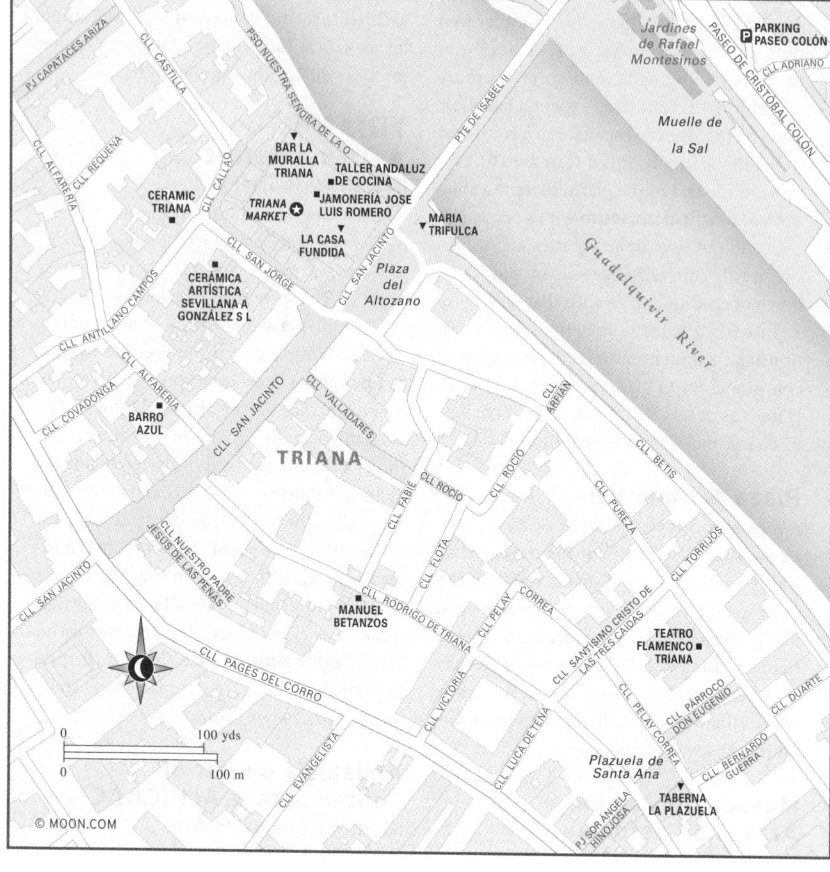

looking to see the newest in today's art world, this is the place to go.

SANTIPONCE

Just north of Seville you'll find the town of Santiponce, home of two impressive sites: the old Roman city of Itálica and the San Isidoro del Campo Monastery. From Seville, it's a short drive north on the SE-30 (30 min; 14 km/9 mi), and both sights are well marked from the main road. A morning visit is best most of the year, as in the hotter months, the exposed ruin of Itálica can be unbearably hot with little shade available. A guided tour makes a lot of sense, for transportation reasons alone, if you haven't rented a car.

Itálica

Avenida de Extramadura, 2; tel. 699/341-142; www.italicasevilla.org; 9am-3pm Tues.-Sat. (or later, depending on season), 9am-3pm Sun.; €1.50

Built around 206 CE, this former Roman economic hub proved important over the years, particularly as it was the birthplace of two Roman emperors: Trajan and Hadrian. Today, the well-excavated archaeological site provides over 52 hectares of space (128 acres) to wander through the public buildings, homes, streets, and plazas that made Itálica, to say nothing of the large semicircle amphitheater. To get the most of an excursion to Itálica, consider a guided tour (€35), particularly as Itálica is about a 30-minute drive from central Seville, and most guided tours include transportation to the Roman ruins. Guided tours typically run about 4 hours.

San Isidoro del Campo Monastery
(Monasterio de San Isidoro del Campo)

Avenida de San Isidoro, 18; tel. 955/624-400; www.juntadeandalucia.es/cultura/enclaves/enclave-monumental-san-isidoro-del-campo; 10am-2:30pm Tues.-Sun.; €1.50

Dating back to the 14th century, the well-preserved monastery boasts a stunning blend of Gothic, Mudejar, and Renaissance architectural styles. The monastery was originally established as a sanctuary for hermits but later evolved into a complex featuring a church, cloisters, chapels, and a magnificent Mudejar-style tower. It played a prominent role in Spanish history, serving as a residence for important religious figures and a place of worship. Today, the Monasterio de San Isidoro del Campo stands as a captivating historical site that offers a glimpse into the complexity of religious worship over the years in Andalusia. Often overshadowed by Itálica and overlooked by day-trippers, this is one of those little roadside gems that rewards the intrepid traveler.

TOURS

Guided Tours

Andalusia Sur Excursions

Calle Zaragoza, 1; tel. 954/211-609 or 664/274-428; www.andalsurexcursiones.com; from €30

This reliable local tour company offers walking tours as well as bus tours to Itálica and day trips from the city center. If you are using Seville as a base to discover Andalusia, it is well worth seeing the discounts on offer when you purchase multiple day trips. Guides are all licensed and have a wealth of information that can enhance your experience in Seville and around. This particular outfit is really good for day trips outside Seville.

All Seville Guides

tel. 606/217-194; www.allsevillaguides.com; from €25

These guides are licensed and run a really fun Monuments Tour, which is a fantastic way to see some of the best hits of Seville, including the Royal Alcázar, the cathedral, and little pockets of the Barrio Santa Cruz neighborhood. This is a join-in group tour and does not include cost of admission to the monuments. Tours run Monday-Saturday at 2pm from Plaza del Triunfo. If you're looking for a privatized tour, guides Elena and Susana offer wonderful, adaptable, professional tours starting at €170 for 2.5 hours. If you want a more bespoke guided experience, having a private guide is highly recommended.

Naturanda

Calle Arfe, 3; tel. 955/220-543 or 654/871-750; www.naturanda.com; from €10

With fun, lively guides and a knack for peeling back the layers of Seville, this guide company is fun for an outing around town, whether on your feet or as a trip out to Itálica. They have multiple offices dotted throughout Seville, so feel free to just walk in and ask questions. One of my favorites is the sunset walk through the María Luisa Park and the Plaza España. They also offer active tours not typically available from other companies.

Boat Tours

Cruceros Torre del Oro

embark from the pier in front of the Torre del Oro; tel. 954/561-692; www.crucerosensevilla.com; cruises offered hourly starting at 11am daily; €25

Set sail on the Guadalquivir, the river that has aided the city throughout the years in gaining prosperity. Follow in the wet footsteps of other explorers, such as Columbus and Magellan, who also set sail from Seville in their quest to discover the world. You won't be sailing quite so far, but there is full bar service, and at sunset the twinkling city lights are magical.

Roman History of Seville and the Ruins of Itálica

amphitheater of Itálica

Seville, with its vibrant culture and rich heritage, boasts a fascinating past deeply intertwined with the Roman Empire. As you wander through the city's ancient streets, you'll uncover remnants of a bygone era that still whisper tales of grandeur and conquest. Delve into the Roman history of Seville and finish your journey with a visit to the magnificent ruins of Itálica.

HISPALIS

Roman Seville was a flourishing metropolis. In the 2nd century BCE, the Roman Republic established Hispalis, a city that would eventually evolve into modern-day Seville. The Romans recognized the strategic importance of this region, situated on the banks of the Guadalquivir River, and transformed it into a prosperous urban center. Hispalis flourished as a hub of commerce, art, and culture, leaving an indelible mark on the city's landscape.

ITÁLICA

Just outside Seville lies the archaeological site of Itálica, a magnificent Roman city that offers a captivating glimpse into ancient life. Founded in 206 BCE, Itálica became a significant Roman enclave and birthplace of two emperors, Trajan and Hadrian. Walking through the vast ruins, you'll discover the grandeur of the Roman forum, the remains of opulent villas adorned with intricate mosaics, and the impressive amphitheater, the third largest in the Roman Empire.

At the heart is the amphitheater. Built during the 2nd century, it is known for its architectural prowess and capacity to hold 25,000 spectators. Walking through the amphitheater brings to life the dramatic spectacles that once captivated the citizens of the Roman Empire. Imagine the roar of the crowd as gladiators battled against one another, or the anticipation of witnessing theatrical performances and wild animal contests. Standing amid the weathered stones, you can't help but feel a profound connection to the past and the stories etched into these ancient walls.

The history of this region is a testament to the enduring influence of the Roman Empire. The ruins of Roman Itálica remind us of the city's architectural treasures and a once-thriving metropolis.

Tapas Tours

No matter the tapas tour, it's impossible not to have a great time out on the town enjoying the many nibbles for which Andalusia is so well known. You can always head out on your own steam and do your own tapas tour, and you will have a great time! Those who want a bit more knowledge and guidance to add a touch of erudition to the patatas brava should check out some of these specialized local outfits.

Not Just a Tourist

https://notjustatourist.com/tours/triana-seville-tapas-tour; €80

Head out into the Triana neighborhood for a more local feel for Sevillian tapas. This is a neighborhood famous for being the birthplace of many flamenco dancers and musicians. With a small group, enjoy a fun night on the town, hopping from bar to bar and sampling regional specialties paired with some local wines.

Sevilla Tapas Tours

tel. 608/636-290; https://azahar-sevilla.com/sevilletapas; from €100

If you're going out for a night on the town tasting tapas with Shawn at Sevilla Tapas Tours, you'll get an insider's view on tapas, tapas culture, and the art of Spanish bar-hopping. You'll also receive another tapas route you can do on your own steam during your stay in Seville. Shawn is a certified sherry educator, so take advantage by ordering up a glass of sherry fino or manzanillo and asking a question or two, or just sign up for the Sherry and Tapas tour, or even consider splurging a touch and going with the Gourmet Tapas tour. Over the course of four hours, you'll get to indulge in some of the finest jamón ibérico de bellota, paired perfectly with lauded vintages of regionally produced Spanish wines. This more bespoke experience will pair your palate with the best chefs in Seville, serving up truly designer tapas (contact for pricing).

All Seville Guides

tel. 606/217-194; www.allsevillaguides.com; €30 per person plus €180 for personal guide

Get in touch with Elena and Susana if you prefer a more personal, tailored tapas experience for you, your friends, and family. For small groups, this can actually be a touch more economical way of having a fun tapas tour without having to join a bigger group. With these guides, you can expect a very local touch with your tapas, mixed with a little history, both regional and familial. This is the choice if you are looking to get away from the crowds and want a more personalized experience of Seville.

Sports and Recreation

You probably already know that Seville is a vibrant city. However, it might come as a surprise just how many choices there are for active travel. Whether you're a fútbol fanatic or a thrill-seeking adventurer, this city offers many possibilities.

The streets come alive with the whir of bike wheels as cyclists explore the charming lanes and picturesque parks. The Guadalquivir River beckons kayakers, offering a serene and refreshing escape as they paddle through its tranquil waters. Football matches ignite an electric atmosphere, with passionate fans cheering on their beloved teams. And when the sun sets, the city's vibrant energy extends to the riverside paths, where joggers and bikers share the scenic route. In Seville, sports and recreation blend seamlessly, creating a dynamic and invigorating atmosphere that is sure to captivate both athletes and spectators alike.

Day Trips from Seville

A few day trips from Seville can only be done by car, while for others you can make use of the good rail service connecting Seville with elsewhere around Andalusia. While many of the destinations do reward overnight stays, we don't always have the gift of time, and in some cases, it might make more sense to use Seville as a home base as you venture out to other destinations during the day. Do make sure to take everything you might need in a day bag, including a refillable water bottle and a portable battery charger for your devices.

If You Like . . .	Destination	Getting There
Islamic and Christian architecture, gastronomic delights	Between Seville and Granada, you'll find **Córdoba**—a city steeped in cultural and architectural richness (page 93).	From Seville, it's about 1 hr by train or car via the A-4 freeway.
Wine tasting, horseback riding, historic cities	**Jerez de la Frontera** is renowned for its sherry production and horse breeding, with a tradition dating back to the 12th century (page 276).	From Seville, it's 1 hr by train or 1 hr by car via the AP-4 toll freeway.
Roman history and the ancient world	Just outside Seville is the Roman city of **Itálica.** This once-thriving capital was a force in the region, and its power can still be felt centuries later (page 58).	From Seville, it's a 30-min drive on the SE-30 due north. Consider a guided tour for this excursion.
Small-town life, picturesque rural villages, and hearty meals	One of the most picturesque pueblos blancos, **Ronda,** is just within a day trip's distance of Seville (page 297).	Ronda is an easy 2-hr drive from Seville on the A-376 and A-375.

PARKS

María Luisa Park

Paseo de las Delicias; tel. 955/473-232; 8am-10pm daily; free

This is the most famous and largest park in Seville. The sprawling, landscaped gardens and famous plazas of the Parque María Luisa, just south of the Royal Alcázar of Seville, provide a natural respite for Sevillians throughout the year. The park encompasses two of the most famous plazas in all of Spain: Plaza de España and Plaza de América.

In the northeast corner is the **Plaza de España.** Made famous by films such as *Star Wars* and *Lawrence of Arabia,* and the series *Game of Thrones,* this picturesque plaza was built in 1928 for the Ibero-American exposition to be held the following year. The tiled alcoves around the semicircle plaza each represent a different region of Spain. Toward the end of the plaza, a small **archaeological museum** holds a permanent collection of Roman antiquities taken from the nearby ruin of Itálica. A shallow moat runs along the plaza, where you can rent rowboats (€6) for a touch of romance.

In the southern corner of the park is the **Plaza de América.** Known locally as "Park of the Pigeons," it is impossible not to want to take a photo with the local flying Sevillians.

Next to the plaza is the neo-Mudejar-style building now housing the **Museum of Popular Arts and Customs,** which houses the most expansive collection of Andalusian ceramics in all of Spain.

There are many shady corners of the park to enjoy a picnic lunch, something of a Sevillian pastime.

Alamillo Park

Cortijo del Alamillo, Isla de la Cartuja; tel. 954/516-141; www.juntadeandalucia.es/avra/parque-alamillo; 7am-late daily; free

Situated on the northern bank of the Guadalquivir River, north of the Triana neighborhood, Parque del Alamillo is a vast natural park with extensive green spaces, forests, and recreational areas. It is a favorite spot for locals and visitors alike, offering opportunities for jogging, cycling, and leisurely walks. The park also features playgrounds, picnic areas, and a lake where visitors can rent rowboats and even take rollerblading classes on the weekends.

Princes Park

Avenida Blas Infante, 2; 8am-8pm daily; free

Located across the street from the fairgrounds for the Feria de Abril, south of the Triana neighborhood, the Parque de los Príncipes is a charming park known for its picturesque setting and peaceful atmosphere. It offers well-maintained gardens, beautiful sculptures, and ample seating areas. The park is perfect for relaxation, leisurely strolls, and shady spots for a quiet escape from the bustling city. Very much a local park where you won't see too many other travelers.

BIKING

If you fancy pedaling around on two wheels, Seville's ample bike lanes and predominantly flat characteristic make this a bike lover's dream. There is a reason it is considered the fourth most bike-friendly city in the world, competing with the likes of Copenhagen and Amsterdam. With over 160 km (100 mi) of dedicated bike lines winding through Seville, it's understandable why bikes are such a popular way to get around and why bike tours are a popular activity.

It is easy enough to rent a bike on your own to scoot around town, though you will want to make sure to bring your helmet with you or pick one up while in town. Quite a few companies offer bike tours, where you'll get a two-wheeled view of the monuments and history of this incredible bike-friendly city. Tours typically run 2.5-3 hours and provide everything you need for a safe experience, including helmets. The tour companies all offer bike rentals as well, though none are as cost-effective as Sevici.

Sevici

Plaza San Francisco; tel. 900/900-722; www.sevici.es; from €2.59/day

If you are looking to bike on your own through Seville, Sevici has over 250 bike stations dotted throughout the city, making it easy to check out and return bikes. Be sure to download the app. They have different rental periods available, starting from one day for €2.59. The first 30 minutes are included. After that, you pay a modest fee of just over €1 for each additional hour. Bike helmets are not included, so be sure to add that to your packing list if you are looking to use bike rentals in Seville.

Elecmove

Calle de Castelar, 9; tel. 954/215-925; https://elecmove.com; 10am-2pm and 4pm-8pm Mon.-Fri.; from €40

For the smoothest pedaling around Seville, check out this outfit by Spanish entrepreneur Sofia Delclaux, the first provider of electric bikes in Seville. Not only can you do some of the highlight tours of Seville in small groups, but with the advantage of e-bikes, you can even do trips farther afield, such as to the Roman ruins of Itálica, without breaking a sweat (and reducing your carbon footprint). For the more adventurous, there are even overnight bike tours into the Andalusian countryside.

1
2

Naturanda

Calle Francos, 19; tel. 955/220-543 or 654/871-750; www.naturanda.com; 9am-9pm daily; from €29

A local agency specializing in day trips in and around Seville, Naturanda has a few offices dotted around Seville. This is the most central. They work with reputable, licensed guides. The bike tours are thoughtfully plotted out, beginning near the Alameda Park before continuing through Triana and ending in the Barrio Santa Cruz. The tour takes about 2.5 hours and does not include entry to the monuments.

Sevilla Bike Tour

Calle Aronja, 8; tel. 677/658-317; https://sevillabiketour.com; 10am-2pm and 6pm-10pm Mon.-Fri.; €30

The choice for families and traditionalists who eschew the use of e-bikes, this is the original bike tour of Seville. Guides are all fun and knowledgeable, as expected, but also really gifted with children. There are a few bikes available for 8 years and up as well as child seats for the younger set. A tandem bike option makes for an unbeatable active couple photo op.

HOT AIR BALLOONS

Glovento Sur

Placeta Nevot, 4; tel. 958/290-316 or 695/938-123; www.gloventosur.com; €175

Prepare to ascend into the skies above Seville! During your one-hour flight, you'll be treated to breathtaking views of Seville's iconic landmarks, including the historic Royal Alcázar, the majestic cathedral, and the winding Guadalquivir River. As you float above this ancient city, you'll also see the picturesque countryside dotted with olive groves and charming villages.

Departing in the morning, typically around 8am, this magical experience begins as you watch the balloons inflate while enjoying a delightful local breakfast. Your flight comes complete with a certificate commemorating your adventure. Private flights are available, starting from €800. This same outfitter offers hot-air balloon rides in several other destinations across Andalusia, including Antequera, Ronda, and Granada.

1: biking along the Guadalquivir River **2:** kayaking on the Guadalquivir River

GOLF

Though not as well known as the so-called "Costa del Golf" (the nickname for the Costa del Sol) along the Mediterranean, Seville has great golf courses to explore. Summers can be dangerously hot, particularly in the afternoon. Plan accordingly.

Real Club Sevilla Golf

Plaza San Francisco; tel. 943/124-301; https://sevillagolf.com; from €100

One of the best golf courses in Spain and all of Europe, the surprising Real Club Sevilla twists and turns, with hidden bunkers, challenging water features, and mature trees hugging the fairways. The course often hosts international competitions, such as the World Cup of Golf and the Andalusian Cup. If you were to golf only one course in Seville, this is the one.

KAYAKING AND PADDLEBOARDING

Discover the tales of Seville's nautical past along the Guadalquivir River, where intrepid seafarers and their expeditions ignited the imagination of a nation and forever transformed the course of world history. Immerse yourself in the captivating narratives that unfold along the banks of the Guadalquivir, allowing the echoes of the past to guide you through the captivating legacy of this iconic city. From the awe-inspiring circumnavigation of Magellan and Juan Sebastián Elcano to the thrilling race to the Indies, Seville's connection to the golden age of Spanish navigation is truly extraordinary. Tours along the river generally last 1.5-2 hours.

Kayak Sevilla

American Garden (across the bridge from the Torre del Oro); tel. 669/247-913; https://kayaksevilla.com; 9am-8pm Mon.-Sat., 9am-3pm Sun.; from €30

If you haven't tried kayaking before, you'll be surprised at just how easy it is. Slip into the water with a small group and paddle down Seville's Guadalquivir River. If you hired a guide, you'll learn a lot about explorers, such as Magellan and Columbus, among others, who all once set sail from Seville to explore the New World. A fun way to dip into Seville and enjoy the near year-round sunshine. Meet your instructor at the Club de Remo and jump into your kayak for a couple hours of fun. Paddleboards are also available. Tours leave around 11am most days.

Naturanda

Calle Francos, 19; tel. 955/220-543 or 654/871-750; www.naturanda.com; 9am-9pm daily; from €35

The local Seville go-to for day tours also has kayaking available. They have double kayaks, making this a good choice for couples or parents with a child. Tours are daily, with departure times differing a bit with the seasons and weather. Knowledgeable guides will get you quickly up to speed on the nautical nature and history of Seville as you paddle up the historic Guadalquivir.

SPECTATOR SPORTS

Soccer (Fútbol)

Soccer, or rather fútbol, holds an unwavering grip on the hearts of Spaniards, and Seville is no exception. In Spain, soccer is more than just a sport; it is a passion that unites people from all walks of life. The country's love affair with the beautiful game is evident in the fervor of the fans, the packed stadiums, and the vibrant atmosphere that engulfs match days. In Seville, home to two renowned football clubs, Real Betis and Sevilla FC, the city pulsates with an electrifying energy as locals proudly don their team colors, filling the stadiums with chants, cheers, and unwavering support.

The football season in Spain typically runs from August to May, following the schedule set by La Liga, the top professional league in the country. During this period, football enthusiasts flock to stadiums across Spain, including Seville, to witness the thrilling matches. The availability of tickets can vary depending on the popularity of the teams and the significance of the match. For high-profile matches and derbies, such as the Seville derby between Real Betis and Sevilla FC, tickets can be in high demand, and it is advisable to purchase them in advance. However, for regular league matches, tickets can often be obtained closer to the match day, either through official club websites and authorized ticket vendors or at the stadium box offices. It should be noted that each football club has a men's and women's team. Women's football, though popular, doesn't share quite the same popularity as the men's, and tickets tend to be more available and far less expensive, starting at €5.

Sevilla FC

Estadio Ramón Sánchez-Pizjuán, Calle Sevilla Fútbol Club; tel. 954/535-353; https://sevillafc.es; from €30

Dating back to its establishment in 1890, Sevilla FC is one of the more storied clubs in Spain. The club has enjoyed both triumphs and challenges, including numerous successes in domestic and international competitions, solidifying its reputation as one of Spain's prominent football clubs. Today, Sevilla FC continues to be a formidable force in La Liga, consistently competing at the highest level and captivating fans with their passionate style of play and unwavering commitment to excellence.

Real Betis Balompié

Estadio Benito Villamarín, Avenida de Heliópolis; tel. 955/463-955; https://en.realbetisbalompie.es; from €30

The young up-and-coming squad—established in only 1907—Real Betis Balompié has long played little brother to Sevilla FC. The team had a lot of early success, winning multiple titles and cups throughout the beginning of the 20th century, but was often relegated to the second division until the 1990s. They have enjoyed recent success, even qualifying for a few European Cups. That said, the green and whites are very much a feisty underdog.

Entertainment and Events

Whether indulging in the lively festivities of the Feria de Abril, witnessing the grandeur of Semana Santa processions, or immersing oneself in the captivating world of flamenco, Seville offers a vibrant entertainment scene that never fails to captivate and enchant visitors.

While some of the festivities, such as the Feria de Abril, are tied to specific times of the year, others, like flamenco, can be enjoyed year-round. If you are looking to enjoy Seville at a particular time of year to coincide with a festival, consult the festival schedule accordingly. Be sure to make reservations well in advance and increase your budget because most accommodations and services will double in price for popular times to be in Seville. Tickets for popular events, particularly rival soccer matches, will sell out quickly, so this is another thing to plan for well ahead of time.

FESTIVALS

April Festival (Feria de Abril)

April

The Feria de Abril in Seville is a weeklong extravaganza that embodies the vibrant spirit and rich cultural heritage of the city. Held annually in April, this iconic festival transforms Seville's fairgrounds (Calle Alfonso de Orleans y Borbón, south of Triana and directly west and across the river from the María Luisa Park) into a kaleidoscope of colors, music, and joyous celebrations. The festivities begin with the traditional lighting of thousands of paper lanterns, creating a magical atmosphere. Throughout the day, the fairgrounds come alive with beautifully adorned casetas (marquee tents), where locals and visitors gather to dance sevillanas, a traditional Spanish dance, and indulge in delicious Andalusian cuisine and drinks. The Feria de Abril is an unforgettable experience, offering a glimpse into the heart and soul of Seville's cultural identity. Horse carriages parade through the streets, adding to the enchantment.

Though the parade fairgrounds are open to the public, only a few of the casetas are. If you are planning on attending the festival, you will want to dress up accordingly. Men typically wear suits while women don their stunning flamenco dresses.

Holy Week (Semana Santa)

Easter week

Semana Santa in Seville is a deeply religious and visually captivating event that takes place in the week leading up to Easter. The city becomes immersed in a solemn yet awe-inspiring atmosphere as elaborate processions wind through the streets.

Majestic floats, known as pasos, are carried by devoted members of religious brotherhoods, accompanied by haunting music and the rhythmic sound of marching footsteps. In particular, the devout brotherhoods who wear pointed hoods as they proceed through the streets can be disconcerting for some travelers because visually they recall the images of white supremacist organizations in the United States. Keep in mind that these brotherhoods have been doing this for centuries in Spain and have nothing to do with white supremacy.

The pasos depict scenes from the Passion of Christ, adorned with intricate artwork and fragrant flowers. Spectators line the streets, watching in hushed reverence as the processions pass by, experiencing the profound devotion and spiritual intensity that characterizes this event. Semana Santa in Seville is a testament to the city's deep-rooted traditions and provides a powerful glimpse into the religious fervor and cultural heritage of Andalusia.

1
2
3
4
Casa de la Memori
TRO CULTURAL FLAM

TOP EXPERIENCE

★ FLAMENCO SHOWS

Seville offers a diverse array of flamenco shows that cater to a variety of tastes and preferences. Venues showcasing this passionate art form range from intimate tablaos (flamenco venues) to grand theaters, and each flamenco show presents its unique charm.

At the renowned **tablaos,** such as Casa de la Memoria, visitors can witness the raw power and emotional intensity of flamenco up close. These intimate settings provide an immersive experience, with exceptional dancers, skilled guitarists, and soulful singers captivating the audience with their fiery performances. The intimate atmosphere allows for a deep connection between the performers and spectators, creating a truly unforgettable evening.

Theaters like Teatro Flamenco Triana showcase flamenco productions on a grander scale. These performances combine the artistry of flamenco with elaborate set designs, vibrant costumes, and talented ensembles. The stage becomes a canvas for storytelling through dance, music, and song, transporting the audience to the heart of flamenco's rich history.

Additionally, some traditional bars in Seville offer spontaneous flamenco sessions known as **juergas.** These impromptu gatherings bring together local flamenco artists and aficionados in an informal setting, where the music flows freely and the passion of flamenco fills the air. These authentic and spontaneous juergas offer a unique opportunity to witness the unfiltered and improvised nature of flamenco.

Barrio Santa Cruz

Casa de la Memoria

Calle Cuna, 6; tel. 954/560-670; www.casadelamemoria.es; 3 shows per night; €22

There is undoubtably a bit of glam with this performance set inside a 15th-century palace festooned with artwork, and rightly so. The Casa de la Memoria hosts a rotating cast of singers, dancers, and guitarists year-round.

Casa de la Guitarra

Calle Mesón del Moro, 12; tel. 954/224-093 or 634/867-658; www.casadelaguitarra.es; 7:30pm and 9pm daily; €20

One of the most affordable flamenco shows in town also offers a free exposition of a wonderful collection of guitars in Spain. Just the thing to set the mood for a traditional flamenco feast for the senses. World-class dancers twirl and guitarists pluck powerful emotions right in the historic center of Seville in a traditional Sevillian home full of rustic charm.

Flamenco Dance Museum (Museo del Baile Flamenco)

Calle Manuel Rojas Marcos, 3; tel. 954/340-311; https://museodelbaileflamenco.com; 5pm, 7pm, and 8:45pm daily; €25

Cristina Hoyos, the world's most decorated flamenco dancer, opened a museum that not only takes the uninitiated through the art of flamenco but also hosts nightly hour-long shows. There are two types of performances: The Dreams show takes place in the outdoor patio, while the more intimate Poems show happens in a 5th-century exposed-stone Roman centenary vault.

Triana

Teatro Flamenco Triana

Calle Pureza, 76; tel. 611/002-330; www.teatroflamencotriana.com; 5:30pm, 7:30pm, and 9pm daily; €25

The most theatrical flamenco in town has performers elevated on a stage in a renovated century-old theater. The seating ensures everyone has a great view of the passionate show. Unlike at other venues, photos are sometimes allowed throughout the show from the top-floor seats. A great event to pair with a

---

1: ceramic art depicting penitents during Semana Santa **2:** Feria de Abril attendee **3:** Casa de la Memoria **4:** flamenco performance

Flamenco Styles

Flamenco music is wide and varied. At different times it can be soulful and somber, lively and playful, or passionate and erotic. This emotional range is conveyed through different styles, or **palos.** In each palo, the basic performers remain the same: guitarist, singer, and dancer, though the number of dancers, singers, and even guitarists can vary according to the musical arrangement of the palo.

Here are a few different palos you'll hear:

flamenco dancers

- **Alegría:** These are happy, 12-beat palos. Often thought of as originating in Cádiz, this is the type of tune that really shows off the dancer's quick footwork.
- **Bulería:** Another light, quick, 12-beat palo, this is usually played toward the end of a performance, with the musicians, dancers, and singers aligned toward the audience in a half circle. The guitarists show off their virtuoso fast hands accompanied by impossibly fast, rhythmic clapping.
- **Fandango:** The palo with the most influence from the Moors, this distinct 3/4 rhythm can be either slow or fast, serious or playful. Of all the palos, this has perhaps the widest emotional range, with the most known fandangos hailing from nearby Huelva.
- **Seguirilla:** Flamenco aficionados consider the seguirilla to be the soul of all flamenco. It is known as one of the oldest palos, if not the oldest. These emotional, tragic, and intense palos are somber and slow, much like their soleá counterparts.
- **Soleá:** Like the seguirilla, this is a slow, soulful performance. The basic 12-beat rhythm is echoed in many of the other flamenco palos.
- **Tango:** The tango in flamenco has little resemblance to the Argentinian tango, though like its Argentinian cousin, it is joyful, sensual, and erotic. Typically, tangos have a fast 4-beat rhythm, though the tempo may occasionally slow down for the dancer. Nearly every city in Andalusia claims its own specific style of tango.

hip dining experience in the trendy Triana neighborhood.

FLAMENCO CLASSES

Seville offers the largest array of venues for taking flamenco classes, allowing you to dive into the heart and soul of this passionate dance form. The city's deep flamenco roots make it an ideal destination to learn from experienced instructors and connect with the vibrant flamenco community. In these classes, you'll have the opportunity to learn the intricate footwork, hand movements, and body expressions that make up flamenco's captivating choreography. Experienced teachers guide you through the rhythms, helping you understand the emotional storytelling behind the dance. The classes not only focus on technique but also provide insights into the cultural significance and history of flamenco. Prices for courses typically start around €30 for a one-hour class but can vary depending on length of class, level of skill, and time of year.

Taller Flamenco

Calle Peral, 45; tel. 954/564-234; https://tallerflamenco.com; 9am-7:30pm daily; prices vary

Taller Flamenco offers a diverse range of classes suitable for all levels of experience, from introductory sessions for beginners to specialized workshops for intermediate and advanced dancers—there is something for everyone. In these classes, students develop their technique, learn intricate choreography, and gain a deeper understanding of the emotional nuances of flamenco. There is a commitment to preserving the authenticity and heritage of flamenco that shines through in their cultural context lectures and demonstrations. Led by experienced instructors, the classes provide a supportive and inspiring environment for students to explore their creativity and immerse themselves in the captivating world of flamenco, for dancing, guitar, and singing. Spanish language lessons are also available.

Manuel Betanzos

Calle Rodrigo de Triana; tel. 954/340-519; www.manuelbetanzos.com; 9:30am-8:30pm Mon.-Fri.; prices vary

Located in the hip Triana neighborhood, this longtime flamenco academy features excellent facilities, including separate dressing rooms for men and women as well as three large studios centered around a bright, charming courtyard. A friendly atmosphere of companionship hums with lots of good energy, along with the personalized and friendly attention of both the office and the cast of teachers. Different classes are available for different levels, including for children. There are also occasional flamenco guitar lessons.

COOKING COURSES

One of my favorite ways of getting to know a culture is through the cuisine, and there is perhaps no better way of doing this than diving into a cooking course. You'll gain a skill to bring back home and share the deliciousness with your family and friends. Whether you want to make paella like a pro or dive into making some light tapas for your next fiesta, you'll find something for every type of cook.

Taller Andaluz de Cocina

Mercado de Abastos de Triana, stalls 75-79; tel. 672/162-621 or 608/503-918; www.tallerandaluzdecocina.com; from €70

This contemporary classic cooking experience is right in the heart of the famous Triana Market. Ariadna and her team have put together something really special for the foodies. Courses not only take you through the local ingredients that make Sevillian cuisine so spectacular but also create a caring, fun-filled cooking experience that is sure to be a highlight for amateur chefs and cooking pros alike. One of the more popular classes involves a short tour of the Triana Market. Whatever you do, you'll come away with some firsthand know-how, a written menu to take home, a full belly, and a big smile.

Seville Food

Calle San Fernando, 2; tel. 611/700-354; http://seville-city.com; €145

Head up to this rooftop terrace and enjoy the views over the cathedral and the rest of Barrio Santa Cruz while Fernando shows you how to whip up not only a classic paella but also a killer sangria that will be sure to be a hit when you show your friends back home. In just under two hours, you'll become an expert paellero. There are more inexpensive cooking courses to be had, though none have this view.

CERAMICS WORKSHOPS

Of the many experiences you may want to indulge in while in Andalusia, creating and decorating your own ceramics is an engaging way to get a feel for the local culture and develop an appreciation for a type of artistry that you've seen all throughout the region.

Arte Crea

Calle Francisco Meneses, 7B; tel. 658/567-413; https://artecreasevilla.es; from €25

Arte Crea is a relaxing, inviting space for all ages and art levels. It will help to have a basic level of Spanish, as classes may be taught with limited English, which can be great for an immersive activity. They also have rock painting and papier-mâché available for child-friendly activities. Though activities can be privatized (contact for pricing), the real fun here is joining in with a group and seeing all your crazy creations.

Barro Azul

Calle Alfarería, 9, Local B; tel. 644/455-624; www.barroazul.es; from €30

With classes in Spanish and English, this is an easy choice for an exploration into local ceramics. Some workshops focus on specific techniques, such as throwing clay or painting tiles, though the choice for most will be the Introduction to Ceramics course or the Ceramicist for a Day course. Both run for about three hours and will include a history of ceramics in Seville as well as the chance to paint tiles using different techniques you'll learn about in the class. Of course, you'll take home a unique souvenir of your own making fired in the kiln.

Shopping

In Seville, shops run the gamut from high-end boutique pop-ups to big box stores carrying household name brands. You might be surprised to know that you can even find a Costco in Seville. However, Seville is best known for textiles, Iberian ham, wine, sherry, and traditional dresses (like the trajes de gitana, the colorful dresses worn for festivals). These items can be found easily throughout Seville in different qualities, particularly around the Barrio Santa Cruz.

CLOTHING

Ricami Veronica

Calle Siepres, 67; tel. 675/046-550; www.ricamiveronicasevilla.com; 10am-3pm and 5pm-8pm Mon.-Sat.; €20

Particularly neat find for the chef in your life. Embroidered aprons and chef hats are wonderfully stitched by hand, on demand. You can ask the lovely artisans here to write something unique for that special someone, and even better, your gift will be light as a feather and roll up neatly in your luggage!

IBERIAN HAM

The famed jamón ibérico makes a tasty addition to any picnic basket. You'll be amazed by the breadth of varieties and prices, and there are plenty of choices for something to snack on. Expect to pay around €5 on up for a nice package of paper-thin-sliced Iberian ham. Although jamón may seem like a great souvenir, the USDA restricts bringing cured meats into the United States.

Corta y Cata

Mercado de la Encarnación, Puesto 10; tel. 955/183-736; https://cortaycata.com; 9am-3pm Mon.-Sat.

When it comes to buying jamón ibérico in Seville, one of my top choices is always the local market. Tucked away beneath the imposing Metropol Parasol sculpture, the Mercado de la Encarnación has been an integral part of local life since 1842. Among the numerous family-run stalls, Corta y Cata stands out as a favorite. The husband-and-wife team behind it expertly prepare and serve some of the finest meat products in the city. Their warm, friendly service and unwavering commitment to quality, not to mention their excellent ham, make it a regular stop for me.

Jechura

Avenida de la Constitución, 22; tel. 634/342-690; 10am-10pm Sun.-Thurs., 10am-10:30pm Fri.-Sat.

Those interested in the many different types of Iberian pork products on offer in Andalusia can check out a wide variety at the small local chain, Jechura, dotted around Seville. This

Traditional Dress of Seville

Depending on the time of year you visit, you may just be lucky enough to see Sevillians coloring the streets in their traditional attire. Sevillians take pride in dressing in their finest traditional clothing, including the traje de gitana for women and the traje corto for men, during festivals such as the Feria de Abril and other special occasions.

traje de gitana dresses

TRAJE DE GITANA AND TRAJE CORTO

The traje de gitana, more commonly known as a flamenco dress, is a very colorful dress. It is typically worn by women during special occasions and celebrations, such as the Feria de Abril. The traje de gitana is a long, flowing dress that is often brightly colored and adorned with ruffles, lace, and other decorative details. It is typically worn with a shawl, high heels, and a flower in the hair. The dress is designed to accentuate the curves of the body and to allow for movement and expression during flamenco dancing.

The traje corto consists of a short jacket, typically made of corduroy or velvet, paired with tight-fitting trousers, typically made of dark fabric. The jacket is often adorned with intricate embroidery or decorative buttons, and it is commonly worn with a crisp white shirt, a vest, and a wide-brimmed hat.

While these outfits are not typically worn on a daily basis, they are a beautiful, iconic part of Sevillian culture and are often seen during flamenco performances and other cultural events throughout the year.

LAS MANTILLAS

During popular religious gatherings, a more sober sort of fashion takes hold of the city. The week of Semana Santa, you are more likely to see women sporting las mantillas, delicate and intricately woven lace pieces that are draped over the head and shoulders, often secured with a comb or decorative pins. A mantilla adds an elegant touch and is commonly seen during religious processions, weddings, and other formal occasions. In Andalusia, particularly in Seville, wearing a mantilla is considered a sign of respect, modesty, and adherence to local Catholic customs and mores.

CAPIROTE

Another distinctive item is the capirote, a pointed hood or cone-shaped head covering traditionally worn during some religious processions and events throughout Spain. Capirote hoods are often associated with Semana Santa processions, where participants, known as penitents (or nazarenos), wear them as a form of religious devotion. These hoods typically feature eye openings and are made of fabric, often in various colors representing different religious brotherhoods or orders.

The capirote serves as a symbol of the wearer's willingness to repent and atone for their sins, embodying a humble attitude during the religious procession. The pointed shape of the capirote is often associated with a desire to lower one's head in reverence and submission to God. Additionally, the capirote serves the practical purpose of providing anonymity to the wearer, allowing them to focus solely on their devotion without drawing attention to their personal identity.

Though images of white supremacists may leap to mind, particularly for American travelers, please do keep in mind that this has been going on for centuries, and the pointed hood in Spain has nothing to do with white supremacy movements in the United States.

branch is right next to the cathedral, making it a convenient little stop. Sandwiches (bocadillos) are readily available as well and can make for a nice pickup for a picnic lunch or quick bite on the go.

Jamonería José Luis Romero

Triana Market, Plaza del Altozano, 58; tel. 954/343-522; 8:30am-3:30pm Mon.-Thurs., 8:30am-4:30pm Fri.-Sat.

Do you know what are the differences between bellota ham, farm bait ham, and bait ham? If you are serious about your Iberian ham, the experts at this excellent little stall in the popular Triana Market are there for you. They work hand in hand with some of the best Iberian pig breeders in Andalusia and handpick all of their products for sale. Tapas are also available, so you can enjoy your jamón with a glass of crisp white while discovering the differences of bellota versus bait ham in person.

CERAMICS

Ceramic Triana

Calle Callao, 14; tel. 954/332-179; www.ceramicatriana.com; 9:30am-8:30pm Mon.-Fri., 10am-8pm Sat.

Easily located just a block into the Triana neighborhood from the Triana Market, this ceramics store kicks off a solid square block of various stores all keeping the tradition of Triana ceramics alive. Though nearly all the ceramicists now live in other neighborhoods and fire their clay creations elsewhere, this is where most are sold to travelers and locals alike. Start here to get an idea for prices, as they're kept very standard, and the shop always has some fun pieces you can easily imagine in that special place back home.

Cerámica Artística Sevillana A González S L

Calle San Jorge, 17; tel. 954/344-564; www.ceramica-agonzalez.com; 10am-2pm and 6pm-9pm Mon., 6pm-9pm Tues.-Fri.

If you know a thing or two about ceramics, head here to find some very high-quality pieces that are truly unique, hand-painted, and would steal the show in nearly every room or garden you might imagine them in. Founded in 1984 by a local ceramicist, this is a family-run shop that has the distinction of having their tiles grace the Palace of Zarzuela, the Monastery of El Escorial, the Royal Cavalry of Seville, the Ronda Bullring, the City Hall of Antequera, Hotel Alfonso XIII in Seville, and Casa Carmona Hotel, among others.

Food

BARRIO SANTA CRUZ

★ Tapas Bars

Empanadillo Bread Square

Plaza Jesús de la Pasión; www.empanadillasdesevilla.es; 8am-10pm Mon.-Fri., 10:30am-10pm Sat.-Sun.; €2

Empanadillos are classic little Andalusian sandwiches, a little like a Hot Pocket but much, much better. They make the perfect sort of little on-the-go pick-me-up. This little walk-up shop has half a dozen types on offer at any given time. It's easy enough to order a few for the road. You'll get discounts the more you order. There is quite a variety here, but the Iberico black pudding and sweet tomato Marcella hits a particular Sevillian note the others miss.

Café Bar Las Teresas

Calle Santa Teresa, 2; tel. 954/213-069; 10am-midnight Sun.-Thurs., 10am-1am Fri.-Sat.; €8

Legs of cured ham dangle from this rustic establishment buzzing with locals. Take a cue from the legs above you and go for some of the thinly sliced Iberian ham. There are seats along the narrow street as well as tables dotted around the café. Busier nights it will be standing room only. This is one of those bars where occasionally some locals will tune up their guitars and offer an impromptu flamenco performance.

Mariscal Café Español

Calle Mariscal, 3; open daily, hours vary according to demand; €8

Traditional homemade tapas and nightly music set inside a typical 18th-century Sevillian house make this a sort of must-visit for an authentic taste of a Sevillian tapas bar. Solo travelers and those wanting to work on their Spanish should try to find a seat at the busy bar, while couples will find tables tucked away in corners throughout the renovated house. Expect homemade food with a focus on everything fresh and traditional.

★ Sal Gorda

Calle Alcaicería de la Loza, 23; tel. 955/385-972; 1pm-4:30pm and 8pm-11:30pm daily; €10

Colorful, modern tapas bar with a focus on plate representation, making for some very delicious and photogenic tapas. Dive into this brightly colored Sevillian bar for some fun fusion tapas introducing some Far East flavors, including edamame and kimchi, alongside traditional dishes, like ajo blanco. The craft beer selection is a refreshing changeup from the ubiquitous Cruz Campos everywhere.

Andalusian

La Trastienda

Calle Alfalfa, 8; tel. 954/210-463; noon-4:30pm and 8:30pm-midnight Tues.-Sat.; €20

Don't let the clean, rather spartan interior with its poor lighting and school cafeteria vibes fool you. This is the go-to for fresh seafood right in the heart of the Barrio Santa Cruz. From mussels, clams, and wonderfully grilled shrimp to rich lobster or the seasonal fresh catch, you'll find something for all seafood-loving diners. Thanks to swift, attentive service and a very convenient location right in the barrio, crowds are occasionally the only barrier to entry here. The menu is priced by kilo, and prices vary with the local markets. In general, you'll do very well asking your waiter what is freshest and asking for a portion or half portion.

Veneria San Telmo

Paseo de Catalina de Ribera, 4; tel. 954/410-600; www.vineriasantelmo.com; 9:30am-4pm and 8pm-midnight Mon.-Sat., 10am-4pm and 8pm-midnight Sun.; €25

Wine aficionados should head here for dinner and pair some popular, tasty Spanish vintages with classic Andalusian offerings. With a focus on local cuisine, the menu boasts an array of dishes, each showcasing the region's gastronomic heritage. One standout dish worth trying is the carrillada ibérica, featuring tender Iberian pork cheeks slow-cooked to perfection, offering a harmonious blend of rich flavors. Complementing the culinary delights is an impressive wine selection, including a robust Rioja that pairs excellently with the carrillada ibérica.

Breakfast and Cafés

Olma Heladaria Artesanal

Cuesta del Rosario, 1; tel. 618/622-666; 1pm-11pm Mon.-Thurs., 1pm-midnight Fri.-Sat., 1pm-8:30pm Sun.; €3.50

When the heat hits, sometimes there is just no better solution than a creamy cool gelato. Luckily, there are plenty of gelato joints for a refreshing bite dotted around town. The artisanal offers at Olma are something else, though! For a real taste of Andalusia, go for La Medina, a wonderful mix of orange, ginger, and cinnamon with a dollop of lemon and mint on top. Plenty of dairy-free options are well-marked and readily available, making this a great stop for the lactose-intolerant crowd.

Panther

Plaza Villasís, 2; tel. 954/721-963; www.pantherorganiccoffee.com; 8:30am-9pm Mon.-Fri., 8:30am-9:30pm Sat.-Sun.; €5

This friendly, organic coffee joint is an easy place to hit up for a light breakfast or afternoon pick-me-up. A great alternative to the ubiquitous coffee joints (like Starbucks) you'll find everywhere. Toasted sandwiches are

LA TRADICIONAL
LA TRADICIONAL
BODEGA BAR TAPAS
Cruzcampo
TAPAS
MENÚ DEL DÍA
1
2
ZAFIRO
BAR ZAFIRO
3
4

made on order, and you can also get a fresh, pesticide-free seasonal fruit.

★ Hispalis Café

Calle Amor de Dios, 1; tel. 651/061-877; 9:30am-7pm Mon., Wed., and Thurs., 9:30am-4pm Tues., 9:30am-8pm Fri.-Sat.; €5

The best espresso in Seville, looked after with care by a true barista. Cold brew is also available and more than welcome on the hot days. Grab a quick nibble and enjoy it at the window bar while people-watching in one of the less touristy parts of old Seville. The small interior can get busy quickly, so best nab one of the few chairs or window seats if available.

Café Catunambu

Calle Serpias, 10; 7:30am-9pm Mon.-Sat.; €6

A classic little stop for churros, a fried dough typically served with thick hot chocolate. A small outside seating allows for people-watching, though most locals stick to hanging out at the counter inside. When they're busy, which is often, service can be quite brisk. Tostadas (toasted bread options for breakfast, typically with olive oil and tomatoes) are also readily available.

Almazen Café

Calle San Esteban, 15; tel. 955/359-764; 9am-4pm Wed.-Mon.; €12

A tiny, bright little breakfast spot with great coffee in the busy Barrio Santa Cruz. Located in a historic building, the café welcomes with its bohemian atmosphere. The interior is adorned with vibrant artwork, cozy seating, and an array of eclectic decorations. You'll find a delightful selection of aromatic coffees, teas, and refreshing juices, all served with attention to detail. The word is out, so it can get a bit busy during the morning breakfast rush.

1: tapas outdoors at a bodega **2:** outside dining **3:** paella **4:** lunch at Triana Market

Avant-Garde

Abantal

Calle Alcalde José de la Bandera; tel. 954/540-000; www.abantalrestaurante.es; 2pm-4pm and 8:30pm-10:30pm Tues.-Sat.; from €100

The Michelin-starred Abantal is a foodie must. Chef Julio Fernández Quintero and his team have put together a creative menu featuring many of the traditional flavor profiles found in the regional cuisine. Arabic heritage is a clear highlight, as is the attention to texture, color, and local provenance. Menus are created by reservation, taking into account any allergies and intolerances. Pair with the local Spanish wines for a memorable dinner experience you will talk about for years to come.

MUSEO

Tapas Bars

La Brunilda

Calle Galera, 5; tel. 954/220-481; www.labrunildatapas.com/carta; 1:30pm-4:30pm and 8:30pm-11:30pm daily; €15

Head to this tiny, unassuming little bar for a contemporary light tapas dinner. It's run by a husband-and-wife team, with a menu featuring some seafood favorites and a wine list with some of Spain's finest vintages. The buñuelos de bacalao (codfish donuts) and lomo de salmón con salsa de chili dulce (salmon loin with sweet chili sauce) are just the right balance of flavorful and delicate for the end of the evening.

TRIANA

Tapas Bars

Taberna la Plazuela

Plazuela de Santa Ana, 1; 8am-4pm Sun., 8am-4pm and 8pm-midnight Mon., Wed., Thurs., 8am-midnight Fri.-Sat.; €5

No-nonsense tavern set along a quiet neighborhood square. Those looking for an authentic contemporary local bar with minimal tourists should make their way here, but keep expectations low for food as only simple tapas are usually available (Iberian ham, local cheese, olives, that sort of thing). Best for a cold drink on the tree-shaded square. Taberna la Plazuela has a welcoming, neighborhoody ambience with low prices.

Bar La Muralla Triana

Triana Market, toward the back, Puente de Isabel II; tel. 954/344-302; https://mercadodetrianasevilla.com/comercio/bar-la-muralla; 7am-5pm daily; €14

A delightful culinary spot tucked away in the lively Triana Market in the quieter area toward the back, conveniently not too far from the public restrooms. One of their standout dishes is the succulent carrillada, featuring slow-cooked pork cheek bursting with flavorful tenderness. Additionally, their tapas selection offers tempting options such as the rich salmorejo soup, expertly fried calamari, and a standout grilled swordfish. Generous portions, so order accordingly!

La Casa Fundida

Triana Market, toward the entrance, Puente de Isabel II; tel. 600/600-147 or 656/557-560; https://mercadodetrianasevilla.com/comercio/la-casa-fundida; noon-5pm daily, 8pm-11:30pm Fri.-Sat.; €18

Set right inside the entrance of the popular Triana Market, La Casa Fundida is a little gem, known for its flavorful creations that beautifully represent Andalusian cuisine. Among their enticing menu, the perfectly grilled octopus stands out as a highlight, offering a tender and succulent seafood delight. Additionally, their tapas selection features wonderfully cool gazpacho, succulent prawns, shrimp croquetas, and a spicy chorizo sausage that showcase the rich flavors of the region.

Andalusian

Maria Trifulca

Puente de Triana, Plaza del Altozano, 1; tel. 954/330-347; www.mariatrifulca.com; 1pm-1am daily; €25

Classy riverside dining with romantic views along the Guadalquivir River. Best as a dinner spot so you can see the river and city alight with a touch of Andalusian charm. The menu showcases a delightful array of dishes, highlighting the finest local ingredients and innovative techniques. From fresh seafood to succulent grilled meats, each plate is beautifully presented. The inviting atmosphere, with its contemporary decor and cozy outdoor terrace overlooking the river, creates a relaxed and enjoyable ambience. Attentive service, an impressive selection of wines and cocktails, a perfect date spot in Seville. Reservations recommended.

Accommodations

Seville offers a diverse range of accommodations to suit every traveler's preferences. You'll want to stay in the central Barrio Santa Cruz neighborhood, where you'll be within walking distance of iconic sites like the Seville Cathedral, Royal Alcázar, and countless charming tapas bars and restaurants. A variety of options add to the allure of staying in this historic neighborhood. Boutique hotels in Barrio Santa Cruz capture the essence of Seville's charm with their intimate atmosphere, personalized service, and unique decor. Traditional guesthouses and charming bed-and-breakfasts provide a more authentic experience, often housed in restored historic buildings adorned with colorful tiles and courtyards. For a touch of luxury, upscale hotels in the area offer stylish rooms, top-notch amenities, and stunning rooftop terraces boasting panoramic views of the neighborhood and the city's landmarks. The narrow winding streets of Barrio Santa Cruz are lined with cozy apartments available for short-term rentals, allowing travelers to live like locals and immerse themselves in the neighborhood's vibrant ambience.

BARRIO SANTA CRUZ

Under €150

Hotel Simon

García de Vinuesa, 19; tel. 954/226-660; www.hotelsimonsevilla.com; €90

A charming Andalusian villa featuring a picturesque central courtyard. While its amenities are basic, lacking a bar, TV, and in-room tea/coffee facilities, the hotel compensates with its authentic ambience and tranquil atmosphere. The cleanliness is impeccable, although the establishment shows a touch of wear and tear. Its prime location places it just a short stroll away from the cathedral and the vibrant restaurant and bar scene of Barrio Santa Cruz. Be sure to ask for rooms situated off the main street if you are sensitive to noise, or pack your ear plugs.

★ Aquitania Home Suite

Calle Martín Villa, 3; tel. 955/287-499; www.aquitaniahomesuites.com; €115

Classic apartments with exposed brick, oozing with charm and kitted out with everything you need for your stay in Seville. A small equipped kitchen has a breakfast bar, cups, plates, utensils, the all-important coffeemaker, and a small fridge. Each apartment has a lounge area for reading or watching TV, while the front desk is helpful making reservations and recommendations around the city. The rooftop pool is refreshing after a hot day of exploration. An awesome value in Andalusia's priciest city.

Soho Boutique Sevilla

Calle Javier Lasso de la Vega, 6; tel. 955/440-851; www.sohohoteles.com/en/hotel-soho-boutique-sevilla; €135

A chic choice in the heart of the Barrio Santa Cruz, this former palace has bright, cheerful rooms with unexpected pops of color reflecting the vibrance of Seville. There are other Soho Boutique properties in Seville, all good, though this is my fave. The rooms are all well appointed and include thoughtful touches, such as locally sourced bathroom soaps and sustainably produced amenities. Helpfully for those of us that work on the go, the room safes are large enough to store most laptops.

€150-300

Amadeus

Calle Farnesio, 6; tel. 954/501-443; www.hotelamadeussevilla.com; €225

Taking inspiration from classical music, the exposed brick, curvy oak tables, and cheerful living spaces might just put you in the mood for a great sonata. If you are so inclined, pianos and a few other instruments are available to play in a public room on the ground floor. The rooftop with views over the cathedral is magical. The staff will ensure that your stay is a symphony of comfort and hospitality. Musicality aside, the location is central and close to shopping, though on a quieter side street in the Barrio Santa Cruz.

★ Las Casas del Rey de Baeza

Plaza Jesús de la Redención, 2; tel. 954/561-496; www.hospes.com/en/casas-rey-baeza; €250

A restored and upcycled Sevillian farmhouse turned gorgeous boutique in the midst of Seville's most popular neighborhood. The hotel's beautiful architecture, with its traditional courtyards and decorative tiles, creates a tranquil and inviting atmosphere. The rooms are tastefully decorated, offering a blend of modern comfort and traditional Spanish style. The staff's warm hospitality and attention to detail make for a truly memorable stay. Plus, the hotel's central location allows easy exploration of Seville's historic landmarks and vibrant neighborhoods. The splurgy choice for your stay in Seville.

Hotel Casa 1800

Calle Rodrigo Caro, 6; tel. 954/561-800; www.hotelcasa1800sevilla.com; €290

A stately hotel with original coffered ceilings and frescoes dating from the early 19th century, though without the stuffy, stately service. Service is friendly to a fault and the location is fantastic, just a short jaunt to all the major monuments and attractions. You would be forgiven if you spent more time than you expected lounging on the panoramic rooftop pool with unobstructed views over the cathedral.

EL ARENAL

Under €150

La Banda Rooftop Hostel

Calle Dos de Mayo, 16; tel. 621/012-891; https://labandahostel.com; €40

For those on more of a shoestring budget or who like the hostel environment when traveling, there are several fun ones to choose from around Seville. For 10 years, though, all the other hostels have been trying, and not quite succeeding, to live up to the ambience of La Banda. Friendly family-style dinners with crafted cocktails and musical performances on the rooftop terrace are a nightly thing, the Seville Cathedral a beautiful backdrop to it all. It's close enough to the Barrio Santa Cruz to be considered a central location.

Information and Services

TOURIST OFFICES

There are several tourist offices (https://visitasevilla.es) dotted around Seville. Make liberal use of these, particularly if you are looking for what shows and events are happening in town. They can tell you where to get tickets. Here are three of the most conveniently located offices in town:

- **Seville Cathedral:** Plaza del Triunfo, 1-3; tel. 954/787-578; 9am-7:30pm Mon.-Fri., 9:30am-7:30pm weekends and holidays
- **Seville Airport:** Arrivals Terminal, Buzón A027; tel. 954/782-035 or 954/782-036; 9am-7:30pm Mon.-Fri., 9:30am-3pm weekends and holidays
- **Santa Justa Train Station:** Avenida Kansas City; tel. 954/782-002; 9am-7:30pm Mon.-Fri., 9:30am-3pm weekends and holidays

HOSPITALS

Seville is a large city with public and private hospitals. For most travelers, the private hospitals will be more likely to provide the sort of service and care you would expect back home (even better, in many cases!), with cost-effective fees and the ability to work with most international insurance programs. At least a few staff speak English. The following hospitals are open 24 hours.

Victoria Eugenia

Avenida de la Cruz Roja; tel. 954/351-400; https://hospitalveugenia.com

Victoria Eugenia is a private hospital that should be able to help with most urgent care.

Vithas Hospital

Avenida Plácido Fernández Viagas, Castilleja de la Cuesta; tel. 954/464-000; https://vithas.es/centro/vithas-hospital-sevilla

Vithas Hospital is another private hospital in Seville.

PHARMACIES

You'll find easily recognizable pharmacies all over the city. The unmissable **Art Deco Pharmacia** (Calle Argote de Molina, 25; tel. 954/224-329; 9:30am-10pm daily) is centrally located, reliable, and generally open on Sunday (unlike many other pharmacies).

POLICE

If your passport is stolen or lost, you must file the appropriate report (loss or theft) at a police station. Remember to notify your embassy as well. If you have been a victim of a crime or need assistance in Seville, head directly to the central **Police Station** (Alameda de Hércules, 39; open 24/7) in the historic district. Most of the law enforcement here speak some English.

POST OFFICES

You will see post offices, or correos, dotted throughout Seville. One of the more convenient ones is **Oficina de Correos y Citypaq** (Jesús del Gran Poder, 86; tel. 954/905-104; 8:30am-8:30pm Mon.-Fri., closed holidays), located in the Museo neighborhood.

BANKS/ATMS

You'll find ATM machines and different banks easily available and scattered throughout the city. Just north of the cathedral is a solid location of banks and ATMs, from Caixa Bank on Avenida de la Constitución to Banco de España on Plaza de San Francisco.

LUGGAGE STORAGE

(Consignas Equipaje)

If you need luggage storage, your accommodation will generally be happy to stow your extra bags for you at no extra cost while you spend time in the city before departure. If for some reason you need a luggage storage solution, check out **Stasher** (https://stasher.com), which offers insured baggage hold for a modest €6 a day per bag at locations dotted throughout the city.

The **Santa Justa train station** has convenient lockers starting at €3.10 a day. Look for the **Consignas** sign on the ground floor.

Transportation

GETTING THERE

Air

Seville San Pablo Airport

SVQ; A-4, km 532; tel. 954/449-000

The Seville San Pablo Airport is a busy international airport with connections to over 40 destinations around Europe and North Africa. It serves as a hub for budget airlines **Vueling** and **Ryanair.** The airport is 10 km (6.2 mi) east of Seville, just off the A-4 autoroute.

TUSSAM bus **route EA** connects the Seville Airport with downtown Seville (1 hr, daily every 12 min or so; €4). Look for the bright sign reading Bus Seville Centro just after passport control before exiting the airport across from all the car rental storefronts. Purchase your bus tickets here. Exit the doors and walk to your right about 40 m (100 ft). There are two ticketing machines next to the bus stop as well, though they are often not functioning. The bus stop is thankfully shaded.

Train

Santa Justa Train Station

Calle Joaquin Morales y Torres; tel. 912/320-320; www.renfe.com; 4:30am-12:30am, Mon.-Sat., 5:15am-12:30am Sun. and holidays

The Santa Justa train station is a 20-minute walk (1.5 km/1 mi) from Barrio Santa Cruz. From here, you can get trains to any major city in Spain. Book tickets ahead of time on the Renfe website for the best price and to ensure a ticket for your preferred departure day and time. Tickets are available about two months before train departure on the Renfe website. Other train ticket resellers, such as www.thetrainline.com and https://rail.ninja, are slightly more expensive, but they offer a smoother user experience and the ability to purchase tickets months ahead of time.

When purchasing tickets, be aware that there are different trains offering a different rail experience. The high-speed train option is a quicker, though more expensive, connection, and train cars are generally air-conditioned and have amenities like power outlets to recharge your devices, a cafeteria car for snacks and drink, more storage space for luggage, and designated seats for travelers with special needs. The slower local lines make more stops, though they are less expensive and have fewer amenities. Traveler tip: If the air-conditioning doesn't seem to be working in your car, head to the cafeteria, where the air-conditioning always works really well.

Car

Avis, Budget, Hertz, Enterprise, Europcar, and Sixt all have rental car offices right in the Seville Airport after passport control. You will also find their offices in the Seville train station. Typically, rental cars are less expensive in Málaga, where last-minute deals can often get you a small four-door sedan for around €10 a day.

GETTING AROUND

Walking

Seville is an extremely walkable, relatively flat city. Most of the major sites of interest can be reached within a 15- to 20-minute stroll. Barrio Santa Cruz even has a few pedestrian-only shopping thoroughfares that are nicely shaded during the warmer months. Keep in mind that heat and sunstroke can be a real concern, so head out prepared with a parasol or sunhat and sunscreen in the warmer months.

By foot, you will be able to best experience Sevillian life. Plenty of buskers and street performers populate the more touristy areas, while often just heading down a quiet street will unveil yet something else magical about this city. Crosswalks are well identified and drivers are respectful of pedestrians, but do keep an ear out for the jangle of horse-drawn carriages, as these sometimes pass a bit closer than is perhaps comfortable. You'll find traffic lights for pedestrians themed for Seville—a flamenco dancer silhouette for the red light and a green guitarist for the green light—at major intersections. Respect the lights and respect your feet; don't forget a comfy pair of walking shoes! No matter the heat, you won't want to head out wearing a pair of flip-flops.

Bus

The **TUSSAM buses** (tel. 955/010-010 or 955/479-000; www.tussam.es; 5:30am-10:30pm daily; €1.40) connect all through Seville. Buses generally run from early to late-ish at night, though each line has a slightly different schedule. The bus is particularly handy when connecting with the airport (EA bus, 1 hr, €4, daily every 12 min or so) and train station (28, 32, C1, and C2 buses).

If you plan on taking the bus often, purchase the tarjeta multiviaje (multitrip card; €1.50 deposit plus €10 minimum; €1.50 deposit returned when ticket returned). Bus trips on the multitrip card run less than €1 a trip. Multiple people can use the multitrip card, so it's a good option for families and friends traveling together.

The tourist travel pass (1-day €5, 3-day €10 plus €1.50 deposit for card, returnable like the multitrip pass) allows unlimited use of transport over the period of the card but is non-transferable and doesn't include a connection to the airport, so it's only a good choice if you really plan on making use of the bus system.

Light Rail

For most travelers, Seville's one-route light rail system, Metro de Sevilla, is not the most practical solution, but it's great for commuters or those opting to stay outside central Seville. The single light rail line is divided into three sections. The "green zone" (trama 1) is the large middle part of the line and the area of most touristic interest, stretching from Blas Infante to Pablo de Olavide. A single ticket (€1.35) in this zone can whisk you from one side of the old city to the other.

Taxi

You'll find taxi stands dotted throughout the city, and flagging one down is generally a piece of cake. €5-7 will get you just about anywhere in central Seville, and on hot days the quick, air-conditioned ride is welcomed relief.

During the Feria de Abril and in peak seasons, taxis can be much tougher to come by.

Car

Driving in Spain is as it is in North America, though with notably more roundabouts and, in central Seville, lots of one-way streets. Signage is of course in Spanish. GPS directions work quite well and, thankfully, parking is easy to find. For most travelers road-tripping through Andalusia, the solution is to find a parking lot and check in your car for the days you are in Seville. As wonderful as a drive through the white villages is, driving in the old cities is more stress than it's worth, even with a great copilot and GPS guiding the way.

Parking

Parking lots in Seville are easy to find. Just follow the big blue signs with a large white letter P! You can also elect to park on the street. In certain neighborhoods there is ample street parking, but do be aware of the local laws because parking may be forbidden on some days. Here are a couple of parking lots I use regularly.

Parking Avenida Roma (Parada de las Delicias; tel. 954/500-552; €24 per day) is an underground car park just off the main thoroughfare running along the east side of the water, near the Torre del Oro. It's a short three-minute walk to the cathedral and Barrio Santa Cruz.

Parking Paseo Colón (Parada de Cristóbal Colón; tel. 954/224-239; €24 per day) is another underground car park right next to the old bullring, also off the main road running on the east side of the water, just a few minutes' walk to Barrio Santa Cruz and the major sites.

Seville's light rail

Sierra Norte de Sevilla Natural Park

Tucked in the heart of the expansive Sierra Morena lies the vast, tranquil expanse of the Sierra Norte de Sevilla Natural Park. A canvas of gently rolling hills is adorned with thick evergreen oak forests. This hidden gem, sparsely populated and extending over 177,484 hectares (438,573 acres), remains a well-kept secret, often bypassed by international travelers but cherished by Sevillians seeking refuge from the city's hustle. A mere 90 km (56 mi) north of Seville, this natural haven beckons locals on weekends and holidays, offering a sanctuary of pristine wilderness.

Within its boundaries, charming villages and towns dot the landscape, each exuding a Moorish charm. Winding, cobbled streets ascend steeply, rewarding travelers with a feeling of being steeped in old-world history. Many of these ancient paths lead to hilltop castles or Mudejar churches, adding a touch of architectural marvel to the serene beauty of the park, where nature and history converge in a landscape that feels both timeless and authentically Andalusian.

VISITING THE PARK

Just over an hour from Seville, though not frequented by travelers, this is an extremely popular park for locals. Though most arrive by car, there is a train that stops in Cazalla de la Sierra, making this one of the most accessible parks in all of Andalusia for those traveling by rail. The park has four proper seasons, with autumn being most impressive as all the leaves change color in the oak forests.

Gateway Towns

Cazalla de la Sierra

Cazalla boasts one of the better-kept churches in the park, **Iglesia de Nuestra Señora de la Consolación** (Plaza Mayor, 2; tel. 954/884-043; 11am-1pm Mon.-Sat.; free), as well as a number of large mansions and monasteries funded from the proceeds of the local liqueur factories and wineries. One of these monasteries, the former Carthusian monastery of **La Cartuja de Cazalla** (Finca La Cartuja; tel. 617/271-024; www.lacartujadecazalla.com; €95), has been transformed into a charming rural stay with unbeatable appeal. In Cazalla you can nearly always find free parking on **Plaza Mayor,** the central square of this hilly village. There are also several options for dining should you need refreshments.

Constantina

The largest town in the park has over 6,500 inhabitants and a history dating back thousands of years. Historically, Constantina was an important Roman settlement. You can feel the medieval charm of its cobblestone roads, particularly in the Barrio la Morería. This is the most interesting section of town and preserves the Moorish heritage of Constantina. **Castillo de Constantina** (Calle Venero; tel. 955/881-297; hours vary; free), the renovated fortress at the top of the hill, dates from the Islamic era and is worth a quick detour, even if you only walk the castle grounds, which are open 24/7. The **Anís La Violetera Distillery** (Calle Mentidero, 2; tel. 955/880-763; www.anislavioletera.com; 10:30am-2pm and 5pm-8pm Mon.-Fri., 10:30am-2pm Sat.; free) is an experience in family-run artisanal distillation that should not be missed. In town you'll find quite a few options for bars and cafés to get a bite to eat.

Visitor Centers

Cortijo El Berrocal Visitor Center

Camino Rural Almadén de la Plata-los Melonares, km 5.5, Almadén de la Plata; tel. 955/952-049; 10am-3pm Thurs.-Sun.

An exhibition center provides information about the park as well as maps, including detailed maps of different walks and activities. Activities not covered in this guide but possible in the park include horse riding, trout fishing, bike rental, and canoeing on the reservoir.

HIKING

Sendero Molino del Corcho

Distance: *9.7 km/6 mi round-trip*
Time: *2.5 hr*
Elevation gain: *104 m/341 ft*
Effort: *moderate*
Trailhead: *Isla Margarita picnic area, Cazalla de la Sierra*

If you fancy a walk along a gurgling river, you'll want to pack a picnic and make for this trail. As with most hikes in this area, if you can do this in autumn, visually it will be stunning with the changing leaves while the summer weather has passed its peak. For this out-and-back trail, consider taking your swimsuit if it's warm enough for a chilling plunge into the river.

Sendero de los Castañares

Distance: *7.5 km/4 mi round-trip*
Time: *2 hr*
Elevation gain: *173 m/567 ft*
Effort: *easy*
Trailhead: *Calle Venero, Constantina*

From Constantina, you will quickly enter a land of sweet chestnut groves (castañares) and make a sloped climb to a hilltop viewpoint overlooking the mountains. The path descends through another forest of oak and olive as it loops back to Constantina. This walk is best done in autumn so you get those bright oranges, reds, and yellows from the changing leaves. If it has rained recently, plan for lots of mud.

GETTING THERE AND AROUND

Train

From Seville, there is a train that stops in Cazalla de la Sierra (1.5 hr; 5 daily; €10), making it possible to get to the park for those hopping on the rails. Once in Cazalla you will be limited to the trails, accommodations, and restaurants in town, as accessing other parts of the park requires a car.

Car

If you have a rental car, you can get to the park by heading east from Seville (1.5 hr; 95 km/59 mi) on the A-4, turning off at Carmona, continuing north on the A-457 to Lora del Río, and then continuing north on the A-455 into the park. There are a series of smaller roads and dirt paths in the park. Park your car to explore the towns and the park on foot.

waterfall in the Sierra Norte de Sevilla Natural Park

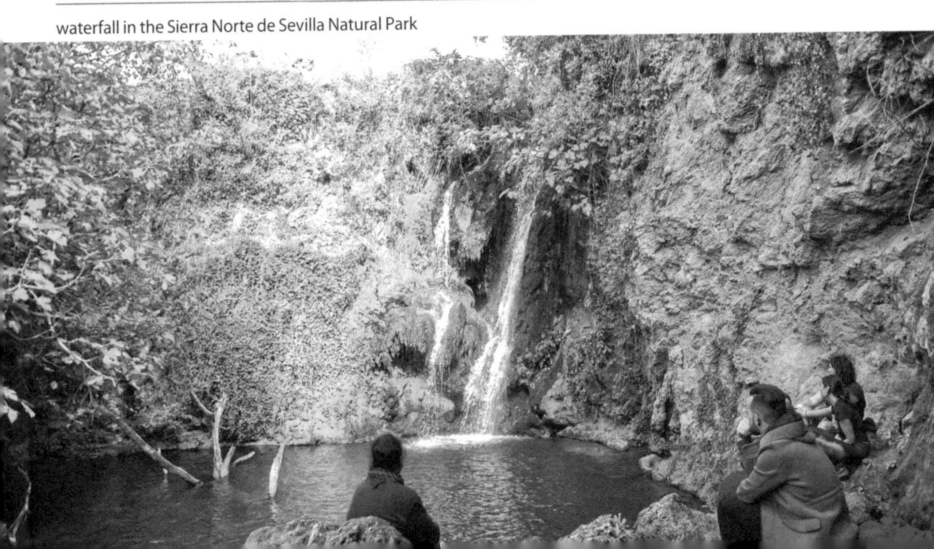

Córdoba, Antequera, and El Torcal Nature Reserve

Smack dab in the heart of Andalusia lies Córdoba, an oft-forgotten-by-travelers city with a history that traces back to the Roman era. Córdoba boasts enduring influences from Moorish and Christian civilizations, and these days, the city offers a true immersion into the heart of Andalusia's rich heritage that is easier to access than in its more touristed sister cities of Seville, Granada, and Málaga.

The crown jewel of Córdoba is the Mosque-Cathedral, an incredible UNESCO World Heritage Site that encapsulates the city's unique history spanning from the Visigoth and Jewish eras through the Muslim and Catholic. It was one of the great mosques of the world during the Islamic era. After the Reconquista, this architectural masterpiece was

Highlights

Look for ★ to find recommended sights, activities, dining, and lodging.

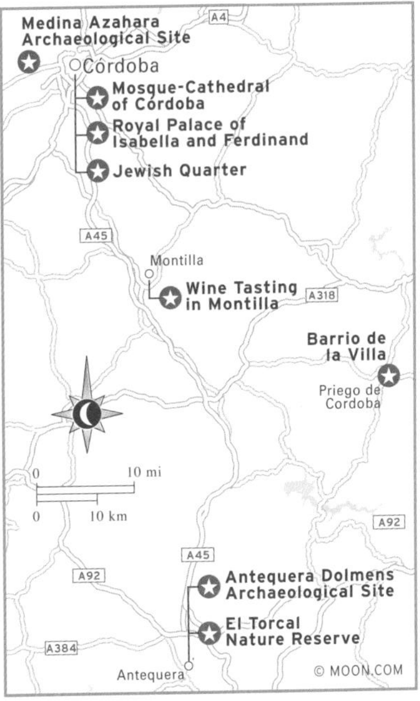

★ **Mosque-Cathedral of Córdoba:** This stunning example of Islamic architecture features a cathedral built within a mosque (page 93).

★ **Royal Palace of Isabella and Ferdinand:** The Alcázar de Los Reyes Cristianos is a historic palace with beautiful gardens and a fascinating history (page 95).

★ **Jewish Quarter:** The old Judería of Córdoba is known for its narrow streets and whitewashed buildings (page 98).

★ **Medina Azahara Archaeological Site:** The ruins of a vast medieval palace city lie just outside Córdoba (page 109).

★ **Barrio de la Villa:** In Priego de Córdoba, the best preserved Islamic-era neighborhood in Andalusia transports you back to medieval Muslim Spain (page 112).

★ **Wine Tasting in Montilla:** Explore the historic vineyards and wineries of the region for an experience that will touch all of your senses (page 119).

★ **Antequera Dolmens Archaeological Site:** These megalithic monuments, dating back to the Neolithic era, are an impressive example of prehistoric architecture (page 123).

★ **El Torcal Nature Reserve:** This stunning park boasts unique limestone formations and hiking trails for all levels (page 128).

transformed into a Christian cathedral. The incongruous blend of Islamic and Gothic architectural elements within its walls tells the captivating story of Córdoba's past.

Make time to wander through the enchanting Jewish Quarter, or "Judería," where meandering streets and whitewashed buildings adorned with cheerful flowerpots create a truly picturesque scene. The Synagogue of Córdoba, one of Spain's oldest, stands as a poignant symbol of the city's rich Jewish heritage. Nearby, the Royal Palace of Isabella and Ferdinand (Alcázar de los Reyes Cristianos), a medieval fortress and palace, boasts meticulously landscaped gardens and awe-inspiring views of the Guadalquivir River. The palace gardens serve as a serene oasis, offering respite from the city's lively streets.

One of Córdoba's most iconic symbols, the Roman Bridge (Puente Romano), gracefully spans the Guadalquivir River, affording an ideal vantage point to marvel at the city's skyline. At the far end of the bridge sits the Calahorra Tower, which today houses a museum that delves into Córdoba's history, including its Islamic and Roman origins.

Every spring, Córdoba bursts into life with the vivid colors of its traditional courtyards, or "patios." The May Patio Festival showcases the creativity and horticultural prowess of Córdoba's residents, providing a unique and culturally enriching experience for visitors. Year-round, Córdoba's culinary scene is a delightful journey of flavors, where you can dig into traditional dishes such as salmorejo, a refreshing cold tomato and bread soup, and flamenquín, a delicious deep-fried ham and cheese roll. Complete your culinary adventure with a pastel cordobés, a local pastry filled with sweet pumpkin or sweet potato.

Córdoba, where history, culture, and gastronomy seamlessly converge, ensures travelers an unforgettable experience, allowing them to dive headfirst into the captivating heritage of Andalusia. And remember, the city's warmth is not just in its weather, but also in the smiles of its people—a truly Spanish alegría (joy) that will leave you with lasting memories. In Córdoba it's all about savoring life and tapas, because, as the locals joke, "A meal without tapas is like a day without sunshine!"

Beyond Córdoba, you can find some truly authentic Andalusian towns, each with its own charm and rich history. Though this area is central Andalusia, it is far less touristed than some other regions, while some spots are more popular with Spanish travelers than international ones. Atop Antequera you will find the impressive El Torcal Nature Reserve and its storied rock formations, while below you can delve into prehistoric megalithic rock formations at the Antequera Dolmens Archaeological Site. The town of Montilla is known throughout Spain for its fine wine, and Lucena was once the Sephardic capital for the region. The mountain towns of Zuheros and Priego de Córdoba offer incredible views and a touch of mountain culture similar in some respects to the white villages, though much less touristed.

For those looking to escape the crowds, this is the region in which to spend some time, connect with locals, and uncover some of the most distinctive history in all of Europe.

HISTORY

Córdoba's origins can be traced back to the Roman era, when it was known as "Corduba." The Romans, skilled engineers and builders, established the city, leaving enduring architectural structures. Among them stands the Puente Romano, a 1st-century bridge that gracefully spans the Guadalquivir River, connecting the city's two banks.

The zenith of Córdoba's architectural prowess arrived during Abd al-Rahman III's rule of the Umayyad caliphate in the 10th century. At this peak, the city was a beacon of culture and refinement in Europe. The Great

Previous: Mosque-Cathedral of Córdoba; Hebrew script in arabesque decoration in the Jewish Quarter; gardens at the Royal Palace of Isabella and Ferdinand.

Mosque of Córdoba, a paragon of architectural engineering, was constructed during this epoch. Its hallmark horseshoe arches, elegant columns, and ornate gilded mihrab create an awe-inspiring sacred space, showcasing the precision of builders. Nearby Medina Azahara also was built during this era, designed to be a symbol of the wealth and power of the Umayyad caliphate of Córdoba. For a brief period, this small city served as the political and administrative center of the caliphate. The construction of Medina Azahara continued over several decades, reaching its peak during the rule of Abd al-Rahman III's son, Al-Hakam II.

The 13th century ushered in a new chapter as Córdoba was reclaimed by Christian forces under Ferdinand III of Castile during the Reconquista. The transformation of the Great Mosque into the Mosque-Cathedral is a testament to the city's complex history. In this architectural marvel, Christian chapels and Gothic features were integrated into the existing Islamic structure, symbolizing the harmonious coexistence of architectural styles—or a disastrous design faux pas. You decide.

The 16th century heralded yet another architectural renaissance, witnessed in structures such as the Royal Palace of Isabella and Ferdinand. These buildings showcase the grandeur of the Spanish Golden Age, still resonating through the city's architectural legacy today.

Córdoba's historic center, a UNESCO World Heritage Site, safeguards this blend of architectural wonders. As you meander through its winding streets, grand palaces, and historic buildings, you'll discover that the city's history isn't confined to textbooks; it's a living, breathing narrative etched into every stone and archway, beckoning you to step back in time and immerse yourself as you meander the charming pedestrian-friendly city.

ORIENTATION

Córdoba is perched along the serene banks of the Guadalquivir River, with a 2,000-year-old Roman Bridge connecting its right and left banks. Its strategic location within the region has historically made it a gateway to Andalusia and, during the age of the great explorers, to the New World. Today's city can easily be divided into two areas to explore: the historic center and greater Córdoba.

The historic center is where most travelers spend their time. Here is where you will find the Mosque-Cathedral, a stunning fusion of Islamic and Christian architecture; the Royal Palace; and the Judería (Jewish Quarter), an iconic neighborhood and labyrinth of narrow streets and whitewashed buildings, reminiscent of Córdoba's medieval past. The centrally located train station here offers easy access to high-speed rail services, connecting travelers to major cities throughout Spain.

Greater Córdoba offers archaeological sites, a few museums, restaurants, and lodging options.

Medina Azahara, an impressive archaeological site, is approximately 8 km (5 mi) west of Córdoba. This historic palace city, built by the Umayyad caliphate, is a short journey from Córdoba's historic center by taxi, rental car, or bicycle.

The often-overlooked town of Antequera lies just south of Córdoba (115 km/72 mi). This area is home to the El Torcal Nature Reserve, a wonderfully unique park and UNESCO World Heritage Site, as well as megalithic stone structures called dolmens. The area around Córdoba includes several other smaller cities and villages worth visiting should your travel time allow, including Lucena, Montilla, Zuheros, and Priego de Córdoba.

PLANNING YOUR TIME

As with much of inland Andalusia, the best times to visit are in the spring and fall, which offer better weather and generally fewer crowds. Córdoba's famous Patio Festival is an annual two-week festival that usually happens in May, and it may be something you want to plan for or plan around, depending on how you feel about crowds. While Córdoba, Lucena, and Antequera are not as

Córdoba, Antequera, and El Torcal Nature Reserve

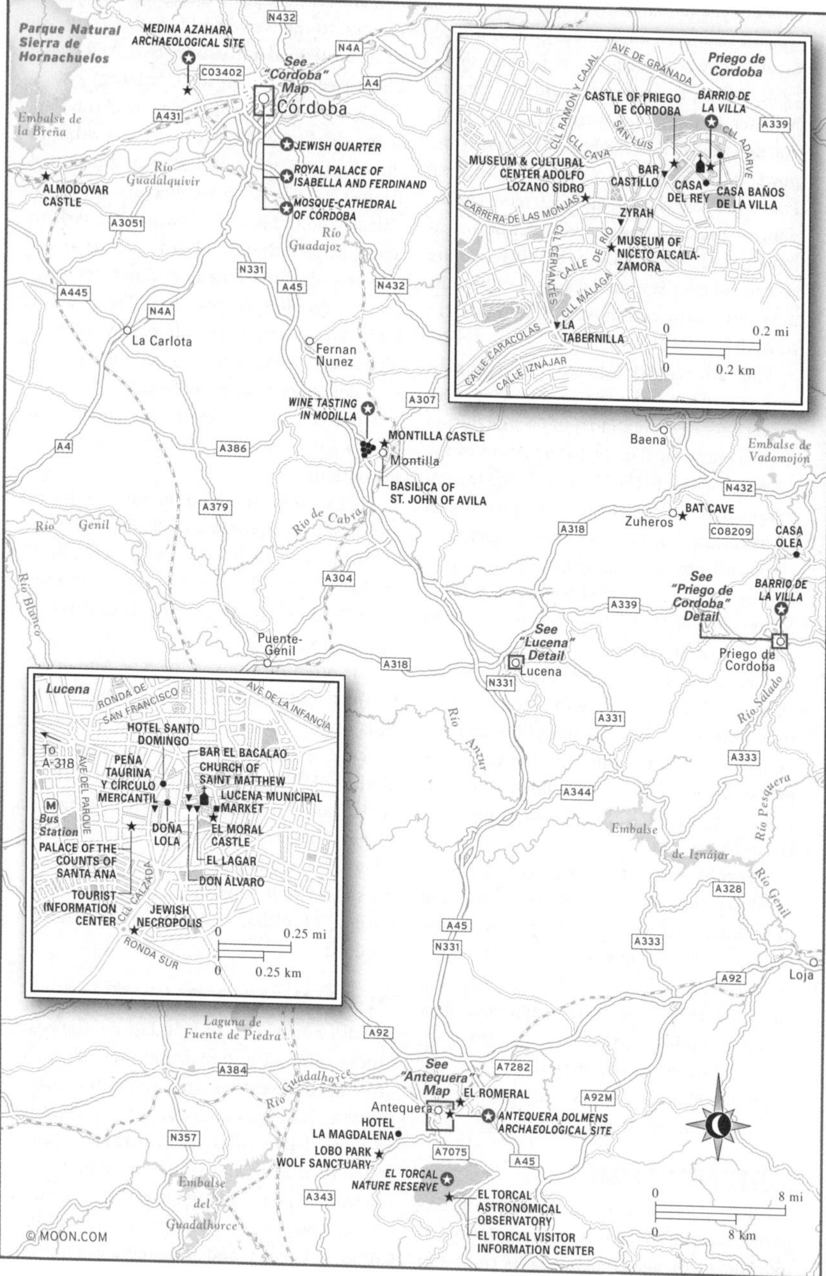
Parque Natural Sierra de Hornachuelos
MEDINA AZAHARA ARCHAEOLOGICAL SITE
See "Córdoba" Map
Córdoba
Embalse de la Breña
JEWISH QUARTER
ROYAL PALACE OF ISABELLA AND FERDINAND
MOSQUE-CATHEDRAL OF CÓRDOBA
Río Guadalquivir
ALMODÓVAR CASTLE
Río Guadajoz
La Carlota
Fernan Nunez
WINE TASTING IN MODILLA
MONTILLA CASTLE
Montilla
BASILICA OF ST. JOHN OF AVILA
Río Genil
Río de Cabra
Río Blanco
Puente-Genil
See "Lucena" Detail
Lucena
Baena
Embalse de Vadomojón
Zuheros
BAT CAVE
CASA OLEA
See "Priego de Cordoba" Detail
BARRIO DE LA VILLA
Priego de Cordoba
Río Salado
Río Anzur
Río Pesquera
Embalse de Iznájar
Río Genil
Loja
Laguna de Fuente de Piedra
Río Guadalhorce
See "Antequera" Map
EL ROMERAL
Antequera
ANTEQUERA DOLMENS ARCHAEOLOGICAL SITE
HOTEL LA MAGDALENA
LOBO PARK WOLF SANCTUARY
EL TORCAL NATURE RESERVE
EL TORCAL ASTRONOMICAL OBSERVATORY
EL TORCAL VISITOR INFORMATION CENTER
Embalse del Guadalhorce
N432
N4A
C03402
A4
A431
A3051
N331
A45
A445
A386
A307
A379
A304
A318
A339
N432
C08209
A331
A333
A344
A328
A92
A384
A7282
A92M
N357
A7075
A343
Priego de Cordoba
AVE DE GRANADA
CLL RAMON Y CAJAL
CASTLE OF PRIEGO DE CÓRDOBA
BARRIO DE LA VILLA
SAN LUIS
CLL CAVA
CLL ADARVE
MUSEUM & CULTURAL CENTER ADOLFO LOZANO SIDRO
BAR CASTILLO
CASA DEL REY
CASA BAÑOS DE LA VILLA
CARRERA DE LAS MONJAS
ZYRAH
MUSEUM OF NICETO ALCALÁ-ZAMORA
CLL CERVANTES
CALLE DE RÍO
CLL MÁLAGA
LA TABERNILLA
CALLE CARACOLAS
CALLE IZNÁJAR
0.2 mi
0.2 km
Lucena
RONDA DE SAN FRANCISCO
AVE DE LA INFANCIA
HOTEL SANTO DOMINGO
BAR EL BACALAO
To A-318
PEÑA TAURINA Y CÍRCULO MERCANTIL
CHURCH OF SAINT MATTHEW
LUCENA MUNICIPAL MARKET
AVE DEL PARQUE
Bus Station
DOÑA LOLA
EL MORAL CASTLE
PALACE OF THE COUNTS OF SANTA ANA
EL LAGAR
DON ÁLVARO
CLL CALZADA
TOURIST INFORMATION CENTER
JEWISH NECROPOLIS
RONDA SUR
0.25 mi
0.25 km
8 mi
8 km
© MOON.COM

frequently overrun by tourists as some of the larger Andalusian cities, you may still run into crowds at popular attractions, such as the Mosque-Cathedral of Córdoba.

Downtown Córdoba is relatively flat and pedestrian friendly. You will want to explore the historic district on foot. However, to explore the region outside Córdoba, including Medina Azahara and Antequera, as well as smaller towns like Lucena, Montilla, and Priego de Córdoba, a rental car offers the easiest, most flexible way to maximize your time. If you're using public transportation, options are listed for connections to/from Córdoba, though be sure to account for extra travel time.

Plan for at least 3-4 days to explore this region thoroughly. In Córdoba, allocate a significant portion of your time to the Mosque-Cathedral, Royal Palace of Isabella and Ferdinand (Alcázar de los Reyes Cristianos), and the rest of the historic center. These landmarks are the heart of Córdoba's historical and cultural heritage. Not far from Córdoba lies the Medina Azahara; dedicate about half a day for its exploration.

Enjoy at least a half day in the El Torcal Nature Reserve to hike through the unique limestone formations along well-marked trails, which offer a surreal landscape for exploring and appreciating the natural beauty of the area.

Spend another half day in Antequera. The Alcazaba and the dolmens of Antequera are must-visit sites, though both only require an hour at most.

If time allows, don't miss the chance to explore the charming towns of Lucena, Montilla, Zuheros, and Priego de Córdoba, each offering its own sort of charm. In smaller towns like these, you will most readily enjoy an authentic atmosphere, visit historical sites, and explore the picturesque streets alongside locals.

Itinerary Ideas

DAY 1: CÓRDOBA

1 Begin your day in Córdoba at the mesmerizing **Mosque-Cathedral,** a stunning blend of Islamic and Christian architecture, and explore the forest of columns and arches.

2 Stroll through the **historic center** around the cathedral, whose charming streets have been designated a UNESCO World Heritage Site.

3 Enjoy a traditional Andalusian lunch at **Bodega San Basilio,** tasting dishes like salmorejo and flamenquín.

4 Visit the **Royal Palace of Isabella and Ferdinand,** with its beautiful gardens and impressive courtyards. Discover its history, including its involvement with the great world explorers.

5 In the evening, experience Córdoba's unique atmosphere by wandering around the **Roman Bridge** and the surrounding area, where the city's historic buildings are beautifully illuminated.

DAY 2: AROUND CÓRDOBA

The best way to explore Medina Azahara and Montilla is by car. You can take a taxi to/from Medina Azahara, but skip Montilla if you're car-less.

Itinerary Ideas

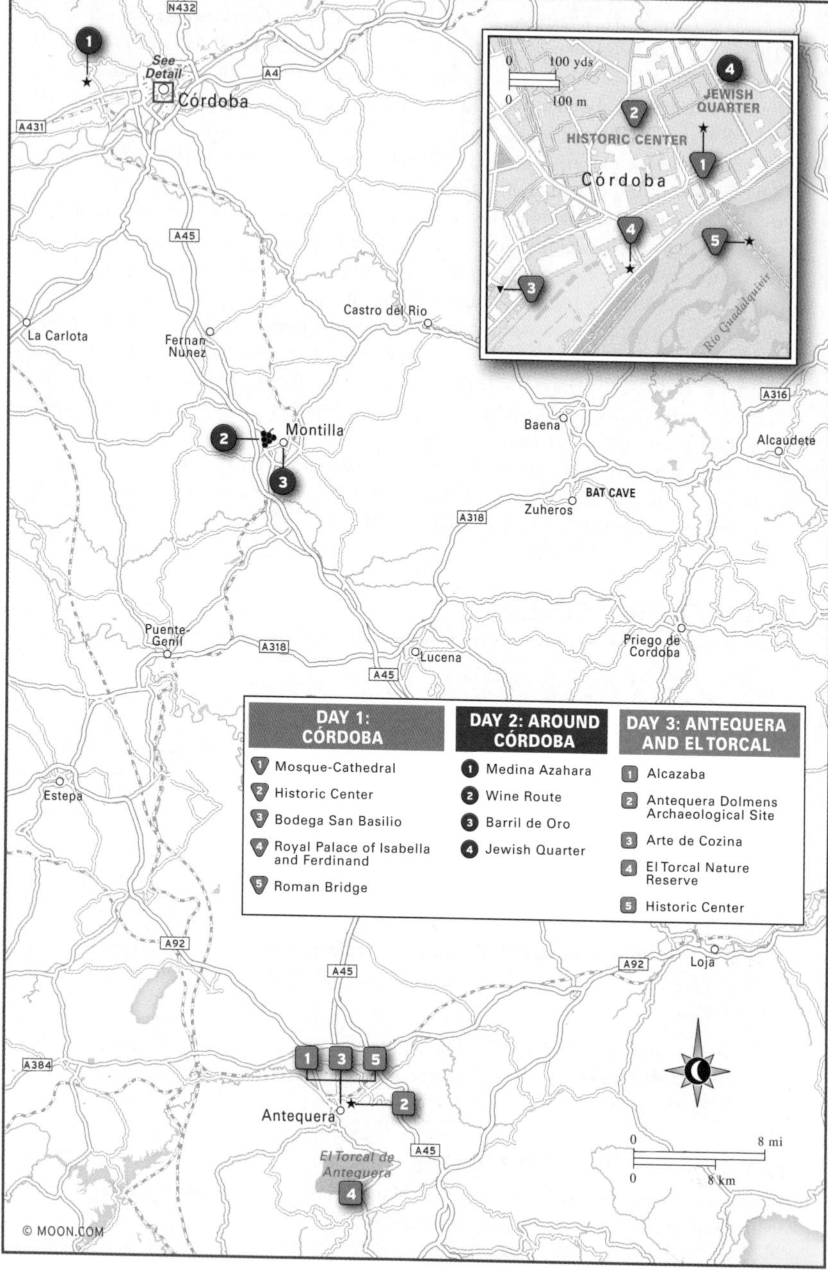
DAY 1: CÓRDOBA
1 Mosque-Cathedral
2 Historic Center
3 Bodega San Basilio
4 Royal Palace of Isabella and Ferdinand
5 Roman Bridge
DAY 2: AROUND CÓRDOBA
1 Medina Azahara
2 Wine Route
3 Barril de Oro
4 Jewish Quarter
DAY 3: ANTEQUERA AND EL TORCAL
1 Alcazaba
2 Antequera Dolmens Archaeological Site
3 Arte de Cozina
4 El Torcal Nature Reserve
5 Historic Center
See Detail
Córdoba
N432
A4
A431
A45
La Carlota
Fernan Nunez
Castro del Rio
Montilla
Baena
Alcaudete
A316
BAT CAVE
Zuheros
A318
Puente-Genil
Lucena
Priego de Córdoba
Estepa
A92
Loja
A384
Antequera
El Torcal de Antequera
JEWISH QUARTER
HISTORIC CENTER
Río Guadalquivir
0
100 yds
100 m
8 mi
8 km
© MOON.COM

1 Spend your morning at the **Medina Azahara,** an archaeological site that offers insights into the city's Islamic history.

2 Afterward, head into nearby Montilla and enjoy some of the region's vintages along the **wine route.**

3 Savor a delicious Andalusian lunch at **Barril de Oro,** enjoying local specialties like rabo de toro (oxtail) and salmorejo.

4 As the day winds down, return to Córdoba and head to the **Jewish Quarter.** Enjoy the vibrant atmosphere and try popping into a bar or two for a sundowner.

DAY 3: ANTEQUERA AND EL TORCAL

From Córdoba, connection to Antequera by bus or train is straightforward, though once in Antequera, you will need to take a taxi to El Torcal.

1 Depart from Córdoba and head to Antequera, a picturesque town with a rich history. Start your day at the **Alcazaba,** an ancient fortress offering panoramic views of the town and surrounding landscapes.

2 Visit the **Antequera Dolmens Archaeological Site,** a collection of megalithic tombs dating back over 5,000 years and a UNESCO World Heritage Site.

3 Enjoy a memorable lunch at **Arte de Cozina,** sampling home-cooked dishes such as porra antequerana and migas.

4 In the afternoon, make your way to **El Torcal Nature Reserve,** a unique natural park known for its otherworldly limestone formations. Hike along the marked trails and marvel at the surreal landscape.

5 As the day comes to an end, return to Antequera for a leisurely evening exploring the town's **historic center.**

Córdoba

SIGHTS

Historic Center

If you only have one day in Córdoba, concentrate your time here, as all the sites are within easy walking distance. The entirety of the historic district is a registered UNESCO World Heritage Site, so there is no lack of antique charm along the many pedestrian thoroughfares and cobblestone streets.

TOP EXPERIENCE

★ Mosque-Cathedral of Córdoba (Mezquita-Catedral de Córdoba)

Calle Cardinal Herrero, 1; tel. 957/470-512; https://mezquita-catedraldecordoba.es; 10am-7pm Mon.-Sat., 8:30am-11:30am and 3pm-7pm Sun.; €13 (bell tower access €3; ascents every 30 min)

Of the sites to see in all of Andalusia, the Mosque-Cathedral of Córdoba lands right at the top of the list, perhaps only overtaken by the Alhambra in Granada. It's a true masterpiece of 10th-century Islamic architecture whose influences are still felt today. Under the rule of the caliph Hisham II at the turn of the 11th century, the expansive mosque took shape. The sight of the galleys' jasper and marble columns gracefully supporting horseshoe arches that seemingly echo on forever strikes awe in travelers and the faithful.

Carved out of the middle of the mosque lies a 16th-century cathedral, "a strange

Córdoba

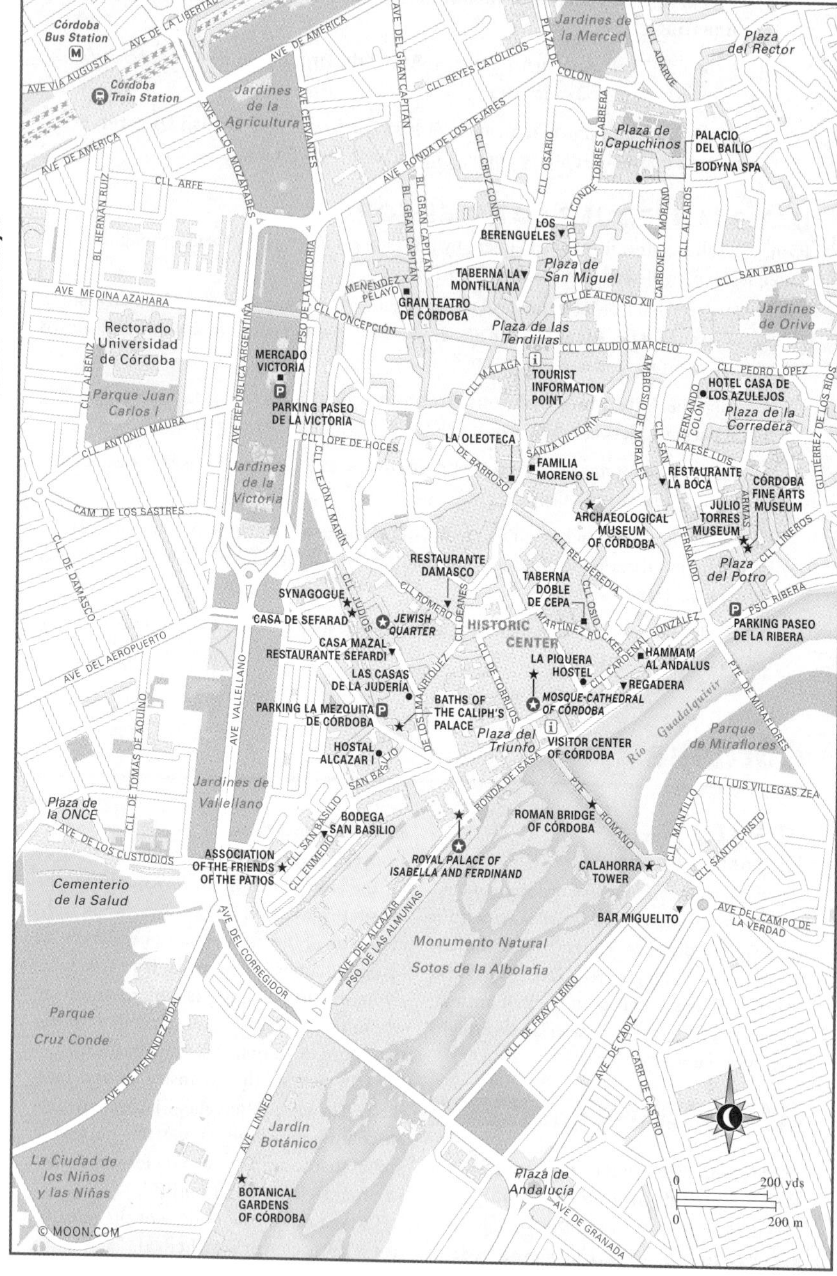
Córdoba Bus Station
Córdoba Train Station
AVE DE LA LIBERTAD
AVE DE AMÉRICA
AVE VIA AUGUSTA
Jardines de la Agricultura
AVE CERVANTES
AVE DE LOS MOZÁRABES
AVE DEL GRAN CAPITÁN
CLL REYES CATÓLICOS
Jardines de la Merced
PLAZA DE COLÓN
CLL ADARVE
Plaza del Rector
AVE RONDA DE LOS TEJARES
CLL CRUZ CONDE
CLL OSARIO
CLL DEL CONDE TORRES CABRERA
Plaza de Capuchinos
PALACIO DEL BAILÍO
BODYNA SPA
CLL ARFE
BL HERNÁN RUIZ
BL GRAN CAPITÁN
LOS BERENGUELES
CARBONELL Y MORAND
CLL ALFAROS
TABERNA LA MONTILLANA
Plaza de San Miguel
CLL SAN PABLO
MENÉNDEZ Y PELAYO
GRAN TEATRO DE CÓRDOBA
CLL DE ALFONSO XIII
Jardines de Orive
AVE MEDINA AZAHARA
PSO DE LA VICTORIA
CLL CONCEPCIÓN
Plaza de las Tendillas
CLL CLAUDIO MARCELO
Rectorado Universidad de Córdoba
MERCADO VICTORIA
CLL MÁLAGA
TOURIST INFORMATION POINT
AMBROSIO DE MORALES
CLL PEDRO LÓPEZ
HOTEL CASA DE LOS AZULEJOS
CLL ALBÉNIZ
Parque Juan Carlos I
AVE REPÚBLICA ARGENTINA
PARKING PASEO DE LA VICTORIA
FERNANDO COLÓN
Plaza de la Corredera
GUTIÉRREZ DE LOS RÍOS
CLL ANTONIO MAURA
CLL LOPE DE HOCES
LA OLEOTECA
SANTA VICTORIA
DE BARROSO
FAMILIA MORENO SL
CLL SAN
MAESE LUIS
RESTAURANTE LA BOCA
CÓRDOBA FINE ARTS MUSEUM
Jardines de la Victoria
CLL TEJÓN Y MARÍN
CAM DE LOS SASTRES
ARCHAEOLOGICAL MUSEUM OF CÓRDOBA
JULIO TORRES MUSEUM
ARMAS
CLL LINEROS
CLL DE DAMASCO
RESTAURANTE DAMASCO
CLL REY HEREDIA
FERNANDO
Plaza del Potro
SYNAGOGUE
CLL ROMERO
TABERNA DOBLE DE CEPA
CLL OSIO
PSO RIBERA
CASA DE SEFARAD
CLL JUDÍOS
JEWISH QUARTER
CLL DEANES
HISTORIC CENTER
MARTÍNEZ RÜCKER
CLL CARDENAL GONZÁLEZ
PARKING PASEO DE LA RIBERA
AVE DEL AEROPUERTO
CASA MAZAL RESTAURANTE SEFARDÍ
HAMMAM AL ANDALUS
LA PIQUERA HOSTEL
REGADERA
LAS CASAS DE LA JUDERÍA
CLL DE TORRIJOS
MOSQUE-CATHEDRAL OF CÓRDOBA
PTE DE MIRAFLORES
AVE VALLELLANO
PARKING LA MEZQUITA DE CÓRDOBA
BATHS OF THE CALIPH'S PALACE
DE LOS MANRIQUEZ
Río Guadalquivir
Parque de Miraflores
CLL DE TOMÁS DE AQUINO
Plaza del Triunfo
VISITOR CENTER OF CÓRDOBA
HOSTAL ALCAZAR I
SAN BASILIO
RONDA DE ISASA
Jardines de Vallellano
CLL LUIS VILLEGAS ZEA
Plaza de la ONCE
BODEGA SAN BASILIO
PTE ROMANO
ROMAN BRIDGE OF CÓRDOBA
CLL MANTILLO
CLL SANTO CRISTO
AVE DE LOS CUSTODIOS
ASSOCIATION OF THE FRIENDS OF THE PATIOS
CLL SAN BASILIO
CLL ENMEDIO
ROYAL PALACE OF ISABELLA AND FERDINAND
CALAHORRA TOWER
Cementerio de la Salud
BAR MIGUELITO
AVE DEL CAMPO DE LA VERDAD
AVE DEL ALCÁZAR
PSO DE LAS ALMUNIAS
AVE DEL CORREGIDOR
Monumento Natural Sotos de la Albolafia
Parque Cruz Conde
CLL DE FRAY ALBINO
AVE DE MENÉNDEZ PIDAL
AVE DE CÁDIZ
CARR DE CASTRO
AVE LINNEO
Jardín Botánico
La Ciudad de los Niños y las Niñas
BOTANICAL GARDENS OF CÓRDOBA
Plaza de Andalucía
AVE DE GRANADA
0
200 yds
0
200 m
© MOON.COM

experiment akin to splicing the head of a bull onto the body of a gazelle," writers Andrew and Suzanne Edwards exclaim in their literary guide, *Andalusia*. As a matter of fact, it took 300 years after Ferdinand III and his forces had taken Córdoba for Christian authorities to be able to change the mosque in any way, such was the respect the new rulers had for this masterpiece of Islamic era architecture. After the cathedral was finished, complete with a beautiful mahogany choir, the overall feeling was that as beautiful as the cathedral might be, it remained a wart on something fine and unique in the world. If anything, the Mosque-Cathedral of Córdoba speaks to the conflict of Islam and Christianity over centuries on the Iberian Peninsula.

Every night, an exclusive one-hour tour at 10pm (€20) illuminates the complex through the lens of art history, paying special attention to its religious significance. This tour is by reservation only through the Mosque-Cathedral.

★ Royal Palace of Isabella and Ferdinand (Alcázar de los Reyes Cristianos)

Calle de las Caballerizas Reales; tel. 957/485-001; https://cultura.cordoba.es/equipamientos/alcazar-de-los-reyes-cristianos; 8:15am-2:45pm Tues.-Sun.; €5, free entry Thurs. from noon

With its sturdy defensive walls, this UNESCO World Heritage Site has served as a fortress, a luxurious palace, and even a prison. The current structure is a remarkable evolution of Cordoban architecture across the ages, built on a mix of Roman, Visigoth, and Arabic remains. The palace was rehabilitated and expanded over the rules of several kings, including Fernando III and his son Alfonso X. Although it's dubbed the "Palace of the Christian Kings," Isabella and Ferdinand only really lived here for about eight years in the early years of the 14th century.

The first thing you'll notice is the palace's rectangular shape, featuring long walls made of solid stone blocks guarded by four hulking corner towers: the Tower of the Lions, the Main Keep, the Tower of the Inquisition, and the Tower of the Doves. In the interior, you'll discover classic courtyards adorned with exotic flowers, aromatic herbs, and ancient trees. The Gothic-style stone cupolas covering the rooms and corridors add a touch of medieval charm. However, the Hall of the Mosaics steals the spotlight. This small Baroque chapel houses a series of Roman mosaics discovered locally. Two courtyards grace the Alcázar, but

Royal Palace of Isabella and Ferdinand

UNESCO World Heritage Sites of Andalusia

Andalusia is a treasure trove of cultural and historical riches that boasts numerous UNESCO World Heritage Sites. The sites are an open invitation to explore the stories of Andalusia's past and its diverse heritage.

El Torcal Nature Reserve

- **Royal Alcázar of Seville:** The Real Alcázar de Sevilla is a magnificent palace complex that exemplifies various architectural styles, including Mudejar, Gothic, Renaissance, and Baroque. The Alcázar has been used by the Spanish royal family for centuries and is still in use today (page 47).
- **Seville Cathedral:** The Seville Cathedral is one of the largest Gothic cathedrals in the world. It was constructed on the site of the former Aljama Mosque after the Reconquista, and it features the famous Giralda tower, which was originally the mosque's minaret (page 47).
- **Córdoba Historic Center:** The entirety of the historic district of Córdoba, including the Roman Bridge, the Calahorra Tower, Jewish Quarter, and the Royal Palace of Isabella and Ferdinand, completes a comprehensive urban site (page 93).
- **Mosque-Cathedral of Córdoba:** The magnificent Mezquita-Catedral uniquely juxtaposes high Islamic and Christian architectural elements. Its forest of pillars and red-and-white arches is a sight that has been captivating visitors for over a thousand years (page 93).
- **Patios of Córdoba:** The flowery patios of Córdoba are a protected heritage site you'll be able to spy throughout the year, though the Córdoba Patio Festival is the best time to see them erupt in bloom (page 103).
- **Medina Azahara Archaeological Site:** Located near Córdoba, Medina Azahara is the archaeological remains of a palatial city that was built during the Umayyad caliphate of Al-Andalus in the 10th century (page 109).
- **Antequera Dolmens Archaeological Site:** Located in the town of Antequera, this site includes three megalithic dolmens: Menga, Viera, and El Romeral. These prehistoric structures are among the most impressive megalithic monuments in Europe (page 123).
- **El Torcal Nature Reserve:** Near Antequera, El Torcal is known for its unique karst landscape, which features stunning limestone rock formations and is a popular destination for nature enthusiasts and hikers (page 128).
- **Alhambra:** The Alhambra in Granada is perhaps the most renowned of Andalusia's UNESCO sites. This stunning palace and fortress complex is the crown jewel of the region (page 143).
- **Generalife gardens:** Along with the Alhambra, the Generalife gardens are an exquisite example of Islamic architecture and design and a reflection of the paradise that awaits us in the next life (page 148).
- **Albaicín:** Facing the Alhambra in Granada, the Albaicín quarter, with its winding streets and whitewashed buildings, is a historical gem in its own right (page 155).

And this is still just scratching the surface! Flamenco music and dance and the Mediterranean diet enjoyed by so many throughout the region have each been named a UNESCO Intangible Cultural Heritage. If you're keeping score, you'll notice that the lesser-visited part of Andalusia that includes Córdoba and Antequera has more UNESCO sites than the rest of Andalusia combined!

the Mudejar-style courtyard is the ultimate showstopper. Its cool marble floors and the soothing sound of flowing water in the channels and ponds offer a refreshing respite even during the scorching summer days.

It was in this palace that Christopher Columbus first discussed exploring a new passage to India with Isabella and Ferdinand during their residence here. A monumental sculpture marking this first-ever meeting can be found in the expansive Islamic-styled palace gardens.

Baths of the Caliph's Palace (Baños del Alcázar Califal)

Calle Saint Máritres; tel. 608/158-893; https://banosdelalcazarcalifal.cordoba.es; 8:15am-2:45pm Tues.-Sun. mid-June-mid-Sept., 8:15am-8pm Tues.-Fri., 9:30am-6pm Sat., 8:15am-2:45pm Sun. mid-Sept.-mid-June; €3

In the "Andalusian Baths," three distinct areas correspond to different periods of renovations: a caliphal bath to the east, a reception hall from the Taifa period, and an Almohad bath to the west. The caliphal bath contains a portico, changing room, cold room, tepid room, and hot room, as well as an oven, woodshed, and service areas. The layout was designed in such a way that the main rooms were hidden from direct view from the outside. As a connecting element between the caliphal and Almohad baths, there is a porticoed hall. In its front space, there was a garden with a central fountain. From this portico, access was granted to the reception hall, built during the 11th century in the Taifa period. The hall was flanked by two small side rooms, one of which served as a connecting space with the 10th-century bath, while the other led directly to the woodshed hallway. In the 12th century, during the rule of the Almohads, the bath underwent its last major expansion. A new private bath was constructed, reusing one of the side rooms of the hall as a vestibule and preserving the use of the old oven. The Almohads included a small pond for users to wash their feet for ablutions. Make no mistake—this is a quick dive into ancient bathing practices. To get the most out of your experience, couple this visit with an Arab-style hammam (spa treatment).

Roman Bridge of Córdoba (Puente Romano de Córdoba)

Avenida de Alcázar; free

It's not every day you can walk across a 2,000-year-old bridge. Originally constructed in the 1st century BCE, this Roman bridge was the only bridge crossing the river until the 20th century. It has been restored and repaired over the years, with most of the current bridge still held up by the 8th-century reconstruction under the Umayyad caliphate.

Calahorra Tower (Torre de Calahorra)

Puente Romano; tel. 957/293-929; www.torrecalahorra.es; 10am-7pm Thurs.-Tues., 10am-2pm and 4:30pm-8:30pm Wed.; €4.50

Across the old Roman Bridge is the Calahorra Tower, used to control passage on the bridge. Over the years, it has served various functions—as a prison for Cordoban nobility, a military barracks, and even a 19th-century all-girls' school. In 1931 it was declared a national monument and is now home to the Living Museum of Andalusia (Museo Vivo de al-Andalus). One of the more important aspects of this small museum is how it highlights positive collaboration among the three Abrahamic religions—Judaism, Christianity, and Islam—in this region of the world and how, through their history, they have helped to inform contemporary Andalusian culture.

Association of the Friends of the Patios

Calle de San Basilio, 44; www.amigosdelospatioscordobeses.es; 10am-2pm daily; free

If you are not so lucky as to visit Córdoba in May during the Patio Festival, be sure to step into this year-round patio celebration to get a feel for the love and care that go into the annual festival. This is a private home that is opened daily just for visitors to experience

Isabella and Ferdinand

Isabella I of Castile and Ferdinand II of Aragon were pivotal leaders in Spain, unifying the country and making their joint reign a true turning point for the nation. In 1469, they tied the knot, uniting the powerful kingdoms of Castile and Aragon. Then, together, they finished the Reconquista, a centuries-long quest to take back the Iberian Peninsula from Islamic rule. In 1492, their campaign ended with the fall of Granada.

As the ultimate patrons of Christopher Columbus, having backed the explorer largely credited with the so-called "discovery of the New World," Isabella and Ferdinand were controversial historical figures. They also stirred things up in the Catholic Church by kickstarting the Spanish Inquisition in their attempt to unify the peninsula under Catholicism. Much of their tales has been fodder for music, plays, novels, and poetry over the years.

statues commemorating Columbus meeting Isabella and Ferdinand

BOOKS

William H. Prescott, one of the first acclaimed American history writers, penned perhaps the most definitive account of the Catholic monarchs in his seminal *History of the Reign of Ferdinand and Isabella, the Catholic, of Spain* (1851). This is an easily found work that has passed into public domain.

Their story also got the novel treatment, with works like *The Queen's Vow* and *The Last Queen* by C. W. Gortner. These historical fiction novels breathe life into the era, with Isabella as the central protagonist.

TELEVISION

Look up *Isabel,* the Spanish TV series that cranks up the volume on their reign and the major events of their time. It's got everything: politics, drama, and challenges that ring true, even today.

FILM

In contemporary film, director Ridley Scott turned toward this Renaissance power couple when he filmed *1492: Conquest of Paradise.* This visual spectacle takes you on a wild ride through Columbus's journey and the unwavering support he received from the Catholic monarchs.

this more intimate side of Córdoba. For green thumbs and garden lovers, this is a can't-miss.

If you are interested in touring more patios, the association offers a couple of interesting patio tours: the San Basilio tour (€10) and the Palacio de Viana tour (€7). These patio tour experiences are open nearly year-round to give visitors a sense of the famed patios of Córdoba (note: you are paying for a guide, not for entrance to the patios). The San Basilio tour is a bit longer with more patios featured, while the shorter Viana tour is best for those without a lot of time, less interest in patios, or just tired feet.

★ Jewish Quarter (Judería)

Take a stroll through the labyrinthine former Jewish Quarter (Judería), a subsection of the historic center of Córdoba, and get a feel for

1: the mihrab in the Mosque-Cathedral of Córdoba **2:** the mosque's restored facade **3:** looking from the gardens and pond to a tower at the Royal Palace of Isabella and Ferdinand **4:** Casa de Sefarad

1
2
3
4
CASA de
sefarad

what life was like a thousand years ago for the Sephardic Jews that once were numerous here. This romantic walk takes you along narrow passages with narrower terraces looking over the pedestrian-only streets, and the occasional fresh breeze carries a whiff of jasmine and citrus. Under the caliphate of Abd al-Rahman III, the Judería thrived, as they were not only great traders, but were entrusted by Abd al-Rahman with the administration of Córdoba and its provinces.

Córdoba Synagogue (Sinagoga de Córdoba)

Calle Judios, 20; tel. 957/749-015; 9am-3pm Tues.-Sun. mid-June-mid-Sept., 9am-9pm Tues.-Sat., 9am-3pm Sun. mid-Sept.-mid-June; free

The Córdoba Synagogue is a rare example of Jewish Mudejar architecture. Built in the early 14th century, it features a square prayer hall with well-kept plasterwork, including star-shaped lattices and Hebrew inscriptions from the Book of Psalms. The highly decorative stucco panels, Hebrew inscriptions, and Almohad-inspired architecture were likely inspired by the Synagogue of Santa María la Blanca in Toledo. This small synagogue has been through a lot. Though not much is known specifically of its Sephardic roots, it is thought that this synagogue may have been a private building or perhaps have belonged to a local trade guild. When the Jews and Muslims were expelled from Spain during the Reconquista in 1492, the synagogue was converted into a hospital for those suffering from rabies before being used as a community center and chapel for a shoemakers' guild. After being rediscovered in 1876, it was declared a national monument. A short visit of 20-30 minutes provides a necessary view into this corner of Spanish history.

Casa de Sefarad

Calle Judios; tel. 957/421-404; 11am-6pm Tues.-Sun.; €4.50

A beautifully restored 14th-century house, once connected by a tunnel to the nearby synagogue, provides the backdrop to explore Andalusia's Sephardic Jewish history. The visit itself will likely take just half an hour, and proceeds all go to maintaining and restoring the house.

Greater Córdoba

Córdoba Fine Arts Museum (Museo Bellas Artes de Córdoba)

Plaza de Potro; tel. 957/015-858; www.museosdeandalucia.es/web/museodebellasartesdecordoba; 9am-3pm Tues.-Sun.; €1.50

In 1862, this 15th-century hospital was wonderfully converted into the museum you see today. For over 150 years this museum has served as a hub of artistic preservation, showcasing local masters from the 15th century through to the 20th century. The collection is small, manageable, and largely Catholic in inspiration. Most rooms have only 10 or so paintings, making the entire experience digestible in a short amount of time.

Julio Torres Museum (Museo Julio Romero de Torres)

Plaza de Potro; tel. 957/470-356; https://museojulioromero.cordoba.es; 8:30am-7:30pm Tues.-Fri., 8am-5:30pm Sat., 9:30am-2:15pm Sun.; €4

Directly across the courtyard from the Córdoba Fine Arts Museum you'll find this small museum dedicated to one of Córdoba's brightest sons, Julio Romero de Torres. This intimate collection of the master's works is perhaps best visited after seeing other works of the era, as in the Fine Arts Museum, to best understand just how subversive and powerful his art was at the time.

Archaeological Museum of Córdoba (Museo Arqueológico de Córdoba)

Plaza Juan Páes; tel. 957/355-517; 9am-3pm Tues.-Sun. mid-June-mid-Sept., 9am-9pm Tues.-Sat., 9am-3pm Sun. mid-Sept.-mid-June; €1.50

Examples of Mudejar Cordoban architecture recovered from various historic sites around the city include some spectacular ones of the palace at Medina Azahara. If you are going to Medina Azahara, you could skip this museum and prioritize a bit more time at the archaeological museum at the ruins. Otherwise, do stop in if you are archaeologically inclined.

Botanical Gardens of Córdoba (Real Jardín Botánico de Córdoba)

Avenida de Linneo; tel. 957/200-018; www.jardinbotanicodecordoba.com; 10am-2:30pm Tues.-Sun.; €3

Visit the gardens that inspire so many of Córdoba's lush patios. These gardens are a refreshing break from the city, offering an array of indigenous and imported plant species. It's popular with locals for picnic outings but not as informative as it could be, so consider this more if you just need some time in a green space, as large green spaces are lacking in Córdoba.

Tours

Hop-On, Hop-Off City Bus Tour

tel. 902/101-081; https://city-sightseeing.com/en/20/cordoba; 9:30am-6pm daily, buses run until 8pm and more frequently during high season; €25

This classic double-decker bus experience has 19 stops at all the major points of interest in Córdoba. If you are using the bus, you will save money packaging your bus ticket with one of the packages including the major sites of Córdoba.

SPORTS AND RECREATION

Biking

Baja Bikes

www.bajabikes.eu/en/cordoba-sightseeing; from €8

If you want to rent a bike and cruise around Córdoba guiding yourself, you'll find a good selection of bicycles as well as an easy check-in, check-out process with this cycling outfitter. It's probably best to just book for a full day (€16). They also offer a standard sort of sightseeing tour with e-bikes available, and their English-speaking guides are always a lot of fun. Tours start at €28.

Wellness and Spas

Hammam Al Andalus

Calle Corregidor Luis de la Cerda, 51; https://cordoba.hammamalandalus.com; tel. 957/484-746; from €60

Plunge into the Arab baths and transport yourself with this deliciously luxurious spa experience. Bathing and massage have been rituals in this part of the world for centuries. What better way to culturally immerse yourself?

Bodyna Spa

Calle Ramírez de las Casas Deza, 10-12; tel. 957/498-993; www.hospes.com; from €60

Located in the Palacio del Bailío, this chic spa has the benefit of using the Roman baths located beneath the hotel, making for an archaeologically intense spa experience. If you were going to splurge on an upscale spa experience while on vacation, dial in here.

ENTERTAINMENT AND EVENTS

Festivals

Holy Week (Semana Santa)

Week before Easter

During Semana Santa in the days leading up to Easter, the streets hum with a sense of devotion, as processions of hooded penitents, carrying elaborately decorated pasos (religious floats), wind their way through the historic center. The air is filled with the haunting melodies of saetas (traditional religious songs) and the scent of incense. Córdoba's Semana Santa is a display of faith and tradition, where the entire city comes out to participate in this weeklong commemoration of the Passion of Christ. Residents and visitors alike gather to witness the solemn beauty of the processions, making this a spiritually enriching experience.

Patio Festival (Festival de los Patios)

May

The Patio Festival in Córdoba is a celebration of the city's vibrant floral heritage and architectural beauty. During this annual event, typically held in May, Córdoba's residents open their homes to the public, allowing visitors to explore hidden courtyards (patios) that are adorned with an exquisite array of flowers and plants. Each patio is a living work of art, a testament to the centuries-old tradition of cultivating flowers in the heart of the city. As visitors wander through the narrow streets of the historic Jewish Quarter (Judería) and other neighborhoods, they are immersed in a sensory delight of colors, scents, and the soothing sound of fountains. The Patio Festival is a true reflection of Córdoba's cultural heritage, offering a unique and enchanting experience that showcases the beauty of these meticulously cared-for spaces.

Córdoba Spring Fair (Feria de Córdoba)

May/June

The Feria de Córdoba, also known as the Feria de Nuestra Señora de la Salud (Our Lady of Health), is a popular annual fair. It typically takes place in late May or early June. The exact dates for the Feria de Córdoba can vary from year to year, as it is based on the lunar calendar. The fair usually begins with a traditional horse parade, known as the "Cabalgata," and continues with a week of festivities that include dancing, music, flamenco performances, fairground rides, and plenty of traditional food and drink.

All-Night Flamenco (Noche Blanca del Flamenco)

June

During the all-night Noche Blanca del Flamenco, the streets, plazas, and venues scattered throughout Córdoba come alive with live performances of flamenco music, singing, and dance. You'll find both established and up-and-coming flamenco artists showcasing their talents. Spectators immerse themselves in the passionate and expressive world of flamenco. This is also an opportunity to witness flamenco performed in a variety of settings, from intimate tablaos to large outdoor stages and open-air public plazas.

Flamenco

Taberna Doble de Cepa

Calleja del Pañuelo; tel. 957/944-673 or 677/747-472; 2 shows daily, 2:30pm and 9pm fall and winter or 2:30pm and 10pm spring and summer; €18

Set in a bright Cordoban patio, this is the most accessible flamenco in town. There are better settings to be had in Granada, Seville, and Cádiz, so no reason to make this a priority in Córdoba, but if you love flamenco and/or Córdoba is the only place you have time to see flamenco, this is the address. The flamenco show in the afternoon seems to be more of an amateur affair, while at night, the flamenco feels more professional. The open patio setting fits with the theme of Cordoban patios, and drinks and tapas are ample and encouraged.

Theaters

Gran Teatro de Córdoba

Avenida del Gran Capitán, 3; tel. 957/480-644; https://teatrocordoba.es/recintos/gran-teatro; prices vary by performance

Cross-check your travel dates with the Gran Teatro de Córdoba's event calendar to see what performances are available. Typically, classical and flamenco guitarists will have weekly performances, as well as nationally famous flamenco groups and other local artists with modern takes on traditional Andalusian music and dance. As part of the annual Guitar Festival in 2015, Bob Dylan performed here. The 19th-century theater itself is something to behold; with an Italian-inspired horseshoe design, sculpted balconies, and lush red curtains, it makes for an ideal venue to enjoy a show.

SHOPPING

Gourmet Goods

La Oleoteca

Calle Ángel de Saavedra, 8; tel. 957/244-101 or 634/951-922; www.oleotecacordoba.com; 10am-

A Peek Inside Córdoba's Beautiful Patios

The origins of the Patio Festival can be traced back to the city's ancient Moorish past, when these courtyards served as private sanctuaries and a vital component of architectural design. The concept of cultivating flowers and plants in inner courtyards was introduced by the Moors, who recognized the aesthetic and functional benefits of creating these cool, lush spaces in the heart of their homes.

Over time, this horticultural practice evolved into a competition among residents, who meticulously decorated their patios with an impressive array of blossoms, herbs, and ornamental features. This rich tradition, with its deep Moorish and Andalusian roots, eventually led to the establishment of the annual Patio Festival, where proud homeowners open their doors to showcase their exquisitely adorned courtyards to the public.

one of the famous flowery patios of Córdoba

PATIO FESTIVAL

The first Patio Festival was organized in the 1920s, and it was established to recognize and showcase the beauty of Córdoba's patios and to promote the conservation of these spaces. Over the years, the festival has grown in prominence and popularity, drawing visitors from around the world who come to admire the stunning floral displays and architectural features.

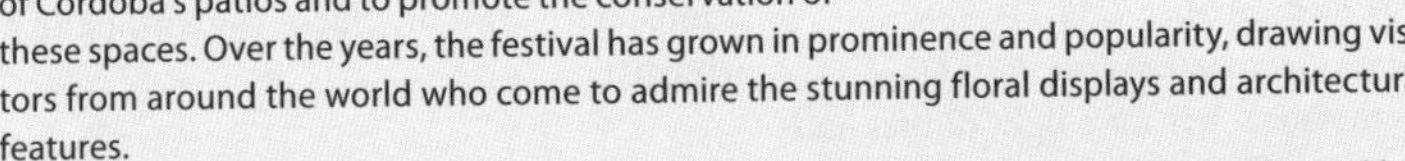

Today, the Patio Festival is an annual event that typically takes place in May. The festival has become an integral part of Córdoba's cultural identity and a UNESCO-recognized tradition that highlights the city's rich history and artistic legacy. An unspoken pact of respect and admiration permeates the festival, fostering an atmosphere of cultural exchange and shared appreciation.

Entrance to these patios during the festival is typically free, reflecting the warm hospitality of Córdoba's people and their desire to share their beloved tradition with the world.

VISITING PATIOS YEAR-ROUND

It you are visiting Córdoba outside of the festival season, different patios are usually open for visitors to explore, as seasonality reflects the ever-changing floral displays within the courtyards. After all, different plants and flowers bloom throughout the year! Check with the local tourism office for patio openings. Also stop by the Association of the Friends of the Patios (page 97). The spirit of the Patio Festival is one of openness and community, where visitors are invited to experience the captivating beauty of these spaces, which are lovingly cared for by the residents.

2:30pm and 5:30pm-8:30pm Mon.-Fri., 10:30am-8:30pm Sat.-Sun.

It is impossible to come to the capital of Spain's famous olive region without tasting its specialty: olive oil. Pop into this friendly shop for an olive oil tasting and perhaps you will develop a new appreciation for this kitchen staple. After a tasting, pick your favorite olive oil to pack home for yourself or give as gifts for those who weren't fortunate enough to come with you on your adventure.

Familia Moreno SL

Calle Ángel de Saavedra, 5; tel. 744/647-176; www.familiamoreno.es; 9:30am-1:30pm and 4:30pm-8:30pm Mon-Fri., 9:30am-1:30pm Sat.

Make a stop here to pick up deliciously thin

slices of jamón ibérico. Ham makes a fantastic, tasty snack to enjoy with wine and bread sticks and savor a taste of Andalusia.

Mercado Victoria

Paseo de la Victoria; 8:30am-midnight daily; www.mercadovictoria.com

It is hard not to love a local market. The covered Mercado Victoria is a much more local affair than the Triana Market in Seville, though every bit as charming. It's bright and airy, with lots of local fruits and vegetables on display. The middle of the market has a few food stalls serving international cuisine, though the real charm is the market itself, with the attached flea market to peruse for local odds and ends.

FOOD

Tapas Bars

Bar Miguelito

Calle Acera Pintada, 8; tel. 957/290-338; www.barmiguelito.es; 11am-midnight Thurs.-Tues.; €12

Pop into this local bar for a light dinner and cool beverage. The influx of locals promises a fun evening. Though Miguelito specializes in fried foods, particularly fish, the grilled calamari is a treat. The expansive terrace is a great low-key spot to relax and do a bit of people-watching.

★ Bodega San Basilio

Calle Enmedio, 12; tel. 957/297-832; 1pm-4pm and 8pm-11:30pm Mon. and Wed.-Sat., 1:30pm-4pm Sun.; €14

If you are ever going to try bull tail (el rabo de toro), this local bodega could just be the joint. Located in San Basilio, this still has the feel of a working-class Córdoba classic, with many locals crowding in for a quick lunch bite or to gather with friends at night. Though you'll likely be one of the few travelers here, you'll be made to feel more than welcome.

Traditional Spanish

Restaurante Damasco

Calle Romero, 4; tel. 631/503-436; noon-5:30pm and 7:30pm-11:30pm Wed.-Mon.; €15

Located in one of the historic old houses of Córdoba, Damasco serves up classic Mediterranean cuisine, including zesty hummus dishes and crisp falafels served alongside Arab-inspired, saffron-slathered baked chicken dishes. Options abound for vegetarians and vegans, though no alcohol is served as it is a halal restaurant.

Taberna La Montillana

Calle San Alvaro, 5; tel. 957/479-518; https://tabernalamontillana.com; 1pm-4:30pm and 7:30pm-11:30pm daily; €20

Creative, contemporary takes on classic Spanish dishes, such as oxtail stew, are served in a surprisingly generous quantity. Save room for dessert. Their torrijas (Spanish-style French toast) is particularly well put together and will put a smile on your face. This is another restaurant that is popular with locals, who come here for the food, the genial atmosphere, and of course the all-Spanish wine list.

Los Berengueles

Calle Condes de Torres Cabrera, 7; tel. 957/472-828; 1:30pm-4pm and 9pm-11pm Tues.-Thurs., 1:30pm-4pm and 8pm-11pm Fri.-Sat., 1:30pm-4pm Sun.; €25

Set around a leafy interior courtyard, this is the sort of local restaurant that caters to the local crowd. They do have a menu in English, though be prepared to order your well-done Spanish classics, like salmorejo and flamenquín, in Spanish. On weekends, you will likely need a dinner reservation. Be sure to ask for terrace seating. This is the place to experience warm, local dining in one of the famous garden patios of Córdoba.

Casa Mazal Restaurante Sefardí

Calle Tomás Conde, 3; tel. 957/246-304; www.casamazal.es; 12:30pm-4pm and 7:30pm-11pm Thurs.-Tues.; €45

This restaurant features a fresh seasonal menu highlighting Judeo-Spanish dishes. A stop here is a wonderful culinary dive into the multicultural heritage of Andalusia. You could dine on a bit more of a budget, but the tasting menu is well worth the price of admission. From a bright, zesty traditional hummus and smoky muhammara (roasted red pepper dip) to a rich couscous with duck confit, there is much to enjoy, to say nothing of the crisp vino de rosas.

International and Fusion

★ Restaurante La Boca

Calle San Fernando, 39; tel. 695/961-862; noon-midnight Wed.-Mon.; €20

Not your typical tapas. The bright, airy interiors and leafy courtyard reflect the lighter fusion food at La Boca, mixing old-school Andalusia with new-school modern touches. Alongside the modern fusion menu, you'll find international foods like burgers, poke bowls, and udon noodles. For vegans, it's great to know that any meat here can be substituted with seitan, tofu, or tempeh. Usually by the time one gets to Córdoba, it is nice to find a break from the tapas bars that seem to largely serve the same menus, especially for vegans, vegetarians, and others with specific dietary restrictions. La Boca caters to these travelers better than just about everywhere else in Córdoba. Don't forget to peruse the all-organic wine list to find the perfect pairing with your lunch or dinner.

Regadera

Ronda de Isasa, 10; tel. 676/025-695; www.regadera.es; 1pm-4pm and 8pm-11:30pm daily; €50

A bright rustic-chic interior with pops of turquoise sets the scene for elevated traditional Spanish cuisine that takes heart in locally sourced legumes and seasonal variety. Cozy, perfectly grilled asparagus with melting Iberian ham, line-caught tempura hake, and glazed suckling lamb are a few of the many highlights.

ACCOMMODATIONS

Under €100

★ La Piquera Hostel

Calle Corregidor Luis de la Cerda, 68; tel. 744/634-598; www.lapiquerahostal.com; €50

Bright. Clean. Airy. Modern. Central. What more could you ask for at this price point? Oh! And there is free coffee or tea waiting for you after a day of exploration! Wonderful! This beautifully restored traditional house maintains its courtyards, while the rooms are refreshingly large and lack that stuffy hostel feel that is all too common. The hostel has 14 rooms, all with air-conditioning (extremely important for those hot summer months).

Hostal Alcázar I

Calle San Basilio, 2; tel. 957/202-561; https://hostalalcazar.com; €50

This dated two-star hotel offers a lot in terms of location, service, and value. The spartan rooms seem mismatched with the rather cluttered common areas, but it adds up to the sort of stay where you feel like you might just be in a local's home. Sure, the rooms could use a refresh, but the beds are comfy and you'll have the amenities (bathrooms, air-conditioning, heating) that you might want for a no-nonsense overnight.

€100-200

Hotel Casa de Los Azulejos

Calle Fernando Colón, 5; tel. 957/470-000; http://casadelosazulejos.com; €125

The House of the Tiles swirls around a brightly tiled traditional Cordoban patio with lots of greenery. This oasis of tranquility is an easy spot to love, particularly for its price point. You'll not only have a beautiful night of sleep, but you can count on Manuel, the owner, to link Córdoba with its imported Mexican heritage from the times of the great explorers who sailed around the globe, bringing with them influences, spices, and cultures that were previously unknown. Count on more than just a few tequila possibilities for nightcaps. The colorful, fun decor adds to the vibrancy of it all. Lower floors tend to be a bit noisier, so it's best to request upper-level floors in this converted townhouse.

Las Casas de la Judería

Calle Tomás Conde, 10, Barrio de la Judería; tel. 957/202-095 or 957/202-085; www.lascasasdelajuderiadecordoba.com; €175

Joining together five traditional palatial houses in the Jewish quarter, this boutique promises an excellent stay with a central location. Over the long renovation, a piece of a Roman road and some Arab amphorae were discovered. You can visit these in the cellars during your stay. Above, you'll find several connected patios with various citrus trees and flowering blooms, offering an intimate look at the famous patios of Córdoba. Unique rooms surround each of these courtyards, offering a clean, quiet stay with all the amenities you would expect. And each of them is vastly different with its own personality and charm. Before booking, check through each room to get a feel for what might be the best fit for you. Don't miss out on the views over Córdoba from the rooftop terraces!

Over €200

★ Palacio del Bailío

Calle Ramírez de las Casas Deza, 10-12; tel. 957/498-993; www.hospes.com/en/palacio-bailio; €200

Built on the foundation of a Roman palace, the ruins of which are still visible beneath the main patio's expansive glass floor, this is a splurge to celebrate your time in Córdoba. It has a classically charming Islamic-inspired garden courtyard, complete with a sizable pool and small cocktail bar, as well as plenty of photograph-worthy public areas; you might not want to leave the property, which is its only real letdown. The on-site restaurant features a contemporary menu highlighting local produce and culture. The ruins are available for residents to visit, and use of the attached underground Roman bath will complete your plunge into historical Córdoba.

INFORMATION AND SERVICES

Visitor Center of Córdoba

Plaza del Triunfo; tel. 957/469-707; www.andalucia.org; 9am-6:45pm Mon.-Sat., 9am-2:15pm Sun. and holidays

Near the Mosque-Cathedral and directly after the Roman Bridge, this modern, centrally located visitor center is easily found and offers friendly help.

Tourist Information Point

Plaza de las Tendillas; tel. 957/471-577; www.turismodecordoba.org; 9am-2:30pm daily

Depending on where you are overnighting in Córdoba, this information point may be more easily accessible than the visitor center to help with morning planning, though remember that it is only open in the morning and early afternoon.

GETTING THERE

Train

Córdoba boasts its own central train station, **Estación de Córdoba** (Glorieta Tres Culturas), which is well connected to major cities in Spain, including Seville (1 hr), Granada (3 hrs), Málaga (1 hr), and Madrid (2 hrs). If you're traveling by train, you can easily reach Córdoba via the modern train station located near the city center. The station is served by high-speed AVE trains and other regional services, making it a convenient choice for travelers arriving in Córdoba by rail. For the most up-to-date train schedules and ticket information, consult the national train operator Renfe (www.renfe.com). Train fares may vary based on demand and ticket class. From the train station, it's about a 2 km (1 mi) walk into the historic center or a 15-minute taxi ride.

Bus

Córdoba's central bus station, the **Estación de Autobuses de Córdoba** (Avenida Vía Augusta; tel. 957/404-040; www.estacionautobusescordoba.es), is conveniently located right across the street from the train station. Quite a few bus companies operate routes connecting Córdoba to neighboring cities, towns, and regions. The regional bus system is best for connecting with smaller towns without train stations. Alsa (www.alsa.es) and Autocares Carrera (https://autocarescarrera.es) have multiple daily connections with towns such as Lucena (1 hr; 72 km/45 mi; €6), Antequera (2.5 hr; 115 km/72 mi; €13), and Priego de Córdoba (2.5 hr; 103 km/64 mi; €14).

Car

Córdoba is connected by the A-4 freeway to Seville (1.5 hr; 140 km/87 mi) and the A-45 freeway to Málaga (1.5 hr; 160 km/100 mi), while Granada is connected by the slower national road, the N-432 (2 hr; 165 km/102 mi) or a combination of the A-45 toward Málaga and A-92 (2 hr, 200 km/125 mi).

Parking

As in other major cities in Andalusia, you likely will want to park your car once you're in Córdoba. A few paid public parking lots are centrally located.

Parking la Mezquita de Córdoba

Calle Cairuan, 1; tel. 957/787-959; www.parkinglamezquita.es; €17/day

This is the most well-located parking garage, though spaces are very small, so it's not for larger cars or large SUVs.

Parking Paseo de la Ribera

Paseo de la Ribera, 1; €14/day

Another good option for downtown parking, this lot is very central, though it also has smaller, tighter spaces to navigate.

Parking Paseo de la Victoria

Paseo de la Victoria; tel. 957/296-345; €13/day

This lot, just on the edge of the historic district, is the best option if you have a larger car or camper.

GETTING AROUND

Walking

Exploring Córdoba on foot offers the most immersive way to embrace the city. The historic city center is a pedestrian-friendly labyrinth of narrow streets and winding alleys, leading you to numerous points of interest. Major attractions, such as the Mosque-Cathedral, the Royal Palace, and the historic Jewish Quarter, are conveniently located within walking distance of each other.

Bus

Córdoba boasts a well-connected public transportation system, offering convenient options for getting around the city and its environs. The urban bus network in Córdoba is managed by Aucorsa (https://aucorsa.es; €1.30), providing extensive coverage throughout the city. Buses are a popular mode of transportation for both locals and visitors, serving as a cost-effective means to reach various neighborhoods and attractions. Bus routes typically operate from early morning until late evening, and they are linked to key locations, including the train and bus stations.

Taxi

Taxis are readily available and convenient, particularly when your feet are tired or you need to reach a specific destination or hop to the other side of town. You can find taxi stands throughout the city or flag down a passing cab on the street. Most journeys within the city limits are relatively short, typically costing less than €10.

1
2
3
4

Around Córdoba

★ MEDINA AZAHARA ARCHAEOLOGICAL SITE

(Conjunto Arqueológico Madinat al-Zahra)

A-431 Almodóvar, km 7; tel. 957/103-637; www.turismodecordoba.org/medina-azahara-1; 9am-6pm Tues.-Thurs., 9am-9pm Fri.-Sat., 9am-3pm Sun. mid-Sept.-mid-June, 9am-6pm Tues.-Thurs., 9am-3pm and 8pm-midnight Fri.-Sat., 9am-3pm Sun. mid-June-mid-Sept.; €1.50

Medina Azahara is an oft-overlooked UNESCO World Heritage Site, one of the four in Córdoba that take you to back to the age of the most powerful Muslim empire of the region. Construction started in 936 during the rule of the first (self-proclaimed) caliph of Córdoba, Abd al-Rahman III, and the glories of Medina Azahara are a mystery largely lost to time. In a surprisingly swift few years, al-Rahman seemingly willed this city into existence. Strategically placed at the foot of a short mountain range with plenty of water to flow for its gardens, and not far from the Guadalquivir River, it was built for Zahra, either his favorite concubine who had died or his new favorite. For a few short years, this city was unrivaled in majesty, with imported marble, red gold inlays, precious and semiprecious stones littered throughout the mosaic-tile, and intricate stucco work typical of the time, the totality of which yielded a unifying vision of incomparable beauty. Rumors of its beauty spread quickly. Unfortunately, the truth of its beauty was lost to history, as the city was razed to the ground over the winter of 1008-1009 by Berber armies from Morocco, just over 70 years after its first stone was laid.

Today, there is a contemporary museum where you can learn much about the art and architecture of Medina Azahara, including many pieces taken from the ongoing excavation. A bus connects from the museum to the top of the hill and entrance of the ruins, where you'll find restrooms and a small café. The ruins themselves are perhaps best viewed with a knowledgeable guide, who can help to bring the city to life so that you might glimpse a bit of its majestic past.

1: archway gate in Medina Azahara 2: a wasp nest-style capital topping a column, a detail unique to Medina Azahara 3: cliffside Zuheros Castle 4: Almodóvar Castle

Getting There

Car

From Córdoba, take the A-431 west (20 min; 8 km/5 mi). There is a free parking lot next to the museum at the foot of the ruins. Be sure to look out for the turnoff just after the Petroil gas station on your right.

Public Transportation

You could take the bus 1 or 2 (40 min; €1.40) from Córdoba, which will let you off at the Petroil gas station. From there it's a hot 700-m (half-mile) walk to the Medina Azahara museum. Returning to Córdoba would travel the same route, though pay attention to bus times as stops are hourly, though not entirely dependable.

For most travelers, it is best to make use of the special Medina Azahara bus that leaves from Avenida Alcázar just next to the Alcázar (departures 11am and 4:30pm Tues.-Fri., 10am and 4:30pm Sat., 10am Sun.; €10, reservations required). This is the most convenient option and allows for 2.5 hours to tour the compound before returning to Córdoba.

Taxi

Taxis are usually readily available from around Córdoba to Medina Azahara (20 min; €15-20). You can find taxis on the edge of the historic center and well-marked taxis stands, or try calling Radio Taxi Córdoba (tel. 957/764 444).

Tours

Medina Azahara (www.medinaazahara.org; €29) offers group tours using the shuttle bus listed above. Tours are approximately 3.5 hours long and capped at 30 people.

The two-hour night tour from Art en Córdoba (www.artencordoba.com; €14) starts at 9pm and includes shuttle bus service from downtown Córdoba. This is maybe one of the most interesting ways to visit the site!

ALMODÓVAR DEL RÍO

Almodóva del Río does not have much in the way of restaurants or accommodations, but it does have the remarkable Almodóvar Castle on the far side of town. This is well worth a stop as a quick trip from Córdoba or linking up with a road trip through the region.

Sights

Almodóvar Castle (Castillo de Almodóvar)

Camino Acceso el Castillo; tel. 957/634-055; https://castillodealmodovar.com; hours vary by season, though generally 11am-2:30pm and 4pm-7pm with extended weekend hours; €10

Plunge into medieval Andalusia in this towering hulk of a castle, a 40-minute drive east of Córdoba. Perched on a tall hill offering commanding views over the region, this is one of the best-preserved examples of Middle Ages castles perhaps in all of Europe. The crenellated tower walls, long interior dining halls, armory, and dungeons should have you reminiscing about playing with your Lego castle when you were a kid. Standard entry comes with a free audio guide in English, which you should make good use of to get the most out of your visit. Guided visits are also available (from €15, 1.5 hr). On the weekends, a fun option for children and young at heart adults is to take the twice-daily theatrical tour led by a faithful steward and knight of the king, who takes you deep into this castle's storybook past.

Getting There

A short drive along the A-431 (40 min; 27 km/18 mi) from Córdoba brings you to the small town of Almodóvar.

ZUHEROS

This intensely hilly town is a true "pueblo bonito" for all the right reasons. You have a picturesque hillside castle fortification and a historic cave, known locally as the "Bat Cave," at the top of the hill, while the town itself makes for an excellent overnight if you are looking for a small, traditional regional pueblo to discover.

Sights

Zuheros Castle (Castillo de Zuheros)

Plaza de la Paz; tel. 957/694-545; https://turismozuheros.es/castillo-palacio-de-zuheros; 10am-2pm and 5pm-7pm Tues.-Sun. Apr.-Sept., 10am-2pm and 4pm-6pm Tues.-Sun. Oct.-Mar.; €4

The castle is the main attraction of Zuheros, beautifully perched and built into an outcropping of stone. The castle itself isn't nearly as large or classically impressive as the Almodóvar Castle. What makes this castle interesting is how it is perched over the cliffside. The origin of Zuheros Castle dates back to the 9th century, when a group of Muslims called the Banu-Himsi settled around the area, which they named "Sujayra." They mixed with the local inhabitants, who converted to Islam. During the caliphate of Córdoba, the castle was part of a walled enclosure with about 30 houses, a mosque, and several towers, playing a crucial role in the trade and exchange of knowledge, sciences, and arts between Córdoba and Granada. The Christian conquest of Zuheros occurred in the early 1240s, and after that, the mosque was converted into a temple dedicated to Santa María. Over time, the castle and palaces fell into ruins, and in the 20th century, some restoration work was done on the towers we see today. Ticket price includes admission to the neighboring archaeological museum.

Archaeological Museum of Zuheros (Museo Arqueológico Municipal de Zuheros)

Plaza de la Paz, 2; tel. 957/694-545; https://turismozuheros.es/museo-arqueologico-zuheros; 10am-2pm and 5pm-7pm Tues.-Sun. Apr.-Sept., 10am-2pm and 4pm-6pm Tues.-Sun. Oct.-Mar.; €4

This is one of those small local museums that give you something to do should you have some time on your hands, such as when stopping for a quick bite in the village as part of a road trip. It has archaeological findings from the Bat Cave, dating from the Paleolithic to late Roman era.

Church of Our Lady of the Remedies (Nuestra Señora de los Remedios)

Calle Horno o Párroco Rafael Linares López, 2; tel. 620/403-409; 6pm-8:30pm daily; free

Next to the castle you'll discover the Nuestra Señora de los Remedios Church, a former mosque with a 13th-century carving of the Virgin Mary.

Bat Cave (Cueva de los Murciélagos)

Carretera Local Cueva de los Murciélagos, km 4; tel. 957/694-545; https://turismozuheros.es/cueva-de-los-murcielagos; hours vary, typically 11am-1:30pm and 4:30pm-5:30pm Wed.-Sun.; €8

This real-life Bat Cave has nothing of the Caped Crusader about it. You won't find Alfred or Bruce. In fact, you probably won't even find a bat, despite its name. During a one-hour tour you'll descend 350 steep steps into the cave, where you'll learn much about how the cave was used in prehistoric times through the Roman era. And before you can say "Holy spelunking, Batman!" you'll ascend another set of 350 steep steps to the exit.

Food and Accommodations

Zuheros Gourmet

Calle Mirador, 19; tel. 957/917-311; 10am-6pm daily; €8

Blissfully air-conditioned, this little market has a small bar where you can enjoy regionally specific cheeses, hams, and olive oils paired with a local beer, vermouth, wine, or sherry. Consider not only having a little snack but picking up goods for the road or souvenirs as well.

Los Palancos

Plaza de la Paz, 1; tel. 957/694-538; 10:30am-midnight Wed.-Mon.; €10

Right across from the church at the top of the hill, near the castle, is Los Palancos. A shaded streetside patio offers continuous service, making it a very welcome stop for those looking for a traditional local lunch of rabo de toro or pork knuckle. Outside of the usual Spanish dining hours, you'll find continuous service, where you can always get a little nibble and a cold drink.

Hotel Zuhayra

Calle Mirador, 10; tel. 957/694-693; https://zercahoteles.com; €60

This simple and clean no-nonsense hotel with lots of Andalusian country charm is right in the middle of the village, near the castle. Nearly all the rooms have commanding views over the village and valley beyond. The service is good, though you will likely have to make use of your Spanish. Thankfully, there is parking on-site, and a small restaurant can take care of breakfast for you.

Getting There

Zuheros is southeast of Córdoba along the N-432 (1.5 hr; 76 km/47 mi). There is limited bus service three times daily from Córdoba.

PRIEGO DE CÓRDOBA

Located about equidistant between the major cities of Córdoba and Granada, this charming, historic city makes for a great midday stop to break up the drive and get a sense of small-town life in one of the region's most beautiful towns. During the Roman era, it was known as "Baxo" or "Bago" and was part of the province of Baetica. The Romans established settlements and cultivated the land, leaving behind archaeological remains. Like much of Andalusia, Priego de Córdoba was ruled by the Moors for several centuries. The Moors contributed significantly to the development of the town's irrigation systems, agriculture, and architecture. In the 13th century, during the period of the Reconquista, the town was captured by Ferdinand III of Castile in 1226, while the 16th and 17th centuries marked a period of great prosperity for Priego de Córdoba. It experienced significant economic growth, thanks to the production of silk and the olive oil industry. It was during this era that construction of the town's most iconic Baroque buildings, including churches, fountains, and mansions, was accomplished. Interestingly, Priego de Córdoba boasts more nationally recognized monuments than any other city or town in the province, making for a beautiful backdrop to your visit and offering numerous attractions that could easily fill up an itinerary for a few days.

Sights

Castle of Priego de Córdoba (Castillo de Priego de Córdoba)

Calle Marqués de Priego; tel. 957/700-625; 11am-2pm and 6:30pm-8:30pm Tues.-Sat., 11am-2pm Sun.-Mon., guided night visits 10pm Fri.-Sat.; €1.50

This is perhaps the most iconic of the monuments in Priego de Córdoba to visit, though if you have seen quite a few other castles along your voyage, perhaps not the most interesting. It's an Arabic fortress that was altered in the 13th century and again in the 15th. It has a prayer tower and a walled interior with seven different towers; two are cylindrical and the rest are quadrangular. An interesting flea market is held on the first Sunday of every month right in front of the castle. The market and some of the views from the castle make this a good stop.

★ Barrio de la Villa

Declared a historical-artistic monument in 1972, Barrio de la Villa is the original urban area on which present-day Priego de Córdoba is based. It is obviously of medieval and Muslim inspiration. Its winding whitewashed and narrow streets lead to the Plaza San Antonio, the town square, which is in the center of the narrow, geranium-lined streets. This part of Priego will likely have you thinking more Morocco, perhaps, than Spain. You could easily spend an hour or so just wandering the streets, taking photos, and peeking into the boutique shops and restaurants that call this neighborhood home. There are not too many neighborhoods still like this in the towns of Andalusia that are this well-preserved. It's well worth a detour if you would like a sense of how some of the medinas (old cities) of North Africa feel.

Church of the Ascension (Iglesia de Nuestra Señora de la Asunción)

Calle Santa Ana, 0; tel. 957/701-817; 11am-1:30pm Tues.-Sun.; €3

This is another wonderful example of a church repurposing the minaret of a mosque for its bell tower. The plain white exterior does not fully prepare you for the intricacy of the Baroque treasure waiting inside. The ornately carved interior is a real masterpiece that will inevitably make you wonder just how all of this gets dusted. The peaceful music puts you in the right mood for spiritual reflection as you tour the small church and take a moment in the pews.

Calle del Río

The picturesque Calle del Río runs north to south. On the southern edge you'll find the **Fuente del Rey,** a popular local park, while the north end connects with **Plaza de Andalucía,** winding right into the Barrio de la Villa. Along this street you'll see some of the most iconic houses and buildings of Priego de Córdoba, most of them constructed in the 18th century. There are a few eateries, pubs, and gastrobars along here as well, fitting in with the hip sort of feel to the town, despite its age and historic importance.

1: Zuheros Castle **2:** flowers in the Barrio de la Villa **3:** looking down the Calle del Río **4:** Priego de Córdoba's town hall

1
2
3
4

Museum of Niceto Alcalá-Zamora (Casa Museo Niceto Alcalá-Zamora)

Calle del Rio, 33; tel. 957/006-224; 11am-2pm and 5pm-7pm Tues.-Sat., 11am-2pm Sun.; €2

Arguably, this is the birthplace of modern Spain. In fact, it was in this home-turned-museum that Niceto Alcalá-Zamora was born. If you were paying attention in your Modern Spanish History class, you might remember that name. Alcalá-Zamora was the first president of the Second Spanish Republic in 1931. This is a museum of the bourgeoisie of the time and how his family and the town of Priego de Córdoba influenced the development of the politician he would become, rather than a museum of his presidency.

Museum and Cultural Center Adolfo Lozano Sidro

Calle Carrera de las Monjas, 16; tel. 957/540-947; 10am-2pm and 6pm-8:30pm Tues.-Fri., 10am-2pm and 5pm-7pm Sat., 10am-2pm Sun.; €2

An ancestral home from the end of the 19th century, donated by the painter's family, this building currently houses a local history museum, a gallery that exhibits various artistic schools in landscape painting, and the Adolfo Lozano Sidro Museum. Lozano Sidro was one of the most appreciated illustrators of the early 20th century. For art lovers, it could be an inspiring little center to enjoy for an hour or so. There's not a lot of info in English, though the exposition detailing the history of Priego from prehistory to the Reconquista needs no introduction.

Food

Bar Castillo

Calle Marqués de Priego, 7; hours vary; €10

After walking around Priego a bit, a fresh drink at the wall of the castle on the little pedestrian-only cobblestone street that once connected the castle to the medieval town is just the ticket. The bar seems to be always open, except when it is not. It's one of those local places and is very much patronized by just about everyone in town. It's a picturesque stop for tapas and a cold drink.

La Tabernilla

Calle Málaga, 70 (on the southeast corner of the Fuente del Rey); tel. 957/542-237; 7am-5pm and 7pm-1am daily; €15

On the stairway overlooking the park, you can belly up to the oldest tavern in town. Dating back to 1901, this local staple offers near-continuous service with the typical sorts of Andalusian dishes you'll find for breakfast (think churros and tostadas), as well as a wide selection of locally sourced tapas with a focus on regional legumes and proteins. The food is delicious and the service swift and kind, though you are stopping in here more for the ambience with locals and of course the stellar views over the park. In the chilly winter months there is a wonderfully heated terrace to take full advantage of the outdoors.

★ Zyrah

Calle del Río, 8; tel. 957/547-023; noon-midnight Tues.-Sun.; €25

Visit this modern vibey wine bar right on the popular Calle del Río if you want an updated take on traditional Andalusian specialties. Service is in English, which is particularly unexpected in a small town. There are several standout dishes, but the duck with smoked burrata is worth the side trip into Priego de Córdoba, and the ibérico, parmesano, and boletus risotto is as mouthwatering as it sounds. You'll typically find mostly locals about, though occasionally a local expat might make their way in. This place is earning quite the reputation, and deservedly so.

Accommodations

Casa del Rey

Calle Real, 20; tel. 671/277-128; www.casadelreypriego.es; €70

This fun little rustic lodging is right in the tight quarters of the old Barrio de la Villa. There are only six rooms, so you'll want to make sure to reserve ahead of time as this is also a popular spot with families from the area looking to spend a weekend or a long week in Priego. More of a B&B than a hotel, it's family-run and simple but charming, with all the amenities you need for a nice stay.

Casa Baños de la Villa

Calle Real, 63; tel. 957/547-274; https://casabanosdelavilla.com; €110

Each room of this quaint, nine-room boutique property nestled in the heart of Priego de Córdoba, near the castle, has a different theme and a unique scent to whisk you away into your Andalusian fantasy. The on-site Moroccan-style baths offer an opportunity to relax after a long day of exploration. Sessions in the baths start from €22.

★ Casa Olea

Apartado de Correos, 281; tel. 696/748-209; www.casaolea.com; €150

The perfect sort of retreat for those needing a break from the busy cities, Casa Olea is about 20 minutes north of Priego de Córdoba (13 km/8 mi) in the wilder part of the Subbética range. A large pool looks out over endless peaks of jagged limestone and shadowy deep gorges. The six guest rooms all have king beds, while the Olivo room has its own private terrace. This is a calm getaway with lots of local hiking and biking available for active travelers.

Getting There and Around

Priego de Córdoba is an easy car ride from Córdoba (1.5 hr; 97 km/60 mi) along the N-432 and a short drive from Zuheros (45 min; 33 km/20 mi) along the same national road that connects with Córdoba. The N-432 continues along to Granada (1 hr; 79 km/49 mi), making Priego de Córdoba a nice lunch stop to explore on a road trip between Córdoba and Granada.

There is a single direct local bus run by Carrera (2.5 hrs; https://autocarescarrera.es; €5) connecting Priego de Córdoba with Córdoba.

Once in Priego, the usual rules apply: Park your car and get ready to explore on foot.

LUCENA

If you loved Seville but didn't love the crowds and wanted something with more local flavor, Lucena ticks a lot of the boxes. Plaza Nueva, Plaza San Miguel, and Calle El Peso form the heart of this proud city, with plenty of local shopping and tapas. Be aware that you might be the only non-Spanish traveler in this overlooked city, which is a shame. Lucena, once known as the "Pearl of the Sefarad," with a rich Jewish epoch spanning over 200 years, offers a unique look into the complex, multicultural history of Andalusia.

Sights

El Moral Castle (Castillo del Moral)

Pasaje Cristo del Amor; tel. 957/503-662 or 605/867-514; https://turismodelasubbetica.es/en/lucena/item/castillo-del-moral-museo-arqueologico-y-etnologico; €3.50

This entirely medieval castle is most interesting for its re-creation of the nearby Angel's Cave, an archaeological discovery of prehistoric importance where *Homo heidelbergensis* (early humans) lived about 600,000-100,000 BCE. The cityscape views over Lucena from the top of the castle should not be skipped, though watch out while you're ascending the towers—the going is narrow and steep while the ceiling is quite low. The lower levels of the castle, including the re-creation of the Angel's Cave, are now a museum for local archaeology and ethnology.

Church of Saint Matthew (Parroquia de San Mateo)

Plaza San Miguel; tel. 957/500-775; https://turismodelasubbetica.es/en/lucena/item/parroquia-de-san-mateo; 7:30am-1:30pm and 6pm-8:30pm Mon.-Fri., 8:30am-1:30pm and 6pm-8:30pm Sat.-Sun.; free

Once the place of the central synagogue of Lucena, and later a mosque, the current church didn't form here until 1498 CE. The outstanding Dome of the Transept (Cúpula del Crucero) is an incredible, ornate example of Andalusian Baroque, sculpted between 1740 and 1772. If you are on the main plaza,

1
2
3
4

you might as well duck in to check out the Dome of the Transept.

Palace of the Counts of Santa Ana (Palacio de los Condes de Santa Ana)

Calle San Pedro, 42; tel. 957/509-990; 10:30am-6pm Mon.-Sat., 10:30am-2pm Sun.; free

This relatively modern 18th-century building once was part of the proud Mora-Saavedra family. Featuring two courtyards and an ornate vaulted ceiling over a grand staircase, this prime example of civil architecture is now a museum dedicated to the amazingly rich history of Lucena, from cave dwellers to the Sephardic Jews, Muslims, Christians, and even more contemporary Spaniards who breathe this history daily.

Jewish Necropolis (Necrópolis Judía)

Calle la Parra, 64; tel. 957/503-662 or 605/867-514; 9am and 9:30am Sat., 9am Sun. mid-June-mid-Sept., 9am and 10am Sat., 9am Sun. mid-Sept.-mid-June; €3.50

Reservations to visit the expansive Jewish Necropolis can be made at either El Moral Castle or the information center at the Palacio de los Condes de Santa Ana. There are three time slots weekly (two on Saturday and one on Sunday). Discovered in 2006, the necropolis is one of the very few (perhaps the only) pre-Inquisition Jewish burial sites discovered in Spain. This is one of those visits made so much better by a good guide. Luckily, Lucena has a few great guides that work with the local tourist office.

Shopping

Lucena Municipal Market (Mercado Municipal de Abastos)

Calle General Chavarre, 4; tel. 957/503-344; https://mercadodelucena.es; 8am-3pm Mon.-Sat.

While Triana in Seville gets all of the attention, smaller markets like the one in Lucena provide a more local experience, with tons of local meats, cheeses, baked goods, and produce. A couple of smaller cafés and bars offer snacks and quick eats. Saturday tends to be a slower market day, so it's better to dive in during the week if possible.

1: Church of Saint Matthew 2: view from El Moral Castle 3: Basilica of St. John of Avila in Montilla 4: Palace of the Counts of Santa Ana

Food

Bar el Bacalao

Lucena Municipal Market; 8am-3pm or 4pm Mon.-Thurs., 8am-5pm Fri.-Sat. €4

Bar el Bacalao is what the bars and restaurants used to be like in the Triana Market in Seville—low key and with surprisingly great, fresh food for a nominal cost. The focus here is on keeping things fresh and local and pairing tapas with a draft beer. There is limited seating, and you'll have to navigate in Spanish to figure out what the freshest of the fresh arrivals is. As the name implies, cod is the local specialty.

El Lagar

Calle Barahona de Soto; 8pm-midnight Tues., noon-4pm and 8-midnight Wed.-Sun.; €5

Hip local wine bar with deliciously shaded patio seating just off the Plaza Nuevo on the south side of the San Mateo Church. Service is swift and friendly. The locally sourced wine is a particular delight; a crisp Andalusian white is just the sort of thing to parch your thirst after a long day of exploration.

★ Don Álvaro

Plaza Nueva, 16; 8am-midnight Mon. and Wed.-Fri., 9am-1pm Sat., 9am-5pm Sun.; €7

On Plaza Nueva, directly in front of the San Mateo Church, there are several places popular with locals, with Don Álvaro being perhaps the flag standard. Pop a squat for a cool beverage and a spot of people-watching. Tapas here are all really standard. You can never go wrong with a small platter of boquerones (anchovies).

Peña Taurina y Círculo Mercantil

Calle El Peso; 8am-1am daily; €10

Calle El Peso, the popular walking strip through Lucena, has a surprising number of tapas joints. Peña Taurina is one of the more popular spots to hang with the locals. There is continuous service, so there is no telling when the crowds will really start, though a good bet is early in the morning and then after the paseo (stroll) in the evening.

Accommodations

Hotel Santo Domingo

Juan Jiménez Cuenca, 16; tel. 957/511-100; €50

Once a convent, this charming property has clean, though basic, rooms that have the typical amenities you would find in most hotels, including en suite bathrooms, safe boxes, towels, soap, 24/7 reception, Wi-Fi, and TVs. This is all set against the charm of the 18th-century patio in hues of pink and red trimmed with white. The property has the feeling of a real grande dame and is a favorite for budget-conscious couples. For those road-tripping through Andalusia, the parking garage is a small blessing.

Doña Lola

Calle Montenegro, 2; tel. 621/231-529; https://lolaalojamientos.com; €62

Well located in central Lucena, this is a modern boutique for independent travelers. You'll have your own fully equipped apartment, from studios to two-bedrooms. The two-bedroom Lola has a private patio and is a great choice for traveling families and friends, while the bunk bed setup in the small double room is a great value and perfect for those wanting a more private hostel feel with a good friend.

Information and Services

Tourist Information Center

Calle San Pedro, 42, in the Palacio de los Condes de Santa Ana; tel. 957/513-282; www.turlucena.com; 10am-2pm and 5pm-8pm Mon.-Sat., 10am-2pm Sun. (hours vary slightly between winter and summer)

The tourist information center can arrange private half-day guided tours (Mon.-Fri.) of Lucena and its monuments in English (€80). Every Saturday at 10am there is an English-speaking group tour for €10 per person. The English-speaking staff are motivated to show off the best Lucena has to offer.

Getting There and Around

There are connections by bus to major cities like Córdoba (12-plus daily; 1.5 hr; 73 km/45 mi; €10) on carriers like Autocares Carrera (https://autocarescarrera.es). Lucena's bus station is located on Calle Miguel Cruz Cuenca. For most travelers, though, it will make the most sense to connect to Lucena by car. There is inexpensive central parking (Plaza Nueva; €12), and the rest of the predominantly flat city can easily be navigated on foot.

MONTILLA

Locally revered for its wines, Montilla is a must-stop for those who enjoy their grapes crushed, fermented, and well aged. There are a few sights to visit while you are in town, though for most travelers the big draws are the wineries dotting the area just around town. Historically, though there is evidence of people living here in prehistoric times, this region was largely unsettled until after the Reconquista. Many of the older buildings date from the 16th century onward, with the majority being built over the last 300 years as the local wine production has brought employment and economic opportunity.

Sights

Montilla Castle (Castillo-Alhorí)

Antiguo Castillo; 10am-2pm Mon.-Thurs., 10am-2pm and 6pm-8pm Fri., 10am-1pm and 6pm-8pm Sat., 10am-1pm Sun.; free

On the north slope of town lies the unmissable medieval castle. The castle itself is undergoing a long period of renovation work. Eventually it will become the Andalusian Wine Museum, which will be a must-stop for wine enthusiasts traveling through. As of this writing, you are going there to admire the views, which are pretty incredible.

Basilica of St. John of Avila (Basílica de San Juan de Ávila)

Calle Corredera, 23a; tel. 957/650-232; www.sanjuandeavila.net; 8am-3pm Mon.-Fri.; free

There are a surprising number of picturesque churches dotted throughout Montilla. Of the many, this is perhaps the one you really should take a moment for. San Juan de Ávila is locally revered as a saint. His remains are entombed in the 18th-century temple, an impressive temple that wasn't finished until near the end of World War II in 1944. Pilgrims make their way annually to pay their respects. Note the impressively carved wood altar.

★ Wine Tasting

Alvear

Avenida de María Auxiliadora, 1; www.alvear.es; 8:30am-6pm Mon.-Fri.; €12

Founded in 1729, this is the oldest winery in Andalusia and the second oldest in all of Spain. For nearly 300 years the Alvear family has been perfecting their lovingly crafted wines. If you can stop by only one winery, this would have to be the one. Tours are available in English. Exact price of the tour depends upon how many and what types of wines you are tasting at the end. All tastings come with cheese, olives, and bread. Advance reservations required.

Cruz Conde

Calle Ronda del Canillo, 4; tel. 957/651-250 or 663/786-183; http://bodegascruzconde.es; 9am-2pm and 4pm-7pm Mon.-Fri., 10am-2pm Sat. Sept.-Apr., 8am-3pm Mon.-Fri., 10am-2pm Sat. May-Aug., tour at noon Mon.-Sat.; €15

Cruz Conde is an award-winning winery founded in 1902. If you plan it right, you can join the tour at noon (daily except Sun.). The English-language tour lasts for 1.5 hours and ends with a tasting that includes some traditional tapas. If you miss out on the tour, the shop is well-priced, so you could cobble together your own wine-tasting experience.

Pérez Barquero

Avenida de Andalucía, 27; tel. 957/650-500; https://perezbarquero.com; 7am-3pm Mon.-Fri., 10am-2pm Sat.; €15

Since 1905 this has been a local favorite. Some of the best wines produced in the region these days come from Pérez Barquero. During a tour, usually about an hour long, you'll likely deepen your appreciation for wines in general and get a nose for some of the flavors coming off these local vines.

Wine Tours

Bacus Travel and Tours

Avenida de Andalucía; tel. 957/022-063 or 670/627-195; www.bacustravel.com; from €18

If you have a deep interest in enology, give Teresa a call! She can arrange wonderful local wine tastings as well as a walking tour of Montilla that will plunge you into the rich history of this town. Some of the more interesting guided experiences take you out in the vineyards and olive groves, where you can touch, feel, and smell this particular terrain for yourself, as well as to some of the historic wine presses in the region.

Food and Accommodations

★ Barril de Oro

Avenida de Andalucía, 26; tel. 669/593-882; noon-5pm and 7:30pm-midnight Tues.-Sat., noon-5pm Sun.; €10

This unpretentious street-side spot at the entrance of town is right next to the roundabout. Black barrels advertise the local "barrels of gold"—what they dub the wine and olive oil from this region—that put Montilla on the map, making it famous throughout Spain. The portions here are particularly generous, so go easy on the menu. One tapa or a half ration and a beverage is good for most people. The tortilla española is particularly well done, as are the flamenpequiño, a smaller version of the traditional flamenquín, and the artichoke hearts stewed with white wine, garlic, and an Iberian ham-infused sauce.

The Montilla Wine Route

The Montilla Wine Route, known officially as the "Ruta del Vino Montilla-Moriles," is dedicated to the wine production of the Montilla-Moriles Denomination of Origin (DO), which is locally known for its unique wines, especially its naturally fortified wine known as Pedro Ximénez. Despite being one of the oldest and genuinely historic wine regions in all of Spain, if not all of Europe, strangely it is one of the least known.

a vineyard in the Montilla-Moriles region

THE ROUTE

The entire route encompasses Córdoba, the provincial capital, as well as Montilla and Moriles, the towns from which the route takes its name. Lucena, Fernan Nuñez, Montemajor, La Rambla, Aguilar de la Frontera, and Puente Genil are the other towns along this route. To get around to the different towns along the route, it is recommended that you rent either a car or a bicycle.

The tourism office in Montilla has a lot of information about the wine route. Online, the Rutas Vino de España website (https://wineroutesofspain.com) has some great info as well for oenophiles.

THE WINES

Montilla-Moriles DO

The Montilla-Moriles DO is primarily known for its production of sherry-style wines. These wines are made from the local Pedro Ximénez grape variety, which is particularly well suited to the region's hot, arid climate and chalky white soil. This grape variety is the only one in the world that produces a wine that is naturally more than 15 percent alcohol by volume. These particular wines are known among aficionados for their complexity, sweetness, and rich flavors.

Pedro Ximénez

Pedro Ximénez is made by drying grapes in the sun, basically turning them into raisins, which intensifies their sugars and flavors. The dried grapes are then pressed and aged in large barrels, which you'll find lining the different bodegas you visit. There are two basic ways the wine is aged in casks: biological and oxidative. The biological wines use a natural flor (yeast) for aging, while oxidative means that the wine has had another artificial increase in alcohol value, as with amontillado wines. There is a noticeable shift in color and bouquet in some of the wines that happens as a part of this process, dubbed oloroso, which is uniquely Andalusian.

Tasting

During a typical flight of wine tasting in the region, you will taste the five major wines characteristic of the Montilla-Moriles DO, beginning with a young wine from the last year before continuing with a fino, an amontillado, an oloroso, and finally ending with the rich finish of the celebrated Pedro Ximénez.

Restaurante Don Quijote

Calle Ballen, 6; tel. 957/651-271; www.restaurantedonquijote.com; 8:30am-4pm and 8pm-midnight Mon. and Wed.-Fri., 8:30am-noon Tues., 8:30am-midnight Sat., 9am-midnight Sun.; €13

Bright and air-conditioned with a shaded outdoor patio, Don Quijote is perfect for quick tapas or for a longer lunch or dinner. You can also duck in for a quick churro break nearly any time before dinner. Service is always swift and friendly. For dinner, there is a set menu available, or you can just order à la carte.

Lujo Pobre

Calle Ancha, 5; tel. 629/811-864; €45

There is nothing poor about this little boutique, despite its name. This is a place to rest up during your adventure through the enological specialties of Montilla. The service is kind and the traditional dinners paired with local fino are excellent. Check out their cellar, where you can even pick up a bottle of some local vintages. If May is around, say hi and compliment her on her artwork, which she displays around the property.

Hotel RB Don Ramiro

Calle Río de la Hoz 4; tel. 957/656-779; https://complejorbdonramiro.es; €75

A touch more modern, this hotel is a very clean, easy, regular no-fuss sort of hotel experience. It's centrally located and within an easy walk to just about everything. Spanish-speaking staff are quite kind, though the downstairs restaurant is lackluster, so don't feel bad about skipping it.

Information and Services

Tourist Office

Calle Iglesia; tel. 957/652-354; www.montillaturismo.es; 10am-2pm Mon.-Thurs, 10am-2pm and 4:30pm-6:30pm Fri., 10am-1pm and 4:30pm-6:30pm Sat., 10am-1pm Sun.

This friendly office provides lots of information about Montilla and its surroundings. If you are planning on exploring the region beyond what's listed in this guidebook, I strongly suggest stopping by for the numerous regionally focused pamphlets, maps, and guides.

Getting There and Around

You'll likely be visiting Montilla by car. Montilla is small enough to walk around, and there is easy street parking as well as an inexpensive parking garage. Montilla is just off the A-45 freeway, south of Córdoba (45 min; 50 km/31 mi) and north of Antequera (1 hr; 75 km/47 mi).

Antequera

This small town has more churches and UNESCO World Heritage Sites than you can shake a stick out, including the stunning El Torcal Nature Reserve. Antequera is where the Neolithic and megalithic meet up with various forms of European Renaissance architecture. The ubiquitous Alcazaba (Muslim-era fortress) towers over all.

During the Reconquista, the royal family of Spain invited fighters from all over Europe, gifting them land in Antequera. The fight brought wealthy families and landowners from all over, each with their small armies to aid in the cause. Soon, each family built their own church in a style from "back home," unwittingly creating a unique sort of city, one that in its church architecture reflects the styles and trends from not only Spain, but also France, Germany, Italy, and other European countries during this era.

Today there are still 28 functioning churches in Antequera, each with its own charm and history. For a smaller-scale town, with the heritage sites and churches it packs a lot of punch in terms of sites to see and experience.

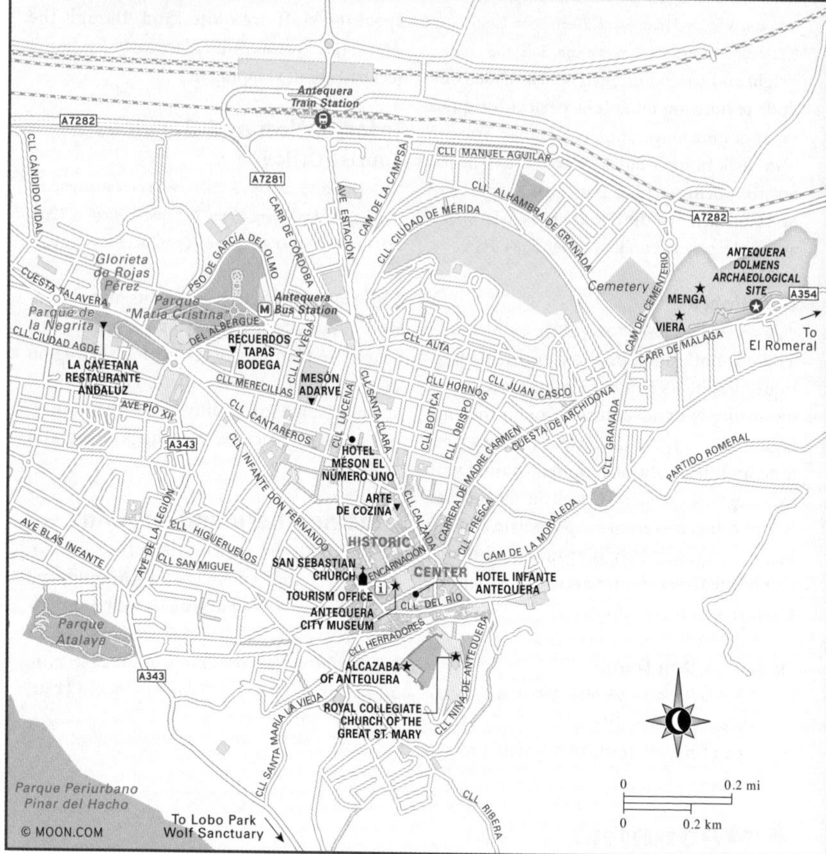

ORIENTATION

Located at the base of the northern face of the Sierra Nevada mountains, the city of Antequera tumbles downhill due north. At the top of the town you'll find the Alcazaba. From there, a steep drop fans out into the historic center of Antequera. Calle Infante Don Fernando is roughly the western border of the historic center, while Calle Calzada/Calle Santa Clara forms the eastern border. Plaza San Sebastián is a good central reference point when you are walking around, as most of the major avenues in Antequera connect there.

El Torcal Nature Reserve is a short drive (15 min; 15 km/9 mi) south of Antequera as you climb into the mountains on the A-7075.

SIGHTS

Alcazaba

Alcazaba of Antequera

Plaza de los Escribanos; tel. 951/700-737; www.andalucia.org/en/antequera-cultural-tourism-recinto-monumental-de-la-alcazaba; 10am-6pm daily; €4

The complex of the Alcazaba of Antequera crowns the hill to the south of the city along the foothills leading up to the El Torcal Nature

Reserve. This hilltop fortress was one of the greatest strongholds of the Islamic era in all of Spain and one of the very last to fall before Granada. Built in the 11th century, complete with gardens and crenellated towers, this is an impressive fortress, though with steep stairs throughout the visit. The free audio guide can make the medieval era of this towering fortress come alive. The views over Antequera and the valley bring home just how strategic of a fortress this was, and make for a fine photo op!

Royal Collegiate Church of the Great St. Mary
(Real Colegiata de Santa María la Mayor)

Calle San Salvador, 2; tel. 952/708-142; 10am-6pm daily; €3

For €6, you can couple the entrance to the Alcazaba complex with a visit to the impressive Real Colegiata de Santa María church just next door. From the courtyard in front of the church you can look down on the 1st-century Roman baths, which are open to the elements, though closed to the public. The church itself is perhaps most impressive from the outside. Like many other 16th-century constructions, there is an interesting mix of Islamic styles with touches of Baroque and Gothic. To get the most out of the visit, the free audio guide is worthwhile, as is the Spanish video with English subtitles that tells the story of the church.

Historic City Center

Antequera City Museum
(Museo de la Ciudad de Antequera)

Plaza Coso Viejo; tel. 952/708-300; https://museoantequera.wordpress.com; 9am-2pm and 4pm-6pm Tues.-Sat., 10am-2pm Sun. mid-June-mid-Sept., 10am-2pm Tues.-Sun. mid-Sept.-mid-June; €3

Housed in the renovated 18th-century Palacio de Nájera, the local museum features a rotating art exhibit as well as collections that highlight the archaeology and ethnology of the Antequera. The rooms are organized by era, taking you from the prehistory of Antequera and its dolmen-building peoples through the Roman and Islamic eras and right up to the 20th century. This is one of the stronger municipal museums in Andalusia.

San Sebastián Church
(Parroquia San Sebastián)

Plaza San Sebastián, 6; tel. 952/841-158; 10am-6pm daily; free

You won't be able to help seeing the tallest, most ornate church of Antequera, located right on the main plaza. Though there are 28 churches in town, this is probably the only "must see" church. From a distance you'll see the gilded El Angelote (the Fat Angel) atop the weathervane of the church bell tower. Nearly all the processions of Holy Week (Semana Santa) pass by here. Considered the most beautiful church by locals, this 16th-century church has a plateresque doorway (built in 1548 by Diego de Vergara) and 60-m-tall (197-ft) brick bell towers that add to the overall splendor. Interiors are a mix of Baroque and neoclassical designs, each overlapping, with a series of altarpieces and paintings that make for an overall grandiose impression.

★ Antequera Dolmens Archaeological Site
(Conjunto Arqueológico Dólmenes de Antequera)

Carretera de Málaga, Tholos de el Romeral; tel. 670/945-453; www.andalucia.org/es/antequera-turismo-cultural-conjunto-arqueologico-dolmenes-de-antequera; 9am-6pm Tues.-Sat., 9am-3pm Sun. fall-winter, 9am-8pm Tues.-Sat., 9am-3pm Sun. spring, 9am-3pm Tues.-Sun. summer; free

These megalithic wonders are some of the most important in all of Europe and the largest on the European continent. If you were thinking that there was something of Stonehenge about these dolmens, you would not be wrong. No wonder these three megalithic structures found themselves on the UNESCO World Heritage Site list. There are three separate dolmens you can visit, with **Menga** and **Viera** being neighbors and **El**

1

2

3

Romeral being a bit of walk or a short car ride away.

These dolmens, among the largest on the continent, are steeped in historical significance, mirroring the enigmatic allure of Stonehenge. Dating back thousands of years, the dolmens of Antequera were meticulously crafted using enormous stones, each weighing several tons. The engineering prowess required to transport and position these massive stones is awe-inspiring. The stones, strategically arranged to create these massive structures, evoke a sense of wonder and admiration for the ancient architects and the communities who envisioned and executed such monumental feats. These colossal stones bear witness to the cultural and technological achievements of civilizations long past.

To delve deeper into the secrets of these megalithic wonders, a small contemporary museum near Menga and Viera serves as a gateway to understanding their creation. Pick up your free ticket and immerse yourself in an informative video that unravels the intricate process behind the dolmens' construction. The museum provides a glimpse into the ancient craftsmanship, shedding light on the tools, techniques, and communal dedication that culminated in the creation of these enduring marvels.

Lobo Park Wolf Sanctuary

Carretera de Antequera, km 16; tel. 952/031-107; www.lobopark.com; guided tours 11am, 1pm, 3pm, and 4:30pm; €13.50 adults, €8.50 children 3-12

Discover this wildlife park in the heart of Andalusia. It is a private park set in a bit of unspoiled nature at the foot of El Torcal, a 15-minute drive southwest of Antequera. You might just look at a wolf eye to eye for the first time in your life. It is home to three different wolf subspecies (European, Alaskan Tundra, and native Iberian wolves). All of these wolves are rescue animals and would have nowhere else to live. The owner is passionate and involved intimately with the raising of the wolves to give them the best natural lives possible. For a howling good time, look out for special "Wolf Howl Nights" (€25/€15), once or twice a month, where the park opens at sunset as the full moon rises. This is a great outing for families and lovers of animals.

1: tower of San Sebastián Church 2: exploring the Antequera Dolmens Archaeological Site
3: Alcazaba of Antequera

SPORTS AND RECREATION

Parks

Parque de la Negrita

Cuesta de Talavera

Parents traveling with young ones should mark this little park and put it at the top of their list. It's all about the location. A restaurant, **La Cayetana Restaurante Andaluz** (tel. 951/830-933; 8am-midnight daily; €15), overlooks the Parque de la Negrita, one of the best play parks in the region for the under 14 set. Features include a large, enclosed slide section with a number of nooks and crannies on the ladders that reach three stories, a kid-friendly zipline, twirling play structures, and plenty of room to run around. The kids can expend their seemingly endless energy while the parents enjoy a cold drink and look on at the restaurant. This is the type of family travel where the kids and their adult chaperones can both engage culturally and have an immersive moment on their level.

ENTERTAINMENT AND EVENTS

Festivals

Semana Santa is celebrated here (as everywhere else in Spain) during the week leading up to Easter with religious processions. Here are a few festivals specific to Antequera.

Spring Fair

June

This is a cultural fair that includes a fair amount of drinking and dancing as well as bullfights and an agricultural element that focuses on local produce and livestock, much like a county fair in North America.

Festivities happen around the city, but are largely centered around the bullring.

Royal Fair of August (Feria Real de Agosto)

August

This festival claims to be one of the oldest and longest-running ferias in the entire country. It includes a romeria, a pilgrimage typically undertaken over the year on foot to Rome, Italy. This is one of the few celebrations done outside the city center during the festival—the rest are around the city center and bullring.

Saints of Antequera: Our Lady of the Remedy and Saint Euphemia (Nuestra Señora de los Remedios)

September 8 and 16

An annual two-part procession honors the patron saints of Antequera, Nuestra Señora de los Remedios, and Saint Euphemia. This is a religious affair that has the usual Catholic pomp, though here it's much smaller than in the surrounding cities and is a more intimate experience. The procession circles around Antequera, beginning and ending at the Nuestra Señora de los Remedios church (Calle Infante Don Fernando, 72) on the 8th and church of Santa Euphemia (Calle Belén, 4) on the 16th.

FOOD

Tapas Bars

Recuerdos Tapas Bodega

Calle Seguro; tel. 640/960-648; 1pm-4:30pm and 8:15pm-11:30pm Thurs.-Sun.; €20

Fresh, light, Mediterranean-inspired tapas at this well-loved local joint will have you singing the praises of Antequeran cuisine. Tapas here are particularly well done. As in many of the restaurants throughout the region, you'll have your choice of serving size. In practice, it's a lot more fun to have the "tapa" or "medio" size and share various dishes with your travel companions. If the weather is fair, the restaurant will fill up, so it's best to call the morning of and reserve a table.

Traditional Spanish

★ Arte de Cozina

Calle de Calzada, 29; tel. 952/840-014; https://artedecozina.com; 1pm-4:30pm and 8pm-11pm Mon.-Sat., 1pm-4:30pm Sun.; €25

This is the sort of place I make sure to visit at least once a year. In the chilly winters, the roaring fire in the enclosed courtyard is something special. There is a stress on local

food at Arte de Cozina

produce, and the chef, Charo Carmona, has more than just a deft hand in the kitchen. She elevates the local cuisine so much so that she's become something of a local celebrity. The focus on regional dishes means things like rabbit are on the menu. You won't find it elsewhere, though in the family homes of Andalusia, rabbit is quite typical. You'll also find a few vegan and vegetarian options as well as seafood, beef, and ham. All dishes feel like abuela's (grandma's) home cooking, but they are presented in a slightly upscale, homey bistro fashion. Even if you just stop in Antequera for lunch, this restaurant alone would make it worth the journey.

Mesón Adarve

Calle Merecillas, 12; tel. 661/563-658; www.mesonadarve.com; 1pm-3:30pm and 7:30pm-10:30pm Tues.-Fri., 1pm-3:30pm Sat.-Sun.; €25

Cozy lighting in an industrial interior makes for the backdrop to a fun date night or easy lunch out. Mesón Adarve has a definite steakhouse vibe. It's quite popular locally for the varied menu, including a few international classics. You will usually find Juan here, and he is an excellent host, always quick with a joke and happy to make sure you have everything you need. Salad lovers should rejoice at the self-branded olive oil gracing the leaves, while lovers of seafood would do well to try the grilled octopus.

ACCOMMODATIONS

Under €100

Hotel Méson el Número Uno

Calle Lucena, 40; tel. 952/843-134; www.hotelnumerouno.com; €45

This breezy little property makes for a fine economical stay while in Antequera, with bright, cheerful rooms full of old-world charm. You'll be within walking distance to everything in town and have a comfy bed to return to. Hot water is plentiful. What the property lacks in amenities it really does make up for in service. You'll likely have to navigate in Spanish, though that should be part of the adventure. The property can be a bit noisy, particularly on the lower floors, so if you are a sensitive sleeper, ask for a quieter room and plan to use ear plugs or noise-canceling headphones.

Hotel Infante Antequera

Calle Nájera, 22; tel. 952/844-982; www.hotelinfanteantequera.com; €70

The rooftop pool is the big draw, with unimpeded views over the impressive rooftops of Antequera. The rooms are all contemporary and modern. Location is central with all of the town within walking distance. Perhaps not the most memorable stay you'll have in Andalusia, but definitely an easy one. Did I mention the rooftop pool?

INFORMATION AND SERVICES

You can pick up street maps and occasionally other flyers at the **tourism office** (Oficina de Turismo; Calle Encarnación, 4A; tel. 952/702-505; http://turismo.antequera.es; 9am-6:30pm Mon.-Sat., 10am-2pm Sun.). If Maria is working, you are in for a treat. She is extremely helpful and will happily point you anywhere in town.

GETTING THERE AND AROUND

Train

Right on the north edge of the city you'll find the main train station, **Estación de AVE de Antequera** (Ave. Estación, 1), with connections to Córdoba (10-plus daily; 45 min; €10), Seville (6 daily connecting through Córdoba; 2 hr; €25), Granada (10-plus daily; 45 min; €12), and Málaga (10-plus daily; 30 min; €9) as well as other destinations. You can walk from the station into Antequera. It's about 20 minutes to the city center and a farther 10 minutes up the steep hill to the Alcazaba of Antequera, though walking around the station is not great as you'll have to walk along a highway for a few minutes without a sidewalk. Taxis are preferable and usually available into town (10 min; €10).

Confusingly, there are two other

train stations in the area associated with Antequera. The first is a boarded-up old train station still pinned on most online maps (like Google Maps) near the new train station. This can cause confusion whether driving or walking to the station. There is another train station, Antequera-Santa Ana, that is 20 km (12 mi) inland from Antequera and used specifically for the high-speed trains. Beware of purchasing train tickets for Antequera-Santa Ana. If you end up there, it will be an expensive taxi ride into Antequera.

Bus

Though for most travelers it is best to come by car or train, bus can be an option, particularly if you are going from smaller town to smaller town. At the Antequera **bus station** (Calle Sagrado Corazón de Jesús, 1), Alsa (www.alsa.es) and Autocares Carrera (https://autocarescarrera.es) have multiple daily connections with towns such as Lucena (30 min; 52 km/32 mi; €5) and Córdoba (2.5 hr; 115 km/72 mi; €13).

Car

Centrally located at the junction of the A-45 freeway (connecting Córdoba and Málaga) and the A-92 (connecting Seville with Granada), Antequera is a small city that should be at the top of the list for road-trippers zooming through Andalusia. Due north you'll find Córdoba (1.5 hr; 117 km/73 mi), while south you run into the Mediterranean and Málaga (1 hr; 55 km/34 mi). If you head east you'll run into Seville (2 hr; 200 km/125 mi), while west is Granada (1 hr; 101 km/63 mi). Sometimes there is parking along the backside of the Alcazaba, but often this is full. There are a couple of well-marked parking garages in town.

★ El Torcal Nature Reserve

The **Paraje Natural El Torcal de Antequera,** with its karstic landscape, holds a special enchantment for observers. It has been designated as one of Europe's most important landscapes, captivating visitors for almost a century since its recognition as a Natural Site of National Interest. This extraordinary place is where the heavens seem to converge with the earth, creating a truly unique and singular environment.

Torcal's fame extends beyond its astronomical significance. Its limestone rock formations contribute to a breathtaking landscape that is considered unparalleled worldwide. Covering an impressive 1,171 hectares (2,894 acres), this natural wonder has even served as a backdrop for science fiction films. Navigating through its labyrinth of rocks, depressions, valleys, passages, landings, and narrow passes can lead one to a sense of being lost in a mysterious world.

El Torcal consists of limestone rock that originated in the depths of the sea during the Jurassic period (250-150 million years ago). The sediments that accumulated on the seabed were cemented together by salts and precipitates produced by marine dissolution. Pushed by tectonic activity, they emerged from the sea to occupy their current location. The subsequent erosion and sinking of the crevices led to the creation of El Torcal's natural "passageways."

There are several geographically diverse parks and reserves of Andalusia. Visually, this is perhaps the most interesting and offers hiking for nearly every age and skill level. Couple this with its location nearly equidistant from the major cities of Andalusia and you have the ideal spot to add some outdoor activity while you drive between cities in the region.

VISITING THE PARK

There are limited facilities available in the park, though you will find a restaurant and

Andalusia Under Water: The Formation of El Torcal

Spanning millions of years of geological history, the region of Andalusia in the Iberian Peninsula is an absorbing narrative of transformation. The geological processes mark the region's topography, geology, and biodiversity in a way that is evident, even to the lay traveler, offering impressive limestone landscapes known as "karst" landscapes.

limestone rock formations

UNDER WATER

Around 200 million years ago, this part of Andalusia was submerged beneath the ancient Tethys Sea, like much of Europe and the Middle East.

In this geological epoch, a striking saga of carbonate sedimentation unfolds, as the seabed transforms into a canvas adorned with the accumulation and deposition of marine organisms' skeletons and shells. Over approximately 175 million years, this accumulation culminates in the stratification of sediments. Over the eons, these sediments undergo processes of compaction and lithification, giving rise to horizontal strata of monumental proportions, measuring thousands of meters in thickness.

TECTONIC FORCES

Fast-forward to the middle Miocene, about 15 million years ago, and we witness a pivotal juncture in geological history. The dynamic convergence of the Iberian Plate, positioned to the north of the Tethys Sea, with the African Plate to the south, initiates a multifaceted geological transformation. In response to tectonic forces, the accumulated sediments experience compression, deformation, and fracturing. Gradually but inexorably, the sediments commence their ascent from the depths of the earth, an ascent that continues today.

WATER, ICE, AND WIND

Over the last 15 million years, this landscape has been at the capricious whims of meteorological processes. In fact, it is the artistry of Mother Nature that carves this karst landscape. Water, ice, and wind combine to sculpt the terrain of El Torcal de Antequera, bestowing upon it a geological masterpiece. The geological signature of this formation is that of a colossal mushroom-shaped fold, distinguished by an expansive, flat crown and steep, truncated flanks, each bordered by significant fractures. Basically, when you visit today's El Torcal, it feels like you're walking on another planet.

The geological design of El Torcal Nature Reserve enhances the intricate process of limestone dissolution. Rainwater, collected on the surface, embarks on a subterranean journey, percolating through the labyrinthine karst landscape. This natural reservoir plays a pivotal role in promoting processes of underground dissolution, ultimately culminating in the resurgence of water along the entire perimeter of El Torcal. Significantly, Nacimiento de La Villa, the most prominent spring, graces the northern expanse of Torcal.

SUBTERRANEAN FEATURES

While the karst landscape captures immediate attention, it is essential to acknowledge the hidden wonders concealed beneath the earth's surface. El Torcal reveals a subterranean realm, boasting a labyrinth of over a hundred caves and chambers, each a masterpiece of the intricate process of limestone dissolution. This subterranean world introduces yet another layer of intrigue to the rich tapestry of El Torcal's geological legacy, presenting an alluring avenue for further exploration and study.

clean bathrooms. The weather will likely be much cooler than wherever you are coming from, so pack accordingly. You should plan at least half a day to visit the park. This should give you enough time to arrive, experience the park through one of the three main hiking routes, and eat in nearby Antequera. Morning visits are suggested in hot summer months, while cooler winter months can lend themselves better to afternoon exploration. Most importantly, keep an eye on the weather, as that will most likely dictate when you go.

Gateway Towns

Antequera

The mountain town of Antequera is a short 30-minute drive (16 km/10 mi) from the park. From Antequera, you follow the A-7075. The road is well signed and there are few turns. From Antequera you will need a rental car to easily reach the park. Local taxis will take you to the park, but getting back to Antequera can be challenging, though not impossible. You can reserve a taxi online or call Taxi Antequera (tel. 687/597-500 or 952/845-555; https://taxiantequera.es). Expect to pay around €25 each way. When reserving, it is best to arrange a pickup time for a ride back to Antequera.

Visitor Centers

El Torcal Visitor Information Center

Carretera A-7075; tel. 617/444-772; www.andalucia.org/es/antequera-servicios-de-informacion-torcal-alto; 10am-7pm daily Apr.-Oct., 10am-5pm daily Nov.-Mar.

This center has clean bathrooms and plenty of information specific to the El Torcal Nature Reserve, including the indigenous flora and fauna of the region and its unique geography. The attached restaurant is the only one located in the park.

Tours

El Torcal de Antequera

tel. 952/243-324 or 637/596-465; www.torcaldeantequera.com; weekends only; €12

Limited guided tours of the park are available. Interestingly, these guided tours focus on areas of the park off limits to the general public. One of the more popular routes is the Route of the Ammonites, which focuses on fossils found in the region. English and Spanish are both spoken for guided tours. Tours all leave from the visitor center and typically take about three hours to cover 5 km (3 mi).

rock formation at El Torcal Nature Reserve

SIGHTS

El Torcal Astronomical Observatory

Calle el Torcal de Antequera, 70, 75; tel. 952/243-324; https://torcaldeantequera.com/en/information/visitors-center/astronomical-observatory; hours vary, generally 10pm-midnight Sat.; €8

With a little planning and some luck with the night skies, you can have a memorable deep-star-gazing experience in the observatory. Thanks to telescopes that can see galaxy formations, nebulae, and star clusters in deep space, the possibility of seeing the heavens unfolds. You will need to reserve ahead of time. Hours vary throughout the year, and what is available to see depends on the weather and the time of the year. March-August are your best bets. Interestingly, diurnal observations of the sun are also available, usually on Sunday, which use a filter so you can see the movements of the sun.

HIKING

The first thing you must account for when hiking El Torcal is the altitude. At over 1,200 m (3,900 ft), the weather is often cooler, wetter, and windier than elsewhere you might be coming from, like Córdoba or Málaga. As you are at a significantly higher elevation, the sun tends to be stronger as well, so don't forget your protective layers and sunscreen.

Otherwise, the terrain is stony and steep in parts. Though hiking boots aren't a necessity, if you are doing any of the longer routes, you would likely be more comfortable with them. Be sure to pack your refillable water bottles and some snacks. For lovers of a good hike, this makes for a great outing with unique landscapes not found elsewhere. In nice weather, the weekends are typically crowded with locals, so it's best to go during the week if possible.

Green Route

Distance: *1.5 km/1 mi round-trip*
Time: *45 min/1 hr*
Elevation gain: *40 m/131 ft*
Effort: *easy*
Trailhead: *upper parking lot*

This easy walk has parts that are accessible, making it possible for those in wheelchairs or in need of walking assistance to experience the start of this walk. The path is well marked. You'll first come to the Hoyo de la Burra, where you'll usually see a mix of wedding photo shoots and meditating yogis. Continue through this moon-like landscape to see a couple of the popular rock formations, such as The Indian and The Sphinx.

Yellow Route

Distance: *3 km/1.5 mi round-trip*
Time: *2 hr*
Elevation gain: *53 m/174 ft*
Effort: *easy-moderate*
Trailhead: *upper parking lot*

This circular route starts at the upper parking lot and finishes at the visitor center right next door. You'll cross the labyrinthine Torcal Alto section of the park. You do have to follow signs carefully. Once you leave the signposted trail, it is easy to get turned around. They don't call it a labyrinth for no reason! The best way to think of this route is as an extension of the green route, as the first and last section of this overlap with it. You'll find a well-marked forked crossing of the routes. The yellow route passes some of the most impressive natural rock formations, such as El Dedo and La Botella.

Orange Route (Torcal Alto)

Distance: *7 km/4.5 mi one-way*
Time: *3.5 hr*
Elevation gain: *263 m/863 ft*
Effort: *moderate-strenuous*
Trailhead: *lower parking lot*

This is the route you would naturally take up from the lower parking lot if you decided against taking the bus. Due to the elevation gain, this is by far the most strenuous hike in El Torcal. From the lower parking lot, near the entrance of the park, a route takes you across grasslands and canals before you begin your ascent. The ascent itself is steep. There is no getting around that. Several viewpoints offer respite as well as incredible views over the mountain range. The route ends at the visitor center.

FOOD AND ACCOMMODATIONS

El Torcal Alto Restaurant

Paraje Natural Torcal de Antequera (next to the visitor center); tel. 667/926-517; 10am-5pm daily; €15

This is the only game in town for food and drinks. Prices might be a touch elevated compared to some central downtown village restaurants, but considering the location, views, service, and overall quality of the food, it seems fair. Stick with the porra antequerana, which promises to warm you up on a cool day, even if it is a cold soup similar to gazpacho. If you are coming off a long hike and want something a bit heartier, it would be hard to beat the pork cheeks in a Malaganian wine sauce with deliciously fried potatoes.

Hotel La Magdalena

Urb. Antequera Golf Finca de la Magdalena (on the edge of the park); tel. 951/060-352; www.hotellamagdalena.com; €125

Tucked in the mountainside just a short 25-minute drive from the El Torcal Visitor Center you can find this convent-turned-five-star hotel. Formerly a 16th-century convent of San Pedro de Alcántara, Hotel La Magdalena today offers rambling luxury with a focus on wellness and good rest. Rustic tiles, exposed wood beams, and the occasional flowery mural take you back to another age. The modern beds and services ensure a pleasant stay. The on-site restaurant has floor-to-ceiling windows with romantic views over the park and valley. The restaurant is a culinary delight, though with the price to match—€75 tasting menu with the possible addition of a €35 supplemental wine pairing.

GETTING THERE AND AROUND

Car

You'll need a car to get to El Torcal. The park is 16 km (10 mi) from the city of Antequera along the A-7075 mountain road.

There is free parking at the foot of the nature reserve and at the visitor center at the top. During busier seasons, the upper parking near the visitor center is often closed, though there is a bus (€2) that offers a quick commute to the top. You could also choose to hike up into the reserve (1 hr; 4 km/2.5 mi).

Granada and the Sierra Nevada

Granada comes as a breath of fresh air, both literally and figuratively. Perched at over 735 m (2,400 ft) alongside the towering Sierra Nevada mountain range, Granada's elevation lifts it above the heat that pummels Andalusia, and cool winds often waft down from the mountains. The city is also home to the University of Granada, the fourth-largest university in Spain, with over 60,000 students. The youthful energy electrifies Granada in ways that are not as present in other parts of the region. This adds up to a progressive feeling throughout this city that embraces its long, rich heritage, most typically exemplified by the Alhambra complex.

Most travelers to Andalusia have the Alhambra at the top of their "must see" destinations, and for good reason. The Alhambra is a

Highlights

Look for ★ to find recommended sights, activities, dining, and lodging.

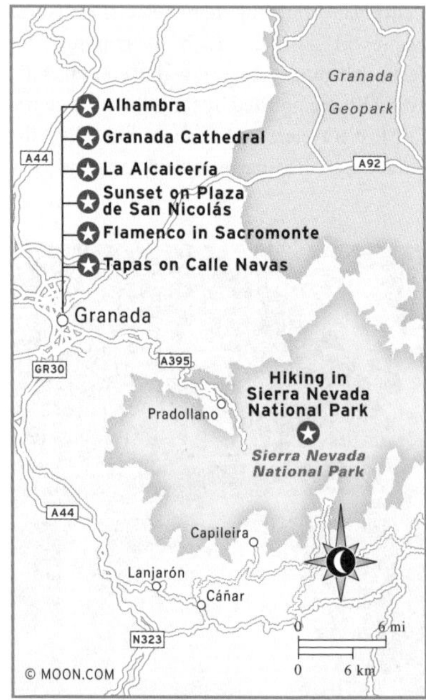

★ **Alhambra:** This UNESCO World Heritage Site is the crown jewel of Granada, if not all of Andalusia, and a testament to the city's rich history and culture. Make sure to book your tickets in advance (page 143).

★ **Granada Cathedral:** A must-visit for architecture and history enthusiasts, this impressive Renaissance-style cathedral is the seat of the Archdiocese of Granada, not to mention the final resting place of the Catholic monarchs, Ferdinand and Isabella (page 152).

★ **La Alcaicería:** This historic market is a great place to shop for souvenirs, especially Moroccan-style ceramics and textiles. Look past the kitsch and practice your bartering skills to land a hand-stitched artisanal treasure (page 152).

★ **Sunset on Plaza de San Nicolás:** The charming Albaicín neighborhood is a maze of narrow streets and alleys lined with whitewashed buildings. Crowning this neighborhood is the Plaza de San Nicolás, which offers breathtaking, lively sunset views over the Alhambra (page 156).

★ **Flamenco in Sacromonte:** This historic neighborhood is known for its unique cave houses, where flamenco shows, though a touch touristy, are irreplicable (page 162).

★ **Tapas on Calle Navas:** Granada is known for its free tapas culture, where a drink always comes with a small plate of food. If you are going out for a night of tapas tasting in Andalusia, Calle Navas is the place to go (page 165).

★ **Hiking in Sierra Nevada National Park:** Keep it active with a beautiful trek through the mountains. The park has paths for hikers of all skill levels, and it's a fantastic way to touch on the natural beauty of the region (page 185).

massive, well-preserved and renovated fortress built beginning in the 11th century and added to over the centuries. Its flowing gardens and ornate architecture are typical of Spain's Islamic era, when various Muslim empires ruled Spain from 711 CE until January 2, 1492, when the emir Muhammad XII (known to the Spanish as Boabdil) ceded Granada to the rulers Ferdinand and Isabella, establishing Catholic Spain as we know it today. Boasting a transportive history you can truly walk through, the Alhambra should top anyone's list of things to experience in Granada.

Granada's hilly, winding neighborhoods reward travelers with scenic views and peeks into local life, not to mention some of the best tapas bars in all of Spain. If you have first visited Seville, Córdoba, Málaga, or perhaps another Spanish city, you might be surprised to find that here you will receive a free tapa with your beverage of choice. Tapas vary widely from bar to bar, and it's somewhat of a Granadian tradition to strike out on the town on a do-it-yourself tapas tour to enjoy the gastronomic variety with friends.

Around Granada you will find a few pueblos (towns) that are worth a visit. These are best done either as day trips from Granada or (my preference) linked with a road trip through Andalusia where you are connecting to or from another destination. Visiting these towns really only makes sense if you are driving, but they do offer glimpses into local life that are missing in the cities. These side trips are also a fun way to break up a drive, with a lunch stop coupled with seeing a slightly off-piste site, such as the fortress at Montefrío or the cathedral at Guadix.

The mountains of the Sierra Nevada are a haven for hikers, bikers, skiers, snowboarders, and those looking for a taste of the outdoors to couple with their Andalusian adventure. Nearly year-round the mountains provide excellent hiking and biking opportunities for all skill levels. The ski resort, the southernmost in all of Europe, has a shorter season than similar resorts in the Alps or Pyrenees, exacerbated by climate change and warmer, drier winters. Though with the magic of snow machines, a winter wonderland is guaranteed for at least a few months out of the year.

HISTORY

Nestled at the foot of the Sierra Nevada, Granada's rich history weaves a vibrant tapestry of cultures, leaving an indelible mark on its architecture, traditions, and atmosphere. From its humble beginnings to its majestic Alhambra, the city's story is one that has been woven through the ages, the warp and weft of it intertwining in surprising, beautiful ways.

Pre-Islamic Era

Granada's strategic location between the Mediterranean and the interior of the Iberian Peninsula contributed to its significance as a trading hub and military outpost, perhaps as far back as 5,500 BCE. There is evidence of inhabitants in the region since the Bronze Age, with archaeological discoveries nearly a yearly occurrence, helping to define the legacy before the coming of the Islamic empires from North Africa. It's understood that Iberians and later the Romans inhabited the area of Granada, though specifics of this era are not well defined.

Islamic Era

The most transformative era in Granada's history, as elsewhere through Andalusia, came during the Islamic rule. Though the fortress structure that is part of the Alhambra was built beginning in the 11th century, it really wasn't until the 13th century, with the rise of the Nasrid dynasty, that Granada began to flower and the iconic Alhambra complex really took form. This inarguable masterpiece of Islamic architecture stands as a testament to their intricate craftsmanship and love for architectural and natural beauty. The

Previous: Nasrid Palaces at the Alhambra; colorful market stalls in La Alcaicería; hiker in Sierra Nevada National Park.

Granada and the Sierra Nevada

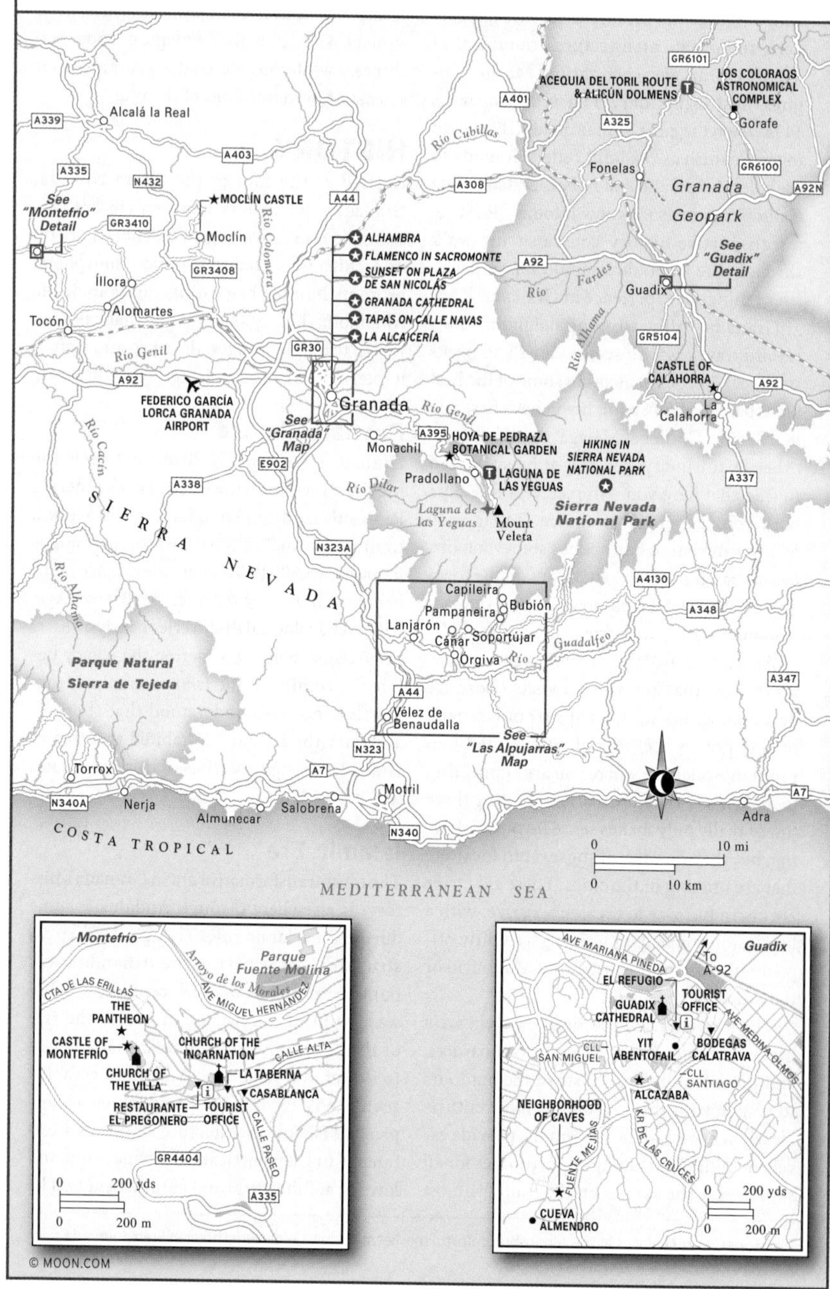

Alhambra's intricate palaces, lush gardens, and delicate stucco work continue to enchant visitors to this day. If Granada is a tapestry, the Alhambra is its centerpiece.

The Reconquista and the Catholic Monarchs

Granada's destiny shifted in 1492, when Catholic monarchs Ferdinand and Isabella completed the Reconquista, reclaiming the city from Islamic rule. If you head up into the Sierra Nevada, you can visit El Puerto del Suspiro del Moro, commonly translated as "The Pass of the Moor's Last Sigh." This is where the emir Muhammad XII (Boabdil) supposedly turned and looked one last time at Granada before continuing on to Morocco after surrendering the city. The Alhambra's transformation into a Christian court symbolized the merging of cultures, resulting in the unique architectural blend that delicately threads together the story of today's Granada. The subsequent centuries brought a flourishing of culture and art. The 16th-century Granada Cathedral stands as a magnificent example of Spanish Renaissance architecture, while the Royal Chapel houses the final resting place of Ferdinand and Isabella.

Modern Identity

Granada's history also shuttles to and fro through its modern streets. The Albaicín, a hilly labyrinthine Moorish quarter, preserves its medieval layout and whitewashed houses, offering a glimpse into the city's past, while the Sacromonte district, known for its cave dwellings, showcases the Romani heritage that has shaped Granada's identity. Walking these streets, you can perhaps glean a deeper insight into the poetry of Federico García Lorca (1898-1936), who was executed by fascists during the Spanish Civil War, or the life of Mariana Pineda (1804-1831), Granada's first feminist, who was put to death for having a flag outside of her house that said "law, liberty, and equality."

Granada Today

As you stroll through the bustling markets, dine on tapas, and gaze upon the Sierra Nevada in the distance, you'll witness the tension of centuries of history that make Granada the captivating city it is today. It doesn't matter whether you're grabbing a bite, exploring the elaborate Islamic architecture of the Alhambra, gazing up at the audaciously gilded Basilica of Saint John, getting lost in the Albaicín's narrow streets, or enjoying a

the Court of the Lions at the Alhambra

local flamenco performance—Granada's history is palpable everywhere, just waiting for your cartouche to add to its intricate weave.

PLANNING YOUR TIME

At the bare minimum, spend two full days in Granada. You will need about one full day to tour the Alhambra and another day to visit the Albaicín and Sacromonte neighborhoods. Three days opens more possibilities, including the Sierra Nevada. If you can add another day or two, you will feel the overall travel experience is less of a whirlwind and you'll have more time for immersive experiences, longer treks, more time on the slopes, or just more tapas.

Unless there is a festival, the nightlife in Granada tends to be fairly quiet. Most bars and restaurants will close up around midnight. During festivals and celebrations everything tends to be open much later, and a rambunctious, convivial sort scene opens up.

Because of the difficulty of connecting different parts of the Sierra Nevada mountain range, it's best to divide this area into two distinct regions: Sierra Nevada National Park on the north face of the mountain range and Las Alpujarras on the south face. From Granada, the winding A-395 will take you into the snow-covered peaks of the Sierra Nevada National Park and its ski resort in Pradollano, where winter sports enthusiasts can indulge in thrilling alpine adventures. To reach Las Alpujarras, you'll take the A-44 freeway south through a valley cutting through the western edge of the national park before exiting on A-348 for Lanjarón to begin your exploration of the villages here.

Itinerary Ideas

DAY 1: ROMANTIC ALHAMBRA

1 Spend your first morning in Granada touring the ancient **Alhambra** (reservations required). With a guide, you can spend about three hours touring the Nasrid Palaces, Palace of the Lions, Generalife gardens, and more. If you are touring on your own, budget a little more time, as you'll likely need to take some time more than once to find your bearings.

2 Break for lunch at the **Restaurant du Parador de Granada,** where you can enjoy views over the Alhambra. Try their ajo blanco, a chilled soup of almonds, garlic, and bread garnished with dried figs and honey.

3 Walk down Cuesta de Gomérez through the **Alhambra Forest** on your way to the Albaicín Bajo neighborhood. Note the sculptures, including a tribute to Washington Irving, and locals walking their dogs.

4 At the bottom of the hill, take a right and continue your stroll on **Carrera del Darro** alongside the trickling Darro River. This is maybe Granada's most romantic street, blending the views up the hill of the Alhambra with the old city. If you need an afternoon pick-me-up, stop for coffee at Oteiza and skip the touristy riverside cafés with bad brew.

5 Cap off your day with a lovely tapas tour. You can never go wrong dining your way down **Calle Navas** in the San Matías neighborhood.

DAY 2: ALBAICÍN ALTO AND SACROMONTE

1 Get out of the central tourist zone and enjoy a light breakfast at **Atypica Coffee.**

2 Visit the nearby **Basilica of Saint John,** perhaps one of the most audacious basilicas in all of Spain.

3 Continue your exploration of Catholic Spain and pay your respects to Ferdinand and Isabella at the **Granada Cathedral.** While you're at it, enjoy the Renaissance architecture and ornate design.

4 Leave the cathedral and duck into the old Moroccan-style neighborhood of **La Alcaicería,** a series of bazaars of trinkets and odds and ends. If you squint, you can just imagine yourself in Marrakesh.

5 Continue the Moroccan magic and explore the charming Tea House Street on your way toward the Albaicín Alto neighborhood. Pull up a barstool and slow it down to a snail's pace in local favorite **Bar Aliatar Los Caracoles.**

6 Take in a lively sunset at **Plaza de San Nicolás,** with stunning views over the Alhambra.

7 End your last night in Granada with dinner in the **Sacromonte** neighborhood.

DAY 3: A DAY IN THE SIERRA NEVADA

Take a drive into the **Sierra Nevada** this morning, enjoying the quick change into forested, mountainous land with winding country roads.

1 Stop in Lanjarón and relax into a thermal spring spa experience at **Relais Termal.**

2 Check into your accommodations in Capileira and stop for a bite at **El Corral del Castaña.**

3 Get in touch with the natural mountainous beauty of **Sierra Nevada National Park** on an active afternoon hike.

4 Tuck into a cozy dinner at **Restaurante Gloria** in the Finca los Llanos at the top of Capileira.

Granada

Granada is a mountainous sort of city where each neighborhood really does carry the weight and style of its past. Unlike Seville, where much of the historic city center blends together over a largely flat land, here in Granada, neighborhoods are distinct, each capturing a sense and an era that is palpable. You'll see this in the architecture and from navigating at street level, making it easy to imagine yourself in the different epochs that define Granada's history.

ORIENTATION

For the purposes of this guidebook, Granada has been divided into five sections: the Alhambra complex, the San Matías neighborhood, the Albaicín Bajo neighborhood, the Albaicín Alto neighborhood, and the Sacromonte neighborhood. It is very helpful in Granada to differentiate between what is uphill and what is downhill. San Matías and the Albaicín Bajo neighborhoods are largely flat and easy to navigate. The Alhambra complex, Albaicín Alto, and Sacromonte

Itinerary Ideas

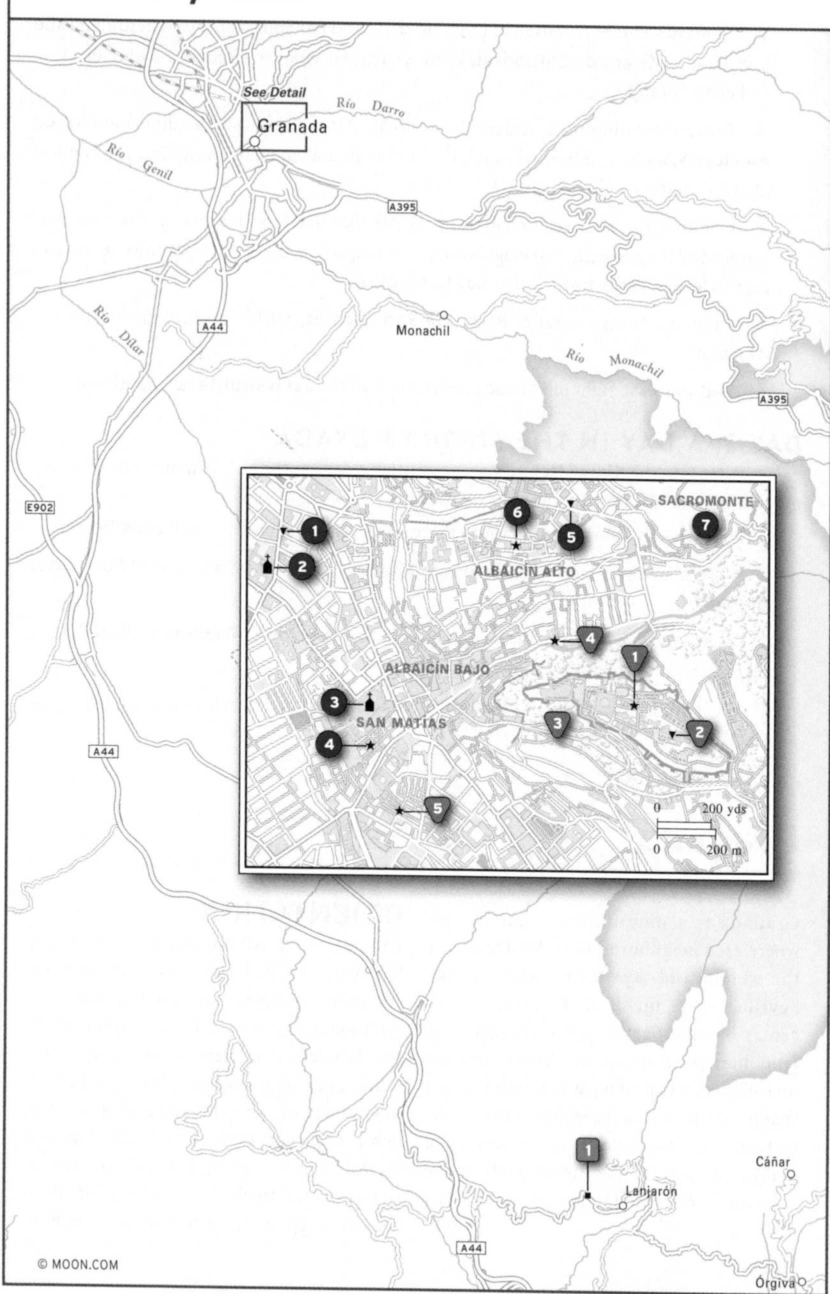

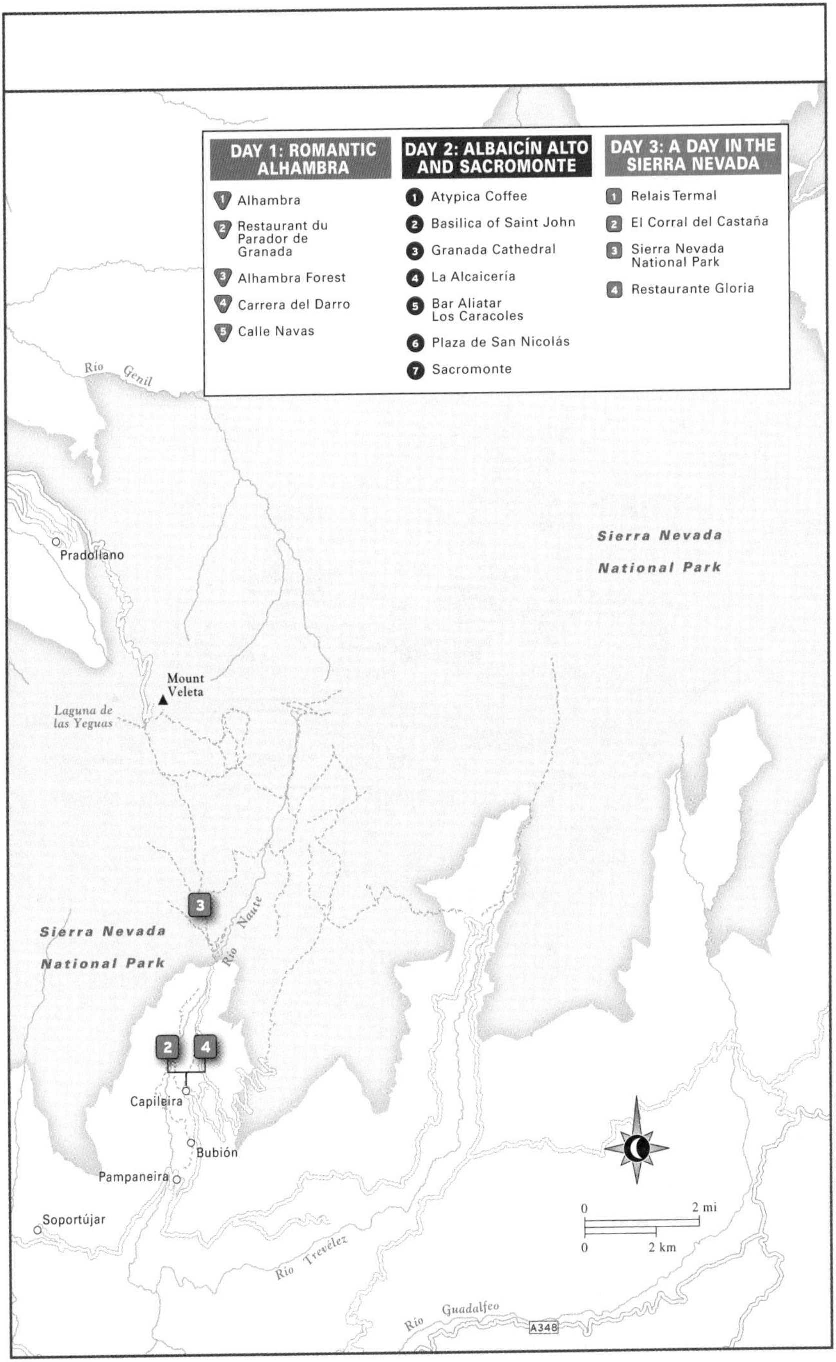

DAY 1: ROMANTIC ALHAMBRA

1. Alhambra
2. Restaurant du Parador de Granada
3. Alhambra Forest
4. Carrera del Darro
5. Calle Navas

DAY 2: ALBAICÍN ALTO AND SACROMONTE

1. Atypica Coffee
2. Basilica of Saint John
3. Granada Cathedral
4. La Alcaicería
5. Bar Aliatar Los Caracoles
6. Plaza de San Nicolás
7. Sacromonte

DAY 3: A DAY IN THE SIERRA NEVADA

1. Relais Termal
2. El Corral del Castaña
3. Sierra Nevada National Park
4. Restaurante Gloria

Río Genil
Sierra Nevada National Park
Pradollano
Mount Veleta
Laguna de las Yeguas
Río Naute
Sierra Nevada National Park
Capileira
Bubión
Pampaneira
Soportújar
Río Trevélez
Río Guadalfeo
A348
0 2 mi
0 2 km

Granada

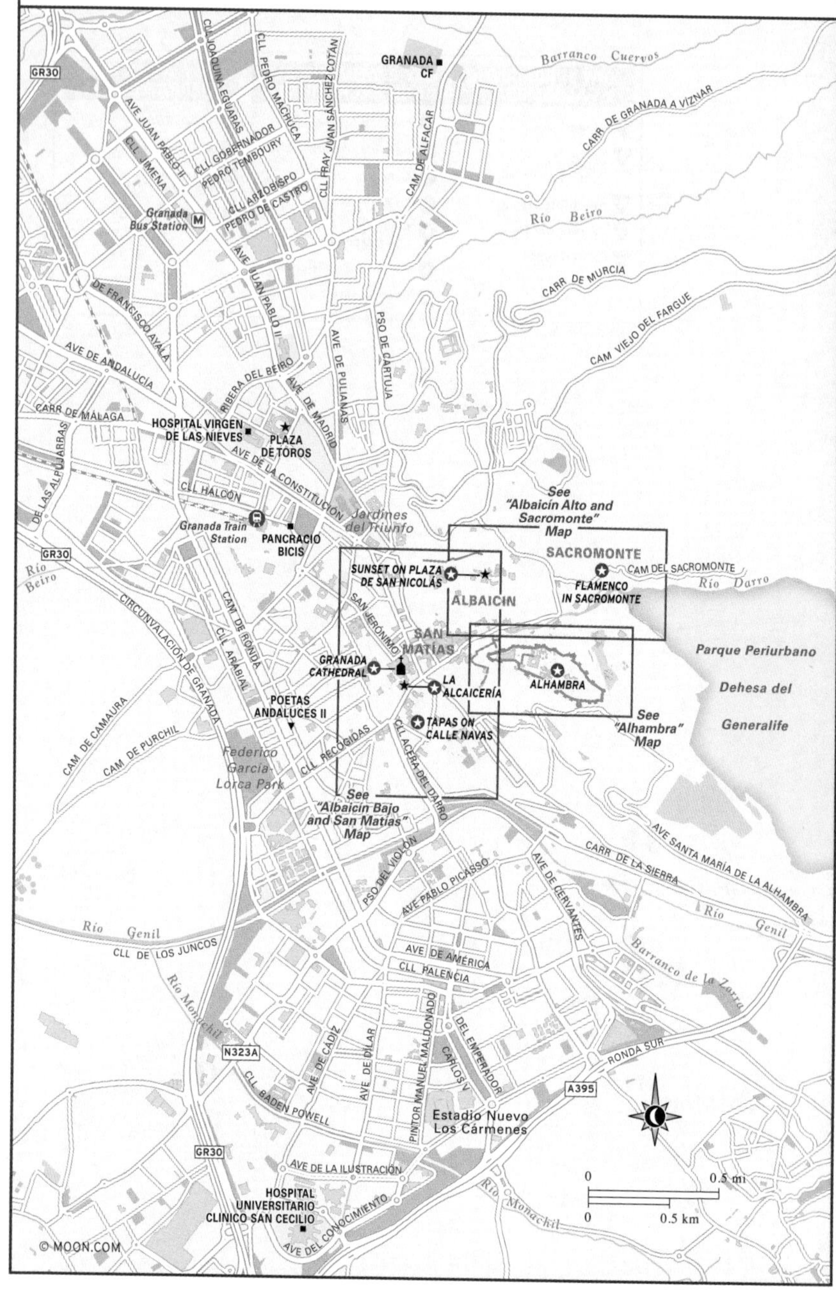
GRANADA CF
Barranco Cuervos
CARR DE GRANADA A VÍZNAR
Río Beiro
CARR DE MURCIA
CAM VIEJO DEL FARGUE
GR30
CLL JOAQUINA EGUARAS
CLL PEDRO MACHUCA
CLL FRAY JUAN SÁNCHEZ COTÁN
AVE JUAN PABLO II
CLL JIMENA
CLL GOBERNADOR PEDRO TEMBOURY
CLL ARZOBISPO PEDRO DE CASTRO
CAM DE ALFACAR
Granada Bus Station
DE FRANCISCO AYALA
AVE DE ANDALUCÍA
RIBERA DEL BEIRO
AVE DE MADRID
AVE DE PULIANAS
PSO DE CARTUJA
CARR DE MÁLAGA
HOSPITAL VIRGEN DE LAS NIEVES
PLAZA DE TOROS
AVE DE LA CONSTITUCIÓN
DE LAS ALPUJARRAS
CLL HALCÓN
Granada Train Station
PANCRACIO BICIS
Jardines del Triunfo
See "Albaicín Alto and Sacromonte" Map
SACROMONTE
CAM DEL SACROMONTE
Río Darro
SUNSET ON PLAZA DE SAN NICOLÁS
ALBAICÍN
FLAMENCO IN SACROMONTE
Río Beiro
CIRCUNVALACIÓN DE GRANADA
CAM DE RONDA
CLL ARABIAL
SAN JERÓNIMO
SAN MATÍAS
GRANADA CATHEDRAL
LA ALCAICERÍA
ALHAMBRA
Parque Periurbano Dehesa del Generalife
POETAS ANDALUCES II
TAPAS ON CALLE NAVAS
See "Alhambra" Map
CAM DE CAMAURA
CAM DE PURCHIL
Federico García Lorca Park
CLL RECOGIDAS
CLL ACERA DEL DARRO
See "Albaicín Bajo and San Matías" Map
AVE SANTA MARÍA DE LA ALHAMBRA
CARR DE LA SIERRA
PSO DEL VIOLÓN
AVE PABLO PICASSO
AVE DE CERVANTES
Río Genil
CLL DE LOS JUNCOS
AVE DE AMÉRICA
CLL PALENCIA
Barranco de la Zorra
Río Monachil
N323A
AVE DE CÁDIZ
AVE DE DÍLAR
PINTOR MANUEL MALDONADO
CARLOS V
DEL EMPERADOR
RONDA SUR
A395
CLL BADEN POWELL
Estadio Nuevo Los Cármenes
AVE DE LA ILUSTRACIÓN
HOSPITAL UNIVERSITARIO CLÍNICO SAN CECILIO
AVE DEL CONOCIMIENTO
0
0.5 mi
0
0.5 km
© MOON.COM

neighborhoods are all found up rather steep hills. Though walkable, they each require a bit of fitness to mount. For many travelers, using taxis is an inexpensive option to summit each of Granada's beautiful hills.

Alhambra

The Alhambra complex includes not only the palaces and gardens, but also a few shops, restaurants, and hotels that are privileged enough to call this neighborhood home. When in Granada, it is nearly impossible to miss, as it dominates the city's southern skyline with a picture-perfect backdrop of the Sierra Nevada looming behind.

San Matías

San Matías is a historic neighborhood beneath the Alhambra complex. The neighborhood abuts the southern edge of the Albaicín Bajo and similarly offers many options for sleeping and eating. You'll find the Granada Cathedral here, as well as the local favorite for nibbling tapas, the Calle Navas.

Albaicín Bajo

The Albaicín Bajo neighborhood connects easily with all the other major neighborhoods, not to mention a wealth of tapas bars, cafés, and restaurants. For many travelers, this will be the most central place to stay for your time in Granada. Note: Most other resources will not differentiate between the Alto and Bajo neighborhoods of the Albaicín.

Albaicín Alto

The Albaicín Alto neighborhood sits tall to the northwest of the Alhambra. The winding streets are a carryover from its Islamic past. Plaza de San Nicolás is the central gathering point, offering unobstructed, classic views over the entire Alhambra complex, and where watching the sun set is something of a rite of passage.

Sacromonte

Sacromonte is perhaps Granada's oldest neighborhood. A series of whitewashed cave dwellings uphill from the Albaicín Bajo, this is the neighborhood most associated with Gitano community (also called Romani). These days the caves are home to flamenco shows accompanied by traditional Andalusian cuisine.

TOP EXPERIENCE

★ ALHAMBRA

"I do not know what to call this land upon which I stand. If what is beneath my feet is paradise, then what is the Alhambra? Heaven?" exclaimed the Spanish Baroque novelist and playwright Lopa de Vega. And when you first ascend to this ancient palace, a masterful work of Islamic design, you may feel what moved Lopa de Vega. There can be little doubt that the Alhambra is the jewel of Andalusia.

Plan on spending at least half a day touring the exquisite remains of this heavenly palace and gardens. If you have the luxury of time, spend an entire day here. The Alhambra is a vast complex, and to make the most of your journey, be very organized with your visit.

Visiting the Alhambra

As the most visited site in all of Spain, tickets to the Alhambra are often sold out weeks, sometimes months, in advance. You will need to organize your stay in Granada (and perhaps all of Andalusia) around the tickets you find available. This is when advance planning really helps, as does a really great guide!

Tickets for the Alhambra should be purchased directly from the website (https://tickets.alhambra-patronato.es) or with a trusted tour company or guide. You will absolutely need to purchase tickets in advance—I can't stress this enough. You will most likely not be able to walk up to the Alhambra and purchase tickets directly from the ticket office for that day. It is best to purchase tickets weeks, if not a couple of months, in advance.

There are multiple ticket options. To visit the entire complex, purchase the Alhambra General ticket (€9). The general ticket provides you access to the entire Alhambra complex from 8am to closing for the day of your ticket, no matter what time you arrive. If for some reason you weren't interested in visiting the palaces, you could purchase the Gardens, Generalife, and Alcazaba ticket (€11) just for the grounds and the gardens. You'll also see ticket options for visiting at night.

When you are purchasing tickets that include the Nasrid Palaces, after you select the date of your visit, you will see a reservation time slot for the Nasrid Palaces. On the day of your visit, you will only have access to the Nasrid Palaces of the Alhambra at this time. Choose wisely! Typically, the early mornings and early afternoons have smaller crowds.

When making reservations, you must get tickets for everyone in your group ages 3 and up, even though minors under 12 are free. Children 2 and under will be given a ticket upon entry.

When you do visit the Alhambra, remember to bring your passport! Your identifying document is needed for entry to the Alhambra.

Group Tours

You can book tours directly with Alhambra Tours (www.alhambra.org; €50), though numerous companies and organizations offer tours and similar price points. Groups are limited to 30 people and will have headsets available to hear the knowledgeable guides. The tours run 2.5 hours and include tickets. If there are not enough of one language group, tours are often carried out in two languages, like Spanish and English. Group tours usually have two times, once in the morning and once in the afternoon.

Private Tours

Private guided tours generally run €175-240 with the additional cost of tickets, which vary seasonally. It is a good idea to contact your guide directly and have them arrange your guided tour with tickets, as purchasing tickets can be complicated. Tours are generally 3-4 hours and will take you through all the major points of the Alhambra, as well as ensure that you don't miss your scheduled time to see the Nasrid Palaces and the Palace of the Lions.

Patricia Bernard Rodrigo (tel. 630/769-080; patriciabernad_7@hotmail.com; €175) is a passionate guide who knows the Alhambra like she knows her own kitchen. She'll help you navigate the Alhambra at a good pace to ensure you've seen everything in about three well-paced hours.

Juan Vera (tel. 667/480-350; €175) is a Granadino with a fun knack for all things Alhambra, historic and folkloric. If you would like your tour of this monument to have a touch of monumental humor, give Juan a call. WhatsApp is preferable to contact him.

Night Tours

A nighttime visit to the Alhambra is a quietly magical experience. Hours vary seasonally (8pm-9:30pm Fri.-Sat. mid-Oct.-Mar., 10pm-11:30pm Tues.-Sat. Apr.-mid-Oct.; from €12), making the warmer months easier to schedule. You choose either a night visit to the Nasrid Palaces or the illuminated visit of the Generalife. These visits can be done on your own, as part of a small group, or privatized. That said, for a first-time visitor, it's better to go during the day first to see everything in daylight before the limited illumination exploration available on a night visit. However, if you forgot to purchase your Alhambra tickets ahead of time, there are often nighttime visits still available, even at the last minute.

Sights

Nasrid Palaces (Palacios Nazaríes)

Because the Nasrid Palaces are the one part of your visit you must be on time for, it makes sense to begin your visit here. The Nasrid Palaces encompass three primary buildings: the Mexuar, the Comares Palace, and the Palace of the Lions (also called Court of the

1: the Alhambra **2:** Plaza de los Aljibes reflection pool **3:** the Court of the Lions **4:** exterior view of the Nasrid Palaces

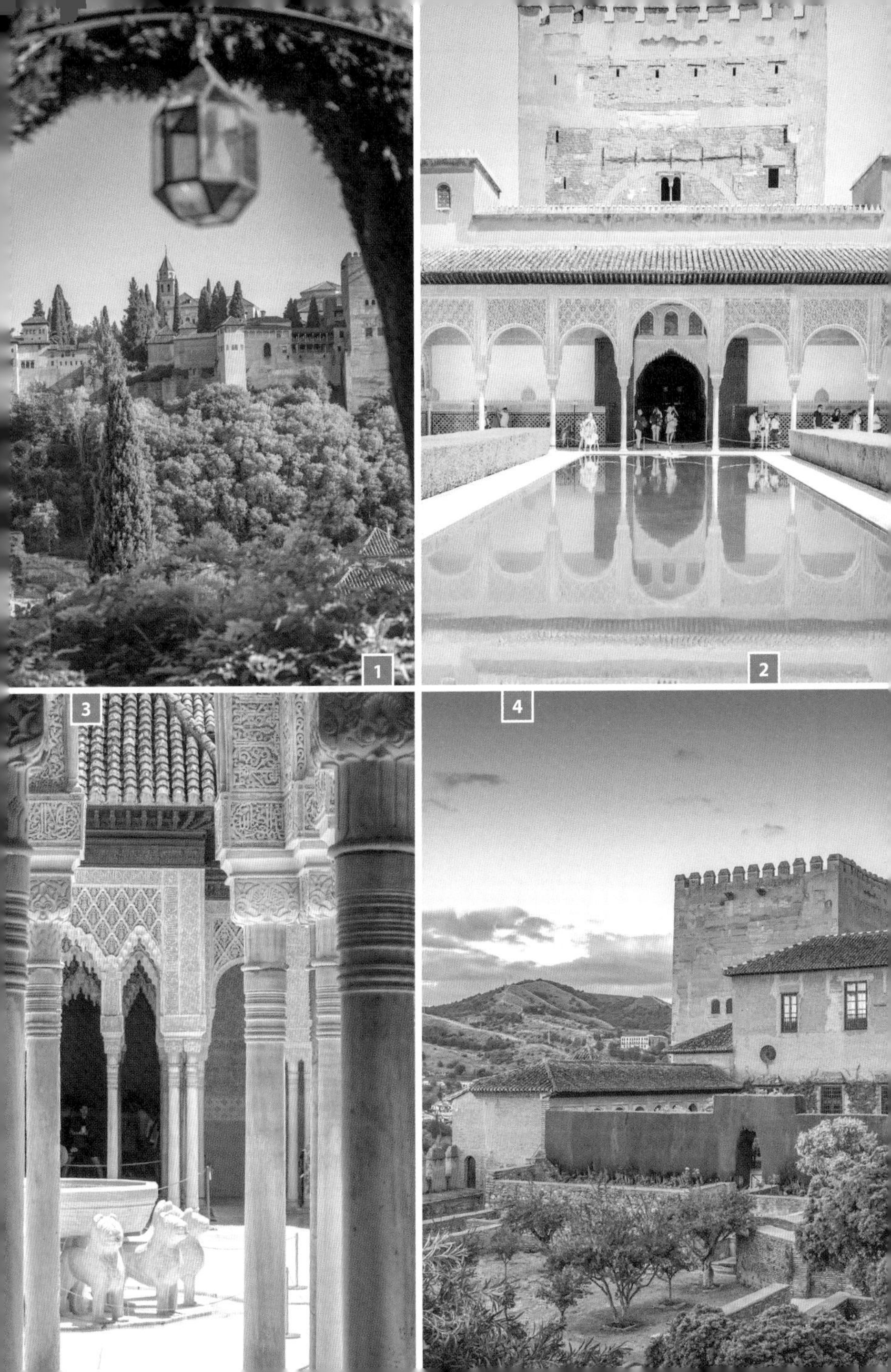

1
2
3
4

Alhambra

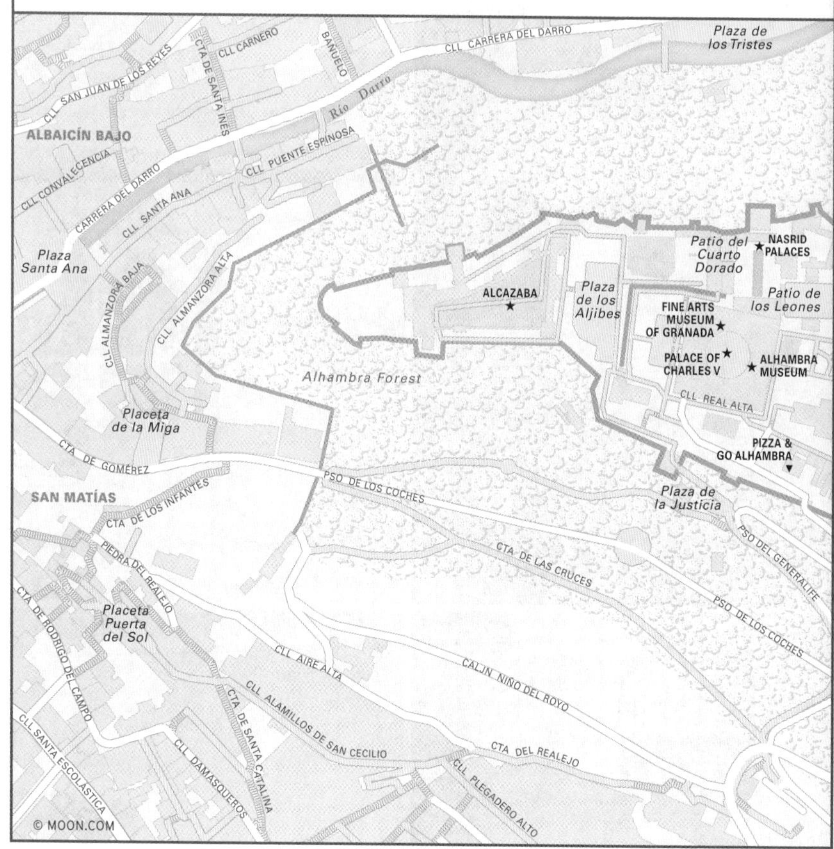

Lions), as well as the Hall of Abencerrajes. Each of these buildings is a masterful work of Islamic art and architecture. Hand-chiseled-and-set colorful mosaic work runs along the bottom half of the walls, while above, delicate stucco work—replete with knotted Kufic and cursive Arabic inscriptions intricately woven into the design—continues to the ceiling, where it meets the geometrically complex, intricately carved, kaleidoscopic cedarwood ceilings. The **Mexuar** is the oldest of these buildings, a great hall once used as a courtroom for the king's ministers. The **Comares Palace,** once the official palace of the sultan, also houses a reflective pool within the Courtyard of the Myrtles, the Hall of Ambassadors, the Hall of the Boat, and the Comares Tower.

The **Palace of the Lions,** however, is one of the most cherished works of Islamic art and architecture in the world. Four halls are arranged around the courtyard of the famed fountain guarded by its statues of lions. To the west is the Hall of Muqarnas, named for its ornamented vaulting, while the Hall of Kings opens to a series of rooms, each with its own ornate vaulted muqarnas ceilings. To the south is the Hall of the Two Sisters, originally known as the Hall of the Great Dome for its elaborate muqarnas dome, which features

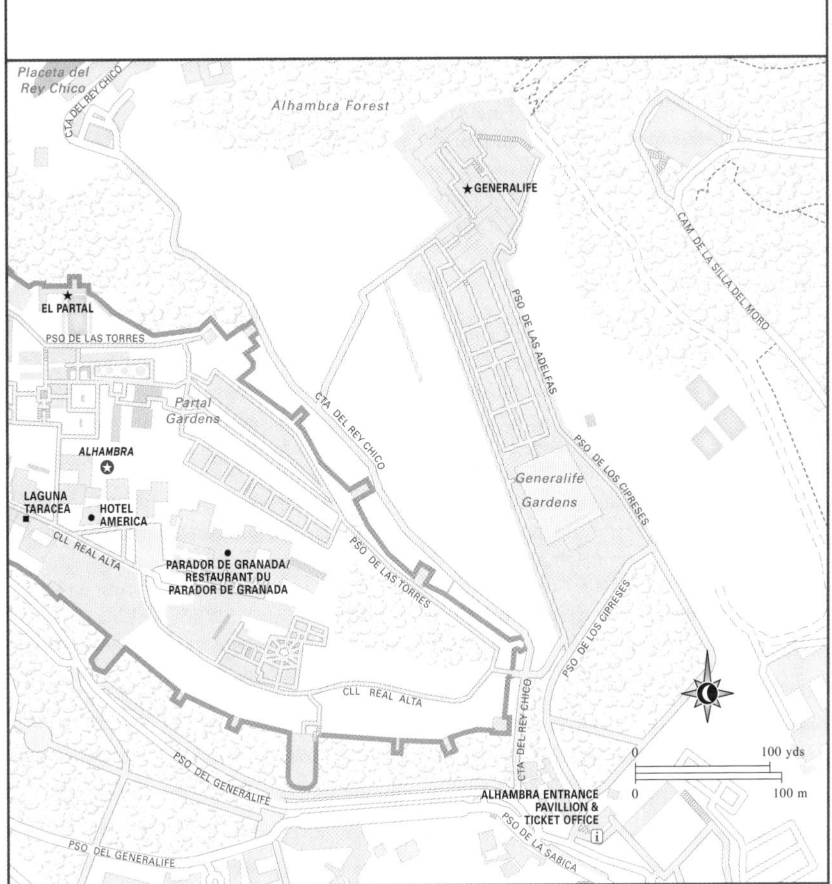

over 5,000 prismatic pieces, each of which serves to lighten the ceiling, giving a feathery weight to this great mass. Past the Great Dome you'll find the Eye of the House of Aisha, or Lindaraja, a small room with some of the most intricate stucco work, mosaics, and carved wood to be found in the entirety of the Islamic world. Named for the 12 mythical white lions that hold the central fountain, the Palace of the Lions is also home to some impressive 13th-century water technology. The lions spurt water from their mouths, feeding four small channels of water. Each channel represents a river of heaven, and the water runs through the palace, cooling each of its rooms.

Palace of Charles V

A ruler has never lived in this Renaissance-style palace. Commissioned by Charles V, the grandson of Isabella and Ferdinand, its construction began in 1527. However, the palace was never completed and in fact was without a roof for 450 years. It wasn't until 1967 that the palace was finally covered. The exterior of the palace gives little clue to the large, round courtyard found within, a ringing example of Renaissance architecture, echoing the circular courtyards of Italy in that era. More interesting than the building itself is what the building has become. On the lower level, you will find the **Alhambra Museum,** which features some smaller fragments of some of the ornate carvings and marble work. The Vase of the Gazelles, one of the few intact vases from the Alhambra during the Islamic rule, is a true standout. On the upper floor, the **Fine Arts Museum of Granada** houses various paintings and sculptures from Spanish artists from the 16th to 20th centuries, while the courtyard itself has a rotating calendar of shows and performances.

Alcazaba

Located on the southwesternmost tip of the Alhambra, the Alcazaba is the military fortress and the oldest part of the Alhambra. Here you can walk through what remains of the soldiers' barracks, public bath, and communal kitchen. Belowground, there are the rims of silos and dungeons, though the most interesting parts of the Alcazaba are the two towers: Tower of Homage (Torre del Homenaje) and Tower of the Candle (Torre de la Vega). From the Tower of the Candle, commanding views over Granada, the Alhambra, the Sierra Nevada, and the rolling Spanish countryside are worth the short climb. It is a tradition for single girls of Granada to climb the tower on January 2 to ring the bell, commemorating the victory of the Catholic monarchs over Granada and ensuring their marriage by the end of that same year.

El Partal

This section of the Alhambra is perhaps the quietest and least visited. The **Partal Palace,** though likely the oldest palace in the complex, is also one of the most damaged, with the decorative ceiling having been dismantled and taken to Germany over a century ago. Around the palace you can find gardens and ponds, as well as four houses without courtyards called the Partal Dwellings. Each of these houses is known for plasterwork as well as mural paintings, which many scholars believe are the only known examples of Nasrid painting in the entirety of the Alhambra, and some of the very few found worldwide.

Generalife

When the weather was too warm or the sultan wanted a bit of quiet, he retreated to the Generalife, the summer palace. Most likely constructed toward the end of the 13th century, the palace was intentionally set to disappear against the backdrop of the extraordinary garden, one of the oldest examples of its kind. Over the years, the palace itself has been whitewashed and plastered over, so the many delicate, lace-like stucco works that once graced its walls are no longer to be found. Still, there are numerous arcades and, if you squint just a bit, you can still see some of the magic of this old palace. The Royal Chamber is best preserved and includes an impressive muqarnas vaulted ceiling, as well as views out to the Albaicín.

However, it is the **gardens** that take precedence. Though influenced over the years by various schools of gardening, the original layout is Moorish in origin, with a stress on the importance of water. While walking up the stairs to the Generalife, you will see rivulets of water streaming down through small channels carved into the banister. This same water seemingly defies gravity as it moves back up and around the gardens. In fact, this water is brought from the river that lies nearly a kilometer downhill. The secret is in the Nasrid technology, the first of its kind, which used a combination of dams and waterwheels to lift the water uphill. Ending your visit of the Alhambra here around sunset provides some contemplative quiet time in the gardens with the water trickling down, not to mention stunning lighting for pictures over the Alhambra and Granada.

Shopping

Laguna Taracea

Calle Real de La Alhambra, 30; tel. 958/229-019; www.lagunataracea.com; 9:30am-6pm Mon.-Fri., 9:30am-2pm Sat.-Sun. winter, 9:30am-7pm Mon.-Fri., 9:30am-2pm Sat.-Sun. summer

1: Alcazaba **2:** Alhambra Museum **3:** Generalife patio garden **4:** traditional artisan working at Laguna Taracea

1
2
3
4

Washington Irving in Granada

Washington Irving commemorative plaque at the Alhambra

Washington Irving is largely considered the first American to have been able to pay for his livelihood solely through his writing. If you haven't come across Washington Irving, you might know two of his most famous literary characters: the Headless Horseman and Rip Van Winkle. A fun factoid involves one of his lesser-remembered creations, his writer pseudonym, Diedrich Knickerbocker. He wrote under this nom de plume, which became a nickname for New Yorkers and, eventually, the namesake of the NBA team, the New York Knicks.

Deft with a pen and a gifted wordsmith, Irving is credited with coining the phrase "the almighty dollar." Unfortunately, he also was one of the first thinkers to popularize the flat earth myth.

In his day, Irving was a bit of a celebrity. Largely owing to this, he was allowed by the Spanish authorities to live in the Alhambra during the summer of 1829. Here, Irving compiled a series of historical notes as well as mythological stories of this abandoned palace, left to the elements, inhabited only by vagabonds and wayward travelers like himself. His compiled notes and stories, both real and less real, comprise his ***Tales of the Alhambra,*** a fundamental publication that put the Alhambra at the forefront of the public's imagination. Copies of *Tales of the Alhambra* are nearly always readily available at the Alhambra in English and translated into other languages. Irving's work is credited with popularizing the Alhambra among writers, thinkers, and romantics of the age and, eventually, spurring international interest in restoring the palace to something resembling its former glory.

Today, plaques around the Alhambra commemorate where Irving lived while in residence at this once-forsaken palace.

Located near the Alhambra, Laguna Taracea is a local institution. Since 1877, it has been re-creating the furniture that decorated the Alhambra 700 years ago. These tables, chairs, desks, and other pieces are still done using old inlay or marquetry (taracea) techniques and processes. This is a once-in-a-lifetime purchase for most, as each of the pieces is completely handmade and designed with a price to match. Even if you don't have the deep pockets for a purchase, this is well worth the stop to admire how the taracea pieces were made and witness for yourself this deeply ornate, artistic process. If you make a purchase, you can ship it directly back home.

Food and Accommodations

Pizza and Go Alhambra

Calle Real de la Alhambra, 2; tel. 958/221-971; 10am-6:30pm daily; €8

There are very few places to eat in the Alhambra, and if you are searching for a quick bite on the go, this is your only option. You can get pizzas by the slice with a cold drink and ice cream. Nothing extraordinary, but it's an okay option if you don't want to sit down at the Parador.

Restaurant du Parador de Granada

Calle Real de la Alhambra; tel. 958/221-440; 1pm-3pm and 8:30pm-11pm daily; €50

Few people can afford to stay at the Parador Hotel, a historic former convent that serves as a boutique four-star property now. However, most can stretch their budget enough to eat here. Lunch service is classic white linens, while things are a bit more casual on the terrace, which is probably where you want to be anyway, since it has unbeatable views over the Alhambra. I'm partial to a light lunch featuring the ajo blanco, a chilled almond and garlic soup, though the haute Spanish cuisine menu has numerous à la carte options.

★ Hotel America

Calle Real de la Alhambra; tel. 958/227-471; www.hotelamericagranada.com; €140

A lovingly restored rustic home with lots of exposed-wood charm in the heart of the Alhambra, Hotel America has an unassuming entrance, with the front door buried behind a bit of bougainvillea. Though technically it's a one-star property, the service is more like a nice three- or four-star accommodation with the feeling of a family-run establishment. Oozing with historical character, it's a quiet sanctuary to get away from the tourist crowds just feet away from the front door of the hotel.

The onsite restaurant (€20; reservations recommended) serves a mix of regional cuisine and international favorites, like cheeseburgers, with friendly service in the open-air patio.

Parador de Granada

Calle Real de la Alhambra; tel. 958/221-440; https://paradores.es/es/parador-de-granada; €650

If you are not familiar with the Parador chain of hotels, they are dotted throughout Spain and are all well-appointed, high-end, state-run hotels in historic locations. The Parador of Granada, located right in the middle of the Alhambra complex, in a former monastery, is splurge-worthy, though you are definitely paying for location, location, location. If you can, avoid the rooms on the first floor as they can be a bit noisy with restaurant and kitchen noise. Rooms all have incredible views out over the Alhambra complex, with some looking at Granada below and others to the valley and mountains beyond.

Information and Services

Alhambra Entrance Pavilion and Ticket Office

Calle Real de la Alhambra; tel. 958/027-971; www.alhambra-patronato.es; 8am-sunset daily; €15

The entrance near the main parking lot is unmissable. You'll usually find people waiting in line, though the line does move quickly thanks to the number of windows. Attendants all speak English. You will need to present your passport to obtain your ticket. If you purchased tickets online, you should have a copy (digital or print) at the ready. Informative maps and audio guides are available and free with your ticket.

Getting There and Around

From historic downtown Granada it is a notable uphill climb to the Alhambra. Luckily there are a few options for getting up and down the hill, though once you are in the Alhambra, you will have to mostly navigate on foot, as the vast majority of the UNESCO World Heritage Site is pedestrian only.

Walking

If you're already in the city center, walking to the Alhambra is a viable option. The journey offers picturesque views and allows you to appreciate the surroundings leading up to this iconic monument.

The best walking route takes you through the small Alhambra Forest: Starting in Plaza Nueva in the San Matías neighborhood, turn right at the edge of the Albaicín Bajo and head uphill along the Cuesta de Gomérez. This route passes beneath the Puerta de las Granadas archway marking the edges of the forest walk, which brings you directly up to the central entrance to the Alhambra.

Another great route is following the Cuesta del Rey Chico to/from the Plaza de los Triestes. This walk follows the monumental Alhambra fortress walls, though it is much more exposed to the sun, making it for a hard climb on a hot day. Either route is about 1.5 km (0.9 mi), and takes 15-20 minutes.

Accessibility

The Alhambra has made efforts to improve accessibility, but it's essential to note that the historic nature of the site poses some challenges. The Generalife gardens and the Nasrid Palaces, in particular, have uneven terrain and steps, making accessibility limited for wheelchair users. However, the Alcazaba fortress and the Palace of Charles V are more accessible, with ramps and paved paths. To enhance the experience for visitors with mobility challenges, the Alhambra provides wheelchairs for loan at the entrance. It's recommended to inquire about these services upon arrival to ensure a more comfortable visit. To maximize accessibility during your visit, consider checking with the official Alhambra website or contacting them directly for the latest information on services and facilities available for visitors with specific mobility needs.

While certain areas present challenges, the Alhambra strives to accommodate all visitors, allowing them to enjoy this historical masterpiece to the best extent possible.

Bus

The convenient C32 Alhambra-Albaicín bus (30 min; €1.40) runs frequently and connects to and from downtown at Plaza Nueva with the top of the hill and entrance to the Alhambra.

Car

Ample parking facilities are available, but it's advisable to arrive early, especially during peak tourist seasons. The main parking for the Alhambra is a short 10-minute drive from downtown Granada.

Taxis are also an option and cost around €5.

OTHER SIGHTS

San Matías

Thought of as Central Granada (Centro Ciudad), San Matías is where you'll find the Granada Cathedral and many other buildings built in the 16th century onward. Unlike the other neighborhoods of Granada, which, to be frank, can start to feel quite touristy, in San Matías there is a healthy mix of tourism and local life. Nibble your way down Calle Navas enjoying some of Andalusia's finest tapas, and you'll see what I mean. Granadinos love old Granada just as much as the average traveler, particularly when it comes to food and drink.

★ Granada Cathedral (Catedral de Granada)

Gran Vía de Colón, 5; tel. 958/222-959; https://catedraldegranada.com; 10am-6:15pm Mon.-Sat., 3pm-6:15pm Sun.; €5

The lavish Renaissance cathedral of Santa María de la Encarnación in Granada is one of the monumental attractions of Granada, and conveniently unmissable right in the center of town. Like many cathedrals dotted around Andalusia, this cathedral was built atop the ruins of a mosque. Work on the cathedral began in 1518, but it would be over 150 years before the cathedral was finished. Most impressive is the stained-glass domed chapel—just don't hurt your neck looking up. In the **Royal Chapel** (Capilla Real de Granada; €6) around the corner, you will find the final resting places of Ferdinand and Isabella, who saw their conquest of Granada as the crowning achievement of their reign. The early Gothic construction sticks out against the Renaissance-style cathedral, though it was the preferred architectural style of Isabella. The queen gets what she wants, even in death. Interestingly, the cathedral was originally much more like the one in Córdoba, with a Christian church amid the columns of the mosque. This was rightly deemed aesthetically egregious, and the current cathedral was built in neo-Renaissance style after the completion of the early Gothic funerary chapel. Entry lines to the Royal Chapel can occasionally be long.

★ La Alcaicería

Reyes Católicos, 12; 24/7; free

At first glance, the small, narrow streets of the La Alcaicería district are very kitschy, full of cheap made-in-China flamenco dresses and various Alhambra refrigerator magnets, but spend a little time exploring this quarter and

Albaicín Bajo and San Matías

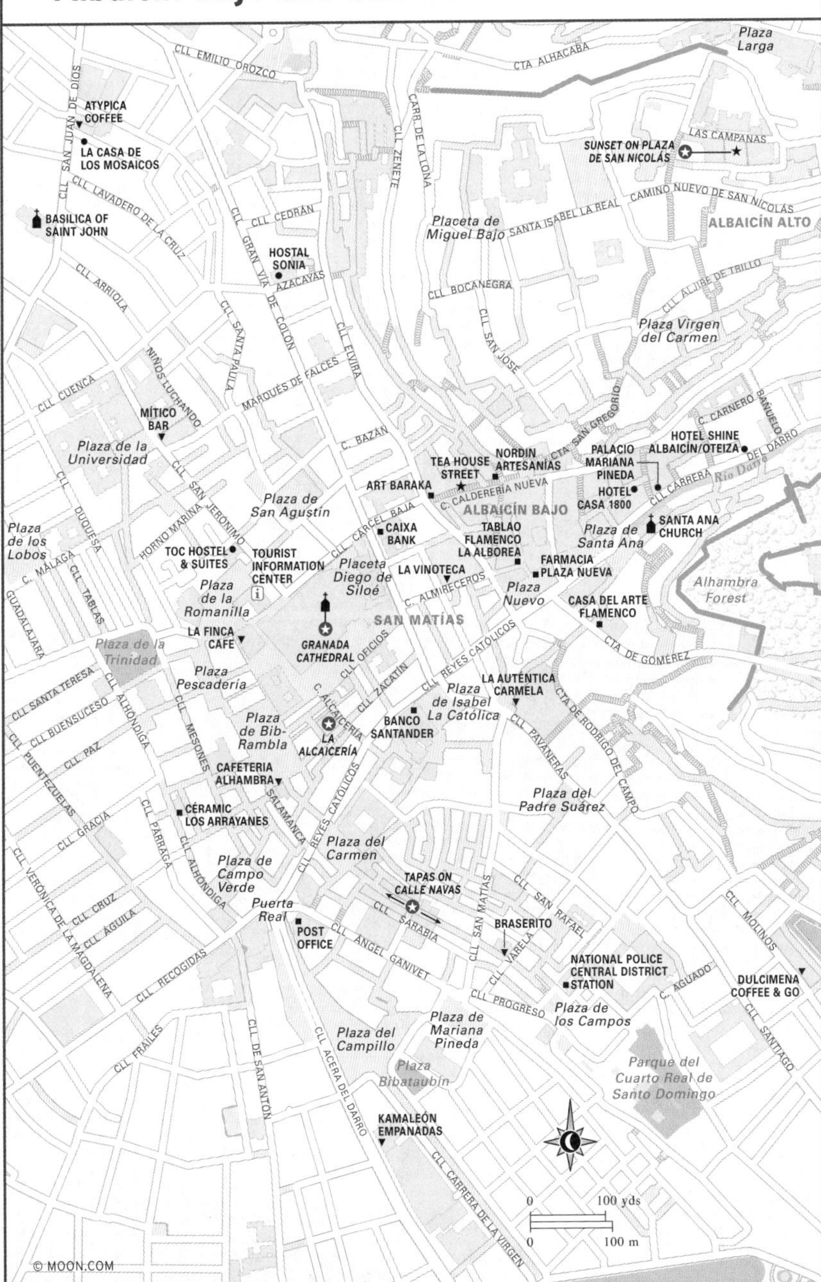

1
2
3

you'll quickly pick up on the fact that this little district has more in common with the souks of Marrakesh than it does with Granada. Delicate hand-spun and hand-painted pottery from Fez and sturdy Moroccan leather bags are piled high in the bazaars. Walking through here, you will undoubtedly hear a peppering of Arabic and be ushered back to the Granada that existed before the Reconquista.

Basilica of Saint John (Basílica de San Juan de Dios)

Calle San Juan de Dios, 17; tel. 958/275-700; https://basilicasanjuandedios.es; 10am-7pm Mon.-Sat., 10am-noon and 1:30pm-7pm Sun.; €7

If you've ever wanted to witness gilded splendor, duck into this ornate basilica. An impressive altarpiece towers over parishioners, covered in floor-to-ceiling gold, all more than likely taken from the supposed New World. The gold continues throughout the church, again from the floors to the vaulted ceilings, overpowering the brilliant Baroque frescoes featuring the Ascension and other themes. Like many of the larger religious structures throughout Andalusia, this basilica was built using the architectural bones of the preexisting mosque, which likely dates from the 13th or 14th century.

Plaza de Toros

Avenida Doctor Oloriz, 25; tel. 653/275-903; https://plazadetorosdegranada.es; hours vary; €8 (tour of the grounds)

Historically a site reserved strictly for bullfighting, concerts are now played at Plaza de Toros throughout the year. Tours are sometimes available depending on the event calendar. See the Seville chapter for information on bullfighting and its place in contemporary Spain (page 55).

Albaicín Bajo

The Albaicín Bajo neighborhood hugs the bottom of the Albaicín Alto and features a couple of Granada's most quintessential roads to meander. When you're strolling the Tea House Street (Calle de la Teterias), you'll be forgiven if you think you've taken a magic carpet ride to Morocco. This isn't exactly a neighborhood bursting with specific sights to see; it is more the experience of strolling old Granada and ducking into the many cafés, bars, and restaurants that make this city so vibrant.

Tea House Street (Calle de las Teterias)

Calle Caldererίa Nueva; 24/7; free

Tea House Street (Calle de las Teterias, or more literally, Street of the Tea Houses) comes to some as a breath of fresh air carrying aromatic herbs and saffron-spiced scents from the Middle East and North Africa. Along this narrow walking route connecting the Albaicín Bajo to the Albaicín Alto you'll feel the "Little Morocco," as many locals refer to this area, with its spice shops, eateries, bazaars, and, of course, tea houses. If you do feel like indulging in a bit of shopping, know that, as in Morocco, haggling is expected. Feel free to bargain hard. The shop owners will only respect you more for it, even if they do seem to sport perma-frowns.

Santa Ana Church (Iglesia de Santa Ana)

Calle Santa Ana, 1; tel. 958/225-004; 11:30am-1:30pm and 6pm-8pm Tues.-Sat., 11:30am-2pm and 6:30pm-7:30pm Sun.; free

Just off Plaza de Santa Ana is another mosque-turned-church in the 16th century, right on the Plaza Nuevo. Iglesia de Santa Ana is one of the better examples of Mudejar architecture found in Granada and is well worth a quick peek, particularly if you haven't seen too many churches of this era yet.

Albaicín Alto

The Albaicín Alto is a steep hill with narrow cobblestone roads open to charming plazas. The traditional homes often have doors ajar

1: Santa Ana Church **2:** La Alcaicería
3: Granada Cathedral

Albaicín Alto and Sacromonte

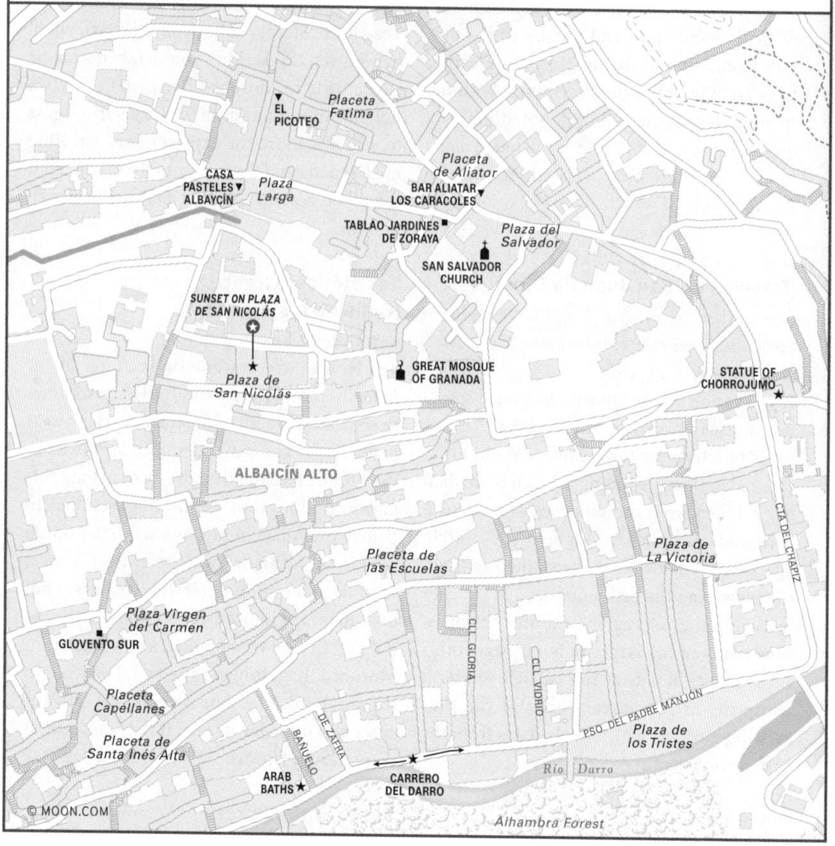

so you can peek at their quaint courtyards to glimpse what life is like in this former Muslim quarter of Granada. While the Alhambra fortress and palace occupied the uppermost, most militarily strategic point, the old city of Granada that makes up today's Albaicín lies just on the neighboring hill, facing the Alhambra to take advantage of the protection it afforded. The hillside placement of the Albaicín neighborhood offers commanding views over to the Alhambra and the rest of Granada below. While strolling through this neighborhood, which once had more than 40,000 residents, keep an eye out for remnants of this once-thriving Muslim city. The streets can be a bit steep with uneven footing, so be sure to wear a good pair of walking shoes.

★ Plaza de San Nicolás

Plaza de San Nicolás; 24/7; free

This always-bustling square atop the Albaicín Alto touts stunning views over the Alhambra on the opposite hilltop, the sprawling city of Granada downhill, and the distant Sierra Nevada as a postcard-perfect backdrop to it all. Though the views are wonderful anytime, and sunset is the most popular time to visit, try to get here shortly after sunrise for even better light and fewer crowds if you want a quieter experience. That said, during sunset

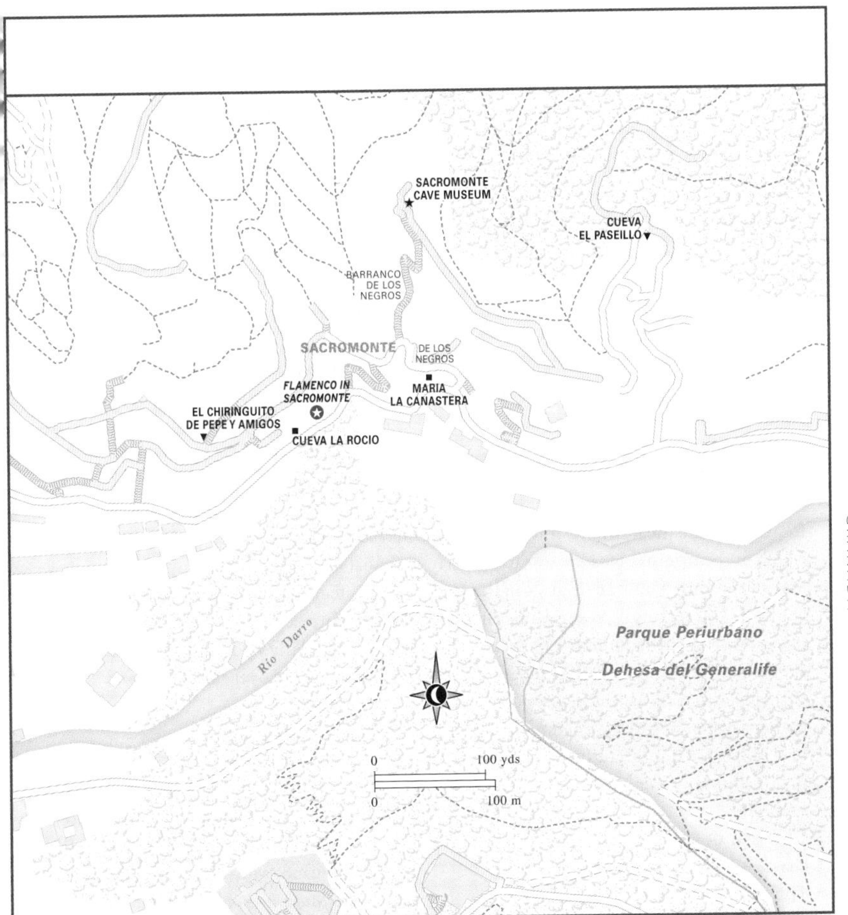

the plaza is more animated, complete with flamenco musicians, couples, and travelers all reveling in the romance, nearly everyone snapping their own sunset photo selfie to capture the moment. For some, this might be one of those experiences that is a touch more fun with the crowds.

Great Mosque of Granada (Mezquita de Granada)

Plaza de San Nicolás; tel. 958/202-526; www.mezquitadegranada.com; 11am-2pm and 5pm-8:30pm daily; free

Just off the Plaza de San Nicolás is the Great Mosque of Granada (Mezquita de Granada). Opened in 2003, this is the first new mosque constructed in Granada since the 1400s. Though relatively new, the architecture adheres to the principles of Islamic architecture as it existed in Andalusia during the period of the Moorish dynasties, complete with a traditional courtyard, an intricate cedarwood-paneled ceiling made of 2,400 individual pieces, and a mihrab with obvious design cues taken from the historic Mosque of Córdoba. Here you can have a more in-depth understanding of Islam and how it was incorporated into the daily lives of the people of Granada, not to mention how Islam is practiced in Spain today. The views from here are just as good as from the square next door, if not better, and it's almost never as crowded. Entrance to the prayer halls is limited to prayer times for Muslims, though the garden, courtyard, and small gift shop are open for all.

San Salvador Church (Parroquia de Nuestro Salvador)

Plaza del Abad, 2; tel. 958/278-644; www.archidiocesisgranada.es/index.php/guia-diocesana/parroquias/parroquia-de-nuestro-salvador; 9am-5pm Tues.-Sun., 6:30pm-7:30pm Mon.; free

The original Great Mosque of Granada, constructed here in the 13th century, was once considered one of the most beautiful mosques in the entire world. After the Reconquista, the mosque was converted into a parish and consecrated for Christian worship while working to indoctrinate the local Muslim population. Much of the original mosque was torn down and a new church built in its place in the 16th century. Interestingly, several inscriptions in Arabic run throughout the church, likely speaking to the ongoing effort to either convert the local Arab-speaking population, or perhaps just owing to the ongoing popularity of Arabic as a quotidian lingua franca during this time.

Carrera del Darro

Carrera del Darro; 24/7; free

This pedestrian-friendly thoroughfare is the most emblematic street in Granada. It is the sort of walk you dream of when thinking of strolling through Europe, and Andalusia in particular. (Note that small mini-buses do run on this road, so pedestrians should be prepared to squeeze to one side of the street whenever one passes through.)

From the **Plaza de los Tristes,** walk downhill onto the Carrera del Darro, a winding cobblestone lane that snakes along the trickle of the Darro River. Stone footbridges crisscross the river, and directly above, the great Alhambra towers over it all. The road ends in an all-too-brief half mile (800 m) at the **Plaza Nuevo,** where you will often find buskers, flamenco dancers, and other street performers. Pop into the 11th-century **Arab Baths** (El Bañuelo; Carrera del Darro, 31; 9:30am-2:30pm and 5pm-8:30pm daily; €5) for a quick look into the only remaining Arab baths in Granada. Information is sparse, so it's best for those with an interest in Arab art and architecture.

Sacromonte

Granada's oldest neighborhood, known for its Romani past, is a series of whitewashed caves in the northern part of the city. It sits atop a steep hill, just like the Alhambra and Albaicín Alto, and has impressive views over the Alhambra. This is a neighborhood to explore on foot. You'll find the main road leading up the hill from the Albaicín Bajo. You may want to take advantage of a quick taxi service to shuttle you up to the top, a particular sort of luxury if you're sporting a couple of sore feet. The primary attractions in the Sacromonte neighborhood are the flamenco shows held daily and nightly in the caves as well as the views over the Alhambra.

Statue of Chorrojumo

Placeta del Peso de la Harina; 24/7; free

If you are walking up from the Albaicín Bajo, you will see at the entry of the Sacromonte neighborhood a statue of Chorrojumo. Who is Chorrojumo, you might ask? His given name was Mariano Fernandez. He created the moniker of Chorrojumo, though he was also known in his time as the King of the Gypsies. Most interestingly, though, Chorrojumo is perhaps the most successful tour guide of all time in Spain. In the latter part of the 19th century, you could find him spinning tall tales of the Alhambra to the romantic travelers of the age, many of them no doubt inspired by the words of Washington Irving. These travelers were lured to Granada with the promise of the old Islamic era of the region and the crumbling ruins that, even today, have a sort of magic about them. Chorrojumo took these

1: traditional ceramic decorations in Albaicín Alto **2:** Great Mosque of Granada **3:** Sacromonte **4:** San Salvador Church

1
2
3
4

travelers under his wing and led them through the Alhambra and the old neighborhoods of Granada. He charged a good amount of money for his services, encouraged travelers to take photos of him dressed up in his Gitano garb, and also created postcards with his own image and sold them to travelers as well.

Sacromonte Cave Museum (Museo Cuevas del Sacromonte)

Barranco de los Negros; tel. 958/215-102; https://sacromontegranada.com; 10am-10pm daily mid-Mar.-mid-Oct., 10am-6pm daily mid-Oct.-mid-Mar.; €5

Take a quick peek inside the whitewashed caves of the Sacromonte Cave Museum (Museo Cuevas del Sacromonte) for a glimpse at what life once looked like here. Along the way, learn how the caves helped to influence the sounds of flamenco music. There are several historical photos and lots of traditional tools and instruments used around the home, with some helpful info in English. If you've made your way here, make sure to take advantage of the viewpoint looking over the Alhambra and snap a few photos of your own.

SPORTS AND RECREATION

Parks

Alhambra Forest

Cuesta de Gomérez; 24/7; free

Just off the Plaza Nueva, this park, popular with walkers and runners, leads directly up to the Alhambra. Though much of the Alhambra is paid-only access, other parts, such as the popular Calle Real de la Alhambra and the Palace of Charles V, can be visited without tickets or fees. A promenade through the park to the Alhambra just feels like something one should do while in Granada, particularly in the morning when the air is fresh.

Federico García Lorca Park (Parque Federico García Lorca)

Calle Virgen Blanca; 24/7; free

Dedicated to the memory of Granada's Federico García Lorca, the famed poet and playwright, this park is the perfect spot for a relaxed morning, cup of coffee in hand. In the middle of the park is the temporarily closed Huerta de San Vicente. This was the summer home for Lorca and his family and features original furnishings and works of art. Plans to reopen the summer home have stalled over the past few years, though hopefully it will reopen soon. While strolling through the park, or perhaps sitting down for a quiet read, this line of Lorca's might ring true: "Granada is the perfect dream and fantasy, forever ineffable . . . Granada will always be more malleable than philosophical, more lyrical than dramatic."

Biking

With its hilly, mountainous terrain, biking in Granada is not for everyone. However, there is ample bike parking around town; after all, Granada is a university town. You won't find many bicycle lanes, though drivers are generally respectful. Bike rentals here are predominantly geared to mountain and trail bikes for exploring the nearby mountains.

Pancracio Bicis

Calle Rector Marín Ocete, 10; tel. 958/055-724; www.pancraciobicis.com; 9:30am-1:30pm and 5pm-8pm Mon.-Fri., 10:30am-1:30pm Sat.

If you are looking for a bike rental for exploring the city or beyond, into the Sierra Nevada, Pancracio Bicis has you covered.

Cycle Sierra Nevada

Calle Mariana Pineda, 13B, Velez de Benaudalla; tel. 684/205-648; www.sierranevada.cc; contact through the website

For a premium experience, consider this outfit, which will deliver a well-conditioned rental bike right to your door in Granada. An official BMC bike rental dealer, they also offer one-week bike tours into the Sierra Nevada starting at €600. Tours tend to have a good mix of uphill and downhill, and with the natural beauty of the mountains, there's a lot to love for cyclists here.

Lorca's Granada: Where Tragedy and Poetry Converge

Granada conceals within its historic streets a treasure trove of cultural richness and artistic inspiration. This picturesque city was not only the canvas but also the muse for Federico García Lorca, the renowned Spanish poet and playwright of the 20th century. Lorca's connection with Granada is an undying love story written in verse. Granada, with its captivating blend of history, culture, and natural beauty, served as the crucible for Lorca's artistic brilliance.

a fountain in Granada with poetry by Federico García Lorca

AT THE ALHAMBRA

At the legendary Alhambra, the majestic palace complex showcases Granada's rich tapestry of history and multicultural heritage. Its ornate halls and enchanting gardens ignited Lorca's poetic imagination.

AT A FLAMENCO PERFORMANCE

Lorca's masterpiece, *Gitano Ballads (Romancero Gitano)*, is deeply rooted in Andalusian culture, particularly the vibrant traditions of the Romani people. To truly become immersed in the essence of these verses, you can attend a local flamenco performance. The passionate rhythms, expressive dance, and soulful melodies of flamenco embody the very spirit of Lorca's poetry, which often explores themes of love, yearning, and the human experience.

IN ALBAICÍN AND SACROMONTE

In the Albaicín and Sacromonte, you venture deeper into Lorca's world. These charming districts served as the backdrop for Lorca's timeless tragedy, *Blood Wedding (Bodas de Sangre)*. The winding streets, framed by the awe-inspiring Alhambra, create an evocative atmosphere that mirrors the intense emotions and drama of Lorca's play.

LORCA'S SPIRIT LIVES ON

It was in these rugged hills surrounding Granada that Lorca, a celebrated figure whose sexuality was often a source of controversy during his era, met his untimely end at the hands of fascist forces during the Spanish Civil War, a stark reminder of the grave consequences faced by those who dared to express their true selves and resist oppression. Lorca's spirit lingers in these solemn landscapes. In the **Federico García Lorca Park,** we can pay homage to him and what he stood for at the monument erected in his memory, reflecting for a moment on the price of artistic freedom.

Soccer (Fútbol)

Granada CF

Carretera de Alfacar; tel. 958/253-300; www.granadacf.es; €40

Granada's premier fútbol (soccer) men's club was founded in 1931. It has never had the success of some of the teams in other big cities throughout Spain, though in 2022 it was promoted to La Liga, and in 2018 it did qualify for the UEFA Europa League. The women's club, founded in 2003, has largely been relegated to the second league, though occasionally it bounces into the top league, La Liga F. Tickets for women's matches start at €5. Notably, the women's club doesn't have the following or support of other clubs around Spain, though the men's club has quite a group of vocal supporters. Things get heated, particularly when rival squads like Málaga or Seville come to town. Plan on a full stadium for these matches.

To purchase tickets, you can either buy direct at the stadium (Calle Pintor Manuel Maldonado; 10am-6pm Mon.-Fri.) or online (www.entradas.granadacf.es). Tickets go on sale only a week before the match, so you won't be able to purchase ahead of time.

FLAMENCO

Though the Sacromonte neighborhood with its charming, whitewashed caves typically highlights the flamenco shows on offer around Granada, and perhaps rightly so, there are flamenco shows to be found year-round throughout the city in traditional tablaos. Though the scenery is different, the performances can be just as good, if not sometimes a touch better, in other spots around the city. In general, you can't go wrong. Sometimes it makes the most sense to choose a performance that is closest to your accommodation.

Albaicín Bajo

Casa del Arte Flamenco

Cuesta de Gomérez; tel. 661/118-951; www.casadelarteflamenco.com/espectaculo-flamenco; 7pm and 8:30pm daily; €20

Just off the Nueva Plaza, this centrally located tablao has year-round nightly performances. A rotating cast of musicians, singers, and dancers ensures that no two evenings are alike. A small, intimate venue that is all-acoustic (no amplifiers or microphones) makes for a memorable evening. If you want to engage all of your senses, consider upgrading your flamenco show with the gastronomic experience (starting at €80), which includes an array of artfully presented local dishes to pair with your flamenco.

Tablao Flamenco La Alborea

Calle Pan, 3; tel. 858/124-931; https://alboreaflamenco.com; 7pm and 8:45pm daily; €18

This small theater sets the stage for the drama of a Granadian flamenco show. Head for the upstairs seating if you want to have tapas and drinks while enjoying the show. Traditionalists will want to stick to the floor to be as close to the performers as possible. The stage itself is one of the better-constructed stages in all of Andalusia, making for a real pop when the dancers and musicians tap or dance on the stage.

Albaicín Alto

Tablao Jardines de Zoraya

Calle Panaderos, 32; tel. 958/206-266; https://flamencogranada.com; 8pm and 10:30pm daily; €25

Flamenco right in the heart of the Albaicín Alto. What more could you ask for? If you want to order drinks and tapas, be sure to come about 30 minutes early. If you can, try to attend the later show. There always seems to be a bit more energy in flamenco shows the later they are into the night, and this is one of the latest shows in a traditional tablao.

★ Sacromonte

One of the popular flamenco legends is that this art form began in the zambras (caves) of Sacromonte, where Arabs once lived, and then the Gitano people (Gypsies) took over the neighborhood after the Reconquista. As a matter of course, the origins of flamenco in Granada's Sacromonte neighborhood are rooted in a synthesis of Arab and Gitano influences. Undoubtedly, it was the Arab communities who inhabited the caves and laid the groundwork for the unique musical and dance traditions. Post-Reconquista, the Gitano population, seeking refuge, integrated their cultural expressions with the existing Moorish musical heritage.

Over the centuries, Sacromonte became a crucible for the development and preservation of flamenco. The caves, once dwelling places, transformed into intimate performance spaces where the profound emotions of flamenco found a home. The symbiotic relationship between the caves' acoustics and the impassioned performances gave rise to a unique artistic expression.

Today, flamenco lives on in these caves in Sacromonte, which host diverse flamenco performers, contributing to the genre's multifaceted landscape and serving as both preservers of tradition and platforms for innovation. Throughout the year different performers rotate through, sometimes playing the tablaos in Granada or even Seville or Cádiz, and other times here, in the old zambras of the Sacromonte. Flamenco performers, even the most well-known ones, often sing the praises of the old zambras and make a point to perform here every year.

Cueva La Rocio

Camino del Sacromonte, 70; tel. 958/227-129; https://cuevalarocio.es; nightly until late; €25

Shoulder-to-shoulder you'll sit in straight-backed wood chairs in this whitewashed cave. It's simple and slightly uncomfortable, as true flamenco should probably be. It's touristy, but at the same time the performances are authentic and powerful. If you are not booking dinner with your show, come about 20-30 minutes early to get the best seats. Dinner is €30 extra and not recommended. Best to come for only the show here.

María la Canastera

Camino del Sacromonte, 89; tel. 958/121-183; www.marialacanastera.com; nightly until late; €62

Zambra María la Canastera is the oldest flamenco establishment in Granada, and María's descendants continue her performances to this day. Because of their location, it is convenient to enjoy "dinner and a show," as this part of Sacromonte is a bit more remote, far on the northern edge of the city. Many of the venues can arrange shuttle service to/from your accommodation. The intimate, passionate nature of flamenco sets these zambras aflame for an unforgettable night.

FESTIVALS AND EVENTS

San Cecilio Festival

February

The San Cecilio Festival, an annual celebration held in Granada, pays homage to the city's patron saint, Cecilio. This culturally rich event takes place in the first half of February and features a diverse array of religious, artistic, and musical activities. Pilgrims embark on visits to the Sacromonte Abbey, a

Zambra María la Canastera

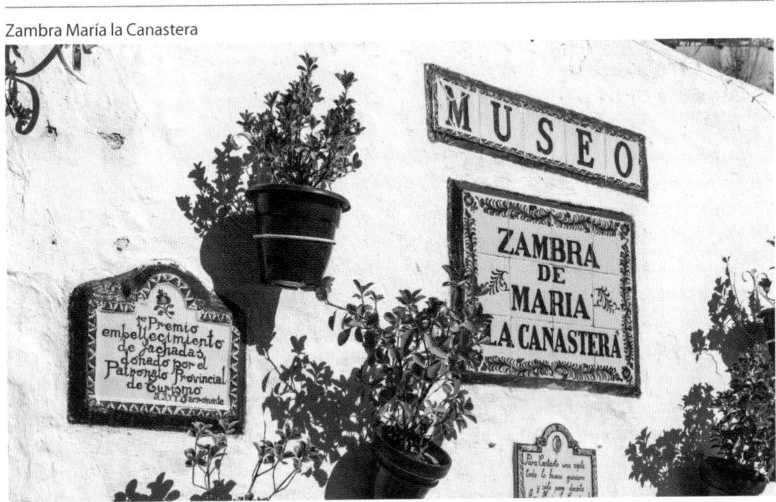

tribute to San Cecilio, while both locals and visitors are treated to traditional Andalusian music and dance performances, solemn street processions, and a delightful selection of regional cuisine. The San Cecilio Festival stands as a testament to Granada's enduring traditions and serves as an exquisite showcase of the city's rich cultural heritage and deep religious reverence.

Holy Week (Semana Santa)

Late March/mid-April

In Granada, Semana Santa, or Holy Week, is an awe-inspiring religious and cultural spectacle. Taking place in the week leading up to Easter Sunday, this solemn procession transforms the city's streets into a living theater of devotion. Confraternities, dressed in distinctive robes and accompanied by hauntingly beautiful music, carry intricate religious sculptures through the winding alleys of Granada. The air is filled with the scent of incense as locals and visitors gather to witness these moving processions, reflecting on the passion and sacrifice of the season. Semana Santa in Granada is a profound and deeply spiritual experience, making it one of the most significant and visually striking celebrations in the city, as elsewhere in Andalusia.

Festival of the Cross (Fiesta de la Cruz)

May 3

Fiesta de la Cruz, the Cross Festival, paints the city with vibrant colors and joyful festivities. This annual event beautifully adorns various locations with meticulously crafted crosses, each a work of art in itself. The streets come alive with processions, traditional music, and fun dancing. It's a time when Granada's rich cultural heritage shines through, as locals and visitors join in the celebrations, indulging in the delicious regional cuisine and sharing in the spirit of unity and tradition. The festival is a delightful blend of religious reverence and communal merriment for all.

Corpus Christi

Late May/early June

The Corpus Christi festival in Granada, Spain, is a grand celebration of religious devotion and cultural heritage. Held on the Thursday following Trinity Sunday, usually in late May or early June, this vibrant event transforms the city's streets into a colorful tapestry of floral displays and intricate, handmade carpets. Locals and visitors come together to create stunning floral designs, or alfombras de flores, that adorn the procession route. The highlight of the festival is the solemn procession of the Eucharist through these exquisite flower carpets, accompanied by traditional music, dance, and elaborate religious displays. Corpus Christi is a visually captivating and spiritually significant experience, demonstrating the city's deep-rooted traditions and artistic prowess.

International Music and Dance Festival

Late June/July; https://granadafestival.org

Held annually during the summer months, this festival transforms the historic city into a vibrant stage for a diverse array of artistic performances. Renowned musicians, dancers, and artists from across the globe converge in Granada, offering captivating shows ranging from classical concerts and flamenco performances to contemporary dance and world music. Against the stunning backdrop of Granada's historic sites, including the Alhambra, this festival celebrates the universal language of music and dance, making it a must-attend event for those seeking a rich cultural experience in the heart of Andalusia.

International Jazz Festival

Early November; www.jazzengranada.es

Held annually in early November, the Granada International Jazz Festival is a harmonious blend of world-class jazz musicians, captivating concerts, engaging workshops, and vibrant jam sessions. This musical extravaganza transforms Granada into a haven for jazz enthusiasts, offering unforgettable performances that span jazz genres from traditional to avant-garde. The festival's intimate jam sessions provide an opportunity for musicians and attendees to share the magic of improvisation in cozy settings. Whether you're a seasoned jazz aficionado or a newcomer to the genre, this festival promises an immersive experience that celebrates the universal language of jazz against the unbeatable backdrop of Granada's historic charm. Programs and specific dates are usually published in October, about a month before the festival.

SHOPPING

San Matías

Céramic Los Arrayanes

Calle Alhóndiga, 16; tel. 958/437-368; 10am-2pm and 5pm-9pm Mon.-Sat.

Easily found right in San Matías, Céramic Los Arrayanes has been specializing in ceramics since 1988. It's been featured often on local media for the care and craft the artisans put into rediscovering the motifs and features of Islamic-era pottery of the region. They offer shipping for purchases, which makes it a touch more enticing of a purchase, knowing that you don't have to slog your souvenirs around while traveling.

La Alcaicería

Reyes Católicos, 12; 24/7 (most shops open early-late)

This historic market, situated in the heart of Granada's old town, is a bustling labyrinth of shops selling Moorish-style ceramics, textiles, leather goods, and other bits and bobs, some made in Morocco and others imported from China. Somehow this is all reminiscent of the city's past as a Silk Road trading center. It's almost impossible to recommend just one shop. They are all similar in offerings and prices. Best to go with your gut, and don't be afraid to bargain for the best price. It's part of the fun—or so they say.

Albaicín Bajo

Calle Caldereria Nueva is a pedestrian thoroughfare connecting Albaicín Bajo with Albaicín Alto. The street is littered with bazaars and tea shops straight out of North Africa. You might feel more like you are in a souk in Marrakesh than in Granada. As a matter of fact, many of the store owners are Moroccan. Expect to haggle! If you're looking for souvenirs and tchotchkes, this is the neighborhood.

Art Baraka

Calle Caldereria Nueva; tel. 640/525-628; 9:30am-11pm daily

On the corner with Calle Elvira, at the bottom slope of the pedestrian thoroughfare, this is a classic bazaar with leather goods, pottery, and lamps from Morocco dangling alongside scarves imported from India. If you wanted to warm up your bartering skills, this is the place.

Nordin Artesanías

Calle Caldereria Nueva, 19; 10am-8:30pm Mon.-Sat., 11am-7pm Sun.

For a spot of illumination, peek inside this little shop specializing in lamps. You'll find lighting fixtures in all types of colors, shapes, and shades.

FOOD

San Matías

★ Calle Navas

If you want to hang out where the local Granadinos hang out, make a beeline for Calle Navas. This beautifully historic street is a backdrop to a plethora of tapas bars found along this pedestrian-friendly thoroughfare. Nearly every tavern has streetside seating, a cool interior, and a delicious little (or sometimes quite large!) tapa that naturally comes free with the order of any beverage. For the most animated experience, head out a little after sunset. You'll find friends and couples from the city, as well as travelers and foodies, all enjoying the competitive tapas culture that has bred more than a few bars and cafés frequented by tastemakers from around the world, including the likes of the late, great Anthony Bourdain.

Braserito

Calle Rosario, 7; tel. 958/221-984; 1pm-4:30pm and 8pm-midnight daily; €10

Braserito is a historic local favorite known for its pimientos (peppers) tapas. As at many local joints, to enjoy drinks and tapas you head straight to the bar. No need to order anything but your drink. Various tapas just magically appear. If you do have food allergies or preferences, this is one of those places where you will need to have your information prepared to let the bartender or waiter know, as they are used to just bringing out whatever is coming fresh from the kitchen. The main seating area is for ordering lunch or dinner off the menu.

Mítico Bar

Plaza de la Universidad; daily 1pm-11:30pm; €10

A truly historic local bar with shaded seating in the public square, Mítico is known for its snails in a spicy sauce. This was one of the first bars ever established in Granada and is proudly patronized by much of the neighborhood for tapas and a cold drink on a hot day.

Cafeteria Alhambra

Plaza de Bib-Rambla, 27; tel. 958/523-929; www.cafeteria-alhambra.com; 8am-2pm and 4pm-9pm daily; €12

Sure, you could order a pizza. But why would you when churros paired with deliciously thick hot chocolate are on the menu? The busy plaza is a great spot to take in the local hullaballoo, while the imposing fountain with its statue of Neptune lives up to its name: Fuente de los Gigantes.

La Auténtica Carmela

Calle Colcha, 13; tel. 958/225-794; www.restaurantescarmela.com/la-autentica; 8am-midnight Mon.-Fri., 9am-midnight Sat.-Sun.; €20

Nestled on the corner of a little plaza close to the cathedral is this unassuming little restaurant with clean lines and exposed brick and stone, though the outside terrace is where it's at for people-watching. The menu features updated Iberian classics highlighting the Mediterranean roots of this regional cuisine. For dinner, nothing is perhaps more cozy than the Iberian rice fluffed with warm chorizo and perfectly prepared asparagus.

Poetas Andaluces II

Calle Pedro Antonio de Alarcón, 43; tel. 958/263-050; www.poetasandaluces.es; 1pm-4:30pm and 9pm-12:30am Thurs.-Mon., 1pm-4:30pm Tues.; €35

For meat lovers, this might just be a poetic Andalusian symphony for your taste buds. Cured Iberian ham, grilled lamb chops, and roast suckling pig are just a few of the highlights of this unassuming little bodega that, like all good poetry, has one foot rooted in tradition and the other pushing the boundaries of the form.

Albaicín Bajo

Kamaleón Empanadas

Carrera del Darro, 13; tel. 630/263-856; 11am-9pm daily; €2

There's maybe nothing more Granadian than picking up a toasty empanada as a light lunch or snack on the go. Luckily, this little joint right on the Carrera del Darro is a quick-bite gem. If you are feeling spicy, order up the picante classic, or the jamón y queso is an easy-to-like favorite.

La Vinoteca

Calle Almireceros, 5; tel. 615/991-761; www.lavinotecagranada.es; 1pm-4:30pm and 7:30pm-11:30pm Sun.-Thurs., 1pm-4:30pm and 7:30pm-midnight Fri.-Sat.; €4

In the Albaicín, toward the end of Tea House Street, you'll find this tapas joint always bustling with a good mix of travelers and locals. It's a cozy-historic vibe without feeling too touristy. Some really nice little notes of years past are tucked around the bar, making it a good stop for the thirsty curious-minded traveler.

Albaicín Alto

Casa Pasteles Albaycín

Plaza Larga, 1; tel. 958/278-997; www.casapasteles.es; from 8am daily, closing times vary; €3

Pop in here for a traditional Spanish lunch

Granadino Cuisine

habas con jamón

Granada has one of the most developed food cultures in all of Spain. There are dishes that show off a proud Muslim heritage, while others are creative takes on regional cuisine using locally found legumes. Here are four quintessential Granadino dishes you should try while visiting the city.

- **Habas con jamón (beans with ham):** This dish ranks among Granada's most iconic culinary treasures. Crafted from locally sourced ingredients available in the markets from March to October, it features fleshy green beans cooked in a pan with delectable pieces of cured ham. For an extra treat, it's often crowned with a fried egg.
- **Berenjenas con miel (eggplant with honey):** Dive into a delightful plate of sliced and battered eggplant served with the sweetness of cane honey. This harmonious blend of flavors is a testament to the region's culinary creativity, stemming back to Andalusia's vibrant period of Muslim rule.
- **Cazón en adobo (marinated fried monkfish):** This dish, featuring bite-size cubes of marinated and fried monkfish, is an Andalusian favorite. Its popularity extends throughout the entire Andalusian region, though it originated in Granada. A must-try for seafood enthusiasts.
- **Piononos:** Piononos are the quintessential sweet treat of Granada. Named in honor of Pope Pius IX, they consist of a delicate, thinly rolled sponge cake forming a delightful circle, generously bathed in syrup. Indulge your sweet tooth with a local favorite steeped in tradition and flavor.

with toasted bread, tomatoes, ham, and, of course, olive oil. It's right in the heart of the Albaicín so you'll immediately feel that friendly neighborhood vibe. You'll also notice a lot of cakes and other sweets. This is probably the area's best pastry shop, known locally for its excellent piononos, a specialty of Granada.

Bar Aliatar Los Caracoles

Plaza Aliatar; tel. 650/877-353; 1pm-4pm and 8pm-11pm Tues.-Fri., 1pm-4pm and 8pm-11:30pm Sat.; €5

A historic tapas joint on the Plaza Aliatar, right at the top of the Albaicín. It can get busy very quickly. Staff are lovely, and though you could have the typical tapas, if you are coming here you should get adventurous with some caracoles (snails), a local delicacy.

El Picoteo

Calle Agua del Albayzín; tel. 958/292-380; www.casatorcuato.com; 12:30pm-4pm and 8pm-11:30pm Thurs.-Sat.; €8

At chill El Picoteo, take a seat, do a spot of people-watching, and enjoy some local tapas with an icy cold jarra of sangria. The daily menu is written at the entrance on a chalkboard. For something more substantial, try one of the seasonal rice dishes flavored with a bit of star of anise and clove. Confusingly, this same restaurant is called Casa Piti on Google Maps.

Sacromonte

El Chiringuito de Pepe Y Amigos

Calle Verea de Enmedio, 57; 10am-midnight Mon.-Fri., 11am-midnight Sat.-Sun.; €5

At the entrance of the Sacromonte

Coffee Shops

If, like me, you find yourself with an overwhelming desire, nay, *need* for a good cup of coffee, Granada is the place. Granada is known best for its tapas, and rightly so, but the third-wave coffee shop scene is not far behind. Here are a few of my favorites.

Atypica Coffee

★ ATYPICA COFFEE

Calle San Juan de Dios, 48; tel. 624/843-319; https://atypica.es; 8:30am-1:30pm and 5pm-9pm Mon.-Sat.; €4

Light, airy, family-run coffee joint with a lightly industrial vibe. Sweets and sandwiches highlight Granada's diverse past and eclectic present. Find cheesecakes and gluten-free brownies alongside spinach-stuffed empanadas and sweets straight out of Morocco. Floor-to-ceiling windows make for great people-watching in the air-conditioned space, though the gorgeous single roast coffee, freshly squeezed orange juice, and friendly service are what will make you come back. It's a bit of a walk from the central tourist area, but it's my main café when I'm in town and a great choice for meeting friendly locals.

OTEIZA

Carrera del Darro, 25; tel. 663/811-516; www.oteizacoffee.com; 8am-8pm daily; €4

There's lots of rustic charm right on the popular Carrera del Darro to go with your flat white. Or, when it's hot out, go for the deliciously chilly cold brew. Service is super friendly and the coffee is top-notch. Indoor seating is limited, so it's best to plan on taking your coffee to go. Various homemade cakes and sweets are available.

DULCIMENA COFFEE & GO

Calle Molinos, 19; tel. 699/634-348; 8am-1:30pm and 3:30pm-6:30pm Mon.-Thurs., 8am-1:30pm Fri.; €5

So . . . there are no bathrooms, no Wi-Fi, and only a couple of tables, but the coffee prepared by barista José is top-notch. For serious coffee lovers only. Well, and those who are feeling a little snacky. They also make some tasty toasted sandwiches that shouldn't be overlooked. If you appreciate expertly pulled espressos and single-origin beans, this may just be your go-to coffee fix in Granada.

LA FINCA CAFE

Calle Colegio Catalino, 3; tel. 658/852-573; 8:30am-8pm Mon.-Fri., 9:30am-8pm Sat.-Sun.; €4

They roast their own beans at La Finca, and you can taste the care in every cappuccino they pour. Tucked down a little alley not far from the Granada Cathedral, this also makes for a great stop for a light breakfast. Flaky croissants, crispy granola, cardamom buns, and other breakfast favorites always highlight the menu.

neighborhood you'll find this classic Gitano bar. Service is simple, as are the tapas, but come here after dark during the week and you'll typically be in for a treat when the locals all congregate and the beer flows fast.

Cueva el Paseillo

Calle Barranco Valparaiso; tel. 958/220-284 or 600/781-860; hours vary; €10

Mariano and his family run a little restaurant out of their cave. Hours vary tremendously and you can't count on it ever being open, but when it is open, it's as charming as charming gets. Food is simple—rice is a staple, along with sausages and tomato salads—and deliciously homemade, but the views down the valley over the Alhambra and the general conviviality can't be beat. If you're coming to Sacromonte and plan on eating here, it's best to call ahead to make sure they're open.

ACCOMMODATIONS

The San Matías and Albaicín Bajo neighborhoods offer many accommodation options. You'll be centrally located with a stay in either neighborhood, though you might also want to consider one of the hotels inside the Alhambra complex (page 151) for a unique experience!

San Matías

TOC Hostel and Suites

Pcta. de Castillejos; tel. 958/322-214; https://tochostels.com/destinations/granada; from €30 (bed in shared room) to €100 (double room, private)

Hip international chain near the cathedral. If you can stretch your budget, you'll appreciate the private rooms. That said, this well-located, lovely two-star option offers a traditional hostel stay in a clean, shared room with other travelers in a bunk bed setup. Female-only dorms are available.

Hostal Sonia

Calle Gran Vía del Colón; tel. 958/206-116; www.hostalsonia.com; €60

This no-frills one-star hostel is centrally located. The best rooms are on the street, though you will want to bring ear plugs, particularly if you are a light sleeper, as the entire property can be a bit noisy. Reception can run a bit hot and cold, though typically staff are quite helpful at directing you around town.

La Casa de Los Mosaicos

San Juan de Dios, 48, Calle Cardenal Mendoza; tel. 958/280-725; www.lacasadelosmosaicos.com; €70

If you prefer a quieter stay a bit away from the crowds, this hotel is an easy choice. It has a bit of a cutesy Airbnb feel with modern rooms and spacious bathrooms, coffee stations, and safes for your valuables. Other than a small, unstaffed lobby, there are no public spaces. You'll use the facing Hotel los Girasoles (not recommended) for check-in and check-out.

Albaicín Bajo

Hotel Shine Albaicín

Carrera del Darro, 25; tel. 958/224-402; www.shinehotels.com; €120

This is a centrally located boutique three-star hotel right on the Carrera del Darro. A welcoming homey-hip enclosed courtyard greets you with hints of Andalusian charm, while the original wood interiors have an unmistakable patina. Walk in here and you feel a sense of history. The rooms offer modernized comfort with firm beds and convenient air-conditioning/heating units, plus a hint of times past felt in the exposed wood ceilings. A nice mix of modern and historic.

★ Hotel Casa 1800

Calle Benalua, 11; tel. 958/210-700; www.hotelcasa1800granada.com; €130

A 16th-century home has been renovated and converted into a charming boutique with 25 rooms, just off the picturesque Calle del Darro. The building was used by King Ferdinand for his military. This property has an elevator (rare!) beyond the short flight of stairs at the entrance. No pool, spa, rooftop terrace, or room service for dinner. No other public spaces. A nearby hammam is highly recommended. Staff will help with reservations for dinner, the hammam, excursions, etcetera, although there's no concierge; just ask at reception.

Palacio Mariana Pineda

Carrera del Darro, 9; tel. 958/216-158; www.palaciomarianapineda.es; €140

This is a restored palace, as the name suggests, with charming exposed wood and brick. It's splurge-worthy for the junior suites with views out over the Alhambra and quaint little terraces that curve out from the rooms, providing a private outdoor space, which might just be the town's most sought-after locale!

And you could have it all to yourself. Service is provided with some really nice warm touches of personality.

INFORMATION AND SERVICES

Tourist Information Center

Calle Cárcel Baja, 3; tel. 958/247-128; 9am-8pm Mon.-Fri., 10am-7pm Sat., 10am-3pm Sun. and holidays

The main tourist info point is right across the square from the cathedral. You can pick up a map of the city and brochures, and get up-to-date information on events happening in town.

Hospitals

For emergencies, dial 112.

As a large city, Granada has multiple hospitals to cater to the health-care needs of its residents and visitors and provide emergency services. **Hospital Universitario Clinico San Cecilio** (Avenida del Conocimiento; tel. 958/023-000) is a major public hospital with emergency services. It's part of the Andalusian Public Health Service, as is the **Hospital Virgen de las Nieves** (Avenida de las Fuerzas Armadas, 2, Beiro; 958/020-000).

Pharmacies

You'll find easily recognizable pharmacies all over the city. A centrally located one is **Farmacia Plaza Nueva** (Plaza Nueva, 4, Albaicín Bajo; tel. 958/222-946; 9am-9pm Mon.-Sat.). Many pharmacies are closed on Sunday, so check before you go.

Police

If your passport is stolen or lost, you must file the appropriate report (loss or theft) at a police station. Remember to notify your embassy as well. If you need police assistance in Granada, visit the **National Police Central District Station** (Plaza de los Campos, 3; tel. 958/808-000; 8am-9pm Mon.-Sat.).

Post Office

It's almost worth writing a few postcards just to have an excuse to pass through the classic **Oficina de Correas** (Puerta Real de España, 2; tel. 958/221-138; www.correos.es; 8:30am-8:30pm Mon.-Fri.), a testament to Spanish old-world architecture.

Banks/ATMs

You'll find ATMs and banks easily accessible and scattered throughout the city. A convenient area of ATMs is just around the cathedral, where you'll find a **Banco Santander** (Reyes Católicos, 36; www.bancosantander.es) with a 24-hour ATM, as well as the main branch of **Caixa Bank** (Calle Gran Vía de Colón, 16; tel. 958/577-700; www.caixabank.es; 8:30am-2:30pm Mon.-Fri., plus 4:15pm-6:30pm Thurs.). In the neighborhoods of Sacromonte and the Alhambra, there are a couple of ATMs near the entrances.

GETTING THERE

Air

Granada is served by the **Federico García Lorca Granada Airport** (Carretera de Málaga, Chauchina; tel. 913/211-000; www.aena.es). This smaller airport has limited connections with travel hubs throughout Europe, though likely you would only use it if connecting with another Spanish city.

Train

From Granada, travelers can connect on the AVE (Alta Velocidad Española) high-speed train from Granada to Madrid (3 daily; 3 hr; €30-80) or Barcelona (1 daily; 6.5 hr; €60-120). There are hourly connections daily from early morning to late night with Seville, Córdoba, and Málaga (all starting around €35).

The **Granada train station** (Avenida de Andaluces, 20; tel. 912/432-343; www.renfe.com) rests on the western edge of the old city. There is a taxi stand right at the exit, which is terribly convenient, particularly if you are not traveling light. Taxis into central Granada are typically €5-8, making it a no-brainer for whisking you quickly to your accommodations. By and large, English isn't spoken, so it's best to have your lodging marked on a map, such as the one in this guide.

Bus

Located on the north edge of the city, an hour or so of a walk from the main areas of the city and even the train station, this is not the most conveniently located **bus station** (Barrio Plan Parcial, 24; www.alsa.es) in Andalusia. It's best to take a taxi to connect with the city center. If you can take the train or drive into Granada, that is preferable to the bus. If you are on more of a shoestring budget or wanted to hit the slopes to go skiing, you would want to make your way here to catch the bus at 8am (9am weekends) to get up to the ski station.

GETTING AROUND

Walking

For the most part, you'll be walking around old Granada. Walks are pleasant, though hilly, and occasionally steeply so. Cobblestones and stairs can make the going difficult for some, while others will relish the feel of old Europe underfoot. Taxis never seem to be too far away, and are never too expensive, so if the legs give out before the spirit does, head to the nearest busy-looking thoroughfare to hail a cab.

Bus

For those relying on the bus, there are a few really nice connections to know about. From Plaza Nueva, the C21 and C32 busses leave about every 5 minutes and take you directly up Calle del Darro and around to the Plaza de San Nicolás in the Albaicín Alto neighborhood. The C30 and C32 busses leave every 10 minutes and connect directly from Plaza Neuva to the Alhambra. Each connection is an easy 15-minute ride. A one-way ticket costs €1.40.

Taxi

Taxis are readily available and will shuttle you through the narrow roads, one-way streets, and pedestrian-only thoroughfares to the top of the Alhambra, Albaicín Alto, and the caves of Sacromonte, or to transportation connections, such as the airport, train station, or bus station. You can always try to hail a taxi, though practically it is often easier to head to the taxi stands at Fuenta de la Batallas, Plaza Nueva, Gran Vía de Colón, or in front of the Jardines del Triunfo. You can also try to call and arrange for a taxi from **Tele Radio Taxi** (tel. 958/280-654) or **Radio Taxi Genil** (tel. 958/132-323), though it's best to have someone with fluent Spanish arrange this for you. A taxi ride will cost a minimum of €4, while €5-6 will get you pretty much anywhere around central Granada and can be a good time and energy saver.

Here are some common taxi fares:

- From Plaza Nueva to the Alhambra: €5
- City center to/from the airport: €27
- City center to the Sierra Nevada ski station: €65

Around Granada

A few places around Granada can add depth to your experience of the region, whether you are interested in visiting some of the smaller towns and getting a feel for rural life or wish to delve into the unique natural beauty of the area. Though public transportation is possible, these places are much easier to access with a car.

To the northwest you'll find the picturesque towns of Moclín and Montefrío. Each of these can work well on a road trip connecting to/from Córdoba or Málaga or on their own as a day trip from Granada.

MOCLÍN

A quick 45-minute jaunt from Granada brings you to the small hillside village of Moclín. Little known, though historically important, Moclín can make a great alternative to Granada as a base for exploring the area, particularly for those who have rented a car and would enjoy a taste of small-town life in the region, to say nothing of the views over Granada, the Alhambra, and the Sierra Nevada during those crisp Andalusian mornings.

Sights

Moclín Castle (Castillo de Moclín)

Calle Mota, 14; tel. 690/778-517; www.andalucia.org/en/moclin-tourisme-culturel-castillo-de-moclin; €2.50

Built during the mid-13th century to safeguard the Nasrid kingdom of Granada, the Castle of Moclín, also called Hins Al-Muqlin, served as a frontier stronghold between Granada and Castile. Throughout the Hispanic-Muslim era, it faced relentless sieges until it finally fell to Ferdinand and Isabella in 1486. Perched atop the highest peak in the region, at an elevation exceeding a thousand meters, the castle boasts an irregular layout, cleverly adapted to the terrain. Its outer walls taper gracefully toward the west and south, blending into the Tajos de la Hoz, where nature itself contributes to its defense. The castle's alcazaba, or citadel, can be accessed via the Camino Real, which remains accessible even today. The grand entrance is marked by the imposing Torre del Homenaje, the tallest tower, affording splendid views of Alcalá la Real. Within the citadel's upper reaches, a significant feature is the vast cistern, of utmost importance during times of siege. Tours are best arranged by phone a day or two before your arrival.

Sanctuary of Cristo del Paño (Santuario Cristo del Paño)

Avenida Santísimo Cristo del Paño; tel. 958/403-032; https://santuariocristomoclin.com; 10:30am-12:30pm and 6pm-8pm Mon.-Wed. and Fri., 11am-1pm and 4pm-6pm Sat.-Sun.; free

For some, this is a deeply spiritual place. Legend has it that during the Reconquista Isabella and Ferdinand brought with them a canvas painting of Jesus that they held up as a banner and proof of victory during their campaign. On July 26, 1486, when Moclín was won, the royals gave this painting to Moclín, where a temple was constructed to house it. At the end of the 17th century, a nearly blind sacristan using a cloth to clean the painting implored god to cure him of his cataracts, and his eyes were miraculously healed. After that, the cult of Christ of the Cloth, or Cristo del Paño, was truly born. From the 18th century on, the legend grew, with many taking the opportunity of the annual local livestock fair on October 5 to make a pilgrimage to this miraculous bit of canvas.

Festivals

Moclín has the typical festivals of Spain, with the **Epiphany celebration** and **Semana Santa** looming large on the calendar.

Its most interesting festival is probably the annual **Cristo del Paño** procession held every October 5. The pilgrimage inspired Lorca to write his work *Yerma*. Every year, thousands of pilgrims gather here and camp in the vicinity. The famed painting of the Sanctuary of the Cristo del Paño, which looks something like a copy of a Titian painting of Christ carrying the cross, is kept in the sanctuary. The devotion to this image, according to the history of Moclín, stems from a miracle through which one of its inhabitants recovered his sight while cleaning the painting.

Food and Accommodations

Breaking Bar la Plaza

Plaza de España, 4; tel. 629/475-721; 8am-6pm Tues.-Thurs. and Sun., 8am-1am Fri.-Sat.; €15

You will find a few small tapas bars and eateries dotted throughout Moclín. Any of them is fine for a little nibble and drink, though if you're looking for a heartier meal, particularly for lunch or for dinner on the weekends, head here for generous portions, swift service, and some real local vibes.

Casa de la Placeta del Rincón

Calle Eras, 12; tel. 644/854-142; http://casadelaplacetamoclin.es; €55

Locally owned and operated, this restored

18th-century building, originally military barracks, has undergone many transformations over the years. The latest renovations brought it up to date, and now it has been repurposed into six apartments, one of which is specially adapted for individuals with disabilities. Each unit is fully equipped with a kitchen, appliances, bathroom, living/dining room, telephone, cable television, and internet access. The property also includes a small store showcasing local products and another featuring antique and period furniture, paintings, and crafts from the region. You'll also find a swimming pool and a solarium that provides romantic views of Moclín and its historic castle. It's a great place for a longer stay or if you don't mind making your own breakfast.

Casa Higueras

Calle Amargura, 16; tel. 663/506-000; www.casahigueras.com; €60

Brits Ian and Andrew bought and restored a traditional village house that they now operate as a quaint little B&B. The house features a large terrace, a garden, and a couple of wood-burning fireplaces to keep the interiors cozy during the cold winter months. The hosts are always on-site and enjoy sharing some of their favorite local places to dine as well as some choice hiking trails. Though it's not a restaurant, they can provide lunch and dinner with a 48-hour notice, using fresh, local ingredients. They only have two guest rooms and guests do not have use of the kitchen. For an apartment rental with kitchen access, check out their sister property in Moclín, **Esperanza 9** (www.esperanza9.com).

Information and Services

For information on Moclín, it's best to check out the city hall website (https://ayuntamientodemoclin.com), though you will have to navigate in Spanish or use a translator.

Getting There and Around

Departing from Granada, get to Moclín by following the A-432 northwest, heading toward Puerto Lope where you'll see the exit for Moclín. This follows the GR-3414 east. Upon reaching Moclín, you'll find parking spaces available to leave your vehicle as you explore the town on foot.

If you are determined to use public transportation, you could make use of the 323 bus that connects with Granada. There are usually four stops in Moclín daily on the private Contreras bus network (https://autocarescontreras.es).

MONTEFRÍO

After the fall of Priego de Córdoba, Benameji, and Alcalá in 1341, Montefrío, along with Moclín, became part of the new line of defense of the Nasrid kingdom of Granada. From 1352 to its conquest in 1486, the castle of Montefrío stood strong against the waves of attacks, which in those years were frequent. Though there are several sites to see in Montefrío, they can all be visited in just a couple of hours, making this a great stop if you're road-tripping through Andalusia on your way to or from Granada.

The entirety of Montefrío is situated around a steep hill leading to the picturesque remains of the castle and its adjoining church, which tower over the whitewashed town. It's a steep walk up the hill to the castle, though it is blissfully shaded by the cliffs and forest. At the foot of the cliff, you will find an interesting graveyard known as The Pantheon.

Sights

Castle of Montefrío (Castillo de Montefrío)

Calle San Sebastián, 62; tel. 958/336-004; www.montefrio.org/paginas/villa.htm; 11am-2pm Tues.-Fri., 11am-2pm and 4:30pm-6:30pm Sat.-Sun.; €2.50

Situated on the southern edge of Montefrío, today's Castle of Montefrío was built on the remains of the old Nasrid castle, whose founding dates to around 1352, during the reign of Abu-Abdallah Yusuf in Granada. The chief architect from the Alhambra selected the location and planned its construction with a triple enclosure, parade ground, arrow slits, battlements, towers, water cisterns, warehouses, and everything necessary to withstand, if needed, a long siege. Even if you are a bit castled-out, the views here are something to behold and worth a climb up the steep, narrow castle steps. Around the castle grounds you can discover the remaining vestiges of the excavated houses and a rock-carved cistern. The enclosing wall shows off the rubble masonry used to construct the walls, all flanked by six towers, all with semicircular designs around a rectangular layout, giving you a good idea of the size and power of this castle in its prime.

Church of the Villa (Iglesia de la Villa)

Calle San Sebastián, 40; 10:30am-2pm Tues.-Fri., 10:30am-2pm and 4:30pm-6:30pm Sat.-Sun.; €2

When the Muslim fortress fell to the Christian monarchs in 1486, the entirety became the manor of the Fernández de Córdoba family. As was the custom of the time, they initiated the construction of a church to adjoin the castle. Work on the church was finished in 1507, with the popular Renaissance style of the time combined with the Mudejar attributes typical of the era and this region. It's worth a quick peek, though don't spend too much time here as there are more impressive churches around Andalusia.

The Pantheon

Calle Arco; 24/7; free

There are 16 niches dug into the cliff as graves that remain from the family pantheons that belonged to the wealthy families of Montefrío. Exact dating has not been established, but it is known that this graveyard was in use between the 17th and 19th centuries. The graves are vaulted and framed by double semicircular arches. They are typically 2 m (6.5 ft) deep by 1.5 m (5 ft) in height and about 1 m (3 ft) wide. Three corpses would usually be buried in each of these tombs, and there are sadly a few smaller tombs for laying children to rest. The Pantheon is the only sort of gravesite like this in the region, which makes this a bit of a morbid curiosity.

Church of the Incarnation (Iglesia de la Encarnación)

Calle Alcalá, 1; tel. 958/336-039; 9:30am-1:30pm Mon.-Sat., 11am-1:30pm Sun.; free

Inspired by the Pantheon of Agrippa in Rome, this is one of the biggest and most important neoclassical churches in Spain. The brainchild of architect Domingo Lois Monteagudo, the

Montefrío from a viewpoint atop the hill

church was constructed between 1786 and 1802. From the main entrance, you walk directly into an enormous circle with a diameter of nearly 30 m (100 ft), echoing the rotunda and its vast dome above. This is the true heart of today's Montefrío and well worth a quick peek inside.

Festivals

The Night of the Lights (La Noche de las Lumbres)

February 1

Though you can expect the usual festivals and holidays as in other parts of Spain, including of course big celebrations for Epiphany and Holy Week, Montefrío is quite special for its Night of the Lights (La Noche de las Lumbres) festival held annually in the dark days of winter on February 1. The Night of the Lights marks the culmination of the olive harvest, when historically the children of the town busily scoured every corner, collecting anything combustible to vie for brilliance and magnificence against the other luminous displays. The most prized possessions were the rondeles, mats traditionally used for pressing olives in oil mills, which, when saturated with oil, ignited into brilliant torches. In the spirit of the event, a variety of meats and cherished local roast sausages are savored and lively circles form, echoing with the tunes of traditional Candelarias songs. Montefrío, viewed from afar, glows with a multitude of lights scattered across the landscape, stretching from the distant farmsteads to the heart of the town.

Food

Casablanca

Plaza Pililla s; €3

For a real local experience, head up and around the corner from the main plaza to this little neighborhood joint. A few tall bar tables are placed outside, making a little terrace. From here, you can see down to the main street. Festive flamenco music chimes in over the speakers, adding to the sort of convivial atmosphere found only in Andalusia. Tapas are pretty run-of-the-mill, so you're coming here more for a beer or wine and less for lunch.

La Taberna

Plaza Virgen de los Remedios; tel. 615/689-319; €4

The popular choice right on the main plaza across from the church, La Taberna can get very busy, particularly during holidays. If the sun isn't too strong, make use of the seating off the plaza and enjoy the views over the church and the fortress on the cliff. As elsewhere in Granada province, expect a free tapa with your drink.

Restaurante El Pregonero

Calle Garcia; tel. 958/336-117; http://restauranteelpregonero.com; 11:30am-5:30pm and 8pm-midnight Wed.-Sun., 11:30am-5:30pm Mon.; €12

If La Taberna is packed, walk a block uphill in the direction of the castle. This little restaurant tucked just off the church plaza always seems to have room somewhere. It features Montefrío's finest dining and most complete local wine list—a surprisingly gastronomic experience, particularly for a town of this size. The pulpo braseado (braised octopus) is particularly well done.

Accommodations

In Montefrío proper, you won't find many decent accommodations, though you will find plenty of apartment rentals to choose from. Instead, consider heading out into the countryside, where a few rural houses have been converted into charming Spanish-style B&Bs.

Huerta Nazari

Huerta Cambil; tel. 958/456-339; www.huertanazari.com; €70

A charming B&B hotel near the town of Alomartes, about 30 minutes from Montefrío, this U-shaped property encloses a delightful garden and swimming pool, which feels like a real luxury in those hot summer months. You'll find a sauna as well as plenty of public spaces for relaxing. English-language communication might be difficult, so it's a better option if you are comfortable speaking (or trying to speak!) Spanish.

Lasnavillasmm

Carretera de Íllora, km 15; tel. 680/573-077; www.lasnavillasmm.es; €88

On the road to Íllora, just over a 10-minute drive from Montefrío, you'll find Marc and Mady's little countryside oasis. For active travelers looking to get some hiking or biking in, this can be a great option as Mady is an avid walker and knows a lot of the great hikes in the area, while Marc is a cyclist and can point you in the right direction for riding. There is an accessible room for wheelchair users. Paella and other local dishes are available on request, including some vegetarian and gluten-free options.

★ Casa Olivar

Barranco del Rayo, Tocón; tel. 474/319-164; www.casa-olivar.com; €80

Located just 25 minutes from Montefrío outside of the town of Tocón, this gem of tranquility nestled in the olive groves is a real rural treat. Hosts Marijke and Carl will leave you feeling pampered. Carl happily advises on restaurants and parking in the area, particularly Granada, and he has a nose for great vintages of wine. An extensive, fresh breakfast is served every morning. If you ask ahead of time, Marijke will happily make a local dinner for you featuring whatever is fresh and delicious at the local markets. All of this kindness is packaged in a lovingly restored traditional whitewashed home featuring four guest rooms and a secondary little house with two more rooms, ideal for friends traveling together or families. The property also has a pool, hot tub, large fish pond, library, and more to help you relax after a long day of exploration. You couldn't ask much more of a rural stay in the region.

Casa del Agua

Arroyo de los Molinos; tel. 958/339-840 or 606/038-652; https://lacasadelagua.org; €90

This restored flour mill, complete with waterwheel, dates from the 16th century. It is hard to argue with the Andalusian countryside charm here. It's a quick 10-minute drive south from Montefrío, peacefully surrounded by fields of oak, olive, and pine. The nights are a starry delight. The on-site organic farm provides seasonal ingredients for breakfast and other meals (inquire ahead of time for pricing and reservations). For couples, the Al Alhambra apartment is perhaps the best setup, though do watch for the low ceiling beams. For some, access to a professional masseuse would be an understandable draw.

Palacio de la Veracruz

Calle Veracruz, 6, Alcalá La Real; tel. 953/581-178; https://palaciodelaveracruz.com; €100

Newly opened in 2020, this boutique hotel is located in the town of Alcalá La Real, just 30 minutes north of Montefrío. Open the door beneath the retro golden age facade into a light, airy, cool interior with lean lines, comfy modern furnishings, and contemporary Art Deco regional touches, such as the decorative cement floor tiles. It's very comfortable for a multi-night or overnight stay and a nice option if you prefer more of a hotel feel but want to be in the middle of a small Andalusian village, able to walk out the front door and explore a little pueblo.

Information and Services

Tourist Office

Plaza de España; tel. 958/336-004; www.turismomontefrio.org; 10am-2pm Tues.-Fri., 10:30am-2pm and 4pm-6pm Sat., 10:30am-2pm Sun.

The Montefrío tourist office has a surprising number of materials for the town and region, though unsurprisingly the majority are in Spanish, pointing to a robust amount of local tourism. Tickets for the castle and tours in English can be booked through the tourist office.

Getting There and Around

You will need a rental car to get to Montefrío as public transport is sparse. From Granada (1 hr; 59 km/37 mi), take the A-92 west toward

Seville. Exit onto the A-335 and continue north directly to Montefrío. Other destinations within a short drive include Moclín (30 min; 24 km/15 mi), Priego de Córdoba (45 min; 35 km/22 mi), Zuheros (1 hr; 71 km/44 mi), and Córdoba (2 hr; 140 km/87 mi). Lucena (1 hr; 68 km/42 mi) and Antequera (1 hr; 85 km/53 mi) are also short drives, making this a good stop to break up a road trip. Once in Montefrío, you'll be out exploring on foot.

Parking

Free central parking is well marked at the main village access, at the obvious bottom of a hill leading up to town. From the parking lot, you can walk up the stairs and ramps leading into the heart of the village to the main plaza. However, if you are only stopping to visit the Castillo de Montefrío and the Iglesia de la Villa and are not planning on having any food or drink, make your way through town and park at the bottom of the cliff. This isn't quite as obvious of a drive, so just follow the signs for the Castillo de Montefrío to find the parking, right next to the unmarked Pantheon gravesite.

Granada Geopark

Recognized by UNESCO in 2020, the geology of the Granada Geopark, found in the eastern part of Andalusia, is one of Europe's great badlands and one of the largest desert regions found on continental Europe. Surrounded by tall mountain peaks, the rivers and channels once had no natural drainage to the sea. Over time, they carved a hydrographic network—an uneven, arid desert landscape, including the Gorafe Desert, with deep canyons and gullies. Of all of Andalusia, this is perhaps the least-visited region. International tourism is still gaining a foothold, though many locals are now discovering it.

Within the 4,722-sq-km (1,823-sq-mi) geopark are several small cities and towns with restaurants, bars, cafés, hotels, and short-term apartment rentals. **Guadix** and **La Calahorra** are two of the more interesting towns.

PLANNING YOUR TIME

Guadix and La Calahorra can be visited as a day trip from Granada, though this area does play host to some unique properties for overnights.

For travelers seeking a touch of adventure, there are quite a few hiking and cycling trails, as well as other activities, though do keep in mind your surroundings. The summers are scorching hot, while in the winter, temperatures will dip below freezing.

GATEWAY TOWNS

Guadix

Nestled in the heart of Andalusia, Guadix is a town that beckons with its larger-than-life presence and a treasure trove of historical wonders. Strolling through its streets you'll discover grand buildings alongside humble dwellings, stately homes, and ornate palaces with intricately designed doorways and ornate coats of arms. Corner towers crowned with brick galleries offer glimpses into Guadix's aristocratic past, evoking an air of nobility that lingers. It is a place of contrasts, charming corners, and magnificent urban features that invite you to delve into its captivating past. From prehistoric times to the Roman era and beyond, this town is a testament to the cultural wealth of Andalusia.

Guadix is home to a remarkable collection of Mudejar-style churches and convents you can visit while having a walk around the city. Three highlights are the Parish Church of Santiago, with its unique doorway, and the historic convent chapels of Santo Domingo and San Francisco, boasting magnificent polychrome structures. All provide a glimpse into the town's religious heritage. Dominating the town's skyline is the medieval Alcazaba of Guadix, one of the largest in the province. This fortress, perched at the highest point, offers panoramic views over Guadix and the surrounding valley.

Guadix even has its moments in the cinematic spotlight, with cinema chairs strategically placed around town to mark the locations where popular movies were filmed. From Spanish productions to the iconic *Indiana Jones and the Last Crusade,* the town's cinematic history adds an extra layer of intrigue as you walk around town playing "Did you see that movie?"

La Calahorra

At the foot of the Sierra Nevada the sleepy pueblo of La Calahorra unfolds beneath the watchful eye of its 16th-century castle. The castle's Mudejar-style interiors offer panoramic desert views from the towers. This is a good alternative to Guadix for staying in the geopark if lodgings around Guadix are full or you just like the idea of a small town. To truly immerse yourself in the town's essence, savor authentic Andalusian cuisine at local restaurants. Indulge in dishes like ajo blanco (a chilled almond garlic soup) and migas (fried breadcrumbs with chorizo), served with the warmth of Andalusian hospitality.

SIGHTS

Guadix

Guadix Cathedral (Catedral de la Encarnación de Guadix)

Plaza Catedral; tel. 692/574-671; www.catedraldeguadix.es; 11am-3pm and 5:30pm-7:30pm Mon.-Thurs., 11am-7:30pm Fri.-Sat., 2pm-7:30pm Sun. (possibly shorter hours in winter); €7 (plus €2 for the tower), entry includes free audio guide in English

The Cathedral of Guadix is a masterpiece that combines architectural elegance with a dash of mystery. Built on the site of a former mosque during the 16th century, it boasts a stunning blend of Gothic and Renaissance styles, thanks to the renowned architect Diego de Siloé from nearby Burgos. As you step inside, you can't help but note the intricacy of its design. With every echoing footstep, the cathedral seems to whisper tales of centuries gone by, including the visit of Queen Isabella and Christopher Columbus. The adjoining tower is a strenuous, narrow steep climb. You'll walk up a helicoidal spiral inspired by the work of Leonardo Da Vinci. Panoramic views over Guadix and the region greet you at the top, making the climb worthwhile for those suckered in by a good view.

Alcazaba of Guadix

Calle la Muralla, 1; tel. 958/662-804; https://guadix.es/servicios-turisticos; 10am last Fri. of every month (only 25 spots available, reserve ahead of time); free

This iron-red crenellated fortress may just have you reminiscing about Marrakesh. The Alcazaba of Guadix, one of the most important of the Nasrid kingdom, stands on the highest point of the Islamic medina (old city). With a construction likely dating back to the very early days of Islamic rule in Spain, the city and its fortress grew over the centuries. The fortress itself is still amazingly well preserved. A walk through the monumental keep and along the walkways easily transports you to a bygone era. It's interesting to think that this fortress served a military role as late as the 19th century. If you are not lucky enough to be in Guadix on a Friday that it's open, you could walk around the Alcazaba, though the neighborhood lacks the charm of elsewhere in town. Entry is limited to 25 people as part of a one-hour guided tour.

Neighborhood of Caves (Barrio de Cuevas)

Barrio de Cuevas; 24/7; free

A train on wheels will take you from the Plaza Catedral to Barrio de Cuevas on the south edge of town. A few cave houses have even been converted to short-term rentals! Right in the heart of Guadix, this is a captivating neighborhood that has a transportive affect, drawing you into a unique world of subterranean living. Centuries-old cave dwellings have been transformed into charming homes, maintaining a constant, comfortable temperature year-round. Wandering through its winding streets, you'll encounter a labyrinthine landscape of cozy cave houses adorned with colorful facades and flower-filled patios, offering an enchanting glimpse into the town's rich cultural heritage. If you are interested in learning more about cave living, the Cueva Museo Centro de Interpretación (Plaza del Padre Poveda; tel. 958/665-569; 10am-2pm and 4pm-6pm Mon.-Sat.; €3) is worth 30 minutes or so of your time.

La Calahorra

Castle of Calahorra (Castillo de La Calahorra)

Plaza del Cardenal Cascajares, 3; tel. 941/130-098 or 606/523-923; www.catedralcalahorra.es; free

Unless you are visiting La Calahorra toward the beginning of your journey, you might just be "castled out" by the time you get here. Luckily, this is one of those castles you could probably skip, though with guided visits in English available (€2), you might get a bit more from this visit than some of the others you've undoubtedly covered by now.

SPORTS AND RECREATION

Hiking

Hiking trails crisscross the geopark. With the park's canyons and shaded river beds, some hikes are less exposed than you might think, though keep in mind the type of territory you'll be covering. With this sort of desert environment, the sun can be sneaky hot, and if you're out after the sun peaks in the winter months, it can be brutally cold. It's best to head out completely prepared for the weather, in any case. Any of the tourist offices can furnish you with a local hiking map with well-marked trails. If you have never hiked on your own in an unfamiliar place, it might be best to go with a guide—you'll likely learn more about the local terrain as well. Contact **Onturi** (tel. 639/782-666; www.onturi.com) for information about guides.

Acequia del Toril Route and Alicún Dolmens

Distance: *2 km/1.2 mi round-trip*
Time: *1 hr*
Elevation gain: *50 m/165 ft*
Effort: *easy*
Trailhead: *Hotel Reina Isabel (Alicún de las Torres)*

This is one of those beautiful walks that the whole family can do. Along a flat, well-kept trail you can discover some of the dolmens, the megalithic stone buildings the area is known for, as well as an impressive gorge. This little hike impresses with its mix of natural beauty and historical human elements.

Closed Castril River

Distance: *2.2 km/1.4 mi round-trip*
Time: *1 hr*
Elevation gain: *110 m/360 ft*
Effort: *easy*
Trailhead: *Castril Town Center*

With adult supervision, this is a hike the entire family can do. You'll walk along a closed river valley and cross a suspension bridge. Following, you duck through a tunnel and arrive at a waterfall. If you do this in hot weather, you can take a dip in the river to cool down before heading back. The easy route is to come back the way you came, or you could make it more of a moderate hike and climb up the Peña de Castril to circle back to town, adding a decent amount of elevation gain.

Fonelas-San Torcuato

Distance: *9.3 km/5.8 mi round-trip*
Time: *2.5 hr*
Elevation gain: *190 m/625 ft*
Effort: *moderate*
Trailhead: *Fonelas (on the A-325)*

This fairly flat out-and-back trail is great for hiking or mountain biking. It's unlikely that you would see many people on this trail, so make sure you come prepared with everything you might need. Keep in mind it's a very exposed trail with little shade. Year-round it can

1
2
3
4

be a nice hike, though in the winter months the sun can be surprisingly strong despite the cool air.

Biking

Onturi

tel. 639/782-666; www.onturi.com; €10

The trails and roads crisscrossing the geopark are inviting for exploration on two wheels. If you are traveling with your own bike, you'll want to either follow the roads or explore the trails, depending on your type of bike. Onturi is the local bike rental office. You can rent by the day and even join in guided biking excursions, depending on your fitness level and ability. If you're going it on your own, the hikes listed are also a good start for a cycling adventure.

Canoeing

Onturi

tel. 639/782-666; www.onturi.com; €8-25

Unless you're packing your own canoe, you will have to contact Onturi for a small group or privatized experience paddling across the impossible blue of the Negratín reservoir. You'll have the opportunity to make quite a few stops to enjoy the views, which you will want to take full advantage of. It might even be a good idea to pack a waterproof camera just for this activity. You'll learn about this unique enclave of the Granada Geopark while paddling along. Canoes are all double and include canoe, paddles, and life jacket.

Hot Air Balloons

Glovento Sur

Placeta Nevot, 4; tel. 958/290-316 or 695/938-123; www.gloventosur.com/zonas-de-vuelo/guadix; €175

Prepare for liftoff! Even if you have been up in a hot air balloon before, this is an experience that promises to be unforgettable. On a one-hour flight you'll soar above the great plains of Spain for views over Granada, the Alhambra, and the ever-so-close Sierra Nevada. Flights leave in the morning, typically around 8am. Certificates of flight come with the journey, as does a local breakfast you enjoy while witnessing the balloons inflating. Private flights start from €800. This same company has rights to fly in a few other destinations around Andalusia, including Antequera, Ronda, and Seville.

1: Guadix Cathedral 2: Granada Geopark, looking out over the badlands 3: hot air balloons 4: La Casa del Desierto

Astrotourism

Los Coloraos Astronomical Complex

Llano del Cocón, Polígono 3, Parcela 31, Gorafe; tel. 669/445-830; https://turismoastronomico.org; €23

Amazingly, over 10 percent of the geopark has ideal conditions for watching the night sky. Four observation domes make up Los Coloraos complex, and you're in a for a night that blends music, nature, gastronomy, and the penetrating art of deep space. The purpose of the center is to offer an interactive, inspirational look at the night sky. As of this writing, food and drink were no longer served because of the pandemic, but by the time of publication, there is real hope that this form of "dining under the stars" will make a return (plan on spending around €150 or perhaps a bit more per person if it does). See the monthly schedule on the website for details, as every month brings something new. Private and fully customized tours are available, while in the main dome there is a nice exhibition of meteorites that will get the star-struck kids and kids-at-heart excited. The astrotourism complex is a 35-minute drive (33 km/21 mi) north from Guadix.

Guided Experiences

Onturi

tel. 639/782-666; www.onturi.com

From contemplative guided walks and canoeing through serene natural parks to more adrenaline-packed activities like e-biking, four-wheeling, canyoning, and (safely) climbing steep cliff faces, the lively group of locals at Onturi have you covered. They specialize in guided experiences only in the geopark and know every square foot of the park like the back of their hand. If you want to know where to find a grove of 150-year-old American redwoods as tall as skyscrapers, the best spot for a starry night sky, or where to find the shaded routes over the badlands on a bright sunny day, this is your outfitter. They will be able to provide gear for or arrange any of these activities.

FOOD

Guadix

Bodegas Calatrava

Calle Tribuna, 12; tel. 666/403-226; 8:30am-4pm and 7:30pm-midnight Mon.-Sat.; €10

A classic Andalusian tavern situated in a charming, vaulted, and wonderfully picturesque cave-like setting, Bodegas Calatrava features a quaint and inviting interior lounge. The diverse menu offers both hearty meals and light snacks as well as a robust tapas selection to complement your drinks at a budget-friendly price, from little plates of delicate Iberian ham to spicy patatas bravos. It's a nice spot for a nibble.

★ El Refugio

Plaza de las Palomas; tel. 689/940-126; noon-4:30pm and 8pm-midnight Mon.-Sat.; €20

Abutting the plaza, reminiscent of the Place de Vosges in Paris with its long arcaded sidewalks, this little gem of a restaurant is a popular local joint. If the weather is fair, everyone makes for the sidewalk seating, enjoying the breeze with their vino tintos and cool cervezas. The menu is varied, though the tostas are particularly well done. Just the sort of thing if you're looking for a light lunch. Dinners are a more elaborate affair highlighting seafood and other favorites. Seasonal oysters on the half shell, artichoke flowers with pâté and egg, and the Segureño lamb lasagna all make for a memorable meal.

La Calahorra

Bar Hogar del Pensionista

Plaza Alamo; tel. 649/124-390; 9:30am-midnight Mon.-Fri., 11:30am-midnight Sat.-Sun.; €10

Simple, though well done, grilled meats, stews, and plenty of French fries grace the menu in this unpretentious pub. I would be surprised if you saw a single non-Spanish person in this little dive. The surprisingly delicious and plentiful mains hit the spot. The service and vibe are all very Andalusian, opening possibilities for warm conversations and new friends over a few afternoon beverages.

Labella

Carretera Aldeire, 1; tel. 958/677-241; 7am-11:30pm daily; €20

This family-run hotel and restaurant makes for a relaxing sit-down meal featuring some local homemade classics, like gratins. A filling wood-fired pizza is sometimes the thing after a busy day of exploration. There is seating on the terrace, though for the warm months you'll want to keep to the cool, rustic indoors.

ACCOMMODATIONS

Guadix

Cueva Almendro

Calle Fuente Mejías, 109; tel. 958/951-017; www.alojamiento-andalucia.es; €65

Several little cave homes have been converted into apartment rentals in the Barrio de Cuevas, each of them pretty similar. You can expect a clean bed in a surprisingly cozy cave. Some have a minimum-stay requirement of two nights or longer. These are independent rentals without breakfast service or other food options, though you will have kitchen access to make your own cave person meals. If you're interested in spending a couple of nights in a cave house, start with Cueva Almendro, as they do have limited English and an accessible website. Find other caves using the usual suspects (Booking.com, Expedia, Google, etc.). Most lack websites and you will likely have to navigate a bit in Spanish to confirm your booking. Parking here is all streetside.

YIT Abentofail

Calle Abentofail, 8; tel. 958/669-281; www.hotelabentofail.com; €80

Just a two-minute walk from the Plaza la Constitución central square in old Guadix, this is a swanky local hotel with an on-site bar and restaurant as well as a rooftop balcony. This is about as nice as it gets in Guadix, as the other local hotels, though often less expensive, show their age. Reception is friendly and knowledgeable and the rooms are clean, if not a touch spartan, with modern facilities. If you are looking for an easy, central location in Guadix, it is hard to fault anything on offer here.

★ La Casa del Desierto

Camino de la Meseta; tel. 665/499-211 or 654/300-419; www.thehouseinthedesert.com; €275

Just when you think the accommodations around Andalusia are incredible, something comes along and ups the ante. This purpose-built 20-sq-m (215-sq-ft) house featuring floor-to-ceiling thermally insulated windows for walls is something to behold amid the geopark's arid desert landscape. Captured and filtered rainwater, an ecofriendly septic system, and a large rooftop solar panel array fully power this completely off-grid one-room private desert retreat. A large plush bed and all the amenities of home kit out what is sure to be a cinematic stay of your Andalusian adventure. You might feel like you're one of the stars speckling the impossibly starry night.

La Calahorra

Hospederia de Zenete

Carretera de la Ragua, 1; tel. 958/677-192; www.hospederiadelzenete.com; €60

Located on the east side of town on the main road connecting with the A-92 freeway, this is a surprising little hotel. Expect warm, friendly service and homey Spanish-style rooms complete with four-poster beds, traditional red tile flooring set against bright mustard walls, and a touch of flowery grandma decor. A large dining hall is sometimes used for gatherings, which can make for a livelier atmosphere than you might wish. This is a good address to keep in your back pocket for that spontaneous road trip through this part of Andalusia. You can almost be guaranteed a room or a comfortable home base to explore the surrounding geopark.

INFORMATION AND SERVICES

Granada Geopark

www.geoparquedegranada.com

The official website for the park is littered with some fantastic information and free downloadable PDFs, including local guides for the towns in the park as well as activities and ideas for the younger set.

Guadix

Tourist Office

Plaza de Catedral; tel. 958/662-804; https://guadix.es/servicios-turisticos; 10am-2pm and 5pm-8:30pm daily

Blue and yellow trains function during office hours, taking visitors around the city to historic points of interest. Come here to arrange a tour of the Alcazaba (last Fri. of every month) and catch the train to the cave houses. The Guadix tourist office is the central office for the entire Granada Geopark and the surrounding towns, including La Calahorra.

GETTING THERE AND AROUND

You'll need a rental car to easily navigate the Granada Geopark. The geopark is a short drive east on the A-92 from Granada (45 min; 54 km/34 mi), which takes you straight to Guadix. La Calahorra is just south of Guadix (20 min; 20 km/14 mi). Once in the park, you'll likely find yourself navigating by car between points of interest, though once you arrive to any town, you'll park and explore on foot.

Sierra Nevada National Park

Just a short, winding 45-minute drive from the historic city of Granada thrusts you into the peaks of the Sierra Nevada mountain range. Nestled within the province of Andalusia, this pristine wilderness is a snowcapped jewel of the Iberian Peninsula. The rugged mountain terrain, serene alpine meadows, and ancient forests serve as a refuge for a diverse range of flora and fauna.

Towering over the region, the Sierra Nevada mountain range is much more than a stunning natural backdrop; it is also a playground for outdoor enthusiasts, from hikers and skiers to wildlife enthusiasts and stargazers. With a mix of trails and, in the winter, Europe's southernmost ski slopes, this is an active traveler's paradise. Skiers and snowboarders will want to take advantage of the ski season, which usually runs from late November into May, while hiking, biking, and more can be done year-round.

However, what truly sets the Sierra Nevada apart is its profound serenity—an attribute that rivals its remarkable natural beauty. Nestled within the Sierra Nevada National Park, a hidden gem cherished by many international travelers, you'll discover an extensive landscape spanning an impressive 85,883 hectares (212,222 acres), making it the largest national park in Spain. Adding to its allure, an additional 89,966 hectares (222,310 acres) are designated as natural parks, creating an expansive, carefully preserved sanctuary totaling 175,849 hectares (434,532 acres).

It's worth noting that UNESCO has recognized nearly the entire region as a biosphere reserve, attesting to the Sierra Nevada's extraordinary ecological significance. The mountain peaks themselves are equally impressive. Mulhacén reigns as the tallest at 3,479 m (11,414 ft), earning its distinction as mainland Spain's loftiest peak. Veleta and Alcazaba proudly stand alongside, at 3,396 m (11,141 ft) and 3,336 m (10,944 ft), respectively.

During the winter season, these lofty heights receive a generous blanket of snow, a captivating sight that lasts from November to May. In fact, the northern slopes of Veleta house the Sierra Nevada ski station—a bustling hub that hosted the prestigious Alpine World Ski Championships in 1996. Yet, despite the region's fame, it's astonishing that you can embark on a day of mountain exploration and scarcely encounter another soul. This stands as a testament to the unspoiled beauty and tranquil allure that epitomize this extraordinary corner of Spain.

PLANNING YOUR TIME

The experience you might have in the national park depends largely on what time of year you visit. Late spring through fall is ideal for hiking and trekking, while winter snows are ideal for snow sports. As you ascend from Granada, the landscape undergoes a captivating transformation. Lush river valleys and dense pine forests gradually give way to rugged mountains, offering breathtaking vistas that seem to stretch endlessly. On the clearest of days, your gaze can extend across the glistening Mediterranean expanse, reaching all the way to the shores of Morocco.

The overwhelming majority of travelers visit the Sierra Nevada National Park on a day trip from Granada, choosing one area of the park to explore, whether that's a hiking trail, a day of skiing on the slopes, or just one mountain village to discover. Nearly everything covered here is less than an hour of driving from Granada, making a day trip exploration feasible. Many Europeans book ski holidays and summer mountain getaways for a week or more at a time, which can make sense for lovers of the outdoors and those with more time. If you can spend a night or two in the mountains, whether at the ski resort or in the more idyllic spots like in Las Alpujarras, you'll be rewarded with crisp mountain nights and, on clear nights, starry nights that stretch out to infinity, to say nothing of the ability to dig a little more into the gastronomic delights of the region.

GATEWAY TOWNS

Pradollano

The town of Pradollano is the main hub for hotels, restaurants, and activities in this region. The feel is very much that of a ski town you might find in the Alps or tucked in the folds of the Rockies. After a good snow, the town transforms into the most vibrant play park in all of Spain. Summers are quieter with some of the hotels and restaurants shuttered for the off season. There are several nice hikes from town, with a few using the ski lift (there are usually a few ski lifts operational June-Sept.).

SIGHTS

Hoya de Pedraza Botanical Garden

Calle Sierra Nevada, km 27; tel. 697/958-939; www.andalucia.org/en/monachil-sierra-nevada-leisure-parks-hoya-de-pedraza-botanical-gardens; 9am-2:30pm Tues.-Sun. Jan.-Nov.; free

As you climb into the Sierras, if you're a garden or plant lover, you will want to make a stop at the jardín botánico. Located just a few minutes from Pradollano on the A-395, this little roadside attraction is full of native plants and others in danger of extinction. Though plants are labeled with their Spanish and Latin names, you won't find too much in the way of English signage. Do use your phone to translate as needed, as the info is pretty good, particularly welcome if you are traveling with kids and want them to interact or learn a thing or two. Keep an eye out for pines, junipers, roses, and a few rare, unique species of mountain flora. And enjoy the top-notch views!

★ HIKING

Laguna de las Yeguas

Distance: *6 km/4 mi round-trip*
Time: *2 hr*
Elevation gain: *81 m/266 ft*
Effort: *easy*
Trailhead: *ski station*

From Granada, follow the A-395 to the Sierra Nevada ski station (45 min; 39 km/25 mi). The trailhead is at the ski station. This is a very easy uphill that makes use of the ski lifts when they are open, usually from late June-August. Take the cable car and chair lift to the top. Give yourself a pat on the back. You're getting a taste of the Sierra Nevada mountains

Sierra Nevada National Park

without having to trek up thousands of meters. This circular hike takes you on a tour of the mountain peak before heading back down via the chair lift.

Los Cahorros de Monachil

Distance: *8 km/5 mi round-trip*
Time: *3 hr*
Elevation gain: *346 m/1,135 ft*
Effort: *easy-moderate*
Trailhead: *behind Restaurante El Puntarron*

This hike is great for the entire family. You'll need to drive to Monachil from Granada (10 min; 14 km/9 mi). This is a straightforward, quick drive. Take the A-395 and get off at the Monachil exit. Follow signs into town. You'll find the trailhead at the back of the Restaurante El Puntarron. The valleys of this loop trail are full of blooming wildflowers and fruit trees in the spring, making it the ideal time to hike. The canyon and suspension bridges at the first or last mile of the loop (depending on which direction you go) are photogenic year-round and can make a nice short family hike of a little over a mile (1.6 km). This is easy, though some of the heights might put some people off, while others may have difficulty ducking under some of the lower rock formations.

Mount Veleta

Distance: *13 km/8 mi round-trip*
Time: *5 hr*
Elevation gain: *866 m/2,841 ft*
Effort: *moderate-difficult*
Trailhead: *Hoya de la Mora*

Take the A-395 from Granada to the town of Hoya de la Mora (45 min; 44 km/27 mi), where you'll find this demanding, though beautiful, hike. The trailhead is well marked in Hoya de la Mora and will take you on a there-and-back trail to the peak of Mount Veleta, mainland Spain's third-highest mountain peak at 3,396 m (11,141 ft). The distinct wedge-like peak is easily visible from Granada on a clear day. Whether you're a peakbagger or just a sucker for a good view, on a clear day you'll be able to see out over the Sierra Nevada and the plains of Spain below. This particular trail is popular with locals and cyclists, so avoid the weekends for fewer crowds. The hike will take you by the 18th-century sanctuary of the Virgen de la Nieves. There are few watering holes, and temperatures here are cool, if not cold, year-round, with snow and ice conditions in winter. It's a trail for confident, seasoned hikers used to high mountain conditions in the winter, making this a difficult hike for most. Outside the winter months, the occasional high winds and strong sun can make the hike seem a touch more difficult than its moderate rating would suggest.

SKIING AND SNOW SPORTS

Sierra Nevada Ticket Center

Pradollano Center; https://sierranevada.es; from €44

With over 100 km (60 mi) of runs, there is a lot for the average skier or snowboarder, though do keep in mind that most runs are reds and blues. Different ski pass formulas are available. Day passes are usually €44, though during peak travel times, like the winter holidays around Christmas, New Year, and the Epiphany (Three Kings Day), prices go up substantially. Passes for 10 days (€485) or longer are available online. All other passes are only available to purchase in person at the ski station. There are two ticket offices, one in Pradollano (8am-4:30pm daily) and one at the Los Peñones parking lot (8:30am-3pm Fri.-Sat., and only if the Virgen de las Nieves chair lift is open).

Mirlo Blanco Fun Park

Pradollano, at the end of the slope El Rio; tel. 958/708-090; 10am-4:30pm daily; €5

Easily accessible from the middle of Pradollano, the Fuente del Mirlo Blanco fun park takes center stage as a haven for family-friendly snowy escapades. This delightful amusement park boasts an array of exciting attractions. For the young ones and those young at heart, there's a selection of thrilling slides and sled runs that promise endless fun. However, the true star of the show

Call of the Wild: The Fauna and Flora of the Sierra Nevada

Nestled in southern Spain, the Sierra Nevada mountain range invites you to delve into its natural beauty. This pristine wilderness is home to a diverse range of flora and fauna that has evolved over centuries.

The rugged terrain of the Sierra Nevada nurtures a variety of plant life, from alpine species to Mediterranean blooms. The ancient Spanish fir forests and vibrant wildflower meadows are highlights of the landscape. The scent of pine trees permeates the air, offering a unique sensory experience.

ibex

The Sierra Nevada provides habitat for a variety of wildlife. Ibexes, Iberian lynxes, and golden eagles are among the remarkable species that call this region home. The melodies of birds, like the western Bonelli's warbler, add to the natural soundtrack of the area.

Recognized for its ecological importance, the Sierra Nevada holds UNESCO Biosphere Reserve status and is designated as a national and natural park. Responsible exploration is encouraged through well-marked hiking trails, preserving the delicate balance of this pristine environment. For those seeking a connection with nature, the Sierra Nevada offers an opportunity to discover its natural beauty and engage with a remarkable array of flora and fauna.

is the Russian Sled, a modern roller coaster specially designed to deliver a unique snow-filled adventure. As you embark on this exhilarating ride, you'll zip through the snowy terrain, navigating a series of purpose-built rails featuring twists, turns, straightaways, and banked curves. It's an absolute must-try experience for the entire family. That said, at €5 per activity, per person, the cost does add up quickly.

Ski and Snowboard Rentals

Blanca Nieve

Local 10, Telecabina Borreguiles; tel. 653/040-560; www.blancanieve.net; €54

Centrally located in Pradollano, Blanca Nieve is where you need to head if you've not packed your gear. You'll find everything you need to get kitted out for a day on the slopes. We're talking not only your skis or snowboards, boots and bindings, but also poles, jackets, pants, gloves, helmets, and even goggles. You could just rent skis and poles for the day (€20), but if you're reading this guide, it's likely that you might be thinking of more of a last-minute addition to your time in Andalusia rather than a full-on ski holiday. It's good to know that the people at Blanca Nieve have you covered. Do hop on their website and book online at least a day or two before you plan on hitting the slopes. It's the best way to make sure you'll have your gear waiting for you on arrival.

FOOD

Pizzeria Titto Luigi II

Calle de la Virgen de las Nieves; 12:30pm-4:30pm and 7:30pm-12:30am daily; €15

What is it about mountain sports that makes you crave pizza? There are quite a number of pizza joints in town, but this answers the question better than the others. It's an easy place to get a wood-fired pizza quickly after a big day on the slopes. The seating, both indoor and out, is unremarkable, so go elsewhere if you want big views over the mountains.

Wild Camping in the Sierra Nevada National Park

If you packed your tent and sleeping sacks and were set on camping as part of your experience through Andalusia, you are in for a treat. The colorful play of light during sunrise and sunset and some brilliant starry nights await. For reaching deep into the park, wild camping is necessary and allowed—and also free of charge—though with some rules and regulations to follow. Here are some things to keep in mind:

wild camping

- Camping is not allowed within 500 m (1,640 ft) of a refuge or mountain road. This is 0.5 km (0.3 mi) away from paved roads.
- Tents can only be set up an hour before sunset and have to be dismantled and packed an hour after sunrise.
- Wild camping in winter is only allowed at elevations over 1,600 m (5,250 ft); in the summer months the rule is above the treeline, which is often more like 2,000 m (6,560 ft).
- You can't camp on private property without the consent of the owners.
- You must notify the Sierra Nevada National Park administrative office in writing (pn.snevada.cam@juntadeandalucia.es), including your name and passport number, how many people are traveling with you, the number of tents, and intended locations for camping.

Besides wild camping, there are campsites in some of the smaller towns that are European in style and can have swimming pools, bars, and cafés, as well as laundry facilities, not to mention cabins and apartments for rent. For a car and tent, expect to pay €15-30, depending on demand.

Terraza Tia Maria

Plaza Andalucía; tel. 958/481-193; 9am-7pm daily; €20

A popular, busy après-ski spot. Service can get a bit overwhelmed during the crush, but if you accept it for what it is, it's one of the best value spots for a bit to eat and drink. Portions are large. The chicken fingers are known locally, mostly for the copious quantity overfilling your plate. Enjoy the views over the mountains and people making their way down while you sip on your beer.

The Sun Deck (El Lodge)

Calle Maribel, 8; tel. 958/480-600; 1pm-4pm daily; €30

The only ski-in/ski-out restaurant offers a varied menu that includes everything from nachos with guac to spaghetti Bolognese, cozy homemade soups, and truffled cheese raclette. It's an easy place to like for lunch on an active day for a swift in-and-out to get back to the slopes, though you do pay for the convenience. You can stay warm between runs with faux-fur throws and the built-in fireplaces. There is even a boot-heating service so you can hang a little longer and maybe enjoy a second cocktail.

ACCOMMODATIONS

Hostal Yeti

Calle de la Fuente del Tesoro, 2; tel. 958/650-758; €60

Within a whisper of the entrances to the slopes of the Sierra Nevada you'll find this warm, comfy hostel with friendly service and a copious buffet breakfast. It's a great value considering the price and location. To make the most of the buffet breakfast, the early bird does get the worm—other travelers tend to swoop in. There is free onsite parking, though it is limited. There is also an on-site equipment rental for gear if needed. Water pressure is a bit weak in the showers, though the water is hot. Hostal Yeti is a popular spot for budget travelers that tends to fill up quickly. Reserve well ahead of time.

Meliá Sierra Nevada

Plaza Pradollano; tel. 912/764-747; www.melia.com/en/hotels/spain/sierra-nevada/melia-sierra-nevada; €250

A chic four-star choice for alpine-style lodgings comes complete with a roaring fire giving a warm welcome in the main hall. It's centrally located right in the middle of Pradollano, so you'll be within walking distance of the bars, restaurants, and different après-ski options throughout town. That said, with the on-site bars, restaurants, and wellness spa, after a day on the slopes you might not leave the property.

El Lodge Ski & Spa

Calle Maribel, 8; tel. 958/480-600; www.ellodge.com; €550

Boasting the only ski-in/ski-out privileged property in town, this is a true five-star getaway that includes a heated indoor/outdoor pool, fitness center, kids' club, four on-site restaurants and bars, and a selection of curated experiences and packages for romantic couples, families, and digital nomads. If you have the budget and are looking for a weeklong getaway, you couldn't do much better than El Lodge. The property has everything you would expect at this level for a mountain retreat. Most of us will have to make do with lunch on the Sun Deck restaurant after a morning of slaloming.

INFORMATION AND SERVICES

Sierra Nevada National Park Administrative Center

Carretera Antigua de Sierra Nevada, km 7, Pinos Genil; tel. 958/026-300 or 958/026-310 (call only, not open to the public); pn.snevada.cam@juntadeandalucia.es

If you are planning on camping in the national park or would like guidance for hiking in the upper elevations, contact the park administration. For camping, it is required to inform them in writing. Send an email including your name and passport number, how many people are traveling with you, the number of tents, and intended locations for camping.

GETTING THERE AND AROUND

If you are coming into the Sierra Nevada, a rental car is almost a necessity. In Andalusia, the best car rentals are going to be found in Málaga, which is a short two-hour drive from the Sierras. See the Málaga chapter for details.

Car

From Granada, it is a straightforward climb into the mountains following the A-395 as it twists and turns east and then southeast from the city. The drive to Pradollano should take about 45 minutes (37 km/23 mi). Just follow the signs.

Parking

Plaza de Andalusia; 24/7; from €15

If you are coming for a day trip or your accommodation does not have parking available, this is the most practical place to park. It is covered, guarded, and has 24/7 access.

Bus

From the Granada bus station, during ski season a bus runs up to the ski station, operated by Autocares Tocina (1 hr; 3 daily Mon.-Fri. starting at 8am, and 4 daily Sat.-Sun. beginning at 9am; €9 round-trip). The bus makes one stop in downtown Granada at the Palacio de Congresos (Paseo del Violón, Zaidín), making this the ideal spot to catch the bus.

Las Alpujarras

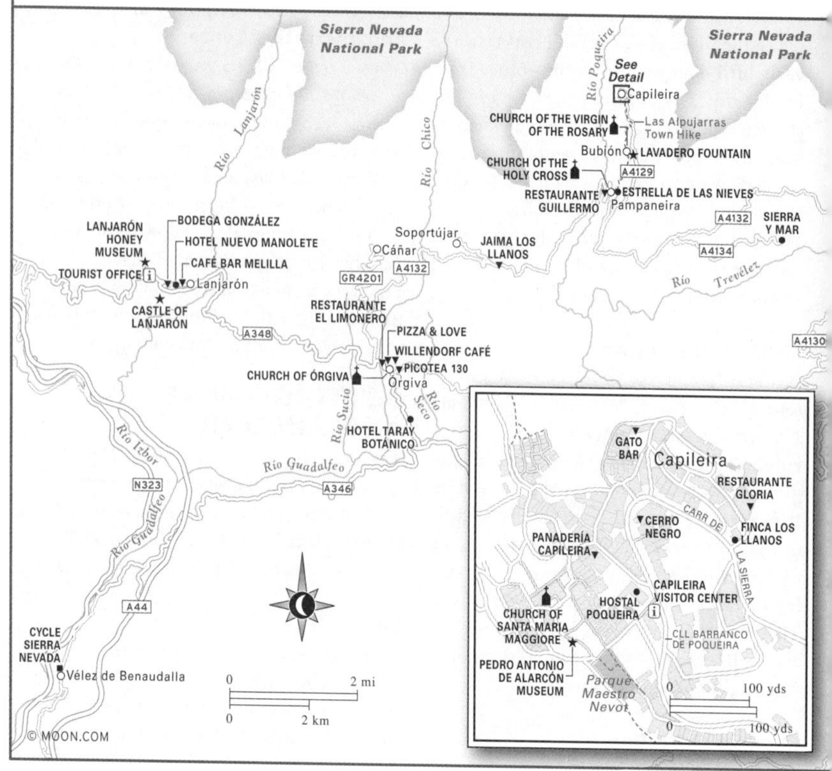

Las Alpujarras

Beyond the biodiversity and activities of Sierra Nevada National Park, you will also find centuries-old traditions and charming villages dotting the landscape, another texture to explore in your time here. The whitewashed villages of Las Alpujarras make for a wonderful mountain getaway, with charming towns full of cafés and tapas bars. A couple of the gateway towns at the base of the mountains are a fine introduction to the local life and culture for those interested in a culturally immersive experience.

ORIENTATION

Two towns, **Órgiva** and **Lanjarón,** connect with the road leading to the mountainous Las Alpujarras region outside of Granada. Órgiva is a busy crossroads town connecting with many villages from the region, while Lanjarón is well known for its thermal spring waters. As you climb into the mountains, you'll discover three villages—**Pampaneira, Bubión,** and **Capileira**—that are the most quintessential villages of Las Alpujarras. They offer incredible mountain and valley views, and each has a central main square with a church and a few restaurants and tapas bars to choose from.

The Spanish Civil War: Granada and Las Alpujarras

During the Spanish Civil War (1936-1939) leading up to World War II, Granada and the neighboring region of Las Alpujarras played significant, perhaps surprising, roles in the conflict.

GRANADA

Granada, renowned for its stunning Alhambra palace and rich Moorish history, was a critical battleground during the Civil War. The city itself was divided between Republican (antifascist) and Nationalist (pro-Franco) sympathizers, leading to intense urban warfare.

The Alhambra, an iconic symbol of Spain's heritage, was used as a military fortress first by the Republicans. After intense fighting, pro-Franco Nationalists continued using the fortress as a base for local operations. The walls of the Alhambra still bear the scars of the conflict. When you're visiting the Alhambra, you can learn about the history of the Civil War through guided tours and occasional exhibitions.

LAS ALPUJARRAS

Las Alpujarras, just a short drive from Granada, was a hotbed of Republican, antifascist, and anti-Franco regime resistance during the Civil War. The area became a haven for leftist militias and anarchist groups who sought refuge in its rugged terrain. Las Alpujarras witnessed intense guerrilla warfare and was a stronghold for these hardy Republicans. The small towns and villages of the region, such as Órgiva and Lanjarón, were key centers of liberal Republican activity.

The memory of the Civil War still lingers in Las Alpujarras, with many locals preserving stories of the conflict passed down through generations. Travelers exploring this region can visit small museums and historical sites that offer insights into the wartime experiences of the people who lived here. Today's natural beauty of Las Alpujarras, with its terraced hillsides and charming villages, provides a striking contrast to the war-torn history of the area.

Though they are all similar in look, design, and offerings, they each do have their own feel. Pampaneira feels a bit more local while Bubión almost feels like it's more popular with Spanish and continental European travelers. By contrast, Anglophones tend to gravitate to the highest village of Capileira, where some of the best hiking trailheads are located.

LANJARÓN

The warm, clean smell of eucalyptus and the buzz of cicadas welcome you to one of Spain's great spa towns. From Granada, you'll enter from the top of town on a main thoroughfare that continues to Órgiva and the rest of Las Alpujarras. Lanjarón tumbles downhill into a series of shops, markets, small hotels, and little boutique shops surrounded by eucalyptus and evergreens. At the lookout point, look for a large FT-44 Galileo cannon. It was last used during the Spanish Civil War, which wasn't all that long ago. As relaxing as this town is, historically it was one of a series of rebel towns that experienced heavy guerrilla warfare as they resisted the fascists that brought Franco to power in the years leading up to World War II.

Like much of Las Alpujarras, Lanjarón is a town where you'll want to get out and enjoy nature. Luckily there are a few great trails, not to mention the thermal spring waters.

Sights

Castle of Lanjarón (Castillo de Lanjarón)

24/7; free

A short walk through the Lanjarón forest brings you to the foot of the Castle of Lanjarón (Castillo de Lanjarón). There is no information available at the castle itself. The original construction dates from the Nasrid dynasty, and it fell with the rest of the area surrounding

Granada to the Christian monarchs, Isabella and Ferdinand, in 1492. Though the castle did have renovations at some time following the Reconquista, today it is little more than an unmarked ruin, though with fantastic views, and it is free to walk around. This is a good marker for a short 30-minute hike from the town.

Lanjarón Honey Museum (Museo de la Miel Lanjarón)

Just north of the Balneario de Lanjarón hotel; tel. 958/770-472; www.apicultoresgranada.com; 10am-2pm Tues.-Sun.; free

You would be forgiven for spending your gastronomic energy on the jamón, tapas, wine, and olive oil Andalusia is renowned for worldwide. That said, the natural floral richness of the Sierra Nevada National Park imparts unique characteristics to the honey produced in this region. It's less a museum than a shop. Jars of single appellation sweet golden deliciousness start around €5. This is one of the more tasty, unique souvenirs to consider leaving room for in your check-in luggage.

Thermal Spas

Relais Termal

Avenida de Madrid, 2; tel. 958/770-452 or 902/104-841; www.balneariodelanjaron.es/relais-termal; from €30

Located in the Balneario de Lanjarón hotel, this high-end thermal spa has much to offer for those looking to experience the pure mountain water. The fault that forms one of the borders of the Sierra Nevada mountains runs through Lanjarón, providing a path for ancient rainwater to filter to the surface. This is the best known local spa with services centered around this mineral-rich spring water. Amazing to think they've been doing this since 1760! A unique way to plunge into the local culture of Las Alpujarras.

Hiking and Biking

Well-marked trails leave right from Lanjarón. Here are a couple of popular ones you could do by foot or on two wheels. There are quite a few more, some of which connect through the mountains to other towns.

Lanjarón Castle (Castillo de Lanjarón)

Distance: *4.5 km/2.8 mi round-trip*
Time: *1.5 hr*
Elevation gain: *238 m/780 ft*
Effort: *moderate*
Trailhead: *tourist office*

Take the trailhead near the tourist office and adjacent parking lot. Located 30 minutes west of Lanjarón, the Castle of Lanjarón is unmissable, sitting atop a tall hill surrounded by steep stone walls. It makes for a great landmark to discover on this loop trail. The hike takes a little over 1.5 hours to complete, making it a good option for nearly everyone.

Forest Trail

Distance: *14.5 km/8.9 mi round-trip*
Time: *6 hr*
Elevation gain: *978 m/3,208 ft*
Effort: *strenuous*
Trailhead: *behind the Lanjarón Honey Museum*

You'll find this trailhead tucked behind the Lanjarón Honey Museum. There are two options, one for hikers and one for mountain bikers. The beginning of the trail is a steep uphill until you reach the Casa Forestal de Tello, which takes you along the left bank of the river valley. Once you cross the bridge, there is about 2 km (1.2 mi) of a narrow cliff-side path on the Cerecillo-Mesquerina trail, which offers fantastic views, but if there is anyone with a fear of heights, watch out! There are a couple of places along the way to fill up water bottles with fresh mountain water.

Festivals

Festival of John the Baptist (Noche de San Juan)

Midsummer

In little Lanjarón, the major festivals and holidays of Spain are celebrated, as elsewhere. If you are here in the summer, see if you can be there on the day of John the Baptist, nicknamed the Water and Ham Festival (Fiestas

Hiking and Trekking in Las Alpujarras

trekker walking along Poqueira Gorge from Capileira

Las Alpujarras is a fantastic region for intense multiday treks. More than 50 villages are connected by a well-trodden and well-kept trail system, and you can easily select hikes of different difficulty levels, depending on fitness and mobility. Pack appropriately for the weather. In winter, cold winds and snow are probable at higher elevations, while year-round, the sun can be sneakily strong.

Before starting out on a longer hike, stop at the nearest **tourist office** and ask about trail conditions. You'll likely have to work on your Spanish because most of the tourist offices are staffed by non-Anglophones. You should also be able to pick up current hiking maps. Before departure, order the **Editorial Piolet** (www.editorialpiolet.com) ***Las Alpujarras* map,** published in a double-sided, multilingual, 1:25,000 format on waterproof paper. This map lists the majority of the better trails in the region, with marked elevations as well as roads, towns, rivers, and lakes.

For any hiking, it's a good rule of thumb to have a **GPS** device or your phone enabled and with an extra battery pack for charging. Signposting isn't always clear or available, though cellular service is available throughout the region.

Do be wary of **ticks** as they can be found throughout the countryside, though the biggest dangers will likely be the weather and the **sun.** Stay hydrated and remember the three S's: sunscreen, sunglasses, and your silly sun hat.

del Agua y del Jamón). The festival involves more Serrano ham than you can shake a leg at, to say nothing of the fun water fights that break out between friends and kids, making this a lighthearted affair with lots of laughs and smiles. Just bring a dry pair of clothes.

Food and Accommodations

Café Bar Melilla

Calle Melilla, 5; tel. 958/770-494; 8am-12:30am Thurs.-Tues.; €3

A favorite with the locals, Café Bar Melilla never seems to disappoint. Though you can find the usual tapas menu throughout the day, make a beeline for the most traditional and delicious of Spanish breakfast treats: churros and hot chocolate. The churros here are an inexpensive, exquisite delight. Dip them in thick, bittersweet hot chocolate for the full Spanish experience. The tostadas and Serrano ham and cheese sandwiches are another win if you're not in the mood for churros con chocolate.

Bodega González

Avenida de Las Alpujarras, 15; tel. 958/770-494; 7am-midnight Tues.-Thurs., noon-midnight Fri.-Sun.; €8

As at many local bars in Granada, there is good value to be had with tapas and drinks. The menu features a wide variety of meats, cheeses, and roast lamb, though not many choices for vegans and vegetarians. It's the sort of place where you can pull up a seat on the patio, enjoy a drink, and watch small-town life unfold.

Hotel Nuevo Manolete

Calle San Sebastián, 3; tel. 958/770-773; www.spainhotels.top/hotel-nuevo-manolete; €50

This centrally located, no-frills hotel has comfy beds, heating and air-conditioning, and available parking in the garage (€5), which makes it an ideal spot for a quick overnight.

Balneario de Lanjarón

Avenida de Madrid, 2; tel. 958/770-452; www.balneariodelanjaron.es; €70

Balneario de Lanjarón is just off the A-348, the main road that weaves through town. The rooms are comfortable and clean enough, and the staff are generally affable, but make no mistake—you are coming here less for the hotel than for the attached thermal springs (Relais Termal).

Information and Services

Tourist Office

Avenida de Madrid, 3; tel. 958/770-462; www.lanjaron.es and www.turismo.lanjaron.es; 10am-2pm and 4:30pm-8:30pm Mon.-Sat., 10am-2pm Sun.

Hikers and cyclists will want to make sure to pass by the office for updated maps of Lanjarón and Las Alpujarras. Maps are generally free. Exhibitions featuring local artisans, history, and culture are occasionally on offer in the exhibition room upstairs.

Getting There and Around

Lanjarón is easily accessible by car from Granada (45 min; 50 km/31 mi). Follow the A-44 south in the direction of Motril. Take the A-348 exit toward Lanjarón and you'll find the town just a few minutes away. Once there, park the car and explore on foot.

Parking

Avenida de Madrid, next to the tourist office; 24/7; free

Perhaps more of a field than a parking lot, still it is a free, safe, central place to park your car whether you're exploring for the day or overnighting.

ÓRGIVA

Known locally as the "Capital of Las Alpujarras," this is the largest city in the region. It sits at a crossroads of the region. Though not perhaps the most picturesque town in this part of Spain, it can be the most practical. You'll find lots of options for restaurants and hotels as well as other daily needs, such as banks, pharmacies, grocery stores, and other essentials. A weekly outdoor municipal market and the Órgiva church are on the main town plaza.

Sights

Church of Órgiva (Parroquia de Nuestra Señora de la Expectación)

Plaza Garcia Moreno, 10; tel. 958/785-210; hours vary; free

When seen from afar, the great ochre towers of Parroquia de Nuestra Señora de la Expectación jut out from the whitewashed village of Órgiva, a striking contrast beneath the Andalusian sun. This local parish, like a few others dotting the region, has a posted schedule for mass, but otherwise, visiting the interior of the church, with its classic Mudejar styling and ornate Baroque altarpiece, depends on the whim of the pastor.

Festivals

Day of the Lord (El Día del Señor)

Friday two weeks before Good Friday

Besides Holy Week and the other traditional holidays, El Día del Señor is one of the more interesting religious processions in Las Alpujarras. On Thursday, the statue of Our Lord of the Expiration is taken from the Órgiva church and paraded around town. This takes place at nightfall and is accompanied by the boom of some loud firecrackers. On Friday at 6pm, another procession begins from the church, this time with a full fireworks display that American travelers would easily associate with the Fourth of July. Brass bands provide the soundtrack for this all-evening festival.

Órgiva Festival

Last weekend of September

This five-day feria (fair) was historically a traveling animal market where locals inspected, bought, and traded livestock. Even today there is still a horse sale where you can see buyers and sellers plying their trade, bartering, and wheeling and dealing. In the evenings, you can partake of a humongous paella for free that is meant for all comers to the festival. Another day is dedicated to making migas with an open fire. Expect lots of beer and wine and general revelry, with music and dancing. The locals use it as an excuse to get dressed to the nines.

Shopping

Outdoor Market (Thursday)

Calle Huerta Palencia, 6; early morning-late afternoon Thurs.; free

One of the joys of exploring the smaller villages and towns of Andalusia is participating in local life. In Órgiva on Thursdays, nearly everyone descends on the local market to pick up their produce for the week, along with some other odds and ends. In addition to fresh fruits and legumes, you'll find colorful herbs, pungent spices, and locally produced olive oil and honey alongside rows of artisans and clothes sellers. For rubbing elbows with locals, it doesn't get much more local than this popular weekly market.

Food

Willendorf Café

Calle Estación, 8; 6:30am-midnight Mon.-Sat.; €5

Friendly service paired with creamy cappuccinos and frothy espressos makes for a great start to breakfast. Go for the simple traditional Spanish tostadas and tuck into one of the cozy couches for a lazy breakfast to kick off your day.

Picotea 130

Calle Prof. Lora Tamayo, 130; tel. 643/545-322; 8am-12:30am Thurs.-Tues.; €15

A more modern bar with a relaxed atmosphere and good rations, this is one of the few cafés or bars in the region where you might want to skip tapas and head straight into some of the main dishes on offer, like paella, stews, and fried octopus. Familiar desserts like carrot cake and cheesecake pair well with a pick-me-up coffee.

Pizza & Love

Calle Libertad, 36; tel. 605/516-546; 7pm-11pm Thurs.-Tues.; €15

Down a quiet alleyway, this authentic pizzeria serves up wood-fired pizzas and delish local tapas, as well as the occasional cocktail or cold beer. Sometimes after a long road trip or hike, a slice of pie is what the doctor ordered. Pizza & Love has lots of great options, particularly if you are vegan, vegetarian, or gluten intolerant! A popular local favorite—too bad it's dinner only.

Restaurante El Limonero

Avenida González Robles, 3; tel. 958/998-260; https://ellimonerodelaalpujarra.com; 8am-5pm and 8pm-11pm Tues.-Sat., 8am-5pm Sun.; €15

A very popular spot with Argentinian flair. The nightly live music is great for some and not for others. Lunches are typically a quieter affair in this family-run restaurant, and you have to love their attention to product and value. As in other popular eateries of this size, if you happen across a large group, it can make the whole experience hectic. If it doesn't look too busy, hop in for one of the more pleasant sit-down dining experiences in town. Though vegetarian options are available, this is a better address for those who appreciate a well-prepared Argentinian steak or Iberian ham.

Accommodations

Ananda's Mundo

Calle Cristo de la Expiración, 4; tel. 681/921-825; http://orgivarooms.com; €40

In the region, this is one of the better budget finds around for solo travelers. It's well located right in the middle of town within easy walking distance of the different bars, cafés, and restaurants. The friendly staff at Ananda's Mundo offer five guest rooms in a charming building with high ceilings and spectacular rooftop views. Single bedrooms are the best value, though they have shared bathrooms. Couples should opt for the more spacious double rooms with attached private living rooms.

★ Hotel Taray Botánico

A-358, km 18; tel. 681/900-115 or 958/784-525; €90

A rustic, rural gem on the outskirts of town toward the Gaudalfeo River, Hotel Taray Botánico is popular with European hikers and rightly so. It's hard to believe that the on-site gardens matured in just over a decade; such is the natural power of this almost-subtropical microclimate, unlike villages farther up in the mountains. This hotel takes full advantage of that climate, making for a wonderful getaway. Meals served in the on-site restaurant nearly always feature fresh veggies and fruits from the gardens. The bungalow-style bedrooms angling out from the main hotel, with their exposed beams and terracotta floors, make for a charming, comfy stay.

Information and Services

Oficina de Turismo de Órgiva

Plaza de la Alpujarra; tel. 958/784-266; www.ayutamintodeorgiva.es; 9am-5pm Fri.-Wed., 9am-noon Thurs.

Staffed by locals that know the region, this tourism office provides maps, guides, and other materials to make your stay in the Alpujarras enjoyable. Of the tourist offices, this seems to be the only one in the region with local hiking materials and maps.

Getting There and Around

From Lanjarón (20 min; 10 km/6 mi) continue east down the A-348 to arrive in Órgiva. The town is big enough that it is a bit of a public transportation hub, though it's likely you'll be in a rental car if you're exploring this region. Alsa (www.alsa.com) runs regular service connecting Lanjarón to Órgiva on the Berja line (20 min; 9 daily; €1.50), with some buses direct and others making one stop in Barreras. On arrival, you'll be walking around, as in other towns. Alsa also operates direct buses from Granada (2 hr; 8 daily; €5), making this a good connection for exploring the region via public transport.

Parking

Calle Huerta Palencia, 6; 24/7, except closed Wed. 3pm-Thurs. 6pm for local market; free

Órgiva's central parking puts you in a secure spot for free right in the middle of town. Note: It is closed to parking from late afternoon on Wednesday until late Thursday, when the parking lot is used for the weekly market.

PAMPANEIRA

The town of Pampaneira feels almost like a working town more than a mountain getaway. You'll find a functioning hydroelectric dam as well as a few turn-of-the-20th-century community wash basins that add to this charm. In a lot of ways, the feel of a working town is true because there are generally fewer foreigners than in other villages, while the 350 or so locals that live here full time keep the vibrant little café and tapas bar scene going. This picturesque town beautifully maintains the distinctive hallmarks of the region that have captivated numerous romantic travelers. Its narrow, cobblestone streets meander steeply, with charming water channels running through their centers. The town's traditional whitewashed houses are delightful, and the tinaos, small connecting corridors between neighboring homes, further enhance its character. Along these inviting streets, a plethora of local craft shops await, adding to the town's charm. Just before sunset, take a stroll down the Paseo Federico García Lorca to really get into the community spirit.

Sights

Church of the Holy Cross (Iglesia de la Santa Cruz)

Plaza de la Libertad, 1; tel. 656/651-371; hours vary; free

Situated at the heart of Liberty Square, the Santa Cruz Church embodies the Mudejar style and dates back to the 18th century (1726-1730), featuring a single nave. Inside you'll find the usual coffered ceiling and wooden altarpieces, while from the exterior, the distinctive ochre hue of its tiles and bricks stands in stark contrast to the predominantly white houses in the town. Facing its entrance is the San Antonio fountain, affectionately dubbed "La Chumpaneira," which holds a local legend about the water's purported properties to aid singles in finding a partner.

Festivals

Sulayr Festival

Summer; https://festivalsulayr.es

Conceived in 2016, this festival is a harmonious convergence of music, cultural heritage, and ecological consciousness. The festival infuses the rugged landscape of the Alpujarras with a rich tapestry of sounds. This auditory journey encompasses a diverse spectrum, weaving together traditional melodies with the vibrant fusion of ethnic and contemporary styles.

Against the backdrop of Pampaneira's picturesque surroundings, the tinaos, emblematic spaces of Alpujarra architecture, serve as the quintessential setting for this extraordinary cultural celebration. These architectural gems, with their distinctive features, create an immersive atmosphere that transcends the conventional concert experience. Musicians and spectators alike converge within these tinaos, fostering a shared space where the boundaries between performer and audience blur, allowing for a uniquely communal encounter with music.

The Sulayr Festival has quickly become a platform for cultural exchange and ecological awareness, highlighting the significance of preserving the natural environment and emphasizing the symbiotic relationship between culture and ecology. Check the festival website for exact dates for this multiday event.

Chestnut Tree Festival (La Mauraca)

November 1

Coinciding with All Saints' Day is a fun local festival called La Mauraca, the Chestnut Tree Festival. This festival is celebrated in other little towns around Granada. Its origins stretch back to Galician settlers who arrived at the end of the Reconquista. The festival died out and was successfully revived in the 1990s. The people of Andalusia love an excuse to get together, laugh, dance, and sing. If there are chestnuts roasting over an open bonfire, it's even better!

Shopping

Flea Market

Town center; Mon.; free

Every Monday, Pampaneira comes alive with a bustling flea market, known locally as rastros. Here, you'll find an eclectic array of offerings, ranging from antiques, artwork, and clothing to toys and household items. If fortune smiles upon you, you might even discover a genuine hand-woven Alpujarran rug (a jarapa) at a remarkably reasonable price—a splendid keepsake to take home as a cherished memento of your visit.

Food

★ Restaurante Jaima los Llanos

Carretera Pampaneira, km 8; tel. 958/999-739; https://jaimalosllanos.com; 9am-5pm Wed.-Sun.; €15

Tucked off the road in the Sierra Nevada just before you reach Pampaneira is this surprising touch of Spanish-Muslim culture, heavily influenced by nearby Morocco. You'll find saffron-laden tajines and Friday couscous on offer alongside classic bocadillos and hummus plates, all with a rustic homey touch. More than just a lunch, they really want to find a way to share the culture of Muslim Andalusian Spain through their delicious, lovingly prepared halal menu, served in their vibrant café and art shop that properly gives off some spiritual vibes.

Casa de la Abuela

Calle Real, 10; tel. 638/471-330; www.portalpujarra.com/casa-de-la-abuela; 11am-6pm and 8pm-11pm daily; €10

Savor a delightful range of dishes that celebrate the simple yet flavorful gastronomy of Las Alpujarras. Culinary excellence meets the heartwarming traditions of the region. One standout dish is the ham croquettes, a culinary masterpiece that originally emerged from the kitchens of Restaurante Casa Julio. These delectable morsels encapsulate the essence of Spanish comfort food, with a crispy exterior giving way to a creamy, ham-infused interior. Another must-try specialty is the renowned migas of Las Alpujarras. These savory breadcrumbs are skillfully prepared to perfection, creating a dish that's as comforting as it is flavorful. Savor the rustic essence of Andalusian cuisine as you indulge in these authentic, time-honored flavors, all lovingly prepared in the heart of Las Alpujarras.

Restaurante Guillermo

Restaurante Guillermo, on the A-432 just after the hydroelectric dam; tel. 958/763-023; 11am-5pm Mon.-Thurs., 9am-8pm Sat.-Sun.; €12

A charming oasis for a leisurely late lunch, Restaurante Guillermo nestles beneath a lush canopy of grapevines. At this cozy family-run restaurant, generous servings are the norm, making it entirely feasible to share a main course. The outdoor patio is a wonderful haven, with graceful shade provided by the overhanging grapevines. As you peruse the menu, my personal recommendations include the mouthwatering grilled meats, a true specialty of the house. And when it comes to dessert, do not miss out on the delectable cottage cheese drizzled with locally sourced honey—an absolute delight for your taste buds! For those seeking a taste of the region's culinary traditions, go for the patatas a lo pobre or the secreto a la brasa, both showcasing the exquisite flavors of locally sourced ingredients.

Restaurante Casa Julio

Avenida Alpujarra, 9; tel. 958/763-322; www.casa-julio.com; 9am-5pm Wed.-Mon.; €10

In Las Alpujarras, Casa Julio is often thought of being the best restaurant, and with good cause. They maybe have the most suggestive tapas and cuisine in the entire Alpujarra. You can feel the art in the kitchen and the love in the service, so that your vacation is a dream and you take with you an unforgettable memory. You'll get a great meal for about €10 each. Think: gazpacho, pork loin and potatoes, and rice pudding; migas alpujarreñas is perhaps the most famous local dish on offer.

Accommodations

Hostal Pampaneira

Avenida de las Alpujarras, 1; tel. 958/763-002; www.hostalpampaneira.com; €50

A small rural hotel featuring 15 comfortable rooms. Each room is thoughtfully appointed with modern amenities, including television, heating, and a private bathroom, which is a real luxury at this level, as well as scenic views of the surrounding landscape. An on-site bar and restaurant feature homemade wine made by the owners. This is a popular stop for hikers and cyclists, particularly as there is secure overnight bike storage. Hostal Pampaneira is one of the best budget options of the three most touristed villages.

Estrella de las Nieves

Calle Huertos, 21; tel. 958/763-981; www.estrelladelasnieves.com; €75

This charming country hotel is housed within an enchanting mountainside stone building with whitewashed walls and with a privileged vantage point overlooking the mountain valley and Poqueira Gorge. A hospitable team gives a warm welcome, and the accommodations themselves are generously spacious and meticulously maintained. Parking facilities are easy to access. It's a good place to hang up your hiking boots after a day of exploring the mountains.

★ Sierra y Mar

Calle Albaicín, 3; tel. 958/766-171; www.sierraymar.com; €80

If you're looking for a getaway and don't mind a 15-minute drive, Angela and Sepp (Giuseppe) run a smooth retreat just a short drive east of Pampaneira. This friendly B&B consists of a series of small houses (casitas) scattered in the hills, each with plush beds and en suite bathrooms. An easy path circles around the property and into the mountains. Here, you'll feel as though time slows down a beat.

Information and Services

Visitor Center (Capileira)

Calle del Barranco de Poqueira, 2, Capileira; tel. 641/213-345; https://informacionturismoalpujarra.com; 10am-2pm and 5pm-7:30pm daily

The only visitor center in the area is in Capileira. This center has a small exhibition that displays some of the traditional ways of life in the mountains. There is also info for guide services and books and maps for sale.

Getting There and Around

From Granada, the charming village of Pampaneira (1 hr; 66 km/41 mi) is the first of three villages in the Alpujarras (alongside Bubión and Capileira) that have captured the fancy of travelers looking for picturesque whitewashed villages. You'll want to have a car to access this part of Las Alpujarras, as public transportation connections are infrequent at best. Leaving from Granada, follow the A-44 southward toward Motril. Look for the A-348 exit for Lanjarón and take it, heading east. The mountainous road is winding and scenic with beautiful vistas and plenty of roadside attractions.

Once in Pampaneira, keep your car parked to explore the small village on foot. There are several trails from here, with a popular hike following the A-348 to connect to Bubión and Capileira by foot.

BUBIÓN

Bubión is the middle child of the three villages in this stretch of the Alpujarras. And like many middle children, it is sometimes overlooked, which is a shame. This village features traditional Alpujarran architecture with whitewashed houses, flat clay roofs, and narrow winding streets. Many of the buildings have been restored and preserved, maintaining the charm of the town. Bubión provides easy access to beautiful natural surroundings, including hiking trails and scenic viewpoints, as well as plenty of options for dining and sleeping—often for a touch less than its sister towns, Pampaneira and Capileira.

Sights

Church of the Virgin of the Rosary (Iglesia de la Virgen del Rosario)

Plaza Pérez Ramón; tel. 958/763-074; hours vary; free

In the lower part of Bubión, where the plaza hosts the Bubión town hall, stands the Church of the Virgin of the Rosary, a Mudejar-style church, simple and austere. Volunteers from the church help with visits, so hours are always uncertain, though if a volunteer is helping out, undoubtedly they will help you and be patient as you take photos. Originally constructed during the 16th century, the church tower endured earthquake damage but was expertly restored by a local architect. Climb inside the tower to discover two bells. The larger one, created in 1771, features an inscription honoring the patron saint, San Sebastián, and the Virgin of Carmen.

Lavadero Fountain

Calle Lavadero, 12; 24/7; free

This humble fountain has a cherished place in the hearts of locals. With four graceful spouts, it delivers high-quality water that draws visitors from as far as Motril. Nearby, the historic Lavadero Alto, dating back to at least 1945, once served as the village's largest washhouse.

1
2
3
4

In recent years, careful restoration has revived the fountain and washhouse, preserving their significance in Bubión's heritage. It doesn't seem much to look at, but there is a lot of local history and pride wrapped up in this fountain.

Festivals

Cultural Week

Mid-August

Cultural Week is a collaborative effort involving nearly all the groups and associations within the municipality. The festival takes place the week preceding the patron saint festivities in honor of San Sebastián and San Antón, occurring on the penultimate weekend of August. Over the past two decades, this festival has evolved into a defining feature of Bubión, emerging as a tourist attraction that supports and showcases local culture. Music concerts, theater performances, solidarity activities, sports tournaments, workshops, hiking routes, guided tours, excursions, and informative talks make for activities for all ages and interests.

Food and Accommodations

★ Restaurante Plaza 6

Plaza Pérez Ramón, 6; tel. 858/990-217; noon-midnight Thurs.-Sun.; €15, reservations recommended

For a mix of local scenery and great food, this might be the best restaurant among these three villages at the top of Las Alpujarras. The rustic interior is as cozy as you might expect, but even the terrace seating is a bit limited. Come a little early for mealtimes or reserve for your best shot at choice seating. Service is as kind and sweet as the chocolate brownies you'll want to leave room for. Hits on the menu include carpaccio de lomo and the ever-popular patatas bravas, which have a real kick. Portions are larger than usual, even for this region, which is saying something.

1: countryside of Las Alpujarras 2: Lanjarón Castle 3: looking up at Capileira from Bubión 4: poolside at Finca los Llanos in Capileira

Las Terrazas Hostel

Placeta del Sol, 12; tel. 958/763-034; www.terrazasalpujarra.com; €45

Those using hostels on their travels have a bit of luxury at Las Terrazas, where the simple single and double rooms have private bathrooms. Though the rooms are simple, they are comfy. The public areas sport lots of rustic charm and, as befitting the name, terraces with incredible views, making for a nice spot to make a new friend or share a bottle with your travel buddy.

Information and Services

The only visitor center in the area is in Capileira. Head there if you're looking for local info, though for hiking, cycling, and other active travel information, it's better to research ahead of time.

Getting There and Around

By car, depart from Granada following the scenic A-44 southward toward Motril. Transition onto the A-348 and head east through the postcard-perfect landscapes of the Alpujarras. Traverse the charming towns of Lanjarón, Órgiva, and Pampaneira before ascending to the doorstep of Bubión (1.5 hr; 70 km/42 mi). Park your vehicle. Plan on exploring by foot or taking one of the trails for a delightful hike connecting neighboring villages or venturing through the rugged mountains.

CAPILEIRA

At an impressive 1,500 m (4,900 ft), Capileira promises to keep you cool even in the hottest summer months, though beware the sun! It is still strong. The town is growing more popular with those looking for fresh mountain air, which is a good thing as now there are a few good accommodations and restaurants.

Nestled between the bars and cafés are vintage shops, wicker shops, artisan shops, and other sorts of knickknacks that give the town a fun, hippie-ish, artsy vibe. Many of the restaurants and bars have odds and ends for sale by local artists and artisans.

Sights

Church of Santa María Maggiore (Iglesia de Santa María la Mayor)

Calle Trocadero; tel. 958/763-074; hours vary; free

This whitewashed parochial church dates from the 16th century. It is not nearly as impressive as the cathedrals or even some of the smaller churches in the area, but it is worth knowing about because the entire town revolves around it. The most interesting time to visit inside would be for Sunday mass with the locals, where you can enjoy Latin liturgy and a Spanish sermon. For most travelers, enjoying its exterior is all you need.

Pedro Antonio de Alarcón Museum (Casa-Museo Pedro Antonio de Alarcón)

Just south of the church; tel. 958/763-051; 10am-2pm Sat.-Sun.; €1

This small local museum shows a typical rural house, including traditional housewares and dress. For one euro, it's a quick, easy museum to pop into, giving you a short peek into the recent local history and culture of Las Alpujarras. It is a short, though enriching, experience.

Hiking

Las Alpujarras Town Hike

Distance: *10 km/6 mi round-trip*
Time: *4 hr*
Elevation gain: *650 m/2,130 ft*
Effort: *easy-moderate*
Trailhead: *Pampaneira*

This popular there-and-back hiking route runs between terraces and old farmhouses, connecting the towns of Pampaneira, Bubión, and Capileira. Start in Pampaneira, the lowest of the three villages, and climb through the chestnut grove in the ravine. It's a gentle climb with peekaboo views of the Mulhacén and picturesque white towns. The trail ends in Capileira, which is a nice stop for lunch, and it's an easy walk downhill back to Pampaneira.

Festivals

In general, Capileira is the most animated of the villages of the Alpujarras. The event calendar (https://capileira.es/eventos) is constantly updated with live music performances and other events.

Virgen de la Cabeza

Late April

Capileira celebrates its patron saint festivities in late April in honor of the Virgen de la Cabeza (literally: Virgin of the Head). This fun, local festival is a long weekend of music, parades, and lots of food. There is even a children's soccer (er, fútbol) championship! This festival has a bit of a county fair feel to it, complete with fairgrounds with amusement park rides.

Food

Panadería Capileira

Calle del Doctor Castilla, 2; tel. 958/763-195; 9am-2pm Tues.-Sun.; €4

For over four decades this bakery has been producing some of the finest breads and baked goods in all of Spain. The wood-fired oven has something to do with it. Their tarta de lata, made with an 18th-century recipe, and their roscos (Spanish donuts) are particularly heavenly. For picnics, pick up a loaf or two of bread. Generally they'll have a few different types on offer, from plain white to whole wheat.

Gato Bar

Calle Castillo; tel. 652/425-910; €15

Gato Bar offers funky mountain fun with its lovely terrace and delicious eats. Service is always friendly and easy-going, and the plates are portioned generously. The food is all sourced locally, including the eggs. Their oven-baked rice meals are the cat's meow. Speaking of cats, as you might imagine with a name like Gato Bar, there are usually a few friendly felines about.

Cerro Negro

Calle del Barranco de Poqueira, 26; tel. 633/367-167; 11am-midnight daily; €20

Cold beers. Barbecued chicken. Gazpacho.

What more could you ask for? The menu is varied, with a focus on meats of the region (kid goat, oxtail, pig cheek, and more) that you wouldn't necessarily find elsewhere. Cerro Negro is easy to find in the middle of town, right off the main square, and with plenty of seating indoors and out, so whatever the weather, you'll likely find somewhere to pull up a chair. The continuous service is a good option; not many restaurants offer it, so if you're pulling in at an odd hour of the afternoon, you'll be able to get a solid meal.

Restaurante Gloria

Finca los Llanos; tel. 958/763-071; https://gloriarestaurantecapileira.com; 1:30pm-4pm and 8pm-10:30pm daily; €30

This is where to go for more of a sit-down meal for date night or when you are tired of tapas. Soups warm the bones and the cod in aioli sauce is a winner. Don't skip dessert. The apple pie would look right at home in a bakery in Paris. There are a few tables outside along the patio, which is preferable if the weather cooperates. The interior is a little cold and could use a refresh.

Accommodations

Hostal Poqueira

Calle del Doctor Castilla; tel. 958/763-902; www.hotelespoqueira.es; €35

Poqueira is a quiet, peaceful sort of hostel with a cool pool to dip in. Bedrooms are dated, as you might expect, but clean and comfy enough. Location is excellent, right in the middle of town so you can easily pop out, walk around, and enjoy the animation on the streets. Be aware that there is no air-conditioning, so in the summer months, you may have to keep the windows open, and you'll get some of that street hubbub, so use noise-canceling headphones or earplugs accordingly.

★ Finca los Llanos

Calle Sierra Nevada; tel. 958/763-071; www.hotelfincalosllanos.com; €75

Sprawling over a few different buildings at the top of town, this rustic finca has everything you need for a mountain getaway. Rooms are simple, though not quite spartan, with charming tile work and modern bathrooms. Views from the upper floors are breathtaking, and the pool isn't just fun for families—it's fun for your tired feet as well. The lobby has a nice little selection of books and cozy loungy couches. Restaurante Gloria is great to have on the property so that you don't feel like you have to wander into town for a bite to eat and can just relax close to your temporary home. Be careful, though—this is the sort of relaxing stay that will get you daydreaming about moving to Las Alpujarras yourself!

Information and Services

Capileira Visitor Center

Calle del Barranco de Poqueira, 2; tel. 641/213-345; https://informacionturismoalpujarra.com; 10am-2pm and 5pm-7:30pm daily

The visitor center at Capileira has some limited information for Capileira, Bubión, and Pampaneira, though surprisingly there isn't a lot of good information for hikes in the area.

Getting There and Around

For venturing to the charming town of Capileira, you'll want to have a rental car. From Granada, follow the A-44 south in the direction of Motril. Take the A-348 and head east through the picturesque landscapes of the Alpujarras region, up past the towns of Lanjarón, Órgiva, Pampaneira, and Bubión before arriving to Capileira (1.5 hr; 73 km/45 mi).

The road offers a delightful blend of mountainous twists and turns, granting you glimpses of the stunning surroundings. Keep an eye out for signposts guiding you to Capileira. Once in Capileira, you'll likely leave your car parked as you walk around town or hike between villages or through the mountains. There is plenty of street parking, and most accommodations have some limited onsite parking.

Málaga and the Southern Coast

Welcome to the Southern Coast, also known as the Costa del Sol—a land of sun, sand, and sea that offers visitors a unique blend of Spanish, British, and Moroccan culture. This region is a perfect destination for those looking to explore the historic cities, charming towns, and stunning coastline of southern Spain along with the exotic flavors and sights of northern Africa.

Málaga's Mediterranean climate and lively atmosphere make it a favorite among travelers seeking a mix of sun, sea, and culture. Málaga boasts a rich history dating back to ancient times, and its impressive landmarks reflect its diverse past. Its lively streets are lined with tapas bars, restaurants, and shops, offering visitors the opportunity to indulge in local cuisine and shop for traditional handicrafts. The city's

Highlights

Look for ★ to find recommended sights, activities, dining, and lodging.

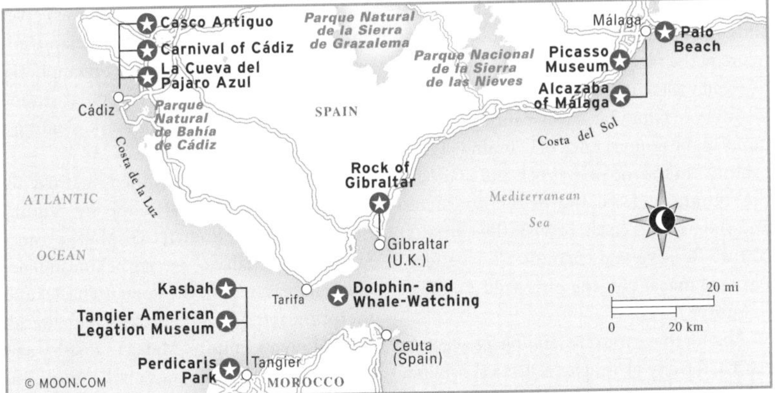

★ **Picasso Museum:** Málaga is the birthplace of the famous artist, and this museum showcases his works, providing insights into his life and career (page 214).

★ **Alcazaba of Málaga:** This historic fortress palace is a must-visit attraction in Málaga. It offers stunning views of the city and the sea (page 218).

★ **Palo Beach:** With miles of pristine coastline, this region features dozens of stunning beaches. Palo Beach is the most convenient to access and enjoyable year-round (page 221).

★ **Rock of Gibraltar:** This iconic landmark offers breathtaking views and is home to the famous Barbary macaques (page 233).

★ **Dolphin- and Whale-Watching:** The waters around Tarifa and Gibraltar are home to several species of dolphins and pilot whales. Take a boat tour to see these majestic creatures up close (page 241).

★ **Tangier American Legation Museum:** Learn about the long history of diplomatic and cultural ties between the United States and Morocco, and view an impressive collection of art and artifacts (page 245).

★ **Tangier's Kasbah:** The kasbah is the heart of Tangier's historic medina, where visitors can wander through narrow streets and alleys, browse local shops and markets, and take in stunning views (page 246).

★ **Perdicaris Park:** Tangier is regarded as one of the garden hubs of the Mediterranean, and the sprawling Perdicaris Park is Tangier's finest (page 251).

★ **Cádiz's Casco Antiguo:** Explore the winding streets of Cádiz's historic center and visit landmarks like Plaza de España and the Torre Tavira (page 260).

★ **Carnival of Cádiz:** Numerous festivals occur year-round along the coast, though the Cádiz Carnival, a vibrant celebration of music, dance, and culture held each year in February, maybe takes the cake (page 265).

★ **La Cueva del Pajaro Azul:** Cádiz is one of the heartlands of flamenco, and visitors can revel in traditional performances set in this cave, which has a soulful history (page 266).

beach promenade, lined with palm trees and overlooking the Mediterranean, is perfect for a leisurely stroll or a bike ride. Pablo Picasso was born in Málaga, so it is no surprise that the Picasso Museum houses an impressive collection of the artist's works, while the Centre Pompidou Málaga features a range of contemporary art exhibitions. In addition to its many cultural attractions, Málaga is also known for its bustling nightlife. The city's bars and clubs offer a lively atmosphere, with many venues staying open until the early hours of the morning.

Head west to discover the British Overseas Territory of Gibraltar, a tiny peninsula that is home to the famous Rock of Gibraltar. Take a cable car to the top of the rock and marvel at the stunning views of the Mediterranean Sea and the African coast, or visit the Gibraltar Nature Reserve and encounter the resident Barbary macaques, the only wild monkeys in Europe.

And for those who are looking for a taste of Africa, the city of Tangier is just a short ferry ride away. Tangier is a city of contrasts, where traditional Moroccan culture meets modern European influences. Take a stroll through the medina (old town) and soak up the sights and smells of the bustling markets, or visit the kasbah (fortress) and explore its labyrinthine streets and alleys.

At the west end of the Southern Coast is the ancient city of Cádiz, the oldest continuously inhabited city in Europe. Cádiz is a place where the past meets the present, with its historic buildings and narrow streets coexisting alongside trendy cafés, bars, and shops. Take a stroll along the seafront promenade and soak up the stunning views of the Atlantic Ocean, or visit the city's cathedral, a majestic Baroque-style building that dominates the skyline.

Spain's Southern Coast is a place where visitors can immerse themselves in a rich tapestry of history, culture, and natural beauty. It is a place where Spanish, British, and Moroccan influences come together to create a truly unique destination where the sun, sand, and sea await you.

HISTORY

Today's thriving port city of Málaga, the capital of the Costa del Sol, has a captivating allure of history that lives in harmony with all the sun-soaked pleasures you would expect from a Mediterranean destination. Various peoples and cultures, from ancient Phoenician traders and Roman conquerors to contemporary wanderers converging on this popular seaside destination, have all left their mark, creating a vibrant patchwork of cultures.

The Phoenicians established the thriving trading port of "Malaka" in the 8th century BCE. Later, under Roman rule, Málaga transformed into "Malaca," leaving behind archaeological treasures like the Roman Theater and the formidable Alcazaba fortress. With the fall of the Roman Empire, Málaga's history saw the rise and fall of various civilizations, including the Visigoths and the Moors, who arrived in the 8th century, leaving an indelible mark on the city's architecture and culture, visible in the Alcazaba's winding alleys and the Gibralfaro Castle.

In the late 15th century, Isabella and Ferdinand captured Málaga, marking the city's transition from Islamic to Christian rule. The splendid Málaga Cathedral, a Renaissance masterpiece, reflects this significant period of transformation. Soon afterward, Málaga's role as a gateway to the Americas during the Age of Exploration brought economic prosperity and played a vital role in Spain's maritime empire, like it did in nearby Seville and Córdoba. Today, the customs house, known as La Aduana, houses the Museo Picasso, celebrating the artistic legacy of Málaga's most famous son, Pablo Picasso.

In contemporary times, Málaga effortlessly

Previous: Cádiz's Casco Antiguo; a macaque monkey in Gibraltar; Moroccan tiles in Tangier's kasbah.

balances its rich heritage with a vibrant, modern spirit. The Picasso Museum and the Centre Pompidou Málaga exemplify the city's commitment to art and culture. Málaga's sun-soaked beaches and lively nightlife showcase its allure, making it the sort of destination where the past and present coexist harmoniously. It's difficult not to succumb to the allure of Málaga when stopping in one of the many tapas bars lining its charming streets or taking in the history and contemporary flair. That blend of culture, heritage, and relaxation mingles right on the shores of the Mediterranean Sea.

ORIENTATION

Running east to west along the Southern Coast of Andalusia, Málaga, Gibraltar, Tarifa, and Cádiz are historic cities and hubs of beachfront activity. **Málaga** is the largest city in the region, boasting an international airport, and, unlike the other cities along the coast, is well-connected to the rest of Spain by train lines. Like most cities in Andalusia, Málaga has a historic center lined with cafés, shops, museums, cathedrals, and monuments, which is the focus for most travelers alongside the eastern hill where you'll find the Alcazaba and Gibralfaro Castle.

Once arrived in Málaga, you'll be traveling by either bus or rental car. Traveling west along the **A7** (freeway) or **AP7** (tolled autoroute), you'll first come to the British enclave of **Gibraltar,** famed for its military history. A bit farther down the coast brings you to the windy, laid-back, kitesurfing mecca of **Tarifa.** From Tarifa, it's an easy 1-hour ferry ride across the Strait of Gibraltar to **Tangier, Morocco,** and the northwest corner of Africa, steeped like its famed mint tea in a blend of history, culture, and mythology. At the far western point of this region are the golden beaches of **Cádiz,** Europe's oldest continuously inhabited city. If you explore this entire region, you'll be sure to add a few stamps to your passport as you'll cross border checks in and out of Gibraltar and Tangier. Though you'll cross into different countries, you'll be amazed perhaps more at their similarities than their differences.

PLANNING YOUR TIME

When planning your visit to this region, consider the best time of year, which is typically during the spring and fall, when the weather is pleasant and the tourist crowds are less overwhelming. You can savor a more leisurely exploration without bumping into too many shoulders. The cities of Málaga and Cádiz, though charming, can be overrun by cruise ship crowds almost any time of year, though only in the main tourist corridors. Savvy travelers can dodge these crowds pretty easily. During popular festivals, like the Feria de Agosto in Málaga, crowds (and a good time!) are unavoidable.

Plan for at least 3-4 days in Málaga. Dedicate at least two full days to Málaga's historical heart, which includes the Alcazaba fortress, the castle, the cathedral, and the Picasso Museum. You'll likely want to have another day to enjoy at the beach or to explore one of the smaller nearby towns as a day trip. For a day trip from Málaga, consider Antequera, Ronda, and Nerja for town visits, or El Torcal Nature Reserve and the Caminito del Rey for hikes.

Gibraltar is best planned as a day trip while you are shuttling between Málaga and Tarifa. A day in Gibraltar will give you enough time to explore the Rock of Gibraltar and meet the famous Barbary macaques. Tarifa, with its renowned windsurfing culture and pristine beaches, is alluring. You could spend a couple of nights in Tarifa if you like the idea of a calm, laid-back town, though for many what makes the most sense is a quick overnight before continuing the journey across the Strait of Gibraltar to Tangier, Morocco, for a weekend of immersive exploration into North African culture.

Not to be outdone, Cádiz, with its beautiful beaches, historic old town, and vibrant atmosphere, is the type of city you could "do in a day," but consider spending at least a couple of nights to let the magic sink in.

Málaga and the Southern Coast

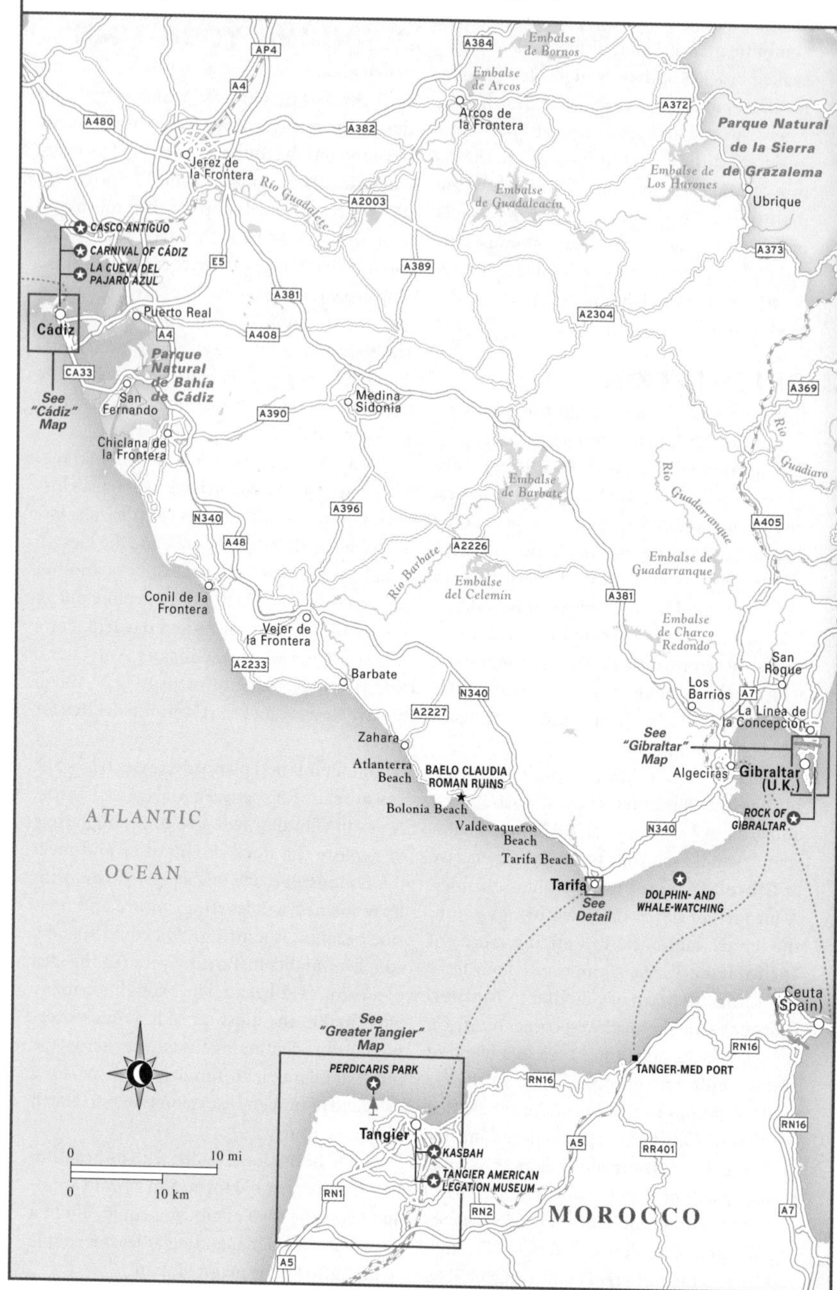

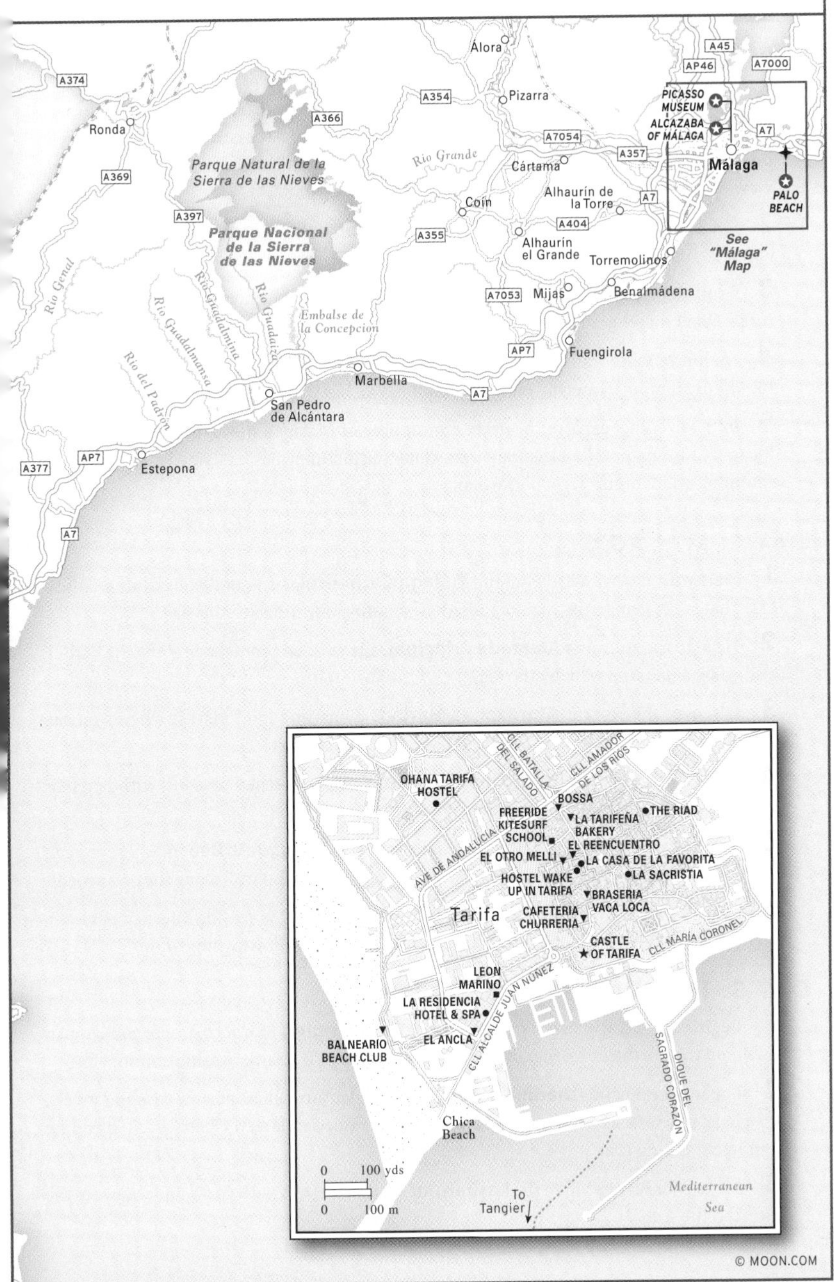

Álora
A45
AP46
A7000
A374
A354
Pizarra
PICASSO MUSEUM
ALCAZABA OF MÁLAGA
A366
Ronda
A7054
A7
Rio Grande
A357
Málaga
Parque Natural de la Sierra de las Nieves
Cártama
A369
Alhaurín de la Torre
A7
PALO BEACH
Coín
A397
Parque Nacional de la Sierra de las Nieves
A404
A355
Alhaurín el Grande
Torremolinos
See "Málaga" Map
Rio Genal
Rio Guadalmina
Rio Guadaiza
A7053
Mijas
Benalmádena
Rio Guadalmansa
Embalse de la Concepcion
AP7
Fuengirola
Rio del Padrón
Marbella
A7
San Pedro de Alcántara
A377
AP7
Estepona
A7
CLL BATALLA DEL SALADO
CLL AMADOR DE LOS RIOS
OHANA TARIFA HOSTEL
BOSSA
THE RIAD
FREERIDE KITESURF SCHOOL
LA TARIFEÑA BAKERY
AVE DE ANDALUCÍA
EL REENCUENTRO
EL OTRO MELLI
LA CASA DE LA FAVORITA
HOSTEL WAKE UP IN TARIFA
LA SACRISTIA
BRASERIA VACA LOCA
Tarifa
CAFETERIA CHURRERIA
CASTLE OF TARIFA
CLL MARÍA CORONEL
LEON MARINO
CLL ALCALDE JUAN NUÑEZ
LA RESIDENCIA HOTEL & SPA
EL ANCLA
BALNEARIO BEACH CLUB
DIQUE DEL SAGRADO CORAZÓN
Chica Beach
0 100 yds
0 100 m
To Tangier
Mediterranean Sea

Itinerary Ideas

DAY 1: MÁLAGA

1 Begin your day in Málaga by exploring the historic **Alcazaba** of Málaga, a well-preserved Moorish fortress. Marvel at its impressive architecture and enjoy panoramic views of the city from its vantage points.

2 Head over to the nearby **Roman Theater,** one of Málaga's archaeological gems. Learn about its history and the ancient ruins surrounding it.

3 Stroll along the scenic **Málaga Park** and enjoy the lush greenery, fountains, and sculptures. Don't forget to visit the beautiful botanical gardens within the park!

4 For lunch, savor traditional Andalusian cuisine at **Restaurante José Carlos Garcia,** indulging in mouthwatering tapas and regional dishes with a focus on seafood.

5 In the evening, explore the lively atmosphere of Málaga's **historic center.** Visit the Picasso Museum or take a leisurely walk along the picturesque La Alameda, known for its shopping and vibrant street performances.

DAY 2: MÁLAGA

1 Start your day with a visit to the **Málaga Cathedral,** a feat of Renaissance architecture that is the gem of the region, though it remains unfinished to this day.

2 Head to the stunning **Alameda Principal,** a tree-lined promenade along the harbor, and enjoy a relaxing walk by the sea.

3 Discover the vibrant **Atarazanas Market,** a bustling food market where you can sample fresh seafood, local produce, and other Andalusian treats.

4 After lunch, take a short trip to **Gibralfaro Castle,** perched on a hill with fantastic views of the city and the Mediterranean Sea.

5 Wrap up your afternoon with a relaxing moment at **Malagueta Beach,** where you can unwind by the sea, enjoy a beachside dinner, or take a leisurely stroll along the promenade.

6 Take the bus to **Tarifa** via Algeciras and overnight at this seaside kitesurfing haven. Get ready to cross continents, from Europe to Africa, the following morning!

DAY 3: TANGIER

1 Begin your day with a ferry ride from Tarifa to **Tangier,** Morocco, where you'll touch down on the northwest corner of Africa in a vibrant, progressive Muslim country.

2 Explore the bustling **medina of Tangier.** Wander through its narrow winding streets, visit local markets, and sit for a coffee or tea on the famed square, the petit socco, spending a moment taking it in.

3 Make your way uphill to the **kasbah,** an ancient fortress with panoramic views of the city and the sea.

4 Enjoy a traditional Moroccan lunch at **Chez Hassan,** savoring the flavors of tajines, couscous, and mint tea.

5 Take a leisurely walk along the beautiful **Tangier Municipal Beach,** known for its scenic views and vibrant street vendors.

6 End your day at one of the centrally located riads in the medina or kasbah, like **Saba's House,** to fully experience the renowned hospitality of the region.

Málaga

ORIENTATION

Málaga is easily divided into five distinct sections, each offering a unique experience: the historic center, the Alcazaba hill, the Soho district, La Malagueta beach area, and the Pedregalejo neighborhood.

The **historic center** serves as the heart of Málaga, boasting historic landmarks, shops, restaurants, and lively plazas. It's easily walkable, providing a fantastic introduction to the city's culture and heritage.

The **Alcazaba hill,** overlooking the city, offers historical sites like the Roman Theater and the Alcazaba fortress. The ascent is steep, but it's worth the effort for panoramic views of Málaga and the Mediterranean. Bus and taxi services are available to shuttle you to the summit of Málaga's tallest hill.

The trendy **Soho district** is known for its vibrant street art, contemporary galleries, and a burgeoning arts scene. Here, you can explore colorful murals and discover the latest cultural trends in a neighborhood that's rapidly evolving. Like the historic center it abuts, it's an easily walkable, primarily flat neighborhood, though with more tapas bars and art galleries than sights to see.

La Malagueta is a coastal haven, offering sun-drenched shores and a vibrant promenade. This is the perfect spot to relax by the Mediterranean and enjoy fresh seafood at the beachside restaurants.

The **Pedregalejo** neighborhood, farther

walking through Málaga's historic district

Itinerary Ideas

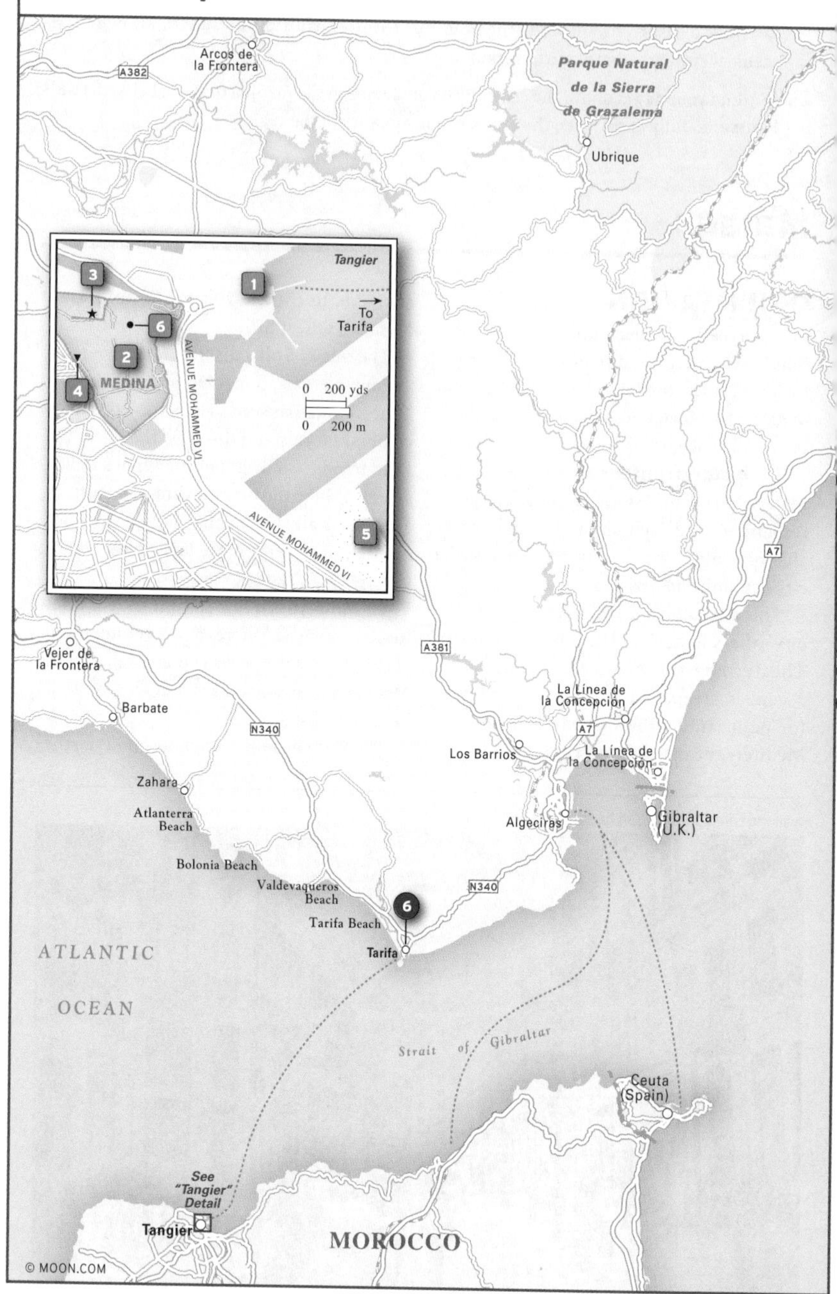

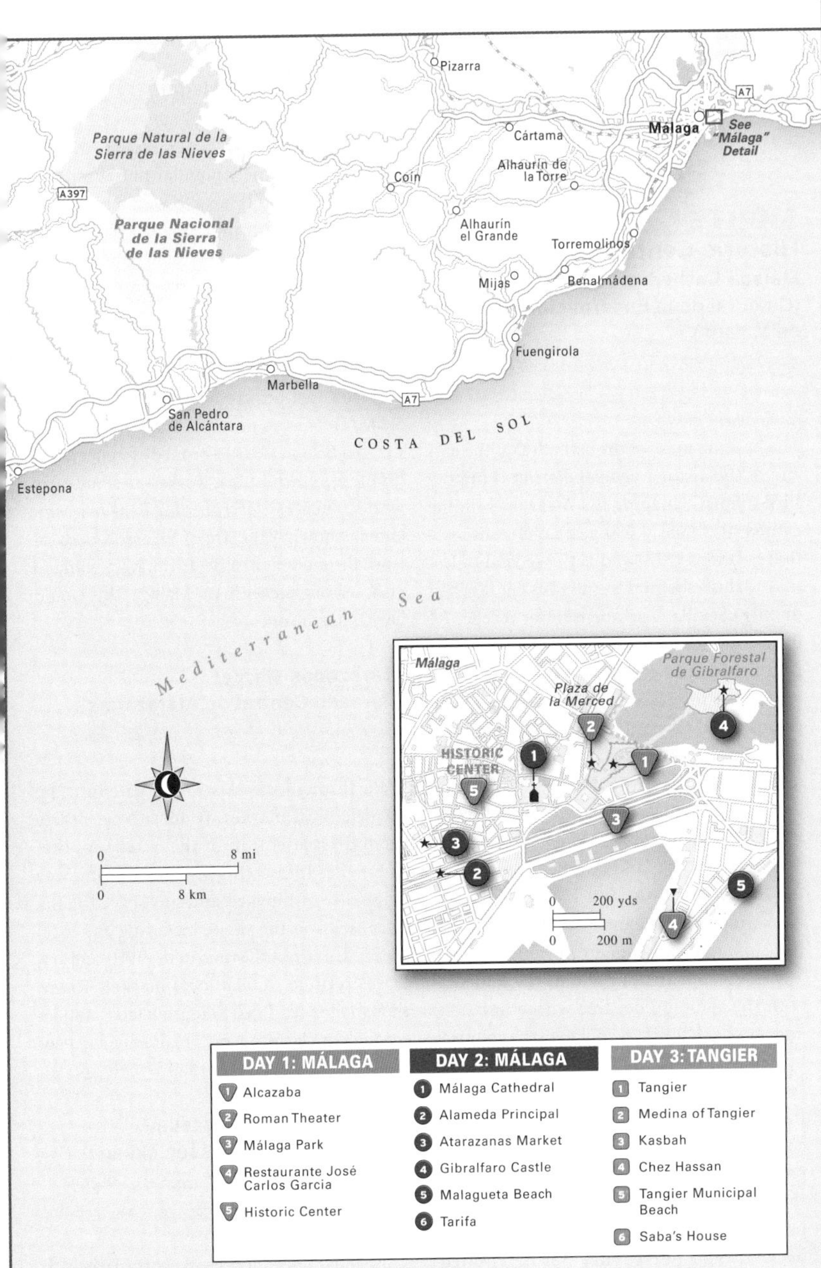
Pizarra
A7
Málaga
See "Málaga" Detail
Cártama
Parque Natural de la Sierra de las Nieves
Alhaurín de la Torre
Coín
A397
Parque Nacional de la Sierra de las Nieves
Alhaurín el Grande
Torremolinos
Mijas
Benalmádena
Fuengirola
Marbella
A7
San Pedro de Alcántara
COSTA DEL SOL
Estepona
Mediterranean Sea
0 8 mi
0 8 km
Málaga
Parque Forestal de Gibralfaro
Plaza de la Merced
HISTORIC CENTER
0 200 yds
0 200 m
DAY 1: MÁLAGA
1 Alcazaba
2 Roman Theater
3 Málaga Park
4 Restaurante José Carlos Garcia
5 Historic Center
DAY 2: MÁLAGA
1 Málaga Cathedral
2 Alameda Principal
3 Atarazanas Market
4 Gibralfaro Castle
5 Malagueta Beach
6 Tarifa
DAY 3: TANGIER
1 Tangier
2 Medina of Tangier
3 Kasbah
4 Chez Hassan
5 Tangier Municipal Beach
6 Saba's House

east along the coast and outside the area considered Malaga's center, is famous for its charming seaside vibe and traditional seafood restaurants. It's a fantastic place to savor the local cuisine while taking in the sea breeze.

West Málaga is where you will find transportation hubs, such as the Málaga Airport and María Zambrano train station.

SIGHTS

Historic Center

Málaga Cathedral (Catedral de la Encarnación de Málaga)

Calle Molina Lario, 9; tel. 617/500-582; 10am-8pm Mon.-Fri., 10am-6pm Sat., 2pm-6pm Sun.; €8 (€12 with roof access)

The hulking mass of the cathedral at the east end of the historic central district is impossible to miss. Hugging the Alcazaba hill, the cathedral is nearly 500 years old (construction began in 1528) and is the second tallest in Andalusia, behind the famous Giralda bell tower in Seville. The north tower reaches 84 m (276 ft). The matching south tower remains unfinished. The funds raised to finish this tower were instead used to aid the American colonies in their fight for independence from Great Britain. A plaque at the bottom of the tower commemorates this. Because of the missing tower, the locals have dubbed this cathedral La Manquita (The One-Armed Lady). This Renaissance- and Baroque-inspired cathedral houses 18th- and 19th-century artworks, including the impressive painting *The Beheading of Saint Paul*, by Enrique Simonet.

Allow about an hour to tour the cathedral with the audio guide (free with admission) and another hour if you opt to make your way up to the rooftops, which are best around sunset for some beautiful panoramic views over the city and Mediterranean. The rooftops are accessible on the hour throughout normal opening times. Keep in mind that to access the rooftops you must ascend and descend a narrow spiral staircase of 200 steps, and larger backpacks or purses may not be allowed. There is limited free access to the cathedral 8:30am-9am Monday-Saturday and 8:30am-9:30am Sunday (without an audio guide).

★ Picasso Museum (Museo Picasso Málaga)

Calle San Agustín, 8; tel. 952/127-600; www.museopicassomalaga.org; 10am-8pm daily; €9.50

This is an extremely popular museum, so it is very likely you'll have to wait a bit before being allowed entrance, due to crowds. The permanent collection of Picasso paintings and sculptures, as well as information on his life and works, is well worth the price of entry as well as the wait in line. Temporary exhibitions are usually fantastic as well. Highlights from Picasso's vast oeuvre range from *Jacqueline Seated* (1954) and *Bust of a Woman with Arms Crossed Behind* (1939)—from different eras of his more known Cubist works—to some early works, such as *Portrait of a Bearded Man* (1895), showing the arc of Picasso's body of work throughout his life. If you were going to visit just one museum on Málaga, this would have to be the one.

Atarazanas Market (Mercado Central de Atarazanas)

Calle Atarazanas, 10; tel. 951/926-010; 8am-3pm Mon.-Sat.; free

Walk through the Nasrid-era gate into the historic local market. It doesn't get nearly the tourist attention of the Triana Market in Seville. Interestingly, this building was originally a shipyard and has served many purposes over the years, including as a local hospital, until, at the turn of the 19th century, it was refitted to be a local market. Today, though the occasional tour group does wander through, it's largely a local market where people are just shopping for their weekly goods.

Carmen Thyssen Museum (Museo Carmen Thyssen Málaga)

Plaza Carmen Thyssen, Calle Compañía; tel. 952/217-511; https://carmenthyssenmalaga.org; 10am-8pm Tues.-Sun.; €8

This stellar collection hosts works largely by Spanish masters. For most, it might be only

Málaga

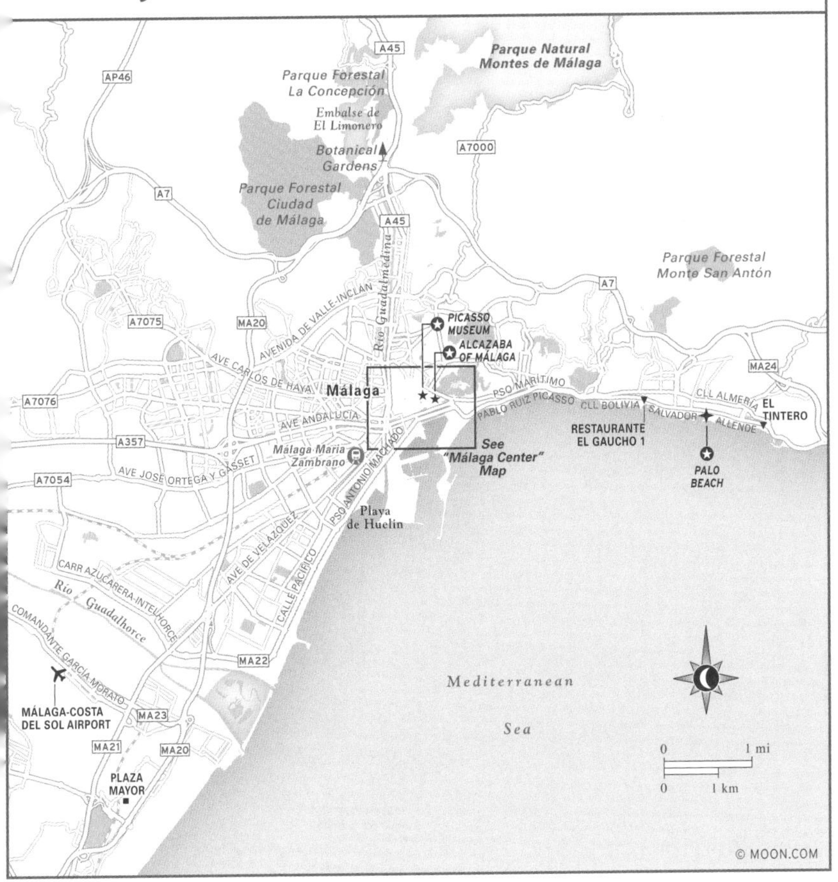

of passing interest, but if you have a love for Spanish artists, this is a well-curated collection of 19th- and 20th-century Spanish art, much of which focuses on rural life in Andalusia. The collection is housed in a beautifully restored 19th-century building, apropos considering the pieces on display. Admission is free on Sunday after 4pm.

Sacred Heart Church (Iglesia del Sagrado Corazón)

Plaza de San Ignacio; tel. 952/210-500 ext. 17; 7am-12:15pm and 6pm-8pm daily; free

This neo-Gothic peachy creamsicle of a church is worth a diversion, for the photo op alone. During the boom of church construction at the end of the 19th century in Málaga, this was the only one built in the historic downtown. Warring F. Strachan, the architect behind the church, was influenced by the cathedral of Toledo, adding more of an Islamic flair to this church that was absent in other churches of this era. The bell towers, in particular, are built to reflect the minarets of mosques that once dotted this landscape.

Málaga Center

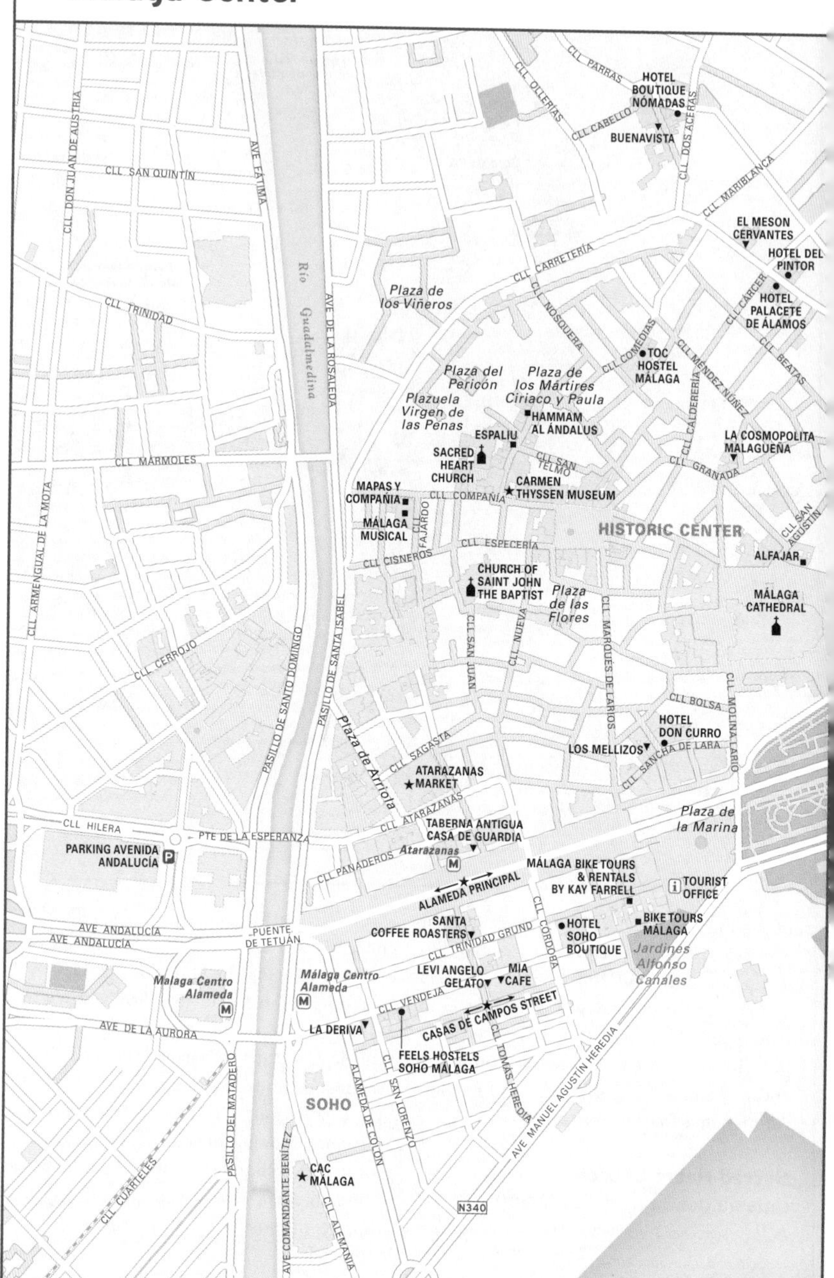

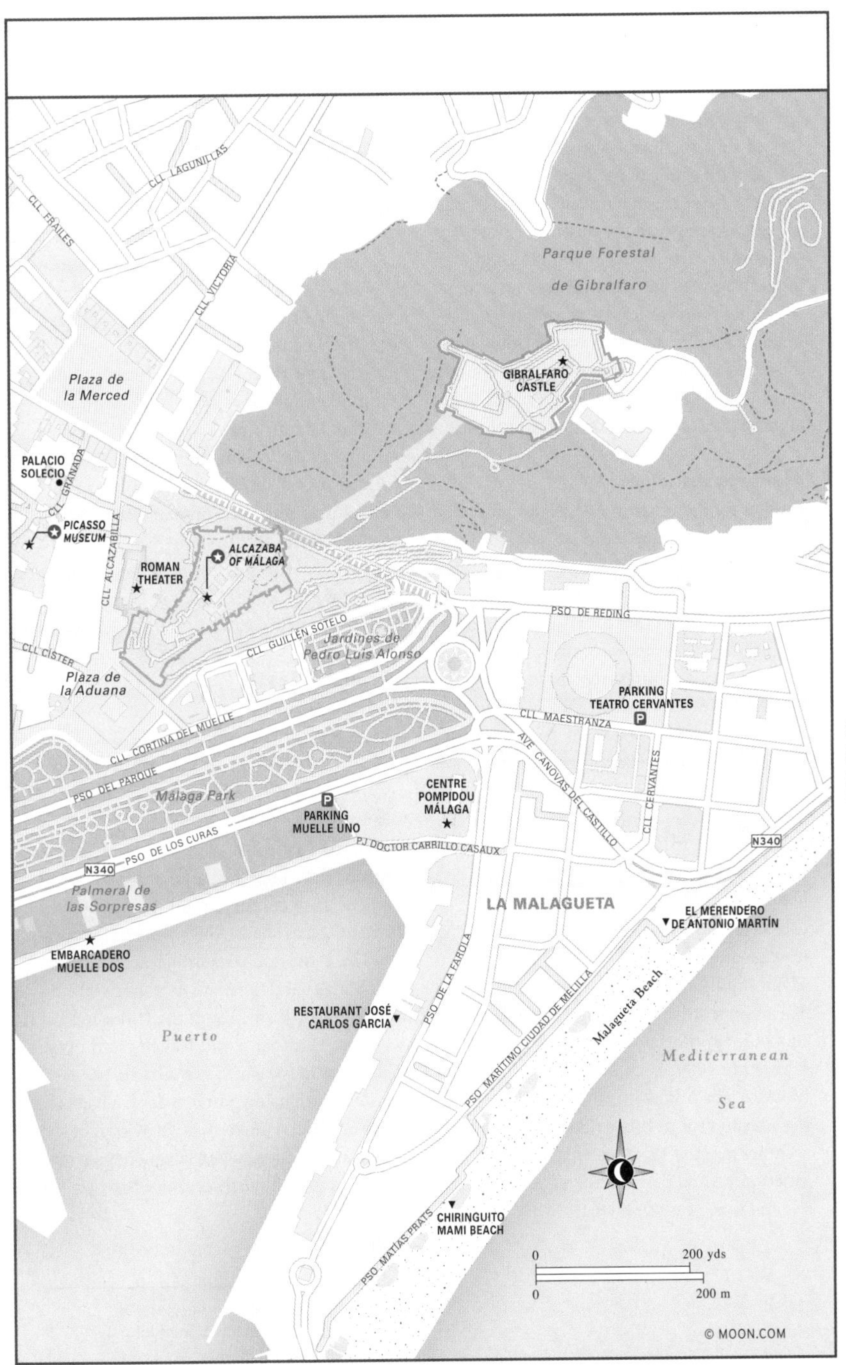

CLL LAGUNILLAS
CLL FRAILES
CLL VICTORIA
Parque Forestal
de Gibralfaro
GIBRALFARO
CASTLE
Plaza de
la Merced
PALACIO
SOLECIO
CLL GRANADA
PICASSO
MUSEUM
CLL ALCAZABILLA
ALCAZABA
OF MÁLAGA
ROMAN
THEATER
PSO DE REDING
CLL GUILLÉN SOTELO
Jardines de
Pedro Luis Alonso
CLL CISTER
Plaza de
la Aduana
PARKING
TEATRO CERVANTES
CLL MAESTRANZA
CLL CORTINA DEL MUELLE
AVE CANOVAS DEL CASTILLO
CLL CERVANTES
PSO DEL PARQUE
Málaga Park
PARKING
MUELLE UNO
CENTRE
POMPIDOU
MÁLAGA
PSO DE LOS CURAS
PJ DOCTOR CARRILLO CASAUX
N340
Palmeral de
las Sorpresas
LA MALAGUETA
EL MERENDERO
DE ANTONIO MARTÍN
EMBARCADERO
MUELLE DOS
PSO DE LA FAROLA
PSO MARÍTIMO CIUDAD DE MELILLA
Malagueta Beach
RESTAURANT JOSÉ
CARLOS GARCIA
Puerto
Mediterranean
Sea
CHIRINGUITO
MAMI BEACH
PSO MATÍAS PRATS
0
200 yds
0
200 m
© MOON.COM

Church of Saint John the Baptist (Iglesia de San Juan Bautista)

Calle San Juan, 3; tel. 952/211-283; 8am-noon and 6pm-8pm daily; free

Iglesia de San Juan Bautista is a Baroque church with a relic of the True Cross that was found by Saint Helena in 326 CE. Don't forget to peek around at the beautifully painted exterior walls in the back. Though the church is interesting, the exterior walls are maybe more so in that they are left from an era when, in Málaga, people and shop owners would paint the exterior walls of their buildings to make them appear as though they were made out of more precious materials than was the case.

Alameda Principal

Known to Malagueños as La Alameda, this wide, tree-lined boulevard is the main thoroughfare, for pedestrians and wheeled traffic alike, from East Málaga to West Málaga. The most picturesque parts of this promenade are in the historic center of Málaga and feature 18th-century buildings along both sides of the street. Numerous orange, ficus, plantain, and palm trees provide shade for passersby, joggers, and cyclists. Some of the ficus trees are over 150 years old!

Alcazaba Hill

Roman Theater (Teatro Romano)

Calle Alcazabilla, 8, next to the Alcazaba; tel. 951/501-115; 10am-6pm Tues.-Sun.; free

The restoration and excavation of this Roman Theater are still very much in progress, as it was built in the 1st century but only rediscovered in 1980. Located right at the foot of the Alcazaba hill, this is the first of the three big sites to visit in this neighborhood. In the summer months, this theater is used for open-air concerts and performances, adding to the general liveliness of Málaga.

★ Alcazaba of Málaga

Calle Alcazaba, 2; www.alcazabamalaga.com; 9am-6pm daily Nov.-Mar., 9am-8pm daily Apr.-Oct.; daily tours in English at 4pm Nov.-Mar. or 5pm Apr.-Oct.; €3.50 (€5.50 combined with Gibralfaro Castle)

What the Alcazaba of Málaga lacks in grandiosity, it makes up in oodles of charm. You won't find the spaciousness of the Alhambra in Granada or the pomp of the Royal Alcázar of Seville. Instead, this brick-built fortress lures you in through its winding passageways, vistas overlooking the sea, and cozy courtyard gardens, inviting you to really imagine what living here must have been like. More than the other Islamic-era fortresses and palaces you might visit, this is the one you can best project yourself actually living within. There is something inherently human-sized and approachable about it. In many ways, it's hard to realize that this fortress predates the other well-known fortresses in Granada and Seville by more than 300 years.

Gibralfaro Castle (Castillo Gibralfaro)

Cam. Gibralfaro, 11; www.alcazabamalaga.com/gibralfaro-caste; 9am-6pm daily Nov.-Mar., 9am-8pm daily Apr.-Oct.; €3.50 (€5.50 combined with the Alcazaba)

Gibralfaro Castle lurks at the summit of the Alcazaba hill, a beast of a fortress that dates from the 10th century, about two centuries after the Alcazaba below was constructed. Views from the ramparts stretch across downtown Málaga and the port. As you're walking the ramparts, think about the three-month siege that Ferdinand and Isabella laid upon the fortress in the world's first battle between two sides both using gun powder—a fun factoid to consider. Hunger was what brought the siege to an end. The brave Malagueños surrendered to the Catholic forces once their provisions had dried up.

1: Málaga Cathedral **2:** Atarazanas Market **3:** looking up at the Church of Saint John the Baptist **4:** Alcazaba of Málaga

Soho District

Contemporary Art Center (CAC) of Málaga

Calle Alemania; tel. 952/208-500; http://cacmalaga.eu; 9am-9:30pm Tues.-Sun.; free

A contemporary art museum at home mellowing in the Soho district vibe, the CAC focuses on contemporary and modern Spanish artists. The art is modern and accessible for most. You're sure to find something you like, but for me this is only the start. What I really appreciated was the size of the gallery and the space to walk around. The white walls added to this openness. You'll find some large-scale canvases here, which makes sense given the sheer scale of the place. The other bonus is that you are very unlikely to have any issue walking around people as you navigate from one piece to the next.

Casas de Campos Street

Calle Casas de Campos

This quintessential Málaga pedestrian thoroughfare cuts right through Soho, connecting with West Málaga on one side and the Malagueta neighborhood on the other. Cafés, bars, restaurants, used clothing stores, boutiques, and more line this street—not a sight per se, but a wonderful, vibrant local stroll.

La Malagueta

Centre Pompidou Málaga

Pasaje Doctor Carrillo Casaux; tel. 951/926-200; https://centrepompidou-malaga.eu; €9

Located in The Cube just outside of the central historic city center, the Pompidou is an oft-overlooked museum that gives its more famous mother museum in Paris a run for its money. The exhibition focuses on modern and contemporary artists, often with a socially charged message. The semipermanent collection is sourced from the museum in Paris and features works by luminaries such as Picasso, Miró, Bacon, Magritte, Frida Kahlo, and Giacometti.

Embarcadero Muelle Dos

Paseo del Muelle Uno

A modern, covered passageway runs along the port, across the busy boulevard from Málaga Park. The lovely seafront walk takes you from the city, past the pier, along an uncovered pathway through shopping boutiques and eateries to the always-busy Malagueta Beach. The passageway, reminiscent perhaps of a whale skeleton, makes for a visual experience as you make your way along the waterfront.

Tours

Málaga a Pie

Plaza de la Marina, 11; tel. 645/641-541; www.malagapie.es; 10:30am-8pm daily; free

This outfitter offers free two-hour guided walks in English daily at 11am, though you are expected to tip. The paid group experience (€18) includes entrance fees and is worth it, particularly during the warm months, when the cool interiors give you a break from the heat.

Victor Garrido

tel. 646/543-566; https://welovemalaga.com; from €50

There is nothing like a friendly, knowledgeable guide to show you around their hometown, and Victor is one of the best. He can take you around some of the more famous sights or show you some of the lesser-visited parts of Málaga and his favorite little hidden gems. His tours can be privatized, or you can join up with a small group. Like a true Malagueño, he loves tapas and wine. Take advantage of his local knowledge and book him for a tapas tour.

SPORTS AND RECREATION

Beaches

Malagueta Beach (Playa de la Malagueta)

This popular city beach is perfect for swimming, sunbathing, and people-watching. However, as it is the closest beach to the historic district, it can get pretty crowded in summer months. If you're looking for fewer crowds, head elsewhere. If you don't mind the crowds, this is a fun beach to meet other vacationers and a few stray locals. It's a well-equipped beach with showers and bathrooms.

★ Palo Beach (Playas del Palo)

This series of small, sandy coves in East Málaga, past the Alcazaba hill, is popular with local families. It's best to take a car as there is ample parking, though you could walk or take the bus. There are a quite a few outdoor barbecues and restaurants, and the water here is much calmer, making it a natural choice for those with young kids. Public bathrooms and showers are readily available. Uniquely, you can still find some excellent seafood shacks lining the beach and serving up whatever comes in fresh that day.

Huelin Beach (Playa de Huelin)

A long, thin stretch of sand in West Málaga is the go-to choice for most locals, as it is within walking distance of many apartment buildings. It has that municipal beach feel to it, with plenty of lifeguards and just enough services, like public bathrooms and showers. Part of the beach is directly beneath the flight path of the Málaga Airport, so expect to see and hear lots of planes.

Maro Beach

(Playa de Maro)

Not the easiest beach to get to, but the more romantic for it. This is only a "those in the know" local type of beach. In fact, the person that told me about this beach made me promise to not write about it. Oops! Sorry, Tara! Anyhow, there is a really nice little café for a light lunch as well as possibilities to rent kayaks.

Parks

Málaga Park

Paseo del Parque; 24/7; free

Málaga's quintessential public park runs right along the edge of the Alcazaba and Malagueta neighborhoods. Despite being alongside an oft-frantic boulevard, the botanical garden manages to be a relaxing stroll right in the midst of the city. The attached Pedro Luis Alonso rose garden is usually a calm place to sit and enjoy the surroundings.

Botanical Gardens (Jardín Botánico Histórico La Concepción)

Camino del Jardín Botánico, 3; tel. 951/926-180; http://laconcepcion.malaga.eu; 9:30am-8:30pm Tues.-Sun. Apr.-Sept., 9:30am-5:30pm Tues.-Sun. Oct.-Mar.; €5.20

The historic botanical gardens of Málaga are a transportive experience. Often overlooked, perhaps because of their location north of the city, they are nonetheless well worth stopping at for any lover of gardens and plants. After hundreds of years of private ownership and caretaking, the gardens were opened to the public in 1990. It was in the 19th century that the gardens first became known throughout Europe, and in 1943 they were declared a Garden of Historical and Artistic Importance. Under the stewardship of the Málaga City Council, the gardens have increased the species of flowers and trees for educational and scientific purposes, making for a brilliant outing with acres and acres of curated flowers, trees, and other flora to discover.

Biking

Bike Tours Málaga

Plaza Poeta Alfonso, Canales 4; tel. 650/677-063; www.biketoursmalaga.com; from €10

There are daily city bike tours, including a wine and tapas tour for small groups. E-bikes are also available, making the tours accessible for more riders, particularly for those wanting to get up one of Málaga's famous hills for the views. The super-friendly team at Bike Tours Málaga is happy to give you all sorts of local insight.

Málaga Bike Tours and Rentals by Kay Farrell

Calle Trinidad Grund, 5a; tel. 606/978-513; https://malagabiketours.eu; 10am-7pm daily; from €9

Rentals include a great selection of Dutch-style city bikes, kids' bikes, tandems, and

Kona trekking bikes. Tours are available, and well-reviewed, though this outfitter really shines with their bike rental service and well-thought-out self-guided bike routes.

Hammams

Hammam Al Ándalus

Plaza de los Mártires, 5; tel. 952/215-018; https://malaga.hammamalandalus.com; €59

Plunge into the traditional Arab baths and be spirited away by the sensual pleasure of the hammam ritual. It's the perfect way to get not only a spot of relaxation and self-care, but also a real cultural experience of a bathhouse you would have found typical in Málaga during the Islamic era.

FESTIVALS

Málaga Film Festival

Spring

The Málaga Film Festival, also known as the Festival de Málaga, Cine en Español, is typically held annually in the spring. The exact dates can vary from year to year, so check the official festival website or reliable sources for the most up-to-date information regarding the festival's schedule and dates for the year you are interested in attending. Typically, the festival lasts for around a week, during which numerous film screenings, competitions, and cultural events take place, celebrating Spanish and Latin American cinema. It is no surprise that the hometown of Antonio Banderas has one of the best film festivals in Europe!

Holy Week (Semana Santa)

Week before Easter

The solemn yet festive atmosphere that envelopes Málaga at this time of year is much like that of other major Spanish cities. The processions happen throughout the week and include the Cristo de la Buena Muerte, the Virgen de la Esperanza, and the Virgen de la Soledad. These figures are often adorned with flowers. The religious brotherhoods also make their hooded walks for penitence during this time.

Virgin of Carmen Festival (Día de la Virgen del Carmen)

July 16

The festival of Nuestra Señora del Carmen, which is celebrated in honor of the Virgin of Carmen, takes place on July 16 each year in Málaga. This is the feast day of Nuestra Señora del Carmen, the patron saint of fishers and sailors. The celebrations include religious services, processions, and other festivities that pay homage to the Virgin of Carmen and seek her protection for those who work at sea. It's a significant and colorful event, particularly in coastal communities, where the maritime tradition is strong. In the main procession, an image of the saint is carried out to sea on a boat, followed by a flotilla of other vessels.

August Festival (Feria de Agosto)

August

This celebration is similar to Seville's Feria de Abril, though in many ways much friendlier. In Málaga, there is no tradition of private family casitas, so everyone is able to go everywhere—and boy do they! You'll find all of Málaga really going all out for the week. Locals often take the week off, and people from all around descend on the city to celebrate. Though people do get dressed up, given the beachside location and general relaxed vibe of Málaga, it is much less dressy an occasion than its Sevillian counterpart.

SHOPPING

Malls

Plaza Mayor

Calle Alfonso Ponce de León, 3; tel. 952/247-580; 10am-10pm daily

This large outdoor shopping mall boasts over 100 shops, with many recognizable name brands, such as North Face and Ray-Ban. If you forgot a summer essential or your luggage was lost, this is one of the easiest places to restock. It's tax-free shopping if you don't

1: The Cube at the Centre Pompidou Málaga
2: Malagueta Beach **3:** Palo Beach **4:** Málaga Park

1
2
Malagueta
3
4

live in Spain (e.g., are traveling to Spain from the United States and are a US citizen—just remember to bring your passport). The mall has easy connections with the urban rail system (Cercanías).

Art and Ceramics

Alfajar

Calle Cister, 1; tel. 952/211-272; www.alfajar.es; 10am-8:30pm daily

Alfajar sells period re-creation pottery and other artwork by local artists. If you are looking for a more bespoke, individual piece to take home, it would be worthwhile to peruse this easy-to-find shop, located just across the street from the Roman Theater.

Books and Music

Mapas Y Compañía

Calle Compañía, 33; tel. 952/608-815; 10am-1:30pm and 5:30pm-8:30pm Mon.-Fri., 10am-2pm Sat.

This is the travelers' travel store, with tons of maps, guides, and more. It's geared toward Spanish speakers, though there is a small selection of English editions, with some classic novels sitting alongside more specialized reads on the history of Andalusia. If you've read *The Shadow of the Wind,* you'll know what I mean when I say it does remind me of the Cemetery of Forgotten Books.

Málaga Musical

Calle Compañía, 33; tel. 952/225-899; www.malagamusical.com; 10am-1:30pm and 5pm-8:30pm Tues.-Fri.

If all the flamenco has inspired you to pick up your own guitar, or maybe just a set of castanets (as they are infinitely more portable), beeline for this iconic music store, founded in 1979. The owners have a reputation for sourcing high-quality instruments from around Spain and internationally. Many contemporary musicians stop in here for their gear, and if you've attended any flamenco shows in the region, there is a good chance the musicians picked up their guitars here.

Jewelry

Espaliú

Calle Mártires, 10; 10am-2pm and 6pm-9:15pm Mon.-Sat.

Created by designer Joaquín Espaliú especially for his own shops, these are all 925-certified sterling silver pieces made in Spain. Most of the pieces on display are small, making them the perfect souvenir or gift to take back home.

FOOD

Historic Center

★ Taberna Antigua Casa de Guardia

Alameda Principal, 18; tel. 952/214-680; https://antiguacasadeguardia.com; 11am-10pm Mon.-Thurs., 11am-10:45pm Fri.-Sat., 11:30am-3pm Sun.; €8-15

Step back in time at this old-school tavern with cask-lined walls, known for its vast selection of wines. This historic bodega, dating back to 1840, preserves its original charm with wooden barrels lining the walls and an authentic ambience. You can savor a glass of traditional Málaga wine alongside classic tapas. The house-cured olives and marinated anchovies are staples. Expect no-nonsense service.

El Mesón de Cervantes

Calle Álamos, 11; tel. 952/216-274; https://elmesondecervantes.com; 7pm-midnight Sun.-Mon. and Wed.-Thurs., 7pm-12:30am Fri.-Sat.; €10-20

El Mesón de Cervantes offers an authentic Spanish tapas experience with a modern twist. It's typically busy with locals and tourists alike. The menu boasts a wide selection of tapas, from traditional patatas bravas to innovative creations like goat cheese-stuffed piquillo peppers. Don't miss the grilled octopus, perfectly tender and bursting with flavor. Be prepared to wait for a table during peak hours.

La Cosmopolita Malagueña

Calle José Denis Belgrano, 3; 1:30pm-4pm and 8pm-11pm Mon.-Sat.; €15-25

La Cosmopolita is a more modern, trendy tapas restaurant that pays homage to

1: August Festival **2:** seafood **3:** Plaza Mayor

traditional Spanish flavor profiles with a contemporary twist. The sleek and stylish interior sets the stage for an extraordinary culinary experience. The tapas menu is an inventive fusion of local and international influences, offering surprises like Iberian pork with sweet potato puree and mango chutney. The bartenders craft cocktails that complement the bold flavors of the dishes—a refreshing change if you are beer and wined out.

Los Mellizos

Calle Sancha de Lara, 7; tel. 952/220-315; https://losmellizos.net; 1pm-4:30pm and 7pm-11:30pm daily; €15-25

Los Mellizos is a seafood lover's paradise, serving up a delectable selection of fresh catches from the Mediterranean Sea. The maritime-inspired decor and vibrant ambience add to the experience. Specializing in seafood tapas, their menu boasts mouthwatering options like garlic prawns (gambas al ajillo), grilled octopus, and paella. One of the best spots in town for seafood tapas.

Buenavista

Calle Gaona, 8; tel. 951/387-464; www.buenavistagastrobar.es; 1pm-4pm and 7:30pm-11pm Mon., Thurs., and Sun., 1pm-4pm and 7:30pm-11:30pm Fri.-Sat.; €20

Buenavista is a hip eatery that reinvents traditional tapas with a creative flair. The stylish decor and chic atmosphere create a trendy backdrop for an unforgettable dining experience. From the tender oxtail croquettes to the melt-in-your-mouth pork cheek confit, every dish is a celebration of flavor and presentation. The extensive wine list includes both local and international selections, and the attentive staff are happy to help you find the perfect pairing. For a modern spin on Andalusian cuisine, Buenavista is a top-notch choice.

Soho District

Levi Angelo Gelato

Calle Tomás Heredia, 11; www.leviangelo.com; noon-12:30am Mon.-Thurs., noon-1am Fri.-Sat., 1pm-12:30am Sun.; €4

Not only is this the best gelato in Málaga, but this is also one of the best gelatos in the world. Don't take my word for it. Levi Angelo's delectably creamy gelato concoctions have been a finalist for the recent Gelato Festival World Masters for the past few years now. All the classic flavors plus some fun takes, like coffee with Bailey's, make this a must-stop for lovers of everything cool and sweet.

Mia Café

Calle Vendeja, 9; tel. 671/447-679; 9:30am-6pm Mon.-Fri., 10am-6pm Sat.; €4

Mia has the best cup of coffee in town, hands down. Just a short walk from the main part of the historic center, this easy-to-miss hole-in-the-wall is an address for serious coffee lovers. Come here for the coffee, but know that the bagel sandwiches are a nice little bonus. There's no outdoor seating and limited indoor seating (I did say this was a hole-in-the-wall, after all), but kind professional baristas will feather your creamy café con leche with panache.

Santa Coffee Roasters

Calle Tomás Heredia, 5; tel. 952/123-456; https://santacoffee.es; 8am-8pm Mon.-Fri., 9am-8pm Sat.-Sun.; €8

A haven for coffee enthusiasts and health-conscious breakfast seekers, this charming local coffee chain boasts a wide selection of ethically sourced and freshly roasted coffee beans, ensuring a flavorful cup every time. Lots of cakes are on the menu, including carrot cake, spinach and cardamom, and vegan chocolate, among some other tasty treats. The breakfast menu features delicious toasted artisanal bread topped with a variety of delectable spreads, from avocado and smoked salmon to almond butter and fresh berries. A nice change of pace from the typical Spanish fare. There's only outdoor terrace seating. There are two other locations in Málaga (Calle Fernán González, 6 and Calle San Agustín, 5), both with slightly different hours.

★ La Deriva

Alameda de Colón, 7; tel. 638/086-529; noon-midnight daily; €20-30

This trendy, vibrant tapas bar captures the essence of today's Málaga. Contemporary decor and a laid-back ambience set the stage for a delightful meal. The tapas menu offers a mix of traditional Spanish dishes and inventive creations. The Iberian pork sliders with caramelized onions are a popular choice, as are the creamy spinach and goat cheese croquettes. Pair your tapas with one of their signature cocktails or a selection from their excellent wine list.

La Malagueta

Chiringuito Mami Beach

Puerto de Matías Prats, 2; tel. 673/121-702; noon-7pm Thurs.-Tues.; €20

Come here for simple seafood grill right on Malagueta Beach. Like at other chiringuitos (beach bars) dotted along the coast of Andalusia, you'll want to stick to freshly grilled seafood for the best dining experience. Always ask what's fresh caught. Service can be a bit slow, particularly during the busy summer months, so plan on a long lunch, relax, and enjoy the views out over the Mediterranean.

El Merendero de Antonio Martín

Plaza de la Malagueta; tel. 951/776-502; 1pm-11:30pm Mon.-Sat., 1pm-4pm Sun.; €40-50

This seaside restaurant, cheekily named a "merendero" (picnic area), is more of a special occasion romantic type of place for the locals and an upscale dining option popular with travelers. The highlights here, beyond the stunning views, are the rice dishes, such as the famous Spanish paella. All rice dishes are accompanied with yolk aioli, roasted garlic, and saffron, making for a delightful experience for your tastebuds. Though the restaurant might be pricey for some, a tapa and drink can be had at the lounge for around €10, which, accounting for the views, is a pretty good bargain.

★ Restaurante José Carlos Garcia

Muelle Uno, Puerto de Málaga; www.restaurantejcg.com; 1pm-4pm and 8pm-11pm Tues.-Sat.; €50-80

Restaurante José Carlos Garcia is a Michelin-starred little culinary marvel, delivering a gastronomic journey. Located in the picturesque Muelle Uno harbor, the restaurant boasts stunning views of the Mediterranean Sea. Chef José Carlos Garcia's innovative approach to tapas elevates traditional Spanish dishes to an art form. Each plate, from the exquisite foie gras with Pedro Ximénez reduction to the delicate sea bass ceviche, is a masterful display of creativity and craftsmanship, featuring top-quality ingredients sourced from the region. Reservations are needed.

Pedregalejo

Restaurante El Gaucho I

Calle Jábega, 56; 9pm-11:30pm Mon.-Thurs., 1:30pm-4pm and 9pm-11:30pm Fri.-Sun.; €10-20

This family-run tavern offers an array of traditional tapas, highlighting the region's finest produce and flavors. The hand-carved jamón ibérico is a must-try. Pair it with a glass of their excellent local sherry for a delicious combo. The menu also features classics like espetos (grilled sardines) and gambas al ajillo (garlic prawns), alongside daily specials that showcase seasonal ingredients. With its rustic charm and Andalusian character, El Gaucho is old-school and caters to the local crowd. There is an El Gaucho II (same owners) closer to the old city center, but I like heading to the original in East Málaga for more local vibes and beachfront goodness.

El Tintero

Avenida Salvador Allende, 340; tel. 650/680-956; https://eltinteromalaga.com; 12:30pm-11:30pm daily; €12-20

This unique seafood spot practices a lively "auction" system, where waiters bring around dishes of freshly caught seafood and announce prices. The first person to raise their hand wins the dish. It's a fun and engaging way to dine, and you can choose from an array of delicious offerings, like grilled fish, fried squid, and garlic prawns. The atmosphere is usually lively, with locals and tourists mingling, and the ocean views add to the vibe.

ACCOMMODATIONS

Historic Center

★ TOC Hostel Málaga

Calle Comedias, 18; tel. 952/911-264; https://tochostels.com/malaga; €18

The centrally located, clean hostel is hands down the best budget deal in town. Female-only dorm-style rooms are great for independent female travelers. If you are on a tight budget, check here for availability before looking into other options.

Hotel Boutique Nómadas

Calle Guerrero, 3; tel. 951/993-452; http://hotelboutiquenomadas.com; €80

A friendly owner is generally on-site at this well-located hotel in a renovated 19th-century building in central Málaga. It's quieter than other options at this level and has lovely turn-of-the-20th-century decor. Rooms are simple, clean, quirky, and fun. Staff are great. There is definitely room for updating, as this is more of a nice budget hotel than a true "boutique" as the name might suggest. Set expectations accordingly and you'll be happy. The rooftop terrace is lovely; relax with a few drinks and enjoy the views.

★ Hotel Palacete de Álamos

Calle Álamos, 20; tel. 952/215-410; www.palacetedealamos.com; €95

With lots of exposed brick as well as a contemporary twist, this hotel has charm for days. It features some of the original medieval walls of Málaga as part of its construction. A few of the rooms have views out over the cathedral, making for a romantic backdrop. Location is central, with the main parking at the marina just steps away and the beach a short five-minute stroll. Wi-Fi is only good in the public areas.

Hotel Don Curro

Calle Sancha de Lara, 9; tel. 952/227-200; www.hoteldoncurro.com; €110

Don Curro is a clean, modest hotel with over 100 rooms. Rooms veer toward simple, masculine lines and have a general revitalized feel about them. The junior suites are a good value for families, and most room categories have possibilities for views. It can be a bit noisy on the street side, so make sure to use your ear plugs if you are a light sleeper.

Hotel del Pintor

Calle Álamos, 27; tel. 952/224-350; www.hoteldelpintor.com; €280

You quickly see why they call this the Painter's House. The red-and-white color scheme recalls flamenco and bullfighting, the passions of Andalusia. The clean, modern, and bright rooms are situated around a classic central courtyard, which will plunge you right into the feeling of old Málaga.

★ Palacio Solecio

Calle Granada, 61; tel. 952/222-000; https://palaciosolecio.com; €300

If you were going to splurge on a property in Málaga, this would be the one. This award-winning boutique is housed in a gorgeously renovated 18th-century palace right in the city center. Not only will you be within walking distance to everything, but when you come back from a long day of exploration, you'll have some of the kindest bespoke service in the region. Do not hesitate to ask for recommendations or some help making dinner reservations and such. You can expect plush towels, baby-soft sheets, and a particularly well-thought-through breakfast service. If you are feeling particularly splurgy and appreciate a good view, the Tower Room (there is only the one) looks out over downtown.

Soho District

Feel Hostels Soho Málaga

Calle Vendeja, 25; tel. 952/222-832; www.feelhostels.com; €25

Just on the edge of the city center, across the street from Parkigrund (paid public parking), and walking distance to the train station, this hostel is in a prime central location. It can get noisy, and the air-conditioning isn't strong enough for the hotter months, but the price is right. Great for solo travelers and those on a budget. Guests are typically the younger backpacker crowd, and there is nearly always a meetup happening somewhere.

★ Hotel Soho Boutique

Calle Córdoba, 5; tel. 952/224-079; www.sohohoteles.com; €250

The local Soho Boutique chain currently owns and operates nine boutique properties in Málaga, so take care to note which one you reserve! Not that any of them are bad—quite the opposite. You could easily have a great stay in any one of them. However, it can be confusing! This is my go-to boutique hotel chain in Spain, and if I had to pick one in Málaga, this would be the one. It's a charming, well-located boutique in Málaga's historic district, with fantastic service and a fun wine cave where you breakfast.

INFORMATION AND SERVICES

Tourist Information Center

Plaza de la Marina, 11; tel. 951/926-020; www.malagaturismo.com; 9am-6pm daily

Conveniently located right next to the port, this tourism office has lots of free maps and guides. You can book guided experiences in English. If you haven't planned much to do in Málaga, stop in here to figure out an activity that might be good for you and your travel companions.

GETTING THERE

Air

Málaga-Costa del Sol Airport

Avenida del Comandante García Morato; tel. 913/211-000

The Málaga-Costa del Sol Airport (AGP) serves as the main international gateway to Málaga and the Costa del Sol region. It is a well-connected airport with flights to numerous destinations across Europe and beyond. Major airlines and budget carriers operate regular flights to and from the airport, making it convenient for travelers from all around the world.

From the airport to downtown Málaga and other locations, you can use various transportation options. The airport is approximately 14 km (8.7 mi) southwest of the city center.

Málaga Airport has a direct **train station** connected to the suburban train network (Cercanías) of Málaga. The train line C-1 connects the airport to the city center and other destinations along the coast, offering a quick and cost-effective option for reaching your destination (€1.80 one-way).

Several **bus** services operate between the airport and the city center. The Airport Express Bus (Line A) offers a convenient connection to the city center, with multiple stops along the way. Other regular bus lines serve different areas of Málaga and neighboring towns.

Taxis are readily available outside the airport terminals, offering a comfortable and direct way to reach your destination. The taxi fare to the city center is typically metered, and the journey takes around 15-20 minutes, depending on traffic conditions.

If you prefer the flexibility of having your own vehicle, many **car rental agencies** (Avis, Hertz, and others) have desks at the airport. Málaga typically has some of the least expensive car rental rates in the region. Often you can find last-minute deals on small sedans for €10 (or less!) a day.

Train

If you are connecting from other major cities in Andalusia, you'll likely be traveling by train. Thankfully, the modern train station, **Málaga María Zambrano** (Calle Cuarteles, 2), is well connected throughout Málaga and near enough to consider walking right into downtown if you're traveling light. The station itself is attached to a contemporary shopping center. Consult the national train operator Renfe (www.renfe.com) for updated schedules. Train costs vary depending on demand.

- Seville (2 hr; 8 daily; €25): There is no high-speed train line to Seville. A couple of trains are even slower (3 hr) and make several more stops.
- Granada (1.5 hr; 3 daily; €20): There are only three daily, all on the newer high-speed trains.
- Córdoba (1 hr; 10-plus daily; €30): Opt for the high-speed train system.
- Madrid (3 hr; 10-plus daily; €50): Opt for the high-speed train system.

Bus

Málaga has a well-connected public transportation system, offering convenient options for getting around the city and the rest of Andalusia. The urban bus network in Málaga is managed by **EMT** (Empresa Malagueña de Transportes; www.emtmalaga.es; €1.30) and provides extensive coverage throughout the city. Buses are a popular mode of transportation for both locals and visitors, serving as a cost-effective means to reach various neighborhoods and attractions. Bus routes typically operate from early morning until late evening, and they are linked to key locations, including Málaga María Zambrano station and the airport (€4).

All buses from around Andalusia arrive to Málaga María Zambrano station. Check updated schedules with Alsa (http://alsa.com) and Avanza (www.avanzabus.com), as they run the most buses in the region. Córdoba (10-plus daily; 2.5 hr; €13), Granada (10-plus daily; 2 hr; €12), and Seville (10-plus daily; 3 hr; €16) are all connected. Take note of the routes down the coast to La Línea (5 daily; 2.5 hr; €21)—use the La Línea bus to cross over to Gibraltar—as well as Tarifa (2 daily; 3 hr; €25) and Cádiz (2 daily; 4 hr; €35), as they are not serviced by train.

Car

Málaga sits at the junction of the A-45 freeway, which runs inland north to Córdoba (2 hr; 161 km/100 mi), and the A-7, which runs east-west along the Mediterranean Coast, connecting with Gibraltar (1.5 hr; 135 km/84 mi), Tarifa (2 hr; 161 km/100 mi), and Cádiz (2.5 hr; 235 km/146 mi).

Parking is generally easy to find throughout Málaga, except during peak tourist seasons. It's advisable to check availability before arrival and inquire with your accommodation about parking options, as many hotels offer parking facilities. Once in Málaga, exploring on foot is convenient, much like elsewhere in Andalusia.

GETTING AROUND

Walking

Exploring Málaga on foot is a delightful way to experience the city's charm and beauty. The historic city center is pedestrian-friendly, with narrow streets and charming alleys leading to various points of interest. Many of the major attractions, including the Málaga Cathedral, Alcazaba, and the Picasso Museum, are within walking distance of each other. The Gibralfaro Castle is a big uphill climb, though the views along the way are unbeatable.

Public Transport

Málaga's public transportation system is efficient and well developed, making it easy to get around the city and its surroundings. You have your choice of a subway system that links to other towns down the coast (as well as the airport) or the local bus.

Bus

EMT operates the bus network in Málaga, offering extensive coverage across the city. Buses are a popular choice for locals and tourists alike, providing a cost-effective (€1.40 per one-way ticket) solution to reach various neighborhoods and attractions. The buses generally run from early morning until late evening, and routes are well connected to key locations such as the airport and train station.

Subway/Suburban Train

Málaga has a modern and efficient suburban train system (Cercanías) that connects the city with nearby towns and resorts along the Costa del Sol. The train is a convenient option for day trips to popular beach destinations like Fuengirola, Torremolinos, and Benalmadena, as well as the Málaga Airport. It runs underground in Málaga, acting as a subway, before coming up for air along its other stops. Fares are decided by zones, with Zones 0 and 1 (€1.80) covering downtown Malaga and the airport and Zones 2 (€2.05), 3 (€2.70), and 4 (€3.60) going farther afield to neighboring towns.

Taxi

Taxis are an inexpensive and readily available option for getting around Málaga, especially when you need to reach specific locations that might not be easily accessible by public transport. You can find taxi stands throughout the city, or simply hail a taxi on the street. Nearly anywhere you want to go around the city will be less than €10.

Car

Driving in the city center can be challenging due to narrow, one-way streets and limited parking options. You'll want to park your car and explore the city by public transport and on foot.

For those looking to drive around Andalusia, Málaga is the best place to rent cars. It has the largest, least expensive selection of automobiles with all the standard companies as well as a few up-and-coming and smaller companies. Often you can rent cars for €10 a day. This is one of those things that you really can usually reserve the week you travel, as long as you are not too picky about the kind of automobile you need. There is almost always a large selection, and last-minute deals are usually available.

Parking

Málaga is the sort of place you'll mostly want to explore by foot. If you do have a rental car, it's best to leave it in a parking lot for your stay. You can find various parking lots and garages throughout the city. Some popular parking options include:

- **Parking Avenida Andalucía** (Avenida de Andalucía)
- **Parking Teatro Cervantes** (Calle Ramos Marín)
- **Parking Muelle Uno** (Muelle Dos, Puerto de Málaga)

Additionally, street parking is available in many areas, but be sure to check local regulations and parking restrictions to avoid fines.

Gibraltar

What is it about Gibraltar that has captured public fascination? A tall rock jutting out of the water? Perhaps it has more to do with once being a place where one set sail across the Mediterranean for Africa. There is the thrill of travel when you think of Gibraltar, though the reality will likely only match up for the most optimistic of travelers. For most, Gibraltar is the sort of destination that one checks off a list, never to return.

Tourism, alongside online gambling and financial services, is one of the pillars of the Gibraltar economy, and you can't help but feel the whole of Gibraltar is a little Disney-fied. It seems otherworldly that you can just walk a few steps from the land of tapas and flamenco and find yourself in jolly old England, the land of high tea, dingy pubs, and fish-and-chips. English is spoken everywhere, so if you have been struggling to get by in Spanish, this will be a welcome reprieve. Otherwise, most everything of interest can be seen in less than a day, making this appropriate for a day trip while you are traveling through Andalusia rather than an overnight.

Gibraltar

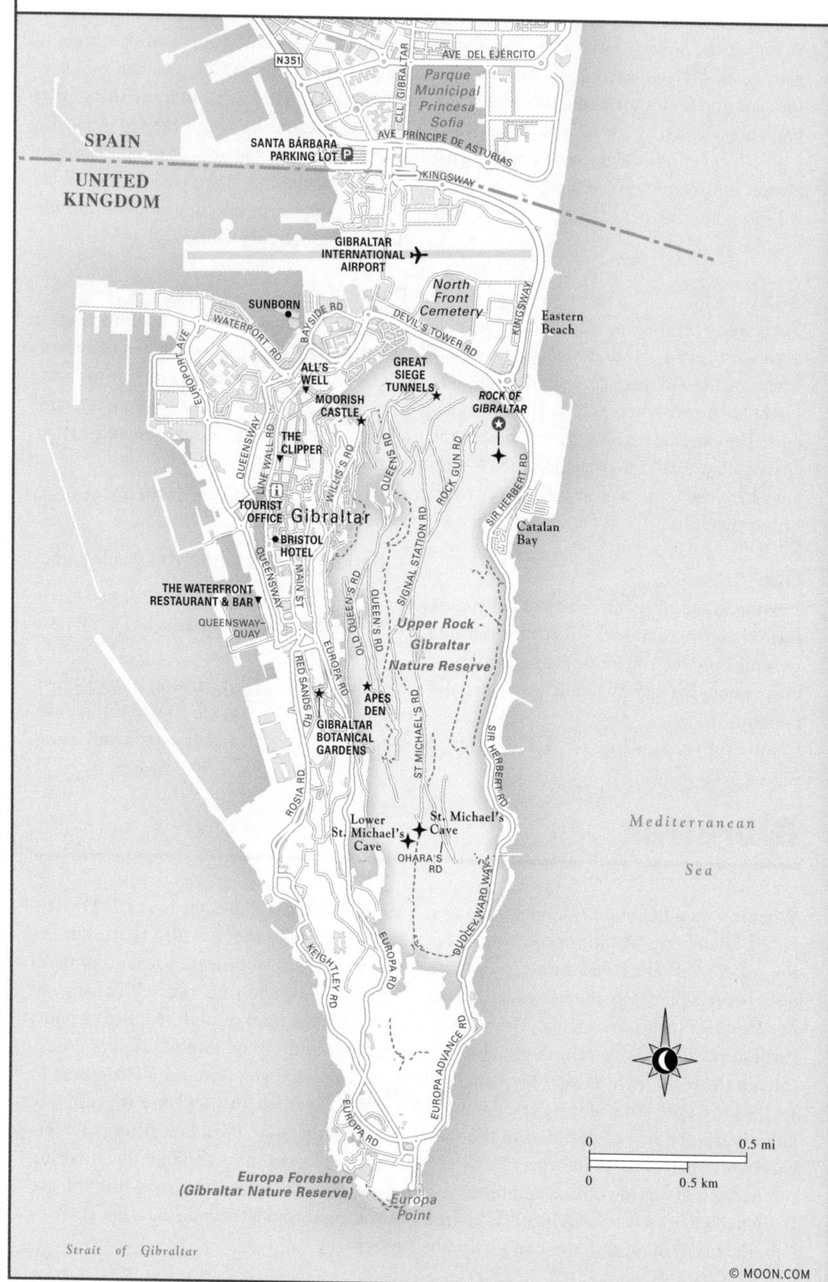
N351
AVE DEL EJÉRCITO
CLL GIBRALTAR
Parque Municipal Princesa Sofia
AVE PRINCIPE DE ASTURIAS
SPAIN
SANTA BÁRBARA PARKING LOT
UNITED KINGDOM
KINGSWAY
GIBRALTAR INTERNATIONAL AIRPORT
North Front Cemetery
SUNBORN
BAYSIDE RD
WATERPORT RD
DEVIL'S TOWER RD
KINGSWAY
Eastern Beach
EUROPORT AVE
ALL'S WELL
GREAT SIEGE TUNNELS
MOORISH CASTLE
ROCK OF GIBRALTAR
QUEENSWAY
LINE WALL RD
THE CLIPPER
WILLIS'S RD
QUEENS RD
ROCK GUN RD
SIR HERBERT RD
TOURIST OFFICE
Gibraltar
SIGNAL STATION RD
Catalan Bay
BRISTOL HOTEL
QUEENSWAY
MAIN ST
OLD QUEEN'S RD
QUEEN'S RD
THE WATERFRONT RESTAURANT & BAR
QUEENSWAY-QUAY
Upper Rock - Gibraltar Nature Reserve
RED SANDS RD
EUROPA RD
APES DEN
GIBRALTAR BOTANICAL GARDENS
ST MICHAEL'S RD
SIR HERBERT RD
ROSIA RD
Lower St. Michael's Cave
St. Michael's Cave
OHARA'S RD
Mediterranean Sea
DUDLEY WARD WAY
KEIGHTLEY RD
EUROPA RD
EUROPA ADVANCE RD
EUROPA RD
0
0.5 mi
0
0.5 km
Europa Foreshore (Gibraltar Nature Reserve)
Europa Point
Strait of Gibraltar
© MOON.COM

NEED TO KNOW

Because you are crossing an international border and entering/exiting the EU and the Schengen Zone, there are a few things that you need to know:

- **Passport:** You need your passport to cross the British border into Gibraltar. US, Canadian, Australian, and British passport holders do not need a special visa and can expect to use their passport to cross the border with no issue. If you are a passport holder from a different country, research what other visa or permission you will need to cross through the UK border, if any.
- **Currency:** Gibraltar uses the British pound (£) as a currency, though euros are accepted just about everywhere (though at an unfavorable rate). It is best to either pay for everything with a credit card or pull a bit of local currency out of the ATMs for your stay in Gib.
- **Electricity:** Annoyingly, Gib uses the British three-prong plug, so you'll likely need another type of adapter to charge your devices.
- **Country code:** The country code for Gibraltar is 350. From any country outside of Gibraltar, you will need to dial this number plus the local eight-digit number to complete a phone call.

ORIENTATION

Gibraltar is an arrowhead-shaped piece of land jutting out from mainland Spain. A heavily enforced border with passport control divides Spain from the UK exclave of Gibraltar. The Rock of Gibraltar towers to the east along the blade, dropping dramatically into the Mediterranean. Nearly all commerce, restaurants, and ports are along the western edge, though a narrow road leads up onto the Rock of Gibraltar, where you'll find all the sites of interest.

In town, it's best to get around on foot. The most popular strips for restaurants and shopping are pedestrian-only. For mounting the Rock of Gibraltar, you could hike (though be prepared for steep elevation gain) or take a tourist van to the top. If you're traveling by bus from Seville or Málaga, look for connections with La Linea, just next to Gibraltar.

SIGHTS

All the sights to see in Gibraltar are on the actual Rock of Gibraltar itself. There is enough to keep you busy for one day, though not longer, and only that if you are hiking. If taking the cable car or a taxi to the top, it is a solid half-day outing. If you time it right, you can visit the Rock of Gibraltar in the morning and then head into town for a pub lunch before continuing your travels.

★ Rock of Gibraltar

Towering above the city of Gibraltar, this pillar of Hercules needs no introduction. Most everything in Gib revolves around this small mountainous rock. Historical military sites include O'Hara's Battery at the very top of the Rock, the small Military Heritage Centre, a cheesy City Under Siege exhibit, World War II tunnels, and the Moorish Castle. All are found along the hiking paths twisting around the Rock, and the highlights are covered here.

It's worth noting that Gorham's Cave Complex is also found on the Rock, and though it is a UNESCO World Heritage Site, this series of four caves providing evidence of Neanderthal civilization of over 100,000 years ago is only viewable from the lookout above.

Cable Car

https://gibraltarinfo.gi/cable-car; 9:30am-7:15pm daily late Mar.-late Oct., 9:30am-6:15pm daily late Oct.-late Mar.; every 10 min; £18 round-trip

It's best to take the cable car to the summit, though keep an eye on the weather. If it's too windy or rainy the cable car won't run. Purchase a combined £32 ticket for the nature reserve and cable car. This way you can take the cable car to the top and hike downhill through the reserve covering most of the Rock of Gibraltar.

1
2
3
4

Apes Den

https://gibraltarinfo.gi; 9:30am-7:15pm daily late Mar.-late Oct., 9:30am-6:15pm daily late Oct.-late Mar.; included in £18 ticket

Undoubtedly the celebrities of Gib are the indigenous Barbary macaques. These monkeys have the distinction of being the only free-living primates in Europe, except for we humans. They are the same species living in the mountain ranges of Morocco. Throughout the years countless tourists have fed these monkeys, and the practice is encouraged (though it should not be) by van drivers who shuttle travelers up and down the Rock. Everyone is looking for that perfect selfie, but it's best to enjoy the macaques from a distance. And do watch your bags and pockets. The monkeys can get grabby looking for food and have been known to snatch loose purses and bags and run away with them. The actual den itself is inaccessible, but there is a viewpoint where the monkeys typically gather at the summit of the Rock.

St. Michael's Cave

https://gibraltarinfo.gi; 9:30am-7:15pm daily late Mar.-late Oct., 9:30am-6:15pm daily late Oct.-late Mar.; included in £18 ticket

This incredible natural cave formation with a series of stalactites and stalagmites will make a spelunker from even the most cave-averse. Colorful lights illuminate some of the most interesting cave formations, really bringing them to life. The cave takes its name from one formation that does look like an angel with outstretched wings. Historically, the cave has been used for thousands of years by locals for different reasons, and with its naturally phenomenal acoustics, it is no surprise that it is used occasionally for concerts in the built-in amphitheater. The cave can be cold, even in the hot summer months, and there will be moisture on the walls, wicking its way through the rock.

1: Rock of Gibraltar **2:** the cable car to the top of the Rock **3:** a macaque monkey **4:** St. Michael's Cave

Moorish Castle

https://gibraltarinfo.gi; 9:30am-7:15pm daily late Mar.-late Oct., 9:30am-6:15pm daily late Oct.-late Mar.; included in £18 ticket

You can see how this small fortress, the oldest building still standing in Gibraltar, was formidable in its day, protecting the area for miles around. The natural protection of the Rock of Gibraltar to its back and a steep slope to its front facing the water made this fortress, with its narrow staircases and slit peepholes, nearly impenetrable. If you are hiking down, this is worth a stop, if only for the commanding views over the port from the crenellated terrace. There isn't too much information available in any language, so it's best to do any research beforehand. The café at the entrance to the castle makes a good stop for a refreshment.

Great Siege Tunnels

https://gibraltarinfo.gi; 9:30am-7:15pm daily late Mar.-late Oct., 9:30am-6:15pm daily late Oct.-late Mar.; included in £18 ticket

The Great Siege Tunnels are a somber reminder of Gibraltar's significant military history. The tunnels were originally dug in 1782, during the (unsuccessful) three-year siege of Gibraltar (the Great Siege) by the French and Spanish during the American Revolutionary War. They were expanded extensively during World War II, becoming a massive tunnel system. Numerous pictures detail the work the excavators and engineers accomplished. It took a great feat of engineering to create a military stronghold to fight against fascist powers.

Lower St. Michael's Cave

www.visitgibraltar.gi/see-and-do/natural-attractions/lower-st-michaels-cave-36; €30

Glimmering with white, gray, and red stalactite columns, this cave was discovered in 1942 during the work on the Great Siege Tunnels. Some say it resembles the Sagrada Família cathedral in Barcelona. The tour is a well-lit speleological experience where you can discover the enormous size of the main chamber of the cave as well as the profusion and variety of calcite formations and a lake of crystal-clear water. It involves some scrambling and light climbing with ropes. Tours must be arranged at least three days in advance through one of the many contacts listed on the website.

Gibraltar Botanical Gardens

Red Sands Road, at the foot of the cable car; tel. 200-41235; 8am-sunset daily; free

A lovely surprise to most travelers, this 6-hectare (15-acre) subtropical garden has been a local secret for over 200 years. First planted in 1816, it is the perfect sort of place to take a saunter. Enjoy the cactus garden and various statues, some dating back to the 18th century. The open-air theater is occasionally used for outdoor concerts and weddings, and the playground and public restrooms make this a good place to take the kids. The small, attached **Alameda Wildlife Park** (€8) houses rescue animals caught from smugglers and is a great place to take little ones to learn about the creatures around us.

TOURS

Guided Tours

Gibraltar Victory Tours

tel. 580-15000; www.gibraltarvictorytours.com

Whether you are looking for a private guided walking tour or a dolphin-watching experience, this local day-tour operator has you covered. Guides are all licensed and there is a good variety of options for different interests and skill levels.

Taxi Tours

Gibraltar Taxi Association

Winston Churchill Avenue; tel. 200-70052; £35

Taxi tours take you to the top of the Rock of Gibraltar. Though a taxi tour company is named here, for the most part they are all interchangeable. A taxi tour isn't the sort of experience you need to book ahead of time. Just book it after crossing through passport control.

BEACHES

The best beaches in Gibraltar are all on its eastern shore with clean, photogenic strips of sand, generally calm sea, and basic infrastructure. That said, given that they face east, you do miss out on sunsets here.

Eastern Beach

East of the airport; free

A bit off the radar, Eastern Beach is one of the nicest strips of sand in all of the United Kingdom. It's just east of the airport, which thankfully does not have a lot of traffic, so you'll have some quiet moments. The Mediterranean waters here are great for swimming and sunbathing and the readily available public restrooms are appreciated.

Catalan Bay

South of Eastern Beach; free

With a stretch of colorful houses hugging the sand beneath the Rock, this is easily Gibraltar's most picturesque beach. But the sun disappears in the mid-late afternoon, casting it in shade.

FESTIVALS

Gibraltar Chess Festival

January/February

Every winter, Gibraltar hosts one of the world's most prestigious chess tournaments, inviting 60 grand masters from all around the world. It's likely one of the most erudite festivals along the coast, with Gibraltar as a fitting, strategic backdrop for the world's most famous war game. Check. Mate.

Gibraltar International Boat Show

April

With spring come yachts and pleasure boats. Though it makes sense that the hulled beauties are the star of this festival, the side tents of fashionable automobiles, dance parties, and nightly music give them a run for their money. Military history buffs will enjoy the display of navy vessels, while the luxury liners and yachts are aspirational for many.

Gibraltar Music Festival

June; www.visitgibraltar.gi; £40

The annual musical festival that rocks Gibraltar's summers is a fun way to celebrate diversity and unity through music. Musical acts from around the world are invited and participate in this fun-loving festival.

FOOD

Pub Fare

The Clipper

Irish Town Lane; tel. 200-79791; 9am-10pm Mon.-Sat., 10am-early evening Sun.; £15

Full of dark wood and darker stouts, this is a popular classic British pub where you can get your fish-and-chips fix over a pint of your choosing. Most nights after 6pm they have a two-for-one deal for mains, which is a nice little cost saver if you're sticking around for dinner. Service is kind, if a touch rushed in the afternoon during the typically busy lunch periods.

All's Well

Grand Casements Square; tel. 200-72987; 10am-10pm daily; £15

All's Well is another nice pub for a fish-and-chips break. The standout feature is the shaded umbrella seating beneath the leafy green on the square, so prioritize dining outside if the weather allows. The menu also features standard Spanish tapas that are done really well. Check out their selection of croquetas.

Seafood

The Waterfront Restaurant & Bar

1 Cormorant Wharf 4/5 Ragged Staff Wharf, Queensway Quay; tel. 200-45666; https://thewaterfrontgib.com; 10am-10pm daily; £50

This picturesque seafood bistro with waterfront ambience has the prices to match the yacht crowd vibes; it's upscale with a hint of pretentious, though not so upscale as to be absurd. It's a good spot for a nicer meal, maybe for a date night or as a special treat for your friend. Stick to the fresh catch, steaks, or sea bass and you'll walk away happy as a clam.

ACCOMMODATIONS

There are no great accommodations around Gibraltar and most travelers will find everything a touch expensive for what it is, particularly when compared with what is available just across the border. For this reason, and the fact that Gibraltar really is quite small, it is best to consider Gibraltar as a day trip from Tarifa or Málaga, ideally when connecting the two destinations. If you do have your heart set on spending the night on Gib, here are a few options.

Bristol Hotel

10 Cathedral Square; tel. 200-76800; www.bristolhotel.gi; £45

The rooms could definitely use a refresh, though the location smack in the heart of Gibraltar is spot on. In the hotter summer, the pool can be a downright necessity. This is a good, not great, budget-friendly option for travelers who just need a clean, comfy place to rest their heads.

Sunborn

35 Ocean Village Promenade; tel. 200-16000; www.sunborngibraltar.com; £200

Perhaps one of the more unique stays along the coast, the world's first five-star cruise ship hotel is permanently moored in Gib. If you ever wanted to stay on a luxury cruise ship without ever setting sail, this is your chance. You'll find all the glitz and glamour of a luxury liner, complete with multiple on-site restaurants, vast swimming pools, live shows, casinos, spas, bars, and more.

INFORMATION AND SERVICES

Gibraltar is a small exclave. You'll find ample information for getting around because tourism, revolving around the Rock of Gibraltar, is the primary economic driver of the town.

Tourist Information Office

13 Jack Mackintosh Square; tel. 200-45000; www.visitgibraltar.gi; 9am-4:30pm Mon.-Fri., 9:30am-3:30pm Sat.

You'll be able to pick up a map of the city, should you need it, as well as information on visiting the Rock of Gibraltar. Do check out the website. It is easy to access, extensive, and quite informative, including not only what to do and see around Gibraltar but also updated travel info and events.

GETTING THERE AND AROUND

Air

Gibraltar International Airport

British Lines Road; tel. 200-12345; www.gibraltarairport.gi

The Gibraltar International Airport (GIB) only serves UK destinations (London, Bristol, and Manchester). If you happen to be coming through the United Kingdom, it may make sense to use the airport here, but for most travelers, Seville and Málaga are much better options for flights.

Bus

La Línea de la Concepción bus station (Ave. de España) is a short five-minute walk from the border. From Málaga there are buses about every two hours (www.avanzabus.com; 2-3 hr, depending on route; €16).

Car

If you have a rental car, it's easiest to park in **La Línea** and walk across the border. If you are driving, follow signs for La Línea. The **Santa Bárbara parking lot** (€10 for the day) is the closest parking lot to the border. Pay for parking only at the official booth. A common hustle is for locals to pose as parking lot attendants and ask you to pay them.

If you do choose to drive in, plan on a long wait, particularly during morning and evening rush hour, as a lot of the workers in Gibraltar live in Spain. Driving in Gibraltar is, thankfully, just like in the rest of Spain. You will not have to change to driving on the left side of the road, as they do in the rest of the United Kingdom, though there is a confusing network of one-way streets to navigate and you will not be allowed to drive to the top of the Rock of Gibraltar.

Tarifa

Tarifa has a touch of that island-vacation vibe to it, especially in the warmer summer months. Interestingly, Tarifa is the southernmost point of continental Europe. It is a picturesque old city with a long history, interesting to walk around and blissfully unscathed by global brands in the old city. You won't find a single Starbucks among its many cafés.

Tarifa's old town is contained within the historic Jerez Gate, fortified walls, and watch towers. The prominent Castle of Santa Catalina, a lazaretto (quarantine area) during the plague, is an unmissable (and inaccessible) site to the west of the port. Just below you will find a block of local bars, restaurants, and tapas joints teeming with locals. Tarifa has a municipal museum (Museo Municipal) and an old church (San Mateo Church), though if you are spending time here, it's likely more for the beaches, the quaint old town, or catching a lift on the ferry to Tangier.

SIGHTS

Castle of Tarifa

(Castillo Guzmán el Bueno)

Calle Guzmán el Bueno; tel. 607/984-871; www.castilloguzmanelbueno.com; 10am-4pm Wed.-Sun.; €4

Lying alongside the Strait of Gibraltar, on the most southerly point of the Iberian Peninsula, this fortress is often dubbed the "last castle in Europe." In fact its strategic position made it, for many centuries, the primary port of entry and departure from the "Old Continent." With a history dating over a thousand years, this castle was declared a Historic-Artistic Monument in 1931. It is the best preserved castle of caliphate origin in Al-Andalus. Just a short walk east of the castle, the **old watchtower** (Torre Miramar; 10am-3:30pm Wed.-Sun.; free) has commanding views across the strait to Africa.

Baelo Claudia Roman Ruins

Ensenada de Bolonia; tel. 956/106-793; www.museosdeandalucia.es/web/conjuntoarqueologicobaelocladia; 9am-9pm Tues.-Sat., 9am-3pm Sun. mid-Mar. through mid-June, 9am-3pm Tues.-Sun. mid-June through mid-Sept., 9am-6pm Tues.-Sat., 9am-3pm Sun. mid-Sept. through mid-Mar.; free

Baelo Claudia is an oft-overlooked, though important, Roman coastal city. At Conjunto Arqueológico de Baelo Claudia, the on-site museum has a really nice collection of Roman sculptures and other artifacts. It's just a short drive from Tarifa (25 min; 23 km/14 mi). Right after visiting the ruins, you can hop over to Bolonia Beach and perhaps see why the Romans loved this little spot along the coast so much.

SPORTS AND RECREATION

Beaches

Chica Beach

This small Mediterranean cove, located between the port and the Isla de Tarifa, offers a familiar, cozy ambience looking out over the boats coming and going from the port. Its cool, crystalline Mediterranean waters are much calmer than the west-facing beaches directly on the Atlantic. As it is a short walk from the old city of Tarifa and with safer water, this is the ideal beach for families with young ones.

Tarifa Beach

Sometimes called locally Playa de los Lances, this long stretch of Atlantic-facing sand to the west of the city is a great spot for sunsets and kitesurfing. Undoubtedly, if there is a stiff breeze you will find the sky littered with colorful kites with boarders hanging on below, occasionally seeming to take flight high in the air before swiftly landing on the next breaker.

Baelo Claudia Roman Ruins

1

2

3

Valdevaqueros Beach

Valdevaqueros Beach often makes appearances on various lists in magazines and on the internet as the best beach in Spain, and for good reason. What stands out the most are the large dune formations—mountains of fine golden sand. Climbing to the top can be tiring, although there are some sections where the sand is hard and very compact, which makes the ascent easier. At the top of the dunes, sea, desert, forest, and mountains converge. This beach is northwest along the coast from Tarifa, just 10 minutes by car.

Bolonia Beach

Crystal clear waters. White, almost tropical sand that follows on a long, easy curve. It's easy to see why this beach is so popular with the locals. You'll need a car to get here, because the beach is about a 25-minute drive (23 km/14 mi) from Tarifa. Do check the wind warnings before you go. The winds tend to kick up the sand, which has the effect of exfoliating the skin.

Atlanterra Beach

Traveling farther afield, you can find the Atlanterra Beach, which extends south from the nearby town of Zahara (1 hr; 48 km/30 mi). This local beach is out of the way, but if you are looking for a more tranquil, family-friendly beach, you can find it here, even in the crazy busy summer months when it seems like every stretch of sand along Spain's southern coast is packed umbrella-to-umbrella with vacationers.

★ Dolphin- and Whale-Watching

Pilot whales, sperm whales, fin whales, orcas, bottlenose dolphins, and striped dolphins all call these waters home. An excursion is a great way to get out on the water and interact with the aquatic nature of the Strait of Gibraltar. Sail as early as possible in the morning for generally calmer waters. Early July is the best season for different species, as their migrating patterns overlap.

The differences between the two companies offering tours are negligible, and both offer English-language tours. You will find **Firmm** (tel. 956/627-008; www.firmm.org; from €45) and **Turmares** (tel. 956/680-741; from €45) at their offices right on the port, each offering 2-3 tours a day, weather depending.

Kitesurfing

Tarifa is a real mecca for kitesurfers worldwide. You'll see them year-round out on the beaches dotting the region, with the long stretch of sand just west of Tarifa one of the most popular spots.

Freeride Kitesurf School

Calle María Antonia Toledo, 12; tel. 601/655-993; https://freeridetarifa.com; €75 on up

Friendly, English-speaking instructors teach at this school. Lessons include the price of gear, insurance, and instruction. The school is located in Hostal Africa, where you can also book a satisfying kitesurfing/yoga getaway, which is all the rage these days in wellness travel circuits.

Scuba Diving

Leon Marino

Calle Alcalde Juan Núñez, 6; tel. 615/066-669 or 629/234-141 or 856/106-888; https://leonmarino.es; from €95

The only scuba diving outfitter in Tarifa offers fun, professional services. Book online for the best rates. The experience includes equipment, insurance, boat ride to the dive site, hot shower, coffee and treat, plus a certificate and a little souvenir to take home.

FOOD

Tapas Bars

★ Bossa

Puerta de Jerez, Calle Silos, 1; tel. 956/685-399; 9am-late daily, breakfast 9am-1:30pm and happy hour 3pm-9pm; €10

1: Chica Beach **2:** interior decor of boutique hotel La Sacristia **3:** gathering for sunset at the Balneario Beach Club

Bossa is tucked right beneath the historic Jerez Gate as you enter the walled city of Tarifa from the north, the farthest point uphill. Impossibly old and rustic, it feels like it has been around for about as long as the city gates. Thanks to the British owners, the atmosphere is that of a friendly neighborhood pub. Though you could visit any time of day, happy hour is maybe the sweet spot, when you can enjoy a cocktail for half price.

Balneario Beach Club

Avenida Fuerza Armadas; tel. 626/884-704; www.balneariobeachclubtarifa.com; noon-11pm Sun.-Thurs., noon-midnight Fri.-Sat.; €10

There is nothing quite like enjoying a cocktail while the sun dips down over the Atlantic Ocean. This is one of the more popular party addresses in town, and for good reason, with the beach right there and the bar right here. If you're spending an evening in Tarifa, it's worth making your way here for a sundowner or two.

El Ancla

Avenida Fuerza Armadas, 15; tel. 956/680-913; 1pm-4:30pm and 9pm-11:30pm Tues.-Sat., 1pm-4:30pm Sun.; €12

Head to this popular local tapas joint, just off the port side boardwalk. You'll find families and friends pulling tables together and enjoying the tapas and the company, making for the lively, friendly kind of atmosphere famous throughout Andalusia. This tapas bar is known locally for its croquetas de choco, a traditional Spanish dish made from cuttlefish that is spiced, shaped into cylinders, coated in breadcrumbs, and deep-fried until crispy and golden brown.

El Otro Melli

Plaza San Martín, 5; tel. 680/402-090; 8pm-midnight Tues.-Fri., noon-4pm and 8pm-midnight Sat.-Sun.; €12

With all the fresh, hip sorts of places around Tarifa, sometimes it's nice to tuck into a classic tapas joint. The tuna meatballs are an easy crowd pleaser, while the patatas bravas are a tapas staple. With the location near the port and right off the main town square, you have a front-row seat to the daily music and general festivities.

Traditional Spanish

El Reencuentro

Plaza la Paz, 4b; tel. 652/749-755; https://el-reencuentro-tarifa.negocio.site; 11am-4:30pm Mon.-Fri., 11am-4:30pm and 7:30pm-11pm Sat.-Sun.; €20

Don't let the shabby chic beach vibes and patio furniture fool you. Right smack in this impossibly quaint plaza in the middle of the historic town center, you've just stumbled on the place to go for paella, a feast fit for friends. Reserve ahead of time. Expect healthy portions and a healthy dose of slow-paced, almost island-lifestyle service. Not bad—just relaxed. So kick back with your cerveza (beer) and soak up the vibes.

Braseria Vaca Loca

Calle Cervantes, 6; 6:30pm-1am Mon.-Thurs., 1pm-1am Fri.-Sun.; €25

Just follow your nose. You will smell this restaurant before you get there, and I mean that in the best of ways. The barbecue goodness tends to waft on the breeze through the narrow streets of this Tarifeña neighborhood. It has quieter outdoor seating than most restaurants because it is tucked off the main pedestrian thoroughfares. Though you could pull up a wood stool and enjoy some time at the medieval bar, on a nice day it would be a shame not to make use of the outdoor seating. The menu focuses on locally raised beef, chicken, and ham. Go for a barbecued steak or the secreto ibérico.

Cafés

Cafeteria Churreria

Calle Sancho IV El Bravo, 34; 7am-1pm Wed.-Mon.

This is a busy local spot for morning churros with a deliciously thick cup of hot chocolate or toast with olive oil and cheese. Other continental breakfast options are available. There is street-side patio seating, but the indoor bar is where all the local action happens.

La Tarifeña Bakery

Calle Nuestra Señora de la Luz, 21; tel. 956/684-015; https://pasterialatarifeña.com; 9am-9pm daily but hours vary

Homemade bread and pastries are served up alongside some delicious chocolates at this utterly unpretentious local bakery. You can find just the sorts of things you might want to pick up for breakfast or lunch on the go, whether you plan on hitting the road, hopping on the ferry, or heading out to the beach. Regionally, this bakery is known for their old "cajilla" of Tarifa—a typical almond sweet of Andalusian tradition made with wheat flour, stuffed with almond paste, and topped with a layer of white glazed sugar.

Markets

Tarifa Municipal Market

Calle Colón, 5; 8am-3pm Mon.-Sat.

This is a good stop for stocking up alongside the locals or for grabbing a quick bite at the Bar el Mercado right in the market.

ACCOMMODATIONS

Under €100

★ Ohana Tarifa Hostel

Calle Trafalgar, 4; tel. 956/680-791; €20

A very short walk just outside the historic city center brings you to a small piece of dormitory-style Hawaiian goodness right here in Andalusia. Very clean, very kind service. And the price is unbeatable. Hostels are often about the people you meet along the way, and you tend to meet the best sort of people here. A great hang for social hostel lovers.

Hostel Wake Up in Tarifa

Plaza la Paz, 3; tel. 660/341-205; €30

The small, clean rooms have limited space. The central location in the middle of old Tarifa is enviable. If you have been using hostels throughout your journey in Andalusia, the English-speaking staff will likely be a breath of fresh air compared to some of the other, often gruffer, service often found in hostels in the rest of the region.

La Casa de La Favorita

tel. 690/180-253; https://lacasadelafavorita.com; €50

Poppy without being annoyingly so, this is a great budget option if you don't need front desk service. The property features an automated check-in, which I haven't experienced too often. It is easiest if your phone is connected to the internet and you use WhatsApp. If you have been using mostly hostels and are traveling with a friend, or could use a quieter, less social property, consider treating yourself here.

★ The Riad

Calle Comendador, 10; tel. 856/929-880; www.theriadtarifa.com; €90

A historic 17th-century home that once belonged to the Comendador, today The Riad is a refreshed boutique accommodation that takes inspiration from Moroccan riads from across the strait. You'll find an indoor plunge pool set against exposed stone and a terrace with Berber throw pillows. Service is friendly and kind, though English can be a bit of a hurdle. There is no breakfast or dinner service as in many other guesthouses, though—the only ding on this otherwise charming accommodation.

€100-150

★ La Sacristia

San Donato, 8; tel. 956/681-759; www.grupolasacristiatarifa.com; €125

A boutique hotel oozing with Moroccan charm sits right in the midst of the old district of Tarifa. If your travel plans include staying in a riad (a Moroccan house that has been converted into a bed-and-breakfast) like the ones available throughout Morocco, this is a great start. Rooms can be a bit cramped, particularly on the top floor, but are still a really good value for the region. Take advantage of the bar and restaurant downstairs.

€150-200

La Residencia Hotel & Spa

tel. 951/022-929; https://laresidenciatarifa.com/en/hotel-spa-tarifa; €180

Bright seafoam green trims the interiors of this beachy getaway. This chic splurge sports stellar views over the port of Tarifa and Strait of Gibraltar over to Morocco, as well as an in-house restaurant and spa services. Rooms are spacious, with lush textiles and service to match. The location right off the port is spot on and within an easy walk of everything you might want to see and do in Tarifa.

GETTING THERE AND AROUND

Getting around Tarifa is easy enough. The town slopes gently downhill to the sea, with everything within about a 20-minute walk. If you aren't driving your own car, getting there can be a bit trickier.

Bus

A handful of buses serve Tarifa from Cádiz, Málaga, and Seville.

From **Cádiz,** connect by bus (1.5 hr; €20) with two daily connections (1pm and 9pm) run by Transportes Generales Comes (www.tgcomes.es) and one daily connection (3:30pm) by Alsa (www.alsa.com).

From **Seville** (3.5 hr; €30), Transportes Generales Comes (www.tgcomes.es) runs four buses a day (8am, 11am, 2pm, and 6pm).

From **Málaga,** you'll want to catch the bus to Algeciras and then transfer to the free bus that runs from the Algeciras port to the Tarifa port. Buses operate from multiple companies every half hour from the Málaga train station, while the port-to-port bus runs once an hour.

Ferry

From Tangier, Morocco

While there's no ferry service connecting Tarifa with other Southern Coast destinations, Tarifa is just a short 45-minute ferry ride from **Tangier, Morocco.** If you are coming from Morocco, the ferry that connects directly with Tangier has an accompanying free bus that connects the Tarifa port with the Algeciras port, where you can find the central bus station with many bus routes connecting throughout Andalusia. The Tarifa ferry terminal is less than a 5-minute walk on the south side of the Old Town.

Tangier, Morocco

Tangier is the first place in Africa many Europeans visit—yet of all the large cities in Morocco it is somehow the least explored, despite its fascinating history and culture. Perhaps this is because it is so far north, removed from the well-traveled paths to Marrakesh and Fez, or maybe because it has retained its reputation as a run-down, seedy port, a carryover from its days as an international zone. Whatever the reason, other than day-trippers who ferry over from Spain for a quick tour, many travelers to Morocco skip Tangier altogether, leaving the city relatively unscathed by some of the mass tourism of other locations. For those with a love of Mediterranean living, this means that Tangier might just be Morocco's best-kept gem.

NEED TO KNOW

Because you are crossing an international border and entering/exiting the EU and the Schengen Zone, there are a few things that you need to know:

- **Passport:** You need your passport to take the ferry into Tangier. US, Canadian, Australian, and British passport holders do not need a special visa and can expect to use their passport to cross the border with no issue. If you are a passport holder from a different country, research what other visa or permission you will need to cross through the Morocco border, if any.
- **Currency:** The unit of currency of Morocco is the Moroccan dirham, listed

in this guide as "DH" and written on official exchanges as MAD. Banknotes come in denominations of 20, 50, 100, and 200 dirhams. Coins are in denominations of 1, 2, 5, and 10 dirhams. In Morocco, cash is king. Many venues and services do not accept credit or debit cards as payment. Euros, and sometimes US dollars, will be accepted in lieu of local currency, though at a less-than-desirable exchange rate.

- **Electricity:** Morocco operates on the continental European 220-volt system, with electronics having two round plugs.
- **Country code:** The country code for Morocco is 212. When in Morocco, it is generally not necessary to dial the 0 before numbers, though if your call does not work the first time, try it with the 0 prior to the number.

ORIENTATION

Tangier lies along a protected bay with most of the city looking north across the Strait of Gibraltar to Spain. Only 14 km (8 mi) separates Tangier from Spain. The Tanger-Ville port, where ferries arrive from Tarifa, is situated right at the foot of the medina. From the port, it's a short stroll across Avenue Mohammed VI to the maze of the medina. The historic kasbah lies uphill to the west, connected directly to the medina. Continuing west, you can discover the Marshan neighborhood as well as Cap Spartel along the Atlantic Coast. To the east is the municipal beach. Directly south and east of the medina is the Ville Nouvelle.

SIGHTS

Medina

Tangier's medina is something of an anomaly in Morocco. It is cleaner than many of the other medinas found around the country. In spots you can feel the tourism vibe, particularly around the central square, the **petit socco.** That said, most of the medina remains residential, with only a few boutique riads. You can feel this "lived in" vibe all around the medina. Perhaps this is the reason why Tangier has provided the backdrop for movies such as *Inception* and *The Bourne Identity.* Though the Tangier medina has shed much of its grubby port town reputation of years past, it still stands in stark contrast to the adjacent, mellow, well-touristed kasbah.

★ Tangier American Legation Museum

8 Rue d'Amerique; tel. 0539/935-317; http://legation.org; 10am-5pm Mon.-Fri., 10am-3pm Sat.; DH20

Close to the aptly named Bab Merican, the Tangier American Legation Institute for Moroccan Studies is the only U.S. National Historic Landmark outside of the United States. The museum itself is a wonderfully restored three-story house dating from the 17th century, featuring tall wood-beamed ceilings, ornate stucco and zellij (mosaic tile) work, and a sprawling outdoor patio. The museum holds a letter from George Washington; many paintings from American, European, and Moroccan artists; and a collection of models re-creating historic battles in the region, including the famed Battle of the Three Kings. A large library specializing in North Africa holds a collection of the first 100 years of the *Tangier Gazette* (a multilingual newspaper that began printing in the 19th century), many antiquarian maps, and travel accounts from the 17th to 19th centuries. Visitors will not want to miss the **Paul Bowles Wing,** a section off the patio dedicated to the life, writing, and music curation of Tangier's most famous expat resident, Paul Bowles, from when he first moved to Tangier in 1947 up until his death in 1999. Guided tours are available (DH50 per person) and are highly recommended to get the most from your visit to one of the most distinctive landmarks in all of Morocco.

Beit Yahoudi Jewish Museum (Assayag Synagogue)

4 Rue Bousselham; tel. 0662/733-266; Sun.-Fri. 10am-5pm; free

Tucked just off Rue as-Siaghin is this lovingly restored synagogue. Opened in 2021, the

Greater Tangier

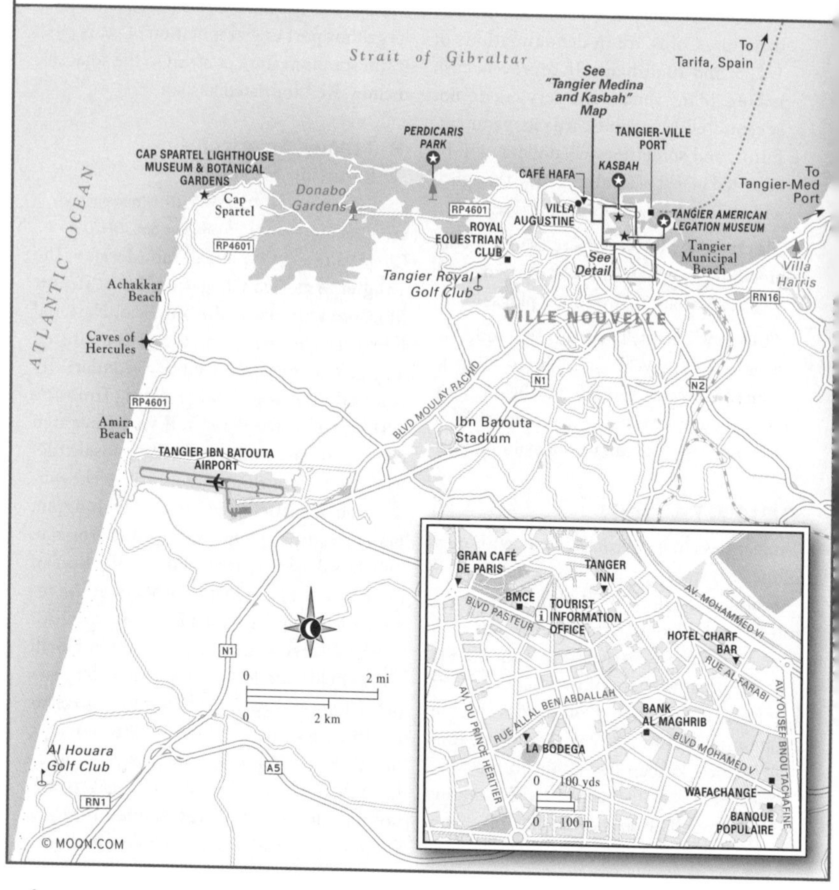

former synagogue is now a Jewish museum dedicated to the memory of the thousands of Tangier Jews that once called this city home. Primarily of Sephardic descent, these incredible people left a mark not only on Tangier, but on the world at large. Discover just how on your own free tour of this little gem of history. Admission is free, but donations are accepted and go to the synagogue's upkeep. There are two other synagogues worth visiting nearby: the **Lorin Foundation Museum** (44 Rue Touahine; tel. 0539/334-696; 11am-1pm and 3:30pm-7:30pm Sun.-Fri.; free) and the **Mosche Nahon Synagogue** (44 Rue Cheikh al Harrak; tel. 0657/433-975; 10am-5pm Sun.-Fri.; free).

★ Kasbah

Towering above the rest of Tangier and standing guard over the Strait of Gibraltar is the splendid kasbah of Tangier. The ancient fortifications that were once in charge of the city's defenses are still largely intact hundreds of years after their erection and, happily, were wonderfully restored from 2016 to 2019. These days, quite a few of the historic buildings and palaces of the kasbah are owned by Europeans and have been turned into private

Tangier Medina and Kasbah

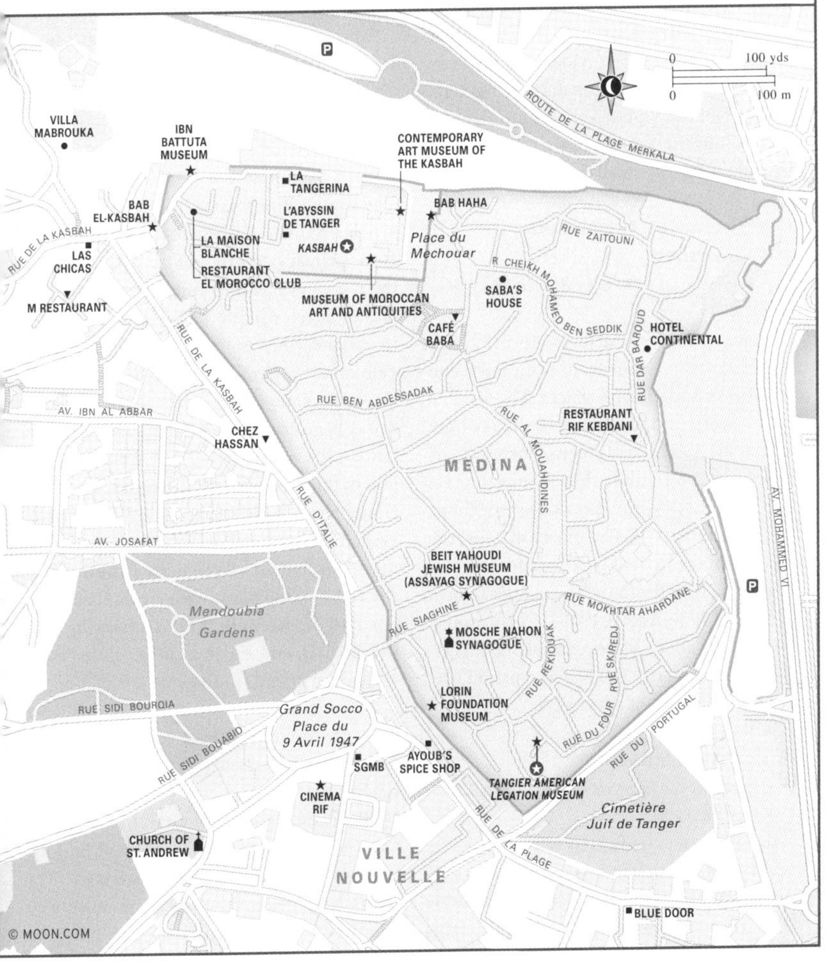

homes or converted into boutique hotels and restaurants.

The two most common entrances to the kasbah are the **Bab el-Kasbah** to the west, off Place du Tabor, and **Bab Haha** (Don't laugh! This gate is actually named for a region around Essaouira) to the east, coming from the medina. **Place du Mechouar** (often referred to as Place de la Kasbah) is next to Bab Haha. There is paid, guarded parking. Touts gather here and will offer to give you a guided tour, though this is unnecessary. The kasbah is small, and to the left of Bab Haha there is a small map highlighting the walk you can do around it.

Museum of Moroccan Art and Antiquities (Musée des Art Marocains et des Antiquités)

Pl. du Mechouar; tel. 0539/932-097; 9am-4pm Wed.-Mon.; 20DH

Just off Place du Mechouar, the Museum of Moroccan Art and Antiquities houses various relics from the Stone Age through the turn of the 20th century, displaying the rich history of Tangier. You can see evidence of the many, many peoples that have inhabited or ruled this region. Not to be missed is a beautiful mosaic taken from the Roman city of Volubilis. Be sure to take a nice stroll through the gardens.

Contemporary Art Museum of the Kasbah

Pl. du Mechouar; tel. 0539/676-081; 9am-4pm Wed.-Mon.; 20DH

Opened in 2021 in the former prison of the kasbah, this museum focuses on more contemporary and modern pieces. The vision of the museum is to function more as a cultural center than strictly a museum. There are various, inclusive exhibits throughout the year, and the museum provides a safe space for expression for artists. The museum collection focuses on the North School of Moroccan art beginning with the foundation of the Tetouan School of Fine Art in 1948. If you want to know more about Moroccan artists, this is a great place to start. The restored prison itself is worth the price of admission.

Ibn Battuta Museum

Borj Naam, Place du Tabor; tel. 0539/339-668; 9am-4pm Wed.-Mon.; 20DH

This museum is dedicated to one of the favorite sons of Tangier and one of the world's truly great explorers, Ibn Battuta. Opened in 2022, the museum makes for a great starting point for your walk through the medina. The architecture of the renovated building, with lots of exposed metal and glass against stone, is beautiful. Considered by many to be the greatest traveler in history, Ibn Battuta went farther than Marco Polo and had just as many adventures along the way.

Ville Nouvelle

Much of Tangier's charm lies in the Ville Nouvelle, unlike in many of Morocco's other cities. Just outside the confines of the kasbah and medina, the city begins its great spread over the hilly landscape, plunging westward to the Big Mountain and beyond into the Atlantic, while to the east it embraces a long stretch of beach and numerous hilly inlets. Tangier truly has a privileged, unmatched topography.

Grand Socco

The southernmost edge of the Grand Socco is now a roundabout, **Place du 9 Avril 1947,** at the primary entrance of the medina, making it a good meeting point for groups. The Grand Socco used to be the largest market in Tangier, where sellers from all over the region came to offer fresh fruits, vegetables, and livestock. Though not quite the large market it was historically, the Grand Socco still has quite a few sellers along Rue d'Italie at the foot of the **Mendoubia Gardens.** From the Grand Socco, it is a straight uphill walk to the kasbah. Back along the Place du 9 Avril 1947, the renovated Art Deco gem, **Cinema Rif,** sits right on the plaza with a café that spills out onto the sidewalk. This is a relaxing spot to kick back and sip on a coffee while you're waiting for friends to show up.

Church of St. Andrew

Rue d'Angleterre; tel. 0539/314-469; roughly 9am-sunset daily

Of the sites around the Grand Socco, perhaps none is as stunning as this functioning Anglican church. Constructed in 1894 on land donated to the British community by King Hassan I and consecrated in 1905, the church features architecture notable for its Andalusian and Moroccan influence. A vision of Tangier's multicultural past can be glimpsed in its halls and around its neighboring gardens, where many expats from Tangier have been buried, including **Walter Burton Harris,** a Tangier legend. In his lifetime, Harris was the local correspondent for *The Times* and was involved in much of the

1: Tangier American Legation Museum **2:** walking through the medina **3:** Grand Socco **4:** Villa Harris

1
2
3
4

political intrigue that gripped Tangier while it served as an international zone. Nowadays, Harris is most known for his travel work, *Morocco That Was*. The grounds are free to access, though DH50 is the going rate for entry to the church and a guided English-language tour with Yassine, the caretaker, which is highly recommended. Attending service, of course, is free and perhaps the best way to get a feel for the vast diversity of Tangier's contemporary resident Christian community.

Cap Spartel

Located just a short 20-minute (12 km/7.5 mi) drive from downtown Tangier is Cap Spartel and the northwest corner of Africa. One of the real charms of Tangier is getting out of the city and into the nearby parks, gardens, and sandy beaches that make this an especially Mediterranean corner of Morocco.

Cap Spartel Lighthouse Museum and Botanical Gardens

Cap Spartel; 8am-9pm daily; DH20

Built in the mid-19th century, this lighthouse was the first built in Morocco, after international pressure. Many commercial ships wrecked along this stretch of coastline, where Mediterranean waters mingle with the cold, dark Atlantic. The museum recounts much of the history of the lighthouse and its keepers through the years. If the winds oblige, the outdoor café and botanical garden are a pleasant diversion.

Caves of Hercules

Route des Grottes d'Hercule, just south of Cap Spartel; tel. 0606/703-374; 10am-5:30pm daily; DH60

The stunning Caves of Hercules (Grottes d'Hercule) are rumored to be the resting place of Hercules after he completed his 11th labor, the Apples of Hesperides (or "The Golden Apple"). After Hercules obtained the golden apple, it is thought he rested in this cave complex near Cap Spartel. However, as interesting (and surprisingly beautiful) as the newly restored cave is, it is also a bit of a tourist trap. Avoid any guides because this cave is simple to navigate on your own. Do look up to see where ancient locals once carved out round stones from the cave walls, used for milling grain. The cave's opening, in the shape of the continent of Africa, looks out toward the Atlantic and is picturesque.

Donabo Gardens

Route du Cap Spartel, km 10; tel. 0539/939-590; www.donabogardens.com; 10am-6:30pm Tues.-Sun.; DH50

Here nature seamlessly weaves together recreation and learning, with a special focus on captivating young hearts and minds. This verdant sanctuary stands as a testament to the history of Tangier's natural beauty, with a forest canopy lovingly preserved from a bygone era. Perched high above, a captivating sea-view balcony reveals the stunning expanse of the Strait of Gibraltar. A meandering path leads you through a delightful maze of themed squares, each with its own unique character. Explore fragrant blooms of the rose garden, immerse yourself in the tranquility of the Moroccan garden, wander through the serene Chinese garden, and marvel at the tenacity of rock garden plants while aromatic herbs infuse the air with their fragrant allure. All around, the whispers of the scrubland and pine forest create a soothing backdrop, punctuated only by the sweet melodies of birdsong. It's a great outing for families and garden lovers. An on-site café serves light lunches and nibbles.

SPORTS AND RECREATION

Beaches

As Tangier is a beach town, there is plenty of free swimming to be had along the Mediterranean and Atlantic Coasts. The Mediterranean beaches, particularly the city ones, are family-friendly and safe places for swimmers, though swimmers must keep well clear of the port. Women, whether alone or in groups, will inevitably be hassled. For a harassment-free beach day, strongly consider spending a few dirhams to reserve one of the cabanas strung out on the Atlantic Coast. There are private beach areas just south of the Caves of Hercules and Cap Spartel. The currents along the Atlantic make it a somewhat more dangerous swimming place, and those with children should exercise caution.

Tangier Municipal Beach

Avenida Mohammed VI, to the east of the ferry terminal; daily; free

The municipal beach of Tangier is a wide stretch of sand tucked right in Tangier Bay. This is the liveliest beach in the region. You can nearly always find camel and horseback riding, acrobats working on their routines, and kids kicking soccer balls around. In the warmer months, lifeguards are on duty. There are free public restrooms available as well as showers to wash off the sand, near the boardwalk (corniche). As this is the busiest beach, it is also where most petty theft and harassment (generally in the form of catcalling) occur.

Achakkar Beach

Atlantic Coast on P4601, between Cap Spartel and the Caves of Hercules; daily; free

The northernmost of the large Atlantic Coast beaches of Tangier, and generally also the busiest, Achakkar has cafés, cabanas, and beach huts catering to those looking for a day at the beach. Within Achakkar, you might find other beach names (Bakkasem Beach, Sun Beach, Mikki Beach), though these are all part of the same long stretch of sand. Outside of the summer months, there are no lifeguards, and there are no public restrooms.

Amira Beach

Atlantic Coast on P4601, just south of the Caves of Hercules; daily; free

The longest stretch of Atlantic Coast beaches is also generally the quietest. Outside of summer, you might share this whole stretch of sand with a couple of fishers and that is it. Undertow can be a concern along this entire Atlantic stretch of beaches, but particularly here. Swim with good judgment as, except in the summer months, there are no lifeguards on duty. No public amenities such as bathrooms and showers are available.

Parks

★ Perdicaris Park

Rmilat on Avenida Mokhtar Gazoulit; 8am-sunset daily; free

Perdicaris Park (Parc Perdicaris) lies just 15 minutes outside the city on the road to the **Caves of Hercules.** The park and its paths

Perdicaris Park

were renovated in 2016-2017 and boast stellar views over the Atlantic, across the strait, and through lush Mediterranean flora. This is a perfect spot for a picnic and a break from the city. There is a juice stand at the entrance of the park, but otherwise food is scarce, so plan accordingly.

You can hire a grand taxi or take bus 5 (DH3.50 per ticket, every 30 min) from Sidi Bouabid by the Grand Mosque (across from the Cervantes Institute in the Iberia neighborhood). If you're driving, take Avenue Sidi Mohamed Ben Abdellah northwest from the big roundabout at the Mohammed V Mosque and follow the road signs for **Rmilat.**

In the middle of the park, where the main walking paths converge, you'll find the former home of Ian Perdicaris, the Greek magnate who once called this expansive park home. After an extensive renovation, his home was opened as a **museum** in 2022 (9am-5pm daily; DH70). Even if you weren't particularly interested in knowing about Perdicaris, the story of his kidnapping, and his life in Tangier in the late 19th and early 20th centuries, the price of admission is worth it just to imagine what it would be like to have this place to yourself.

Villa Harris

Boulevard Mohammed VI; 2 km (1.2 mi) east of Tangier along the beach; daily; free

Now a beloved public park, this villa was once the domain of Walter Burton Harris, a journalist (and likely spy) who used his home here as a base of exploration for the rest of Morocco. Beneath shady palm trees and colorful birds of paradise, there is a system of zigzagging paths alongside well-equipped playgrounds for the kids. Harris's old house in the middle of the grounds has been renovated by the state and is now a museum of contemporary Moroccan art (tel. 0773/074-502; 10am-6pm Wed.-Mon.; DH10). Immediately across the boulevard from the park is beach access, while parking (DH5) is readily available in the parking lots and along the streets.

Horse and Camel Riding

Royal Equestrian Club

Route California, Socco Alto; 8am-noon and 3pm-7pm Tues.-Sun.; DH50 for a pony ride

The Royal Equestrian Club is a Tangier institution that offers pony and horse rides. Many locals come out here on the weekends and after school hours to visit with the horses and walk through the park-like club.

Tangier Municipal Beach

Tangier Municipal Beach; sunrise-sunset daily; DH10-20

On Tangier Municipal Beach, horse and camel rides are always available when the weather is fair for DH10-20, though you will likely be quoted much more. Bargain, gallop along the beach, and remember to take a picture.

Achakkar Beach

Achakkar Beach, Atlantic Coast; sunrise-sunset daily; DH10-20

Along the Atlantic Coast, there are usually camels available to ride on a lookout just south of Achakkar Beach. This is one of the more photogenic camel riding opportunities in the north.

Golf

Tangier Royal Golf Club

Route de Boubana; tel. 0539/938-925; www.royalcountryclubtanger.com; DH400

This golf club offers a challenging 18-hole course over 65 ha (160 acres) just 3 km (1.8 mi) away from the middle of Tangier at the foot of the Old Mountain near Socco Alto. Established in 1914, this was one of the first golf courses in the Mediterranean basin and is one of the oldest in Africa.

Al Houara Golf Club

Houara, Route du Asilah; tel. 0539/409-509; DH600

If you'd rather be out with the old and in with the new, the Houara Golf Club, designed by golf legends Vijay Singh and Graham Marsh, was inaugurated on September 1, 2022. It features long, wide holes abutting the Atlantic Coast where strong winds often add to the challenge and rocky, Martian-like terrain is the norm.

Hammams

Traditional hammams in the medina are great places to meet locals. You can wash for DH10 or so, though all hammams cater to either men or women or have separate hours for the genders. Check with your lodging to find the closest local hammam in the medina. Otherwise, the higher-end hammams are the answer for couples and travelers who are uncomfortable with the local hammams and their unfamiliar social etiquette.

L'Abyssin de Tanger

22 Rue Tenaker, kasbah; tel. 0539/932-817; www.abyssindetanger.com; by reservation only; DH250

Renovated by an architect with an eye toward design, this rambling kasbah house is a fantastic example of a traditional Moroccan hammam, and it abuts a true rarity in Tangier: a heated indoor swimming pool. Though lacking the views of some other places, the experience here more than makes up for it in comfort, charm, and service. My favorite hammam in Tangier, hands down.

La Tangerina

19 Riad Sultan; tel. 0539/947-731; http://latangerina.com; by reservation only; DH250

La Tangerina is a wonderful traditional hammam in the style that was once common in the homes of the wealthy, who wouldn't use the public hammam. It supports up to four people, and couples are welcome. The 45-minute traditional hammam includes a body scrub using rhassoul (clay soap). Massages are also available. Afterward, be sure to lounge on the terrace for spectacular views over the strait.

Cooking Courses

Blue Door

106 Rue de la Plage; tel. 0808/679-797 or 0612/020-210; www.bluedoorcuisine.com; 9am-5pm daily, reservations required; DH600

Roll up your sleeves and get to work slicing, dicing, and laughing your way through your own Moroccan tajine. Over the course of a few hours, you'll have a meaningful, engaging experience that goes far beyond the culinary. You'll break bread with the local women working here. Over a wonderful spread of Moroccan fare, including tea, bread and the tajine you just made, you'll get to know more about your culinary teachers, where they come from, and gain that little window into their everyday lives, making this one of the more culturally enriching activities you can do not only in Tangier, but in all of Morocco. Check the website for availability.

SHOPPING

Gourmet Goods

Ayoub's Spice Shop

Rue Gzenaya, Old Medina near Bab Gzenaya; 9am-10pm daily

This classic Moroccan spice shop is our family's go-to for fresh saffron, cumin, essential rose oil, argan oil, and the famous ras-al-hanout spice mix that flavors so many of the tajines Morocco is known for worldwide. One of the best souvenirs to take home is Moroccan spices.

Handmade Goods

Las Chicas

52 Rue Kacem Guennon, near the Bab el-Kasbah; tel. 0539/374-510; 10:30am-7:30pm Mon.-Sat.

Perched just outside the kasbah is this chic boutique where you can find all sorts of items carefully curated and all made in Morocco, including jewelry, linens, furniture, mirrors, paintings, ceramics, and candles, all signed by their young creators and designers.

ENTERTAINMENT AND EVENTS

For the most up-to-date information on the festivals happening throughout the year, check out the monthly *Tanger Pocket* (www.tangerpocket.com), a predominantly French-language publication, available online and at most restaurants and hotels.

Festivals

Tanjazz Festival

www.tanjazz.org; Sept.; DH200

Since 2000, Tangier has celebrated its musicality annually with the biggest music festival in north Morocco, Tanjazz: Festival de Jazz de Tanger. Helped with support from the local Lorin Foundation, the festival brings acts from around the world for a five-day celebration of music in September, with everything from big band to swing, Delta blues to Moroccan fusion. With tame crowds and a sophisticated air, Tanjazz evokes the city's long history of cultural and musical fusion. Passes are DH200 a day or DH1000 for the length of the festival.

Mediterranean Short Film Festival

www.ccm.ma; Oct.; free

Movie buffs and cineastes should check out the Mediterranean Short Film Festival of Tangier, organized by the Centre Cinématographique Morocain, which runs for a week in early October. Films range far and wide, with a selection of 46 films from 18 different countries. Films are linguistically diverse, with offerings usually in English, Arabic, French, Spanish, and other languages.

NIGHTLIFE

Tangier is famous for its nightlife. During the summer, the young and hip (and wannabe young and hip) flock to the numerous nightclubs and bars along Tangier's long beachfront. Be warned: Drinking is not cheap in Morocco. Most bars and nightclubs in this neighborhood boast loads of security and can help you get taxis back to your accommodations at the end of the night. Prostitution is a concern, and some nights it can feel as though the club is packed solely with them and their escorts. The clubs are best enjoyed in groups, and usually open Thursday-Saturday nights, though hours and days are generally expanded in the busy summer months. It might be worth contacting the club to make a reservation for the night. This can make things smoother at the door.

Most of the historic bars in Tangier are not for the faint of heart. With few exceptions, they are male-dominated, very smoky, and rough around the edges. That said, with the offering of solid tapas, there are a few bars well worth a visit.

Hotel Charf Bar

25 Rue al Farabi; noon-midnight daily; DH25

Perhaps the best remaining tapas bar in Tangier is Hotel Charf Bar. You won't find a nonsmoking section, but you will find plenty to eat as long as you sit and drink. If you ask to go upstairs, you'll be treated to panoramic views of the Mediterranean Sea and Spain. Best of all, in true tapas-style whatever is put in front of you to eat is free. Grilled sardines, Moroccan salads, fried calamari, and whatever else is fresh in from the port that day will find its way onto a plate for you. Kick back, sip on a bottle of suds, and imagine you're buddying up to the bar with Jack Kerouac. The downstairs corner bar is about as authentic of an experience of Tangier bar-hopping as it gets.

Tanger Inn

1 Rue Magellan; 11am-11pm daily; DH20

Soak in the literary history of Morocco at Tanger Inn. Knowing your barstool once supported the likes of Federico García Lorca, Tennessee Williams, and Jean Genet can add a bit of erudition to your beverage of choice. Located just uphill from Avenue Mohammed VI and the beach, this area can be a little sketchy at night, so it's best to travel in groups or have a taxi drop you off and pick you up.

La Bodega

Rue Allal Ben Abdellah, near the Hotel Chellah; 11am-2am daily; DH25

This tapas bar doesn't disappoint, with Iberian ham, queso manchego (cheese), boquerones (anchovies), and numerous other Andalusian specialties on offer. Quieter on weekdays and during happy hour, the bar picks up toward the end of the week. It's one of the cleanest bars in Tangier, catering more to the business and tourist crowd than locals, and is also a comfortable spot for women looking for a beer, cocktail, or glass of wine. With the decor of deep reds and sharp black, as well as the occasional live music, including flamenco, performed here on the weekends, there is a real Andalusian vibe to be had.

FOOD

Though Tangier hasn't developed the culinary reputation of elsewhere in Morocco, the typical Tanjaoui fare is a fusion of Moroccan and marvelous Mediterranean flavors with touches of the Spanish cuisine you've likely tried elsewhere in Andalusia. Restaurants offer fresh, delicious dishes in a variety of cuisines, catering to both locals and travelers.

Medina

Café Baba

Rue Zaitouni; 7am-11pm daily; DH10

Farther up the medina toward the kasbah is the historic Café Baba. Founded in 1941, this café serves up some mean mint tea and heavy Turkish-style coffee, with views over the medina and the water from the indoor balcony. Most clients, including kings of Spain and Sweden as well as the Rolling Stones and filmmaker Jim Jarmusch, come here not for what's served but for the "smoke what you like" policy. Of all the cafés, this might be the most difficult to find. Ask for directions around Bab Haha if you're having trouble.

Restaurant Rif Kebdani

14 Rue Dar el-Baroud, downhill from the Hotel Continental; tel. 0539/939-497; noon-11pm daily; DH50

Known locally as Dar Baroud, this is a good break from the street food and quick snack vendors in the medina. The usual mix of lamb, chicken, and meatball tajines, as well as Moroccan salads and pastilla (a meat or seafood pie), are on offer, though you really want to stop in here for the rather theatrical service set in the beautifully tiled courtyard and open kitchen.

★ Chez Hassan

Rue Kasbah, at the bottom of the hill; tel. 0613/769-293; noon-midnight daily; DH100

This is a fantastic hole-in-the-wall restaurant located just down the hill from the Bab el-Kasbah and easily found just outside the medina, a short walk up from the Grand Socco. The charismatic proprietor, Hassan, serves up fresh seafood and traditional seasonal regional dishes. Tajines are made to order, so be prepared to wait for a few extra minutes. You can pick from a selection of fresh fish, chicken, beef, and vegetarian options, but you should consider the shark tajine—it's one of a kind. Snag a seat on the patio for some unbeatable people-watching.

Kasbah

Restaurant El Morocco Club

1 Rue Kachla; tel. 0539/948-139; http://elmoroccoclub.ma; noon-3pm and 7pm-midnight Tues.-Sun.; DH200

Just outside the medina is this reincarnation of the iconic residence designed by famous American architect Stuart Church and frequented by the Beats and Mick Jagger during their sojourns in Tangier. Dishes are French-Moroccan fusion and include chicken with bakoula (a sort of cooked spinach-like vegetable) and grilled sardines lathered in charmoula (a Moroccan olive oil sauce with coriander, cumin, garlic, and paprika). The downstairs **Piano Bar,** though a bit small, can be a real treat with live music, competent cocktails, and fresh oysters served starting at 8pm.

M Restaurant

31 Rue de la Kasbah, Palacio Aharrar; tel. 0539/334-666; www.riadmokhtar.com; noon-3pm and 7pm-11pm Mon.-Sat., reservations required; DH250

Located on the ground floor of Riad Mokhtar (not featured in this guide, but also worth a stay), this elegant though casual restaurant offers up a tasty fusion of Moroccan and international dishes. The open-air garden courtyard is best for fine weather, when candlelit evenings turn up the charm, while the classic Moroccan interior is cozy for those colder winter months. Fresh, creamy seafood risottos and charbroiled steaks are served, alongside some classic Tangier staples, like caliente, a savory chickpea pie. Strictly Moroccan dishes are available, though you will need to give a minimum 48-hour notice with your reservation. The terrace-level pizza restaurant has wonderful views over Tangier and the bay, but it is only open on good weather days during the high season.

Marshan

★ Café Hafa

Rue Hafa; 8:30am-11pm Mon.-Fri., 8:30am-2am Sat.-Sun.; DH20

In Marshan, close to the Phoenician tombs, Café Hafa is a must-do experience. William Burroughs, Paul Bowles, Tennessee Williams, the Beatles, and countless others have stopped by Café Hafa to sip on a mint tea and look out over the Mediterranean to Spain. Kids from the local schools come here to do homework, and young men get together to play Parcheesi ("par-cheese" in the local vernacular). The tapping of their dice clinking across the glass top of the game board blends into the background with the wind, the surf, and the inevitable one or two bees that find your mint tea as delicious as you do. At night, there is often music. If anyone smokes anything other than a cigarette, a strict "don't ask, don't tell" policy should be adhered to.

Ville Nouvelle

Gran Café de Paris

Place de France; 7am-11pm daily; DH15

The centrally located Gran Café de Paris has a rich literary history and, even now, is considered somewhat of a hot spot for local writers. The colonial decor inside is mostly maintained, with plush leather seats. Grab a spot on the terrace, order a freshly squeezed orange juice, recharge, and people-watch.

ACCOMMODATIONS

Medina

Hotel Continental

36 Rue Dar El Baroud; tel. 0539/931-024; DH400

One of the most storied hotels in Tangier, if not the world, Hotel Continental is sure to leave you with your own tall tale. Winston Churchill and many other notables stayed in this 19th-century National Heritage site—and it doesn't seem as though much has changed since then. Beds are often uncomfortable, breakfast can be a hit-or-miss affair, and the electricity cuts on and off sporadically. Otherwise, the service is friendly, rooms are clean, and the long terrace (overlooking the port and strait) and the outer dining room (with its sculpted ceiling and stained-glass windows) are stellar, though the dinner doesn't quite live up to the surroundings. How could it? This is one of the better-value stays in all of Morocco.

Saba's House

Mohammed Ben Seddik (61 Rue Cheikh), Place Amrah; tel. 0539/331-387 or 0539/371-578; www.riadsabashouse.com; DH2,500

The only real luxury five-star boutique riad found in old Tangier, this is an Art Deco lover's dream. Walk into the covered courtyard featuring a full, fashionable bar complete with a baby grand and paintings and sculptures from owner Roya Lamine's personal collection. An elevator ushers you up to your room, one of just six bright, colorful rooms, each themed around a celebrity who was known to retreat to Morocco. The terrace with views out over the Strait of Gibraltar makes coffee something of a morning ritual. The location, right at the top of the medina, next to the kasbah, is ideal for exploring the old city.

Kasbah

L'Abyssin de Tanger

22 Rue Tenaker; tel. 0539/932-817; www.abyssindetanger.com; DH1,000

This wonderfully cozy, maze-like riad was expertly renovated by an architect. The common areas are spacious, perfect for families and friends, with a real "home away from home" feeling. The terraces offer wonderful views, and the rooms, though perhaps a touch on the small side, are well appointed and have just enough character to make them truly charming. All that said, you're really staying here for the heated indoor pool.

La Maison Blanche

Rue Ahmed Ben Ajiba; tel. 0661/639-332; www.lamaisonblanchetanger.com; DH1,100

A carefully wrought restoration and remodel over the course of many, many years crafted this gem of a riad. Deceptively simple, clean lines give way to small details throughout the property, each one thought out and tied into the Mediterranean history of Tangier. Each room is themed and decorated a bit differently. Those who don't mind a few flights of stairs would be well rewarded by taking up residence in the Ibn Battuta room just off the terrace, while others might want to splurge for the foliage-inspired Moulay Ismail suite, where movie star Daniel Craig stayed while filming the 007 film *Spectre*. Breakfast and Wi-Fi are included with your stay. Dinner is available as well, on request.

Marshan

★ Villa Augustine

Avenida Mohammed (7 Avenida Hadj); tel. 0661/457-900; https://houseofaugustine.com; DH2,250

Villa Augustine is an intimate, artsy five-bedroom villa that opened in February 2023 and really funnels the charm of Tangier's interzone era, updating it for a new generation. A bespoke art collection is set against sand greens, highlighted with canary yellows and rich Mediterranean blues. The location offers up unobstructed sea views, and a charming indoor-outdoor pool has just the right amount of quirk to round out a boutique experience in one of Morocco's newest designer accommodations, put together by noted hotelier and interior designer Willem Smit. With the kasbah a quick 5-minute walk away and the Grand Socco just 10 minutes from the front door, it's a great base for exploration for couples and friends. A homemade arrival dinner included with your stay highlights the best of regional Moroccan cuisine.

Villa Mabrouka

1 Sidi Bouknadel; tel. 0808/526-436; https://villamabrouka.com; DH3,500

The former private home of renowned fashion designer Yves-Saint Laurent and his partner, Pierre Bergé, was opened by designer Jasper Conran in 2023 as a boutique hotel experience. Featuring 12 distinct rooms spread over the large, gardened property, complete with the original pool dug out of the stone hillside and magical Mediterranean views, this is an aspirational destination hotel for most. Prices are elevated over the summer, Tangier's busiest season, generally doubling and sometimes tripling in price, and three-night stays are mandatory for all weekends and during the high season. For most, it would be best to stop in for lunch or a sundowner and enjoy the property, without having to pay the YSL tax.

INFORMATION AND SERVICES

The city code for Tangier and the area is 39, so all fixed phone numbers begin with this number followed by 05. All land lines will begin with 3905. Other numbers beginning with 06 or 08 are mobile phone numbers. This is a good trick to know because most people and businesses in Morocco have their cell phones connected to WhatsApp, making communication over your data plan, eSIM, or Wi-Fi connection free.

Tourist Information Office

29 Boulevard de Pasteur; 9am-4:30pm Mon.-Fri.

Located on the busy Tangier boulevard, a short walk outside of the medina, this info center is a good resource for those looking for opportunities outside of organized excursions as well as up-to-date information on local events.

Currency Exchange

In practice, it's best to just use the ATMs, readily available throughout Tangier. There are a couple of banks on the Grand Socco: **SGMB** and **BMCE** (8:15am-3:45pm Mon.-Fri.). Otherwise, head down Avenue Pasteur and Boulevard Mohammed V to find a string of banks. **Banque Populaire** (corner of Blvd. Mohammed V and Rue Allal ben Abdellah; 8:15am-3:45pm Mon.-Fri.) exchanges travelers checks and has a handy 24-hour exchange ATM. **WafaChange** (across from Banque Populaire on Blvd. Mohammed V; 8am-6pm Mon.-Fri., 9am-1pm Sat.) is the only bank with weekend hours. The state-run **Bank al Maghrib** (Blvd. Mohammed V; 8am-3pm Mon.-Fri.) will generally cash travelers checks.

GETTING THERE

Air

Tangier Ibn Battuta Airport

tel. 539/393-649; www.onda.ma/Nos-Aéroports/Aéroport-Tanger-Ibn-Batouta

The Tangier Ibn Battuta Airport (TNG) is on the south side of the city (25 min; 15 km/9 mi). Budget airline **Ryanair** (www.ryanair.com) operates direct flights from Seville (1 hr; 3 weekly) and Málaga (45 min; 3 weekly) with additional flights added during peak travel season (summer). **Iberia** (www.iberia.com) offers direct connections with Málaga (45 min; 4 weekly). If you book in advance, you'll have a good chance of landing a very inexpensive ticket, making this perhaps the most practical way for many travelers to connect into Morocco, though without the romance of the ferry across the strait.

Airport Taxis

The taxis that service the airport, also known as **grands taxis,** are well regulated, with rates posted at the taxi stand just outside the airport. DH150 is the going rate for a convenient transfer directly into downtown Tangier.

Day-Trip Tours

In Tarifa, you'll find numerous join-in day trips to Tangier priced around €79. These are okay deals as they do include the cost of your round-trip ferry ticket (€71), as well as a half-day guided tour of the old medina and lunch. Without exception, these tours take you into bazaars, where you are expected to shop for souvenirs (and the guide makes his commission), so buyer beware.

If you are looking for a more culturally immersive experience, considering booking your own private guide. Guides start from 800-1,200DH a day, depending on what you want to do and see. When contacting local guides, using WhatsApp is preferable. Here are a couple of reputable local guides you can contact:

- Abdelmajid Domnati; tel. 0666/902-980
- Abdellatif Chebbi; tel. 0661/072-014

You can also reach out to my travel company, Journey Beyond Travel (www.journeybeyondtravel.com), and we will put you in contact with a great guide.

Ferry

From Tarifa, Spain

Tangier is just a 45-minute ferry ride from Tarifa, Spain. Getting on the ferry is as easy as hopping on a bus, though you will go through passport control because you are entering/exiting Spain and the Schengen Zone.

Daily ferries connect directly from Tarifa to the convenient port of **Tanger-Ville,** right at the foot of the Tangier medina. It is easy to walk on and walk off the ferry, duck through passport control, and continue your exploration, much like crossing the border at Gibraltar. Though you can purchase ferry tickets ahead of time, in practice it is easier to just purchase tickets on arrival to the port for the next departure. This gives you the most flexibility in your travel.

Tickets are available online (www.frs.es) and right at the ferry terminal for single passengers (€40/DH420), cars (€180/DH1,920), and caravans (€190/DH2,050). Make sure to arrive at the ferry 30 minutes prior to departure if you are walking on. If you are taking an automobile (not recommended for short trips to Tangier), get there at least an hour early. Take special care if purchasing tickets online to select Tanger-Ville (not Tanger-Med). They are two different ports in and around Tangier serving two different cities in Spain.

From Algeciras, Spain

If there are high winds, the ferry routes between Tarifa and Tangier will stop running. This is the only time I would advise trying the larger ferries connecting Algeciras to the **Tanger-Med port,** about an hour drive east of Tangier. Even then, I would only do this if you need to cross immediately. Though tickets are generally less expensive than for the Tarifa-Tangier ferry, the travel time is usually doubled, if not tripled, with longer lines and longer travel times on bigger, older, slower ferries.

A free bus coordinates with ferry arrivals/departures in Tarifa, connecting the ferry terminal with the Algeciras ferry terminal. The Algeciras ferry terminal is a short walk across the busy Avenue la Marina to the bus station (Estación de Autobuses de Algeciras; Calle San Bernardo 1B; 15 min; 1 km/0.6 mi). At the Tanger-Med port, a shuttle bus connects the ferry terminal at the port with downtown Tangier (hourly; 45 min; DH5).

GETTING AROUND

Walking

The medina and kasbah are large pedestrian-only zones, only accessed by foot. The hills can be steep as well, so bring a good pair of shoes and strongly consider using walking sticks.

Taxi

Red city taxis, which are also known as **petits taxis,** can shuttle you around town, though outside the train station the drivers will often try to get you to agree on an exorbitant price rather than use the counter, as they legally should. Feel free to demand the counter be used, and if a driver ever disagrees, simply refuse to take the taxi. Most taxi rides should cost DH15-20.

Bus

City buses (DH3.50) owned by Alsa (http://alsa.ma) run dependably 7am-9pm daily around Tangier. The handiest for travelers looking to explore the western edges of Tangier is bus 5, which runs every 30 minutes from Sidi Bouabid by the Grand Mosque (across from the Cervantes Institute in the Iberia neighborhood) past Perdicaris Park and all the way to Cap Spartel.

Segways

Segways have also been taking Tangier by storm; try **MobilBoard** (Ave. Abi Jarir Tabari; tel. 0606/000-311; www.mobilboard.com/tanger; DH170 for 30 min). The most enjoyable Segway ride is perhaps the circuit on the new waterfront pedestrian-only boulevard (1 hr, DH300). Helmets are available (and recommended). It's best to reserve a few days in advance.

Cádiz

Despite the occasional glut of cruise ship crowds, Cádiz is an easy city to love. The vibrant old city makes for a great exploration on foot, and there are just enough attractions for a couple of days, although you could stay longer to soak in the beachy vibes. Cádiz does sport some of the best beaches in all of Spain, and the city prides itself on being the oldest city "still standing" in the West. History here dates back continuously to over 3,000 years ago. It's easy to get a sense of this history after just a few moments in the ancient city.

ORIENTATION

The **Old City,** known as the **Casco Antiguo,** is a maze of narrow streets, historic squares, and old-world architecture. Landmarks like the Cádiz Cathedral, the Torre Tavira, the historic castle, and more are all found here. Most travelers will focus their time in this part of Cádiz soaking in the cultural heritage

Cádiz

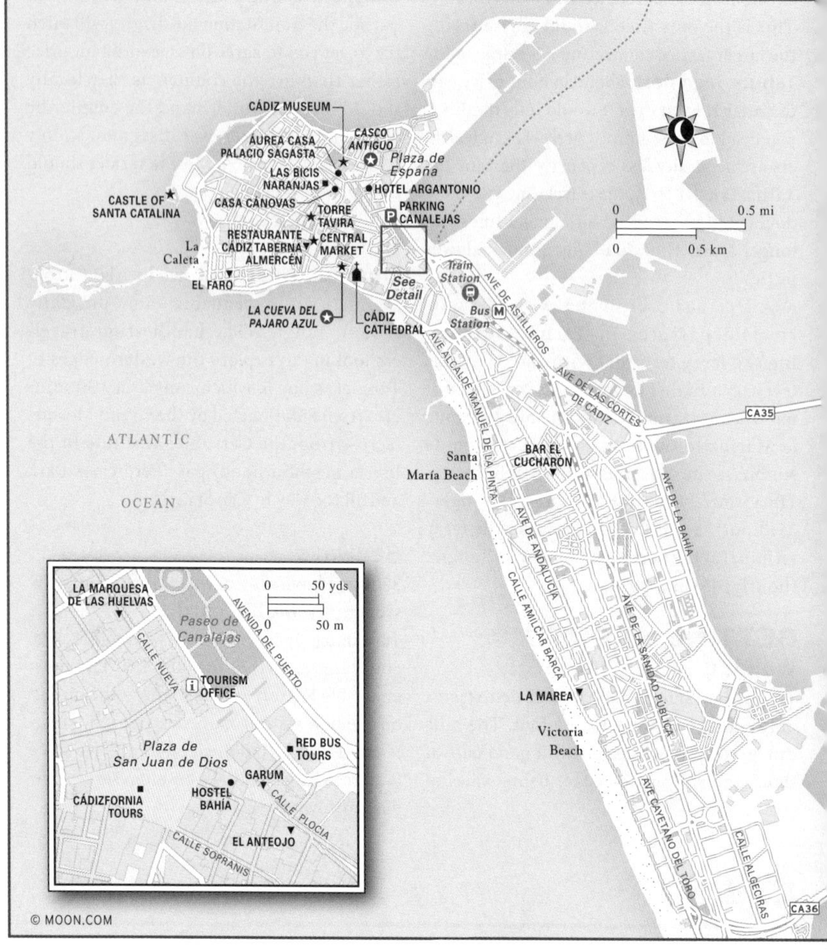

and sights, wandering through its charming streets to uncover hidden taverns, vibrant markets, and enchanting squares. Helpfully, the train station and bus station are right at the northeastern corner of the Casco Antiguo.

To the east of the Casco Antiguo lies the **New City,** or Ciudad Nueva, which offers a more contemporary atmosphere. Here, you'll find modern amenities, bustling commercial districts, beautiful promenades along the waterfront, and some of Europe's best beaches. Expect wide avenues, shops, restaurants, and a vibrant nightlife scene, though there are no real sights in this part of the city.

SIGHTS

★ Casco Antiguo

Plaza de España

Plaza de España; 24/7; free

Whatever is going on in Cádiz begins or ends on this plaza, whether it's a casual sunny day of business-as-usual or a vibrant local festival.

On a typical day you'll see groups of travelers, beach bums, buskers, vendors, and backpackers shuttling by while friends gather for a drink in the square or in one of the local cafés. This completely pedestrianized public square with its monument to the constitution has become a source of pride for the locals.

Cádiz Cathedral (Catedral de Cádiz)

Plaza de la Catedral; tel. 956/807-459; www.catedraldecadiz.com; usually 10am-7pm Mon.-Sat., 2pm-6pm Sun.; €7

The impressive neoclassical cathedral of Cádiz plays host to several important relics and paintings from churches and monasteries from around Spain. Take advantage of the audio guide to get the most out of your visit. Downstairs you'll find a memorial for the composer Manuel de Falla, while upstairs you can take a sloping ramp to the top of the bell tower. The views are fantastic, perhaps the best in Cádiz, though the bell rings every 15 minutes and wow is it loud!

Castle of Santa Catalina (Castillo de Santa Catalina)

Calle Campo de las Balas; tel. 956/226-333; 11am-8pm daily; free

In 1596 King Philip II sent Cristóbal de Rojas, one of his trusted engineers, to shore up the defenses of Cádiz, at this time a strategic port town not only for trade, but for the powerful Spanish armada. The castle of Santa Catalina formed the defenses Rojas built using a star-shaped plan with an interior courtyard and simple functioning locks. Today, the fortress has been transformed into a multipurpose culture and leisure space complete with exhibition halls that always have something interesting on display, as well as arts and crafts workshops and a rotating concert series.

Torre Tavira

Calle Marqués del Real Tesoro, 10; tel. 956/212-910; www.torretavira.com; 10am-8pm daily May-Sept., 10am-6pm daily Oct.-Apr.; €7

Perhaps the most iconic views of Cádiz are had from the top of the Torre Tavira, the most famous of Cádiz's many watchtowers. At Torre Tavira you are at the highest point in town at 45 m (150 ft) above sea level. It was named after Don Antonio Tavira, the tower's first watchman, who used his telescope to track ships laden with goods coming from the Americas. Only so many people are able to go up the tower at a time, so you may have to wait if there are crowds or tours are coming through. It is best to make a reservation ahead of time to visit the tower. Though everyone comes for the views, you should stick around and check out the camera obscura, one of the largest installed in the entire world, which makes for another incredible viewing experience.

Cádiz Museum (Museo de Cádiz)

Plaza de Mina; tel. 856/859-000; 9am-8:30pm Tues.-Fri., 9am-4pm Sat.-Sun.; €1.50

This converted neoclassical Franciscan convent houses a diverse collection that spans centuries of history, art, and culture. Explore archaeological treasures, including Phoenician, Roman, and Moorish artifacts that connect with the region's ancient past. The fine arts section showcases masterpieces by celebrated Spanish artists like Zurbarán and Murillo, which is what the museum is best known for. Additionally, ethnographic aspects of Cádiz and its people are on display, shedding light on local traditions and customs.

Port of Gadir: The Bluebird Cave (Puerto de Gadir: La Cueva del Pajaro Azul)

Calle San Juan, 37-39; tel. 856/386-838; www.cuevadelpajaroazul.com; 10am-7pm daily; €8

Discover the Phoenician Port of Gadir (Puerto de Gadir), also known as the Bluebird Cave. It was named after a popular local smuggler with the same nickname. The port is why many believe Cádiz is the oldest city in Europe. This is a small site and one best visited with a guide who can point out details

1

2

3

and bring the history of this old cave, a dry dock dating to at least 300 BCE, to life.

Plaza de San Juan de Dios

Plaza de San Juan de Dios; 24/7; free

The most emblematic square in Cádiz with the Baroque town hall perpetually holding court. This is where buskers play and locals and travelers mingle under the warm Andalusian sun. You'll find a handy tourism information kiosk here as well as quick access to a few different pedestrian streets that lead into the old city. From this plaza, it's a really nice 10-15-minute walk up the charming Calle San Francisco that connects with Plaza de España near the docks.

Central Market (Mercado Central)

Plaza de la Libertad; tel. 956/214-191; 9am-3pm Mon.-Sat.; free

There is nothing like hitting up a local market to get a real sense for the day-to-day life of the locals. The main market of Cádiz is great for fruits, veggies, and fresh seafood, as well as locally produced sweets, dried fruits, nuts, and cured meats, particularly the ham that the region is so known for. As in the markets in Seville, Málaga, and elsewhere, you'll be able to munch on some tapas or sandwiches and quaff a beverage should you wish.

Tours

Red Bus Tours

Plaza San Juan de Dios; tel. 900/920-092; €25

A double-decker hop-on, hop-off red bus circles Cádiz and makes 14 stops. A two-day pass includes unlimited rides plus a one-hour walking tour in English and Spanish (12:30pm daily). This is an easy way to get up and down the long, thin city and enjoy a ride along the water. It's not often that bus tours are the most convenient way to get around town, but it really works for Cádiz.

1: city street in Cádiz **2:** view from Torre Tavira
3: Plaza de San Juan de Dios

SPORTS AND RECREATION

Beaches

Cádiz is an easy beach-lover's destination to couple with your Andalusian exploration. There are three main beaches in Cádiz, each easily accessible whether you walk, take a taxi, or connect with the red buses. These are some of the cleanest urban beaches in all of Europe.

La Caleta

Avenida Duque de Nájera, northwest corner of old Cádiz; 24/7; free

Located at the northwestern corner of Cádiz's Casco Antiguo, this swooping moon of sand is iconic beach bumming in all its European glory. Views of the San Sebastián and Santa Catalina castles to the north and south frame the view west over the rippling curls of the Atlantic Ocean. A fine palm-tree-lined boardwalk, nearby cafés and restaurants, readily available beach umbrellas, on-site showers to wash off, well-protected from strong winds, and a few colorful small fishing boats complete the scene. Throw in a golden sunset and you have yourself a contender for one of the best public beaches in Spain, if not all of Europe.

Santa María Beach (Playa de Santa María)

Paseo Marítimo, just south of the old city; 24/7; free

Known for its lush, soft sand, the Playa de Santa María is a short walk or ride from the Casco Antiguo in the newer part of the city. Though it's a popular local beach, Gaditanos often won't show up until after work, so it's likely you'll have smaller crowds for most of the day. There are larger waves here, which some may prefer, and the beach is another very clean municipal beach, though lacking the facilities (namely: bathrooms) that you can find at other beaches.

Victoria Beach (Playa de la Victoria)

Paseo Marítimo, just south of the Playa de Santa María; 24/7; free

DE CORAL
6€ '99
1
2
3
4

Restaurants, bars, showers, and even bathrooms can be found right on and off the beach here, which has lifeguards, making it the ideal choice for many locals and Spaniards on vacation. This is the longest stretch of beach around, and, as at neighboring Santa María, you can expect wavier waves and sandier sand than at La Caleta. There are places set aside for sports like soccer (ahem, pardon me, fútbol).

Playa de la Victoria continues right into Playa de la Cortadura, making them effectually the same long beach running along the CA-33 road, the two making a razor-thin isthmus connecting Cádiz to the European continent.

Walking Tours

Red Bus Tours

Plaza de San Juan de Dios; tel. 900/920-092; 12:30pm daily; 1 hr; included with €25 bus package

If you booked the two-day red bus package, a one-hour bilingual English and Spanish walking tour of the old town of Cádiz is included. It leaves from the information kiosk in the plaza at 12:30pm daily. During this short street walk you'll touch on the highlights of Cádiz, including the market, cathedral, and Torre Tavira. This walking tour makes sense for most travelers.

Cádizfornia Tours

Plaza de San Juan de Dios; tel. 695/555-557; www.cadizforniatours.com; 10:30am and 1:30pm daily; 1.5 hr; free (tipping encouraged)

If you are skipping the red buses, then you might want to take advantage of the free walking tours by Cádizfornia Tours. Tours leave from the tourist information kiosk on the plaza and hit the main highlights. Guides love to share their favorite spots to grab tapas as you head through the neighborhoods of the old city. Tours end at La Caleta beach, so pack swimwear and enjoy the beach after your tour.

1: Central Market **2:** Santa María Beach **3:** Carnival of Cádiz **4:** Cristina Aldón, one of Andalusia's premier flamenco dancers

Adriane (Adri) Anderson

tel. 0618/036-628; from €160

Spanish-American Adriane Anderson has been leading tours through her hometown of Cádiz for years. Adri, as her friends call her, is a natural hostess who wants to really show off her favorite hidden gems and foodie bites around town. Her tours are all private and customized, though they usually include some nibbles and drinks. If you're looking for a more bespoke sort of experience in Cádiz, contact Adriane and arrange the Cádiz of your dreams.

Biking

Las Bicis Naranjas

Calle Sagasta, 9; tel. 956/907-671; www.lasbicisnaranjas.com; 10am-2pm and 5pm-9pm Mon.-Fri., 10am-2pm and 7pm-9pm Sat., 10am-1pm and 8pm-9pm Sun.; from €5

If you want to explore the city on two wheels, head here to the home of the orange bikes and get pedaling. You can rent new, well-maintained bicycles by the hour (€5) or day (€15). Go with the day rental so you can enjoy pedaling out to the beaches and perhaps even some of the neighboring towns. Bike tours also available. The popular city bike tour runs three times daily (11am, 4pm, and 6:30pm; €32), though there are other offerings. Check the website for details.

ENTERTAINMENT AND EVENTS

Festivals

★ Carnival (Fiesta de Carnaval)

40 days before Easter (starting in February)

The Carnival of Cádiz is one of the most famous and beloved in Spain. It is a grand celebration characterized by elaborate costumes, satirical performances, music, and street parades. The chirigotas (witty musical groups) and comparsas (satirical troupes) take center stage with their humorous and politically charged performances. The streets of Cádiz fill with people of all ages in colorful and creative costumes. Many participants dress in elaborate outfits, some with a political or humorous twist, adding to the festive atmosphere. You'll find an array of characters, from traditional jesters to contemporary pop culture references. Expect most accommodations to double or triple in price during this time. The Carnival season culminates in the Gran Cabalgata (Grand Parade), where participants showcase their imaginative costumes and choreography, and the entire city becomes one giant party.

Carnival of the Flames (Carnaval de las Viñas)

Late February/early March

Celebrated in nearby El Puerto de Santa María and coinciding with the Carnival season, this quirky, fiery Carnival is similar to the one in Cádiz in that participants dress in colorful costumes and create satirical floats. However, in El Puerto de Santa María they famously set fire to a King Momo float, making a spectacular display that symbolizes the end of the Carnival season.

Holy Week (Semana Santa)

Easter Week

Like many Spanish cities, Cádiz observes Holy Week with solemn religious processions, but it also has its distinctive flair. The city's narrow streets and historic settings create a unique backdrop for the processions, with iconic religious sculptures and ornate floats on display. The processions take place in the week leading up to Easter Sunday. It's not as well known as Semana Santa in Seville or Málaga, so the experience feels more local.

Flamenco

★ La Cueva del Pajaro Azul

Calle San Juan 37-39; tel. 856/386-838; www.cuevadelpajaroazul.com; 9pm Sat.; €32

For one of the best flamenco shows in Andalusia, head to this historic cave. Despite being limited to only 32 seats, with some having views obscured by the support columns of the cave, somehow it all adds to the authentic charm of this performance. Shows are accompanied by tapas and locally produced sherry or wine. Besides the old-world surroundings, the acoustics of the tablao contribute to how the music, stomps, and taps of the dancers reverberate through the cave, making for a performance that will shake your soul. Usually there is only one performance per week, on Saturday, though in busier seasons other performances may be available.

FOOD

You can expect a nice variety of cuisine in Cádiz, particularly given how small the old city really is. There is a focus on seafood, understandable given its seaside locale. Calle San Fernando and Calle Plocia are both really nice strips of bars, cafés, and restaurants that make for a wonderful short walk for tapas. Outside of the old city, you'll find local joints that have a bit more bang for the buck but are a commute from the main areas of interest.

Casco Antiguo

Garum

Calle Plocia, 6; tel. 856/534-604; 8:30am-4pm and 8pm-11pm Mon.-Sat.; €10

Garum is equally nice for a relaxed traditional Spanish breakfast of tostadas (toasted bread) or local tapas. There are only a few little tables outside, though the more local experience is indoors anyhow. The quality tapas include salad, croquettes, and stews, which are all particularly well done. Come here either in the morning or in the evening to have the most local experience and friendliest service.

La Marquesa de las Huelvas

Calle San Francisco, 38; tel. 610/249-989; 8:30am-midnight daily; €12

For a light breakfast with some freshly squeezed orange juice and some great people-watching, this café right along the busy Calle San Francisco hits the spot. Pull up a stool at the large corner windows, sip on your cappuccino, and try a slice of one of their fabulous, spiced cakes. Tapas later in the day are a bit disappointing. Best to stick to breakfast.

El Anteojo

Calle Plocia, 13; tel. 956/076-888; 1pm-4:30pm and 8pm-11:30pm Tues.-Thurs., 1pm-11:30pm Fri.-Sat., 1pm-4:30pm Sun.; €12

This is the kind of joint Andalusia really excels at. With the white linens and attentive service, you could consider this for a casual date night. Equally, it's the sort of place you can just take a seat at the bar and make small talk with the barkeep, or enjoy your tapas, the breezy Cádizian air, and the passersby. Stick with the fresh seafood, though traditional tapas, like jamón ibérico, are also an easy-to-please nibble to have with your beverage.

★ Restaurante Cádiz Taberna Almercén

Plaza Libertad, Calle Robles; tel. 856/581-353; 1pm-5pm and 8:30pm-midnight Mon. and Thurs.-Sat., 1:30pm-5pm Sun., 1pm-5pm Tues.; €15

Don't let the exposed brick fool you; this is about as quintessentially Gaditano as it gets, with a focus on fresh seafood, well spiced and cooked just right. Typically you'll find sushi-grade red tuna on offer that is seared to perfection, while fresh salads and a really surprising beet salmorejo round out a fine dining experience at a great value. It can get busy here right next to the municipal market, so try to come right at opening. Limited outdoor seating. Service is quick and affable, so you normally won't have to wait too long for a table. And the wait is worth it!

El Faro

Calle San Félix, 15; tel. 956/211-068; www.elfarodecadiz.com; 1pm-4:30pm and 8:30pm-11:30pm daily; €25

A visit to El Faro guarantees a memorable culinary experience. This legendary eatery, celebrated for decades as a bastion of Mediterranean cuisine, is for seafood lovers. It's cozy, classic, and unassuming, with picture-lined walls that would look at home anywhere in Spain. Fish and seafood freshly caught daily are expertly prepared, with highlights including the beloved tortillitas de camarones—shrimp fritters. The menu also features exquisite dishes like sea urchin filled with shrimp tartare and oxigarum, an ancient fish sauce with sherry vinegar. El Faro has a reputation, and it does live up to it, but it can also be busy. Reserve in advance or be open to eating at the bar.

New City

★ Bar El Cucharón

Calle Francisco García de Sola, 13; tel. 679/320-297; noon-4pm and 8:30pm-11:30pm Tues.-Sat., 1pm-4pm Sun.; €10

When you're done with the beach, head inland a few blocks to this trusty spot for a wonderfully local dining experience. You'll find the typical tapas menu here: local ham, cheese, and artichokes among other choices. Gluten-free possibilities are on the menu, with the surprising addition of a gluten-free beer option. Food is standard Andalusian tapas, though done very well, and more importantly, the fun, friendly service is typically more welcoming than at places more often frequented by tourists.

La Marea

Paseo Marítimo, 1; tel. 956/280-347; www.lamarea.es; 1pm-5pm and 8pm-midnight daily; €30

The inviting, spacious terrace of La Marea sets the scene for sunset dining over the long stretch of Playa de la Victoria. This charming spot is a paradise for seafood lovers, renowned for its arroces, a delightful variation of paella brimming with intense flavors. For a more interactive culinary experience, diners can choose their selection from a captivating display of fresh lobsters, red snappers, and squids, elegantly presented on ice. When in season, don't miss the opportunity to savor the exquisite bluefin tuna, available in juicy steaks or delicious tacos—a culinary experience you shouldn't miss.

ACCOMMODATIONS

All the accommodations listed are in the old city, as this is the most central for most places of touristic interest.

Under €100

Hostal Bahía

Calle Plocia, 5; tel. 956/259-061; https://hostalbahiacadiz.com; €50

You don't often find such sweet service in a budget hostel. Rooms are clean and thankfully have air-conditioning (not always a given at this price point!), and the location right next to the town hall makes for a great place to lay your head after a day of exploration. However, it really is the five-star service that sets this hostel apart. Make good use of the staff for recommendations and general pointers for getting around.

★ Hotel Argantonio

Calle Argantonio, 3; tel. 956/211-640; www.hotelargantonio.com; €90

There are few truly small, quaint, boutique hotels at a great value in Cádiz, but Hotel Argantonio is the rare exception. Housed in an artfully restored 18th-century manor, it looks across the Strait of Gibraltar to Morocco for its design cues. This kind of chic property would feel right at home in Tangier. The public rooms have the feeling of a cozy library, while the gurgling mosaic fountain in the central courtyard sets the ambience. On the rooftop you'll have fantastic views over Cádiz to enjoy with a sip of cool sherry fino. The service is friendly, elevated, and wonderfully over the top at this price level. Comfy, stylish rooms round out what is perhaps the best-value stay in town. Reserve ahead of time for best rates.

€100-200

Áurea Casa Palacio Sagasta

Calle Sagasta, 1; tel. 856/632-900; www.eurostarshotels.co.uk/aurea-casa-palacio-sagasta.html; €150

A Baroque 18th-century mansion and former British embassy has been transformed into a 38-room boutique property complete with spa. The rooms are all unexpectedly modern with contemporary bathrooms, many of them with walk-in Italian-style showers. The property itself has a lot of charm, while the indoor pool is a really nice touch, making for great public lounging spaces.

Casa Cánovas

Calle Cánovas del Castillo, 32; tel. 956/227-984; https://hotelcasacanovas.com; €175

Velvet and checkerboard marble decorate this stately house turned small hotel. High attention is paid to details throughout, with plush textiles that feel like fluffy cotton balls and large soaking tubs that might as well be your own private sea. Service more than lives up to the rest of the property: personal yet professional, always engaging, and always ready with a great recommendation. You'll likely feel that you've landed at a property that is 3-4 times more expensive. It really does feel that nice. Location, right in old town and just minutes from the beach and main plazas, seals the deal, making it the "must-stay" hotel in Cádiz. Splurge for rooms with balconies and views over old Cádiz. The glittering night views are special.

INFORMATION AND SERVICES

Tourism Office

Avenida Cuatro de Diciembre de 1977; tel. 900/920-092; 9am-7pm Mon.-Fri., 10am-2:45pm Sat.-Sun.

Head to the tourism office if you want to take advantage of the red bus tours. It might be a good idea to pick up a city map, too. It can come in handy. There is another convenient travel information kiosk in the plaza near the town hall (Plaza San Juan de Dios). Meet up there for most walking tours.

GETTING THERE

Unless you are arriving by cruise ship, you'll likely come into Cádiz by train (from Seville or Jerez de la Frontera) or bus (from Tarifa). Both stations are conveniently right next to each other by the Plaza de Sevilla and the ports on the eastern side of Cádiz's old city.

Train

From Seville, take a train (1.75 hr; 12-plus daily; €15) via Renfe (www.renfe.com). This is by far the quickest, most convenient route. It connects through Jerez de la Frontera (30 min; 12-plus daily; €7).

Amazingly, Spain's robust train network scoots across an isthmus and right up to the old city of Cádiz. The **Cádiz train station** (Plaza de Sevilla; tel. 912/432-343; www.adif.es; 6am-11:30pm daily) is basic without a lot of services, but the convenience is undeniable. You'll find a café, signboard, and not much else.

Bus

From Tarifa, you'll connect by bus (1.5 hr; 3 daily; €20). There are two daily connections run by Transportes Generales Comes (www.tgcomes.es), which leave Tarifa at 8am and 5:30pm, and one daily connection by Alsa (www.alsa.com), leaving Tarifa at 3:15pm.

You'll likely arrive at Cádiz's **bus station** (Avenida Astilleros, 302; tel. 956/257-415; http://estacionautobusescadiz.es) if you are using the bus network to travel to/from the pueblos blancos or down to Tarifa to connect with Tangier. The easiest way to find the bus station is to walk right into the train station and follow the signs. Like the train station, it is very basic.

Car

Cádiz isn't the kind of city you'll want to drive around. It's best to park your car while you are there. A convenient underground parking is right near the port: **Parking Canalejas** (Avenida del Puerto, 1; tel. 956/285-061; 24/7; €15/day).

GETTING AROUND

Cádiz is relatively small and easily walkable. Taxis can whip you around town should you need them. Cobblestone streets, uneven sidewalks, and all the other European pedestrian charms await. In Cádiz, it's a really good idea to pack a pair of flip-flops to wear for the beach. You never know when a sandy seaside stroll will magically pop its way into your day.

Red Bus Tours

Plaza San Juan de Dios; tel. 900/920-092; €25

Red double-decker hop-on, hop-off buses circle Cádiz, making 14 stops. The bus basically runs up and down the outer boulevards of Cádiz, stopping every 400 m (0.25 mi) or so. The two-day pass includes unlimited rides. It's not often that bus tours are the most convenient way to get around town, but it really works for Cádiz. The pass also includes a walking tour, offered daily.

Taxi

Taxis are available and connect easily around the city, though there are parts of the old city that are pedestrian-only where taxis are not allowed to enter. €5-7 will get you pretty much anywhere around the old city.

Jerez de la Frontera and the White Villages

Nestled among the hills and olive groves of Andalusia, the white villages, or pueblos blancos, offer a charming and authentic glimpse into traditional rural life in Spain. These whitewashed villages, with their narrow streets and flower-filled balconies, are scattered across the Sierra de Grazalema Natural Park and the surrounding hillsides.

Jerez de la Frontera is an incredibly popular town known as the birthplace of Andalusian horse culture and sherry, a fortified wine from which the town derives its name. It often serves as a day trip or a stopover from Seville or Cádiz.

Other noteworthy white villages include: Arcos de la Frontera, Zahara de la Sierra, Setenil de las Bodegas, and Ronda. Each has its

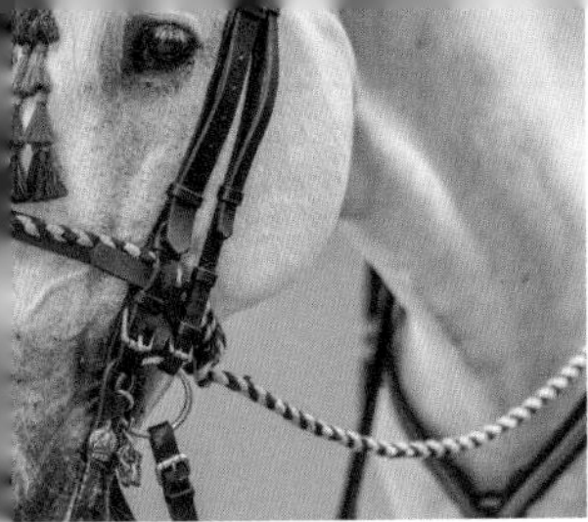

Highlights

Look for ★ to find recommended sights, activities, dining, and lodging.

★ **Bodegas González Byass:** Jerez de la Frontera is famous for its sherry wine, and visitors can tour sherry bodegas, like González Byass, to learn about the production process and sample different varieties (page 278).

★ **Royal Andalusian School of Equestrian Art:** In Jerez de la Frontera, one of the most prestigious riding schools in the world offers stunning horse shows and tours of their facilities (page 280).

★ **Zahara de la Sierra's Medieval Village:** This picturesque village is situated atop a hill, with a medieval castle and stunning views of the surrounding countryside (page 291).

★ **Setenil de las Bodegas:** Uniquely, many of the buildings in this white village have been constructed directly into the surrounding cliffs, providing a glimpse into a small-town experience you're not likely to find elsewhere (page 294).

★ **Puente Nuevo:** There might not be a more emblematic bridge in all of Spain. Spanning across a deep gorge, this sets the scene for Ronda (page 298).

★ **Olive Oil Tasting at LA Organic:** After just an hour at LA Organic, you will come away feeling like an expert in all things olive oil. Expertise has never been so delicious (page 300).

★ **Hacienda Stay:** Just outside of the larger villages and in some of the smallest towns lie quaint traditional haciendas that make for an unforgettable, homey accommodation experience (page 306).

★ **Sierra de Grazalema Natural Park:** Numerous hikes for nearly all ability levels make for an engaging outdoor experience that plunges you into the natural beauty of the region (page 307).

★ **Caminito del Rey:** This easy, cliff-hugging hike is perhaps the most iconic in Spain. In parts, it will seem as though you are defying gravity (page 313).

Jerez de la Frontera and the White Villages

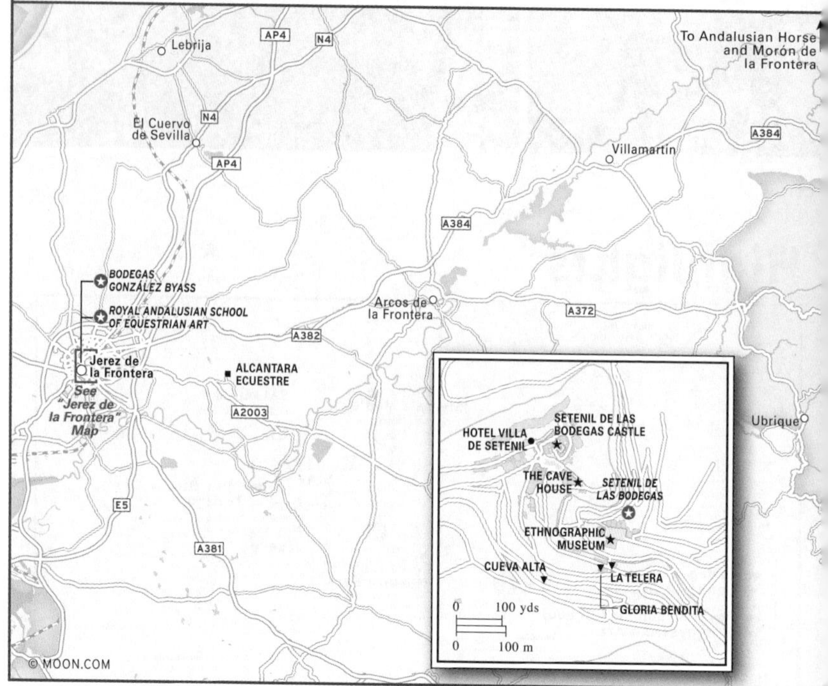

own unique character and history. Some boast medieval fortresses, Roman ruins, and ancient churches. Most of the villages are built into the sides of hills, while others, like Setenil de las Bodegas, are carved directly into the rock face. The region is also famous for its traditional crafts, such as handmade pottery and woven baskets. Visitors can often watch artisans at work in their studios.

With so many villages dotting the mountain landscape, it's no surprise that this area boasts some of the best hiking in the region. The Sierra de Grazalema Natural Park offers numerous opportunities to plunge into the region's mountains, while the iconic Caminito del Rey is one of those easy-going hikes through an incredible landscape that will leave you breathless in admiration. Birdwatching and horseback riding are also popular activities, as is sampling the local cuisine, such as hearty stews and sweet pastries made with local honey and almonds.

You should circle a visit to at least one of the famous white villages of Andalusia if you're looking to experience an authentic side of Spain during your travels. The simple, laid-back lifestyle, stunning landscapes, and rich history are easy to appreciate. With their natural beauty and peaceful atmosphere, I like to think of the pueblos blancos as the little diamonds of Andalusia, scattered through the rugged mountain terrain—tiny glittering jewels that add a touch of sparkling romance to your journey.

HISTORY

Jerez de la Frontera, the white villages (pueblos blancos), and the two parks in this region—Sierra de las Nieves and Sierra de Grazalema—are significant historically and

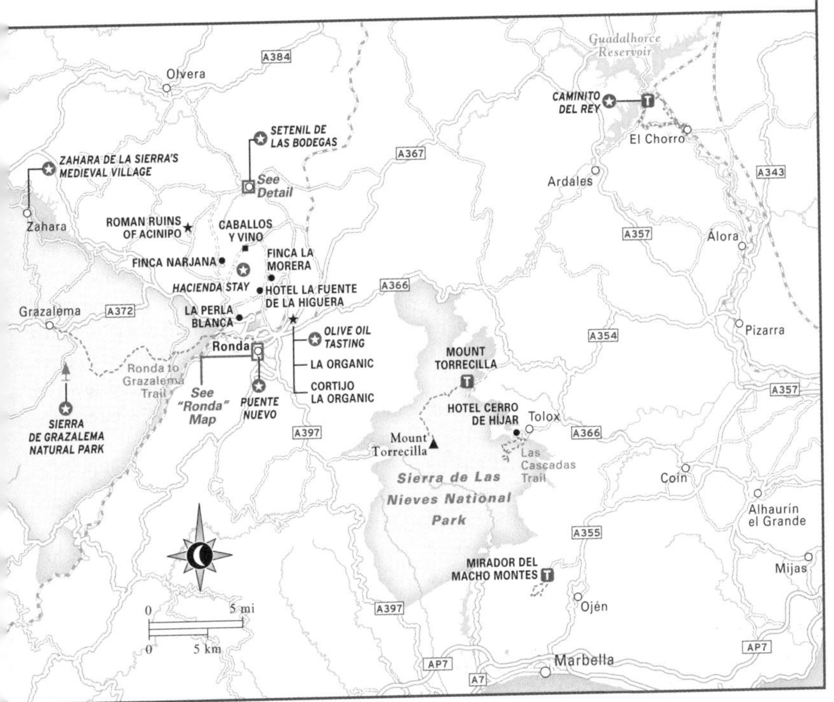

for the vast mountainous Andalusian landscapes they provide.

Jerez de la Frontera, literally "Sherry of the Border," was first historically a strong military outpost of the Islamic era. It wasn't until the 13th century that Jerez de la Frontera fell to Christian forces. Alfonso X of Castile, known as Alfonso the Wise, was a medieval monarch who played a pivotal role in the cultural and intellectual development of Jerez and the broader Iberian Peninsula. Alfonso X was not only a king but also a poet, scholar, and patron of the arts. He fostered a court culture that attracted scholars from across Europe, contributing to the flourishing of science, literature, and music during his reign in the 13th century.

Over the subsequent centuries, the ascendancy of Jerez as a hub of viticulture and trade catalyzed its economic prosperity. The cultivation of vineyards and the production of sherry wine emerged as the lifeblood of the city's economy, fostering trade networks that stretched across Europe and beyond. Enter Manuel María González Ángel, a prominent entrepreneur and visionary. González Ángel was instrumental in shaping Jerez's modern identity as a center of sherry production. In the late 19th and early 20th centuries, he founded the renowned Bodegas Tio Pepe winery, which became one of the most iconic sherry producers in the world. González Ángel's innovative approaches to winemaking and marketing helped elevate Jerez's

Previous: Setenil de las Bodegas; Andalusian stallion; Caminito del Rey.

reputation as a premier wine-producing region while producing what is perhaps the first true worldwide brand. The brand, Tio Pepe, was named after González Ángel's uncle, José María Ángel y Vargas, known affectionately as Tio Pepe (Uncle Pepe). The iconic Tio Pepe logo was created a few years later, in 1934, by Luis Pérez Solero, a man clearly ahead of his time in terms of style, simplicity, and effective marketing. There is maybe no other city more linked to a single brand of alcohol than Jerez de la Frontera is to Tio Pepe.

The famous white villages, characterized by their whitewashed architecture, blend Moorish and Christian architectural styles, their hilltop locations having served strategic roles throughout the ages, serving different rulers during different eras and wars. These days, they are a haven of small-scale tourism.

In terms of natural significance, the Sierra de las Nieves National Park and Sierra de Grazalema Natural Park are characterized by limestone formations, deep gorges, and underground rivers, and both are home to a diverse range of plant and animal species, including the rare Spanish fir. As you might expect, these parks offer opportunities for outdoor exploration. That said, perhaps the most iconic experience you can have follows the footsteps of the Spanish king Alfonso XIII, who in 1921 christened the trail now famously known as Caminito del Rey, to the east of the parks near the Guadalhorce Reservoir.

PLANNING YOUR TIME

For an immersive exploration, allocate a minimum of 3-5 days to fully savor the sights, culture, and nature in this captivating region.

The white villages are best visited outside of the hot summer months. Optimal seasons for exploration are spring and fall, when the weather is delightful and tourist crowds are generally thinner. While the smaller towns in this region are not typically inundated with tourists, you can expect busier moments at renowned attractions like Ronda's Puente Nuevo or even the Caminito del Rey, so strategic planning can make a difference. It's good to keep in mind that this region doesn't face the same tourist congestion as some of the larger Andalusian cities. Ideally you could work them in as stops on the way to Cádiz or opt for an overnight, particularly in Jerez, so you could enjoy a more relaxed town atmosphere to fully appreciate the more rural aspects of Andalusia.

In Ronda, take a day to experience the awe-inspiring Puente Nuevo and explore the historic old town. If you travel at a quicker pace, you could add in a side trip to another white village. However, with another full day, you could visit a couple more white villages and be more immersive with your travel. These towns each offer their unique charm, perfect for soaking in an authentic ambience, exploring historical landmarks, and wandering picturesque streets alongside locals.

The surrounding parks, Sierra de Grazalema and Sierra de las Nieves, are a paradise for nature enthusiasts. To truly appreciate their beauty, plan another day for hiking through the pristine landscapes, discovering hidden caves, and taking in the remarkable biodiversity. The thrilling Caminito del Rey, a dizzying walkway bolted into the side of a sheer rock cliff, requires another half day.

Itinerary Ideas

DAY 1: JEREZ DE LA FRONTERA

1 Enjoy a walk through the historic center of Jerez, remembering to sip your way through a sherry tour at **Bodegas González Byass.**

2 Be amazed at an early afternoon showing of Baroque dressage at the **Royal Andalusian School of Equestrian Art.**

3 Enjoy a traditional Spanish lunch at **Tabanco El Pasaje,** trying a variety of tapas and regional dishes at one of Jerez de la Frontera's most delightful restaurants.

4 In the evening, take yourself out for a self-guided tapas tour along the **historic local sherry route.**

5 Take in the golden illuminated streets of the **city center** and enjoy the lively ambience and vibrant nightlife.

DAY 2: THE WHITE VILLAGES

1 From Jerez, head out as early as possible to explore the white villages, a cluster of charming Andalusian towns. Set your sights on the charming village of **Setenil de las Bodegas,** known for its unique houses built into the cliffs.

2 Savor a traditional Andalusian lunch at **Gloria Bendita,** trying dishes like carrillada or churros with chocolate.

3 Back on the road, drive toward Ronda, a white village perched on a dramatic gorge. Explore the awe-inspiring **Puente Nuevo,** a symbol of the town, which has breathtaking vistas of the Tajo de Ronda.

4 Make your way to Ronda's old town to stroll through its historic streets, filled with charming shops, cafés, and stunning architecture, such as the **Casa del Rey Moro.**

5 Enjoy a leisurely walk along **Alameda del Tajo,** a lush park offering more panoramic views of El Tajo canyon, often beautifully illuminated at night.

6 Savor a relaxing dinner with incomparable views at **Albacara,** the Hotel Montelirio's restaurant.

DAY 3: HIKING THE CAMINITO DEL REY

1 Get ready for an exhilarating day on the **Caminito del Rey,** a renowned trail that promises adventure and scenic beauty. Make sure to book your tickets in advance. Spend the morning following the narrow walkways and suspension bridges, offering thrilling views of the rugged gorge.

2 Take a picnic lunch out to the **Guadalhorce Reservoir.** Enjoy the water, the sun, and the locals who frequent the area when the weather is fair.

3 After a memorable day of hiking, return to your accommodation in Ronda for a leisurely dinner at **Las Tablas,** or continue on to Córdoba, Antequera, Málaga, or Granada.

Itinerary Ideas

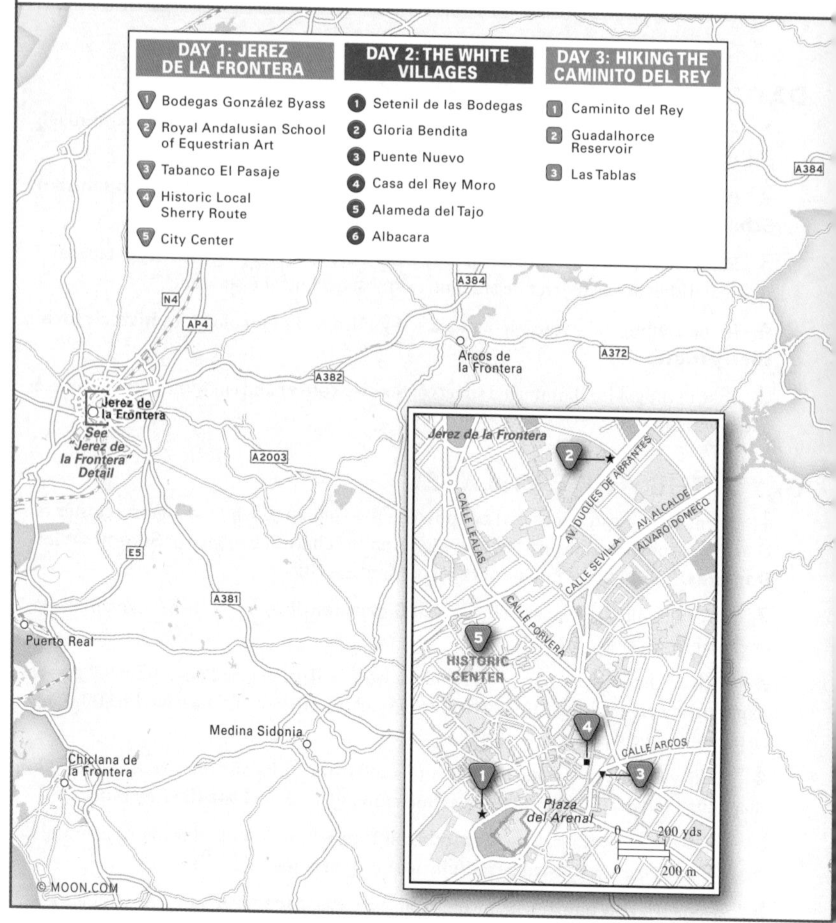

Jerez de la Frontera

Jerez de la Frontera is renowned throughout Spain for its sherry production. In fact, "jerez" literally means sherry, a fortified wine you'll undoubtedly get a taste of while enjoying the historic buildings, flamenco music, and equestrian traditions that make Jerez de la Frontera uniquely Andalusian. The pleasant old town, with its Moorish fortress and cathedral, is much smaller in size than Seville, making Jerez a great day trip from Seville or a stop you can make while connecting to Cádiz or Ronda. That said, because it's a central hub for wine enthusiasts, horse aficionados, and those seeking the authentic sounds of flamenco, overnight stays allow for a more distinctive experience.

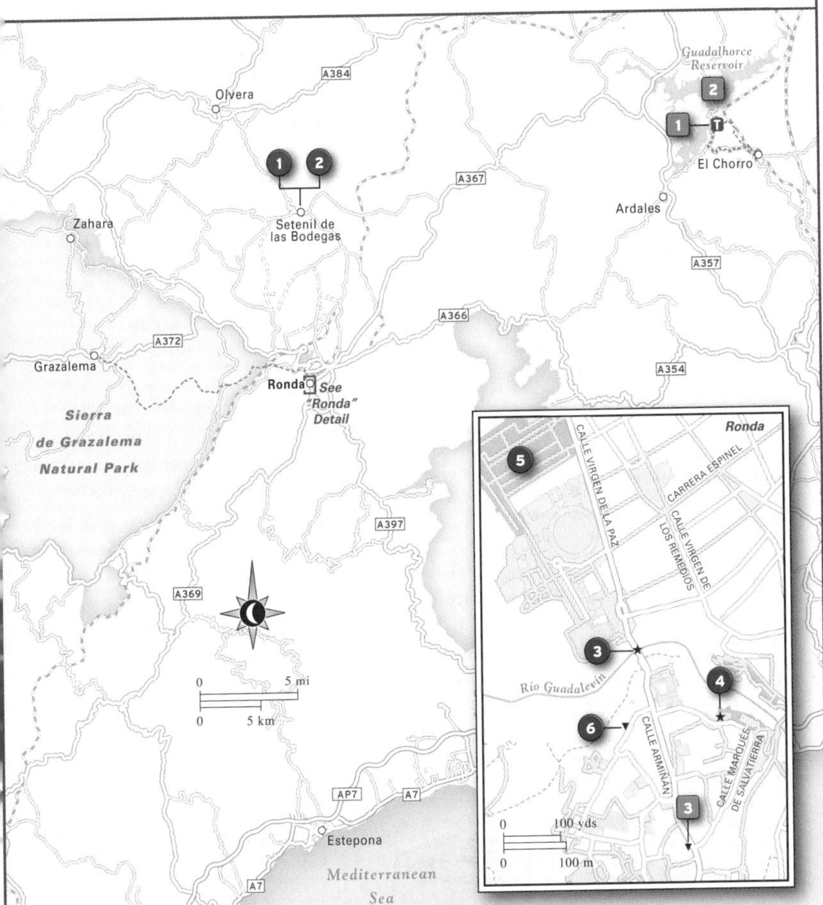

ORIENTATION

Located on the A-4 freeway and conveniently on the train line between Seville and Cádiz, Jerez de la Frontera is a predominantly flat town, easy to explore on foot. Within just a few minutes' walk, the concentrated historic center gives you access to the fortress, cathedral, and main square (Plaza del Arenal), as well as the González Byass winery, which are most of the major attractions of Jerez. However, the Royal Equestrian School is located well north of the historic center, and the train station is on the eastern edge of town.

SIGHTS

Historic Center

Jerez de la Frontera Fortress (Alcázar de Jerez de la Frontera)

Calle Alameda Vieja; tel. 956/149-955; www.jerez.es/webs-municipales/conjunto-monumental-del-alcazar; 9:30am-5:30pm Mon.-Fri., 9:30am-2pm Sat.-Sun.; €5

The long, winding history of the fortress of Jerez de la Frontera begins here in the 12th and 13th centuries, when the original fortress was built while the area was under the rule of the Almohad dynasty, who ruled here from their seat in Marrakesh, Morocco. When Jerez fell to Christian forces, the fortress continued its use, though by the 16th century, it was abandoned and, at one time, even used for farmland. The Islamic gardens you see today date from the 1980s. Over the last few decades, restoration work has been carried out, including on the minaret, to make the entire fortress more closely resemble what it would have looked like in those first centuries after its original construction. In the courtyard there is not a lot of shade, so visit as early in the day as possible.

Cathedral of San Salvador (Catedral de Nuestro Señor San Salvador)

Plaza Encarnación; tel. 956/169-059; www.catedraldejerez.es; €7

You would be forgiven if you thought that the cathedral of Jerez had a former Islamic minaret that was refashioned into a bell tower, similar to the cathedrals found in Seville and Córdoba. However, you would be mistaken. This couldn't be further from the truth. In fact, before the cathedral was built, the entire mosque that once graced this part of town was razed. The current bell tower was constructed in the 16th century, long after the Reconquista and long after there was any Muslim rule in the land. Likely this bell tower was built as an homage to the cathedral in Seville or possibly just to follow the fashionable Mudejar-style architecture of the time. Pope John Paul II visited in 1980 to elevate this from a church to a cathedral.

★ Bodegas González Byass

Calle Manuel María González, 12; tel. 956/357-016; www.tiopepe.com; €20

González Byass's Tio Pepe was the first ever registered brand in Spain. A short train trip through their delightful property brings you through a vine grove, past a private home, and through an expansive garden with flora from the Americas and beyond. You arrive at the oldest part of the property, where old tools and methods are explained. Harvest is in August, fermentation in November. A sherry tasting with tapas greets you at the end. This is one of the most historic wines and brands in the entire world.

Jerez de la Frontera Fortress

Jerez de la Frontera

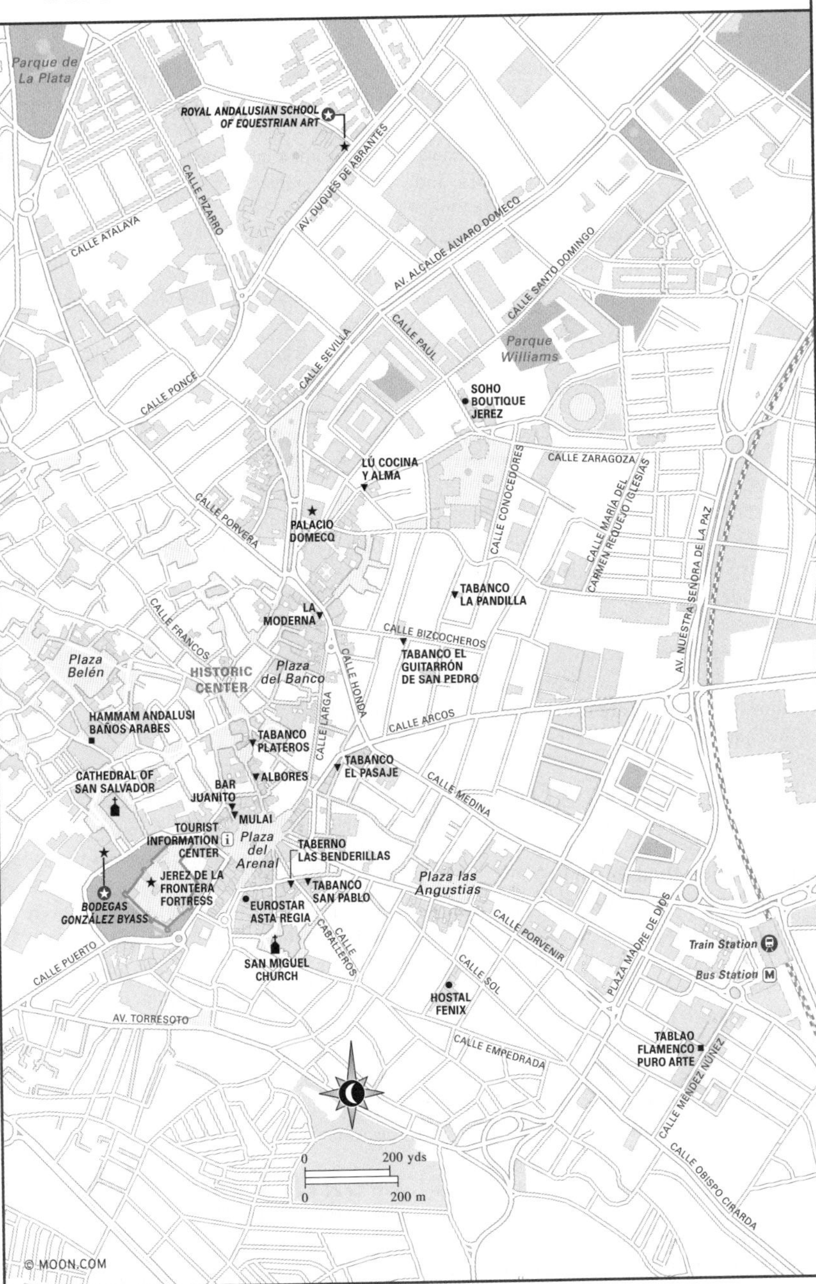
Parque de La Plata
ROYAL ANDALUSIAN SCHOOL OF EQUESTRIAN ART
CALLE PIZARRO
AV. DUQUES DE ABRANTES
CALLE ATALAYA
AV. ALCALDE ÁLVARO DOMECQ
CALLE SANTO DOMINGO
CALLE PAUL
Parque Williams
CALLE SEVILLA
CALLE PONCE
SOHO BOUTIQUE JEREZ
LÚ COCINA Y ALMA
CALLE ZARAGOZA
CALLE CONOCEDORES
CALLE MARÍA DEL CARMEN REQUEJO IGLESIAS
CALLE PORVERA
PALACIO DOMECQ
AV. NUESTRA SEÑORA DE LA PAZ
TABANCO LA PANDILLA
LA MODERNA
CALLE FRANCOS
CALLE BIZCOCHEROS
TABANCO EL GUITARRÓN DE SAN PEDRO
Plaza Belén
HISTORIC CENTER
Plaza del Banco
CALLE HONDA
CALLE LARGA
CALLE ARCOS
HAMMAM ANDALUSI BAÑOS ARABES
TABANCO PLATEROS
TABANCO EL PASAJE
CATHEDRAL OF SAN SALVADOR
ALBORES
BAR JUANITO
CALLE MEDINA
MULAI
TOURIST INFORMATION CENTER
Plaza del Arenal
TABERNO LAS BENDERILLAS
JEREZ DE LA FRONTERA FORTRESS
TABANCO SAN PABLO
Plaza las Angustias
BODEGAS GONZÁLEZ BYASS
EUROSTAR ASTA REGIA
CALLE PORVENIR
PLAZA MADRE DE DIOS
CALLE CABALLEROS
Train Station
SAN MIGUEL CHURCH
CALLE PUERTO
CALLE SOL
Bus Station
HOSTAL FENIX
AV. TORRESOTO
CALLE EMPEDRADA
TABLAO FLAMENCO PURO ARTE
CALLE MÉNDEZ NÚÑEZ
CALLE OBISPO CIRARDA
0
200 yds
0
200 m
© MOON.COM

Barrio de Santiago

This is the most popular neighborhood in Jerez. Its traditional Andalusian architecture, patios full of flowerpots, old churches, traditional shops, and sumptuous civil buildings make this a fine neighborhood to stroll around. It holds the main square, **Plaza del Arenal;** the largest concentration of restaurants, tablaos, eateries, bars, and shops; and Calle Larga, the primary pedestrian shopping thoroughfare connecting the historic city center with Calle Sevilla and the Royal Equestrian School.

San Miguel Church (Iglesia de San Miguel)

Plaza San Miguel; hours vary; €5

This Gothic beauty has a wonderfully distressed sandstone facade. Though easy to manipulate, sandstone has the unfortunate effect of weathering with the rain, wind, and sunshine. However, the protected interiors do display some spectacular details, typical of Mudejar interiors of the era, though not many are quite as well preserved. Hours of operation vary greatly according to the whims of the priest, who, by all accounts, does not enjoy it when there are too many visitors to the church.

Greater Jerez de la Frontera

★ Royal Andalusian School of Equestrian Art (Fundación Real Escuela Andaluza del Arte Ecuestre)

Avenida Duque de Abrante; tel. 956/318-008; www.realescuela.org; shows noon-1:30pm, days vary; €24

The horses here, originally bred for war, have found a much more peaceful occupation. At the Royal Andalusian School they preserve the art of Baroque horsemanship. If you want to understand an elemental aspect of Andalusia, you must attend one of the shows and witness the intelligence of the horses and the respect they are given by not only their riders, but the audience. Even for those not acquainted with the equestrian arts, it is easy to enjoy a 90-minute show and be impressed by the patience and skill of horse and rider as they perform their dressage. When many of the horses gather and perform in unison, it is something to behold, like a ballet with horses. Check the website for the schedule and tickets. Though it is an easy, flat walk from the historic center of Jerez (30 min), with the strong sun, a quick taxi ride (8 min; €5) is often preferable.

Palacio Domecq

Plaza Aladro, 2; tel. 673/923-640; https://palaciodomecq.com; tours run hourly on the hour 10am-7pm Tues.-Sat. and 10am-1pm Sun.; €15

Baroque architecture permeates this private house from Jerez's most wealthy family. If you are interested in all things Baroque, it is worth the 10-minute walk from the historic center, though make sure to coordinate with tour start times as all visits are guided visits. In part, this explains the elevated (for Andalusia) admission cost. You'll be led around and also have an audio guide to take with you, which is quite informative. For architecture and history buffs, this would be a must-stop, though others could give it a pass.

TOURS

Walking Tours

Group tours are often narrated in two Spanish and English, making the tour take twice as long. Unless explicitly stated, tours will not enter any of the monuments, such as the cathedral or fortress.

Private tours are strongly preferable to maximize your time in Jerez. **Discover Costa de la Luz** (tel. 618/036-628; www.discovercostadelaluz.com; from €160) offers some stellar private tours that are well paced and fully customizable. Ask for Adriane, an American-Spanish woman who specializes in walking tours of the region and loves spotting the next best foodie joint.

SPORTS AND RECREATION

Horseback Riding

Jerez de la Frontera is the birthplace of the

What Is Dressage?

Baroque equestrianism on display

Andalusia has a rich equestrian heritage that dates back centuries. The entire region is closely associated with the Andalusian horse breed, known for its elegance, intelligence, and agility. Originally bred for war, these strong, versatile horses are particularly well suited to the demands of dressage, a highly skilled form of horse riding and training that emphasizes the harmonious and precise execution of a series of predetermined movements.

Key aspects of dressage include:

- **Communication between rider and horse:** Effective communication between the rider and the horse is paramount. Riders use subtle weight shifts, leg aids, and rein cues to convey instructions to the horse.
- **Precision movements:** Riders guide their horses through a sequence of movements, known as a dressage test, which includes a combination of circles, turns, transitions, and specific gaits such as walk, trot, and canter.
- **Collection:** Horses are trained to carry more weight on their hindquarters, allowing for greater balance and agility. This is known as "collection" and is a fundamental concept in dressage.
- **Suppleness and flexibility:** Dressage emphasizes the development of the horse's athleticism and flexibility. The goal is to demonstrate a horse that is light in the rider's hands and moves with fluidity.
- **Judged competitions:** Dressage competitions, often held in arenas with specific dimensions, are judged based on the precision, smoothness, and overall quality of the horse's performance. Each movement is scored, and the combination of rider and horse with the highest score wins.
- **Levels of difficulty:** Dressage tests are divided into levels of difficulty, from basic movements for beginners to more advanced and intricate maneuvers for experienced riders and horses.

Dressage is not only a competitive sport and an Olympic discipline but also an art form that celebrates the partnership between horse and rider. In Andalusia, dressage serves as a means of preserving traditional horsemanship practices, and institutions like the Royal Andalusian School of Equestrian Art play a crucial role in passing on the knowledge and skills associated with classical dressage to future generations.

REAL ESCUELA ANDALUZA
DEL ARTE ECUESTRE
PICADERO ALVARO DOMECQ
1

2

3

Spanish thoroughbred horse. The allure of these magnificent animals extends across all provinces of Andalusia. Numerous stud farms, stables, and riding schools throughout the region serve as havens for these elegant and internationally renowned equines. Many of these establishments, situated on sprawling farms, estates, or within hotels, offer not only accommodations but also excellent facilities for horse enthusiasts. Visitors to these venues can partake in a variety of experiences, including horseback riding on the estate, embarking on outings of varying lengths, engaging in pony clubs tailored for the little ones, taking scenic rides in horse-drawn carriages, enrolling in riding classes at any skill level, or witnessing captivating equestrian and carriage displays.

Alcantara Ecuestre

Carretera Cortes, km 10, Cañada Albadalejos, Cuartillos; tel. 658/914-673; www.alcantaraecuestre.com; €70

Master horseman Alfonso Lopez de Carrizosa offers private one-hour lessons for riders of all levels in the art of dressage, particularly Andalusian dressage (doma vaquero). There are also numerous half-day tours available, whether you want to ride through a forest of Spanish pines, enjoy a relaxing horseback tour on a lake, or even sip local sherry on a bar-to-bar tour. The training is fun and lighthearted, and no matter what your riding level, you're guaranteed to learn something, as well as come away with a greater appreciation for the thoroughbred horses of Andalusia.

Andalusian Horse

Calle Utrera, Morón de la Frontera; tel. 652/821-878; www.andalusianhorseriding.com; €75

Whether you are looking for a half-day or multiday experience on a Spanish thoroughbred, this kind, warm-hearted outfitter can get you saddled up. On horseback you can dive into the Andalusian countryside, exploring the beauty of the rural parts of the region. The ranch is a little over an hour away by car in nearby Morón de la Frontera, off the A-8126.

Hammams

Hammam Andalusi Baños Arabes

Calle Salvador, 6; tel. 956/349-066; www.hammamandalusi.com; 10am-2pm and 4pm-8pm Mon.-Thurs., 11am-9pm Fri.-Sun.; €30

Get into the Andalusian spirit with a traditional hammam, like something you might experience in Morocco these days. Historically, these Arab baths were what the locals did for hundreds of years. This is great for couples and friends. There is nothing quite so luxurious as steaming into history in one of these historic baths.

ENTERTAINMENT AND EVENTS

Festivals

Horse Fair (Feria del Caballo)

May

This is the most famous festival in Jerez de la Frontera. It is a weeklong event featuring equestrian shows, flamenco performances, traditional music, dancing, and, of course, the exhibition of magnificent Andalusian horses. The fairground is transformed into a lively spectacle of lights, colors, and festivities. Because of its popularity, accommodations will double or even triple in price, the bars and taverns will be crowded, and reservations will be nearly mandatory at restaurants. Even with all the inconvenience, it is still a festival worth marking on your calendar.

Bulería Festival (Fiesta de la Bulería)

August

Dedicated to the flamenco style known as bulería, this festival brings together flamenco artists, musicians, and aficionados for performances, workshops, and events celebrating this unique and lively form of flamenco all around the city. You'll find performances

1: Royal Andalusian School of Equestrian Art 2: San Miguel Church 3: Bodegas González Byass

in public squares and in the many taverns around town.

Harvest Festival (Fiesta de la Vendimia)

September

The festival celebrates the grape harvest and the renowned sherry wines for which Jerez is famous. Events include grape-stomping, traditional flamenco performances, and wine tastings at the local bodegas. It's a fun, low-key festival, particularly if you have developed a taste for Andalusia's finest fortified wines.

Tapas Festival (Feria de la Tapa)

October

Foodies, and their bellies, will be happy in the autumn as the annual festival celebrating tapas marches through town. Local bars and restaurants participate in this culinary delight by offering a variety of tapas at special prices. It's very much an Andalusian food fair, with all the Iberian ham and queso manchego you can nibble.

Flamenco Shows

Tablao Flamenco Puro Arte

Calle Madre de Dios, 10; tel. 660/030-420; 4pm and 10pm; €30

You'll find this tablao just kitty-corner from the train station. It has a real authentic feel and generally fewer crowds than you'll see in neighboring Seville or Cádiz, particularly for the 10pm show when the locals tend to come out.

FOOD

Andalusian

Mulai

Calle Pescadería Vieja, 2; tel. 695/251-017; https://mulaijerez.com; noon-midnight Sun.-Thurs., noon-1am Fri.-Sat.; €25

This little seafood restaurant is fittingly smack dab in the old fish market just off the central Plaza de Arenal. Patio seating spills out into the quaint courtyard complete with the draped fishnet decor that your Andalusian adventure has been sorely missing. This is an Andalusian restaurant with an Asian soul, featuring fresh local catches brought in from nearby Cádiz. Artichokes graced with kimchi, bright tempura-battered hake, and wild red tuna with a citrus soy sauce dressing are just a few of the highlights. Head here for a break from traditional Spanish cuisine.

Albores

Calle Consistorio, 12; tel. 956/320-266; www.restaurantealbores.com; 8am-midnight Mon.-Sat., noon-midnight Sun.; €30

Sleek, modern, hip. This is the kind of place where you want to take your travel partner and split a bottle of vintage Spanish vino tinto and then cap the night with a glass of your preferred local sherry. The service can be Andalusian relaxed (read: slow), though if you're not in a rush, you can happily pick over lightly battered and fried shrimp with spinach and pistachio and succulent glazed beef medallions. Consider going family-style and sharing a few dishes.

★ Lú, Cocina y Alma

Calle Zaragoza, 2; tel. 695/408-481; www.lucocinayalma.com; 1pm-3pm and 8:30pm-10pm Tues.-Sun.; €150

Foodies may well want to make a journey to Jerez simply for this culinary experience. The transformation of traditional Jerezano dishes into contemporary jewels with *une petite touche de haute cuisine française* is an experience par excellence. The entire dining area circles around the kitchen, leaving no question as to what the centerpiece of this culinary Andalusian spectacle is. Masterful cuisine by one of the world's finest chefs, Juanlu Fernández, is set against a jazzy, poppy, colorful Art Deco background that blends well with the avant-garde cuisine.

Tapas Bars and Cafés

La Moderna

Calle Larga, 67; tel. 956/321-379; 7am-1am Mon.-Thurs., 7am-midnight Fri.-Sat.; €5

A super-friendly local breakfast spot

The Sherry Tavern Route (Ruta de los Tabernos Jerez)

If you want to get in touch with some locals and enjoy local sherries, this route through town will have you quaffing some of Jerez's best sherry at six different historic taverns. It's a fun night out for those who love to imbibe and would enjoy some time out on the town. To complete this entire route, which has been a local pastime since 1936, you would have to do it Thursday, Friday, or Saturday because a few of the tabernos and tabancos are closed on other days.

Here is a list of the taverns that make up the historical local sherry route in the order that makes the most walking sense from start to finish:

Tabanco El Pasaje

- **Tabanco La Pandilla** (Calle Los Valientes, 14; page 285)
- **Tabanco El Guitarrón de San Pedro** (Calle Bizcocheros, 16)
- **Tabanco Plateros** (Calle Algarve, 35)
- **Taberno Las Benderillas** (Calle Caballeros, 12)
- **Tabanco San Pablo** (Calle San Pablo, 12)
- **Tabanco El Pasaje** (Calle Santa María, 8; page 285)

Though you could do this route in daylight hours, it's much more fun as a self-guided sherry and tapas evening tour.

specializing in tostadas, a toasty Spanish staple. Rickety chairs, little tables that would be at home in a Parisian café, and long windows looking out over the busy pedestrian-friendly Calle Larga make for a spot that is equally good to catch up with a friend or break your fast solo and enjoy a spot of people-watching.

Tabanco La Pandilla

Calle Los Valientes, 14; tel. 956/343-248; 12:30pm-3:30pm and 8pm-12:30am Tues.-Sat., 1pm-5pm Sun.; €5

The indoor garden patio makes for a pleasant indoor-outdoor space while the fantastic hulk of an antique cash machine at the long bar takes you back in time. This is generally the quietest of the taverns on the sherry route, unless there is a big fútbol match on, in which case, it can get rowdy. There are lots of colorful caricatures by a local artist and friend of the establishment, and on Wednesday nights there is an English-language meetup here with a cast of characters, both local and of the expat variety.

Tabanco El Pasaje

Calle Santa María, 8; tel. 956/333-359; www.tabancoelpasaje.com; 12:30pm-3:30pm and 8pm-12:30am Tues.-Sat., 1pm-5pm Sun., flamenco shows 2pm, 8pm, and 9:30pm daily; €5

This beautiful divey little local spot is centrally located. Daily flamenco shows give a nice vibrancy to an otherwise often sleepy Jerez. The later the show, the more local it tends to be. The afternoon show can get crowded with day-trippers from Cádiz and Seville. If you're following the sherry route in the evening, it makes sense to time it so you can see the later flamenco show here, though you will want to reserve ahead of time for front row seats as there are only two tables at this little tavern. El Pasaje serves a nice selection of local sherries right out of the cask and tapas as well.

Bar Juanito

Calle Pescadería Vieja, 8; tel. 627/456-989; 12:30pm-3:30pm and 8pm-12:30am Tues.-Sat., 1pm-5pm Sun.; €12

Just up the street from Plaza de Arenal on a quaint, quiet street, this is one of those bar/restaurant combos where you could sit and have a meal or just have a quick drink at the bar, perhaps with a tapa or two. The bar might be preferable, particularly for solo travelers or adventurous couples looking to work on their Spanish. Typically you'll find this jam-packed with locals. If you are considering dinner or want a table, it is best to reserve. The menu is meat-heavy, featuring traditional dishes highlighting some of the sherry from the area, such as kidneys (riñones al Jerez) and cabbage (berza jerezana).

ACCOMMODATIONS

Under €100

★ Hostal Fenix

Calle Cazón, 7; tel. 956/345-291; €45

A 19th-century manor house has been beautifully restored into this unpretentious, friendly two-star hotel. It's an easy walk to everything of interest. The bar downstairs will even give you a free welcome drink. The rooms are clean with all the basic amenities, while the property itself has Andalusian ambience emanating from the decor. This inexpensive hotel feels like it punches above its weight, particularly considering the location, which is about as central as it gets. It can be a bit noisy at night, as it is central and has older single-pane windows, so do wear earplugs or noise-canceling headphones if you're a light sleeper.

Soho Boutique Jerez

Calle Nuño de Cañas, 1; tel. 956/327-230; www.sohohoteles.com/destinos/hotel-soho-boutique-jerez-4; €85

When traveling in the old world, I find it nice to tuck into a real old-world hotel. And this vintage grande dame is easy to enjoy and hits all those notes, particularly if you have a thing for Grand Budapest styling and dated decor. Housed on a former winery, the entire building and staff have charm a-plenty. The on-site parking is especially nice if you rented a car, though it's not as centrally located as some of the other choices in town. During the hot months, the swimming pool is a great escape from the afternoon heat.

€100-200

Eurostar Asta Regia

Calle San Agustín, 9; tel. 956/327-911; www.eurostarshotels.com/eurostars-asta-regia.html; €120

A fantastic location right off the Plaza de Arenal makes it a quick walk to just about everything you'll want to see and do in Jerez. The rooms are modern and a little business-y, which clashes with the classical facade of the hotel. It's a good option for those who just want an easy, no-frills accommodation with a few extras, like a gym, business center, and rooftop swimming pool.

INFORMATION AND SERVICES

Tourist Information Center

Plaza de Arenal; tel. 956/149-863 or 956/338-874; www.turismojerez.com; 9am-2:30pm Mon.-Fri., 10am-2pm Sat.-Sun.

The English-speaking staff here can quickly get you up to date with local festivals and events as well as free walking tours through the historic center of Jerez.

GETTING THERE AND AROUND

Train

Right on the eastern edge of the city, Jerez's historic **train station** (Plaza de la Estación; tel. 956/149-990 or 912/320-320) is one of the prettiest in Andalusia. It's about a 30-minute walk from the station into the city center. Taxis can swiftly transport you into town (10 min; €10). The train operators are Adif (www.adif.es) and Renfe (www.renfe.com). Daily connections to Seville (10-plus daily; 1 hr; €15) and Cádiz (10-plus daily; 45 min; €5) conveniently make Jerez a possible day trip from either destination or a place to stop while in transit between the two. Other train connections require switching trains in Seville or Córdoba.

Bus

The **bus station** is on Plaza de la Estación near the train station. Connecting to Jerez by car or train is often preferable, though bus services offer an alternative, especially for journeys to smaller towns, such as Ronda (1 daily; 2.5 hr; €15) and Arcos de la Frontera (10-plus daily, 45 min; €5) with Transportes Generales Comes (www.tgcomes.es).

Car

Jerez de la Frontera is a quick drive on the A-4 freeway from Seville (1 hr; 91 km/57 mi) and Cádiz (30 min; 32 km/20 mi), while Arcos de la Frontera (30 min; 34 km/21 mi) takes you inland toward the mountains, as does Ronda (1.5 hr; 115 km/72 mi). Parking is easy enough to find throughout Jerez, except if there is a local festival on. Check the calendar before arrival and inquire with your hotel about parking, as most hotels do have parking.

Walking

Jerez de la Frontera, a predominantly flat town, is easy to explore on foot. The sights within the historic center are within just a few minutes' walk of each other. The farthest major points of interest are the Royal Andalusian School of Equestrian Art (about a 20-minute walk north the historic center) and the train station (about a 30-minute walk east of the historic center); these may be easier to reach by taxi.

The White Villages

TOP EXPERIENCE

There are dozens of white villages, or pueblos blancos, to discover in Andalusia. Each has individual charm. Some are so small just a handful of families still populate them and there might only be one little roadside eatery. Others are larger and have a more obvious history, with tapas bars, restaurants, hotels, and lively festivals that attract people from all over. I've focused on just a couple of the white villages that make the best introduction to the region's charming small-town life.

ORIENTATION

Arcos de la Frontera is 88 km (55 mi) south of Seville and a quick 35 km (22 mi) east inland from Jerez de la Frontera. It is on the western edge of Andalusia's Baetic System of mountain ranges and the Sierra de Grazalema Natural Park. The historic area of the city makes a long rectangle built on a cliff overlooking the Guadalete River. Like nearly all Andalusian towns, it's best explored on foot. The walk from Plaza Boticas in the middle of town along Calle Callejas is one of the more picturesque walks you can take, and you'll see the best of Arcos de la Frontera along the way.

To the east of Arcos, **Zahara de la Sierra** and **Setenil de las Bodegas** are connected by easy-going national roads. Many other, smaller white villages serve as gateway towns to the natural parks, such as Grazalema.

Ronda stands dramatically on the Tajo de Ronda gorge, offering captivating views of the surrounding landscapes, with the Puente Nuevo spanning the gorge, connecting the "new" and "old" parts of Ronda together. The town lies equidistant between two parks of Andalusia: Sierra de Grazalema Natural Park to the west and Sierra de las Nieves National Park to the east. Each of these parks has a series of smaller towns that are part of the park system.

ARCOS DE LA FRONTERA

Known for its panoramic views of the Guadalete River valley, Arcos de la Frontera, with whitewashed buildings cascading down the hillside, is a trip into a more rural aspect of Andalusia. As you explore, you'll encounter the remnants of Moorish influence, from ancient gateways to the iconic castle that crowns the town. The Mudejar-style Church of Saint Peter and Gothic-style Basilica of Santa María stand as a testament to the Reconquista, while the Plaza Boticas invites you to savor the ambience of a traditional Spanish square.

Arcos de la Frontera, smaller in scale compared to its bustling neighbors, offers a more intimate Andalusian experience. Stroll through its charming streets, where vibrant bougainvillea drapes over wrought-iron balconies and locals engage in the unhurried pace of daily life in this charming pueblo blanco.

Sights

Old Town

The historic center of Arcos de la Frontera is rife with small monumental buildings, churches, and whitewashed village charm. You could pop into the Mayorazgo Palace (Calle Núñez del Prado), the Hermitage of San Antonio Abad (Calle San Antonio Abad, 12), or the Convent-Hospital of San Juan de Dios (Calle Corredera, 5), but the real charm of Arcos de la Frontera is on its streets, enjoying the many archways and viewpoints over the frontier from which it takes its name.

Two of the most picturesque viewpoints are the Mirador de Abades and the Mirador Plaza del Cabildo. A stop at either of these viewpoints promises commanding views over the river valley. There are several main squares dotted around this pueblo, though Plaza Boticas is perhaps the most traditional where you can really step in and get a feel for local life.

Church of Saint Peter (Iglesia de San Pedro)

Calle Maldonado, 15; tel. 956/702-264; 10:30am-1:30pm and 5pm-7pm Mon.-Fri., 11am-6pm Sat.-Sun.; €2 (additional €2 for tower access)

Of the surprisingly many religious buildings in tiny Arcos de la Frontera, this grand church is one of the more interesting. Like many of the large churches, the tower, likely the former minaret of a mosque during the Islamic era, offers panoramic views over the town and plains beyond. The church itself has been reformed over the centuries with vaulted ceilings and historic paintings on display.

Church of Santa María of the Ascension (Basílica Menor de Santa María de la Asunción)

Plaza del Cabildo; tel. 956/704-529

This church features an unfinished tower—construction halted following the earthquake of 1755. That said, the tower is still the main attraction. It is a late-Gothic masterpiece of architecture with all the star-ribbed vaulting and complex support structures you can imagine. The main altarpiece, a true Renaissance jewel, hugs a Gothic mural painting as well as the incorrupt mummy of Saint Félix.

Festivals

As in nearly all towns, you can expect festivals during the week leading up to Easter (Semana Santa). A small-town fair, the San Miguel Festival (Sept. 28-30) is dedicated to its patron saint.

Living Nativity Festival (Belen Viviente)

Last Saturday before Christmas

The village annually transforms into a living nativity scene, captivating visitors in the historic Plaza del Cabildo and nearby narrow streets. This one-day spectacle turns the picturesque pueblo blanco into one of

1: Church of Saint Peter **2:** Church of Santa María of the Ascension **3:** Arcos de la Frontera

1
2
3

the largest Christmas events in Spain, challenging the notion that Andalusia is only for summertime revelry. Iconic corners serve as enchanting backdrops for the nativity scenes, with candle-lit streets and lanterns creating a timeless ambience. This immersive experience, spanning about 30 scenes, narrates the Christmas story from the visitation to the birth, offering a leisurely two-hour stroll through the old town's captivating narrative. Arcos de la Frontera's Belen Viviente is a sensory feast, transporting visitors back in time and showcasing the town's rich cultural heritage during the winter season.

Food and Accommodations

El Mirador de Isabel

Calle Murete, 5; tel. 617/278-090; 10:30am-11:30pm Tues.-Sun.; €10

El Mirador de Isabel is a really easy place to love for a shady terrace lunch or relaxed dinner. Continuous service means you can stop by anytime for a cold drink and tapas. Standards from the traditional menu include egg tortillas and rich ensaladas. You'll likely get a mouthwatering whiff of this family-run restaurant before you turn onto the street.

Meson los Murales

Plaza Boticas; tel. 678/064-163; 9am-midnight Fri.-Wed.; €12

Though distant Valencia is known as the paella capital of Spain, this friendly joint might just give it a run for its money. Saffron-kissed rice combines with a complex, delicious mix of veggies, chicken, and shellfish that feel right at home in this little plaza.

El Convento

Calle Maldonado, 2; tel. 956/702-333 or 956/704-128; www.hotelelconvento.es; €65

Centrally located with architectural charm, a large terrace with expansive views, and down-home friendly service, El Convento is a classic Spanish two-star accommodation with an array of creams and pastels to sooth your senses. The location makes exploration on your own steam easy as pie. Some will appreciate the more modern furnishings in some of the bedrooms while others might be put off a touch by the clash with the otherwise period-appropriate reformed traditional Spanish dwelling.

La Casa Grande

Calle Maldonado, 10; tel. 956/703-930 or 658/295-422; www.lacasagrande.net; €85

After a stay with Elena at her wonderfully appointed hacienda guest house, you will be guaranteed to come away with a real insider's knowledge on the Andalusian ideal of Mediterranean living. The heart of the house is a traditional Andalusian patio with marbled columns and stone capitals with a cozy library adjacent. A stay here is an invitation to relax, rest your soul, and breathe in a different, slower-paced way of life. Breakfast, complete with freshly squeezed orange juice, kicks off most days here, followed by pensive walks and hushed conversations. There are only a handful of rooms in this charming boutique accommodation, so reserve well in advance. If you can, book La Penúltima room, which features views over the valley as well as handmade tiles from Fez, Morocco, in the shower.

★ Botánico Arcos

Calle Cuesta de Belén, 8; tel. 856/005-833; http://botanicoarcos.es; €95

Massimo and Sergio are exemplary hosts. Massimo prepares delicious breakfasts and bakes rolls himself, to go with the morning latte, fresh orange juice, and yogurt with fruit. They will also provide a delish multicourse homemade dinner on reservation, should you wish. Just let them know ahead of time. Sergio is a designer, and the decor reflects his eclectic stylings, while Massimo's green thumb is evident just about everywhere you turn, with vibrant, drought-tolerant plants adding life to this wonderful getaway. This modern take on a classical guest house has all the touches of home you might want, with a boho-chic atmosphere that feels like you are getting much more for your money than what they charge.

Information and Services

Tourist Information Center

Calle Cuesta de Belén, 5; tel. 956/702-264; www.turismoarcos.es

The tourist center is right in the historic town hall. Stop for updated maps, festival info, and if you want to get out to some of the rural hiking available in the region. Helpful, service-oriented staff will help you get the most out of your time in Arcos.

Getting There and Around

You'll likely be getting to Arcos de la Frontera with your rental car. Jerez de la Frontera (30 min; 34 km/21 mi) is a short drive away. There is parking just outside of the historic city center. You'll have to park your car and then walk around the cobblestoned streets.

ZAHARA DE LA SIERRA

Zahara de la Sierra may be the best-preserved mountain fortress and medieval town in the region. It is an impressive arrival, but do know that you will have to climb the steep slopes of the small mountain, Peñón Rodado, by foot to see the heights of this wonderful little pueblo from the vantage point of the castle, which unsurprisingly towers over the entire valley. From here, you'll look out over the olive groves and the peaks of the mountain range surrounding you at the north edge of the Sierra de Grazalema Natural Park. The name Zahara comes from the Arabic zahra, which means "flower." And if you can make it here in the spring, you'll see why. The entire countryside seems speckled with colorful blooms.

Sights

★ Medieval Village

tel. 623/475-906; 8:30am-2pm and 6pm-9:30 daily summer, 8:30am-dark daily winter; €3.50

With remains dating from the 13th-15th centuries, the medieval town of Zahara is one of the best preserved in all of Andalusia. Situated at the top of the Peñón Rodado, the remains of the **Castle of Zahara,** the largest building in the Medieval Village, include the keep and several walls, while abutting the castle are a few houses and several cisterns. Guided visits in English are usually available outside of August. A small parking lot on the backside of the Medieval Village saves you a long walk uphill, though of course if you are looking to explore the rest of Zahara, you'll have to walk up the hill anyway to get back. If you want to discover medieval life and a period-specific castle in the small towns of Andalusia, this is the spot.

Church of Santa María de la Mesa (Iglesia de Santa María de la Mesa)

Plaza de Zahara; tel. 956/123-014; hours vary, typically 10am-2pm and 5pm-8pm daily; free

The colorful facade of this small but beautifully Baroque 18th-century church pops against the cliff and monotone castle towering above. The church actually dates from the 18th century, so it isn't the oldest building you'll see in town, but it might be the prettiest. Part of the church has now been converted into the Interpretation Center of the Medieval Village, a small museum that tells the history of Zahara de la Sierra.

Chapel of San Juan de Letrán and the Torre del Reloj

Calle Boquete San Juan, 1; 10am-noon daily, 3 people maximum at a time; free

This is a small 20th-century church in the main town, downhill from the Medieval Village perched on the crown of the hill. You would think it wasn't really of much interest, but the 16th-century **Torre del Reloj** is something to note. Attached to the chapel, this tower was built in stone masonry. The four-pitched roof rises to a height of about 15 m (50 ft). If you've been working on your Spanish, you probably already translated its name as literally meaning "Tower of the Clock." This name comes from the introduction of a pendulum clock, which made its home on the upper floor of the tower right at the start of the 20th century.

1

2

3

4

Food and Accommodations

La Era

Calle San Juan, 8; tel. 618/020-204; 11:30am-1am Wed.-Sat., 11:30am-5pm Sun.; €10

Moroccan-inspired floor tiles and large windows in the restaurant that open onto the valley stretched out below make for a wonderful backdrop for a later morning or afternoon snack. Head inside when the weather isn't cooperating or if you prefer a vast landscape. Head out to the streetside patio if the weather is fine and you prefer your tapas with a spot of people-watching. The continuous service is fast and friendly, while the tapas include the standards you might expect, such as olives, anchovies in vinegar, queso manchego, and thin-sliced Iberian ham.

El Gallo

Calle San Juan, 8; tel. 662/129-384; https://mybakarta.com/El-gallo; 9am-11pm daily; €10

This rustic tapas café and bar right next door to La Era feels like it has been around about as long as the Medieval Village, if you could just take away the televisions. Quite a few locals patronize this joint, lending it an authentic air and an unbeatable atmosphere for a calm little moment as you make your way through the pueblos blancos.

La Cabaña

Calle Ronda, 5; €12

Just off the main pedestrian thoroughfare, Calle de San Juan, La Cabaña is usually a touch quieter. The beautiful brick and plaster facade gives way to a deliciously cool, rustic interior or outdoor seating on the streetside terrace. If you want to feel like you're really away from the tourist crowds and keeping as local as can be, it's likely you won't find another tourist here and will be the only English speaker around. Tuck in for a cold beer, and if a fútbol match is on, count on it being a rowdy time.

1: Zahara de la Sierra and the Church of Santa María de la Mesa **2:** Chapel of San Juan de Letrán **3:** café in Zahara **4:** Restaurants dot the medieval streets of Zahara de la Sierra.

★ Hostel Marques de Zahara

Calle San Juan, 3; tel. 956/123-061; €55

This is an incredible find for those who prefer hostel stays. The converted historic building once belonged to a wealthy local family. The rooms are larger than usual, making them very comfortable to share with a friend. Like the rest of the property, they are cozy and just oozing with medieval charm. Santiago is the manager, and he will be happy to help point you around the village and even introduce you to like-minded travelers or tell you about his favorite little spots to get a bite and a cold drink. You might think you'll only spend a night here, but with this sort of service and charm at this price, you could easily spend a week or two.

Getting There

Bus

Zahara de la Sierra is accessible by bus, though connections and times are limited. There's a once-daily service to Ronda (1.5 hr; €5) with TG Comes (www.tgcomes.es). The primary bus station in Zahara de la Sierra is in the town center, making it convenient for travelers to arrive by bus from nearby locations. Be sure to check the bus schedules and routes in advance, as they may vary depending on the season.

Car

Zahara de la Sierra is easily accessible by car, offering a picturesque drive through the Andalusian countryside. From Jerez de la Frontera, it's a beautiful mountain drive (1 hr; 86 km/53 mi). From Seville (2 hr; 124 km/77 mi) and Ronda (45 min; 35 km/22 mi) via the A-376 and A-382 highways, you'll have a scenic route through the mountains as you approach the Sierra de Grazalema Natural Park. The town's historic center is not accessible by car, so leave your vehicle in designated parking areas outside the town and explore on foot.

Getting Around

Once in Zahara de la Sierra, exploring the town is done on foot. The historic center is compact, and its narrow streets and alleys are perfect for leisurely strolls. The town's most iconic landmarks, including the Castle of Zahara and the Church of Santa María de la Mesa, are within walking distance of each other, though it is a steep, hilly town with the castle at the very tippy top.

★ SETENIL DE LAS BODEGAS

Known for its extraordinary architecture, the town's most distinguishing feature is its whitewashed houses that are not merely built alongside the cliffs but fully integrated in the natural rock formations along both banks of the Trejo River, providing an unconventional urban landscape. After the Christian conquest, settlers ingeniously integrated their homes into the natural rock formations, shaping the town's distinctive character. Unlike with many troglodytic dwellings in Andalusia, the residents of Setenil did not excavate the rock; they adapted the existing recesses.

Recently, this wonderfully unique pueblo has become popular with a few bus tour companies that stop here in the afternoons. So expect some crowds if you overlap with the bus visits. In practice, it's never too bad, but if you want a quieter village experience, plan on arriving early in the morning before the buses arrive or later in the afternoon when the buses have all left. Better yet, enjoy an overnight in Setenil with a tranquil dinner and breakfast the following morning.

If you have time to venture out, just southwest of the town you'll find the ancient Roman ruins of Acinipo, a historic site that includes a Roman theater.

Sights

Setenil de las Bodegas Castle (Castillo de Setenil de las Bodegas)

Calle Villa, 32; tel. 675/651-705; 24/7; free

Though the imposing castle of Setenil de las Bodegas is closed, the views from around the castle are unbeatable. From here, you can see how the land is split by the river and how the rocks were incorporated into the village architecture. Worth the climb? You be the judge.

Ethnographic Museum (Museo Etnográfico de Setenil)

Calle Vilchez, 28; tel. 681/931-991; 10am-1pm Mon.-Wed., 10am-3pm Sat.-Sun.; €1

This tiny museum has a small collection that includes tools and traditional outfits of the region. It does give some perspective on how and why the early inhabitants of Setenil built their houses into the rock faces and is a short, inexpensive visit.

Calle Cuevas del Sol and Calle Cuevas de la Sombra

The distinct character of Setenil is exemplified by two parallel streets: Calle Cuevas del Sol and Calle Cuevas de la Sombra; both pedestrian thoroughfares host a delightful array of artisan shops and tapas bars. Along Calle Cuevas del Sol, you'll discover dwellings ingeniously carved into the natural limestone rock, reminiscent of a troglodytic lifestyle dating back to prehistoric times. Traces of soot-stained chimneys and lime residues left by the town's ancient inhabitants provide a tangible connection to the past. Meanwhile, Calle Cuevas de la Sombra offers a striking, if not surprising, contrast. This street plunges you into a tunnel of natural limestone rock that shelters an entire street of houses, bars, and restaurants.

Calle Cuevas del Sol and Calle Cuevas de la Sombra form a loop that you can easily explore clockwise or counterclockwise. Most travelers will begin their exploration on the eastern edge of Setenil de las Bodegas where several streets converge and, unfortunately, many buses unload day-trippers from Seville and Cádiz.

Calle Herrería

Another emblematic street, Calle Herrería, is often considered one of the most beautiful

1: Setenil de las Bodegas Castle **2:** Houses and businesses are built into the rock formations in Setenil.

1

2

and romantic of all the Andalusian streets. With its Instagram-ready sign reading "bésame en este rincón" (kiss me in this corner), aptly and discreetly tucked away in a little corner, perfect for a quick tryst, this main pedestrian street climbs up toward the castle, connecting it with the river and town below. Walking along Calle Herrería, between its limestone facades and geraniums, plunges you into a surreal world somewhere between prehistory and romantic literature.

The Cave House

Calle Herrería, 15; hours vary; €1

There are very few cave houses open to the public. Antonio owns one of the cave houses along Calle Herrería, between the Plaza de Andalucía and the Trejo River. This is a very quick, though interesting glance at how houses were integrated into the rocks surrounding Setenil. Hours vary greatly and depend on when Antonio is home, likely watching the History channel.

Roman Ruins of Acinipo

MA-7402, between Ronda and Setenil de las Bodegas; 24/7; free

The highlight of Acinipo is the remarkably preserved and reconstructed theater. This ancient Roman theater, with its semicircular seating area and stage, is the most well-preserved feature of the site. Other notable structures include the Iron Age House, Boathouse, and Residential Building. All illuminate what typical life here was like during the Roman period. There is free parking and free entry, so it's worth a stop if you're traveling between Setenil de las Bodegas and Ronda, though there are better-preserved, more informative Roman ruins elsewhere, such as Seville. That said, there is something profound about seeing these ruins in this particular landscape—rolling hills, dry grasslands, scattered stone remnants, and some fluffy sheep grazing in the distance—that really brings home the timeless beauty of the Andalusian countryside.

Guided Tours

Tuk-Tuk Tours

tel. 681/934-166 or 681/934-161; www.rutassetenil.es/index1.html; €9

A fun way to get around and explore Setenil is by tuk-tuk. It's obviously an imported concept, but on some of the steep hills, if mobility is a concern or you are just plain tuckered out from your exploration of Andalusia, this is an amusing option to scoot around town and make the most of your time. Reservations are recommended though not totally necessary. Usually one of the tuk-tuks is available at the bottom of town on Calle Cuevas del Sol. Do be wary of annoying other travelers, though. If you are going through the busiest streets, the tuk-tuks can be aggressive in how they navigate the crowds. Best to take one of the circuitous routes to the top of town.

Food and Accommodations

Cueva Alta

Calle Cantareria Alta, 22; tel. 600/273-668; www.cuevadesetenil.com; hours vary; €5

Billed as the longest, deepest of all the caves of Setenil, this former home has been opened into a small tapas bar and shop where you can purchase local products. Lovers of the vino will find wines by 3 Cuevas, a local winery best known for their rich, spicy red wines. The hours here are very, very loose, so it's best to give a call to see if they're open before you climb the hill to the shop.

★ Gloria Bendita

Calle Ronda, 38; tel. 675/651-705; noon-midnight Wed.-Mon.; €12

Gloria Bendita lacks the obvious charm of some of the other cafés and bars, which is probably why it's popular with locals. If some of the other bars and restaurants seem too busy or too touristy for your taste, head here for an authentic experience that probably hasn't changed much in about a hundred years. This is one of the very few places in Setenil where they still serve tapas. Most other places have moved on to selling larger plates of food. So if you prefer to continue your tapas-tasting experience through Andalusia, this is the joint. It helps that the tapas and atmosphere are on point. The smoked bacalao and the carillada, a local snail specialty, are worth a little callout.

La Telera

Calle Cuevas de la Sombra, 1; tel. 644/330-717; 1pm-8pm Sun.-Thurs., 1pm-midnight Fri.-Sat.; €25

La Telera has shaded seating alongside the river, which erupts into flowers over the summer as the water dries. It's just a few steps into the popular Calle Cuevas de la Sombra before you dive into the busy part of the street. An obvious sort of place to like, it's touristed, though rightly so. Fantastic views along the river are just the right sort of backdrop to a lazy lunch or dinner of prawn tacos or oxtail stew.

Hotel Villa de Setenil

Calle Callejón, 10; tel. 646/842-171; www.hotelsetenil.com; €65

Basic, if a touch spartan, this two-star hotel has a fantastic location. The views from the rooms overlooking town are lovely, particularly at night when the city lights twinkle on. Staff are courteous and rooms are basic, though comfortable. If you're considering an overnight stay in Setenil, this is likely the spot. You'll be hard-pressed to leave the terrace, though. You can quench your thirst and take in the sunset here. Including breakfast with your reservation is the correct decision so you can enjoy the terrace even more!

Getting There and Around

Bus

Although Setenil de las Bodegas is a relatively small town, it's very well-connected to neighboring areas by bus. You can check the latest schedules and routes at the website of the official Córdoba bus station (Estación de Autobuses de Córdoba; tel. 957/404-040; www.estacionautobusescordoba.es). Several bus companies operate routes connecting Setenil to nearby towns, cities, and regions. Popular bus companies serving Setenil include Alsa (www.alsa.es) and Autocares Carrera (https://autocarescarrera.es), offering multiple daily connections to towns like Lucena, Antequera, and Priego de Córdoba.

Car

Setenil de las Bodegas is easily accessible by car. You can look forward to a scenic Andalusian countryside drive whether connecting from Jerez de la Frontera (1.5 hr; 105 km/71 mi), Ronda (20 min; 13 km/8 mi), Seville (1.5 hr; 140 km/85 mi), or Málaga (1.5 hr; 160 km/100 mi). If you're traveling from Seville, take the A-374 highway, which will lead you directly to the town. From Málaga, you can reach Setenil by taking the A-374 and A-372 highways. Public parking options in the town make it convenient for visitors to explore its charming streets and attractions. There is a free public parking lot at the top of the village and two more below.

RONDA

Ronda straddles the past and present, much like its iconic Puente Nuevo bridge, connecting new and old. Perched dramatically on the edge of the Tajo de Ronda gorge, this most famous of the white villages blends history and natural beauty in a way that is truly special. As in much of Andalusia, its ancient Moorish origins merge with its Christian heritage, obvious to the most lay observers as you wander through town. This is less a destination of sights and things to do than it is a place where you'll find yourself immersed in the local day-to-day culture, discovering the quotidian pleasures of country life. That said, there is a surprising amount of things to see that can easily fill up a day.

Sights

Old Town

Ronda has the type of historic old town that draws you in. There are numerous cobblestone pathways to wander, each seeming to lead to the **Alameda del Tajo,** a 19th-century park with impressive views from the west of town looking over the sheer cliff face.

It's in this park that you'll find the **Mirador de Ronda,** a structure built out over cliffs that gives you the sensation of floating in thin air. Unsurprisingly, the town branches out from the **Plaza España,** with the iconic bridge connecting the older north with the "new town" to the south, over the gorge. Though most monuments and sites of interest are found in old Ronda, the new town does lay claim to the **Alminar de San Seabastián** as well as a few restaurants and shops. Together, the two halves of Ronda make a unique historic center that straddles the gorge.

★ Puente Nuevo

Plaza España; tel. 649/965-338; 9:30am-7pm Tues.-Fri., 10am-2pm and 3pm-6pm Sat., 10am-3pm Sun. (hours vary slightly in winter); €2.50

The "new bridge" finished in 1793 is the most famous site in Ronda and probably the most popular in the region. Though most travelers drop off in Plaza España and cross the bridge to the south side near the Casa del Rey Moro, it is infinitely more interesting to hike down and look up at the bridge from below. Access to the lower part of the bridge (€2.50, payable only by card) takes you into this 18th-century marvel. This is one of those attractions that you really don't need to pay the entrance fee to enjoy, though. There is another path you can take down to admire it from below—or better yet, stop at the bottom of the gorge when you are driving into Ronda and save yourself the hike up!

Bullring of the Royal Cavalry of Ronda (El Real Maestranza de Caballería de Ronda)

Calle Virgen de la Paz, 15; tel. 952/874-132; www.rmcr.org/intro; 10am-6pm daily; €9

This bullring was finished in 1785, making it one of the oldest in Spain and a national heritage monument. Today, this is much more than a bullring, though bullfights do happen occasionally during the season. This is a multifaceted place that now includes an equestrian riding school, an EU-recognized school teaching classical dressage. The exhibitions on display tell the history of horsemanship and the importance of the bull in Andalusia. Though English-language signage is limited, there is an audio guide in English (and other languages) that you can make good use of and that will supplement the Spanish with plenty of information to make this more than worthwhile for an hour or so visit. Like this, you can learn much more about the intertwined

restaurants overlooking the bridge in Ronda

Ronda

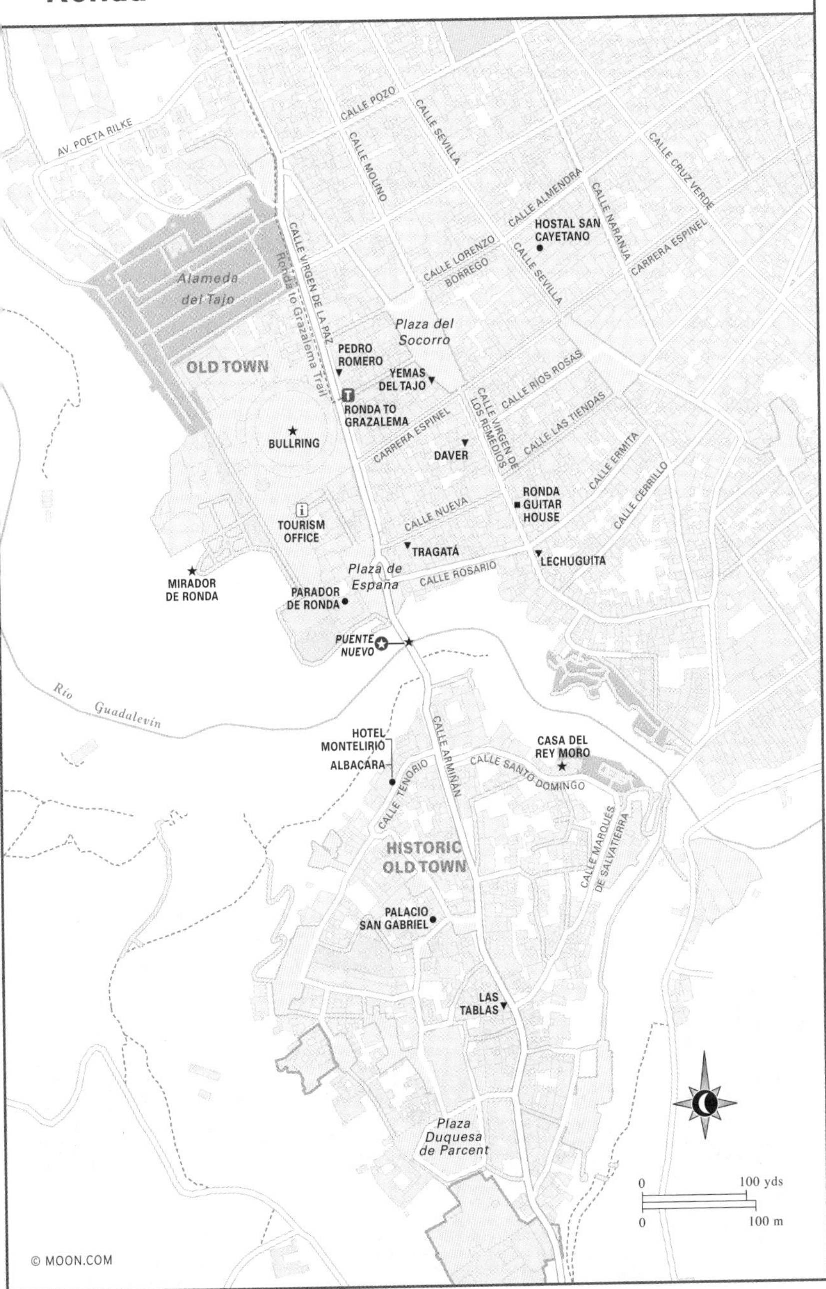
AV. POETA RILKE
CALLE POZO
CALLE SEVILLA
CALLE MOLINO
CALLE CRUZ VERDE
CALLE ALMENDRA
CALLE NARANJA
HOSTAL SAN CAYETANO
CARRERA ESPINEL
CALLE VIRGEN DE LA PAZ
Ronda to Grazalema Trail
CALLE LORENZO BORREGO
CALLE SEVILLA
Alameda del Tajo
Plaza del Socorro
PEDRO ROMERO
YEMAS DEL TAJO
OLD TOWN
RONDA TO GRAZALEMA
CALLE RIOS ROSAS
CALLE VIRGEN DE LOS REMEDIOS
CALLE LAS TIENDAS
BULLRING
CARRERA ESPINEL
DAVER
CALLE ERMITA
CALLE CERRILLO
RONDA GUITAR HOUSE
CALLE NUEVA
TOURISM OFFICE
TRAGATÁ
LECHUGUITA
MIRADOR DE RONDA
Plaza de España
CALLE ROSARIO
PARADOR DE RONDA
PUENTE NUEVO
Río Guadalevín
CALLE ARMIÑÁN
HOTEL MONTELIRIO
ALBACARA
CASA DEL REY MORO
CALLE SANTO DOMINGO
CALLE TENORIO
CALLE MARQUÉS DE SALVATIERRA
HISTORIC OLD TOWN
PALACIO SAN GABRIEL
LAS TABLAS
Plaza Duquesa de Parcent
0
100 yds
0
100 m

history of the horses and bulls that are so emblematic of Andalusia.

Casa del Rey Moro

Calle Cuesta de Santo Domingo, 9; tel. 668/503-050; www.casadelreymoro.org; 10am-8pm daily; €10

For whatever reason, the name of this site is a true misnomer, as a Moorish ruler never lived here. The building dates from the 18th century, long after the Reconquista. Even its Islamic gardens are recent, designed by a Frenchman in the early 20th century. However, there is one important historic element of its construction. When armies besieged Ronda, they always targeted the water supply first. Armed with this knowledge, in the 14th century Ronda's king, Abomelic, ordered steps carved into the gorge walls to transport water from the river. Restored in 1911, the staircase originally had 365 steps descending to the river below, but today fewer than 300 remain, making it a formidable descent, with uneven and dimly lit sections. Today's Casa del Rey Moro abuts Abomelic's stairway.

TOP EXPERIENCE

★ LA Organic

Between Ronda and Campillos, km 39.5 on the A-367; tel. 650/887-247; 11am-9pm Wed.-Sun.; www.laorganic.es; €20

If you have ever wanted to learn how to differentiate between a mild olive oil (blend 80% arbequina, picual, and hojiblanca) and an intense one (100% picudo), you would be hard-pressed, or rather "cold-pressed," to find a better place to dive into the art of this golden delicious staple of the Mediterranean diet. Here you will discover how the terrain, the olive, the sun, the rain, and more go into squeezing this famous Mediterranean oil that has become a kitchen standard worldwide. Tastings feature organic olive oil from olives grown and tended to in the vast olive grove. Tastings last about 45 minutes and include the ability to harvest olives, mill the oil, package, and even personalize your own label. Along the way, you'll undoubtedly learn quite a bit about organic farming.

olive groves at LA Organic

Olive Oil in Andalusia

olive oil press in Jerez de la Frontera

Andalusia is a major producer of olive oil, locally known as "liquid gold" for the generational wealth it has produced, and olive tree cultivation is primarily geared toward the production of this incredibly valuable commodity. The olives harvested from the trees are pressed to extract olive oil. The region is renowned for its high-quality extra virgin olive oil, which is both used domestically and exported worldwide. In addition to olive oil production, olives themselves are a staple in the Andalusian diet. They are used in various dishes, salads, and snacks. You'll find marinated olives of different varieties just about everywhere, and as common little tapas in most restaurants and bars.

Different varieties of olives are grown in Andalusia, each contributing to the diversity of flavors in the produced olive oil. Some well-known varieties include:

- **Picual:** An extra virgin olive oil that is characterized by a spicy, bitter flavor and is thought to be the best olive oil for cooking. This is the most produced olive oil in Spain.
- **Picudo:** An herby, fresh aroma is the headline for this olive oil variety. This variety is very abundant throughout Andalusia and is commonly used.
- **Hojiblanca:** A well-established, sweet and spicy olive oil in Andalusia that is famed for its intense aroma.
- **Arbequina:** Much harder to find in the rest of Spain, this is a sweeter olive oil without any pronounced bitterness or spice.

Vast olive groves are a characteristic feature of the Andalusian landscape. These groves can range from small family-owned orchards to large commercial plantations. The sight of endless rows of olive trees is a defining aspect of the region's rural scenery, particularly around Córdoba.

Olive harvesting in Andalusia typically takes place in the autumn months, usually from October to December. The traditional method involves shaking the branches to make the olives fall onto nets spread beneath the trees. Mechanical harvesters are also used in larger orchards. While modern technology has been incorporated into olive cultivation in Andalusia, some traditional practices persist. Stone mills, known as "molinillos," are still used in some mills for grinding olives, and traditional presses may be employed in smaller, artisanal operations.

It's no surprise that the olive oil industry is a major contributor to the economy of Andalusia. The region accounts for a significant portion of Spain's total olive oil production, and Spanish olive oil, in turn, is a key player in the global market. As you might imagine, this industry is facing some harsh realities in light of climate change. For multiple years now olive production has been in decline, though Spain is still the largest producer of olive oil in the world.

The rolling Andalusian fields endlessly dotted with olive trees are often associated with the region's identity, so much so that visiting olive groves and enjoying an olive oil tasting are sometimes integrated into cultural and historical tours.

Guided Tours

Tourism Office

Paseo de Blas Infante; tel. 952/187-119; www.turismoderonda.es; 10:30am and 6pm Mon.-Thurs.; €10

Ronda is the sort of city where an easy guided tour helps to bring its importance and history alive. After the bridge, bullring, and the long steps down to the river at the Casa del Rey Moro, there isn't too much else to see and do for travelers. With a guided tour, you can squeeze a bit more out of your Ronda experience and learn from a local exactly what makes this small city so darn charming.

Parks

Alameda del Tajo

Calle Virgen de la Paz; 8am-10pm daily; free

This 19th-century tree-lined park is as romantic as they come. From balconies suspended over the cliff you can enjoy jaw-dropping views. Located right next to the bullring, this is a popular walk for just about everyone in town.

Horseback Riding

Caballos y Vino

Lugar Partido Rural Los Frontones, 771; tel. 622/247-757; from €60

A short drive north of Ronda on the route to Setenil de las Bodegas takes you to Sandra's lovely country homestead. As a certified horse trainer, she leads horseback tours in the region in small groups of 2-4 people on safe, reliable horses. This is maybe one of the more authentic ways to discover the Andalusian countryside. Options include rides for beginners and longer treks for seasoned horsefolk.

Live Music

Ronda Guitar House

Calle Virgen de los Remedios, 23; tel. 660/280-720; www.rondaguitarmusic.com; concerts daily Mar.-June and Sept.-Nov.; €18

If you'd like a little Spanish guitar concert before you head out to dinner (and let's be honest, who wouldn't?), reserve an evening with Paco and Lucy. This intimate experience promises great music with a skilled master who is equally knowledgeable of the history of Spanish music, incorporating many styles into the performance and occasionally detouring to wax philosophical on the importance of music and the connections it has the power to create.

Festivals

As in just about every other town and city in Spain, you can expect the find a procession and weeklong festivities for Semana Santa, the Holy Week leading up to Easter, as well as festivities around Christmas and Three Kings Day (Epiphany). Here are a few other particular festivals that Ronda is locally famous for.

Carnival

February/March

One of the better Carnival festivals in Andalusia, Ronda's Carnival usually takes place in late February or early March, during the week leading up to Lent. In Ronda, you'll discover a vibrant celebration complete with a fun parade that includes locally made floats, like what you might see during Mardi Gras in New Orleans. It's a colorful, bright time to visit Ronda, involving lots of music and a good time had by all.

Ronda Romántica

May

This celebration of Ronda's romantic past rings in the month of May. At one time, this was known as the greatest festival in all of Andalusia, with people descending on the town from all around Europe to don costumes of the locals, particularly the bandits the region was once well known for. Though not quite as popular as in its heyday, this is still quite the production, with concerts, markets, and fairs highlighting local arts and crafts.

Feria de Ronda

Last week of August/first week of September

This lively fiesta is a magic week to spend in Ronda. You can expect lots of music and an emphasis on the equestrian culture that is so valued in the region. It is a fun-filled week with lots of dancing, music, and games for kids of all ages. One of the more emblematic festivals in Spain, this particular one includes the Goyescas, inspired by the artist Goya, where men and women sport costumes inspired by this 18th-century period. There is even a fashion contest to determine the best costume, which includes special attention to the elaborate hairstyles of the day. Though this festival dates from the 15th century, it was dedicated to Pedro Romano, a local celebrity and one of the world's greatest matadors, in the 1950s.

Food

Yemas del Tajo

Plaza del Socorro, 3; tel. 952/872-273; 9am-9pm daily (hours vary with season and demand); €5

For some pick-me-up pastries, this is a classic spot for yemas, a pastry of egg yolk and powdered sugar that originates from Ronda. You generally purchase these bite-size morsels of sweet goodness a dozen at a time. They make a nice local treat to pack for hikes in the region or just a quick stop as you are walking around town, though if Ronda is busy, this place tends to get flooded as it is close to Plaza España.

Daver

Calle Virgen de los Remedios, 6; 9am-9pm Tues.-Sun. (hours vary with season and demand); €5

This local favorite is a quieter spot for pastries, including yemas, as well as a strong espresso to go with them. There's just something about yemas and a strong espresso that is so quintessentially Ronda. The café has a sweet 1950s sort of vibe to it, with friendly service. It never seems to get overly busy, so you can take your time picking through the colorful pastries and get a nice variety to take with you.

★ Lechuguita

Calle Virgen de los Remedios, 35; 12:30pm-4pm and 8pm-11pm Mon.-Sat.; €10

This is one of those little places you almost hesitate to write about. It's a no-nonsense, traditional tapas bar popular with locals. At around €1.50 per tapa, you can't go wrong. To order, you make a mark on a paper that lists all the tapas and note how many tapas you want. Give this paper to the bar and they'll get your tapas sorted out. It's a great place to experiment and try lots of little tapas, if you haven't already. There is sometimes a short line to get in, and understandably so, given the great food and service with loads of charm at a bargain basement price.

Tragatá

Calle Nueva, 4; tel. 952/877-209; http://tragata.com/home; 1pm-4pm and 8pm-11pm Tues.-Sat.; €25

Industrial chic meets squid sandwiches. You'll find creative, contemporary tapas rooted in Andalusian flavor profiles. This is one of those addresses that is for the culinarily adventurous. You'll find yourself rubbing shoulders with lots of locals who have exhausted traditional tapas and are looking for the next thing. If you enjoy wine pairings, the staff here are particularly adept with their local vintages. The updated decor is fresh and clean, though nothing special. You're coming here for a culinary adventure more than anything else.

★ Las Tablas

Calle Armiñán, 46; tel. 671/425-069; 1pm-4pm and 8pm-11pm Tues.-Sat.; €30

If you cross the bridge and walk just a couple of blocks, you'll come across this wonderful local spot. If Ronda feels shoulder-to-shoulder with travelers, as can sometimes be the case, try this typical eatery across from the Alminar de San Sebastián. Here you'll find far fewer tourists and dive immediately into a local vibe. Spanish classics are done really well, and some modern options and salads are also on offer. Las Tablas is great choice for those looking to get a little off the beaten path and work on their Spanish.

Pedro Romero

Calle Virgen de la Paz, 18; tel. 952/871-110; www.rpedroromero.com; noon-4pm Mon. and Wed.-Sat.; €30

Across from the bullring, this is the most classic Ronda restaurant; come here for the oxtail.

There is an argument to be made that if you haven't dined at Pedro Romero's, you haven't been to Ronda. Sure, it gets busy with tourists, but it is equally busy with locals. The rustic dining rooms plus a menu featuring some savory Andalusian classics, like the aforementioned oxtail, adds up to an authentic experience drenched in history that you won't find elsewhere.

Albacara

Calle Tenorio, 8; tel. 952/161-184; 12:30pm-4pm and 8pm-11:30pm daily; €30

Fantastic food with fantastic views out over the El Tajo gorge. A few of their specialties include shrimp meatballs with cockle sauce and duck liver mi-cuit with pistachio jam and a reduction of Ronda wine, though in truth, you're really coming here for the view. As such, it's perhaps a better idea for lunch, particularly on a clear day, when you can see out over the countryside, though if you time it right for sunset, that can be quite a special moment.

Accommodations

Hostal San Cayetano

Calle Sevilla, 16; tel. 951/156-067; www.hostalsancayetano.com; €30

A pleasant two-star lacking in any pretension, the hostel is just a few minutes by foot to anywhere in town, and though the rooms are small by local standards, they are clean and comfortable. The staff are helpful and genuinely interested in sharing stories and perspectives. If you are a social backpacker type, this is the spot to hang your pack up for a few days while exploring locally.

★ Palacio San Gabriel

Calle Marqués de Moctezuma, 19; tel. 952/190-392; www.sohohoteles.com/destinos/hotel-soho-boutique-palacio-san-gabriel-4; €100

Of the few boutique hotel companies, Soho Boutique tends to get it right, running well-equipped hotels with charming historic interiors in great locations. Palacio San Gabriel is no exception. Pedro, the manager, always seems to be around and is quick with a joke and to help you get around Ronda, pointing you in the direction of his new favorite tapas joint. It's clean, quiet, and central, with just a touch of charm and great service. If you are traveling out of the busy seasons, look out for deals; you can often find nice double rooms at a substantial discount, making a stay here even more appealing.

★ Cortijo LA Organic

Between Ronda and Campillos, km 39.5 on the A-367; tel. 650/887-247; www.laorganic.es/cortijo; €200

A traditional 19th-century Andalusian cortijo (farmhouse) has been restored by Stefano Robotti, architect and collaborator of the architect Philippe Starck. This stylishly minimalist house incorporates Spanish country living lush with olive groves and lavender. You'll need a car to stay here. For road trippers, this hits a lot of the notes for a fine getaway or home base for local exploration. Happily, if you have an electric car, they have a couple of charging stations so you can fill up overnight. The on-site restaurant serves up an organic breakfast, making for a tasty start to your day, while the rooms are plush and cozy with relaxing views over the countryside.

Hotel Montelirio

Calle Tenorio, 8; tel. 952/161-184; www.hotelmontelirio.com; €250

Friendly, professional staff run this classic Andalusian hotel. It's a good substitute for the Parador hotel, as it hits many of the same notes, though it comes in at a lower price point. Still, at this level, you won't be lacking for much and you'll be central in Ronda, making exploration on foot easy.

Parador de Ronda

Plaza de España; tel. 952/877-500; https://paradores.es/en/parador-de-ronda; €350

You could do an entire four- or five-star trip around Spain using only the Parador hotels and never be disappointed. The locations are unbeatable, and nearly all of them are in historic buildings central to a major attraction.

This one is no different, perched as it is right on the cliff next to the bridge. Service is warm, though professional, and the rooms all offer the sort of old-world touch that will have you dreaming you're traveling in the 1920s.

Information and Services

Tourist Information Center

Paseo de Blas Infante; tel. 952/169-311; 10am-7pm Mon.-Fri., 9:30am-2pm and 3:30pm-7pm Sat., 9:30am-3pm Sun.

The information center is staffed with friendly locals and offers lots of maps and other information for the region. Walking tours in English start from here.

Getting There

Bus

Ronda offers a central bus station conveniently located in the heart of the town, the **Estación de Autobuses de Ronda.** This station serves as a transportation hub for connecting to various nearby towns and regions. Several reputable bus companies, such as Alsa and Autocares Sierra de las Nieves, provide daily routes to destinations including Málaga (1.5 hr; 112 km/70 mi; €10) and Marbella (1.5 hr; 65 km/40 mi; €8), making it a suitable option for exploring the region.

Car

Ronda is well connected by road, with the A-374 and A-369 highways providing access to nearby towns and cities. From Jerez de la Frontera, Ronda is an easy drive (1.5 hr; 115 km/77 mi) east on the A-382, which becomes the A-384 before you turn onto the A-374. If you're driving from Seville, you can reach Ronda via the A-375 (2 hr; 120 km/75 mi). Alternatively, if you're coming from Málaga, take the A-366 (1.5 hr; 105 km/65 mi).

Getting Around

Ronda's charming historic center is not designed for heavy vehicle traffic, so park your car in one of the town's public parking areas to explore the town comfortably on foot. Just remember to pack your good walking shoes!

Parador de Ronda

☆ Top Haciendas in the Pueblos Blancos

If you have a bit more time on your hands and are looking for a peaceful Spanish countryside getaway, or maybe even a spot for that next destination get-together, take a long look at some of the haciendas and fincas dotting the countryside surrounding Ronda. Without fail they are architecturally charming, with lines and curves that stand out in whitewash and stone against a forested background, dramatic cliffs, rolling pastures and terraced vineyards, veggie patches, and olive groves. These stays are marked by homemade food and hospitality, much like staying at a countryside, family-run bed-and-breakfast.

traditional hacienda in Ronda

LA PERLA BLANCA

Fuente La Higuera, 11, Ronda; tel. 711/047-612; www.laperlablanca.com; €110

A classic hacienda stay at an accessible price point with kind service, La Perla Blanca is just a 10-minute drive from Ronda. There is a lot to like, especially the setting on a private vineyard. In hot months the pool is sure to see a lot of use. The rooms lack some of the pizzazz of their more upscale counterparts but are still a fantastic value. On-site wine tastings can be had, and if you book direct through the website, breakfast is complimentary.

HOTEL LA FUENTE DE LA HIGUERA

Partido de los Frontones, Ronda; tel. 952/165-608; www.hotellafuente.com; €150

A 15-minute drive from Ronda will land you in this family-friendly hacienda. Formerly an olive mill, this beautifully situated house rambles around a well-manicured lawn, gardens, and the requisite pool. In the nicer months dining happens out on the terrace, though a cozy fireplace ensures warm toes for cold nights of indoor dining. There is a large library on-site, and in true family fashion, you'll often find yourself walking in, through, and past a busy kitchen. Food is a real highlight, both breakfast and dinner. Rustic touches and soft linens make for a comfy stay. The classic suite is worth the splurge should you fancy a view and a private terrace.

FINCA NARANJA

Lugar Partido Rural Peñacerrada, Ronda; tel. 650/452-313; www.fincanaranja.com; from €4,100 per week

An old farm that has recently had a makeover into a luxury house spread over 6 hectares (15 acres), Finca Naranja boasts four private suites, a large pool, and sunset views that will make your eyes water. It's an ideal spot for couples traveling together or larger families. Equidistant from Ronda or Setenil de las Bodegas (25 minutes from either town), this fashionable finca is a weekly rental (starting at €4,100 in the winter and vaulting to €6,800 for more in-demand spring and summer months) and comfortably fits 8 people, though up to 12 is possible.

FINCA LA MORERA

Lugar Partido Rural Ribera de los Frailes, 41, Ronda; tel. 659/457-473; https://fincalamoreraronda.com; €950 per night, 2-night minimum

A short 15 minutes from Ronda brings you to the immaculately gardened setting of this finca. The lush, inviting organic gardens give way to a multifunction tennis court and pool spaces on the outside. Inside you'll discover six double bedrooms, each with its own bathroom, and plenty of options with twin or king-size beds. The upper floors boast exposed wood ceilings. Throughout there is a sense of space and charm of the old world. For larger families or groups of friends, this is a stellar option for a Spanish hacienda getaway or even a backdrop for a wedding.

★ Sierra de Grazalema Natural Park

Emerging dramatically from the Mediterranean, the Sierra de Grazalema mountain range unfolds as a rocky landscape dominated by oaks and rugged sandstone soil. Remarkably, this terrain is a direct continuation of Morocco's Rif Mountains just across the Strait of Gibraltar. As you ascend, the resilient fir tree, a common sight in Cádiz, Málaga, and northern Morocco, steadfastly roots itself in the higher elevations. The park boasts exclusive flora, including the Grazalema poppy and the "relojillo recoder" geranium. Keep your eyes peeled for mountain goats, otters, stags, genets, and badgers. The caves harbor colonies of bats. Meanwhile, bird enthusiasts will be thrilled by the diverse raptors calling these mountains home.

VISITING THE PARK

Gateway Towns

Grazalema

The town is a haven for nature lovers, nestled right in the Grazalema Natural Park. It is celebrated throughout Spain for its preservation of traditional architecture, including houses owned by wealthy noble families. Most of these structures were built in the 18th century, featuring arcades with bedazzling tops crowned with images of the Virgin Mary and coats of arms decorating their entries, which signifies their affiliation with the Brotherhood of the Santisimo Sacramento, the Brotherhood of Veracruz, or the Brotherhood of La Santa Caridad. Each of these brotherhoods were cloth manufacturers, from which Grazalema first gained notoriety, the weft and weave that form the cloth of its past.

There are not really any prominent sites to visit in Grazalema, but the charming old hamlet itself offers a delightful stroll. The main square hosts the Church of Nuestra Señora de La Aurora, dating back to the 17th century in a late Renaissance style with elements of early Baroque. Another intriguing church, the Parroquia Nuestra Señora de La Encarnación, boasts Mudejar origins and was initially constructed in the early 17th century. However, it underwent reconstruction in the 18th century after damage inflicted by the French during the War of Independence and partial destruction in the Civil War. Despite its original architecture being reduced to a small chapel, the church now houses significant sculptures, including San Atanasio, the town's patron saint.

Grazalema is best approached as a village to base yourself for exploring the surrounding park.

Visitor Centers

Grazalema Tourist Center

Plaza de los Asomaderos, 3, Grazalema; tel. 673/300-323; www.turismo.grazalema.es; 10am-2:30pm and 3pm-5:30pm Wed.-Sun.

Just off the convenient El Mirador parking lot you'll find the local visitor center for the park. This center has the most recent hiking guides and maps for the park for sale in their office. English-speaking help is rare, but there are some English-language guides usually on hand.

Tours

Sue Eatock

tel. 666/999-421; natureplus.grazalema@gmail.com

If you are looking for a cultural tour of Grazalema village or a guided walk through the park, British expat Sue Eatock has made Grazalema her home and has been living here since 2005. A fantastic outing with her covers the circular route to visit both Zahara de la Sierra and Grazalema villages, where you will take an occasional breath to appreciate the incredible mountain scenery and spy some of the flora and fauna of the region.

HIKING

Llanos del Endrinal

Distance: *2.9 km/1.8 mi round-trip*

Andalusia Is for the Birds

Bird-watchers are treated to a spectacular array of avian wonders gracing the skies of the Sierra de Grazalema Natural Park. The park, renowned for its conservation efforts and diverse ecosystems, is home to quite a captivating ensemble of birds.

griffon vulture

The **griffon vulture,** boasting one of Europe's largest breeding colonies, shares the airspace with the critically endangered **Spanish imperial eagle,** a symbol of ongoing conservation endeavors. Majestic eagles, both the Spanish imperial and the **short-toed snake eagle,** contribute to the aerial ballet, showcasing their hunting prowess.

Down in the rocky terrain, the **black wheatear** adds a contrasting touch with its striking black and white plumage, perfectly adapted to the mountainous surroundings. The elusive **Eurasian eagle-owl,** a nocturnal hunter, awaits the evening to reveal its large, tufted ears. Meanwhile, the **blue rock thrush** hangs out in the rocky outcrops with its vibrant blue and orange hues, and the **Eurasian crag martin** performs agile feats in the skies above.

Deep in the coniferous forests, you might spy a **common crossbill** navigating the trees with its unique crossed bill, extracting seeds from pinecones. The **Eurasian griffon,** a cousin to the griffon vulture, and the golden eagle, a regal presence in the skies, contribute to the park's ecological tapestry. Completing this avian ensemble is the **peregrine falcon,** the fastest bird in flight, soaring overhead with unmatched swiftness.

Each of these inhabitants of Grazalema adds a feathery layer of fascination to the park's vibrant biodiversity, making it a haven for bird-watchers and nature enthusiasts alike. As you traverse the park's trails and vistas, look up for its winged residents.

Time: *1.5 hr*
Elevation gain: *241 m/790 ft*
Effort: *moderate*
Trailhead: *Grazalema town entrance*

This moderate circular path plunges you quickly into the heart of the mountains. Along this relatively short hike, you'll be able to see several limestone rock formations typical of the park, as well as a great plain and a few sinkholes. There is a small forest of pine trees along part of the hike that provide shade, where you'll almost assuredly come across grazing cattle. It's a really nice hike if you are looking to get out after breakfast and want to return to Grazalema by lunch.

Arroyo del Fresnillo

Distance: *6.4 km/4 mi round-trip*
Time: *2.5 hr*
Elevation gain: *288 m/944 ft*
Effort: *moderate*
Trailhead: *Mirador El Tajo (Grazalema)*

Full disclosure: Though this trail does call for you to do a full loop, it's almost better to follow the trail clockwise from the lookout and Grazalema, hike out to the Arroyo del Fresnillo, continue to the main road if you want (CA-9123) to reach the Mirador El Tajo for a fantastic view out over the mountains and forest, and then turn back. You'll be at about the halfway point when you get to the road, and if you turn right and complete the circle, you'll just follow the main road back. It's much more pleasant to do this trail as an out-and-back. Either way it will be around 2-2.5 hours, a moderate hike you can do in half a day with no problem.

Ronda to Grazalema

Distance: *25.6 km/16.1 mi one-way*
Time: *8 hr*
Elevation gain: *949 m/3,113 ft*
Effort: *strenuous*
Trailhead: *Ronda or Grazalema*

This point-to-point trail is a challenge largely for the length, though if you are coming from Ronda to Grazalema, toward the end of the walk is where you will have most of your elevation gain. You'll cut through the countryside on trails that cross through valleys, farmlands, and forest. Use your GPS for this hike and make sure to have sunshade and plenty of water. There are not too many places for refreshments or water along the way.

BIKING

Grazalema Biking Adventures

Calle Doctor Mateos Gago, 9, Grazalema; tel. 633/267-250; www.grazalemacycling.com

This is the outfitter for any biking adventure you might want to put together in the park, but you will have to call or check the website ahead of time. It is by appointment only, so make sure to organize with them ahead of your arrival. Once there, Ana can get you fitted on quite a few different styles and types of bikes, all of them new and well taken care of, as well as direct you on some of her favorite biking routes.

SPAS AND THERMAL BATHS

Spa & Wellness Grazalema

Calle de la Laguneta, Grazalema; tel. 956/132-016 or 663/085-193; 11am-2pm and 5pm-8:30pm Wed.-Sun.; €18

Opt for a massage (from €25) if your legs could really use it, but the big draw here is the 90-minute thermal bath circuit for €18. A steaming good deal! If you have spent a few days hiking around the region, treat yourself to the thermal bath and/or a massage, giving your legs and feet their little own mini-vacation.

SHOPPING

Queseria de La Abuela Agustina

Plaza Pequeña, 7, Grazalema; 10am-2:30pm and 4pm-8pm daily summer, 10am-12:30pm and 3:30pm-7pm daily winter

I would be remiss if I didn't include one of my favorite little cheese, wine, and charcuterie shops in all of Andalusia! This is the perfect

hikers in the Sierra de Grazalema Natural Park

little pit stop to stock up on cheesy goods before or after a hike. Their selections of local sheep and goat cheese are particularly delightful. They are used to helping travelers pack up for a delicious picnic.

FOOD AND ACCOMMODATIONS

Cafeteria Rotacapa

Calle las Piedras, 9, Grazalema; tel. 856/586-066; 8:30am-2pm and 3pm-8:30pm daily; €5

Isn't it always time for coffee and cake? If you agree, this friendly, bright local café will hit the spot. Expect homemade daily goodness with your café con leche. If the sounds of lemon meringue, chocolate wafer, or creamy cheesecake are music to your ears, tuck in here and enjoy.

★ Cádiz el Chico

Calle Corrales III, 47, Grazalema; tel. 637/762-665; €20

Floral patterns add to the abuela-chic vibes of this local standard. It's popular with French hikers and was written up in the Michelin. You would be correct in assuming they do something right here. Reservations are highly encouraged. The menu has quite a few variations that are well-done classics, but you should really come here for the stewy wild jabalí (boar) served over potatoes and topped with sweet raspberry sauce. It is wildly delicious, and this is the dish this restaurant hangs its sombrero on.

La Maroma

Calle de Santa Clara, Grazalema; tel. 956/132-279; www.lamaromagrazalema.com; €20

Uphill from the town center (centro urbano), this is a good option for those looking to keep local when travelers crowd the other spots around town. Summer nights are made for their outdoor terrace. La Maroma is a local gastrobar, where reservations are encouraged. Head here if you're craving something lighter and perhaps more contemporary. The light toast layered with lightly sautéed peppers, salmorejo, and crispy ham is just heaven to pair with a chilled vino tinto after a hot day.

★ Casa de las Piedras

Calle las Piedras, 32, Grazalema; tel. 611/127-053; €60

A charming old home has been lovingly restored and converted into this no-frills, rustic bed-and-breakfast. Downstairs you'll find a restaurant and bar as well as a heavily wooded salon with a grand fireplace. You might expect the cold in the winter, but even in the fall and spring it can get quite nippy, and the fireplace is a welcome gathering place to warm your bones. It's centrally located and near everything in the village with rooms that are clean, comfortable, and have private bathrooms. Staff are very kind and family friendly.

GETTING THERE AND AROUND

You need a car to reach Grazalema. Grazalema is a short drive from Ronda (45 min; 34 km/21 mi) on the A-372, which serves as a gateway to the region. Seville (2 hr; 116 km/72 mi) is farther afield, though the A-375 makes for a picturesque journey through the Sierra de Grazalema Natural Park.

From Málaga, the A-357 and A-367 highways provide efficient access to the park's southern reaches.

Grazalema is a compact town that invites strolling its narrow streets lined with whitewashed houses adorned with flowers on foot to really soak in the charm. Most of the attractions, shops, and restaurants are within walking distance of each other.

Sierra de Las Nieves National Park

The Sierra de las Nieves, or the "Mountain Range of the Snows," takes its name from the fact that the peaks of this range are often covered in snow during the winter months. Pack accordingly! The park was designated as a UNESCO Biosphere Reserve in 1995, highlighting the park's ecological importance and its role in conserving biodiversity. You'll find a wide variety of plant and animal species present in the park. It is particularly known for its diverse flora, including Mediterranean pine forests and unique species like the Spanish fir *(Abies pinsapo)*, which is endemic to this region. The park is also home to a range of wildlife, such as mountain goats, eagles, and vultures. This is a popular destination for outdoor enthusiasts. You can explore its hiking trails, enjoy bird-watching, even go rock climbing, and enjoy various adventure sports, not to mention the ample opportunities for picnicking and camping—something of a local pastime.

There are well-marked trails, and visitor centers dotted around the park provide information and further guidance for exploring the area.

A total of 12 municipalities are integrated into the Sierra de las Nieves National Park, including Ronda, and nine towns still preserve the physiognomy inherited from the melting pot of cultures that have made themselves felt in these lands: Alozaina, Casarabonela, Tolox, El Burgo, Yunquera, Monda, Guaro, Istán, and Ojén. The Sierra de las Nieves region borders to the south with the western Costa del Sol, to the east with the Guadalhorce Valley, to the west with the Serranía de Ronda, and to the north with the region of Guadalteba.

The region offers a wide range of activities related to active tourism, including traditional hiking, horse riding, all-terrain or bicycle routes, canoeing, canyoning, caving, and climbing, among others.

VISITING THE PARK

The park is easily accessible from towns like Ronda and Málaga. From Ronda, the A-366 cuts along the eastern border of the park, connecting with towns like Ojén and Tolox (remember to turn onto the A-355 toward Marbella), while the A-397 skirts the western edge, connecting with the A-7 coastal freeway that links together Tarifa, Gibraltar, and Málaga.

Gateway Towns

Ojén

Ojén is a picturesque town that only becomes more beautiful as you climb into the local caves at the top of town, the Cuevas de Ojén. From here, you'll have unobstructed views over Ojén and the Mediterranean, which is not all that far away. Perhaps the largest town in the national park, it has pharmacies, banks, and quite a few restaurants and lodging options.

Tolox

Traditional whitewashed homes circle the Plaza los Poyos in Tolox, where you can find the town church, San Miguel, which has the classic Mudejar stylings known throughout the region. Tolox has several local bars and restaurants.

Visitor Centers

Tolox Tourism Office

Calle Garcia Rey, 1, Tolox; tel. 952/487-333; www.toloxturismo.com; 11am-2pm and 5pm-8pm Wed.-Sat., 11am-2pm Sun.

In Tolox you will find the local tourism office for the national park. You can find updated maps and guides here for the park as well as information on the history of Tolox.

HIKING

Mirador del Macho Montes

Distance: *6.9 km/4.3 mi round-trip*

Time: *2.5 hr*
Elevation gain: *376 m/1,233 ft*
Effort: *moderate-strenuous*
Trailhead: *Refugio de Juanar (near Ojén)*

This is a popular local trail and you'll likely encounter a trail runner or two along the way. On this circular hike you have a choice to either ascend or descend the steepest part of the hike. If you go clockwise you'll tackle this steep ascent on your way up toward the beginning of your hike, while if you go counterclockwise, you'll have a steep, rocky descent as the last part of your hike. Other than this patch, the rest of the hike is fairly easy, offering spectacular views over the national park and a refreshing walk through a eucalyptus forest, though the rock formations of the Mirador del Macho Montes are the highlight.

Mount Torrecilla

Distance: *20.5 km/13 mi round-trip*
Time: *8 hr*
Elevation gain: *670 m/2,200 ft*
Effort: *strenuous*
Trailhead: *Puerto Saucillo (near Tolox)*

This is perhaps the most iconic hike in the national park, taking you to one of the tallest peaks around. The hike is well marked and only steep toward the very end as you get to the summit. This is a there-and-back trail, though from the summit, there are several trails you can pick and choose from that all rejoin the primary trail back to Puerto Saucillo for a bit of variety. The first couple of miles of the trail are in a pine forest, but after that, you are exposed to the elements on rocky terrain. Be sure to pack accordingly, including a large water bladder and windbreaker. The trailhead at Puerto Saucillo is about a 40-minute drive from Tolox (22 km/14 mi). Though not technical or particularly challenging, this is a strenuous trail just based on distance.

Las Cascadas

Distance: *9.8 km/6.1 mi round-trip*
Time: *5 hr*
Elevation gain: *565 m/1,853 ft*
Effort: *strenuous*
Trailhead: *Tolox*

Mountain goats, pine forests, beautiful rock formations, and the plunging waterfalls for which this trail is named highlight the scenery you can expect to encounter on this route. There is a lot of beauty to be had along the circular trail. It's a solidly challenging hike with some steep climbs and a part where you are on a narrow ravine, so be cautious if prone to vertigo or you have an acute fear of heights. Use your poles.

FOOD

Ojén

Boca Bistro

Calle Carrera, 13; tel. 747/766-353; 4pm-midnight Mon., Tues., and Fri., 1pm-midnight Sat.-Sun.; €15

Boca Bistro near the church is a fantastic option for a tapas lunch, particularly for seafood. Go for the tuna tataki or, if you're a bit more adventurous, the perfectly seared scallops. Though indoor dining is available, this is a place you'll want to head to when the weather is fine to sit on the street-side patio and take in local life while enjoying your favorite beverage. In the colder months, outdoor heaters do a magnificent job of keeping the chill off.

Tolox

Bar Mancilla

Plaza los Poyos, 5; hours vary, usually morning-3pm and 6pm-midnight; €10

On Plaza los Poyos you'll find Bar Mancilla, which features local wines, traditional tapas, and nice views over town. It's a good people-watching spot while you're sipping on local wine and enjoying traditional tapas. As at many tapas bars in smaller towns in Andalusia, hours vary tremendously according to the whim and sleep habits of the owner/manager. The upstairs terrace is the place to be as long as it's not too hot out.

ACCOMMODATIONS

Ojén

Refugio de Juanar

Sierra Blanca, Ojén; tel. 690/702-046 or 952/881-000; www.elrefugiodejuanar.com; €50

This rustic, unfussy, well-run inn is a good base, with terracotta and wafer brick backdropping the heavy wood furnishings typical of traditional Andalusia. Homey mountain food will keep you energized for your exploration of the surrounding park. The onsite restaurant features local game, including pheasant and venison, as well as an extensive wine list to help you cozy up to the open fireplaces warming your bones in those cold winter months. Numerous trailheads lead right from this property into the national park.

Tolox

★ Hotel Cerro de Híjar

Cerro de Híjar, Tolox; tel. 952/112-111 or 607/205-170; www.cerrodehijar.com; €85

A unique hacienda with its heart in sustainable travel, this is one of the few accommodations in the region that have been certified by Europarc for their ecofriendly operations. The property includes a pool, restaurant, and spa. The double rooms are a great value for a quick overnight considering the amenities available, while for longer stays, families, or friends traveling together, the suites should be considered. The restaurant (1:30pm-3:30pm and 8:30pm-10pm daily; €25) carries on the sustainability ethos with an organic menu featuring local legumes, seafood, and wines, though some easy international favorites like spaghetti and burgers are also available for those diminutive fussy eaters.

GETTING THERE AND AROUND

You will want to have a rental car to explore the national park. Once in the park itself, most of the exploration will be done on footpaths. If you are looking to explore the national park as a day trip or as a stop connecting overnights in two towns (like Ronda and Málaga), there are parking places and hiking trails just off the A-366.

To get from Ronda to Ojén (1.5 hr; 69 km/43 mi), follow the A-397 south toward Marbella and the coast before turning on the A-7 (or AP-7) to Marbella and then up the A-355. For Tolox (1.5 hr; 54 km/34 mi), follow the A-366 east toward Málaga from Ronda and turn on the A-7250 on the exit marked for Tolox.

★ Caminito del Rey

TOP EXPERIENCE

Hidden amid the captivating landscape of Andalusia, Spain, lies a unique adventure hike dubbed the Caminito del Rey. This daring trek takes you through the rugged terrain of El Chorro Gorge, near the town of Álora, offering a hiking experience like no other. Initially constructed in the early 20th century to grant access to hydroelectric plant maintenance workers, the trail's reputation grew increasingly perilous over time. Recent renovations have breathed new life into the Caminito del Rey, turning it into an exhilarating attraction for intrepid hikers.

HISTORY

The history of Caminito del Rey is a tale of industrial progress and royal presence. In 1866, a railway line connecting Córdoba and Málaga via the rugged gorge was completed. Soon after, a hydroelectric station at El Chorro emerged on the scene, facilitating the region's development. Fast forward to 1921, when a transformative addition took place: the installation of a walkway along the gorge, bridging the gaps between the waterfalls of Gaitanejo and El Chorro. This ingenious solution enabled workers and essential materials to traverse the expanse with ease.

The trail acquired its moniker, "Caminito del Rey," or King's Path, from a momentous event in 1921 when King Alfonso XIII

1
2
3
4

inaugurated the El Chorro dam and strolled along this very pathway. Caminito del Rey is an abbreviated form of El Camino del Rey, both referring to the same location, so don't fret if you encounter the slightly different name in various sources.

Despite its initial promise, access to Caminito del Rey was sealed in 2000 due to safety concerns, stemming from poorly maintained footbridges and a tragic history of accidents. However, after an extensive restoration effort, this iconic trail was once again unveiled in 2015, ready to be explored and appreciated by adventurers from around the world.

GEOLOGY

The home of the Caminito del Rey is El Chorro Gorge, located in the Cordilla Baetic range, northeast of the Sierra de las Nieves National Park. This impressive canyon features sections with walls that soar thousands of feet in the air and narrow spans less than 10 m (33 ft) wide. The rock formations mainly consist of limestone and dolomites from the Jurassic period, with traces of Miocene rock outcrops in the area. What truly stands out is the vertical layering of these limestones, sculpted by the river's erosion over time. These are easily observed, even by non-geologically minded folk.

The gorge boasts around 20 caves, some perched hundreds of feet above the river. Their formation has been influenced by the gradual shaping of the Guadalhorce River, which has steadily deepened the gorge in successive stages.

Among the diverse geological features in this area, you'll find conglomerates, calcarenites, and Miocene sediments. Some parts even hold fossilized remnants of whales.

FLORA AND FAUNA

Look up and you may be fortunate enough to catch a glimpse of magnificent birds like griffon vultures, Egyptian vultures, or golden eagles soaring above. Vultures have clusters of nests hugging the cliffside on part of the trail. On the ground look out for lizards, sheep, foxes, Iberian ibexes, and badgers.

1: The Caminito del Rey is open to kids eight years and over. **2:** path along the cliff face **3:** hiking the Caminito del Rey **4:** looking down from the suspension bridge

VISITING THE CAMINITO DEL REY

Purchasing Tickets

All tickets are tied to date and time. It's best to purchase tickets on the official website (www.caminitodelrey.info) at least 2-3 weeks before your planned travel dates. You will have to register on the website to complete your ticket purchase.

Tickets are available three months out. General admission tickets (€10) go quickly while tickets for guided hikes (€18) are usually available, though these often sell out for popular times. Guided hikes are with groups of up to 30 people. All admission fees include hard helmets, which you are expected to wear throughout your hike. Kids younger than eight years old are not allowed on the trail. Kids eight and over may be required to show identification.

Tickets do not include the shuttle bus (€2.50), which is payable by cash only.

If you neglected to purchase tickets online, you can sometimes purchase tickets at the ticket office at the Caminito del Rey trailhead, though this is risky—tickets are often sold out.

Visitor Reception Center

Puerto de las Atalayas, just off the MA-5403, 2.6 km (1.5 mi) south of the north access of the trail; http://caminitodelrey.info; 8am-6pm daily

The visitor reception center (Centro de Recepción de Visitantes) is situated directly west about 2.6 km (1.5 mi) south along the MA-5403 from the tunnel access of the main trailhead. The center offers a brief glimpse into the history and geography of the Caminito del Rey, as well as restrooms and a snack machine in case you didn't come prepared.

Currently, you cannot buy tickets to access the Caminito del Rey at the visitor center.

Reserve and purchase your ticket through the official website or directly at the northern access of the Caminito del Rey at the ticket office. Tickets often sell out, so it is highly recommended to purchase them online through the website in advance.

HIKING

Distance: *7.7 km/4.8 mi one-way*
Time: *3 hr*
Elevation gain: *105 m/345 ft*
Effort: *easy-moderate*
Trailhead: *Caminito del Rey Tunnel (off the MA-5403)*

Safely hugging the cliff faces, the "trail," comprising narrow wooden walkways bolted into the cliff face and a rocky suspension bridge, provides spellbinding views of the untamed surroundings. You can't help but feel a pump of adrenaline on this experience, which combines a thirst for adventure with a deep appreciation of nature. As you traverse this path, clinging to sheer cliffs high above the Guadalhorce River, you have to admire the courage it took for locals to use a much-less-safe version of this path to commute to their job at the hydroelectric plant.

The Caminito del Rey takes you on a one-way journey, from north to south, commencing in the municipality of Ardales and concluding in Álora. The trek offers a one-of-a-kind opportunity to wander along pathways suspended over 100 m (320 ft) above the vertical cliff faces. The trail guides you through an array of natural wonders, from cliffs to canyons and a vast valley. One of its most astonishing segments is the passage through Desfiladero de Los Gaitanes, a gorge sculpted by the Guadalhorce River, with awe-inspiring walls towering 700 m (2,300 ft) high.

Despite the height and apparent scale of the hike, the path is largely flat with a handful of short stairways. It can be considered an easy hike for most and a must-do for hikers of just about every skill level.

GETTING THERE AND AROUND

You'll need a rental car to get to the Caminito del Rey. There are several parking options. The visitor reception center at Puerto de la Atalayas has the largest parking lot and is central for the shuttle buses connecting the trailhead and the end of the trail. Another solid option is to park at the end of the trail in El Churro and take the shuttle bus to the trailhead in Ardales so you finish the hike at your car.

Parking

North Parking

Ardales; €2

This parking is nearest the trailhead, by the Restaurante El Mirador Ardales. It is popular in warm weather with locals who also come to enjoy time in the reservoir. Parking is payable only in cash in person.

Visitor Reception Center

Puerto de las Atalayas, just off the MA-5403, 2.6 km (1.5 mi) south of the north access of the trail; http://caminitodelrey.info; 8am-6pm daily; €2

The largest parking lot in the area is easy to find just off the MA-5403 road leading up to the Caminito del Rey. It's possible to package this parking cost with your ticket online. You'll need to take the shuttle to the trailhead and then from the end of the trail back here.

South Parking

El Churro; free

This might be the smartest option. Not only is parking free, but if you park here and take the shuttle to the trailhead, you will end up back at your car, making for a pleasant circular journey.

Shuttle Bus

The shuttle bus connects the three main parking lots at the visitor center, El Churro, and Ardales near the trailhead. The shuttle costs €2.50 per person. You must pay for your ticket in cash to the driver on the bus. The shuttle bus is not included in your ticket price

Preparing to Hike the Caminito del Rey

Though the Caminito del Rey is a relatively easy hike for most, there are several things to remember to prepare yourself and make the most of your experience, including several practical considerations.

- **Height sensitivity:** It's essential to be aware that the trail is not recommended for those with a fear of heights.
- **Ticket reservation:** Purchase tickets in advance to secure your spot.
- **Early arrival:** Plan to arrive at the parking area in Ardales at least 30 minutes ahead of your scheduled hike.
- **Timely reservations:** To avoid parking and trail congestion, choose earlier time slots for your hike and avoid weekends.
- **Supplies:** Bring an ample supply of water and snacks for sustenance along the way.
- **Mandatory helmet:** A helmet is mandatory for safety, and it must remain on throughout the hike. These are supplied to you as you enter the trail.
- **Restricted accessories:** Leave selfie sticks, tripods, and similar items in your vehicle, as they are not allowed on the trail.
- **Restroom locations:** Restrooms are available only at the trail's starting and ending points.
- **Age limit:** The hike is open to children eight years and over. Carrying children of any age or pets is not permitted.
- **Weather consideration:** Be aware that the trail may be temporarily closed in bad weather conditions.
- **Shuttle bus:** Keep small change handy for the shuttle bus service. The shuttle bus at the end of the trail is cash only (€2.50).
- **Clothing:** As for attire, opt for comfortable clothing and sturdy footwear like trainers or walking boots. Flip-flops or high heels are not suitable for the trail.
- **Seasonality:** During the summer, use sunscreen and wear a hat for sun protection. In the winter, layer your clothing and consider bringing gloves, as shaded sections of the hike can get quite chilly.

and you cannot purchase tickets online. The shuttle runs 7:40am-8pm with the entire route running about 15-20 minutes.

GUADALHORCE RESERVOIR

On the west side of the MA-5403, across the street from the tunnel leading to the Caminito del Rey trailhead, lies the Guadalhorce Reservoir, a popular spot for locals for a swim and a picnic lunch, particularly in the hot summer months. There are numerous viewpoints and well-signed footpaths around the reservoir. If you wanted to extend the afternoon with a nice walk or plunge in for a refreshing swim, this is one of the best spots in the region. The clear, slightly salty water is renowned locally for being great for your skin. In late summer and into the fall it will be warmer than the Mediterranean. Kayak and paddleboat rentals are usually available starting from around €20. There are a few cafés and restaurants on the road if you need bathrooms or didn't pack a picnic. The beaches are rocky, so wear wet shoes or flip-flops for the most comfort.

Background

The Landscape

GEOGRAPHY

The Coast

Stretching along the southern Iberian Peninsula, the Andalusian coast boasts more beaches than you can dream. The Mediterranean Sea to the south and the Atlantic Ocean to the west influence the climate, creating an environment that is beach-worthy nearly year-round. Starting from the easternmost point at the Strait of Gibraltar and extending to the west, this coastal region encompasses renowned cities such as Málaga, Gibraltar, and Cádiz. The coastline features a mix of golden

beaches, dramatic rock formations, busy ports, and smaller fishing villages offering largely temperate climes. The weather tends to be cooler and more moderate toward the west, gradually becoming warmer and drier as one moves eastward.

From the historic port city of Málaga to the vibrant coastal town of Cádiz, the Andalusian coast is popular with Europeans and Spaniards seeking some fun in the sun, and rightfully so. You'll find the occasional fishing villages alongside the busier cities, though sadly much has been poorly and overly developed to cater to the wave of summertime tourists and cruise ship crowds.

The gastronomy is heavily influenced by its coastal location, as you would expect, with an abundance of seafood mixed in with local favorites alongside plenty of olives and citrus fruits.

The Mountains

Inland, Andalusia is graced by a spectacular mountainous terrain that adds to the region's geographical diversity. The Baetic System, or Sistema Bético, is a complex system of mountain ranges known for its diverse and rugged landscapes, including high peaks, deep valleys, and limestone formations.

The Baetic System comprises several main mountain ranges.

Sierra Norte de Sevilla: Located to the north of the city of Seville, this range is characterized by rolling hills and valleys and is where you will find the Sierra Norte de Sevilla Natural Park, just an hour from the medieval urban hustle of Seville.

Sierra Nevada: This is one of the most well known and significant ranges in the Baetic System. It includes the highest peak in continental Spain, **Mulhacén,** standing at 3,479 m (11,414 ft) above sea level, as well as the Sierra Nevada National Park and the Alpujarras region. You'll find Europe's southernmost ski station on these slopes. Its snowcapped peaks provide a stunning backdrop to cities like Granada.

Sierra de Grazalema: Known for its limestone peaks, deep gorges, and stunning landscapes. It is home to the Sierra de Grazalema Natural Park and is a haven for hikers, mountain bikers, and bird watchers. It's one of the more rustic regions of all of Andalusia, where you will find the most picturesque white villages tucked into its many nooks and crannies.

Sierra de las Nieves: Recognized for its ecological importance, featuring a variety of ecosystems, including Mediterranean forests, rocky landscapes, and high mountain areas, this is an impressive mountain system that descends almost directly into Gibraltar. Here you will find the Sierra de las Nieves National Park and a few great walks.

These mountain ranges are blessed with rich biodiversity, diverse ecosystems, and a mix of Mediterranean and alpine climates. Their geology has been shaped by tectonic activity, resulting in a complex array of mountains, valleys, and plateaus. However, this significance isn't only geological. There is much about these mountains that is culturally and historically important, with various archaeological sites and towns scattered throughout the region. More than that, the Baetic System and the Rif Mountains in Morocco and Algeria on the continent of Africa are considered part of the same orogenic system. Together, they form the Gibraltar Arc or Baetic-Rif Arc, a complex tectonic region that extends from the Iberian Peninsula to North Africa. This geological structure is a result of the convergence between the African and Eurasian tectonic plates.

The Badlands

To the east of Granada, bordering the provinces of Murcia and Valencia, lie the badlands. Characterized by their unique erosional

Previous: A shepherd herds his sheep across the dry countryside.

feature over the millennia, they tell their own intricate story of the earth's history as shaped by wind and water. In the Granada Geopark in the areas nearest the Sierra Nevada, the soft sedimentary rock showcases the impact of erosion on the landscape. Here you will encounter steep slopes, deep canyons, and a network of intricate gullies carved by the forces of nature that create striking formations that expose the geological layers representing various periods in the earth's history. These exposed layers serve as a natural timeline, offering a glimpse into the dynamic processes that have shaped the region over millions of years.

One notable feature of the badlands is the presence of erosion-resistant ridges and pinnacles that stand as silent sentinels amid the sculpted landscape. These formations, often referred to as "hoodoos" or "fairy chimneys," contribute to the geopark's otherworldly scenery while the semi-arid climate contributes to a diverse ecosystem, featuring resilient plant species and adapted wildlife.

In addition to their geological significance, they provide valuable opportunities for paleontological exploration. The exposed sedimentary layers may contain fossils, offering insights into ancient ecosystems and contributing to our understanding of the region's rich natural history.

CLIMATE

Andalusia features a diverse climate that often surprises newcomers. While the area is generally categorized as having a "Mediterranean climate," the nuances across the region reveal a varied weather tableau that can be thought of as coastal, desert, and mountainous.

The true Mediterranean climate is found along the Strait of Gibraltar across the Southern Coast along the Mediterranean and Atlantic, in places like Málaga and Cádiz. Summers are warm, averaging around 30°C (86°F), and winters are mild, hovering around 16°C (61°F), with spring and autumn bridging the gap. Winters, however, mark the wet season, especially along the coast. Cities like Málaga accumulate rainfall in the winter, with averages of 10-13 cm (4-5 in) per month, tapering to around 5 cm (2 in) per month in spring and fall. Moving east over the Sierra Nevada, the region becomes notably drier.

Inland you'll discover the more desert climes of Seville and Córdoba, where temperatures range 15-30°C (59-86°F), averaging 17°C (62°F) in winter and 30°C (86°F) in summer. The semi-arid desert climate occasionally encounters the chergui, the hot Saharan winds that can push temperatures well beyond 32°C (90°F). It is not uncommon for there to be stretches of two or three weeks at a time where temperatures are over 38°C (100°F). During these summer months, Córdoba is locally known as the "frying pan of Europe."

In the mountains there is a more varied seasonal cycle. Four distinct seasons bring cold temperatures, occasional snow, and heavy rain showers in winter, especially above 1,200 m (4,000 ft). Nights at these elevations frequently dip below freezing. Spring and fall emerge as the optimal seasons for exploring these regions, featuring moderate temperatures and a lower chance of rain. Granada, nestled in the eastern part, sees lighter rainfall, emphasizing the arid influence of the mountains. While winters remain mild, it's wise to pack accordingly, as nights can be chilly and dip below freezing.

ENVIRONMENTAL ISSUES

Andalusia, like most everywhere else in the world, faces a range of specific environmental challenges and issues. Generally, Andalusia has been vulnerable to the impacts of climate change, including rising temperatures, altered precipitation patterns, and the increased frequency of extreme weather events. These changes can have significant implications for agriculture, water resources, and ecosystems.

Water Scarcity

Andalusia is characterized by a semi-arid to arid climate in many areas, particularly inland. This has led to several challenges related to water scarcity. Increasing demand for water, coupled with periodic droughts, puts pressure on water resources.

Deforestation and Habitat Loss

Urbanization, agriculture, and infrastructure development contribute to deforestation and habitat loss in Andalusia. This poses a threat to the region's biodiversity, including native plant and animal species.

Air Pollution

Urban areas in Andalusia, especially larger cities like Seville and Granada, face challenges related to air pollution. Vehicle emissions, industrial activities, and other sources contribute to the presence of pollutants in the air.

Waste Management

Increasing levels of waste generation, including plastic waste, pose challenges for waste management in the region. There are several sustainable waste disposal practices and recycling initiatives to mitigate the environmental impact, though there is a long way to go.

Tourism Pressure

While tourism is a significant economic driver for Andalusia, it can also contribute to environmental challenges, particularly regarding water resources and plastic waste. In turn, these have caused damage to environmental and cultural heritage sites. Practicing sustainable tourism is a way you can work to lessen your travel footprint!

Plants and Animals

TREES

The region's climate varies from coastal areas with a Mediterranean climate to more inland areas with a continental climate, influencing the types of trees that thrive there. Here are some common trees found in Andalusia.

Cork oak *(Quercus suber)*: These trees are notable for their thick, corky bark. The cork harvested from these trees is used in various industries, including wine production and as cork material for stoppers and other products.

Holm oak *(Quercus ilex)*: Holm oaks are evergreen trees that thrive in the Mediterranean climate. They are well adapted to the region's conditions and are often found in natural landscapes as well as cultivated areas.

Cypress (*Cupressus* spp.): Cypress trees, with their tall, slender form, are commonly used in landscaping and can be found in both rural and urban areas.

Aleppo pines *(Pinus halepensis)*: Pine forests, dominated by Aleppo pines, are common in some parts of Andalusia, especially in the mountainous areas. These trees contribute to the region's biodiversity and play a role in preventing soil erosion.

Citrus: In the more temperate coastal areas, you'll find citrus orchards with orange *(Citrus sinensis)* and lemon *(Citrus limon)* trees. These fruits are an essential part of Andalusian agriculture.

Almond *(Prunus dulcis)*: Almond trees are cultivated in Andalusia for their nuts. The region is known for its almond orchards, and almond blossoms add a touch of beauty to the landscape during the flowering season.

Carob *(Ceratonia siliqua)*: Carob trees are native to the Mediterranean region and are cultivated in Andalusia. The pods produced by these trees have various uses, including as a chocolate substitute and in the production of animal feed.

Eucalyptus (*Eucalyptus* spp.): While not native, eucalyptus trees are found in some areas of Andalusia, particularly in plantations. They were introduced for their fast growth and are used in the production of timber and paper.

Olive *(Olea europaea)*: Andalusia is renowned for its olive groves, and olive trees are a ubiquitous sight in the region. The olives produced in Andalusia are used to make high-quality olive oil, a significant part of the region's agricultural economy.

FLOWERS AND PLANTS

Andalusia's diverse climate contributes to a rich variety of flora. Here are a few notable flowers and plants that you can find in Andalusia.

Bougainvillea (*Bougainvillea* spp.): With its vibrant and colorful bracts, bougainvillea is a common sight in Andalusia, adorning gardens, streets, and buildings.

Jasmine (*Jasminum* spp.): Jasmine is appreciated for its fragrant white flowers. It is often used in gardens and balconies, adding a delightful scent to the air.

Lavender (*Lavandula* spp.): Lavender's aromatic purple spikes are well suited to the region's climate. It's often cultivated for its scent and is used in various products like essential oils and sachets.

Rosemary *(Rosmarinus officinalis):* This fragrant herb is commonly found in Andalusian landscapes. It's not only used in culinary applications but also appreciated for its ornamental value.

Iris (*Iris* spp.): Wild irises can be found in natural settings, adding a splash of wildflower color to meadows and hillsides.

Almond blossoms *(Prunus dulcis):* In late winter and early spring, almond trees burst into bloom with beautiful pink or white blossoms, creating a stunning landscape.

Aloe vera *(Aloe barbadensis miller):* Known for its medicinal properties, aloe vera is cultivated in Andalusia for its succulent leaves. It's used in various skin-care products.

Basil *(Ocimum basilicum):* Basil is not only a popular culinary herb but is also grown for its aromatic leaves in gardens and pots.

Cacti and succulents: In the drier areas of Andalusia, various cacti and succulents are well-adapted to the arid conditions.

Wisteria (*Wisteria* spp.): Wisteria vines with cascading clusters of purple or white flowers are often planted for their decorative appeal.

Geraniums (*Pelargonium* spp.): Geraniums are popular for adding color to gardens and balconies with their bright and varied blooms.

Oleander *(Nerium oleander):* Oleander is a hardy, though poisonous, evergreen shrub with colorful flowers, commonly found in gardens and along roadsides.

Wildflowers: Andalusia's diverse landscapes, including mountain ranges and natural parks, boast a variety of wildflowers, such as poppies, daisies, and thistles.

VEGETATION ZONES

Andalusia, being a region with diverse topography and climates, exhibits multiple vegetation zones. The primary vegetation zones in Andalusia are influenced by factors such as altitude, proximity to the coast, and the overall climate.

Coastal dunes and wetlands: The coastal areas of Andalusia feature dune systems with vegetation adapted to sandy conditions. Additionally, wetlands and salt marshes along the coast support a unique set of plants adapted to brackish water, including halophytes and salt-tolerant species.

Riverine vegetation: Along rivers and streams, vegetation has adapted to the moist conditions. Willows, poplars, and other riparian species thrive in these areas, creating lush habitats.

Mediterranean scrubland: This is the dominant vegetation zone, and it covers a significant portion of Andalusia. It consists of low, dense shrubs adapted to the Mediterranean climate, such as lavender, thyme, rosemary, and various aromatic herbs.

Urban vegetation: In urban areas, you'll find a mix of ornamental plants, street trees, and green spaces. Parks and gardens are often adorned with flowering plants and trees.

Cork oak and holm oak forests: These forests are common in the mountainous areas of Andalusia. Cork oak and holm oak are evergreen trees that form dense woodlands. These forests are economically important, as cork from cork oaks is harvested, and holm oak acorns are a food source for wildlife and Iberian pigs.

Pine forests: In higher elevations and mountainous areas, pine forests are dominated by species like Aleppo pine and Scots pine. These forests play a role in preventing soil erosion and are home to many bird species.

Alpine vegetation: In the highest elevations, particularly in the Sierra Nevada mountain range, you'll find alpine vegetation, including hardy plants adapted to colder temperatures, such as various grasses, sedges, and alpine flowers.

MAMMALS

Horses and bulls. These are often the first two mammals travelers think of when they think of Andalusia, and rightly so. These two are embedded in much of the local culture and history. The Andalusian horse, known for its elegance and agility, is a breed that originated in the Iberian Peninsula. These horses have played a significant role in Spanish history and are admired for their strength and versatility. They are often associated with traditional equestrian events such as dressage. Toros bravos, or brave bulls, are raised specifically for their aggressiveness and use in bullfighting.

Beyond the horses and bulls, there are a few other mammals to look out for. The Iberian lynx is one of the most endangered wild cat species in the world. Andalusia is a critical habitat for this elusive feline. Conservation efforts are underway to protect and restore the population of the Iberian lynx in the region. If you are in the mountains, there is a decent chance you will spot the Iberian ibex, or Spanish ibex. This is a wild goat species native to the Iberian Peninsula that inhabits rocky mountainous areas, including the Sierra Nevada.

In the grasslands, scrublands, and agricultural areas, the European rabbit is commonly found, hunted, and served for dinner. It plays a crucial role in the region's ecosystems, serving as prey for various predators.

Brave Bulls

The toro bravo, or brave bull, is an iconic symbol of Spain, and it is closely associated with the practice of bullfighting. Andalusia is home to many ranches that breed and raise the famous toros bravos. They are primarily known for their strength, agility, and distinctive appearance. These bulls have a muscular build, a convex profile, and sharp, upward-pointing horns. The breed is well-adapted to the harsh conditions of the Spanish landscape.

The brave bulls are the stars of traditional Spanish bullfights, known as corridas. The bullfighting spectacle involves a matador facing the bull in a series of ritualized encounters that culminate in the matador attempting to bring down the bull with a well-placed sword. The bulls' bravery and strength are central to the spectacle. Bulls are selectively bred for their aggressive and combative nature in the bullring. Traits such as their ability to charge, to respond to the movements of the matador, and to exhibit bravery during the fight are essential.

In recent years, there has been increased attention to the conservation of the Spanish fighting bull breed. Some organizations and ranches work to preserve the genetic diversity of bulls and ensure the continuation of this cultural tradition. Bullfighting, including the breeding and use of the brave bulls, is a controversial practice, with strong opinions both in favor of its cultural significance and against it due to animal welfare concerns. The debate surrounding bullfighting continues to be a topic of discussion in Spain and beyond.

Pigs

The Iberian pig, native to the Iberian Peninsula, is a prized breed known for its exceptional meat quality and unique flavor. Iberian pigs are typically black or dark gray, with a slender and elongated body. They have black hooves, which is a distinctive feature, though their most recognizable trait is the large, floppy ears that almost cover their eyes.

One of the most significant factors influencing the flavor of Iberian pork is the pig's diet. In particular, pigs raised for high-quality Iberian ham are often fed a diet that includes acorns (bellotas). This gives the meat a rich, nutty flavor. The montanera (fattening season) is a crucial period when Iberian pigs are released to graze on open pastures and feed on fallen acorns. This natural diet contributes to the marbling and distinct taste of their meat.

Perhaps the most famous product derived from Iberian pigs is jamón ibérico (Iberian ham), a cured ham that is a delicacy in Spanish cuisine. Jamón ibérico is often classified into different grades based on the pig's diet and lifestyle, with the highest quality associated with pigs that have exclusively fed on acorns during the montanera.

SEALIFE

Over 500 marine species inhabit the Mediterranean coast. Numerous marine centers dotted along the Mediterranean coast delve deep into the sealife of the region. A well-known pod of orcas is found along the Strait of Gibraltar and into the Mediterranean. They have caused havoc in recent years, breaking rudders from pleasure boats, yachts, and fishing vessels. Several vessels have been disabled because of this behavior, likely a form of play on the part of the orcas. The Mediterranean monk seal, one of the rarest seal species, can occasionally be spotted along the coasts of Andalusia.

BIRDS

Andalusia's wetlands and seasonal lakes attract large flocks of pink flamingos. These elegant birds use the marshes and lagoons as breeding and feeding grounds, creating a spectacular sight for bird watchers, usually in the spring and fall months, while in the summer you can look for the European bee-eater, a colorful migratory bird known for its vibrant plumage and distinctive feeding behavior of catching insects, including bees, in flight. Year-round you will find the Spanish imperial eagle, also known as the Iberian imperial eagle, a large bird of prey native to the Iberian Peninsula.

REPTILES

It wouldn't be a trip to Andalusia if you didn't see the Andalusian wall lizard. This species is endemic to the Iberian Peninsula and is adapted to a variety of habitats, including rocky areas and scrublands. It has a long, slim body around 6 cm (2.5 in) in length. They mostly feed on different invertebrates, like beetles, flies, and ants. It's one of over 30 lizards you can find in Andalusia, including the common (and adorable!) Mediterranean wall gecko. If you look closely, you might just discover the European chameleon; however, as it is known for changing color and blending in with its surroundings, you'll have to look very carefully!

Of the few indigenous snakes, you are most likely to come across the Montepellier snake and viperine snake. Neither is harmful to humans, though both can grow several feet in length.

AMPHIBIANS

In the rivers you'll likely see the heads of Moorish terrapins, a freshwater turtle, bobbing in the water. European pond terrapin and Greek tortoise sightings are rare in the lakes and rivers. Along the Mediterranean, encounters with loggerhead sea turtles are unlikely though have been known to happen.

INSECTS AND ARACHNIDS

In the cities, you likely won't spot anything more than common ants and spiders. In some parts of the old cities, you might run across a few cockroaches. It is in the countryside where you'll usually find some more interesting bugs. The European mantis is common, as is the Spanish moon moth, a large moth known for its decorative coloration. You can find Iberian honeybees, blue-winged grasshoppers, and Spanish festoons, a butterfly with brightly colored yellow and black wings. Meanwhile, you might glimpse a tarantula wolf spider lurking in a hole in the ground or step near a camel spider, which sounds scary, but these eight-legged beasts are entirely harmless, at least to humans.

While relatively uncommon, the black widow spider can be found in Andalusia. It is venomous, and its bite can be harmful to humans.

History

Andalusia offers plenty for armchair historians, from fossils and findings of Paleolithic period human activity to a busy timeline of warring ideologies, communities, and nations that have all found reason to plant their proverbial flags in this diverse, uniquely situated corner of the world. Andalusia's history straddles empires from Europe, Africa, and even the distant Middle East, and it informs what the region is today.

ANCIENT CIVILIZATION

The Iberians, an ancient pre-Roman civilization, played a pivotal role in shaping the cultural and archaeological landscape of Andalusia during the formative period of the first millennium BCE. The origin of "Iberian" as a name is thought to have roots in the pre-Roman languages spoken by the indigenous people of the region. The Iberian Peninsula derives its name from these early inhabitants, and the term "Iberian" has been used by historians and archaeologists to refer to both the people and the cultural and archaeological aspects associated with this ancient civilization.

This indigenous group inhabited the region, leaving discernible evidence in the remnants uncovered at archaeological sites, particularly exemplified by the ancient dolmens in the city of Antequera, which revealed a trove of artifacts showcasing the sophistication and intricacy of Iberian culture. Among these findings, distinctive pottery and intricate metalwork have been unearthed, attesting to the advanced artistic and technological achievements of the Iberian society. The dolmens of Antequera stand in testament to the complexity of their societal organization and urban development.

As the Iberians thrived in Andalusia, their historical narrative intersected with the arrival of the Carthaginians, adding another layer to the region's cultural narrative. The Carthaginians, a maritime power originating from the ancient city of Carthage in North Africa, established coastal settlements and trading posts along the Andalusian coastline. This encounter between the Iberians and Carthaginians engendered a dynamic cultural exchange, influencing artistic expression, trade practices, and societal dynamics in Andalusia. The coastal settlements became pivotal hubs for economic activities, facilitating the exchange of commodities and ideas between the indigenous Iberians and the seafaring Carthaginians. Consequently, this interplay of civilizations during the first millennium BCE laid the foundation for the diverse cultural exchange that would continue to evolve through subsequent historical epochs.

UNDER ROMAN RULE

The 800-year epoch of Roman dominion over Andalusia, spanning from the 3rd century BCE to the 5th century CE, was a transformative period, characterized by profound socio-cultural, economic, and architectural developments. Following the Roman conquest of the Iberian Peninsula, the establishment of thriving urban centers, monumental infrastructure, and the assimilation of Roman cultural elements played a pivotal role in shaping Andalusian society. One of the foremost

Historical Timeline

Paleolithic Period (2.5 million-10,000 BCE)	Evidence of human presence in Andalusia dates to the Paleolithic period, with cave paintings and artifacts found in places like St. Michael's Cave in Gibraltar.
Neolithic Period (10,000-2,000 BCE)	Agricultural practices and the establishment of settled communities mark this period. The Antequera Dolmens Archaeological Site, a UNESCO World Heritage Site in the province of Málaga, comprises megalithic structures believed to date back to this era.
Phoenician and Carthaginian Period (circa 9th-3rd centuries BCE)	Phoenician traders and settlers establish coastal colonies, such as Gadir (modern-day Cádiz), contributing to early urbanization.
Roman Period (circa 3rd century BCE-5th century CE)	Andalusia is annexed into the Roman Empire, leading to the construction of cities, roads, and infrastructure. Under the Romans, Andalusia was known as Baetica, a prosperous Roman province. Two Roman emperors, Trajan (reigned 98 CE to 117 CE) and Hadrian (reigned 117 CE to 138 CE), hailed from Itálica, modern-day Santiponce, near today's Seville.
Visigothic Period (5th-8th centuries)	After the fall of the Roman Empire, the Visigoths take control of the Iberian Peninsula, including Andalusia.
711 CE	General Tariq ibn Ziyad crosses the Strait of Gibraltar with his army, storming into Andalusia from Morocco, quickly establishing the Umayyad caliphate.
Islamic Period Begins (8th-15th centuries)	The Umayyad caliphate establishes control over Andalusia in the 8th century. Construction of the Córdoba mosque begins in 785 during the rule of the Umayyad caliph Abd al-Rahman I and is expanded on over successive Muslim rulers.
Caliphate of Córdoba (10th century)	A period of cultural and intellectual flourishing, with Córdoba as a center of learning and commerce, likely the most powerful city in Europe.
Taifa Kingdoms (11th century):	The caliphate breaks into smaller kingdoms after the decline of successive rulers.
Almoravid and Almohad Dynasties (11th-13th centuries)	Amazigh (Berber) dynasties from Morocco take control of parts of Andalusia.

Nasrid Kingdom of Granada (13th-15th centuries)	The last Muslim stronghold in the Iberian Peninsula, with the famous Alhambra palace of Granada, is gradually conquered during the Reconquista.
Reconquista and Christian Period (13th-15th centuries)	Over a period of two centuries, the Christian reconquest of Andalusia from Muslim rule takes place with the beginning of construction on the Seville Cathedral in 1402, marking a new chapter.
1492	The Catholic monarchs, Ferdinand II of Aragon and Isabella I of Castile, complete the Reconquista with the capture of Granada. Also, Christopher Columbus sets sail from Andalusia and reaches the Americas.
Spain's "Golden Era" (15th-17th centuries)	Also thought of as the "Age of Exploration," beginning with the fall of Granada and successful return of Columbus, Spain's Golden Age is powered by its expansion into the Americas and around the world.
Early Modern Period (17th–18th centuries)	Andalusia experiences economic growth through trade, particularly with the Americas. Seville becomes a major trading hub and world power.
19th Century	Napoleonic invasion: Andalusia faces occupation by French forces during the Peninsular War.
Spanish Civil War (1936-1939)	Andalusia played a significant role in this conflict as the fascist Franco regime takes control of Spain.
Post-Franco Era	After the death of Francisco Franco in 1975, Spain transitions to a democratic monarchy. Adolfo Suarez becomes Spain's first democratically elected prime minister in 1976.
2010	Spain's national men's soccer team wins its first World Cup.
2014	King Juan Carlos I, citing personal reasons, abdicates in favor of his son, who accedes to the throne as Felipe VI.
2023	Spain's national women's soccer team wins its first World Cup.

exemplars of Roman influence is the ancient city of Itálica, situated in today's Santiponce, close to present-day Seville, which emerged as a bastion of Roman civilization in the heart of Andalusia.

The archaeological remnants of Itálica showcase the architectural grandeur and urban planning prowess of the Romans. Commencing as a military encampment during the Second Punic War, Itálica burgeoned into a flourishing city, characterized by expansive residential quarters, public spaces, and majestic structures such as the amphitheater, which stands as one of the largest of its kind in the Roman world. The mosaic-laden floors of domestic dwellings in Itálica, adorned with intricate designs and motifs, underscore the sophistication and artistic refinement that permeated Roman society. You'll find pieces of the old Roman empire in Cádiz, Málaga, and Córdoba and scattered throughout the Andalusian countryside.

The Romanization of Andalusia extended beyond monumental constructions to encompass economic practices, governance, and cultural assimilation. The establishment of agricultural estates, known as latifundia, heralded a shift in land management and production techniques. The implementation of Roman legal and administrative frameworks further solidified the integration of Andalusia into the broader Roman Empire. The proliferation of Roman gods in the religious pantheon of the region attests to the syncretic amalgamation of indigenous beliefs with those of the conquering power.

Nevertheless, the decline of the Roman Empire in the 5th century CE heralded a new era, marked by the successive waves of Visigothic and Islamic influences that would come to define the subsequent epochs of Andalusian history.

VISIGOTH TAKEOVER

The Visigothic presence in Andalusia, spanning from the 5th to the early 8th century CE, is another significant chapter. Following the decline of the Roman Empire, the Visigoths, a Germanic tribe, established their dominion over the Iberian Peninsula, and Andalusia became an integral part of their realm. The Visigothic era was marked by a fusion of Germanic and Roman influences, resulting in a unique socio-cultural amalgamation.

The Visigothic rulers, based primarily in Toledo, faced the challenge of governing a diverse population that included both indigenous Iberians and the conquerors themselves. This period witnessed the codification of Visigothic law under King Recceswinth, known as the "Liber Iudiciorum," which blended Roman legal principles with customary Visigothic laws. The Visigoths also played a role in the religious evolution of the region, with the conversion to Nicene Christianity.

Despite their political consolidation, the Visigothic rule in Andalusia was not without internal strife and external pressures. The emergence of religious controversies, including debates over Arianism and Catholicism, underscored the societal complexities within the Visigothic kingdom. Furthermore, the Visigoths faced external threats, notably from the Byzantine Empire in the east and the expanding Islamic forces from the south.

The Visigothic dominion in Andalusia came to an abrupt end in 711 CE with the Islamic Umayyad conquest led by Tariq ibn Ziyad. The Battle of Guadalete, with the death of the Visigoth king Roderic, as well as much of the Visigothic nobility, marked the culmination of the Visigothic defeat. This led to the establishment of Islamic rule in the region and the commencement of the Islamic era in Andalusian history.

ISLAMIC RULE OF ANDALUSIA

Beginning with the arrival of Tariq ibn Ziyad in 711 CE, the page turns to the Islamic rule imported across the Strait of Gibraltar. The rule took hold around much of the Iberian Peninsula and lasted until 1492 CE. These 781 years of rule are renowned as a remarkable epoch in the region's history, characterized by a flourishing civilization marked by significant advances in science, philosophy, arts, and architecture. The establishment of Islamic governance allowed Andalusia to become a vibrant center of Islamic culture under various caliphates, emirates, and taifas.

Córdoba, as the capital of the Umayyad caliphate of Al-Andalus, emerged as a preeminent cultural and intellectual hub in medieval Europe. The Great Mosque of Córdoba, an architectural masterpiece, exemplified the fusion of Islamic and Western aesthetics, featuring intricate horseshoe arches, ornate decoration, and a vast hypostyle prayer hall. The city's streets buzzed with scholarly activities, as Córdoba became a beacon of learning, home to illustrious thinkers like Averroes and Maimonides.

Under the rule of Abd al-Rahman III, Córdoba reached its zenith in the 10th century. The caliphate of Córdoba was a beacon of religious tolerance, fostering an environment where Muslims, Christians, and Jews coexisted, contributing to a rich tapestry of cultural exchange. Under al-Rahman III, the self-proclaimed caliph, a new city was born: Medina Azahara, with an unrivaled network of irrigation and gardens thought to be one of the most beautiful in the world—though like all flowers, it was fated to wilt. In less than a hundred years, Medina Azahara was abandoned and the caliphate disintegrated into smaller taifas (independent Muslim principalities).

From the 11th century, there was a marked period of political fragmentation, but it also saw the flowering of arts and sciences in various centers like Seville and Granada. The Alhambra, a palatial fortress in Granada, stands as an enduring testament to Nasrid artistry of this time, featuring intricate geometric patterns, arabesques, and serene courtyards.

The Islamic rule of Andalusia, known as Al-Andalus, lasted until the completion of the Reconquista in 1492, when the Catholic monarchs Ferdinand and Isabella recaptured Granada. The fall of Granada marked the end of Muslim rule in the Iberian Peninsula. Despite its conclusion, the Islamic period of Andalusia continues to shape the region's identity, and its influence on the European Renaissance thought and knowledge, through translations of Arabic works and the preservation of classical knowledge, is unrivaled.

RECONQUISTA

In a chapter running parallel with the Islamic rule of Spain, we have the equally long history of the Catholic-minded Reconquista. The Reconquista unfolded over centuries, marked by shifting alliances, territorial disputes, and battles that shaped the geopolitical landscape of medieval Iberia. Key milestones include the Battle of Covadonga in 722 CE, often considered the starting point of the Reconquista, and the capture of Toledo in 1085 CE by Alfonso VI of Castile, symbolizing the first reclamation of a significant Islamic stronghold.

As the Reconquista progressed, Christian kingdoms such as Castile, Aragon, and León expanded their territories southward, capturing major cities like Córdoba (1236 CE) and Seville (1248 CE). The culmination of this gradual Catholic Christian advance occurred with the capture of Granada in 1492 CE by the Catholic monarchs Ferdinand and Isabella. The fall of Granada marked the end of Muslim rule in the Iberian Peninsula and the completion of the Reconquista. The Catholic monarchs' entry into Granada, symbolized by the surrender of the Nasrid ruler Boabdil, marked a transformative moment in Spanish history, laying the groundwork for the unification of Spain under a Catholic monarchy and the onset of the Age of Exploration. The Reconquista's impact extended beyond military conquest, shaping the socio-cultural dynamics and religious identity of the Iberian Peninsula until today.

GOLDEN AGE

Spain's Golden Age, the Siglo de Oro, was a period of remarkable cultural, economic, and political flourishing that occurred in Spain during the 16th and 17th centuries. This era is renowned for its significant contributions to literature, art, philosophy, and exploration, making Spain a global powerhouse during this time. The Golden Age is often said to have commenced in the late 15th or early 16th century with the reign of Ferdinand and Isabella, shortly after the completion of the Reconquista in 1492, and extended through the 17th century. During this period, Spain experienced a remarkable expansion of its overseas empire, particularly in the Americas, where Spanish explorers and conquistadors, including Christopher Columbus, Hernán Cortés, and Francisco Pizarro, played pivotal roles in exploring and conquering vast territories.

This was also when the Spanish Inquisition (1478-1834) flourished, prosecuting over 150,000 people and executing around 5,000 of these as heretics. The Spanish Inquisition was originally formed to regulate the religious adherence of those who converted to Catholicism from Judaism or Islam following royal decrees and forced conversions, as the Islamic rulers failed and a stricter Catholic rule took hold. Between 1492 and 1610, more than three million Jews and Muslims fled Spain or were exiled, with many finding their way south, back over the Strait of Gibraltar to modern-day Morocco.

Culturally, the Golden Age is characterized by a flourishing of the arts and literature. It was an age of great Spanish writers, with luminaries like Miguel de Cervantes, the author of *Don Quixote,* considered one of the greatest works of world literature. Playwrights like Lope de Vega and Pedro Calderón de la Barca made significant contributions to Spanish drama, creating enduring masterpieces. The visual arts also thrived, with painters like El Greco and Diego Velázquez leaving their mark on the art world.

Despite the cultural and economic prosperity, the latter part of the Golden Age saw Spain involved in conflicts such as the Thirty Years' War and the decline of its global influence. The death of the last Hapsburg monarch, Charles II, in 1700 marked the end of the Golden Age and the beginning of a new chapter in Spain's history.

18TH AND 19TH CENTURIES

After the Hapsburg rule, Spain underwent a complex series of transformations. The Bourbon Reforms of the 18th century aimed at modernizing the state, influenced by Enlightenment ideas, but faced resistance. The Napoleonic Wars and the subsequent Spanish War of Independence led to the loss of Spanish colonies in the Americas and contributed to nationalist sentiments.

The 19th century was marked by political instability, with conflicts between liberals and conservatives, the turbulent reign of Queen Isabella II, and economic challenges. Attempts at industrialization and modernization were hindered by the loss of colonies and slow economic growth. The late 19th and early 20th centuries witnessed the Regenerationist movement advocating for reforms, and a cultural flourishing known as the Generation of '98 reflected on Spain's identity.

Spain's defeat in the Spanish-American War in 1898 resulted in the loss of its remaining colonies, and the country faced economic difficulties that carried into the 20th century.

20TH-CENTURY WARS

World War I (1914-1918)

Spain remained officially neutral during World War I. While the conflict had profound economic repercussions globally, Spain avoided direct military involvement. The Spanish government pursued a policy of nonintervention, maintaining diplomatic neutrality and seeking to benefit economically from supplying goods to both Allied and Central Powers. Spain's neutrality allowed it to avoid the devastation experienced by many European nations during the war.

Spanish Civil War (1936-1939)

The Spanish Civil War was a pivotal moment in Spain's modern history. It began in 1936 when General Francisco Franco led a military uprising against the democratic Second Spanish Republic. The conflict was characterized by deep political divisions between

Republicans (supporting the republic) and Nationalists (supporting Franco's uprising). Franco received support from Nazi Germany and fascist Italy, while the Soviet Union and international brigades backed the Republicans. The war ended in 1939 with Franco's victory, leading to the establishment of a dictatorial regime that lasted until his death in 1975. The Spanish Civil War is often seen as a precursor to World War II, with some ideological and geopolitical parallels.

World War II (1939-1945)

During World War II, Spain, under Franco's authoritarian rule, officially remained neutral. Franco sought to keep Spain out of the conflict, emphasizing the country's recovery from the devastation of the Spanish Civil War. However, despite its declared neutrality, Spain leaned toward the Axis Powers, particularly Germany and Italy. Economic and diplomatic ties were established with the Axis, and the Blue Division, a Spanish volunteer unit, fought alongside the Germans on the Eastern Front against the Soviet Union. While Spain did not actively engage in combat, its stance during World War II was controversial, and the country faced diplomatic isolation after the war.

FRANCO ERA

Known as the Francoist regime, this was a period marked by political authoritarianism, social conservatism, and diplomatic isolation. After Spain's neutrality in World War II, Franco aimed to consolidate power domestically, fostering a centralized, authoritarian government. The regime suppressed political dissent, banned opposition parties, and imposed strict censorship, creating an environment of political repression. The Falange Española, a far-right party, was a key component of the regime, and Franco held absolute power as head of state and government.

Economically, Franco pursued a policy of autarky, emphasizing self-sufficiency and protectionism. This approach, influenced by the regime's isolation after World War II, led to a closed economy with limited international trade. The economic policies were characterized by state intervention, particularly in heavy industry, and a focus on economic self-sufficiency.

Socially, the Francoist regime promoted a conservative agenda rooted in traditional Catholic values. Civil liberties were restricted, and social policies were conservative, including limitations on divorce, contraception, and women's roles in society. The Catholic Church played a significant role in supporting and legitimizing Franco's rule. The regime also suppressed regional identities, imposing a centralized Spanish identity and limiting autonomy for regions with distinct languages and cultures.

Diplomatically, Spain faced isolation due to its perceived sympathy toward the Axis Powers during World War II. However, as the Cold War unfolded, Franco shifted to a policy of neutrality, distancing Spain from ideological alignment and seeking economic and diplomatic support from the West, particularly the United States.

Franco's death in 1975 marked the end of the regime and initiated a period known as the Spanish Transition. His legacy remains a subject of historical debate, with opinions on his rule ranging from those who view him as a stabilizing force during a tumultuous period to others who criticize the authoritarian methods and social conservatism of his regime.

CONTEMPORARY TIMES

After Franco's death, Spain underwent the Spanish Transition, a process of democratization, with a new constitution adopted in 1978 and the establishment of a constitutional monarchy under King Juan Carlos I. The transition marked a departure from authoritarianism, paving the way for Spain's modern democratic era.

When the 1978 constitution was established, it outlined the framework for a parliamentary monarchy and set the stage for democratic governance. The transition also involved political negotiations and compromises between diverse ideological factions. Key political figures, including Adolfo Suárez, Spain's first democratically elected prime minister (1976–1981), played crucial roles in shaping the democratic path for Spain. The establishment of regional autonomies and the recognition of linguistic and cultural diversity became integral to the new political framework, addressing historical regional grievances.

Spain's entry into the European Union in 1986 marked a significant milestone, symbolizing its integration into the broader European community. The post-Franco era witnessed economic liberalization, modernization, and increased global engagement. Social changes, including advancements in women's rights and LGBTQ+ rights, reflected broader societal shifts.

Spain's post-Franco era has been characterized by sustained economic growth, political stability, and cultural vibrancy. The country's commitment to democratic values, human rights, and regional autonomy has solidified its place as a key player in European and global affairs.

Government and Economy

GOVERNMENT

Organization

Andalusia is an autonomous community within the Kingdom of Spain, governed by a parliamentary system under the Spanish constitution. The regional government operates within a framework that includes an executive branch, a legislative assembly, and a judicial system. The president of the regional government is the head of the executive branch, overseeing the Council of Government, while the Andalusian parliament serves as the legislative body. The judiciary functions independently.

Political Parties

Spain, as a whole, is a constitutional monarchy with a parliamentary system. The political landscape in Andalusia is diverse, with various political parties participating in regional governance. The regional parliament consists of representatives elected by the Andalusian people, and political parties like the Spanish Socialist Workers' Party (PSOE), People's Party (PP), and others play significant roles. In most towns and cities, the PSOE is the most popular party, though in recent years the PP, a conservative party, has gained support.

Elections

Elections in Andalusia follow the Spanish electoral system. The Andalusian parliament is elected by proportional representation, and the political party or coalition with the majority forms the regional government. Elections are crucial in shaping the political direction of the region, with various parties vying for representation.

ECONOMY

Andalusia has a diverse industrial sector, including manufacturing, technology, and renewable energy. Agriculture plays a crucial role in the economy, with the fertile plains and favorable climate supporting the cultivation of olives, citrus fruits, vegetables, and other crops. Traditional practices alongside modern initiatives contribute to the economic vitality of the region.

Tourism is a major economic driver for Andalusia, which attracts visitors with a rich cultural heritage, historic cities, and scenic landscapes. Despite its tourism, Andalusia is still one of the poorest regions of Spain. Most of the wealth is concentrated in the cities of Seville and Málaga, and this is very much apparent. The rural regions have the least

Iberian Ham (Jamón Ibérico)

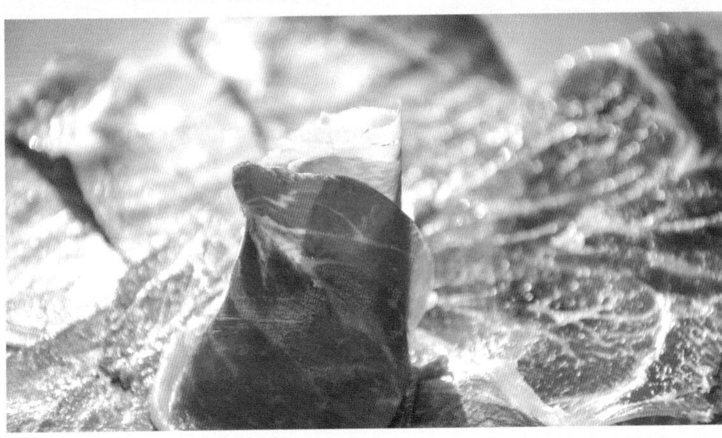

jamón ibérico

Iberian ham is a delicacy highly appreciated for its rich, nutty flavor, and the marbling of fat gives the meat a smooth texture. The curing process enhances the taste, and the resulting hams are often enjoyed thinly sliced as tapas (appetizers), common throughout Spain.

The Iberian pig is known for its dark skin, slender legs, and the ability to store fat within its muscle tissues. The two main breeds associated with jamón ibérico are the purebred Iberian pig (black hooves) and the crossbred pig (crossed with Duroc or another breed, with white hooves).

One of the key defining factors in the flavor profile of jamón ibérico is the pig's diet. Traditional production methods involve allowing the pigs to roam freely in oak forests and feed on a diet largely composed of acorns (bellotas). This acorn-rich diet contributes to the unique taste and marbling of the meat. The curing process is meticulous and time-consuming. The hams are salted and then air-dried for an extended period, sometimes up to several years. During this time, the hams undergo a gradual curing and aging process in carefully controlled conditions.

TYPES OF IBERIAN HAM

Iberian ham is often classified based on the purity of the Iberian breed and the feeding regimen. The highest quality is often given to hams from purebred Iberian pigs that have been acorn-fed during the montanera (fattening season).

- **Jamón ibérico de bellota:** This is considered the highest-quality Iberian ham. Pigs used for this type are free-range and primarily feed on acorns during the montanera.
- **Jamón ibérico de recebo:** Pigs are fed a combination of acorns and supplementary feed.
- **Jamón ibérico de cebo de campo:** Pigs are raised in the open but are not free to roam as widely as those producing bellota hams. They are typically fed a combination of grains and grass.
- **Jamón ibérico de cebo:** Pigs are raised in a more confined environment and are fed a diet of grains and commercial feed.

amount of wealth, with jobs related to agriculture being most common.

Agriculture and Food Products

Andalusia is known as the "Orchard of Europe" due to its fertile lands and favorable climate. The agricultural sector is a cornerstone of the region's economy, producing crops such as olives, citrus fruits, tomatoes, and cereals. Olive oil, in particular, is a major export, with Andalusia being a global leader in its production. Beyond primary agricultural production, Andalusia has a robust agri-food processing industry. Olive oil mills, wineries, and food processing plants are integral to the transformation of raw agricultural products into market-ready goods.

Fishing

The extensive coastline along the Mediterranean and the Atlantic Ocean supports a thriving fishing industry. Andalusian ports, including those in Cádiz, play a crucial role in the processing and export of fish and seafood products.

Tourism

The stunning landscapes, historical landmarks, and vibrant culture make Andalusia a prime tourist destination. The tourism industry encompasses a wide range of services, including hospitality, guided tours, and cultural experiences. Cities like Seville, Granada, and Córdoba attract millions of visitors each year, contributing significantly to the local economy.

The region has seen significant growth in tourist numbers over the years, contributing substantially to the local economy. Andalusia welcomed 12.1 million international travelers in 2019. By 2023, it had nearly matched these numbers, 11.8 million, after the global pandemic. If Andalusia were a country, it would be 25th worldwide in terms of popularity of international travel.

Renewable Energy

Andalusia is a leader in renewable energy production, especially in the field of solar power. Vast solar farms harness the region's abundant sunlight to generate clean energy. Wind energy projects also contribute to the sustainable energy mix, aligning with Spain's commitment to renewable resources.

Aerospace and Technology

The aerospace industry has a notable presence in Andalusia, with companies specializing in aircraft manufacturing and technological innovation. Aerospace research centers and industrial parks, such as the Aerospace Technology Park (Aerópolis) in Seville, foster advancements in the sector.

Automotive Manufacturing

The automotive sector is a key player in Andalusia's industrial landscape. The region hosts several automobile manufacturing plants, contributing to Spain's position as one of Europe's top car producers. Companies like SEAT, a Spanish car manufacturer, have production facilities in Andalusia.

Textiles and Apparel

Textile and apparel manufacturing have a historical presence in Andalusia. The industry includes the production of clothing, textiles, and accessories, with a focus on both traditional craftsmanship and modern design.

Logistics and Transportation

Given its strategic location as a gateway between Europe and Africa, Andalusia plays a vital role in logistics and transportation. Ports, airports, and a well-developed road network facilitate the movement of goods and people.

Cultural and Creative Industries

The rich cultural heritage of Andalusia contributes to a vibrant creative sector. Industries such as art, design, film production, and cultural events play a role in shaping the region's identity and attracting cultural tourism.

People and Culture

DEMOGRAPHY AND DIVERSITY

The population of Andalusia is ethnically diverse, with influences from various historical periods, including Moorish rule, Roman occupation, and subsequent interactions with other Mediterranean cultures. This diversity is reflected in the cultural heritage, traditions, and architecture of the region. While the majority of the population in Andalusia is Roman Catholic, the region has historical connections to Islam, Judaism, and other religious traditions. The legacy of religious diversity is evident in the architecture and cultural practices. The Gitano community, also known as the Romani people (formerly called Gypsies, a term some find derogatory), has a historical presence in Andalusia. They have contributed to the cultural richness of the region, and their influence can be seen in various aspects of Andalusian life.

SUBCULTURES

It's little surprise that Andalusia, with its long history and cultural richness, is home to subcultures that reflect its diverse landscapes, traditions, and influences. From the passionate rhythms of flamenco in the south to the mountainous traditions of the Alpujarras, each subculture contributes to the vibrant mosaic that defines Andalusian identity.

- **Flamenco culture:** Flamenco, with its soul-stirring music, expressive dance, and heartfelt singing, is not just an art form but a way of life in Andalusia. Seville, Jerez de la Frontera, and Granada are hubs where flamenco aficionados and artists converge.
- **Romani influence:** The Sacromonte neighborhood in Granada is synonymous with the Gitano culture of Andalusia. Known for its cave dwellings and intimate flamenco performances, Sacromonte provides a unique glimpse into the Romani way of life.
- **Moorish heritage:** The legacy of Al-Andalus and the Moors, who once ruled Andalusia, is still evident in the architecture of the Alhambra as well as the intricate tilework and geometric patterns that adorn many buildings.
- **Alpujarras mountain culture:** The Alpujarras, nestled in the Sierra Nevada mountains, harbor a subculture shaped by the remote location. Whitewashed villages, terraced fields, and a slower pace of life characterize this region.
- **Fishing communities:** Andalusia's extensive coastline is dotted with fishing communities that have preserved their maritime traditions. Many coastal towns, such as Cádiz and Tarifa, offer a glimpse into the life of fishers and the culinary delights of fresh seafood.
- **Equestrian culture:** Jerez de la Frontera, in particular, is renowned for its equestrian traditions. The Royal Andalusian School of Equestrian Art preserves the art of classical dressage, and events like the Feria del Caballo highlight the importance of horses in Andalusian culture.
- **Olive oil culture:** Many of the towns around Córdoba, such as Lucena, offer a subculture centered around the cultivation and production of this liquid gold. Olive groves stretch across the landscape, and the region celebrates its olive oil heritage.
- **Semana Santa traditions:** Semana Santa (Holy Week, Easter Week) is a time of profound religious significance in Andalusia. Cities like Seville and Málaga host processions, blending religious fervor with artistic expressions through elaborate floats and traditional attire.

- **Bullfighting tradition:** The corrida de toros, or bullfighting, is deeply ingrained in Spanish tradition and has a notable presence in Andalusia. Cities like Ronda and Seville host iconic bullrings where this controversial art form continues to be a part of cultural discussions.

RELIGION

The dynamics of faith in Andalusia underwent significant shifts during the Christian Reconquista. The gradual Christian reconquest of the Iberian Peninsula from Muslim rule led to changes in religious demographics. Córdoba's grand mosque was transformed into a cathedral, symbolizing the transition from Islamic to Catholic Christian influence, a decision that remains controversial to this day. For centuries Muslims and Jews were forcibly converted to Catholicism, killed, or fled for their lives.

The Abrahamic Faiths of Andalusia

The roots of Abrahamic faiths in Andalusia trace back to the early centuries of the Common Era, when diverse communities coexisted in relative harmony. During the Roman and Visigothic periods, Jews, Christians, and later Muslims found a shared space on the Iberian Peninsula, contributing to a multicultural milieu. It was in the early days of the Common Era, during the period of Roman rule, when it's thought Catholicism likely first arrived to the Iberian Peninsula. Early Christian communities established themselves in various regions of Spain, initially facing periods of both acceptance and persecution under Roman rule. With the conversion of Emperor Constantine to Christianity in the early 4th century, Christianity gained official status within the Roman Empire, further facilitating its spread throughout Spain. By the end of the Roman era and the subsequent Visigothic rule, Christianity, particularly Catholicism, had become firmly established as the dominant religion in the region, laying the foundation for its enduring influence in Spanish history and culture.

The transformative era of Al-Andalus (711–1492) witnessed a flourishing of knowledge, arts, and sciences under Islamic rule. Córdoba, the capital, became a beacon of intellectual enlightenment, where scholars from different faiths engaged in a vibrant exchange of ideas. The Umayyad caliphate's tolerance allowed Christians and Jews to participate in the cultural renaissance, fostering an environment where the works of Aristotle, Plato, and Galen were translated, preserved, and expanded upon.

The Jewish community, particularly during the Islamic era, played a pivotal role in the intellectual and cultural development of Andalusia. Jewish scholars like Maimonides emerged as key figures, contributing to philosophy, medicine, and literature.

Since the Reconquista, Catholicism has exerted a significant influence on both societal norms and individual beliefs, though today Andalusia lives in a concept of "convivencia," or coexistence, going back to what had defined much of Andalusia's rich history. Amid political and religious changes, there were instances of mutual influence, where traditions and knowledge from each Abrahamic faith blended. This cultural syncretism is evident in the architecture, art, and literature of the region, something many Andalusians today are quite proud of. The Semana Santa processions, with their heavy Catholic overtures, intermingle with the architectural remnants of Islamic rule and festivals celebrating the Muslim heritage. Recently, there has been a newer reclamation of Andalusia's long Jewish history, preserved in the narrow alleys of ancient Jewish quarters. Through the ebb and flow of religious dominance, the Abrahamic faiths of Andalusia have gone from the early days of shared spaces and the intellectual zenith of Al-Andalus to outright war and bloodshed. These days, you'll find more of an appreciation for the interconnectedness of Judaism, Christianity, and Islam than anything else.

LANGUAGE

Spanish (Castilian) is the official language spoken in Andalusia. However, the region is known for its distinct accent and local variations in language, contributing to the linguistic diversity of Spain.

Arabic Influence

The influence of Arabic on Spanish, in general, is quite significant and can be traced back to the period of Islamic rule in the Iberian Peninsula. While some Arabic words have evolved in form and pronunciation over time, others have been preserved relatively unchanged in Spanish. A great example of an Arabic word that has evolved over time is Gibraltar, the name of the British territory west of Málaga. In fact, the original Arabic name is Jabal Tariq (Mount Tariq), named after the general who stormed into Andalusia and began the period of Islamic rule, Tariq Ibn Ziyad. Jabal Tariq was shortened to "Jabaltar" and eventually what we know today as Gibraltar.

Other common place-names you might think of as Spanish have Arabic roots. As an example, you probably know the city of Guadalajara. In fact, this is a fully Arabic name. In Arabic, "guad" (origin: ouad) means "river" and "al-ajara" (origin: al-hijara) means "the rocks." Thus we have "River of the Rocks." Any name you say beginning with "guad" in Spanish, you can understand originally meant "river" in Arabic.

In fact, anything with an "al" prefix stems from the Arabic definite article. You find that "al" has been retained in many Spanish words, such as "alcohol," "almohada," and "alcalde" (mayor). Many place-names in Spain and other Spanish-speaking regions start with "al," such as Almería, Alhambra, and Albacete.

Other common ways in which Spanish has Arabic origins include words related to science, mathematics, architecture, agriculture, and daily life. Examples include "azúcar" (sugar), "aceituna" (olive), "alcohol," "almohada" (pillow), and "naranja" (orange); some of them, like "alcohol," we even use in English.

LITERATURE

During the period of Islamic rule in Al-Andalus (711-1492), the region experienced its first flourishing literary culture. Arabic literature, in particular, reached great heights with the works of poets, philosophers, and scholars. Notable figures include poets like Ibn Zaydun and Wallada bint al-Mustakfi, as well as philosophers such as Ibn Rushd (Averroes). Andalusian Arabic poetry featured muwashshahat, a form of strophic poetry with a refrain, and zajal, a type of rhymed prose poetry. These poetic forms often explored themes of love, nature, and mysticism.

The Jewish community in Andalusia also made significant contributions to literature during this era. Jewish poets like Solomon Ibn Gabirol and Judah Halevi produced philosophical and religious poetry in Hebrew, often influenced by the cultural milieu of Al-Andalus. The philosophical works of Maimonides are some of the most important pieces of Jewish literature ever written and were composed during this era as well.

In the Christian period following the Reconquista, epic poetry known as mester de juglaría (poetry of the minstrels) celebrated heroic deeds and chivalry. Later, mester de clerecía (poetry of the clergy) emerged, characterized by didactic and moral themes. From this vein of thought, we have *Don Quixote*, penned by Miguel de Cervantes, whose famous duo, Don Quixote and Pancho Sanchez, roamed much of Andalusia.

The 19th century saw the rise of Romantic and costumbrismo literature in Andalusia. Writers like Gustavo Adolfo Bécquer, a Romantic poet, and Serafín Estébanez Calderón, a costumbrista writer, captured the essence of Andalusian landscapes and customs in their works. It was at the very beginning of this era that Washington Irving famously made his way to Granada, where he stayed at the Alhambra and wrote about his time there in his *Tales of the Alhambra*.

A prominent literary movement known as the Generation of '27 emerged in the 20th century. This group of poets, including Federico

Spaghetti Westerns in Andalusia

You've probably heard of "spaghetti westerns." These are a subgenre of western films typically associated with Italian productions, but they were often filmed in various locations, including Andalusia. Andalusia's rugged landscapes, with their desert-like terrain and unique architecture, provided an excellent backdrop for these films, offering a convincing stand-in for the American Wild West.

One of the most famous instances of Andalusia being used as a filming location for spaghetti westerns is the Tabernas Desert, located in the province of Almería. This desert region became known as the "Spanish Hollywood" due to its extensive use as a filming location for numerous westerns during the 1960s and 1970s.

Films like Sergio Leone's *A Fistful of Dollars* (1964), *For a Few Dollars More* (1965), and *The Good, the Bad and the Ugly* (1966), iconic examples of the spaghetti western genre, were partially or entirely filmed in Andalusia. The barren landscapes and architecture of Andalusia, with Moorish-style buildings and old Spanish villages, lent an authentic and visually striking backdrop to these films.

The success of these films helped establish Andalusia as a prime destination for filmmakers seeking to re-create the American West on a budget. The region's affordability made it an attractive alternative to filming in the United States. And some things never change! Even today, many Hollywood productions film in Andalusia, citing its lower cost and striking visuals as reasons. The town of Guadix pays homage to this with a number of director's chairs playfully dotting the city, reminders of the Hollywood heritage of the region.

García Lorca and Rafael Alberti, revitalized Spanish poetry with avant-garde and surrealist influences. Lorca, in particular, celebrated Andalusian folk traditions in his works. At the same time, José María Pemán was making his mark as a poet and in journalism. Just a decade later, the Generation of '36, a group of intellectuals who lived through the Spanish Civil War, brought us María Zambrano. Her philosophical works explore themes such as humanism, exile, and the relationship between reason and passion.

Andalusia continues to be a source of inspiration for contemporary writers. Authors like Antonio Muñoz Molina, a recipient of the Prince of Asturias Award for Literature, and Juan José Millás explore diverse themes in their works. Expats like Chris Stewart, author of *Driving over Lemons,* have equally found inspiration from these lands.

VISUAL ARTS

Alhambra and Islamic Art

The Alhambra in Granada is a treasure trove of Islamic art and architecture. The intricate tilework, geometric patterns, and arabesque designs of the Alhambra's **Nasrid Palaces** are visual marvels that reflect the artistic achievements of Al-Andalus.

Baroque and Renaissance

The **Seville Cathedral,** a UNESCO World Heritage Site, is a stunning example of Gothic and Baroque architecture. Its altarpiece, the largest in the world, is a masterpiece of Renaissance art.

Flamenco Costumes

The visual arts in Andalusia extend to the world of flamenco, where elaborate costumes play a crucial role in the dance performances. Intricate patterns, vibrant colors, and symbolic accessories are integral to the visual spectacle of flamenco.

Pablo Picasso

Born in the city of Málaga in 1881, Picasso spent his formative years in Andalusia before becoming one of the most influential artists of the 20th century. The vibrant colors and geometric patterns of Andalusian folk art, as well as the Moorish art and architecture he encountered, were heavy influences in Picasso's early work.

Contemporary Art Scene

Located in Seville, the **Centro Andaluz de Arte Contemporáneo (CAAC)** is a contemporary art center housed in a former cartuja (monastery). It showcases works by modern Andalusian artists and provides a platform for experimental and innovative art forms.

The **Contemporary Art Center (CAC) of Málaga** is a hub for modern art, featuring works by both local and international artists. It contributes to Málaga's evolving identity as a cultural center.

MUSIC AND DANCE

Flamenco

Flamenco, perhaps the most iconic musical and dance form associated with Andalusia, originated in the region's cultural melting pot, drawing influences from Romani, Moorish, Jewish, and Andalusian folk traditions. Flamenco is characterized by passionate and emotive singing (cante), intricate guitar playing (toque), rhythmic handclaps (palmas), and expressive dance (baile). The dance often includes percussive footwork and intricate hand, arm, and body movements.

Sevillana

The sevillana is a traditional Andalusian dance style that is often performed during festivals and celebrations, especially in Seville. It is a joyful and festive dance performed in pairs or groups. Sevillanas are accompanied by a specific style of music with lyrics that often celebrate Andalusian traditions, love, and daily life.

Zambra

Zambra is a dance form with Moorish origins, reflecting the historical influence of the Moors in Andalusia. It is characterized by sensual and intricate movements. The music accompanying zambra often features Arabic influences, including the use of instruments like the oud.

Essentials

Transportation

GETTING THERE

Air

Seville, Granada, and Málaga are larger cities with airports that are well connected throughout Europe. Tangier (Morocco) and Gibraltar (United Kingdom) also have airports. Tangier is well connected throughout Europe while Gibraltar has limited service only with the United Kingdom. Most European travel hubs are 1-4 hours away from any of the cities in this guide.

There are money exchange offices and ATMs just beyond the

customs area in each airport. It's a good idea to exchange or pull out some local currency before heading out of the airport.

From North America

Nearly all flights from North America connect to Andalusia via larger European travel hubs, and many of the least expensive flights connect in Spain at either Madrid or Barcelona for a short layover via **Iberia** (www.iberia.com). Limited direct flights connect North America with the city of **Málaga,** which has seasonal nonstop service via New York City and occasionally other East Coast cities. For budget travelers and those looking to break up their trip in Europe, it's sometimes worth booking a less expensive round-trip ticket to and from Europe, such as to Madrid, and then purchasing a separate ticket via one of the low-cost carriers directly into one of the destinations in Andalusia. Or consider cutting your carbon cost by taking the high-speed train down from Madrid and continuing by rail.

From Europe

Andalusia is extremely well connected with nearly all major airports in Europe. **Ryanair** (www.ryanair.com) and **Transavia** (www.transavia.com) are two common budget airlines to connect inexpensively between European hubs and Seville, Granada, Málaga, or Tangier.

From Australia and New Zealand

There are no direct flights to any city in Andalusia from Oceania. Most flights will connect you with a travel hub, such as Doha or Dubai. Many travelers coming from Australia and New Zealand bookend their trips to Andalusia with longer stays elsewhere in Spain, such as Madrid and Barcelona. The quickest, most direct, and often least expensive flight into Andalusia from Sydney or Auckland is via **Qatar Airways** (www.qatarairways.com) with a stopover in Doha. This flight is still over 24 hours long, so be sure to pack a pillow.

From South Africa

There are no direct flights into any destination in Andalusia from South Africa. Common cities for layover include Doha, Istanbul, Paris, Madrid, and Rome.

Train

Continental Europeans have a few modes of transport available to them beyond airplanes, including travel by train, though one should not underestimate just how big of a country Spain is. On the high-speed train line it takes seven hours to get from Barcelona to Málaga, while a city like Paris is a farther seven hours, making for a long day to ride the rails. Madrid is just 2-3 hours to connect with Córdoba, Seville, Granada, and Málaga.

For most travelers, the national train run by **Renfe** (www.renfe.com) is the most convenient way to connect to the larger cities in Andalusia. Do be aware that there are two types of train services: local and high-speed. The local lines are often less expensive, but they can take much longer to reach your destination. Most travelers will likely want to take advantage of the high-speed rails that connect the major cities and destinations quickly and efficiently.

Tickets for trains are easily purchased online using your credit card, and the website is navigable in English (www.renfe.com/es/en), making for a smooth process. Outside of peak periods, you can generally purchase tickets in the stations for the next departure, making for a very flexible experience. However, during peak travel times, such as popular holidays like Feria de Abril and Semana Santa, trains can quickly fill up, and sometimes even first-class tickets are not available. When planning your journey to and through Andalusia, be sure to check the holiday calendar and be prepared to buy tickets ahead of time.

Previous: a high-speed train and slower regional train.

Bus

Arriving into Andalusia via bus is impractical for all but the most dedicated bus travelers. You can connect into Andalusia direct by bus from Madrid (6.5 hr, 4 daily, 531 km/330 mi) and Lisbon (6 hr, 3 daily, 463 km/288 mi). **Alsa** (www.alsa.com) is the most reliable bus operator in the region. Longer connections with other destinations in Europe are possible. See your bus operator about schedules and bus changes.

Boat

From Spain, it is easy to take the ferry to and fro across the Strait of Gibraltar into Morocco. Cars, camper vans, and walk-ons are all served by numerous ferry companies shuttling back and forth throughout the day. The quickest ferry crossing, at 35 minutes, is also the most convenient, running between Tarifa and Tangier. This service connects directly from the port in Tarifa to Tangier's port, within a two-minute walk of Tangier's old medina. However, this passage is occasionally closed if the seas are particularly stormy. Ferries operated by **FRS** (DFDS; www.frs.es) usually leave every two hours, though in slower seasons they'll leave 3-4 times a day. A typical four-door sedan with one passenger costs around €360 round-trip. It is not possible to cross the strait with a rented car.

Ferries also service Tangier across the strait from Algeciras and Gibraltar. These ferries take much longer to cross the strait and to load passengers and cargo. Additionally, they make port at the Tanger-Med station (not Tangier-Ville), about a 45-minute drive from Tangier. This port is also used by freight trucks and construction equipment, slowing the entire boarding process. The crossing from either Algeciras or Gibraltar will take an entire day with loading and unloading the ferry, customs, and additional drive time in Morocco. Prices are a little less than the crossing at Tarifa, but not enough for most travelers to justify the extra time and hassle.

You do cross an international border when arriving or departing Morocco via ferry. Coming into Morocco, you will be asked to fill out a customs form on board the ferry. When arriving, you will show this form along with your passport to a customs officer aboard the ferry. To avoid waiting in a long line for everyone on the ferry to pass through passport control, it's best to arrive immediately to the customs officer and present your passport and form. If a line has already formed by the time you enter the ferry, relax, enjoy the trip, and wait until the ferry has almost arrived to Tangier to have your passport checked. There's no reason to spend the entire ferry ride waiting in a customs line!

Car

If you have your own car in Europe or the United Kingdom, you can drive into Spain. It is straightforward enough. UK drivers can take ferries directly into continental Europe and head south from there. Do keep in mind that driving throughout continental Europe is opposite from the United Kingdom. All traffic proceeds on the right lane with the oncoming traffic on the left.

GETTING AROUND

Whether you are driving or riding the rails, getting around Andalusia is straightforward. Do spend some time before your travel familiarizing yourself with your preferred mode of travel.

Train

Connecting between major cities is easy on **Renfe,** the national rail (www.renfe.com). Ticket prices vary depending on traffic, usually ranging €20-50 for standard fare, as well as if you are taking a slower local commuter train or the high-speed line, AVE (Alta Velocidad Española). There are more than 12 daily connections between all major cities in Andalusia, with all connections taking less than two hours on the high-speed rail line AVE.

Do pay attention to the length of time your connection takes when purchasing your ticket. Slower local trains will take twice as long, or longer, making lots of stops at smaller towns en route. Trains can run late occasionally but are generally punctual.

Car

Driving in Andalusia is largely easy, particularly connecting from city to city. The downtowns, though generally well-signed, can be confusing with lots of narrow one-way streets. For the most part, drivers are likely more aggressive than what you are used to back home.

Freeways (autoroutes) are usually in great condition. The speed limit on the autoroutes is typically 100 or 120 kph (62 or 75 mph). Freeways are denoted by A or AP. A freeway such as the A45 is free of charge, while you will have to pay a toll to enjoy the AP46. Tolls are easily paid by credit card. You can also use small change.

Electric charging stations are copious, though a bit tricky to decipher for the uninitiated. If you feel comfortable using your cell phone and a new app, such as Easy Charging (https://easycharging.app/spain) or Iberdrola (www.iberdrola.es), you can pretty easily find charging stations as you travel about. Most have a fee, though the cost is negligible, with a full charge often costing less than €5. This is an effective way to mitigate some travel costs.

If you opted to rent a traditional car, you have the choice of diesel or unleaded. Either is priced by the liter, with variable prices ranging around €1.50-2 per liter. It will generally cost €60-70 to fill up the tank of most standard automobiles.

Rules and Documentation

Australians, Americans, Canadians, Europeans, and South Africans can rent a car with the same driver's license you carry from back home. There is no need to have your valid driving license or permit translated to Spanish (i.e., you do not need a so-called International Driver's License). Rules and regulations vary from rental company to rental company. Make sure to read the fine print and understand what you need for your rental.

Car Rental

It's usually best to arrange your car rental before arrival. Be sure to request an automatic transmission if you need one, because many rental cars are manual. Málaga, in particular, has a very competitive car rental market. Often you can rent a small car for less than €10 a day.

Rental insurance is required, and it comes included with car rentals. Check with your insurance provider at home to see if rentals are covered overseas. Some credit cards offer rental insurance if you use their card to rent a car. If your home auto insurance or credit card covers the rental insurance, you might be able to get the insurance that is included with the rental waived—it's worth inquiring. Spending a little extra on travel insurance is always a good idea.

Hertz (www.hertz.com) and **Avis** (www.avis.com) and other major rental companies have locations at the major airports in Seville, Granada, and Málaga.

Driving Tips

You won't see many police on the side of the road or any speed traps. Nearly all driving citations are by video and are electronically sent. If you rent a car and receive a speeding ticket (a common occurrence), the amount is less if you quickly pay. Pay careful attention to your speed.

Parking tickets are the other bane of many a road tripper through Andalusia. Parking is almost always metered in the cities, with signage usually only in Spanish. Take care to not only pay properly, but also, if you are street parking, to make sure your proof of payment is posted as instructed to avoid the unpleasantness of a citation.

Bus

A hodgepodge of overlapping private companies connect the cities and villages of Andalusia by bus. Regular and frequent services connect the main towns, with both day and overnight options available to and from Madrid. Buses are the primary mode of

Your Packing List for Andalusia

Every traveler's packing list is going to be a bit different, but when traveling to Andalusia, you will want to give strong consideration to the region's climate. Here is a short packing list of essentials and a few tips to help you before you board your flight.

CLOTHING

- Lightweight and breathable clothing for the warm, sunny climate
- Comfortable walking shoes for exploring historical sites and cobblestone streets
- Swimwear for beach visits, hotel pools, or spas
- A light jacket or sweater for cooler evenings, especially in mountainous areas or during winter
- Sun hat and sunglasses to protect yourself from the strong sun
- A scarf or shawl for covering your shoulders when entering religious sites

TRAVEL ESSENTIALS

- Passport with at least six months of validity
- Your ETIAS registration or necessary visa
- Travel insurance to cover interruptions in your travel
- Printed and/or digital copies of your itinerary and accommodation reservations
- RFID travel wallet and/or secure pouch for valuables
- This guidebook!

HEALTH AND SAFETY

- Prescription medications and a copy of your prescriptions translated to Spanish with common names of medications (not brand names like Advil or Tylenol)
- Basic first-aid kit with essentials like pain relievers, antiseptic, and blister bandages
- Sunscreen with a high SPF, as the sun in Andalusia can be intense
- Reusable filtered water bottle to stay hydrated

TECHNOLOGY

- Camera or smartphone for capturing the stunning landscapes, architecture, and food

public transportation to the surrounding villages, and the various private bus companies manage the bus and coach services. While most depart from the main bus terminals in towns, some have their own dedicated bus stations. For inter-town travel, tickets can be obtained from the bus company's ticket sales window. These tickets serve as both a reservation for the bus and, in some cases, the allocation of a specific seat. Passengers typically have their tickets checked by the bus driver as they board, although for shorter journeys or

- eSIM for your smartphone so you can easily stay connected and use your preferred map app while exploring
- Cables and portable charger for your electronic devices
- Plug adapter for European-style electrical outlets

TOILETRIES

- Toothbrush and solid toothpaste
- Small soap bar in plastic bag or holder for use in rural bathrooms
- Any other personal grooming items you may need

MISCELLANEOUS

- Lightweight daypack for carrying essentials during day trips
- A good book or e-reader for downtime
- Travel pillow for a more comfortable travel experience
- Earplugs or noise-canceling headphones for a quieter sleep
- Small umbrella or rain jacket, as rain can occur, especially in the winter months
- Foldable or telescopic walking sticks for hiking and even around town
- Journal for recording your travel experiences
- A small pen or pencil for writing and filling out forms

When deciding what to pack, aim for comfort over fashion. Andalusia is a walking sort of destination, especially in the cities and countryside. You'll want to have a very comfortable pair of walking shoes. Keeping your feet healthy will aid immensely in your exploration of the region. Often the mornings will be cooler, and then it gets downright hot in the afternoons, so layering and staying hydrated are key things to consider while packing.

When traveling on trains, there is usually (though not always) room for large rolling luggage. As usual in Europe, packing as light as possible will make it easier to navigate the cobblestone streets and public transport. There are plenty of pharmacies and grocery stores where you'll easily be able to find replacements for things like sunscreen, pain relievers, toothpaste, or most other toiletries and over-the-counter medications you may have left at home.

in-town travel, it's common to pay the driver directly. Larger towns and cities will have multiple connections a day, while it isn't uncommon for some of the smaller villages to only have one or two connections a day.

Alsa (www.alsa.com) is perhaps the biggest company with the most connections, though their buses don't travel everywhere. **Comes** (www.tgcomes.es), **Contreras** (https://autocarescontreras.es), and **Linsur** (https://linesur.com) are a few of the other companies you will find.

To Drive or Not to Drive: That is the Question

driving toward the Southern Coast

A road trip through Andalusia offers the ultimate in flexible exploration of Spain's southern landscapes, historic cities, and vibrant culture. The freedom of the road allows for the discovery of remote villages and hidden gems, providing an authentic taste of Andalusian life. The region's diverse terrain, from the beaches of the Costa del Sol to the Sierra Nevada mountains, promises a scenic, dynamic journey.

However, the charm of Andalusia's roads comes with challenges. Navigating narrow, winding streets in ancient cities like Granada or Seville can be tricky. Finding parking in historic city centers is often difficult, and the intense summer heat can make long afternoon drives uncomfortable, even with the air-conditioner blasting. Street signs are uniformly in Spanish with little, if any, English-language signage.

Despite these challenges, many travelers find the benefits of flexibility and autonomy outweigh the drawbacks. The roads and freeways connecting cities and towns are generally in good, if not great condition and there are plenty of stops along the way with clean restrooms, readily available gas, charging stations if you're going electric, and roadside cafés. The opportunity to explore Andalusia at your own pace, discovering scenic viewpoints and charming villages along the way, adds spontaneity and authenticity to your journey. Ultimately, the decision to drive through Andalusia depends on your desire for self-guided exploration, comfort in driving in a foreign country, and tolerance for the challenges inherent with discovering old Europe.

Bike

Bicyclists share the road with the drivers and can be seen training throughout Andalusia, along the coast, up the mountains, and over the plains. Mountain biking has grown increasingly popular with European and North American travelers. It's a pleasant way to get around to otherwise inaccessible areas, and the roads are generally quieter than those found back at home. Biking is safe enough when sharing the road with vehicles, as long as bicyclists stick to the shoulder, though a helmet and lamp are highly recommended. Bikes are allowed on trains, though on an extremely limited basis. If traveling by train with your bike, make sure to reserve your bike spot.

Taxi

Unlike buses, taxis provide door-to-door service, offering a personalized and efficient means of transport, though at a cost. Fares are typically determined by a combination of distance and time. Around cities this cost is more than reasonable, with most fares ranging €5-10 to get just about anywhere around town.

Expect to pay north of €100 if leaving the city. A good rule of thumb is to expect to pay €150 per hour if hiring a taxi to take you from one city to the next.

Most taxis accept cash, and some also offer card payment options. Unlike with buses, there is no need for reservations or ticket purchases. Passengers can simply hop in, state their destination, and pay upon arrival.

While taxi services are generally more prevalent in urban centers, they provide a vital option for travelers seeking flexibility and direct routes, especially in areas where bus services may be limited. Though most taxi drivers have some limited English, expect a mostly Spanish-speaking service.

Tours and Tour Operators

If you are looking for travel experts to do the heavy lifting for putting together the trip of a lifetime and ensuring you get the very best of Andalusia on your terms, while maximizing your travel time, consider one of these tour outfitters.

Journey Beyond Travel

www.journeybeyondtravel.com/world

Full disclosure: The author of this guidebook is the owner of this bespoke tour outfitter. Chances are that if you like what's in this book and are looking for a tour operator agency to tailor a tour just for you and your friends in Andalusia, my company Journey Beyond Travel would probably be a great fit for you. If you plan on traveling for a week or more in this region, check out the website, and if you like what you see, send a note to the team at Journey Beyond Travel and let them know you're contacting Lucas through this guidebook.

Tailormade Andalucía

http://tailormadeandalucia.com

This British-Spanish collective offers some wonderful excursions and can put together multiday tours or single-day excursions. They have some wonderful connections throughout the region, though they may veer a touch more to British travel tastes than what some travelers may wish. You can talk to Sam there. Be clear with what you're looking for and without a doubt they'll be able to help you reach your travel goals in Andalusia and throughout Spain. A really easy group to work with.

Toma & Coe

https://tomaandcoe.com

Another wonderful outfitter that is a British-Spanish mixed group with wonderful service. They are an all-inclusive LGBTQ+ agency and put together some tasteful, fun, culturally immersive experiences. If Manni Coe is around, ask him about his book, *brother. do. you. love. me.*, a heartrending memoir about him and his brother. Like Tailormade above, Toma & Coe can put together day trips and multiday excursions for you. What I really like about Toma & Coe is that they are a small team that focuses almost exclusively on Andalusia.

Rick Steves' Europe

www.ricksteves.com/tours/spain/andalucia

This company runs a popular small-group 10-day bus tour through Andalusia, though it's worth noting that this tour dodges the Mediterranean coast. For those looking to join in a bus tour, this is probably the first one to look at, though there are countless others with varying levels of price and service. That said, if you want to join the Ricknicks, they're a fun gang for a group tour of the region and the tour itself nails the highlights of the region at a great pace.

IMT Bike
www.imtbike.com/tours/andalucia-southern-spain/andalucia-southern-spain-tour
For those who prefer to make their adventures powered on two wheels, IMT Bike runs a really fun motorcycle tour. Accommodations include motorcycle-friendly four- and five-star hotels and Parador luxury hotels. The ride includes your pick of a variety of BMWs. Sorry—no hogs. You are guaranteed to hit some scenic drives that buses and many self-guided driving tours would likely miss.

Visas and Officialdom

PASSPORTS AND VISAS

ETIAS Visa Waiver

In 2025, the European Union is introducing a new security screening through the European Travel Information and Authorization System (ETIAS). This is an easy-to-obtain visa waiver and will be a **requirement of entry** for passport holders from the **United States, Canada, Australia,** and **New Zealand.**

Apply online at the **ETIAS website** (https://etias.com) with your valid passport and €7, payable by credit card. People under the age of 18 or over the age of 70 are exempt from paying the €7 processing fee. The ETIAS visa waiver is valid for three years from the date of issue, but it is tethered to your passport, so if your passport is set to expire within those three years, you would have to reapply for the ETIAS visa waiver after you obtain your new passport.

You can travel to the EU as many times as allowed with your travel papers over the three years your ETIAS visa waiver is valid. It is a good idea to apply for the ETIAS before purchasing any tickets or booking accommodations. Though most applications will take less than three days to process, it is possible that it could take up to a month if you need to submit additional information.

Additionally, travelers may be subject to health or other entry requirements, so it's advisable to check the latest information before departure with your embassy or consulate.

United States

For citizens of the United States planning to visit Spain, with your ETIAS visa waiver you are allowed the customary 90 days within a 180-day period of travel within the Schengen Zone. A valid passport is mandatory. Ensure your passport has at least six months of validity beyond your planned departure date and that you have your ETIAS visa waiver if required.

Canada

Canadian citizens, like US citizens, will need their ETIAS visa waiver and can enjoy Spain for short stays of up to 90 days within a 180-day period. A valid passport is necessary, and as a precaution, it should have at least six months of validity beyond your intended departure date.

EU/Schengen

Citizens of European Union (EU) and Schengen Area countries enjoy free movement within the Schengen Zone, which includes Spain. No visa is required for short stays. However, a valid passport or national ID card is necessary. Travelers should be mindful of potential changes to travel regulations and check for any specific entry requirements.

Australia and New Zealand

Australian and New Zealand citizens can travel to Spain for stays up to 90 days within a 180-day period. A valid passport with at least six months of validity is required coupled with an ETIAS visa waiver.

South Africa

South African citizens need a Schengen visa for entry into Spain. It's essential to apply for the visa well in advance of your planned travel dates. Along with the visa application, ensure your passport has at least three months of validity beyond your intended departure date. Familiarize yourself with the specific requirements and procedures for a Schengen visa.

If you are a passport holder from another country not present here, check your nearest Spanish consulate or embassy for updated visa information. All travelers should remember that visa and entry requirements vary by country and are subject to change. It is crucial to check with the respective embassies or consulates for the most up-to-date information before planning your trip.

Following this guidebook, you may leave the EU/Schengen Zone if you cross into either Gibraltar (UK) or Morocco. Though South African travelers will need to apply for a visa, travelers from the United States, Canada, Europe, Australia, and New Zealand need only present a valid passport to cross into either Gibraltar or Morocco.

CONSULATES AND EMBASSIES

All consulates and embassies serving travelers are either in Madrid or Barcelona.

- **United States:** Calle Serrano, 75, Madrid; tel. 915/872-200; https://es.usembassy.gov. For US citizens, there is a smaller consulate near Malaga (Ave. Juan Gómez "Juanito", 8, Edificio Lucia 1, Fuengirola), though this is for non-urgent services and is geared toward expats living in this region of Spain.
- **Canada:** Plaça de Catalunya, 9, 1st and 2nd floors, Barcelona; tel. 932/703-614; www.Canada.ca/Canada-And-Spain
- **Australia:** Torre Espacio, Paseo de la Castellana, 259D, Madrid; tel. 913/536-600; https://spain.embassy.gov.au
- **New Zealand:** Pinar 7, 3rd floor, Madrid; tel. 915/230-226; www.mfat.govt.nz/en/countries-and-regions/europe/spain
- **South Africa:** Edificio Lista, Calle Claudio Coello, 91-6, Madrid; tel. 914/363-780; www.dirco.gov.za/madrid/en

Recreation

BEACHES

If you were looking for beaches, you've circled the right place on the globe. For the most part, there are three types of beaches here: urban, active, and chill. Urban beaches, like around Cádiz, Málaga, and Tangier, tend to have a lot going on, though it's hard to resist those long strips of sand just minutes away from the historic downtowns! Along the Atlantic Coast, particularly around the west coast of Tangier and in Tarifa, you'll find more active beaches with larger waves and steady winds, which are perfect for many water sports. Meanwhile, to reach some of the quieter, more secluded beaches, mostly tucked along the Mediterranean, you will need a car. For the best ones, you will need to be up for a little hike to get to the quietest spots.

BIKING

With diverse terrain and favorable weather, the region caters to both mountain bikers and road cyclists. Cycle through the scenic paths of the Sierras, winding through olive groves and villages, or tackle challenging ascents in the Alpujarras. Andalusia's well-maintained cycling routes offer a mix of cultural richness and natural beauty. Whether you prefer a leisurely ride through vineyard-laden valleys or an adventurous descent from the heights of Ronda, Andalusia promises biking experiences for every cyclist. Urban cycling, particularly in Seville, is a treat. Bike companies can fit you for a rental bike if needed.

HIKING

Andalusia, with its diverse landscapes, is a haven for hikers. From the rugged Sierra Nevada peaks to the inspirational trails of the Alpujarras, the region offers a variety of options for hikers of all levels. Explore the famed Caminito del Rey for a thrilling cliffside adventure, or wander through the ancient cork oak forests of Sierra de Grazalema Natural Park and the family-friendly stony sculptures of El Torcal. For experienced hikers and beginners, Andalusia provides numerous trails to connect with nature. You'll want to pack comfy shoes and the proper seasonal gear.

ROCK CLIMBING

With all the mountainous terrain, it is no wonder that there is a lot of rock climbing to be had. Rock climbing falls outside the scope of this book, but if you are a peak-bagging cragswoman or -man, check out the section **Climb Europe** has on the 650+ routes around El Churro near the Caminito del Rey: https://climb-europe.com/rockclimbingshop/rock-climbing-spain-el-chorro. You'll find some info on the different popular routes and pitches as well as resources for making a memorable climb.

SKIING AND SNOW SPORTS

If you like your recreational thrills on the colder side, you'll want to make your way up into the Sierra Nevada outside of Granada. Here you'll find a little winter wonderland complete with a cozy ski station with dozens of runs for skiers and snowboarders of all levels. Families from around Europe travel here during winter months, so other family-friendly activities abound, from sledding to snowman-building. Trails for cross-country skiers crisscross the mountains as well, making for other ways to enjoy the frigid mountains.

WATER SPORTS

For the most part, the major water sports tend to congregate at the mouth of the Strait of Gibraltar where the Mediterranean meets the Atlantic. The near-constant winds and larger surf make it a paradise for kitesurfing and windsurfing, in particular. There are swoops of beach where regular surfing and bodyboarding are possible. In calmer waters, largely in the Mediterranean, paddleboarding, snorkeling, and kayaking are popular pastimes, with gear often for rent at different pop-up beachfront shops in the summer months. Boating, waterskiing, wakeboarding, parasailing, and fishing are present whenever there is good weather, though largely setting sail from larger port towns, like Málaga. Inland along the rivers and lakes, you'll often find kayaking, canoeing, and paddleboarding.

Food and Drink

Get ready for a culinary fiesta! Spain is renowned for having an approachable, varied cuisine with a history that goes back thousands of years—and Andalusia is at the heart of it. From hearty mountain cuisine to freshly caught seafood and complexly spiced dishes that date from the Islamic era, you're sure to find something to tickle your taste buds.

WHERE TO EAT

From Michelin-starred contemporary restaurants and rustic tapas bars that have been serving up jarras (jugs) of cerveza (beer) for hundreds of years, to third-wave coffee joints and mouthwatering street eats, there's no shortage of culinary delights to discover throughout Andalusia.

Regional Specialties

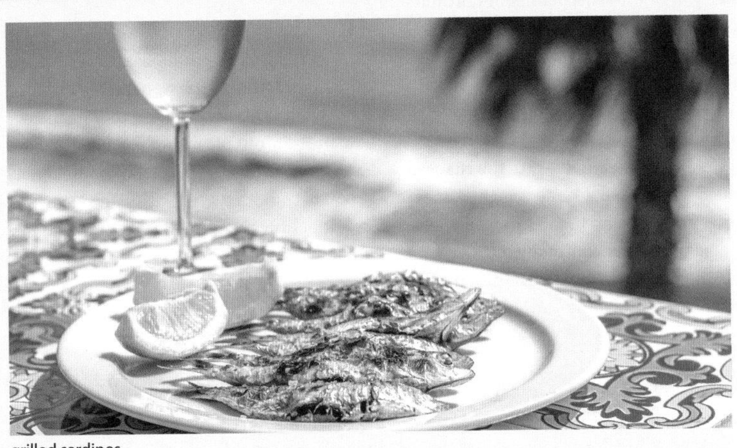

grilled sardines

Featuring a wild mix of flavors inspired by the diverse landscapes, Andalusian cuisine is sure to please:

SOUPS

- salmorejo: a chilled tomato soup
- rabo de toro: a slow-cooked oxtail stew

SEAFOOD

- espetos: grilled sardines
- gambas al ajillo: garlic shrimp

SWEETS

- piononо: sweet rolled pastry
- yemas del tajo: egg cakes

WINE AND SHERRY

- manzanilla
- Pedro Ximénez

Restaurants

Andalusia's restaurants are the real deal—whether you're into Michelin stars or hole-in-the-wall treasures, we've got your cravings covered. Most restaurants are open for lunch and dinner services.

Tapas Bars

Ready for a tapas tour? Dive into the chaos of Andalusia's tapas bars. Grab a plate, try everything, and soak up the loud, lively vibes. Many tapas bars offer continuous service with many being open from breakfast until the last customer closes down the bar.

Markets

Trade your grocery list for a market stroll. The traditional markets, like Triana Market in Seville and Atarazanas Market in Málaga, are like food carnivals—fresh, local, and buzzing with life. Markets are generally open from the morning through the afternoon, and so are best for breakfast or lunch. You'll find a number of stalls with bites to eat and tapas, though most of these markets are given over to fruits, legumes, dried meats, cheeses, and other local artisanal goods.

Street Food

Craving adventure? Grab a calamari sandwich from a beach shack or surrender to churros with chocolate. You'll find street vendors in the cities and along the beachfront promenades.

MENUS

You won't necessarily find menus everywhere you go. Some tapas bars operate without a menu, while others will have elaborate menus in Spanish. More often you'll see English in the cities, though don't necessarily count on it. It's best to come prepared with some menu basics. Hopefully the phrase guide in this book will help!

MEALTIMES

In Andalusia, lunch is often the biggest meal of the day while dinner is typically some light tapas, often followed by what seems like a never-ending party. Embrace the siesta lifestyle, where we close shop in the afternoon and come back stronger for the evening. Siesta now, fiesta later!

TIPPING

Tipping is not as common in Andalusia or the rest of Europe. Similar rules apply as in most European destinations. You can round up or leave about 10 percent, maybe a bit more, in fancier joints. If you are joining in a group or private guided experience, you should expect to tip anywhere from €5-20. You'll sometimes see tip jars in cafés, though this is not standard.

Accommodations

MAKING RESERVATIONS

Planning your stay in Andalusia is a breeze. Whether you prefer the comfort of a hotel, the sociable atmosphere of a hostel, the homely charm of a B&B, or the independence of a vacation rental, it's wise to make reservations in advance, especially during peak seasons. Secure your spot, so you can focus on the beauty of Andalusia.

HOTELS

Andalusia offers a diverse range of hotels catering to various budgets and preferences. From luxurious resorts to cozy boutique establishments, you'll find accommodations that match your style. There are recommendations provided throughout for different styles. Check amenities, location, and reviews to ensure a comfortable stay.

HOSTELS

For budget-conscious travelers or those seeking a more communal atmosphere, hostels in Andalusia provide a wallet-friendly option. Offering shared dorms or private rooms, hostels offer a social vibe and are often located in central areas, making exploration convenient.

B&BS AND VACATION RENTALS

Experience the warmth of Andalusian hospitality by opting for a bed-and-breakfast. Alternatively, choose a vacation rental for added privacy and a home-like feel. Many charming options are scattered across cities and rural areas, allowing you to tailor your stay to your preferences. The hacienda and finca stays in the rural areas are particularly noteworthy.

CAMPING

Nature lovers can immerse themselves fully by exploring Andalusia's camping options. Whether you prefer beachside campgrounds or mountain retreats, camping facilities are available for those seeking a closer connection to the great outdoors, though do be aware of local laws and regulations, particularly around free camping.

LOCATION RECOMMENDATIONS

Choosing the right location is crucial for an enjoyable stay in Andalusia. In cities like Seville, Granada, and Málaga, central accommodations in the historic center provide easy access to major attractions. For a tranquil escape, consider the serene landscapes of the Alpujarras, the sailor charm of a coastal village like Tarifa, or the rustic wonder of some of the interior countryside stays. Tailor your location to your desired pace and experiences.

Conduct and Customs

Understanding some of the basic local conduct and customs can go a long way in helping you have a more immersive, friendly, and interactive experience. Embrace the slower pace of life and savor the art of conversation, a cherished aspect of social interactions. Though Andalusians are famed for being warm and friendly, there are some protocols and things you should know before you go!

GREETINGS

Greetings hold significance in Andalusian culture. A warm handshake is a common way to begin, and close friends may exchange a friendly kiss on both cheeks. Don't be surprised if conversations include personal questions—it's a sign of genuine interest. And if you are deep in a friendly conversation, don't be surprised if you are held by the elbow or shoulder. It's a warm sign of friendship and genuine interest.

Essential Spanish Greetings

Mastering a few essential Spanish greetings enhances your interaction with locals. Nearly everyone you meet will offer up a kindness by way of greeting. Here are some key phrases to keep in your linguistic arsenal:

- ¡Hola!—Hello!
- ¿Cómo estás?—How are you?
- Encantado.—Nice to meet you.
- Buenos días.—Good morning.
- Buenas tardes.—Good afternoon/evening.
- Hasta luego.—See you later.

EATING TIMES

Throughout Andalusia, locals likely have a different eating schedule than you. Breakfast is usually a quick affair between 8am-10am, often at a local café. Lunch is usually taken from 1pm-3:30pm, and is usually the largest meal of the day. Dinner is anywhere from 9pm or later, generally featuring lighter bites, like tapas with friends.

SMOKING

Smoking is prevalent in Andalusia. It is common to see people enjoying a leisurely cigarette in outdoor areas. If you are a smoker, please keep to designated smoking areas and be mindful of those who may not appreciate smoke in enclosed spaces. If you're a nonsmoker, it's a good idea to communicate your preferences politely. Most locals will happily move or put out their cigarette if you feel bothered. The same can't be said of some of the other nationalities traveling through. They can be downright rude if you politely let them know their cigarette is bothering you.

DRESS

Andalusians take pride in their appearance, and dressing well is considered a sign of respect. In urban areas, casual wear is generally acceptable, but in more formal settings or rural locations, opting for slightly more polished attire is appreciated. When visiting churches or religious sites, modest dress is essential.

Health and Safety

EMERGENCY NUMBERS

In case of any urgent situation, familiarize yourself with these essential emergency numbers, though keep in mind that you may need a Spanish-speaker present as not all emergency services have English speakers on hand 24/7:

- Emergency services (general): 112
- Police (local): 091
- Medical emergency: 061
- Fire department: 080
- Roadside assistance: tel. 902/222-222
- Tourist helpline: tel. 902/102-112

POLICE

Andalusia's police force ensures the safety of residents and visitors. In nonemergency situations, contact local police using the number 091.

MEDICAL SERVICES

Accessing medical assistance is crucial, and Andalusia provides a network of medical services. In case of a medical emergency, dial 061 to request immediate assistance.

PHARMACIES

Pharmacies are readily available in Andalusia, offering a range of over-the-counter and prescription medications. Look for the green cross symbol to locate the nearest pharmacy. If you're in need of a drug, it is best to have the generic name.

CRIME

Andalusia, in general, is a safe destination, but it's wise to remain vigilant. Follow these general safety tips:

- Secure your belongings: Keep valuables secure and be cautious in crowded areas.
- Use reliable transportation: Opt for official taxis or reputable ride-share services.
- Emergency contacts: Keep a list of emergency numbers and your accommodation address handy.
- Awareness: Stay aware of your surroundings, especially in unfamiliar areas.

Practical Details

MONEY

Spain is part of the European Union (EU), so plan to spend euros wherever you go. It is a good idea to have a designated travel ATM and/or credit card, which hopefully gives you some perks but, most importantly, does not charge fees for foreign transactions. Most cards not designated for travel have fees for any transaction not in your home currency. These charges can quickly pile up.

Many businesses, from hole-in-the-wall restaurants to charming family-run hotels, will take contactless payment via your debit or credit card, phone, or watch. However, many tapas bars, churro joints, and street sellers are cash-only businesses. It is also a good idea to have some smaller denominations on hand for tips because tipping via debit or credit card payment is not standard.

Budgeting

Spain has long been regarded as one of the more budget-friendly countries in Europe. The region of Andalusia is even more friendly to the pockets than much of the rest of the country. Travelers will be comfortable at just about every level of travel. A comfortable budget for most travelers sharing a room is around €100 a day. This should cover you for a comfy accommodation, meals, and museum and monument admission, as well as an occasional experience or two. Budget-minded travelers and thrifty rail riders can often get by on much, much less. Boutique and luxury-minded travelers taking advantage of private guided services and unique lodging experiences may spend €500 or more per person, per day on bespoke services, transportation options, and more.

Exchange Rates

Fluctuation in exchange rates between the euro and other currencies may have a major impact on your travel expenditures. You will want to check the exchange rate against your home currency to have an idea about it before you travel. It helps to be conservative here.

Banks and ATMs

CaixaBank, Banco de Sabadell, EuroCaja Rural, and Unicaja are just a few of the reputable banks found around Andalusia. You will find ATMs at the airports, in the train stations, and dotted conveniently throughout all major cities and most smaller towns.

Debit and Credit Cards

For taking out euros from local ATMs, fees include cash withdrawal fees, out-of-network withdrawal fees, currency conversion fees, and dynamic currency conversion (DCC). The last of these is always avoidable. When paying or withdrawing money, you will be faced with an option of completing the DCC transaction in your home currency or in euros. Always choose euros to avoid the extra DCC fee from your bank or card issuer.

Cash withdrawal fees vary from bank to bank, running €1-6 per transaction. Your home bank or card issuer will also likely charge a fee for cash withdrawal, so it is best to take out the maximum amount (usually around €200) per transaction.

COMMUNICATIONS

Phones and Cell Phones

The country code for Spain is 34. From any country outside of Spain, you will need to dial this number plus the local nine-digit number to complete a phone call.

If you want to keep connected while abroad, it is best to contact your cell phone carrier at home about an international plan. Many providers now offer affordable international plans for travel. If you have a locked phone, this is likely your best option. Overall, the cellular network throughout the region is quite robust.

If your cell phone is unlocked and has the ability to have an eSIM card, consider getting one for your travels. Airalo (www.airalo.com), Holafly (https://esim.holafly.com), eSIM Card (https://esimcard.com), and Nomad (www.getnomad.app) are among companies offering cost-effective plans for international data with your cell phone. These can be a bit tricky to set up if you are not tech savvy. You often will have to download an app and scan a QR code or dig into your menus in places you likely might not be familiar with to activate your new eSIM in your settings. The benefits far outweigh the costs, so even the less tech-inclined would do well to figure out this technology that can be a lifesaver while traveling around unfamiliar territory.

If you venture into Tangier, Morocco, or Gibraltar, United Kingdom, both covered in this guide, you will want to consider a multi-country eSIM or cellular plan. Of the companies offering eSIM cards, Airalo has perhaps the most robust network with an interesting global plan for as little as 9 USD for 1 week.

Internet Access

Many coffee shops and nearly every accommodation will have free Wi-Fi access so you can keep connected on the go, though the connection may be slower than what you're likely used to.

OPENING HOURS

In Spain, typical opening hours for businesses can vary based on the type of establishment, the region, and cultural norms. However, there are some general patterns to keep in mind:

- **Retail shops:** Shops and retail stores typically open around 10am or 10:30am Monday-Saturday and close for a siesta break between 2pm and 5pm. Many shops close early on Saturday, often around 2pm or 3pm. Most stores are closed on Sunday.

- **Supermarkets:** Supermarkets generally have longer opening hours, often 9am-9pm or later Monday-Saturday, especially in urban areas.

- **Restaurants:** Restaurants usually serve lunch 1pm-4pm, with variations. Dinner service typically starts around 8pm or 9pm, with many restaurants staying open until midnight or later.

- **Bars and cafés:** Cafés may open as early as 7am for breakfast. Bars and cafés often stay open throughout the day, serving coffee, snacks, and drinks. Many bars are lively in the evenings, with some staying open until the early morning hours.

- **Banks:** Banks usually operate 8:30am-2pm Monday-Friday. Some banks may open for a brief period in the afternoon. ATMs are available 24/7 and are commonly used for transactions outside regular banking hours.

- **Museums and attractions:** Cultural institutions may be closed on Monday. Opening hours vary but generally range 10am to 6pm or 7pm.

- **Pharmacies:** Pharmacies often follow regular business hours Monday-Saturday, but one in each area may remain open for emergencies during the siesta and on Sunday.

It's important to be aware that during the traditional siesta period (afternoon break), especially in smaller towns and rural areas, some businesses may close for a few hours, particularly 2pm-5pm. Larger cities and tourist areas may have more businesses operating continuously throughout the day.

PUBLIC HOLIDAYS

Spain, and Andalusia in particular, is known for having a good time. Perhaps this is due to the number of public holidays, which largely follow the liturgical Catholic calendar.

- New Year's Day (Año Nuevo)—January 1
- Epiphany (Día de los Reyes)—January 6
- Holy Week (Semana Santa)—the week leading up to Easter
- Good Friday (Viernes Santo)—Friday before Easter Sunday
- Labor Day (Fiesta del Trabajo)—May 1
- Assumption of Mary (Asunción de la Virgen)—August 15
- National Day (Día de la Hispanidad)—October 12
- All Saints' Day (Día de Todos los Santos)—November 1
- Constitution Day (Día de la Constitución)—December 6
- Immaculate Conception (Inmaculada Concepción)—December 8
- Christmas Day (Navidad)—December 25

OPPORTUNITIES FOR STUDY AND VOLUNTEER WORK

Andalusia's universities offer a range of courses for international students. Consider enrolling in exchange programs through your university at home or directly applying to universities in cities like Seville, Granada, or Málaga.

If you are looking to improve your Spanish, language schools in Andalusia, like **Escuela Montalban** (www.escuela-montalban.com), provide immersive Spanish language courses. These programs often include cultural activities to enhance language learning. Many organizations and schools offer short-term courses focusing on Andalusian culture, history, and arts. These can be excellent for those interested in gaining a deeper understanding of the region. The **Erasmus+** program (https://erasmus-plus.ec.europa.eu) facilitates student exchanges within Europe. Many universities in Andalusia actively participate in this program.

Those considering volunteering can look at organizations such as **Volunteering Solutions** (www.volunteeringsolutions.com), **Projects Abroad** (www.projects-abroad.net), and other local NGOs that offer volunteer programs in areas like community development, education, and environmental conservation. Various programs, such as the **North American Language and Culture Assistants Program** (www.educacionyfp.gob.es/eeuu/convocatorias-programas/convocatorias-eeuu/nalcap.html), allow participants to work as language assistants in schools, providing valuable support to local teachers. Organizations like **Greenheart Travel** (https://greenhearttravel.org) and **WWF** (www.worldwildlife.org) often have volunteer opportunities focused on environmental conservation and sustainable practices. Some programs offer opportunities for volunteers to assist in health-care settings, providing support to medical professionals and gaining valuable experience. Volunteering on organic farms or participating in agricultural projects can be a rewarding experience, especially in rural areas.

TOURIST INFORMATION

Tourist Offices

In most destinations you will find a helpful tourist office offering updated info. Often they are stocked with books, pamphlets, and maps for travelers. Even better, many of them have good connections for guided tours and

Andalusia's Festival Calendar

Feria de Sevilla attendees

There are more festivals in Andalusia than you can shake a stick at. Many of them, such as Corpus Christi, hold religious significance. Keep in mind that there are many, many minor festivals, such as candlelight festivals (also known as "Noche de las Velas" or "Night of the Candles"), which are extremely popular. Streets are illuminated with thousands of candles, creating a magical and enchanting atmosphere. Festivals like these take place throughout the year in the cities and villages throughout Andalusia.

JANUARY

- **Festival de la Matanza** (Antequera): Celebrating the traditional pig slaughter, the festival includes tastings of local products, music, and cultural events.
- **Feria de la Virgen de la Paz** (Ronda): A traditional fair honoring the patron saint of Ronda, featuring music, dance, and a lively parade.

FEBRUARY

- **Festival de la Tapa** (Granada): A culinary festival where local establishments offer a variety of tapas at special prices.
- **Fiesta de Carnaval** (Cádiz): The renowned Carnival of Cádiz, known for its colorful costumes, street performances, and lively atmosphere.
- **Festival de Flamenco de Jerez** (Jerez de la Frontera): This festival celebrates the art of flamenco, for which Jerez is well known. The event includes flamenco performances, workshops, and competitions, drawing flamenco enthusiasts and artists from around the world.

MARCH/APRIL

- **Feria de Sevilla** (Seville): Seville's iconic fair featuring flamenco, horse parades, traditional costumes, and lively casetas (tents).

MAY

- **Festival de los Patios** (Córdoba): A celebration of Córdoba's famous courtyards, adorned with flowers and open to the public during this festival.
- **Feria del Caballo** (Jerez de la Frontera): Jerez's Horse Fair is one of the most important equestrian events in Spain. The fairgrounds come alive with colorful casetas (tents), traditional flamenco music and dance, and various equestrian activities. It's a celebration of Andalusian culture, especially the region's renowned sherry and horsemanship.
- **Corpus Christi** (Granada and other cities): A religious procession with intricate carpets made of flowers and colored sawdust lining the streets.

JUNE

- **Festival de Verdiales** (Málaga): A folk music festival celebrating the traditional verdiales music and dance of the Málaga region.
- **Feria de San Juan** (Cádiz): A midsummer fair featuring music, dancing, and fireworks, celebrated along the beaches of Cádiz.

JULY

- **Feria del Carmen y la Sal** (Cádiz): A maritime-themed fair in honor of the Virgen del Carmen, featuring processions, concerts, and traditional events.

AUGUST

- **Feria de Málaga** (Málaga): A weeklong fair with processions, music, dancing, and traditional food, transforming the city into a lively celebration.
- **Real Feria de Agosto** (Antequera): A traditional fair with horse shows, bullfights, flamenco performances, and a lively atmosphere.

SEPTEMBER

- **Feria de la Raza** (Málaga): A cultural fair celebrating Hispanic heritage with music, dance, and traditional Andalusian activities.
- **Feria de San Miguel** (Arcos de la Frontera): Arcos de la Frontera celebrates its patron saint, San Miguel, with a lively fair featuring music, dance, and traditional Andalusian activities. The fair attracts locals and visitors alike, creating a festive atmosphere in the town.

OCTOBER

- **Fiesta de los Patios en Otuño de Córdoba** (Córdoba): Similar to the May festival, this event showcases the beauty of Córdoba's patios with colorful displays of flowers.

NOVEMBER

- **Festival de Cine Europeo** (Seville): An annual film festival showcasing European cinema, attracting filmmakers and cinephiles from around the continent.

other experiences you can enjoy to round out your journey and make the most of your precious travel time.

Sightseeing Passes

Make the most of your Andalusian adventure by considering sightseeing passes. These passes often grant access to top attractions, historical sites, and museums at discounted rates. Not only do they help you save on entrance fees, but also they can streamline your itinerary, allowing you to explore with ease. These are available at most tourism offices.

Maps

Andalusia's diverse landscapes beckon exploration, and having reliable maps is essential. Whether you're navigating the winding streets of historic cities, trekking through natural reserves, or planning a coastal escape, detailed maps provide a valuable resource. Ensure you have both digital and physical maps for your journey, enhancing your ability to navigate this captivating region. Both Apple Maps and Google Maps work well navigating the cities and driving point-to-point, while AllTrails can help you in the backwoods. Just keep your phone charged and remember the battery pack.

Traveler Advice

ACCESS FOR TRAVELERS WITH DISABILITIES

When traveling to Andalusia with disabilities, careful planning is key. While accessibility is improving, it's recommended to inquire about wheelchair-friendly facilities, accessible accommodations, and specific services tailored to your needs. Major tourist sites often provide assistance, and contacting them in advance can ensure a smoother experience. That said, for some things, stairs are just unavoidable given the age of some of the buildings, monuments, and cities.

TRAVELING WITH CHILDREN

For families traveling with children, Andalusia offers a warm, welcoming environment. Likely your children will be more looked after and nicely attended to than they are back home! Many accommodations cater to families, providing child-friendly amenities. Plan visits to family-friendly attractions like parks, zoos, and interactive museums. Restaurants typically accommodate families, offering local dishes in smaller portions. Remain vigilant in crowded areas and ensure children are aware of their surroundings for a safe and enjoyable experience. Consider sticking an AirTag or Tile on your toddler . . . just in case.

WOMEN TRAVELING ALONE

Andalusia is generally safe for solo female travelers, but taking precautions is essential. Choose accommodations in well-reviewed, safe neighborhoods. Opt for reliable transportation options, and avoid poorly lit or secluded areas at night. Familiarize yourself with local customs, and consider dressing modestly, especially in more traditional areas. Exercise caution in crowded places, and keep belongings secure for a worry-free solo journey.

SENIOR TRAVELERS

Andalusia has a large population of people over 65. That said, you may not find many of the customary comforts of back home. Sidewalks sometimes seem like an afterthought and there are often more stairs than you might be used to. If you are reasonably fit, none of this should pose a problem.

LGBTQ+ TRAVELERS

Andalusia is one of the most progressive areas of Europe. You will likely encounter little, if any, negative stereotyping or discrimination. The destinations are all quite welcoming to the LGBTQ+ community. As usual, the cities tend to be more progressive than the rural destinations, but even then, most rural destinations have their own thriving local communities.

TRAVELERS OF COLOR

While the region is generally open minded and inclusive, it's essential to be aware of certain considerations to ensure a positive experience. Biracial couples may receive a bit more attention, particularly in more rural or traditional areas. This is often out of curiosity rather than anything negative, and locals are generally friendly and welcoming. When it comes to accommodations, most hotels and establishments are accustomed to hosting guests from various backgrounds. In cities like Seville, Granada, and Málaga, you'll find a cosmopolitan vibe where diversity is celebrated. As in any destination, it's advisable to be culturally aware. Understanding local customs, greetings, and traditions can foster positive interactions, so as to not, for example, mistake the hooded and cloaked penitents during processions in Semana Santa as having anything to do with racist white supremacist organizations. While Andalusia is generally safe, it's recommended to remain vigilant in crowded areas and take standard precautions for personal safety.

Resources

Glossary

abierto: open
aseos: toilet
avenida: avenue
banco: bank
barrio: neighborhood or quarter
calle: street
caña: smallest size of beer
catedral: cathedral
cerrado: closed
estación: station
iglesia: church
mercado: market
museo: museum
playa: beach
plaza: square
salida: exit
tapear: to "do tapas"/go out for tapas

Spanish Phrasebook

PRONUNCIATION

It's worth noting that the "c" sound, when the letter comes before e or i, is pronounced differently in Spain than in South America. In Spain it is "lisped"—for example, the word *gracias* is pronounced GRA-thee-as.

Vowels

- **a** like ah, as in "hah": agua AGwa (water), pan PAN (bread), and casa CA-SA (house)
- **e** like eh, as in "help": mesa MEH-sa (table) and tela TEH-la (cloth)
- **i** like ee, as in "need": diez dee-ES (ten), comida ko-MEE-dah (meal), and fin FEEN (end)
- **o** like oh, as in "go": peso PAY-soh (weight), ocho OH-choh (eight), and poco POH-koh (a bit)
- **u** like oo, as in "cool": uno OO-noh (one), cuarto KOOAHR-toh (room); when it follows a "q" the u is silent

Consonants

b, d, f, k, l, m, n, p, q, s, t, w, x, y, z, and **ch** pronounced almost as in English; **h** occurs but is silent—not pronounced at all—e.g., *hola* (hello) is pronounced oh-la and *hielo* (ice) is pronounced ee-el-oh

- **c** like k as in "keep": cuarto KOOAR-toh (room), caliente KAL-ien-tay (hot); c is lisped before e and i—for example, gracias GRA-thee-as.
- **g** like g as in "gift" when it precedes "a," "o," "u," or a consonant: gato GAH-toh (cat), hago AH-goh (I do, make); before e or i, pronounce g like h as in "hat": giro HEE-roh (money order), gente HEN-tay (people)
- **j** like h, as in "has": jueves HWE-ves (Thursday), mejor meh-HOR (better)
- **ll** like y, as in "yes": me llamo me YA-mo (I'm called), ellos AY-yohs (they, them)
- **ñ** like ny, as in "canyon": año AH-nyo (year), señor SEH-nyor (Mr., sir)

r is lightly trilled, with tongue at the roof of your mouth: pero PEH-rrrro (but), tres TRRRES (three), cuatro KOOAH-trrrro (four)

rr like a Spanish r, but with much more emphasis and trill. Let your tongue flap. Practice with burro (donkey), carretera (highway), and ferrocarril (railroad)

v like b as in "baby": vino BEE-no—the v can often be pronounced as a b or a v interchangeably, so listen for words like vino and vale BALLAY (ok)

Note: The single small but common exception to all of the above is the pronunciation of Spanish **y** when it's being used as the Spanish word for "and," as in "Penelope y Javier." In such cases, pronounce it like the English ee, as in "keep": Penelope "ee" Javier (Penelope and Javier).

ESSENTIAL PHRASES

hello hola
good-bye adios
Nice to meet you. Encantado/a (m/f).
please por favor
thank you gracias
You're welcome. De nada.
Excuse me. Perdón.
I don't speak Spanish. No hablo español.
Do you speak English? ¿Habla inglés?
Where is the bathroom? ¿Dónde están los servicios?
yes si
no no
big grande
little pequeño/a
cold frío
hot cálido

TRANSPORTATION

bus autobús
train tren
Where is . . .? ¿Dónde está . . .?
How far is it . . .? ¿Qué tan lejos esta?
What time does the bus leave? ¿A qué hora sale el autobús?
Where can I buy a ticket? ¿Dónde puedo comprar un billete?

ACCOMMODATIONS

hotel hotel
apartment piso
room habitación
key llave
shower ducha
soap jabón

FOOD

I would like . . . Quisiera . . .
The check please? La cuenta, por favor
I'm a vegetarian. Soy vegetariano/a.
Cheers! ¡Salud!
beer cerveza
bread pan
breakfast desayuno
cash efectivo
coffee café
dinner cena
glass vaso
ice hielo
lunch comida
restaurant restaurante
water agua
wine vino

WEATHER

What is the weather like? ¿Qué tiempo hace?
It's hot/cold today. Hoy hace calor/frío.
It's raining today. Hoy esta lloviendo.

SHOPPING

money dinero
shop tienda
I'm just looking. Sólo estoy mirando.
How much does this cost? ¿Cuánto cuesta?
Do you take credit cards? ¿Aceptan tarjetas de crédito?

HEALTH

I need to see a doctor. Necesito ver un médico.
I need to go to the hospital. Necesito ir al hospital.
I am diabetic. Soy diabético/a.
I am pregnant. Estoy embarazada.

I am allergic to . . . Soy alérgico a . . .
pain dolor
fever fiebre
headache dolor de cabeza
stomachache doloar de estómago
toothache dolor de muelas
nausea náusea
vomiting vómito
medicine medicina

NUMBERS

0 cero
1 un/uno/una
2 dos
3 tres
4 cuatro
5 cinco
6 seis
7 siete
8 ocho
9 nueve
10 diez
11 once
12 doce
13 trece
14 catorce
15 quince
16 dieciséis
17 diecisiete
18 dieciocho
19 diecinueve
20 veinte
100 cien (to)
1,000 mil
1,000,000 millón

TIME

What time is it? ¿Qué hora es?
It's one o'clock Es la una.
It's two o'clock. Es las dos.
It's 6:05. Son las seis y cinco.
morning mañana
afternoon tarde
evening noche
night noche
yesterday ayer
today hoy
tomorrow mañana
now ahora
later más tarde
earlier antes
day día
week semana
month mes
year año

DAYS AND MONTHS

Monday lunes
Tuesday martes
Wednesday miércoles
Thursday jueves
Friday viernes
Saturday sábado
Sunday domingo
January enero
February febrero
March marzo
April abril
May mayo
June junio
July julio
August agosto
September septiembre
October octubre
November noviembre
December diciembre

Suggested Reading

LITERATURE

The Alchemist, by Paolo Coelho. This bestselling novel follows the journey of Santiago, a shepherd boy, as he embarks on a quest to discover his personal legend and fulfill his dreams. Set against the backdrop of Andalusia and across the strait into Tangier and through the Sahara Desert, the novel is a philosophical and inspirational tale about destiny, pursuing one's dreams, and the alchemy of life.

The Barber of Seville, by Gioacchino Rossini. A comic opera that is a lively and humorous tale of love, disguise, and mischief. Set in Seville, it follows the escapades of Figaro, the barber, as he helps Count Almaviva woo the beautiful Rosina, navigating through various comedic twists and turns.

For Whom the Bell Tolls, by Ernest Hemingway. This classic novel is set during the Spanish Civil War. The story follows an American dynamiter, Robert Jordan, as he joins a guerrilla group to blow up a bridge. The novel explores themes of love, duty, and the brutality of war against the backdrop of the Spanish conflict.

Granada, by Radwa Ashour. Radwa Ashour's historical novel weaves together the tales of various characters living in Granada during the Nasrid dynasty. Through intricate storytelling, Ashour captures the essence of the city's rich history, its multicultural past, and the profound impact of the Reconquista on its inhabitants.

Selected Poems, by Federico García Lorca. This collection showcases the poetic brilliance of Federico García Lorca, one of Spain's most celebrated and influential poets of the 20th century. His verses, deeply rooted in Andalusian folklore and symbolism, explore themes of love, nature, and the human condition with a rich and evocative language.

NONFICTION

The Alhambra Revealed: The Remarkable Story of the Kingdom of Granada, by Michael B. Barry. A full-color book with lots of illustrative pictures and maps. A wonderful guide taking us deep into the beginnings and up to today.

Andalucia: A Literary Guide for Travelers, by Andrew and Suzanne Edwards. The guidebook for book junkies. Andrew and Suzanne take you on an erudite voyage through the history of Andalusian literature.

Andalus: Unlocking the Secrets of Moorish Spain, by Jason Webster. This is a historical exploration that delves into the legacy of Moorish Spain, revealing the cultural, architectural, and intellectual contributions of the Moors to the region.

The Autobiographical Trilogy, by Laurie Lee. Laurie Lee's autobiographical trilogy, consisting of *Cider with Rosie, As I Walked Out One Midsummer Morning,* and *A Moment of War,* chronicles his coming-of-age in the English countryside, his adventures in 1930s Spain, and his experiences as a soldier in the Spanish Civil War.

Colonial al-Andalus: Spain and the Making of Modern Moroccan Culture, by Eric Calderwood. A very interesting academic work that straddles the Strait of Gibraltar, showing the culture intertwining between Andalusia and Morocco.

Death in the Afternoon, by Ernest Hemingway. Probably Hemingway's best known nonfiction work. This book delves into the world of Spanish bullfighting and provides a detailed examination of the cultural significance and rituals surrounding this controversial tradition.

Driving Over Lemons, by Chris Stewart. This is a laugh-out-loud memoir recounting the Stewarts' move from England to a remote farm in the Alpujarras region of Andalusia. The book reflects on the challenges and joys of adapting to rural Spanish life and farming.

Duende, by Jason Webster. Explore the concept of "duende," a mysterious and passionate force in Spanish culture. The book takes readers on a journey through flamenco, bullfighting, and the landscapes of Andalusia, unraveling the essence of this elusive and captivating phenomenon.

Granada: Light of Andalucia, by Steven Nightingale. Nightingale explores the enchanting city of Granada, delving into its history, culture, and the profound impact of the Alhambra. The book offers a poetic and immersive journey through the landscapes and heritage of Andalusia.

The Life and Work of Pablo Picasso, by Leonie Bennett. A touching biography for young readers that provides an insightful look into the life and artistic journey of the renowned Spanish painter, Pablo Picasso. The book explores Picasso's influential role in shaping modern art in a way that's accessible for readers ages 6 and up.

Moorish Spain, by Richard Fletcher. A very readable history of the culture and rule during the Islamic era and a good starting point for anyone interested in exploring this era of Andalusia.

Tales of the Alhambra, by Washington Irving. A collection of essays, sketches, and stories inspired by Irving's experiences in the Alhambra palace in Granada, Spain. Through vivid storytelling, Irving captures the allure of the Moorish architecture and the cultural legacy of the region.

HIKING GUIDES AND MAPS

La Alpujarra: Valles de Lanjarón, Poqueira, Trevélez y Taha de Pitres, by Piolet Maps. A tear-proof, waterproof map at 1:40,000 scale, nicely sized for walks through the region.

Parque Natural Sierra de Grazalema: Guía del Excursionista, by Manuel Becerra Parra. You will be hard-pressed to find this on Amazon, but if you are in Grazalema pick up a copy of this excellent hiking guidebook for all of your park exploration. There are many walks and hikes of different ability levels nicely mapped out, though descriptions are all in Spanish with no English-language version available.

Sierra de Grazalema Parque Natural, by Editorial Penibetica. If you were looking for a smaller foldout map of the Grazalema region, this is the map. At 1:40,000 scale, it has a number of well-signed, easily followable hiking routes.

Sierra Nevada: La Integrale de los 3,000, by Piolet Maps. A standard tear-proof, waterproof, 1:25,000 scale map that will see you hiking through the Sierra Nevadas.

Suggested Films, Shows, and Series

Star Wars, Game of Thrones, Indiana Jones, and countless other series and movies have used parts of Andalusia as a picturesque backdrop for adventure. Here are a few other programs to watch that promise to take you into Andalusia in ways that hopefully transcend the celluloid experience of a Hollywood blockbuster.

Belmonte. Juan Sebastían Bollaín. Follow the life of Spain's most famous bullfighter in this captivating documentary.

Paco de Lucía: A Journey. Curro Sánchez. Documentary about the legendary guitar genius Paco de Lucía and his contributions to flamenco music.

Rick Steves' Europe: Andalusia: The Best of Southern Spain. Simon Griffith. In his no-nonsense manner, travel guru Rick Steves takes us on a spectacular visual tour of Andalusia, hitting all the highlights.

South from Granada (al Sur de Granada). Fernando Colomo. A light-hearted romantic comedy that takes you into the Alpujarras, giving you a peek of the region, as well as of the type of comedy appreciated by most Andalusians.

When the Moors Ruled Europe. Timothy Coepstake. This documentary argues that the Moors weren't conquerors as much as welcomed liberators who entered Europe with technology and a way of life that was appreciated by the locals and improved their way of living.

Internet Resources

You can leverage travel market websites like booking.com, expedia.com, skyscanner.com, kayak.com, viator.com, tourradar.com, and others to search for things like accommodations, flights, rental cars, and even experiences like guided tours. However, you will often get a better price (and better service) if you book direct. This goes for airlines as well as accommodations and experiences.

GENERAL TRAVEL AND TOURIST TIPS

Andalusia Official Page

www.andalucia.org

This is Andalusia's official tourism portal, covering locations and sights across the region.

Michelin Guide

https://guide.michelin.com/en/es/andalucia/restaurants

I travel through my stomach and the Michelin Guide is a great compass! Happily they have an entire section updated and dedicated to Andalusia.

Spain Traveller

www.spain-traveller.com

A great resource for trip planning in Spain.

Andalucia.com

www.andalucia.com

An unofficial, outdated website for the region that can be useful, particularly if you find yourself house hunting—and travelers to the region are known to do so!

Rome2Rio

www.rome2rio.com

Rome2Rio is a fantastic website to leverage in the early planning stages to know your options for getting from point A to point B, including links to suggested train, bus, plane, and even ferry tickets.

SEVILLE

Seville City Guide

https://sevillecityguide.com

A robust online guide for Seville that is kept up-to-date with seasonal tours and activities.

Welcome to Seville

https://welcometoseville.com

This website has quite a few good itineraries to explore the city, including a five-day deep-dive in Seville with some interesting ideas for day trips to the surrounding area.

CÓRDOBA

Spain Traveller

www.spain-traveller.com/en/cordoba

Córdoba has far fewer online resources than other destinations in the region. Luckily, Spain Traveller does a really good job, complete with a 40-page guide that has a nice self-guided walk you could download for free.

GRANADA

Alhambra.org

www.alhambra.org

If you are going to the Alhambra, which if you are reading this, you likely are, you'll want to make good use of this website for some updated info and additional historical and background information on Andalusia's crown historic monument.

MÁLAGA

Malaga.com

www.malaga.com

A very useful website that has become a mini travel marketplace over the years.

TRANSPORTATION

Renfe

www.renfe.com

The national train network official website. Though notoriously a little tricky to navigate, the updated version has an English-language option, and now international credit cards usually work without hassle to purchase your tickets.

Trainline

www.thetrainline.com

A slightly more streamlined, easier-to-navigate website to purchase your train tickets, though with a small additional service fee added on to the base ticket price. This is best if you're looking to connect through rail into the rest of Europe for a single voyage or one round-trip.

Eurail

www.eurail.com

The classic Eurail Pass is available here in different levels for different travel types and journey lengths. This is best if you are planning on traveling outside of Spain and connecting through Europe on a multi-stop adventure.

APPS

Your phone already has apps for things like maps and your camera, real basics for travel. Additionally, you should download the app for your airline to help with tickets, purchases, and customer support. If you used a travel marketplace, like booking.com or Airbnb.com, you would want to have the app downloaded and make sure your reservations are in your account.

Here are a few other apps you might not have thought about.

Google Translate

You will want to download Google's translator app to use just in case your Spanish isn't quite up to the task or if you catch yourself in a sticky situation.

Duolingo

A really fun way to learn some Spanish on your phone. Entertaining and great for the flight over and while in transit.

Maps.me

This app is great! You can download maps of cities ahead of time when you have an internet connection. You can navigate using just your phone's GPS. If you are not opting to have a local data plan while you travel, this is a must.

TripIt

For organization junkies, this is a fantastic app. You can just forward all of your email confirmations for your trip and the app will organize them for you in an easy-to-grasp itinerary with all your important details in one place.

Index

DE

F

G

H

IJK

L

MNO

P

VWYZ

List of Maps

Front Map

Welcome to Seville, Granada & Andalusia

Seville

Córdoba, Antequera, and El Torcal Nature Reserve

Granada and the Sierra Nevada

Málaga and the Southern Coast

Jerez de la Frontera and the White Villages

Photo Credits

All images © Lucas Peters except: title page photo: Eugene2 | Dreamstime.com; page 5 © (left middle) Tupungato | Dreamstime.com; page 6 © Perszing1982 | Dreamstime.com; page 8 © Cleop6atra | Dreamstime.com; page 10 © (bottom) Anibaltrejo | Dreamstime.com; page 12 © Delstudio | Dreamstime.com; page 14 © (top) Diego Grandi | Dreamstime.com; (bottom) Poike2017 | Dreamstime.com; page 17 © (bottom) Arenaphotouk | Dreamstime.com; page 21 © (top left) Matokmet | Dreamstime.com; (top right) Shootdiem | Dreamstime.com; page 23 © (bottom) Freefly | Dreamstime.com; page 24 © Sborisov | Dreamstime.com; page 25 © Sean Pavone | Dreamstime.com; page 26 © (top) Mistervlad | Dreamstime.com; page 31 © Mereltuk | Dreamstime.com; page 33 © Dziewul | Dreamstime.com; page 36 © (bottom) Nito100 | Dreamstime.com; page 37 © Valery Bareta | Dreamstime.com; page 38 © Lviani | Dreamstime.com; page 43 © Mardzpe | Dreamstime.com; page 50 © Sokolovsky | Dreamstime.com; page 51 © (top) Malajscy | Dreamstime.com; (left middle) Lachris77 | Dreamstime.com; page 56 © (left middle) Jiss | Dreamstime.com; (right middle) Alfredosaz | Dreamstime.com; page 64 © (top) Joserpizarro | Dreamstime.com; page 68 © (bottom left) Kovalenkovpetr | Dreamstime.com; page 85 © Joserpizarro | Dreamstime.com; page 86 © Vlad2003 | Dreamstime.com; page 87 © (top right) Irinywka | Dreamstime.com; page 95 © Yury | Dreamstime.com; page 96 © Rpulham | Dreamstime.com; page 99 © (bottom right) Efesenko | Dreamstime.com; page 108 © (bottom) Digicomphoto | Dreamstime.com; page 116 © (bottom) Joserpizarro | Dreamstime.com; page 120 © Barmalini | Dreamstime.com; page 124 © (top left) RudiErnst | Dreamstime.com; (bottom) Mmeeds | Dreamstime.com; page 130 © 2circles | Dreamstime.com; page 134 © (top left) Sborisov | Dreamstime.com; page 145 © (bottom right) Diegograndi | Dreamstime.com; page 149 © (top) Bpperry | Dreamstime.com; page 154 © (top left) Dudlajzov | Dreamstime.com; (top right) Sborisov | Dreamstime.com; (bottom) Madrugadaverde | Dreamstime.com; page 159 © (top) Efesenko | Dreamstime.com; (left middle) Lunamarina | Dreamstime.com; (right middle) Dudlajzov | Dreamstime.com; (bottom) Diegograndi | Dreamstime.com; page 161 © Jmorat00 | Dreamstime.com; page 163 © Anibaltrejo | Dreamstime.com; page 167 © Jackf | Dreamstime.com; page 185 © Barmalini | Dreamstime.com; page 187 © Bjornd | Dreamstime.com; page 188 © Jesterec | Dreamstime.com; page 193 © Whpics | Dreamstime.com; page 200 © (top right) Saiko3p | Dreamstime.com; page 205 © (top right) Huertas19 | Dreamstime.com; page 223 © (top) Diegograndi | Dreamstime.com; (left middle) Sbostock | Dreamstime.com; (right middle) Nito100 | Dreamstime.com; (bottom) Kotangens | Dreamstime.com; page 225 © (top right) Vitalyano | Dreamstime.com; (bottom) Vitaliybilyak | Dreamstime.com; page 234 © (bottom right) RudiErnst | Dreamstime.com; page 239 © Lilimarmeloart | Dreamstime.com; page 249 © (top left) Saiko3p | Dreamstime.com; (bottom left) Saiko3p | Dreamstime.com; page 262 © (bottom) Snovitsky | Dreamstime.com; page 264 © (top left) Shootdiem | Dreamstime.com; (bottom left) Admin12247 | Dreamstime.com; page 271 © (top right) Escapa777 | Dreamstime.com; page 278 © Efesenko | Dreamstime.com; page 282 © (bottom) Tinamou | Dreamstime.com; page 289 © (top left) Maui01 | Dreamstime.com; (top right) RudiErnst | Dreamstime.com; (bottom) Dudlajzov | Dreamstime.com; page 292 © (top) Diegograndi | Dreamstime.com; (left middle) Diegograndi | Dreamstime.com; (bottom) Jovannig | Dreamstime.com; page 295 © (top) Gorelovs | Dreamstime.com; (bottom) Jovannig | Dreamstime.com; page 301 © Dudlajzov | Dreamstime.com; page 305 © Arenaphotouk | Dreamstime.com; page 306 © renaphotouk | Dreamstime.com; page 308 © Belizar | Dreamstime.com; page 309 © Joserpizarro | Dreamstime.com; page 351 © Barmalini | Dreamstime.com

FULLY REVISED AND UPDATED
MOON
CAMINO DE SANTIAGO
SACRED SITES, HISTORIC VILLAGES, LOCAL FOOD & WINE
BEEBE BAHRAMI

MOON
Amalfi Coast
WITH NAPLES, CAPRI & POMPEII

MOON
Seville, Granada & Andalusia
WITH CÓRDOBA, MÁLAGA, AND TANGIER

MOON
Azores

MOON
Provence & the French Riviera

MOON
Iceland
WITH A ROAD TRIP ON THE RING ROAD

MOON
Croatia & Slovenia
WITH MONTENEGRO

MOON
Greek Islands & ATHENS

MOON
Portugal
WITH MADEIRA & THE AZORES

MOON
Prague, Vienna & Budapest

MOON
Norway

MOON
Rome, Florence & Venice

MOON
Scotland

MOON
Southern Italy
WITH SICILY, PUGLIA, NAPLES & THE AMALFI COAST

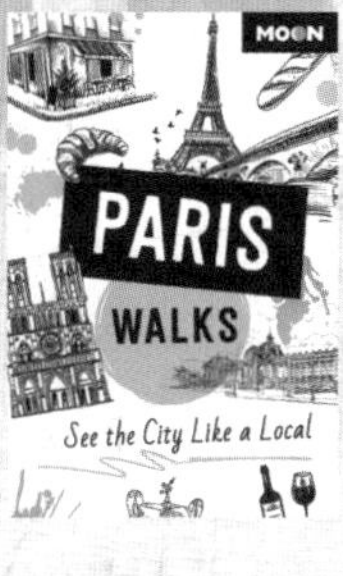

Canada

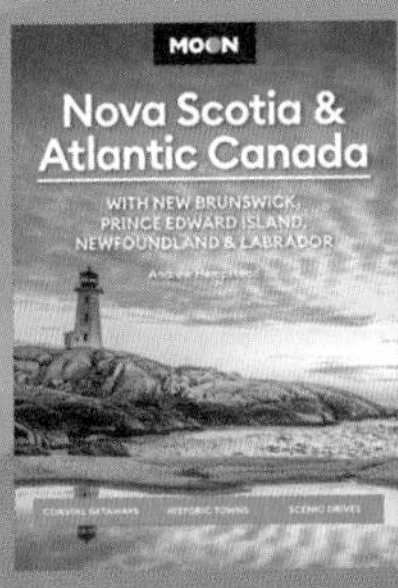

Europe, Middle East & Africa

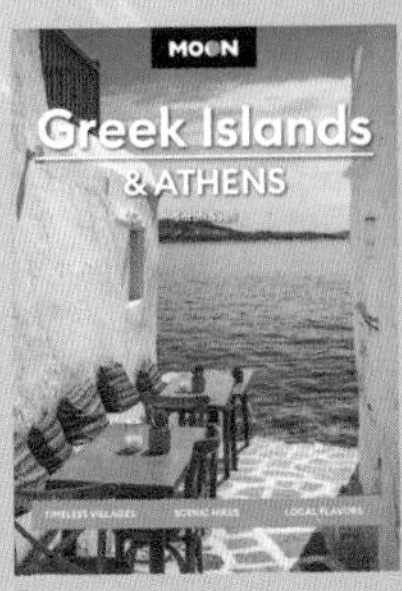

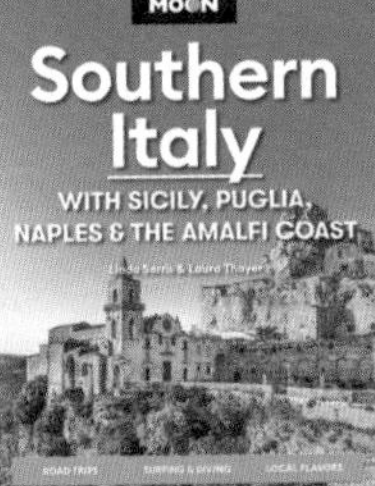

MAP SYMBOLS

Highway
Primary Road
Other Road
Unpaved Road
Pedestrian Route
Stairs
Trail
Ferry
Railroad

City/Town
State Capital
National Capital
Highlight
Site
Accommodation
Restaurant/Bar
Other Site
Information Center

Parking Area
Church/Synagogue/Mosque
Winery/Vineyard
Park
Golf Course
Train Station
Metro/Tram Stop
Airport
Airfield

Trailhead
Unique Feature
Unique Feature Hydro
Waterfall
Camping
Mountain
Ski Area
Glacier

CONVERSION TABLES

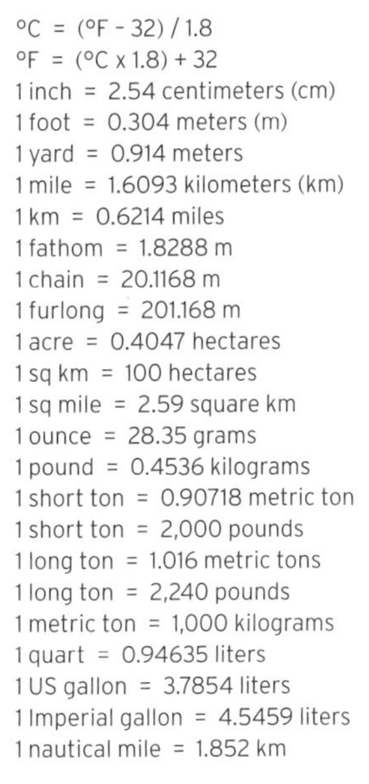

°C = (°F - 32) / 1.8
°F = (°C x 1.8) + 32
1 inch = 2.54 centimeters (cm)
1 foot = 0.304 meters (m)
1 yard = 0.914 meters
1 mile = 1.6093 kilometers (km)
1 km = 0.6214 miles
1 fathom = 1.8288 m
1 chain = 20.1168 m
1 furlong = 201.168 m
1 acre = 0.4047 hectares
1 sq km = 100 hectares
1 sq mile = 2.59 square km
1 ounce = 28.35 grams
1 pound = 0.4536 kilograms
1 short ton = 0.90718 metric ton
1 short ton = 2,000 pounds
1 long ton = 1.016 metric tons
1 long ton = 2,240 pounds
1 metric ton = 1,000 kilograms
1 quart = 0.94635 liters
1 US gallon = 3.7854 liters
1 Imperial gallon = 4.5459 liters
1 nautical mile = 1.852 km

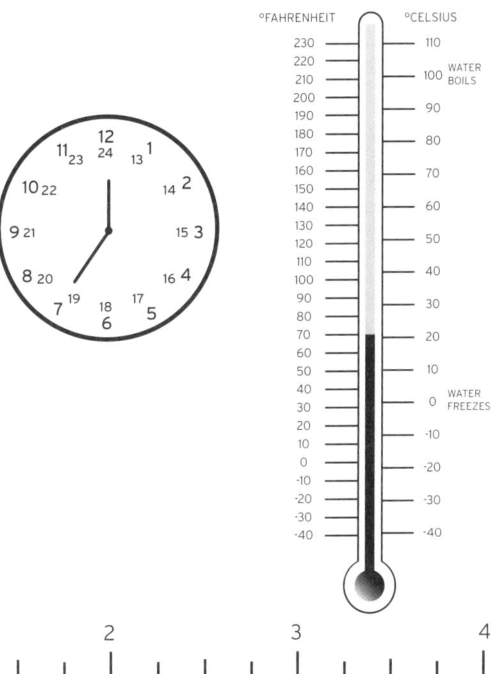

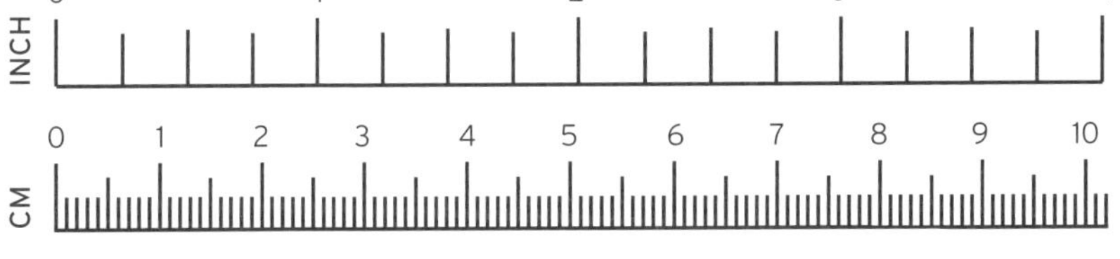

MOON SEVILLE, GRANADA & ANDALUSIA
Avalon Travel
Hachette Book Group
555 12th Street, Suite 1850
Oakland, CA 94607, USA
www.moon.com

Editor: Vy Tran
Managing Editor: Hannah Brezack
Copy Editor: Deana Shields
Graphics and Production Coordinator: Ravina Schneider
Cover Design: Toni Tajima
Interior Design: Avalon Travel
Map Editor: Kat Bennett
Cartographers: John Culp, Abby Whelan
Proofreader: Ann Seifert
Indexer: Courtney Packard

ISBN-13: 979-8-88647-064-2

Printing History
1st Edition — November 2024
5 4 3 2 1

Front cover photo: the Alhambra palace, Granada. Jon Arnold Images Ltd / Alamy Stock Photo
Back cover photo: Roman bridge in Córdoba. © Olgacov | Dreamstime.com

Printed in China APS